Wiley
CMAexcel Learning System
Exam Review 2018

About IMA® (Institute of Management Accountants)

IMA®, the association of accountants and financial professionals in business, is one of the largest and most respected associations focused exclusively on advancing the management accounting profession.

Globally, IMA supports the profession through research, the CMA® (Certified Management Accountant) program, continuing education, networking, and advocacy of the highest ethical business practices.

IMA has a global network of more than 90,000 members in 140 countries and 300 professional and student chapters. Headquartered in Montvale, N.J., USA, IMA provides localized services through its four global regions: The Americas, Asia/Pacific, Europe, and Middle East/India. For more information about IMA, please visit www.imanet.org.

Wiley CMAexcel Learning System Exam Review 2018

Self-Study Guide

Part 2: Financial Decision Making

 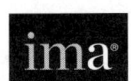

Cover Design: Wiley
Cover Illustration: © jeremykramerdesign/iStockphoto

Copyright © 2018 by Institute of Management Accountants. All rights reserved.

Published by John Wiley & Sons, Inc., Hoboken, New Jersey.
Published simultaneously in Canada.

These materials are copyrighted and may not be reproduced in any form or used in any way to create derivative works. Any reproduction, reuse, or distribution of CMA Learning System® materials without prior written permission from the Institute of Management Accountants (IMA) is illegal and a material violation of the *IMA Statement of Ethical Professional Practice*.

Any Certified Management Accountant (CMA) or CMA candidate who reproduces, reuses, or distributes CMA Learning System® materials or content in any form without prior authorization from IMA is subject to legal action and will be reported to the Institute of Certified Management Accountants (ICMA) and immediately expelled from the IMA and CMA program.

It is your responsibility to ensure that any CMA exam review materials that you are using have been provided to you through authorized channels or personnel. If you are in doubt about the authenticity of your materials or question the means by which they have been provided to you, contact IMA customer service at (800) 638-4427 in the U.S. or +1 (201) 573-9000.

This material is designed for learning purposes and is distributed with the understanding that the publisher and authors are not offering legal or professional services.

No part of this publication may be reproduced, stored in a retrieval system, or transmitted in any form or by any means, electronic, mechanical, photocopying, recording, scanning, or otherwise, except as permitted under Section 107 or 108 of the 1976 United States Copyright Act, without either the prior written permission of the Publisher, or authorization through payment of the appropriate per-copy fee to the Copyright Clearance Center, Inc., 222 Rosewood Drive, Danvers, MA 01923, (978) 750-8400, fax (978) 646-8600, or on the Web at www.copyright.com. Requests to the Publisher for permission should be addressed to the Permissions Department, John Wiley & Sons, Inc., 111 River Street, Hoboken, NJ 07030, (201) 748-6011, fax (201) 748-6008, or online at www.wiley.com/go/permissions.

Limit of Liability/Disclaimer of Warranty: While the publisher and author have used their best efforts in preparing this book, they make no representations or warranties with respect to the accuracy or completeness of the contents of this book and specifically disclaim any implied warranties of merchantability or fitness for a particular purpose. No warranty may be created or extended by sales representatives or written sales materials. The advice and strategies contained herein may not be suitable for your situation. You should consult with a professional where appropriate. Neither the publisher nor author shall be liable for any loss of profit or any other commercial damages, including but not limited to special, incidental, consequential, or other damages.

For general information on our other products and services or for technical support, please contact our Customer Care Department within the United States at (800) 762-2974, outside the United States at (317) 572-3993 or fax (317) 572-4002.

Wiley also publishes its books in a variety of electronic formats. Some content that appears in print may not be available in electronic books. For more information about Wiley products, visit our web site at www.wiley.com.

Library of Congress Cataloging-in-Publication Data

ISBN 978-1-119-47913-0 (Part 2)
ISBN 978-1-119-47899-7 (Part 2 ePDF)
ISBN 978-1-119-47906-2 (Part 2 ePub)
ISBN 978-1-119-47900-0 (Part 1)
ISBN 978-1-119-47910-9 (Part 1 ePDF)
ISBN 978-1-119-47912-3 (Part 1 ePub)

Printed in the United States of America

10 9 8 7 6 5 4 3 2 1

Contents

Acknowledgments of Subject Matter Experts	ix
Candidate Study Information	xi
How to Use the Wiley CMAexcel Learning System	xv
Create a Study Plan	xix
Introduction	1

Section A
Financial Statement Analysis — 3

Topic 1:	Basic Financial Statement Analysis	5
Topic 2:	Financial Ratios	17
Topic 3:	Profitability Analysis	57
Topic 4:	Special Issues	81
Practice Questions: Financial Statement Analysis		99

Section B
Corporate Finance — 109

Topic 1:	Risk and Return	111
Topic 2:	Long-Term Financial Management	129
Topic 3:	Raising Capital	183
Topic 4:	Working Capital Management	201
Topic 5:	Corporate Restructuring	235

| Topic 6: | International Finance | 247 |

Practice Questions: Corporate Finance — 267

Section C
Decision Analysis — 273

Topic 1:	Cost/Volume/Profit Analysis	275
Topic 2:	Marginal Analysis	291
Topic 3:	Pricing	309

Practice Questions: Decision Analysis — 338

Section D
Risk Management — 349

| Topic 1: | Enterprise Risk | 351 |

Practice Questions: Risk Management — 365

Section E
Investment Decisions — 367

Topic 1:	Capital Budgeting Process	369
Topic 2:	Discounted Cash Flow Analysis	385
Topic 3:	Payback and Discounted Payback	405
Topic 4:	Risk Analysis in Capital Investment	411

Practice Questions: Investment Decisions — 423

Section F
Professional Ethics — 431

| Topic 1: | Ethical Considerations for Management Accounting and Financial Management Professionals | 435 |
| Topic 2: | Ethical Considerations for the Organization | 453 |

Practice Questions: Professional Ethics — 471

Essay Exam Support Materials — 473

Essay Exam Study Tips — 476

Examples of Essay Question Answers — 478

Practice Essay Questions and Answers — 488

Answers to Section Practice Questions — 593

Appendix A: Time Value of Money Tables — 649

Appendix B: ICMA Learning Outcome Statements—Part 2 — 653

Bibliography and References — 667

Index of Learning Outcome Statements — 671

Index — 689

Acknowledgments of Subject Matter Experts

The Wiley CMAexcel Learning System (WCMALS) content is written to help explain the concepts and calculations from the Certified Management Accountant (CMA) exam Learning Outcome Statements (LOS) published by the Institute of Certified Management Accountants (ICMA).

Wiley would like to acknowledge the team of subject matter experts who worked with us to produce this version of the WCMALS. IMA would also like to acknowledge this team of subject matter experts, who worked together in conjunction with IMA staff to produce this version of the WCMALS.

Content Contributor for 2018 Edition

Marjorie E. Yuschak, CMA, is fortunate to have enjoyed multiple careers. She had a 21-year career at Johnson & Johnson developing expertise in cost/managerial accounting, financial reporting, and employee stock option programs while working in the consumer, pharmaceutical, and corporate segments of the business. Following that she was an adjunct professor of accounting and faculty advisor to Beta Alpha Psi at the Rutgers Business School, New Brunswick. Marj is an author for John Wiley & Sons, Inc. She continues to facilitate the CMA Review courses at Villanova University, which she has done for over six years and she is currently an adjunct professor of accounting at The College of New Jersey. She has a consulting business providing coaching for accounting, communication skills, and small business management. Marj is a member of the Raritan Valley Chapter of the IMA in New Jersey. In addition, she is a Certified Trainer in both AchieveGlobal and DDI (Development Dimensions International) and a member of ATD (the Association for Talent Development).

Prior Content Contributors

Meghann Cefaratti, Ph.D., is an associate professor in the Department of Accountancy at Northern Illinois University. She completed her Ph.D. in Accounting at Virginia Tech. Professor Cefaratti teaches financial accounting and assurance services. Her primary research interest involves auditors' fraud risk assessment judgments. Her dissertation was recognized by the AAA Forensic and Investigative Accounting Section in 2011. Additionally, her research has received awards from the Accounting and Information Systems Educators Association and has been published in the Journal of Information Systems, Journal of the Association for Information Systems, Journal of Forensic and Investigative Accounting, and Internal Auditor. She is a former auditor for the Air Force Audit Agency (AFAA) where her audit coverage included Andrews Air Force Base, MD, the Pentagon, and various Air National Guard installations. Prior to working with the AFAA, she worked as a tax associate for PricewaterhouseCoopers in Baltimore, MD.

Gary Cokins, CPIM, is an internationally recognized expert, speaker, and author in enterprise and corporate performance management (EPM/CPM) systems. He is the founder of Analytics-Based Performance Management LLC (www.garycokins.com). He began his career in industry with a Fortune 100 company in CFO and operations roles. Then for 15 years he was a consultant with Deloitte, KPMG, and EDS (now part of HP). From 1997 until 2013 Gary was a Principal Consultant with SAS, a business analytics software vendor. His most recent books are *Performance Management: Integrating Strategy Execution, Methodologies, Risk, and Analytics* and *Predictive Business Analytics*. He graduated from Cornell University with a Bachelor of Science degree in industrial engineering/operations research in 1971 and went on to earn his MBA from Northwestern University Kellogg in 1974.

Daniel J. Gibbons, CPA, Associate Professor of Accounting, has been employed by Waubonsee Community College since 2001. Prior to starting his career in education, he worked in Accounting and Finance for approximately 21 years. He has a Bachelor of Science degree in Accounting from Northeastern Illinois University and a Master of Science degree in Finance from Northern Illinois University. He is a resident of Naperville, IL.

Joseph Kastantin, CPA, CMA, MBA, ACCA, is a Professor of Accountancy at the University of Wisconsin-La Crosse and an alum of KPMG Central and Eastern Europe having worked from 1997–2008 in both full time and part time capacities with KPMG Central Europe in the department of professional practice and training. Kastantin served on the board of directors and audit committee of the North Central Trust Company (now Trust Point) for three years and as chairman of the board of La Crosse Funds, Inc. for four years. Additionally, he served as president and board member for several not-for-profit entities, as CEO of a small manufacturing company, business manager for an auto dealership, controller for a textile wholesaler, and as sole practitioner in public accounting. He has more than 30 published journal articles and books. His most recent publications are on fraud and a practical guide to impairments under IFRS and US GAAP. He served nearly ten years on active duty with the US Army (SFC E-7) with tours in Korea and Vietnam and was an instructor and MOS test writer at the US Army AG School.

Candidate Study Information

CMA Certification from ICMA

The Certified Management Accountant (CMA) certification provides accountants and financial professionals with an objective measure of knowledge and competence in the field of management accounting. The CMA designation is recognized globally as an invaluable credential for professional accountancy advancement inside organizations and for broadening professional skills and perspectives.

The two-part CMA exam is designed to develop and measure critical-thinking and decision-making skills and to meet these objectives:

- To establish management accounting and financial management as recognized professions by identifying the role of the professional, the underlying body of knowledge, and a course of study by which such knowledge is acquired.
- To encourage higher educational standards in the management accounting and financial management fields.
- To establish an objective measure of an individual's knowledge and competence in the fields of management accounting and financial management.
- To encourage continued professional development.

Individuals earning the CMA designation benefit by being able to:

- Communicate their broad business competency and strategic financial mastery.
- Obtain contemporary professional knowledge and develop skills and abilities that are valued by successful businesses.
- Convey their commitment to an exemplary standard of excellence that is grounded on a strong ethical foundation and lifelong learning.
- Enhance their career development, salary qualifications, and professional promotion opportunities.

The CMA certification is granted exclusively by the Institute of Certified Management Accountants (ICMA).

CMA Learning Outcome Statements (LOS)

The Certified Management Accountant exam is based on a series of Learning Outcome Statements (LOS) developed by the Institute of Certified Management Accountants (ICMA). The LOS describes the knowledge and skills that make up the CMA body of knowledge, broken down by part, section, and topic. The Wiley CMAexcel Learning System (WCMALS) supports the LOS by addressing the subjects they cover. Candidates should use the LOS to ensure they can address the concepts in different ways or through a variety of question scenarios. Candidates should also be prepared to perform calculations referred to in the LOS in total or by providing missing components of a calculation. The LOS should not be used as proxies for exact exam questions; they should be used as a guide for studying and learning the content that will be covered on the exam.

A copy of the ICMA Learning Outcome Statements is included in Appendix B at the end of this book. Candidates are also encouraged to visit the IMA website to find other exam-related information at www.imanet.org.

CMA Exam Format

The content tested on the CMA exams is at an advanced level—which means that the passing standard is set for mastery, not minimum competence. Thus, there will be test questions for all major topics that require the candidate to synthesize information, evaluate a situation, and make recommendations. Other questions will test subject comprehension and analysis. However, compared to previous versions, this CMA exam will have an increased emphasis on the higher-level questions.

The content is based on a series of LOS that define the competencies and capabilities expected of a management accountant.

There are two exams, taken separately: Part 1: Financial Reporting, Planning, Performance, and Control, and Part 2: Financial Decision Making. Each exam is four hours in length and includes multiple-choice and essay questions. One hundred multiple-choice questions are presented first, followed by two essay questions. All of these questions—multiple-choice and essay—can address any of the LOS for the respective exam part. Therefore, your study plan should include learning the content of the part as well as practicing how to answer multiple-choice and essay questions against that content. The study plan tips and the final section of this WCMALS book contain important information to help you learn how to approach the different types of questions.

Note on Candidate Assumed Knowledge

The CMA exam content is based on a set of assumed baseline knowledge that candidates are expected to have. Assumed knowledge includes economics, basic statistics, and financial accounting. Examples of how this assumed knowledge might be tested in the exam include:

- How to calculate marginal revenue and costs as well as understand the relevance of market structures when determining prices
- How to calculate variance when managing financial risk
- How to construct a cash flow statement as part of an analysis of transactions and assess the impact of the transactions on the financial statements

Please note that prior courses in accounting and finance are highly recommended to ensure this knowledge competency when preparing for the exam.

Overall Expectations for the CMA Candidates

Completing the CMA exams requires a high level of commitment and dedication of up to 150 hours of study for each part of the CMA exam. Completing the two-part exam is a serious investment that will reap many rewards, helping you to build a solid foundation for your career, distinguish yourself from other accountants, and enhance your career in ways that will pay dividends for a lifetime.

Your success in completing these exams will rest heavily on your ability to create a solid study plan and to execute that plan. IMA offers resources to support you during this process—we encourage you to register as a CMA candidate as soon as you begin the program to maximize your access to these resources and tools and to draw on these benefits with rigor and discipline that best supports your unique study needs. We also suggest candidates seek other sources if further knowledge is needed to augment knowledge and understanding of the ICMA LOS.

For more information about the CMA certification, the CMA exams, or the exam preparation resources offered through IMA, visit www.imanet.org.

Standard and pronouncement changes in authoritative literature have an issuance date, an effective date, and possibly an early adoption date. These changes will be eligible for testing on the CMA examinations one year after the effective date. The contents of this curriculum reflect standards that are currently eligible for testing.

Updates and Errata Notification

Please be advised that our materials are designed to provide thorough and accurate content with a high level of attention to quality. From time to time there may be clarifications, corrections, or updates that are captured in an Updates and Errata Notification.

To ensure you are kept abreast of changes, this notification will be available on Wiley's CMAexcel update and errata page. You may review these documents by going to www.efficientlearning.com/cma/support/updates.

How to Use the Wiley CMAexcel Learning System

This product is based on the CMA body of knowledge developed by the Institute of Certified Management Accountants (ICMA). This material is designed for learning purposes and is distributed with the understanding that the publisher and authors are not offering legal or professional services. Although the text is based on the body of knowledge tested by the CMA exam and the published Learning Outcome Statements (LOS) covering the two-part exams, Wiley CMAexcel Learning System (WCMALS) program developers do not have access to the current bank of exam questions. It is critical that candidates understand all LOS published by the ICMA, learn all concepts and calculations related to those statements, and have a solid grasp of how to approach the multiple-choice and essay exams in the CMA program.

Some exam preparation tools provide an overview of key topics; others are intended to help you practice one specific aspect of the exams such as the questions. The WCMALS is designed as a comprehensive exam preparation tool to help you study the content from the exam LOS, learn how to write the CMA exams, and practice answering exam-type questions.

Study the Book Content

The **table of contents** is set up using the CMA exam content specifications established by ICMA. Each section, topic, and subtopic is named according to the content specifications and the **Learning Outcome Statements (LOS)** written to correspond to these specifications. As you go through each section and major topic, refer to the related LOS found in Appendix B. Then review the CMALS book content to help learn the concepts and formulas covered in the LOS.

The **Learning Outcome Statements Overviews** provide a quick reference to the LOS as well as key points to remember within them. These sections should not replace the in-depth discussion of the material that is in this book. However, these overviews do serve as a refresher on what has been learned and can be used as a tool to reinforce the knowledge that you have obtained.

The **knowledge checks** are designed to be quick checks to verify that you understand and remember the content just covered by presenting questions and correct answers. The answers refer to the appropriate sections in the book for you to review the content and find the answer yourself.

The **practice questions** are a sampling of the type of exam questions you will encounter on the exam and are considered complex and may involve extensive written and/or calculation responses. Use these questions to begin applying what you have learned, recognizing there is a much larger sample of practice questions available in the Online Test Bank (described in the next section).

The WCMALS also contains a **bibliography and references** in case you need to find more detailed content on an LOS. We encourage you to use published academic sources. While information can be found online, we discourage the use of open-source, unedited sites such as Wikipedia.

Suggested Study Process Using the WCMALS

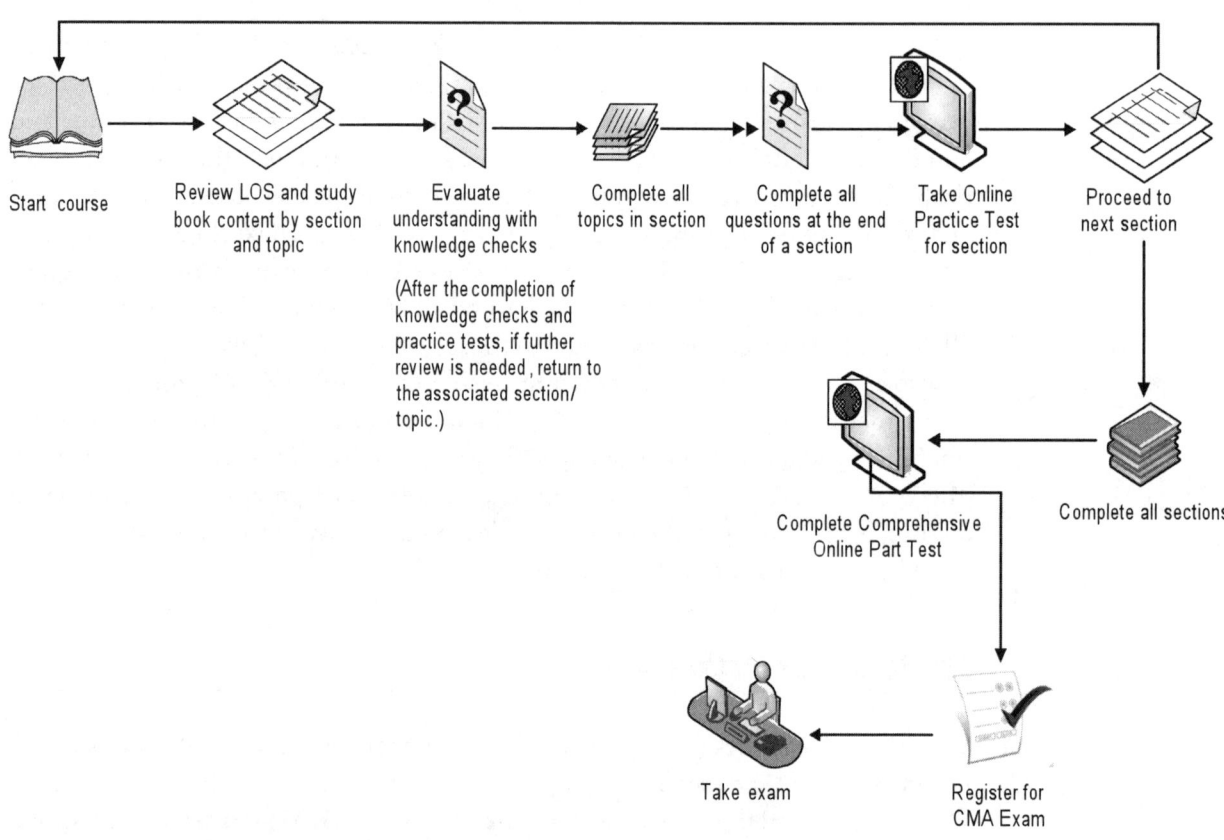

WCMALS Book Features

The WCMALS books use a number of features to draw your attention to certain types of content:

Key terms are **bolded** where they appear in the text with their definition, to allow you to quickly scan through and study them.

 Key formulas are indicated with this icon. Be sure you understand these formulas and practice applying them.

Knowledge checks at the end of each topic are review questions that let you check your understanding of the content just read. (They are not representative of the type of questions that appear on the exam.)

 Study tips offer ideas and strategies for studying and preparing for the exam.

 Practice questions are examples of actual exam questions. Presented at the end of each section, these questions help you solidify your learning of that section and apply it to the type of questions that appear on the exam.

 LOS icons appear in the body of the Sections to highlight where we address each Learning Outcome Statement within the text.

Online Test Bank

Included with your purchase of the Wiley CMAexcel Learning System Part 2 book is an Online Test Bank made available to you through www.wileycma.com. This test bank includes **six section-specific tests** that randomize questions from a selected section only. The course also includes **a comprehensive Part 2 test** that emulates the percentage weighting of each section on the actual Part 2 exam. All questions are drawn from a bank of more than 780 questions, so that each time you repeat the test, you will receive a different set of questions covering all the topics in the section. All the multiple-choice questions provide feedback in response to your answers. Your scores will be recorded so that you can track your progress over time.

It is suggested that you integrate the Online Test Bank throughout your study program instead of leaving them until the end. The section-specific tests are designed for you to practice questions related to the section content—read and learn a section and then practice the online questions related to the section. This also will help you identify if further study of the section content is required before moving to the next section.

The comprehensive Part 2 test is designed to help you simulate taking the actual CMA exam. Try the comprehensive Part 2 test after you have studied all the Part 2 content. You can take this exam multiple times. Each time you will receive a different combination of questions. It is recommended that you set up your own exam simulation—set aside four hours in a room without interruption, do not have any reference books open, and work through the comprehensive part exam as if you were taking the real exam. This will prepare you for the exam setting and give you a good idea of how ready you are.

In addition, sample essay questions are provided that simulate the testing environment. The correct answer is provided which will enable you to self-score your answer.

You are strongly encouraged to make full use of all online practice and review features as part of your study efforts. Please note that these features are subscription based and available only for a specific number of months from the time of registration.

Learn to Write the CMA Exam

The four-hour CMA exam will test your understanding of each part's content using both multiple-choice and essay questions. This means you must learn to write two types of tests in one sitting. The WCMALS books contain tips, instruction, and examples to help you learn to write an essay exam. Be sure to study the Essay Exam Support Materials section so that in addition to practicing with the Online Test Bank, you also learn to respond to the part content in essay format.

Create a Study Plan

Each part of the two-part CMA exam uses a combination of a multiple-choice format and an essay format to test your understanding of the part concepts, terms, and calculations. Creating a study plan is an essential ingredient to planning a path to success. Managing your plan is critical to achieving success. The next tips and tactics are included to help you prepare and manage your study plan.

Study Tips

There are many ways to study, and the plan you create will depend on things such as your lifestyle (when and how you can schedule study time), your learning style, how familiar you are with the content, and how practiced you are at writing a formal exam. Only you can assess these factors and create a plan that will work for you. Some suggestions that other exam candidates have found helpful follow.

- Schedule regular study times and stay on schedule.
- Avoid cramming by breaking your study times into small segments. For example, you may want to work intensely for 45 minutes with no interruptions, followed by a 15-minute break during which time you do something different. You may want to leave the room, have a conversation, or exercise.
- When reading, highlight key ideas, especially unfamiliar ones. Reread later to ensure comprehension.
- Pay particular attention to the terms and equations highlighted in this book, and be sure to learn the acronyms in the CMA body of knowledge.
- Create personal mnemonics to help you memorize key information. For example, CCIC to remember the four ethical standards: Competence, Confidentiality, Integrity, and Credibility.
- Create study aids such as flash cards.
- Use index cards, and write a question on one side and the answer on the other. This helps reinforce the learning because you are writing the information as well as reading it. Examples: What is _____? List the five parts of _____.
- In particular, make flash cards of topics and issues that are unfamiliar to you, key terms and formulas, and anything you highlighted while reading.
- Keep some cards with you at all times to review when you have time, such as in an elevator, while waiting for an appointment, and so on.

- Use a flash card partner. This person does not need to understand accounting. He or she only needs the patience to sit with you and read the questions off the flash card.
- As test time approaches, start to eliminate the questions you can easily answer from your stack so you can concentrate on the more challenging topics and terms.
- If particular topics are difficult, tap into other resources such as the Internet, library, accountant colleagues, or professors, to augment your understanding.
- Use your study plan—treat it as a living document and update it as you learn more about what you need to do to prepare for the exam.
- Use the knowledge checks in the book to assess how well you understand the content you just completed.
- Use the Online Test Bank to test your pability to answer multiple-choice practice questions on each section's content as you finish it. After completing the first 40 questions presented, review areas in the book that you were weak on in the practice test. Then try the section test again.
- Be sure to learn how to take a multiple-choice question exam—there are many online resources with tips and guidance that relate to answering multiple-choice exams.
  - Make an attempt to answer all questions. There is no penalty for an incorrect answer—if you don't try, even when you are uncertain, you eliminate the potential of getting a correct answer.
  - Create your own "simulated" multiple-choice trial exam using the full part Online Practice Test.
- Learn to write an effective essay answer.
  - Use the Essay Exam Support Materials section of this book. This content shows a sample grading guide and includes a sample of a good, a better, and a best answer in addition to some helpful tips for writing an essay answer.
  - Learn how points are awarded for an essay answer so that you can ensure you get the most points possible for your answers, even when you are very challenged by a question.
  - Practice essay responses using the questions in the WCMALS book as well as the Online Test Bank.
- Be sure to access the Online Test Bank and its Essay Questions until you are comfortable with the content.

Ensure you are both well rested and physically prepared for the exam day as each exam is four hours in length with no break for meals. Learning how to answer a multiple-choice and essay exam and being mentally and physically prepared can improve your grade significantly. Know the content and be prepared to deal with challenges with a focused, confident, and flexible attitude.

Introduction

Welcome to Part 2: Financial Decision Making of the Wiley CMAexcel Learning System.

This Part 2 *Self-Study Guide* is composed of six sections:

Section A: Financial Statement Analysis focuses on important ratios and other analytical tools used to evaluate an organization's financial health, including coverage of special issues, such as foreign currency fluctuations, off–balance sheet financing, U.S. GAAP versus IFRS, and fair value accounting.

Section B: Corporate Finance examines key concepts in corporate finance, including risk and return, working capital management, raising capital, corporate restructuring, and international finance issues.

Section C: Decision Analysis reviews fundamental information about the decision-making process, including relevant cost analysis, cost/volume/profit analysis, pricing concepts, and marginal analysis. It also addresses the assessment and management of risk—risk identification and exposure, and risk mitigation strategies.

Section D: Risk Management focuses on enterprise risk management (ERM). ERM provides a comprehensive approach to risk identification, assessment, and response.

Section E: Investment Decisions begins with an overview of the capital budgeting process and then reviews principles used to evaluate investment alternatives—discounted cash flow analysis, payback and discounted payback, ranking investment projects, and risk analsyis.

Section F: Professional Ethics focuses on ethical considerations for the organization, with discussion of the provisions of the U.S. Foreign Corrupt Practices Act and the IMA *Statement on Management Accounting (SMA)*, "Values and Ethics: From Inception to Practice." In addition, this section presents the *IMA Statement of Ethical Professional Practice* in the context of the ethical demands an individual will face within an organization.

SECTION A

Financial Statement Analysis

While financial statements summarize the past performance of an organization, they also can provide users with valuable insights into future performance. Financial statement analysis is performed by stockholders and creditors and is also an important tool for management accountants and financial analysts to use to better understand their company's competitive position.

Financial statements can be analyzed to identify trends in key financial data, compare financial performance across companies, and calculate financial ratios that can be used to assess a company's current performance as well as its prospects for the future. In addition, the management accountant should be familiar with the analytical techniques used by external investors to evaluate their company.

This section focuses on important ratios and other analytical tools used to evaluate an organization's financial health, including coverage of special issues, such as foreign currency fluctuations, off-balance sheet financing, fair value accounting, and U.S. generally accepted accounting principles (GAAP) versus International Financial Reporting Standards (IFRSs).

TOPIC 1

Basic Financial Statement Analysis

IN THE UNITED STATES (US), COMPANIES are required to prepare general purpose financial statements in accordance with the Accounting Standards Codification (ASC). This requirement extends to issuers as defined by the US Securities and Exchange Commission (SEC). Separate SEC reporting requirements are integral to the ASC.

According to Statement of Financial Accounting Concepts No. 8—*Conceptual Framework for Financial Reporting*, "The objective of general purpose financial reporting is to provide financial information about the reporting entity that is useful to existing and potential investors, lenders, and other creditors in making decisions about providing resources to the entity. Those decisions involve buying, selling, or holding equity and debt instruments and providing or settling loans and other forms of credit.

"Many existing and potential investors, lenders, and other creditors cannot require reporting entities to provide information directly to them and must rely on general purpose financial reports for much of the financial information they need. Consequently, they are the primary users to whom general purpose financial reports are directed.

"General purpose financial reports are not designed to show the value of a reporting entity; but they provide information to help existing and potential investors, lenders, and other creditors to estimate the value of the reporting entity."

In order to evaluate companies, financial analysts examine financial statements in different ways; they may create variants of financial statements, such as common-size statements, and consider other issues that may affect the company's performance. Moreover, a financial analyst is expected to be able to prepare base-year statements to enable trend analysis and review the growth rates of the various elements of the financial statement.

According to the Financial Accounting Standards Board (FASB) in Concept Statement #8, "existing and potential investors, lenders, and other creditors need information to help them assess the prospects for future net cash inflows to an entity.

"To assess an entity's prospects for future net cash inflows, existing and potential investors, lenders, and other creditors need information about the resources of the entity, claims against the entity, and how efficiently and effectively the entity's management and governing board have discharged their responsibilities to use the entity's resources."

Additionally general purpose financial reporting may include as required by the ASC a mixture of original cost, adjusted cost, or fair value measures. Financial analysts then start with the general purpose financial statements and the various measures they contain and principles that apply to produce variations so they can help specific users to assess the prospects for future net cash inflows to an entity and the risks of those prospects.

READ the Learning Outcome Statements (LOS) for this topic as found in Appendix B and then study the concepts and calculations presented here to be sure you understand the content you could be tested on in the CMA exam.

Common-Size Statements

Common-size statements recast all items in a particular financial statement as a percentage of a selected (usually the largest and/or most important) item on the statement. These statements can be used to:

- Compare elements in a single year's financial statements.
- Analyze trends across a number of years for one business.
- Compare businesses of differing sizes within an industry (such as Wal-Mart to Target).
- Compare the company's performance and position with an industry average.

Common-size statements are useful when comparing businesses of different sizes because the financial statements of a variety of companies can be recast into the uniform common-size format regardless of the magnitude of individual elements. Some analysts may wish to compare two companies that are not in the same industry or to compare two conglomerates with widely diverse lines of business. An example would be comparing JP Morgan Chase with Exxon Mobil. Granted that both are very large companies by any measure. But the means of generating revenues and the types of assets that these two giants hold are significantly different. These differences may require the analyst to adjust the common-size financial statements to deal with and make sense of these differences.

Comparing common-size statements of companies within an industry or with common-size industry average statistics of that industry can bring to light variations in account structure or distribution that require the analyst to explore and explain the reasons for differences.

Vertical Common-Size Statements

In **vertical common-size statements**, a base amount (generally total assets on the balance sheet and net sales on the income statement) is valued at 100%, and the elements within the statement are expressed as a percentage of the base amount. Figures 2A-1 and 2A-2 are sample vertical common-size statements for the balance sheet (statement of financial position) and income statement of ABC Company.

Figure 2A-1 Vertical Common-Size Balance Sheet for ABC Company

Assets

Total current assets	$350,000	70%
Net fixed assets	150,000	30%
Total assets	$500,000	100%

Liabilities and equity

Liabilities:		
Total current liabilities:	$200,000	40%
Long-term liabilities:	50,000	10%
Total liabilities	250,000	50%
Shareholders' equity:		
Common stock, $ par value	25,000	5%
Additional paid-in capital	100,000	20%
Retained earnings	125,000	25%
Total shareholders' equity	250,000	50%
Total liabilities and equity	$500,000	100%

Figure 2A-2 Common-Size Income Statement for ABC Company

Sales	$250	100%
Cost of goods sold	120	48%
Administrative expense	85	34%
Other expenses	10	4%
Earnings before interest and taxes	$35	14%

As demonstrated in Figures 2A-1 and 2A-2, common-size statements can be created for both the balance sheet and the income statement. Analysis of common-size income statements is useful because each item in it is related to the central value of sales. Most expense items are affected to some extent by sales volume. Even fixed costs can vary with sales volume although the variation may appear like a step. For example a factory with one assembly line may treat the assembly line as a fixed cost. However if sales growth is desirable or planned requiring one or more additional assembly lines, then the added assembly line costs may be referred to as step-variable costs rather than fixed costs. However be aware that on the CMA exam it is likely that the candidate will need to assume that within the relevant range of activity (sales for example) that fixed costs are presumed not to change with activity. Therefore, it is helpful to know what proportion of the sales dollar each of the various costs and expenses represents. Such common-size statements are used to compare two or more different companies.

There are salient differences between the common-size statements across different industries. Typically, companies within the same industry display similar traits in their common-size statements, but companies in different industries display different traits. Different traits include financial statement format, captions level of summarization, etc.

Figure 2A-3 shows common-size statements of four different industries, illustrating the divergence in these statements across industries. As can be seen, the composition of the assets varies widely in the following industries: computer manufacturing, retail, finance, and pharmaceuticals.

Figure 2A-3 Common-Size Balance Sheet Across Industries

	Manufacturing	Retail Trade	Finance and Insurance	Health Care and Assistance
Cash Equivalent	3%	7%	3%	10%
Marketable Securities	0%	0%	9%	0%
Accounts/Notes Receivable	21%	9%	7%	11%
Inventories	6%	25%	0%	1%
Prepaid and Others	4%	5%	7%	6%
Investments	33%	8%	65%	15%
Property, Plant, and Equipment	12%	26%	1%	26%
Goodwill and Intangibles	12%	11%	1%	25%
Other Assets	9%	9%	7%	7%
Total Assets	**100%**	**100%**	**100%**	**100%**
Liability and Equity				
Short-Term Payables	11%	16%	4%	4%
Short-Term Debt	7%	10%	2%	5%
Other Current Liabilities	9%	10%	14%	12%
Long-Term Debt	23%	22%	15%	47%
Other Liabilities	13%	10%	19%	15%
Total Liabilities	**63%**	**68%**	**54%**	**83%**
Total Equity	**37%**	**32%**	**46%**	**17%**
Total Liability and Equity	**100%**	**100%**	**100%**	**100%**

Source: Internal Revenue Service Statistics of Income (SOI) 2012. For illustration purposes only.

It is worth focusing on the variations that are apparent in a few of the accounts. For example, accounts receivable comprises 9% of the total assets for the retailer primarily because a retailer (such as Wal-Mart or Target) has most of its sales in cash or on credit cards. However, as expected, inventories are 25% of the total assets for the retailer, much more so than in any other industry. Moreover, companies in the financial industry (such as a bank or insurance company) possess little or no inventory.

Investments are the most significant account for companies in the financial industry, but this account is 8% for retailers. The business model of financial companies, and in particular investment banks, is to hold investments that yield a high return. Therefore, it is not surprising that investments are about 65% of the total assets. Leaders in the Health Care and Assistance and Manufacturing industries have investments in smaller companies in their respective industries, though the investment amount comprises a smaller proportion of their total assets than for financial companies.

It is interesting to note that the retailer and the health care and assistance company have a significant proportion of their assets in plant, property, and equipment. This signifies that retailers own most of their stores rather than leasing them. Similarly, the health care and assistance companies have a significant proportion of their assets tied up in their means of production (plant and equipment). The investment in plant, property, and equipment is minuscule for the financial institution, primarily because its assets are mostly composed of investments, and they do not require manufacturing plants or machinery and equipment to function. Often, traditional manufacturers have a significant proportion of their assets in plant, property, and equipment. However, during the past several years in which outsourcing production has dramatically increased, the portion of PPE in relation to total assets is decreasing for manufacturers.

The common sizing of liabilities and equities provides some interesting insights as to how these companies are financed. The manufacturing and health care and assistance companies obtain 63% and 83% debt financing. The retail trade and finance and insurance industry also obtains debt financing for more than 50% of its assets.

Similar inferences can be drawn through common sizing of the income statement. Different industries have different cost structures and profit margins. Comparing the various categories of common-size expenses—such as cost of sales, research and development (R&D) expense, advertising expenses, and general overhead—provides validation of the differing business models across industries. For example, a retailer has a higher proportion of cost of sales than a health care and assistance company, which traditionally has a very small cost of sales relative to its total sales, signifying a high profit margin. Similarly, while the R&D expenses for a health care and assistance company are high, they are nonexistent for a retailer.

Such analysis and ability to draw inferences is critical in conducting common-size analysis. The mechanical aspect of developing common-size statements is of limited usefulness unless the analyst is able to make inferences and identify issues of concern based on the expectations formed through experience and knowledge. The skill set necessary to make inferences from financial and non-financial data is useful in auditing as well. In auditing, the focus is on determining whether certain analytical relationships are within an expected range. Those that are outside the expected range usually will require investigation.

Horizontal Common-Size Statements

A **horizontal common-size statement**, also called a **variation analysis** or **trend analysis**, compares key financial statement values and relationships for the same company over a period of years. The increase or decrease in each of the major accounts is shown as a percentage of the base-year amount and hence is sometimes referred to as the base-year financials. As illustrated in Figure 2A-4, such an analysis sets the base year at a value of 100% and then shows subsequent years in relation to increases or decreases over the base year.

Figure 2A-4 Horizontal Common-Size Statement (Variation or Trend Analysis)

	Year 0	Year 1	Year 2	Year 3	Year 4
Sales	$200,000	$210,000	$250,000	$260,000	$300,000
Base-year multiplier	100%	105%	125%	130%	150%
Cost of sales	$100,000	$110,000	$130,000	$150,000	$160,000
Base-year multiplier	100%	110%	130%	150%	160%

Note in Figure 2A-4 how cost of sales is growing faster than sales. This can be inferred through a simple computation of percentage growth in cost of sales and comparing it to the percentage growth in sales. Horizontal or trend analysis helps the analyst examine relationships to detect strengths and weaknesses. In this example, management needs to focus on controlling costs. This analysis can reveal trends in the direction, rate, and magnitude of change. Further analysis also can examine trends in related areas, such as a disparity between an increase in sales and a proportionately greater increase in receivables. Changes can be divided between year-to-year changes and longer-term trends.

By reading across each row in the horizontal analysis, one can quickly spot any unusual change in a particular account from the previous year. Any large changes or a reversal of a trend (a decrease after years of increases) signals issues that have to be further investigated and analyzed. The horizontal analysis provides an initial and quick overview of the financial statements, but it is by no means the final step of a thorough analysis. The purpose of horizontal analysis is primarily attention directing, in that it quickly and efficiently directs attention to the accounts that appear to be anomalies requiring further investigation.

The analyst must use caution in interpreting results using horizontal common-size statements. Changes between years can be expressed in actual dollar amounts but are much more commonly expressed as percentages. When using percentages, the analyst must keep in mind the size of the basis for comparison. For example, a 400% increase in net income might sound remarkable until you learn that last year's income was $1,000.

Expressing change as a percentage also loses meaning when the base is zero or below or the new value is zero. For example, if a company's net income in year 1 has a negative value and in year 2 has a positive value, there is no way to express the change as a percentage. In a case such as this, a comparison must be made by examining the raw numbers.

Another use of horizontal analysis is in cost control. Companies that are experiencing sales growth may tend to disregard controlling expenses. As a result, fixed expenses, which consist of overhead and other indirect expenses, may rise due to a lax management approach or step variable costs. Horizontal analysis can identify the fixed expenses that are increasing over time as sales are increasing. While it is possible that the increase in fixed expenses is justified due to inflation or growth of operations and facilities, an investigation could identify wastage or overconsumption of these resources and provide a means to increase profitability by limiting these expenses.

If changes between years are expressed in actual dollar amounts, the analyst must also bear in mind the relative conditions with which the firm started. For example, an increase in sales of $100,000 in a year has a different meaning for a company that began with sales of $10,000 than it does for a company that began with sales of $2,000,000.

Data across a number of years also can be presented as averages. This method mitigates the effect of unusual fluctuation in data for specific years. That is, a rolling average over two or three years could be used as input to the horizontal analysis. In that way, an unusual year that affects multiple averages and trends could be spotted even when large variations in data are present. For additional reading, if you search for the name Charles Fung you should find an article titled "Analytical Procedures." This article is brief, concisely written, and quite understandable even though it was written to an IFRS audience.

Basic Financial Statement Matters to Remember

There are four basic financial statements. It is said that certain information in each financial statement articulates with the next financial statement and that for this reason the financial statements often are prepared in the following order:

- Income statement–net income flows into the statement of changes in equity or retained earnings.
- Statement of changes in equity or retained earnings–ending retained earnings flows into the stockholders' equity section of the balance sheet.
- Balance sheet–changes in the beginning and ending caption amounts in the balance sheet, net income from the income statement and other changes in equity or retained earnings are used to prepare the statement of cash flows.
- Statement of cash flows is prepared last.

The income statement has certain expected captions depending on the nature of the reporting company and its industry. This example is in the multiple step format.

- Net sales
- Cost of goods sold

- Gross profit
- Operating expenses
- Other income/expense
- Income from continuing operations
- Discontinued operations
- Income before income tax
- Income tax expense
- Net income

The general format of the cost of goods sold displayed on the income statement is summarized as follows. There are other formats as well:

Beginning inventory
   + Net purchases (purchases − returns, discounts, and allowances)
   + Freight in
   = Cost of goods available for sale
   − Ending inventory
   = Cost of goods sold

Remember that cost of goods available for sale can only correctly be allocated to two financial statement captions: ending inventory on the balance sheet and cost of goods sold on the income statement.

Knowledge Check: Basic Financial Statements

The following questions are intended to help you check your understanding and recall of the material presented in this topic. They do not represent the type of questions that appear on the CMA exam.

Directions: Answer each question in the space provided. Correct answers and section references appear after the knowledge check questions.

1. In a common-size balance sheet, the inventory account as a percentage of total assets is expected to be highest for companies in
   - ☐ a. the finance industry, such as Citibank.
   - ☐ b. the airline industry, such as United Airlines.
   - ☐ c. the retail industry, such as Wal-Mart.
   - ☐ d. the pharmaceutical industry, such as Pfizer.

2. Which of the following statements regarding common-size statements is true?
   - ☐ a. Common-size statements for two companies, with both showing a 100% increase in profits, show that both companies would make equally attractive investments.
   - ☐ b. Horizontal common-size statements can be made only for companies with at least 10 years of operational data.
   - ☐ c. Common-size statements can be used to compare companies of different sizes.
   - ☐ d. All of the above are true.

3. You are analyzing changes in the reporting company's financial statement caption amounts from last year to this year. The reporting company's ending inventory increased by 10% from last year to this year. Which of the following could rationally explain changes in other financial statement amounts caused by the increase in inventory? Select all that apply.
   - ☐ a. Accounts receivable increased.
   - ☐ b. Accounts payable decreased.
   - ☐ c. Sales increased.
   - ☐ d. Cash increased.
   - ☐ e. Retained earnings decreased.
   - ☐ f. Accounts receivable decreased.
   - ☐ g. Accounts payable increased.
   - ☐ h. Sales decreased.
   - ☐ i. Cash decreased.
   - ☐ j. Retained earnings increased.

4. True or false: All ratios should compute the denominator value as a simple average of the beginning and ending amount that is part of that ratio.

Knowledge Check Answers: Basic Financial Statement Analysis

1. In a common-size balance sheet, the inventory account as a percentage of total assets is expected to be highest for companies in [See *Vertical Common-Size Statements*.]
   - ☐ a. the finance industry, such as Citibank.
   - ☐ b. the airline industry, such as United Airlines.
   - ☑ c. the retail industry, such as Wal-Mart.
   - ☐ d. the pharmaceutical industry, such as Pfizer.

2. Which of the following statements regarding common-size statements is true? [See *Common-Size Statements*.]
   - ☐ a. Common-size statements for two companies, with both showing a 100% increase in profits, show that both companies would make equally attractive investments.
   - ☐ b. Horizontal common-size statements can be made only for companies with at least 10 years of operational data.
   - ☑ c. Common-size statements can be used to compare companies of different sizes.
   - ☐ d. All of the above are true.

3. You are analyzing changes in the reporting company's financial statement caption amounts from last year to this year. The reporting company's ending inventory increased by 10% from last year to this year. Which of the following could rationally explain changes in other financial statement amounts caused by the increase in inventory? Select all that apply. [See *Common-Size Statements*.]
   - ☐ a. Accounts receivable increased.
   - ☑ b. Accounts payable decreased.
   - ☑ c. Sales increased.
   - ☐ d. Cash increased.
   - ☐ e. Retained earnings decreased.
   - ☐ f. Accounts receivable decreased.
   - ☐ g Accounts payable increased.
   - ☑ h. Sales decreased.
   - ☑ i. Cash decreased.
   - ☐ j. Retained earnings increased.

   (Some may disagree with this solution):

   The increase in ending inventory could rationally explain: b. an accounts payable increase, c. an anticipated sales increase, h. an unanticipated sales decrease, i. a cash decrease. An increase in ending inventory could result in an increase in accounts payable since inventory is usually purchased on account. End of year purchases of inventory for which we have taken delivery are most likely going to result in an increase in accounts payable since the payable would be due in the following year. On the other hand, if the inventory purchases were paid in cash, an increase in ending inventory could result in a decrease in cash. An increasing ending inventory could also arise from an unexpected decline in sales.

If your solution differs from this one, wage an argument that might persuade a colleague that you are right and the solution is wrong.

4. True or false: All ratios should compute the denominator value as a simple average of the beginning and ending amount that is part of that ratio. [See *Financial Ratios*.]

False. It is generally true in practice that when a ratio includes an income statement amount in the numerator and a balance sheet amount in the denominator, the denominator amount should be first computed as a simple average of the beginning and ending figure that forms the denominator. The purpose is to smooth the effect of large increases or decreases in the year-end denominator amount.

TOPIC 2

Financial Ratios

RATIOS ARE COMPARISONS, across time or to benchmarks, of relationships between financial statement accounts or between financial statement accounts and nonfinancial data. An example of a relationship between financial statement accounts is accounts receivable turnover where net credit sales are divided by the simple average of beginning and ending accounts receivable. An example of a relationship between a financial statement account and nonfinancial data is earnings per share, in its simplest form net income divided by weighted after common shares outstanding. Ratios provide incremental information about the financial health of the company beyond the raw amounts presented in the financial statements. Financial ratios are commonly used for three types of inferences: inferences on liquidity, solvency, and operations; inferences on capital structure; and inferences on profitability.

READ the Learning Outcome Statements (LOS) for this topic as found in Appendix B and then study the concepts and calculations presented here to be sure you understand the content you could be tested on in the CMA exam.

Liquidity/Solvency Ratios

Liquidity is a relative measure of the proximity of current assets and current liabilities to cash and is an indication of company's ability to meet its short-term obligations. Since most of the liabilities of a company are paid in cash, a good measure of this ability is how rapidly a company can convert its other assets into cash, if the need arises. Note that two exceptions need to be understood: Unearned revenue represents amounts already collected from the customer but the earning process for that amount is not complete; deferred income tax is not paid as such until the deferral evolves into calculation of the current income tax liability, which is paid. Financial analysts focus on short-term, medium-term, and long-term liquidity, given the time horizon of when the debt has to be paid. When the time horizon is short, only a few types of assets can be converted quickly to cash; hence only those are used in computing the short-term liquidity ratios. As the time horizon increases, more and more assets can be sold or realized through collection of cash and converted to cash; hence those are incorporated in the computation of medium- and long-term liquidity.

Solvency is the ability of a company to meet its long-term obligations as they come due or the ability of a company to meet its long-term fixed expenses and to meet long-term expansion and growth. In essence, it measures the extent to which a company has enough assets to cover its liabilities. Solvency often is confused with liquidity, but it is not the same thing. Various account combinations, primarily ratios, are used to measure both liquidity and solvency, and some of these key ratios are illustrated throughout this topic.

Working Capital Analysis

Working capital is a measure of a company's ability in the short run to pay its obligations. It looks at short-term financial health. Working capital is calculated as shown:

Working Capital = Current Assets − Current Liabilities

Working Capital Ratio = Net Working Capital / Total Assets

Working capital is also referred to as net working capital (NWC).

Current assets are defined as cash or other current investments, such as inventory and accounts receivable (A/R), that can be converted to cash within a year. **Current liabilities** are obligations that will be paid within a year, such as accounts payables, income tax payable, notes payable, and interest payables. A positive value of working capital indicates that there are enough current assets to cover current obligations. Current measures of working capital can be compared to measurements from previous periods to determine if there has been a change that should cause concern.

To examine working capital, we compare two companies:

- AEW, Inc. has $1,000,000 in current assets and $500,000 in current liabilities. AEW's working capital is $500,000 ($1,000,000 current assets − $500,000 current liabilities).
- KF, Inc. has $20,000,000 in current assets and $19,500,000 in current liabilities. KF's working capital is also $500,000 ($20,000,000 current assets − $19,500,000 current liabilities).

Obviously, there is a difference between working capital of $500,000 for AEW, with $1,000,000 in current assets, and KF, with $20,000,000 in current assets. In order to understand what working capital of $500,000 means for a company's liquidity, the analyst should study the current ratio, quick (acid-test) ratio, and cash ratios to examine relationships between current assets and current liabilities.

Current Ratio

The **current ratio** measures the degree to which current assets cover current liabilities. A higher ratio indicates greater ability to pay current liabilities with current assets, thus greater liquidity.

$$\text{Current Ratio} = \frac{\text{Current Assets}}{\text{Current Liabilities}}$$

Using the numbers from the example:

- AEW has a current ratio of 2 ($1,000,000 / $500,000). AEW has sufficient current assets to pay its current liabilities twice.
- KF's current ratio is 1.026 ($20,000,000 / $19,500,000); KF has sufficient current assets to pay current liabilities only once.

AEW and KF have the same working capital, but AEW is better positioned against uncertainty if it is not able to obtain additional assets (via sales) in the near-term future. KF must generate additional current assets before the next cycle of debt obligations is due. It appears that AEW is more liquid than KF.

There are limitations to using the current ratio to assess liquidity. Because cash is normally the only acceptable means of payment, it is important to consider the composition of current assets and determine whether those listed as current assets can be converted to cash readily.

For example, if most of the current assets are composed of prepaid expenses, then the current ratio overstates the liquidity of the company because the prepaid expenses cannot be converted to cash to settle the liabilities.

Furthermore, the current ratio cannot predict or indicate patterns of future cash flows, nor can it measure the adequacy of future liquidity. For example, if there is a significant amount of accounts receivable (A/R) from one customer and that customer files for bankruptcy, there would be significant delay in receiving the payment. Even though the current ratio is high because of the receivables, the debt-paying ability of the company is compromised due to the noncollection of a significant receivable.

The current ratio examines only the current relationship between current assets and current liabilities. Problems with liquidity will affect other aspects of the company's financial situation and ultimately may affect the company's ability to pay long-term obligations (solvency) or use its assets efficiently (operating activity). Traditionally, for a company in the manufacturing industry, a current ratio of 2.0 or above is considered healthy. However, in the current economic environment of e-business, a lower current ratio is acceptable.

Quick (Acid-Test) Ratio

The **quick ratio**, or **acid-test ratio**, examines liquidity from a more immediate aspect than does the current ratio by eliminating inventory and prepaid expenses from current assets. The quick ratio removes inventory because it turns over at a slower rate than receivables or cash and assumes that the company will be able to sell the items to a customer and collect cash. Although there are a few different ways to compute the quick (acid-test) ratio (by making adjustments to the numerator), the formula listed next is the one that is used on the CMA exam.

Especially with accounts receivable, caution must be exercised when the accounts receivable balance includes material receivables with unusual trade terms or material receivables from officers, shareholders or employees of the company, and any other related parties to the reporting entity. The issue is that with other-than-normal term accounts receivable, the pattern of collection and the risk associated with collection may differ from normal accounts receivable. One or more practical exercises included at the end of this topic may include other-than-normal receivables as part of current assets. These exercises should force candidates to consider the liquidity of non-normal accounts receivable within the context of the quick ratio or acid-test ratio.

$$\text{Quick (Acid-Test) Ratio} = \frac{\text{Cash} + \text{Marketable Securities} + \text{Accounts Receivable}}{\text{Current Liabilities}}$$

Current assets include cash equivalents and marketable securities. Cash equivalents include money in petty cash, checking accounts, savings accounts, and other similar accounts. Marketable securities are highly liquid short-term investments, which generally can become cash in a very short time (several minutes). A typical guideline for a reasonable quick ratio is 1 or greater, but this may vary by industry. The quick ratio, like all ratios, should be judged by comparing it to the firm's past values for the ratio and to the values for similar companies and industry averages. Although the quick ratio is a strong indicator of liquidity, it is not perfect. In reality, qualitative information, such as credit terms with suppliers and customers, is a useful indicator of liquidity.

The current ratio, quick ratio, and working capital calculations are by far the most common liquidity measures; however, several other ratios give analysts further information. Among these are the cash ratio and the cash flow ratio.

Cash Ratio

The **cash ratio** analyzes liquidity in a more conservative manner than the quick ratio, by looking at a company's immediate liquidity. The cash ratio compares only cash and marketable securities to current liabilities, eliminating all current accounts receivables and inventory from the asset portion. When using this formula, cash and cash equivalents are used for the term "cash" in the numerator.

$$\text{Cash Ratio} = \frac{\text{Cash} + \text{Marketable Securities}}{\text{Current Liabilities}}$$

To apply the cash ratio to AEW's and KF's financial information:

AEW has $1,000,000 in current assets, which includes $250,000 in cash and $300,000 in marketable securities. The remaining current assets include receivables and inventory. AEW's cash ratio is calculated as shown:

$$\text{AEW Cash Ratio} = \frac{\$250,000 + \$300,000}{\$500,000} = \frac{\$550,000}{\$500,000} = 1.1$$

KF's cash and cash receivables total $2,000,000, and its marketable securities total $9,000,000. Remaining current assets represent receivables and inventory. KF's cash ratio is calculated as shown:

$$\text{KF Cash Ratio} = \frac{\$2,000,000 + \$9,000,000}{\$19,500,000} = \frac{\$11,000,000}{\$19,500,000} = 0.564$$

A firm generally is not expected to have enough cash equivalents and marketable securities to cover current liabilities. Although this limits the usefulness of the cash ratio, the ratio is helpful for companies that have slow inventory turnover or slow collection of receivables. A cash ratio that is too high may indicate that a company is not using its resources productively in its operations. A cash ratio that is too low, however, could indicate a problem with meeting current liabilities. Some companies have either a revolving credit line agreement or an overdraft facility with their bank that allows the company to draw proceeds on demand from the credit line or to go into an overdraft that was previously agreed with the bank. These agreements will result in interest expense charges on the resulting amounts owed to the bank. The existence of either a revolving credit agreement or an overdraft facility is disclosed in the notes to the financial statements but will normally only appear on the balance sheet when amounts are in fact owed to the bank because of these agreements. Analysts need to consider the extent to which the company has access to such agreements for short-term financing. Access to such agreements may allow the company to keep much lower amounts of cash and marketable securities than would otherwise be expected. Another limitation of the cash ratio is that it contains marketable securities, and those may have to be liquidated to pay the debt. As the value of marketable securities is volatile (changes day to day), this ratio (computed based on year-end prices), may not be valid over a longer time horizon.

Cash Flow Ratio

The **cash flow ratio** measures a firm's ability to meet its debt obligations with cash generated in the normal course of business.

$$\text{Cash Flow Ratio} = \frac{\text{Operating Cash Flow}}{\text{Current Liabilities}}$$

The numerator amount normally will be operating cash flow shown on the current period statement of cash flows.

A higher operating cash flow ratio indicates a greater likelihood that the firm will be able to meet its obligations with cash generated from normal business operations. This ratio measures the ability of the company to meet its short-term obligations based on cash generated in the normal course of business. A deteriorating cash flow ratio, over time, indicates impending liquidity problems. If a company has a net operating cash outflow, this calculation would not be done because it is not valid.

Sensitivity Analysis on Liquidity Ratios

When analyzing the ratios, it is important to gauge how sensitive these ratios are to changes in their components. An increase in the numerator of a ratio will increase the value of the ratio, whereas an increase in the denominator of a ratio will reduce the value of the ratio, and vice versa. Since a higher number is preferable for these ratios, a decrease in the numerator or an increase in the denominator adversely affects the ratio and inferences made.

Thus, an increase in liabilities would adversely affect the ratio, whereas an increase in current assets or cash flows (the term in the numerator) would improve the ratios. The amount of increase or decrease in a particular ratio depends on the value of the ratio.

It should be noted that an equal increase in both the numerator and the denominator of the ratio would worsen the ratio, if the ratio is greater than 1. This may seem counterintuitive so you may find it helpful to think through the example that appears below. Similarly, an equal decrease in both the numerator and denominator would improve a ratio that is greater than 1.

Sometimes companies use this mathematical fact to improve the appearance of the liquidity ratios. As an example, paying off current liabilities right before the balance sheet date would improve the current and the quick ratios.

For example: Company Q has current assets of $1,000,000 and current liabilities of $600,000, yielding a current ratio of 1.67.

$$\text{Current Ratio} = \$1,000,000 / \$600,000$$
$$= 1.67$$

If the company were to pay off $200,000 of current liabilities just prior to preparing its financials, the current assets will reduce to $800,000 and the current liabilities will reduce to $400,000, improving the current ratio to 2.0.

$$\text{Current Ratio} = [\$1,000,000 - \$200,000] / [\$600,000 - \$200,000]$$
$$= \$800,000 / \$400,000$$
$$= 2.0$$

It is important to note that when companies engage in such activities for the sole purpose of improving the financial ratios, it is called **window dressing**, and the behavior may be ethically questionable. Analysts without access to inside information from the company may only be able to speculate on whether window dressing has been used. A careful inspection of increases in especially short-term debt shortly after the reporting period ends would raise the likelihood that the debt paydown followed early in the next period by a new incurrence of debt are related transactions.

Capital Structure Analysis

In addition to assessing a firm's ability to meet its short-term obligations, it is important to evaluate its ability to pay long-term debts as they mature. Doing this requires comparing the amount of long-term obligations and the company's ability to generate cash in the long term. This ability is greatly affected by the amount of long-term debt the company has in relation to equity.

Capital structure is the mix of long-term debt, on which interest and principal payments must be made, and equity, in the form of common and preferred stock, which the firm uses to finance operations. The capital structure affects both the risk and returns of the firm and is directly related to leverage. Leverage is also sometimes referred to as gearing.

Financial leverage is the use of debt (fixed cost funds) to increase returns to owners (stockholders). Debt that is too low may result in a company not being able to take full advantage of opportunities. Debt that is too high may affect the company's ability to weather difficult economic times and continue to pay its obligations as debt or interest payments come due. There is no standard guideline or optimal leverage number; it varies by industry and firm.

Firms have a mix of debt and equity financing. Debt holders, including financial institutions and corporate bond investors, are often, but not always, promised a return based on the stated interest rate for the debt. There are costs associated with issuing debt and equity. Debt is usually cheaper but the cost will increase as the firm's ratio of debt to equity increases. Most companies maintain a balance of debt and equity based on the cost of capital for each and the level of risk they wish to maintain.

Debt as Leverage

A company uses leverage in two ways: financial and operating.

Financial leverage is raising capital through debt rather than equity. While debt holders are entitled to interest, the owners share the earnings of the company. Hence, when a company can earn a higher rate of return on its invested capital through its operations than the interest rate on its debt, it could increase the return for its investors by financing the growth of company operations through borrowed capital.

Operating leverage is the existence of fixed operating costs. Because these costs are fixed, the higher the percentage of operating leverage, the greater the effect changes in sales revenues have on operating income.

The focus on leverage in this section is on financial leverage. The cost of financial leverage is the interest expense on debt which must be paid regardless of sales.

Degree of Operating Leverage

Business risk is often measured by the degree of operating leverage (DOL). DOL is defined as the percentage change in operating income given a percentage change in sales. DOL is caused by the organization's cost structure (the relationship of fixed and variable costs).

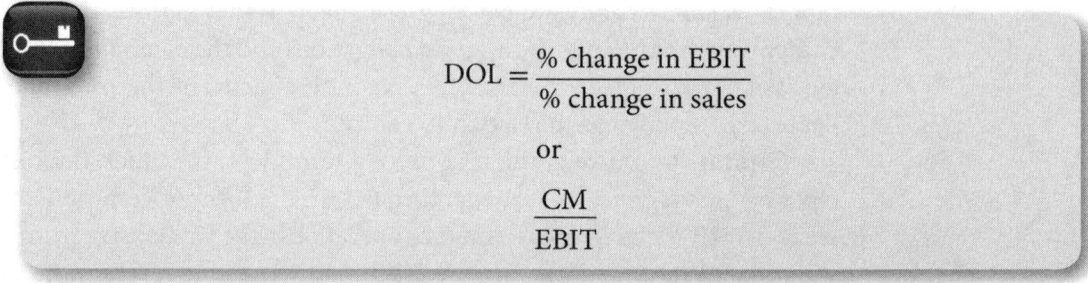

$$DOL = \frac{\% \text{ change in EBIT}}{\% \text{ change in sales}}$$

or

$$\frac{CM}{EBIT}$$

Contribution margin (CM) is calculated by taking sales less all variable costs. Earnings before interest and taxes (EBIT) equals CM less fixed costs.

For example: If a company has sales of $500,000, variable costs of $250,000, and fixed costs of $125,000, its DOL is calculated as shown:

$$DOL = CM/EBIT = (\$500,000 - \$250,000)/(\$500,000 - \$250,000 - \$125,000)$$
$$DOL = \$250,000/\$125,000 = 2$$

A DOL of 2 implies that every 1% increase in sales will result in a 2% (2 × 1%) increase in EBIT. Also, every 1% decrease in sales will result in a 2% (2 × 1%) decrease in EBIT. Companies with a high DOL often have a high degree of business risk. For example, a manufacturing company with excess capacity and high DOL will increase net income with one additional sale. That opportunity for high variability in net income is defined as increased business risk.

Degree of Financial Leverage

Financial risk is often measured by the degree of financial leverage (DFL). DFL is defined as the percentage change in net income (NI) divided by the percentage change in EBIT or as the ratio of EBIT divided by EBT. Financial leverage increases by increasing the balance between tax-deductible debt payments (interest) relative to nondeductible equity payments (dividends). Increasing DFL will increase net income but exposes the company to a higher risk of default on the debt instruments, which increases financial risk.

DFL is calculated by:

$$DFL = \frac{\text{\% Change in Net Income}}{\text{\% Change in EBIT}}$$

or

$$DFL = \frac{EBIT}{EBT}$$

Assume that the company used in the DOL example has interest payments of $25,000. Its DFL is calculated as:

$$DFL = \$125,000/(\$125,000 - \$25,000)$$
$$DFL = \$125,000/\$100,000 = 1.25$$

A DFL of 1.25 implies that every 1% increase in EBIT will result in a 1.25% (1.25 × 1%) increase in NI. Also, every 1% decrease in EBIT will result in a 1.25% (1.25 × 1%) decrease in NI.

Financial Leverage Ratio

On the CMA exam, the **financial leverage ratio** is computed as:

$$\text{Financial Leverage Ratio} = \frac{\text{Assets}}{\text{Equity}}$$

A higher ratio implies that the assets of the company are financed primarily through debt. A financial leverage ratio of 2.0 reflects that the liabilities of the company are equal to the equity. A ratio of greater than 2.0 implies that liabilities are larger than equity; a ratio of less than 2.0 implies higher equity than the liabilities of the company.

Financial leverage has a magnifying effect on both positive and negative earnings. When the earnings are positive, a marginal percentage change in revenue translates to a greater percentage change on earnings per share or on return on equity measures.

Likewise, since the servicing of debt is a fixed cost, leverage also has a magnifying effect on losses. If the financial leverage ratio, for example, is 3.0 and the company experiences a loss, it will experience a greater percentage loss in net income than the percentage decline in revenue. An increase in the financial leverage ratio, therefore, represents not only an increased opportunity for leveraging returns but also an increased risk of magnifying any losses, which may jeopardize the company's ability to meet long-term debt.

Ratio Analysis on Debt/Liabilities

Analysts can examine capital structure by comparing debt to assets (asset-based analysis) or to equity (equity-based analysis). Various stakeholders evaluate capital structure ratios (also known as leverage ratios) in different ways. For example, creditors or potential creditors wish to see low debt ratios, whereas stockholders and managers seek optimal debt levels, using as much debt in a firm's capital structure as can be managed effectively. Optimal debt ratios vary by industry. Firms in noncyclical industries, for example, tend to have higher debt ratios than those in cyclical industries. When performing cross-sectional analysis, therefore, one should compare only firms in the same industries.

The three primary ratios used to measure leverage are debt to total assets ratio, debt to equity ratio, and times interest earned (interest coverage) ratio. These and other debt ratios are reviewed next.

Total Debt to Total Capital Ratio

The **total debt to total capital ratio** measures the proportion of debt compared to the total capital of a corporation. It is a measurement of the financial leverage of a corporation.

$$\text{Total Debt to Total Capital Ratio} = \frac{\text{Current Liabilities} + \text{Long-Term Liabilities}}{\text{Total Debt} + \text{Total Equity}}$$

Companies can finance their operations through either debt or equity. This ratio provides an understanding of how a company is financing its operations and provides insights into the financial strength of the company. The higher the ratio, the higher the debt being used to finance the operations of the company. Thus a higher ratio typically means financial weakness of the company and increases the default risk.

Debt to Equity Ratio

The **debt to equity ratio** also measures the firm's ability to pay long-term debt and how well long-term creditors are protected. It measures the relationship of debt to equity when financing asset purchases. For example, a debt to equity ratio of 2 indicates that a firm historically has paid two parts debt to one part equity when financing asset purchases. The lower the ratio, the less reliant the company is on debt.

$$\text{Debt to Equity Ratio} = \frac{\text{Total Debt}}{\text{Equity}}$$

The debt to equity ratio can be compared to previous years' records for the same company. It also can be compared to competitors' and industry averages. A higher ratio indicates that the firm is more highly leveraged, and there is a higher risk of bankruptcy.

Long-Term Debt to Equity Ratio

The **long-term debt to equity ratio** compares long-term debt only to shareholders' equity.

$$\text{Long-Term Debt to Equity Ratio} = \frac{\text{Total Debt} - \text{Current Liabilities}}{\text{Equity}}$$

A company with a low long-term debt to equity ratio has the ability to raise debt capital if it is needed. Its fixed financing costs are lower because there are lower interest payments. However, the firm's return on capital probably will be lower because it is not using debt to its full capacity. Additionally, the interest expense from debt is tax deductible whereas dividend payments, at least in the United States, are not tax deductible.

Debt to Total Assets Ratio

The **debt to total assets ratio** measures the proportion of assets financed through debt.

$$\text{Debt to Total Assets Ratio} = \frac{\text{Total Debt}}{\text{Total Assets}}$$

This ratio shows the percentage of assets financed by creditors and indicates how well creditors are protected in case the company becomes insolvent.

A lower debt to total assets ratio indicates a better position for creditors, because the company has enough assets to cover long-term debt obligations. A higher ratio, which indicates that creditors are not as well protected, may make it more difficult and expensive for the company to issue additional debt securities.

An unusually low debt to total assets ratio is also problematic, because debt may be a cheap source of capital to finance growth.

Fixed-Charge Coverage Ratio

The **fixed-charge coverage ratio** measures a company's ability to satisfy fixed financing expenses, such as interest and leases. The fixed-charge coverage ratio is calculated as shown:

$$\text{Fixed Charge Coverage} = \frac{\text{Earnings Before Fixed Charges and Taxes}}{\text{Fixed Charges}}$$

Note: Fixed charges include interest, required principal repayment, and leases. Earnings before fixed charges and taxes are equal to the earnings before interest and taxes + fixed charges.

Times Interest Earned (Interest Coverage) Ratio

The **times interest earned ratio** measures a firm's ability to pay interest through its operations.

$$\text{Times Interest Earned Ratio} = \frac{\text{Earnings Before Interest and Taxes (EBIT)}}{\text{Interest Expense}}$$

If the ratio is sufficiently high, the firm should be able to meet its interest obligations. When combined with the debt ratio, the times interest earned ratio gives an analyst a strong indication of a firm's ability to manage debt effectively—or, in other words, to remain solvent.

The combination of a high debt ratio and low times interest earned ratio (when compared to industry averages) is a signal of poor solvency. If, however, a firm has a slightly higher debt ratio along with a higher times interest earned ratio, an analyst should have less worry.

Cash Flow to Fixed Charges Ratio

The **cash flow to fixed charges ratio** measures a firm's ability to satisfy fixed charges, such as interest and leases, from the cash flow generated through the normal operations of the business. The cash flow to fixed charges ratio is computed as shown:

$$\text{Cash Flow to Fixed Charges Ratio} = \frac{(\text{Cash from Ops.} + \text{Fixed Charges} + \text{Tax Payments})}{\text{Fixed Charges}}$$

Note: Cash from operations is after tax. Fixed charges include interest, required principal repayment, and leases.

Capital Structure and Risk

Increases in debt create higher fixed costs for interest and principal payments. A higher debt to equity ratio presents a less favorable position for the ability to pay long-term debt. Likewise, decreases in equity, as a result of redemption of stock or losses from operations, would also result in a higher debt to equity ratio and higher risk for the company's ability to pay long-term debt. Increases in equity, such as those from profits, without corresponding increases in debt would lower the debt to equity ratio, increasing the company's position for long-term debt-paying ability.

The capital structure of a firm is related to the "risk" of the firm, particularly bankruptcy risk. An increase in the amount of debt worsens the capital structure, and increases the possibility of bankruptcy. This is because higher debt means higher interest payments and payment of the principal, requiring a higher amount of cash flows to meet these obligations. Any strain on the cash flow is more dangerous for firms with higher debt because they still have to meet the debt payments.

Off–Balance Sheet Financing

Off–balance sheet financing is a form of financing in which large capital expenditures are kept off an organization's balance sheet through various classification methods. Organizations often use off–balance sheet financing to keep their debt to equity and leverage ratios low, especially if the inclusion of a large expenditures would violate debt covenants. Four of the common techniques employed to achieve off–balance sheet financing include transfer of accounts receivable, variable interest entities, leases, and joint ventures.

Transfer of Accounts Receivable

If the entity requires cash prior to the time that cash would normally be realized from accounts receivable collections, the entity can transfer the receivables to a financier such as a bank or a factor. The bank or factor charges one or more fees to the company in exchange for providing the company with the required cash. Note that the word *transfer* is used. A transfer can be a sale, with or without recourse, or it can be pledging of receivables as collateral for a loan. If the transfer is a sale without recourse, then the company actually gives up the receivables in exchange for cash less the fees charged by the financier.

If the transfer is a sale with recourse, then the company still has responsibility for some of the risks of ownership of the receivables. For that reason the transfer cannot be recognized as a sale until the risks of ownership are resolved.

If the transfer is a transfer of collateral in exchange for a loan, then the company continues to recognize the receivables, disclosing in its notes to the financial statements that the receivables are collateral for a loan and also recognizes a new loan liability.

In each of the transfers described above, the possibility of incurring a liability without recognizing the liability arises, thus resulting in off–balance sheet financing.

Variable Interest Entities

Variable interest entity (VIE) is a term used in the ASC to refer to an entity (the investee) in which the investor holds a controlling interest that is not based on the majority of voting rights. It is closely related to the concept of a special purpose entity. The importance of identifying a VIE is that a company needs to consolidate such entities if it is the primary beneficiary of the VIE. Prior to the ASC guidance on VIEs, companies were able to form SPEs that circumvented consolidation. The main concern with SPEs is to determine if it meets the requirements for consolidation as a VIE. If it does, then the primary beneficiary of the VIE consolidates the VIE. At that point many of the off–balance sheet aspects of the SPE become moot because the entity is included in the consolidated financial statements.

The CMA LOS does not directly refer to VIEs but it briefly mentions SPEs within the context of the possibility of keeping certain assets, liabilities, revenues, and expenses out of the reporting entity's financial statements.

Leases

Lease accounting is in the process of dramatically changing, particularly from the lessee's accounting and reporting perspective. In this topic we briefly mention the fact that lease accounting will change sometime in the next two years. Until that time, the CMA requirements will be based on the extant lease accounting and reporting standards.

Firms usually use leases to obtain the right to use an asset without having to show the asset and the corresponding liability on the balance sheet. If the firm were to purchase the asset, it would have to either use cash or borrow more money to pay for the asset, thus converting short-term assets into long-term assets, recognizing a new liability and thus worsening the company's short-term liquidity, reducing its short-term liquidity ratios. If the firm were to use long-term financing to purchase, it would worsen the debt to equity or other solvency ratios. So both liquidity and solvency would be damaged.

To avoid some of these adverse consequences within the financial statements, firms will sometimes lease the asset. Generally accepted accounting principles (GAAP) require that a determination be made on whether the lease is a capital lease. When the lease meets one of the four conditions established for capital leases, the transaction is recorded by recognizing both the asset (actually a right of use of the asset) and a lease liability. The lease payments are then split between liability reduction and interest expense. Additionally the leased asset is depreciated as if it were PPE. Only if the lease is determined not to be a capital lease, will it then be classified as an operating lease. An operating lease for the lessee is an executory contract. Neither an asset nor a liability is recognized. The lease payments are accrued and paid each period and an expense account is debited while either cash or accrued liability is recognized. The lease obligation is reported only in the notes to the financial statements, thus off-book financing is achieved.

Joint Ventures

A **joint venture** is a business entity that is owned, operated, or jointly controlled by a small group of investors with a specific business purpose. Sometimes a corporation is a partner in a venture, which allows it to be active in management and involved in decision making but not report the venture on the financial statement of the corporation. An investment in a corporate joint venture that exceeds 50% of the venture's outstanding shares must be treated as a subsidiary investment, leading to consolidation in the financial statement. However, firms sometimes are careful to hold less than 50% (say, 48.5%) of outstanding shares to avoid such consolidation, thereby providing off–balance sheet financing.

Recall, however, the previous discussion about VIEs being consolidated by the primary beneficiary. If it is determined that the joint venture is a VIE then it must be consolidated, in which case the assets and liabilities, revenues and expenses, of the joint venture are accounted for and reported by the primary beneficiary. If the joint venture is not a VIE then consolidation normally is not required and the normal alternative accounting and reporting is the equity method.

The equity method recognizes the investor's proportionate share of revenues, expenses, gains, losses, and elements of other comprehensive income but does not record the assets and liabilities of the joint venture. Thus the investor has off–balance sheet assets and liabilities. The investor recognizes an investment in the joint venture, which is accounted for also in accordance with the equity method.

Operating Activity Analysis

Another way to analyze liquidity is to focus on the management of key current assets, namely inventory and A/R. A manager who is successful in managing inventory and collecting A/R in a timely manner will also improve liquidity. Operating activity analysis is done over a period of an operating cycle, which is the time that elapses between when goods are acquired and when cash is received from the sale of the goods.

Accounts Receivable Turnover Ratio

The **A/R turnover ratio** measures the average number of times that receivables from sales are collected during a year.

$$\text{Accounts Receivable Turnover Ratio} = \frac{\text{Credit Sales}}{\text{Average Gross Accounts Receivables}}$$

An underlying assumption of this ratio is that sales occur evenly throughout the year, hence average A/R can be estimated using the average of beginning and ending A/R balances. This is a simple average method. When sales are seasonal, or uneven, the beginning and ending balances may not be representative of the average A/R balance. This is one of the reasons that most retailers have a fiscal year ending on January 31 and not December 31, because the sales in that industry are seasonal.

A/R turnover also can be analyzed in days instead of times per year. There are two conventions used for number of days in a year—360 and 365. When performing calculations, be consistent and state your assumptions. **Note:** The CMA exam uses the 365-day convention in all formulas requiring an assumption for the number of days in a year.

Days' sales in receivables (also known as average collection period) measures the liquidity of receivables. A financial analyst compares days' sales in receivables with the company's credit terms to determine how efficiently the company manages its receivables. If a company's credit term is 30 days, days' sales in receivables should not be substantially over 30 days. If significant differences are found, attention should be focused on collections policies and/or credit policy. As is the case with many ratios, the analyst should examine extreme values in days' sales in receivables. For example, a firm with exceptionally low days' sales in receivables may have excessively tight credit policies that can result in lost sales.

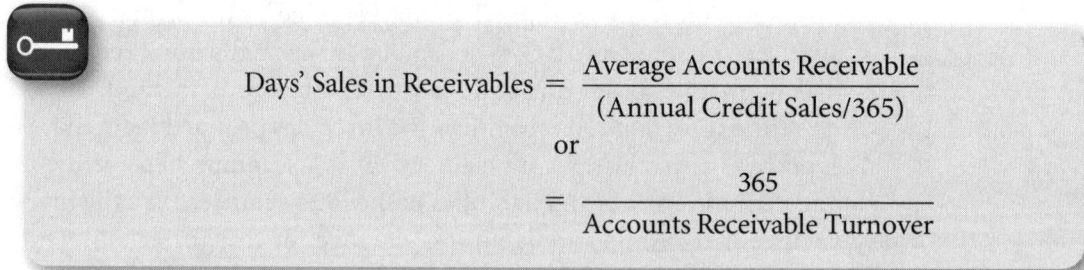

$$\text{Days' Sales in Receivables} = \frac{\text{Average Accounts Receivable}}{(\text{Annual Credit Sales}/365)}$$

or

$$= \frac{365}{\text{Accounts Receivable Turnover}}$$

The ratios provided by the IMA for the CMA exam state "credit sales" be used in the denominator. But in practice the sales figure is usually net sales. It may be useful to look for hints in the CMA exam questions or in the data set used for this ratio to determine whether to use gross sales or net sales.

The financial analyst must also make a distinction between cash sales and credit sales; only credit sales should be included in these ratios. Further, days' sales in receivables is not relevant for primarily cash businesses, such as fast food restaurants. If cash sales are included, liquidity will be overstated. An increase in the amount of time it takes to turn over receivables indicates deteriorating liquidity.

Inventory Turnover Ratio

The **inventory turnover ratio** measures the average number of times that inventory was sold during a year. Inventory is one of the most significant assets in determining liquidity, because the inventory account often is more than half of the total current assets. The inventory of a retailer is the merchandise available for sale. In a manufacturing environment, inventory includes raw materials, work in process, and finished goods. Only the finished goods inventory (if a number is separately available) should be used in computing this ratio. All three inventory categories must be disclosed in the notes if material.

As with A/R, inventory turnover can be calculated as times per year or as number of days of turnover. As previously noted the average inventory here is a simple average.

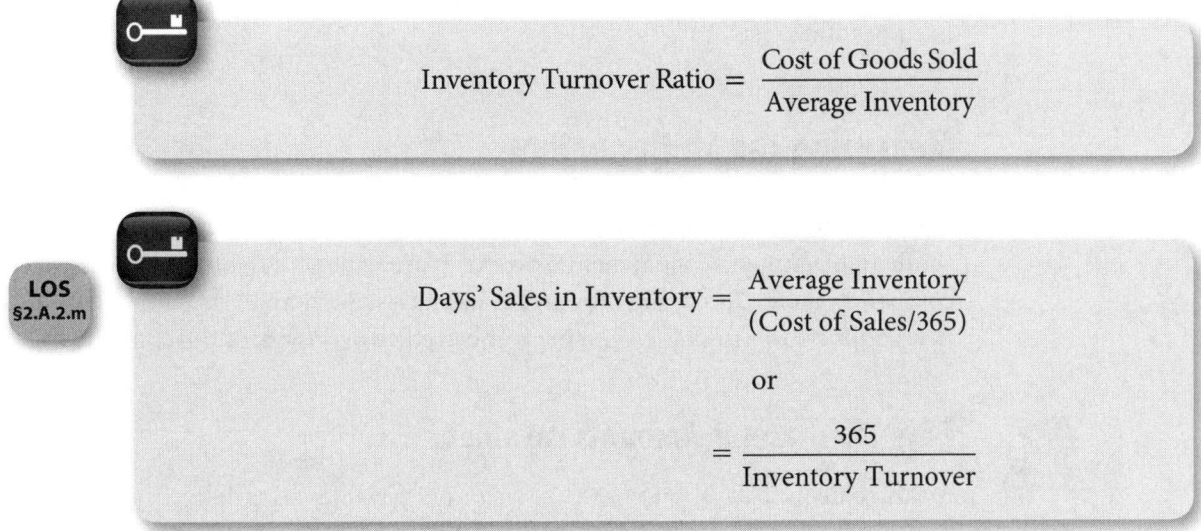

$$\text{Inventory Turnover Ratio} = \frac{\text{Cost of Goods Sold}}{\text{Average Inventory}}$$

$$\text{Days' Sales in Inventory} = \frac{\text{Average Inventory}}{(\text{Cost of Sales}/365)}$$

or

$$= \frac{365}{\text{Inventory Turnover}}$$

If sales are fairly constant, a lower number of days or a greater number of turnovers of inventory indicates better inventory control and stronger liquidity. Generally, successful companies are those that are able to keep their inventory low with high turnovers while still meeting customer orders on a timely basis. Inventory management usually involves supply chain management technique. The concept is to reduce the company's inventory on hand requirements by reducing ordering/delivery times. This change alone improves inventory turnover.

$$\text{Operating Cycle} = \text{Days' Sales in Receivables} + \text{Days' Sales in Inventory}$$

The operating cycle indicates how quickly the company will receive cash once inventory is acquired or a product is manufactured (this depends on the type of business). A shorter operating cycle translates into improved liquidity.

Other Turnover Ratios

Even though the inventory and receivable turnovers are common and widely used, other turnover ratios may be useful in certain industries. These are the *total asset turnover ratio* and the *fixed asset turnover ratio*. For these, total sales are divided by either average total assets or average fixed assets to obtain the turnover ratio.

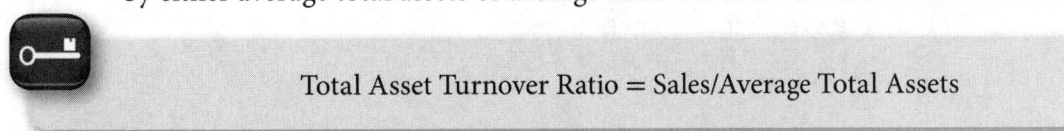

$$\text{Total Asset Turnover Ratio} = \text{Sales}/\text{Average Total Assets}$$

> Fixed Asset Turnover Ratio = Sales/Average Net Plant, Property, and Equipment

In capital-intensive industries with significant investments in fixed assets, it may be useful to determine the relationship between sales and the investment in fixed or total assets.

Measuring the Ability to Pay

Any judgment regarding payment of current liabilities should be made in light of the degree of urgency of payment. Several measurements can be made to assess the company's policy in paying off current liabilities. Such analysis could be used by new suppliers to assess the timeliness and creditworthiness of the company.

Days' Purchases in Accounts Payables

Measurement of days' purchases in accounts payables usually indicates the payment terms that the company has with its suppliers, assuming that the company is not in default on its payments.

$$\text{Days' Purchases in Accounts Payables} = \frac{\text{Average Accounts Payables}}{(\text{Credit Purchases}/365)}$$

or

$$= \frac{365}{\text{Payables Turnover}}$$

Outside analysts may find it impossible to determine credit purchases. A reasonable approximation is to substitute total purchases instead of credit purchases. Total purchases can be estimated by adjusting the cost of goods sold by the changes in inventory balance. A large ratio would indicate that the company either has good relationship with its suppliers and enjoys liberal payment plan or is delinquent in making payments. Further investigation of the credit terms with its major suppliers would provide a reasonable assessment of which of these is true for a particular situation. A larger number than the firm's credit terms would indicate past-due obligations.

The formula also uses average accounts payables, which is the current-year plus the prior-year ending accounts payables divided by 2 (assuming even purchasing patterns throughout the year).

Earnings per Share

Earnings per share (EPS) is an important measure that investors use to determine whether to purchase a security. It is used as a basis for comparison in the price earnings and earnings yield ratios.

EPS expresses net income on a per-share basis. Notice in the formula that preferred dividends are subtracted from net income because preferred dividends take priority in payout and are not available to common shareholders.

$$\text{Earnings per Common Share} = \frac{\text{Net Income} - \text{Preferred Dividends}}{\text{Weighted Average Number of Common Shares Outstanding}}$$

Earnings Yield Ratio = EPS / Current Market Price per Common Share

Market-to-Book Ratio = Current Stock Price / Book Value per Share

Price to Earnings Ratio = Market Price per Share / Earnings per Share

Price to EBITDA Ratio = Market Price per Share / EBITDA per Share

For example: If Company Q has $1,000,000 in net income and an average of 1,000,000 shares of common stock outstanding, it has generated $1 in earnings per share.

That is the simplest case. If the number of shares outstanding fluctuates during the year, the weighted average requires a calculation based on the fraction of the year each share was outstanding.

For example: To take a slightly more complicated case, if there were 800,000 shares outstanding from January through June and 1,200,000 shares outstanding between July and December, the weighted average would be calculated as shown next:

800,000 Shares (Jan. – June) × 6 Months / 12 Months = 400,000 Shares

1,200,000 Shares (July – Dec.) × 6 / 12 = 600,000 Shares

Weighted Average Shares Outstanding (Jan. – Dec.) = 400,000 Shares + 600,000 Shares
= 1,000,000 Shares

Diluted Earnings per Share

Calculating earnings per share (EPS) of common stock outstanding becomes more complicated if the various factors that may dilute the EPS by spreading the earnings over other types of stock-related securities are considered, such as stock options, warrants, some convertible bonds, and preferred stocks.

For example: At some time during the year Company Q issues a convertible bond issue that results in 100,000 shares of new common stock. The company now has 1,100,000 shares of common stock outstanding but no new earnings so the previous stockholders are sharing the company's earnings with 10% more stockholders. This results in a diluted EPS of $0.91 per share ($1,000,000 / 1,100,000), which is lower than the EPS of $1.00 previously calculated.

Similar situations can occur when certain options or warrants are exercised, are but in such a case, the current shareholders get a prorated allocation to prevent dilution of their investment.

$$\text{Diluted EPS} = \frac{\text{Net Income} - \text{Preferred Dividends}}{\text{Diluted Weighted Average Number of Common Shares Outstanding}}$$

Diluted EPS adjusts common shares by adding shares that may be issued for convertible securities and options. This is a pro forma calculation sometimes referred to as "as-if converted."

For example: Company CBA has net income for the year of $50,000,000 and pays out $5,000,000 in dividends on its preferred stock. On January 1, it has 2,000,000 shares of common stock outstanding; it issues another 2,000,000 on April 1 and a final 1,000,000 on August 1. There is an outstanding stock option for 50,000 shares and a "diluted" $1,000,000 convertible bond issue (with a yield when it was issued of more than two-thirds of the average yield on AA corporate bonds at that time). Assume that each $1,000 bond is convertible into 1,000 shares.

Its weighted average common stock outstanding is calculated as shown:

Weighted Average Common Stock Outstanding
= (2,000,000 × 3/12) + (4,000,000 × 4/12) + (5,000,000 × 5/12)
= 3,916,666 Shares

In addition to the stock and the option on 50,000 shares, there are 1,000 convertible bonds outstanding ($1,000,000 in bonds worth $1,000 each). These bonds could be exchanged for 1,000 shares of stock for each $1,000 worth of bonds, adding 1,000,000 shares of common stock to the outstanding amount and saving the firm the amount of after-tax interest that would have been payable to the bondholders. Because the shares of stock underlying those bonds appear in the denominator as if the bonds had been converted, the numerator has to add in the amount that would be saved on interest by the conversion of bonds into stock. Assuming that the bonds have a coupon rate of 5% and would have matured in one year from the date of conversion, the firm would save $30,000 ($50,000 minus taxes paid at a 40% rate).

Putting the weighted average common stock, option, and convertible bonds outstanding into the equation as the divisor under net income minus preferred dividends plus interest expense after tax savings due to conversion of the bonds on outstanding convertible bonds, we get:

$$\text{Diluted EPS} = \frac{\$50{,}000{,}000 - \$5{,}000{,}000 + \$30{,}000}{3{,}916{,}666 + 50{,}000 + 1{,}000{,}000}$$

$$= \$11.08 \text{ per Diluted Share}$$

EPS is the most commonly cited statistic in investing. The amount is a theoretical allocation of net earnings available to common shareholders on a per share basis. Some regard EPS as being a highly condensed income statement. Of course that probably is an overstatement. A higher EPS relative to other companies may well translate into a solid return on investment (ROI) through dividends, price gains, or both. If EPS rises over successive accounting periods, creditors and investors look favorably on the company, and management is assured that its policies are succeeding. If EPS begins falling, the reverse is true because the firm begins to look like a bad investment and a credit risk.

Dividend Payout Ratio

The **dividend payout ratio** is a near complement to the percentage of shareholders' equity. However, it considers EPS on a diluted basis, which is a more conservative measure than only comparing earnings against currently outstanding shares of common stock.

$$\text{Dividend Payout Ratio} = \frac{\text{Common Dividend}}{\text{Earnings Available to Common Shareholders}}$$

Dividend Yield

The **dividend yield** is a measure of the cash return realized by the investor, against the current market value of the stock, by the payout of the dividend. This ratio is helpful to investors seeking income from their securities investments.

$$\text{Dividend Yield} = \frac{\text{Annual Dividends per Share}}{\text{Market Price per Share}}$$

Some companies hold earnings to generate growth (growth stocks), whereas others pay out a majority of earnings in the form of dividends (income stocks) and the market price of common stock trades according to factors in the investment market. Therefore, no generalizations can be made about the appropriate dividend yield on a share of common stock.

Sustainable Equity Growth

Although some companies fail because of ever-declining revenues, companies also fail by attempting to grow too fast. Many small businesses, in particular, go under because they take on a contract with deadlines that cannot be met with their current staff, equipment, capital, and expertise. The **sustainable growth ratio (SGR)** indicates the maximum earnings growth a firm can have without resorting to other means of financing.

The key to sustainable growth is to retain sufficient earnings to reinvest in growth rather than paying out too much of earnings as dividends. The SGR can be calculated as 1 minus the dividend payout ratio multiplied by return on equity (ROE).

Sustainable Growth Rate = (1 − Dividend Payout Ratio) × ROE

If the firm pays out dividends at a rate of 30% of earnings, for example, it retains the other 70% (1 − 30% = 70%). The resulting increase in shareholders' equity will also earn a rate of return and can continue to generate growth in earnings. Ability to take on debt grows as shareholders' equity grows, allowing more borrowing without dangerous changes to the ratio of debt to total assets or debt to equity. If a firm grows at a rate greater than its sustainable growth rate, it will need additional capital from debt or equity. Unfortunately, not all firms can access the money needed to survive in that situation.

Return on Capital Investment

An important question concerning calculations of invested capital is: How well did the company do with the capital it had to work with? **Return on investment (ROI)** and **return on assets (ROA)** are measures of a business's efficiency in using its assets to create profits. The analyst compares ROI to alternative uses of the invested capital as well as the return realized by similar businesses. A relationship exists between risk and reward of investments. An investment can yield a small return, such as interest on U.S. Treasury securities, with virtually no risk (known as the riskless rate of return). However, riskier investments (those with more volatile returns) require higher returns in order to justify the higher risk. ROI measures relate the reward (income) to the amount of capital used to generate income (investment).

Components of Return on Capital Investment

The previous section explored ratios related to capital structure, which is understood as the relative amounts of debt and equity that firms use to build and operate a business. Creditors will analyze the liquidity and solvency of a firm to determine its ability to meet its financial obligations.

In addition to the creditors, the owners or the shareholders are the other important stakeholders for the firm. The analysis of how well the firm is meeting the needs of the owner is significant, and many measures exist to perform the analysis. One common way is to focus on the return on capital investment (ROCI) to measure how productively the firm employs its debt and equity.

There are myriad ways to assess ROCI and at least three ways to name it:

1. ROI is, simply, return on investment—essentially the degree of profit in relation to the capital deployed by the business.
2. ROA is return on assets—essentially the same set of factors as ROI (although calculations may vary the individual factors).
3. ROE is return on equity—essentially the degree of profit in relation to equity, which is less than total investment or total assets because it leaves leverage (debt) out of the picture.

While considering which measure is most applicable, a fundamental issue is: Return to whom? The response to the "whom" determines which of the measures is most informative. For example, when the "whom" are all stakeholders, the appropriate measures are the total assets or total invested capital. When focusing on the owners, however, the applicable measure would be the ROE.

Definitions of Invested Capital

Defining *invested capital* presents difficulties for the analyst, because there are differing views on how the elements of assets and profits should be defined. Invested capital (used in ROA or ROCI) can be defined as all assets, modified investment basis, or shareholders' equity only.

Analysts who use the modified investment basis to calculate ROCI or ROA believe that some components can skew the results. These analysts remove elements from total assets or make determinations of whether to use book value or market value for certain assets. The next elements of financial statements may be modified or not included in the investment base, depending on the analyst's preference:

- **Unproductive assets.** Unproductive assets include such items as an idle plant, surplus inventories, and goodwill. Some consider other intangible assets to be unproductive, but this would usually be inaccurate as intangibles such as patents, copyrights, trademarks, and capitalized development costs, when utilized, are productive.
- **Depreciable assets.** Assets that can be depreciated, such as buildings and equipment, will carry lower values on the books as they are depreciated, resulting in higher ROI against the same earnings.
- **Preferred shareholders' book value.** Some analysts exclude preferred shareholders' book value because, during liquidation, preferred shareholders are entitled only to the book value of the preferred shares, not to the total returns of the business.

Since the value of assets changes over the course of the year, the most appropriate measure may be at the beginning, ending, or the average. The choice can vary widely; however, when the absolute value of the assets is large relative to the changes in assets, the choice usually does not lead to a material difference in the ratio. Usually, though, most analysts average the value of the assets over the period—that is, the average of the beginning and the ending value. Note that while there may be various approaches to calculating ROI, ROA, and ROE, the formulas listed in this text are the ones that are tested on the CMA exam.

Profitability Analysis

The numerator of the return ratio is some measure of earnings or profits. The measure selected for the numerator should match the investment base in the denominator. For example, if total assets are used in the denominator, the income to all providers of the capital, including interest, ought to be included in the numerator. Thus, interest is usually added back to the net income when computing the ROA, which leads to a popular measure known as **earnings before interest, taxes, depreciation, and amortization (EBITDA)**.

The CMA Exam 2015 Ratio Definitions document is very important to your preparation and ultimate success on the CMA exams, especially as it relates to Financial Ratios. Be sure when you read a data set and related question that you clearly understand which investors are the subject of the question and what those investors' interests are. When return on common equity capital is computed, net income after deductions for interest and preferred dividends is used. The final ROI always must reflect all applicable costs and expenses, including income taxes, particularly when the return on shareholders' equity is computed. Profit is realized when an organization is generating more resources than it consumes during the course of a year. Profit is the amount by which revenue from sales exceeds the costs required to achieve those sales, and the profit margin is the percentage of revenues represented by that excess of revenues over costs. Revenues and costs, however, are measured by various criteria.

Profit margins are commonly calculated using one of three different profit measures:

1. **Gross profit**, which equals net sales revenue minus the cost of goods sold (COGS). Note that the term *net sales revenue* is used here. These three measures are from the income statement and are not ratios although ratios are derived from these measures. In other ratios the term *sales* or *revenue* is used. The IMA's CMA Exam Ratio Definitions document uses *sales* and this should guide your use on the exam.
2. **Operating income**, which equals gross profit minus various administrative expenses, not including interest or taxes (because they are not part of operations). Operating income is sometimes called earnings before interest and taxes (EBIT).
3. **Net income**, which reduces revenues by all expenses—cost of goods, operating expenses, and interest and taxes.

The discussion that follows looks at the profit margin calculations that relate each of these to net sales. Net sales are calculated by taking revenue minus discounts, allowances, and refunds on returned items.

The cost of sales analysis is a key to analyzing the profitability of a business. The COGS represents a large expense for merchandising and manufacturing businesses. Changes in the COGS in such industries have a large impact on profits. The COGS as a percentage of sales revenue is the single most significant cost category.

The gross profit margin percentage is a measurement of gross profit as a percentage of sales:

$$\text{Gross Profit} = \text{Sales} - \text{Cost of Sales}$$

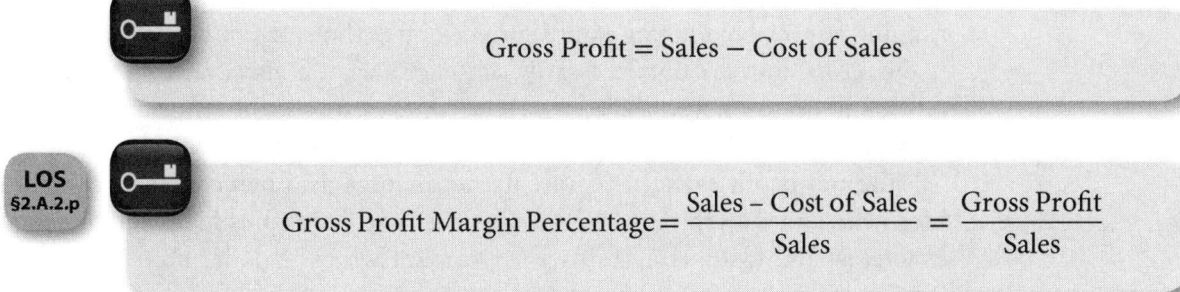

$$\text{Gross Profit Margin Percentage} = \frac{\text{Sales} - \text{Cost of Sales}}{\text{Sales}} = \frac{\text{Gross Profit}}{\text{Sales}}$$

For example: Consider Company A, which realizes $10,000,000 in sales, with a COGS of $4,500,000 and gross profit of $5,500,000. That $5,500,000 represents 55% of net sales ($5,500,000 / $10,000,000 = 55%). Thus, Company A's gross profit margin for the period is 55%.

As with all financial ratios, the gross margin derives its meaning by comparison to performance of the company in past years as well as by comparison to industry averages. One of the things an analyst will look for is the trend of the gross profit margin: Is it increasing, decreasing, or remaining steady? An increase in gross profit margin indicates that the firm is doing a better job of managing the cost of sales, while a decrease would indicate that the cost of sales is increasing.

The analyst must also look for reasons that explain changes. Here are some reasons that gross profit margin may decrease:

- Sales prices have not increased at the same rate as the change in inventory costs.
- Sales prices have declined due to competition.
- The mix of products sold has changed to more products with lower profit margins.
- Inventory is being stolen. (If this is the case, the cost of goods will be higher against the same sales.)

The **operating profit margin** is the ratio of operating income to sales.

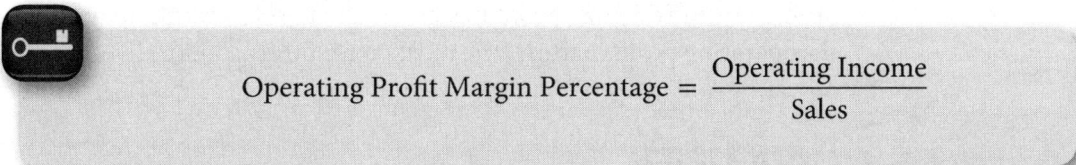

$$\text{Operating Profit Margin Percentage} = \frac{\text{Operating Income}}{\text{Sales}}$$

For example: Consider Company A, which realized $10,000,000 in sales, with a COGS of $4,500,000 and a gross profit margin of 55% of net sales. If Company A also had operating expenses of $3,500,000, its operating profit margin would be 20%, or ($10,000,000 − [$4,500,000 + $3,500,000]) divided by $10,000,000.

In addition to making a judgment about the absolute amount spent on operational expenses, investors and analysts would compare the operating margin as it changed over time and in relation to the gross margin. If the operating margin were to fall in relation to gross margin (indicating increasing expenses in the numerator), the cause would clearly be in the area of operations expenses, because COGS figures in both calculations. There may be reasons for a steady gross margin and a falling operating profit margin, such as a one-time expense for opening new stores or running a special marketing campaign. As long as those activities generate revenue in the future, they are not necessarily cause for alarm. If, however, expenses rise in relation to net sales, it would be wise to study the expenses contributing to the rise to be certain that they are not indicators of inefficient operations.

The **net profit margin** represents net income as a percentage of sales. Net income includes all the expenses in the other two ratios plus financial items such as interest and taxes. (Interest is a net amount which includes both interest and investment income as well as interest expenses.)

$$\text{Net Profit Margin Percentage} = \frac{\text{Net Income}}{\text{Sales}}$$

If Company A were to add provision for income taxes of $500,000, offset by net interest income of $50,000, its net income would be $1,550,000.

Income Statement

Sales	$10,000,000
COGS	4,500,000
Gross Profit	5,500,000
Operating Expenses	3,500,000
Operating Income	2,000,000
Net Interest Income	50,000
Income Before Tax	2,050,000
Income Tax Expense	500,000
Net Income	$1,550,000

The net profit margin would be 15.5% ($1,550,000/$10,000,000). Like operating profit margin and gross profit margin, the net profit margin may also diverge from the operating profit margin. The most common reason for divergence between the operating and net profit margins is an increase in tax rates or interest expenses.

Expense Analysis

Every company has expenses beyond the COGS. Major expenses for a company include:

- *Selling expenses.* These include advertising, marketing, and sales commissions.

- *Administrative expenses.* These include salaries, insurance, telephone, and write-off for bad debts. Salaries are usually the largest single expense for most businesses, particularly in service industries.
- *Depreciation expense.* Capital equipment, such as buildings and equipment (tangible assets), are depreciated over the life of the asset rather than expensed at the time of purchase.
- *Amortization.* Costs of intangible assets, such as the purchase of a software system, patents, or trademarks, are written off during the expected lifetime of the asset.
- *Maintenance.* Maintenance and repair of fixed assets have both fixed and variable costs. These activities can be postponed to save costs temporarily, but too much delay is a sign that assets may deteriorate before the end of their useful life.
- *Financing expenses.* These expenses include interest the company pays on debt.
- *Income taxes.* The effective tax rate may vary significantly from the statutory tax rate. Analysts may want to analyze the reasons for these differences.

Return on Investment

Return on investment (ROI) measures profitability by dividing the net profit of the business unit by the investment in assets made to attain that income. ROI is also called the accounting rate of return or the accrual accounting rate of return.

$$\text{Return on Investment (ROI)} = \frac{\text{Income of Business Unit}}{\text{Assets of Business Unit}}$$

It is important to note that the formula used to calculate ROI may have many variations as to how to derive profit for the numerator and assets for the denominator. However, the formula shown here is the one that is tested on the CMA exam.

ROI is expressed as a percentage, and the greater the percentage, the greater the return on investment. ROI is a popular measure of profitability because it combines revenues, investments, and costs all in one figure.

When ROI uses average total assets in its investment denominator, it becomes *ROA*, which shows how successful a company is at making a profit, using a given level of assets. Firms that are more efficient with their assets are more likely to be profitable.

When ROI uses ownership interest for the investment denominator, it is called *ROE*. ROE is calculated only for common equity because preferred stockholders have a set return that is the preferred dividend rate.

Return on Assets

Calculation of ROA in its simplest form, as shown next, uses net income and the value of all assets. ROA is essentially the same set of factors as ROI, although calculations may mix and match the factors differently.

$$\text{Return on Assets (ROA)} = \frac{\text{Net Income}}{\text{Average Total Assets}}$$

Net income is the bottom line of the income statement, and it includes revenue from sales reduced by all expenses: COGS, operating expenses, other expenses (offset by other income), provision for income taxes, loss (or income) from discontinued operations (net of tax), and extraordinary items (net of tax). The extraordinary reporting of items ended after 12/15/2015. However, extraordinary item reporting may continue for a few years until the change is fully implemented; extraordinary item reporting will no longer be tested after 2016. The effects on this ratio from changes in accounting principles are reported in retained earnings net of income tax effects. So this adjustment to ROA deviates from how the change is reported in the financial statements. Net income includes even the effects of changes in accounting principles (also net of tax). The effects are reported retrospectively to the earliest periods affected or to retained earnings for the earliest period of change.

Average total assets are calculated as the sum of assets at the beginning and ending of the period divided by 2.

ROA may be the most frequently cited measure of the success of firms except for EPS. ROA and ROE can be used to rank firms in the same industry; the higher the ratio, the greater the firm's success in making its total assets productive. The ROA ratio increases as income rises and the average asset value during the period remains the same. If, however, the firm increases the amount of its assets, the ratio will decline unless profits go up proportionally.

The ROA has two components: return on sales and the asset turnover ratio. Return on sales is a profitability measure, and the asset turnover ratio is an operational measure. The two can be multiplied to yield the ROA.

Separating ROA into these two components simplifies the analysis of the change in return on asset measure from one period to the next. Was the return on asset decrease due to a reduction of profit margin (return on sales) or because of employing a larger asset base (decrease in asset turnover ratio)? When a firm replaces its depreciated assets with brand-new ones, the asset base increases without necessarily increasing sales; this causes the asset turnover ratio to decrease, resulting in a lower ROA. However, since normal replacement of worn-out assets is a normal course of business, such decreases in ROA need not cause concern. This concept is developed more fully in the DuPont model.

DuPont Model for ROA

The term *DuPont model* does not appear in the CMA Exam Ratio Definitions document. However, the model can be very beneficial in solving the ROA and may be useful in helping you understand how changes in net income, average total assets, and sales can have an impact on ROA. This conceptual understanding will be beneficial in solving exam questions. The **DuPont model** breaks apart the simpler formula for ROA and instead calculates ROA by multiplying the net profit margin by asset turnover. There is also a revised version of the model that focuses more on ROE than ROA. We will look at the version for ROA first and then at the modified model that calculates ROE.

Here's how the DuPont model turns ROA measured as net income divided by total assets into profit margin times asset turnover. Sales are inserted into the equation as shown:

$$ROA = \frac{\text{Net Income}}{\text{Average Total Assets}} = \frac{\text{Net Income}}{\text{Sales}} \times \frac{\text{Sales}}{\text{Average Total Assets}}$$

ROA is composed of two components: net profit margin and total asset turnover:

Net Profit Margin = Net Income / Sales

Total Asset Turnover = Sales / Average Total Assets

Therefore:

ROA = Net Profit Margin × Total Asset Turnover

Net income divided by sales is the net profit margin. And sales divided by average total assets is total asset turnover. Note that net income divided by sales is also called net profit margin. Sales divided by average total assets is also called total asset turnover.

For example: If Company A has total assets of $1,000,000 and net income of $200,000, its ROA, calculated the simpler way, is 20%: ($200,000 / $1,000,000 = 20%). Assuming sales of $2,000,000 and calculating by the DuPont method produces the same result:

Net Profit Margin = Net Income / Sales
= $200,000 / $2,000,000
= 10%

Total Asset Turnover = Sales / Total Asset
= $2,000,000/$1,000,000
= 2 Times

ROA = Net Profit Margin × Total Asset Turnover
= 10% × 2 Times
= 20%

When analyzing ROA, it is useful to look at both profit margin and total asset turnover. Profit margin tells how much money the firm is earning in relation to revenues, that is, how well management did at controlling costs during the accounting period. Asset turnover is the ratio of annual sales to the asset base and it shows how well management did at using assets efficiently.

For example: If there are two companies with a 10% profit margin and total assets of $1,000,000, the one with higher sales per year will be more attractive. Turnover (efficient asset usage), in other words, magnifies the value of a given profit margin and thus is an essential point of focus.

It is also true that a high profit margin can at least partially mask problems with turnover. That is why management would want to watch both the profit margin and the turnover carefully rather than looking at only the ROA calculated by the simpler formula.

If ROA weakens (the ratio goes down), management might consider any of these actions:

- Cut expenses by improving productivity through automation or reducing discretionary spending, thus increasing net profit.
- Reduce assets by improving inventory control, for example, or speeding up receivables (without reducing sales).
- Boost sales while maintaining the profit margin and level of assets.

Both profitability and asset utilization determine the return realized on a company's assets. Financial leverage shows the extent of the use of leverage to magnify returns.

A higher ROA value indicates a more efficient use of assets to generate profits. A higher ROA (compared to the previous year) could result from increased net income, a lower asset value, or both. For example, if assets are lower in the second year of comparison yet income remains the same (the denominator is a lower value), the ROA ratio would increase. Conversely, if net income decreases, or assets increase, or both, the ROA ratio would decrease, indicating a less efficient use of assets to generate profits.

Calculating Return on Common Equity

ROE measures the return made on the common shareholders' equity rather than return on total assets.

$$\text{ROE} = \frac{\text{Net Income}}{\text{Average Equity}}$$

Because ROE focuses on the return to the common shareholder, the denominator is no longer average total assets but equity. Usually shareholders' equity includes the book value of common shares outstanding (including paid-in capital from common stock) plus retained earnings. (It also excludes treasury stock, which is being held by the company instead of shareholders.) For simplicity, shareholders' equity is equal to total assets minus total liabilities if there is no preferred stock issued.

The net income is the income available to common shareholders after deduction of all payments to bondholders and preferred shareholders. Bond interest and preferred dividends are paid before dividends on common stock. That is one of the meanings of "preferred" in preferred stock. If a firm is successful, ROE should be greater than the cost of equity capital. Moreover, ROE provides a means of comparing the investment opportunities in different companies. Higher ROE ratios suggest better returns for common stockholders.

DuPont Model for ROE

The DuPont model for calculating ROE helps users better understand the reasons for a change in ROE over a period of time. It is a function of Return on Assets (ROA) and Financial Leverage.

Recall the standard ROE calculation:

$$ROE = \text{Net Income} / \text{Average Equity}$$

ROE can also be calculated as shown:

$$ROE = (\text{Net Income} / \text{Average Total Assets}) \times (\text{Average Total Assets} / \text{Average Equity})$$

$$ROE = ROA \times \text{Financial Leverage}$$

The relationship of average total assets to average stockholders' equity is called the equity multiplier (financial leverage) because of its power to boost return to stockholders without requiring more equity. If the firm in our example had 45% of its assets in stock and 55% in debt, for example, the **financial leverage ratio** would be calculated this way:

$$\text{Financial Leverage Ratio} = \frac{\text{Assets}}{\text{Equity}}$$

Financial Leverage Ratio = $1,000,000 / $450,000 = 2.22

The ROE would then become:

$$ROE = ROA \times \text{Financial Leverage} = 20\% \times 2.22 = 44.4\%$$

If the firm's assets were composed 100% of common equity, the ROA and ROE would be the same. (The multiplier would become 1.) But when all the ROA goes to stockholders, who contribute only 45% of the capital, the ROE goes above the 20% ROA. The company, in this instance, is using leverage productively.

Financial leverage also is referred to as the equity multiplier. That is, it is the factor by which return on equity grows faster than the ROA, for a small increase in profitability. From the shareholders' point of view, return on equity increases as the firm borrows more money (as long as the money earns an income greater than the interest costs) rather than raising cash through issuance of more shares.

Another way of saying the same thing is that increased leverage increases ROE, to the benefit of shareholders, without necessarily increasing ROA. To be productive for the firm, then, the increased leverage needs to be accompanied by positive ROA. It is up to financial managers to determine the best mix of debt and equity to keep the company competitive in the marketplace and attractive to shareholders and creditors.

An alternative, and more thorough, method of computing the financial leverage is by listing all sources of capital, various forms of debt, preferred stock, and common stock. Then the amount paid to each one of those stakeholders in terms of interest, preferred dividends, and so on, is added together. Short-term liabilities, such as accounts payable and unearned revenue, are not included because they represent interest-free loans. The cost of capital then can be computed by dividing the amount paid to a particular source of capital by the amount of capital provided by that source. When the financial leverage is being used appropriately, the common shareholder earns the highest rate of return.

This is an indicator that management is effective in raising capital for its operation and maximizing the returns to the owners/shareholders.

Knowledge Check: Financial Ratios

The following questions are intended to help you check your understanding and recall of the material presented in this topic. They do not represent the type of questions that appear on the CMA exam.

Directions: Answer each question in the space provided. Correct answers and section references appear after the knowledge check questions.

Use the next financial statements for XYC Company to answer questions 1 through 9. Management of XYC Company has determined that the note receivable–related party is due to be collected on January 31, Y3. All indications are that collection will occur as planned.

XYC Company Balance Sheet	December 31, Y2	December 31, Y1
ASSETS		
Current assets:		
Cash and short-term investments	$24,628	$36,125
Trade receivables, net of $30K allowance	429,949	385,273
Other receivables	18,941	15,210
Note receivable—related party	80,532	
Inventory	252,567	215,619
Prepaid insurance	7,500	7,500
Total current assets	**$814,117**	**$659,727**
Fixed assets:		
Property and equipment	209,330	209,300
Less accumulated depreciation	(75,332)	(63,402)
Net fixed assets	**133,998**	**145,898**
TOTAL ASSETS	**$948,115**	**$805,625**
LIABILITIES AND EQUITY		
Current liabilities:		
Accounts payable	$175,321	$165,200
Accrued expenses	2,500	1,200
Current portion of long-term debt	36,000	36,000
Line of credit	145,000	111,993
Total current liabilities	**$358,821**	**$314,393**
Long-term debt:	117,343	120,000
Total current and long-term liabilities	**$476,164**	**$434,393**
Shareholders' equity:		
Common stock, $1 par value	$100,000	$100,000
Additional paid-in capital	50,000	50,000
Retained earnings	321,951	221,232
Total shareholders' equity	**$471,951**	**$371,232**
TOTAL LIABILITIES AND SHAREHOLDERS' EQUITY	**$948,115**	**$805,625**

Note: Y1 and Y2 dividends per share $1 paid $.25 per quarter; 100,000 shares of common stock outstanding.

XYC Company Income Statement

	YTD Actual	
	December 31, Y2	December 31, Y1
INCOME		
Sales, net	$1,986,456	$1,822,326
Less:		
Cost of goods sold	1,187,652	1,020,503
GROSS PROFIT	$ 798,804	$ 801,823
Operating expenses:		
Operating expenses, combined	$ 556,732	$ 546,698
Total operating expenses	$ 556,732	$ 546,698
Operating income (loss)	$ 242,072	$ 255,125
Other income (expense):		
Interest expense	($16,453)	($16,523)
Other income (expense)	(2,600)	(1,900)
Income taxes	(22,300)	(23,646)
Total other income (expense)	(41,353)	(42,069)
NET INCOME (LOSS)	$200,719	$213,056

LOS §2.A.2.y

1. What is XYC Company's working capital for Y2 and for Y1? _____

2. What is XYC Company's current ratio for Y2 and for Y1? _____

3. What is XYC Company's acid-test ratio for Y2 and for Y1? _____

4. What is XYC Company's cash ratio for Y2 and for Y1? _____

5. What is XYC Company's debt to total assets ratio for Y2 and for Y1?
   _____

6. What is XYC Company's debt to equity ratio for Y2 and for Y1? _____

7. What is XYC Company's times interest earned ratio for Y2 and for Y1? _____

8. What is XYC Company's financial leverage ratio for Y2? _____

9. What is XYC Company's fixed assets to equity capital ratio for Y2 and for Y1?
   _____

Use the following information to answer questions 10 and 11:

XZ Company has $1,000,000 in net sales in the accounting period. Assume that all sales are credit sales. Its cost of goods sold is $500,000, its average inventory is $100,000, and its average accounts payable are $150,000. Its terms of credit are 30 days, and its average receivables from sales are $100,000.

10. Calculate XZ Company's inventory turnover ratio. _____

11. Calculate XZ Company's accounts receivable turnover ratio. _____

12. Assume that in year 1, a company has sales of $500,000, variable costs of $300,000, and fixed costs of $100,000. What is its degree of operating leverage (DOL)?

    ☐ a. 2.00
    ☐ b. 1.25
    ☐ c. 2.50
    ☐ d. 2.08

13. Assuming that the company in question 12 has interest payments of $20,000, what is the company's degree of financial leverage (DFL)?

    ☐ a. 2.00
    ☐ b. 1.25
    ☐ c. 2.50
    ☐ d. 2.08

Use the next financial statement for Breeze-Eastern Corp Solutions to answer question 14.

Breeze Eastern, Corp
Breeze Eastern Balance Sheets (values in 000's)

Period Ending:	3/31/Y3	3/31/Y2	3/31/Y1
Current Assets			
Cash and Cash Equivalents	$22,806	$6,021	$6,688
Short-Term Investments	$0	$0	$0
Net Receivables	$30,827	$28,799	$22,712
Inventory	$19,427	$18,909	$17,790
Other Current Assets	$1,681	$1,868	$1,506
Total Current Assets	$74,741	$55,597	$48,696

Long-Term Assets

Long-Term Investments	$0	$0	$0
Fixed Assets	$9,498	$10,132	$10,486
Goodwill	$402	$402	$402
Intangible Assets	$0	$0	$0
Other Assets	$8,516	$9,465	$9,540
Deferred Asset Charges	$3,821	$4,197	$4,289
Total Assets	$96,978	$79,793	$73,413
Current Liabilities Accounts Payable	$12,329	$10,675	$9,592
Short-Term Debt and Current Maturities	$0	$0	$0
Other Current Liabilities	$5,938	$5,214	$5,070
Total Current Liabilities	$18,267	$15,889	$14,662
Long-Term Debt	$0	$0	$0
Other Liabilities	$11,596	$13,420	$15,679
Total Liabilities	$29,863	$29,309	$30,341

Stockholders' Equity

Common Stocks	$102	$101	$100
Capital Surplus	$100,454	$98,707	$97,113
Retained Earnings	($26,437)	($41,344)	($46,985)
Treasury Stock	($7,041)	($6,983)	($6,972)
Other Equity	$37	$3	($184)
Total Equity	$67,115	$50,484	$43,072
Total Liabilities & Equity	$96,978	$79,793	$73,413

14. Compute the following ratios for years ending 3/31/Y3 and 2/31/Y2.

Current ratio   _____   _____
Acid-test ratio _____   _____
Cash ratio   _____   _____

Knowledge Check Answers: Financial Ratios

1. XYC's working capital for Y2 is $455,296 ($814,117 − $358,821); its working capital for Y1 is $345,334 ($659,727 − $314,393). [See **Working Capital Analysis**.]

2. XYC's current ratio for Y2 is 2.269 ($814,117 ÷ $358,821); its current ratio for Y1 is 2.098 ($659,727 ÷ $314,393). [See **Current Ratio**.]

3. XYC's acid-test ratio for Y2 is 1.54; its acid-test ratio for Y1 is 1.39. [See **Quick (Acid-Test) Ratio**.]

$$Y_2 = \frac{\$24{,}628 + \$429{,}949 + \$18{,}941 + \$80{,}532}{\$358{,}821} \qquad Y_1 = \frac{\$36{,}125 + \$385{,}273 + \$15{,}210}{\$314{,}393}$$

4. XYC's cash ratio for Y2 is .069 ($24,628 ÷ $358,821); its cash ratio for Y1 is .115 ($36,125 ÷ $314,393). [See **Cash Ratio**.]

5. The debt to total assets ratio for Y2 is .502 ($476,164 ÷ $948,115); the debt ratio for Y1 is .539 ($434,393 ÷ $805,625). [See **Ratio Analysis on Debt/Liabilities**.]

6. The debt to equity ratio for Y2 is 1.009 ($476,164 ÷ $471,951); the debt to equity ratio for Y1 is 1.17 ($434,393 ÷ $371,232). [See **Debt to Equity Ratio**.]

7. The times interest earned ratio for Y2 is 14.555; the times interest earned ratio for Y1 is 15.326. [See **Times Interest Earned (Interest Coverage) Ratio**.]

$$Y_2: \frac{\$200{,}719 + 16{,}453 \text{ (Interest)} + 22{,}300 \text{ (Taxes)}}{\$16{,}453} = \frac{\$239{,}472}{\$16{,}453}$$

$$Y_1: \frac{\$213{,}056 + 16{,}523 \text{ (Interest)} + 23{,}646 \text{ (Taxes)}}{\$16{,}523} = \frac{\$253{,}225}{\$16{,}523}$$

8. The financial leverage ratio for Y2 is 2.008. Financial leverage is calculated by taking total assets and dividing by total equity. Total assets in Y2 is $948,115. Total equity in Y2 is $471,951. Therefore, $948,115 / $471,951 equals 2.008. [See **Financial Leverage Ratio**.]

9. The fixed assets to equity capital ratio for Y2 is .284 ($133,998 ÷ $471,951); the fixed assets to equity capital ratio for Y1 is .393 ($145,898 ÷ $371,232). [See **Financial Leverage Ratio**.]

10. XZ's inventory turnover ratio is 5 ($500,000 ÷ $100,000). [See **Inventory Turnover Ratio**.]

11. XZ's accounts receivable turnover ratio is 10 ($1,000,000 ÷ $100,000). **[See Accounts Receivable Turnover Ratio.]**

12. Assume that in year 1, a company has sales of $500,000, variable costs of $300,000, and fixed costs of $100,000. What is its degree of operating leverage (DOL)? **[See Degree of Operating Leverage.]**

    - ☑ **b.** 2.00
    - ☐ **b.** 1.25
    - ☐ **c.** 2.50
    - ☐ **d.** 2.08

    Explanation: DOL = CM/OI = (Sales − Variable Costs) / (Sales − Variable Costs − Fixed Costs) = ($500,000 − $300,000) / ($500,000 − $300,000 − $100,000) = $200,000 / $100,000 = 2.0

13. Assuming that the company in question 12 has interest payments of $20,000, what is the company's degree of financial leverage (DFL)? **[See Degree of Financial Leverage.]**

    - ☐ **a.** 2.00
    - ☑ **b.** 1.25
    - ☐ **c.** 2.50
    - ☐ **d.** 2.08

    Explanation: DFL = EBIT / EBT = $100,000 / ($100,000 − $20,000) = 1.25

14. Use the next financial statement for Breeze-Eastern Corp Solutions to answer the question.

    Breeze Eastern, Corp Balance Sheets (values in 000's)

Period Ending:	3/31/Y3	3/31/Y2	3/31/Y1
Current Assets			
Cash and Cash Equivalents	$22,806	$6,021	$6,688
Short-Term Investments	$0	$0	$0
Net Receivables	$30,827	$28,799	$22,712
Inventory	$19,427	$18,909	$17,790
Other Current Assets	$1,681	$1,868	$1,506
Total Current Assets	$74,741	$55,597	$48,696
Long-Term Assets			
Long-Term Investments	$0	$0	$0
Fixed Assets	$9,498	$10,132	$10,486
Goodwill	$402	$402	$402
Intangible Assets	$0	$0	$0
Other Assets	$8,516	$9,465	$9,540
Deferred Asset Charges	$3,821	$4,197	$4,289
Total Assets	$96,978	$79,793	$73,413

Current Liabilities Accounts Payable	$12,329	$10,675	$9,592
Short-Term Debt and Current Maturities	$0	$0	$0
Other Current Liabilities	$5,938	$5,214	$5,070
Total Current Liabilities	$18,267	$15,889	$14,662
Long-Term Debt	$0	$0	$0
Other Liabilities	$11,596	$13,420	$15,679
Total Liabilities	$29,863	$29,309	$30,341
Stockholders' Equity			
Common Stocks	$102	$101	$100
Capital Surplus	$100,454	$98,707	$97,113
Retained Earnings	($26,437)	($41,344)	($46,985)
Treasury Stock	($7,041)	($6,983)	($6,972)
Other Equity	$37	$3	($184)
Total Equity	$67,115	$50,484	$43,072
Total Liabilities & Equity	$96,978	$79,793	$73,413

Compute the following ratios for years ending 3/31/Y3 and 2/31/Y2. [**See Working Capital Analysis.**]

Current ratio	**4.09**	**3.50**
Acid test ratio	**2.94**	**2.19**
Cash ratio	**1.25**	**.38**

TOPIC 3

Profitability Analysis

PROFITABILITY IS A FIRM'S ABILITY TO GENERATE EARNINGS over a period of time with a given set of resources. It is analyzed by examining the elements of revenues, the cost of sales, and operating and other expenses.

There are a number of ways an investor can look at return on his or her investment. Some returns involve the price of the stock as it trades in the securities markets. Although there are actions a company can take to make its stock more attractive to investors, return on market price depends on when each investor purchases and sells the stock. Thus, the analyst of a company's financial and operating performance cannot make this calculation for the individual investor. An analyst, can, however, examine how the investor's contribution to the company performed on a per-share basis. This can be done by measuring earnings per share and the dividend yield.

READ the Learning Outcome Statements (LOS) for this topic as found in Appendix B and then study the concepts and calculations presented here to be sure you understand the content you could be tested on in the CMA exam.

This topic is the logical extension of the previous two topics. The analysis in the previous two topics is at a more detailed level. For example, you might confirm from a calculation of inventory turnover that there is a problem with more dollars being lodged in inventory than is warranted by the current levels of sales. Therefore, action should be taken before slow-moving inventory becomes obsolete inventory or before code-dated items go past their expiration dates and have to be discarded rather than being sold.

The analysis described in this topic might first alert you to a degradation in return on investment (ROI). An analysis of the decomposition of ROI might lead you to the conclusion that the firm's assets are being underutilized, and you could use various turnover ratios introduced in the previous topic to determine whether the problem might be with investments in inventory or accounts receivable or fixed assets. Thus, this chapter discusses analysis at a very high level.

Return on Investment

The principal objective of for-profit businesses is to invest funds into resources like inventory and fixed assets so that the business might earn profits for its owners to adequately compensate them for the risk they expose themselves to with their investment. Thus, several of the measures to be discussed might be characterized generically as a return on investment.

Recall from the previous topic, Financial Ratios, that the return on investments ratios in their various forms may be performed by analysts that substitute book value of certain assets for fair values (or market values or replacement cost). Specifically, analysts who use the modified investment basis to calculate ROI or ROA believe that some components can skew the results. These analysts remove elements from total assets or make determinations of whether to use book value or market value for certain assets. On the exam, you will be given book value or fair value to solve this equation. If given both, use the book value.

$$\text{Return on Investment (ROI)} = \frac{\text{Income of Business Unit}}{\text{Assets of Business Unit}}$$

Two very specific types of return on investment are described: **return on assets (ROA)** and **return on equity (ROE)**.

We approach these return metrics through a group of concepts referred to as the **DuPont model** or **DuPont analysis.** It was conceived by managers in the DuPont Corporation almost a century ago. That makes it one of the most enduring concepts in the business world.

Return on Assets

Calculation of ROA in its simplest form, as shown next, uses net income and the value of all assets.

$$\text{Return on Assets (ROA)} = \frac{\text{Net Income}}{\text{Average Total Assets}}$$

The genius of the DuPont model is that the managers realized that management must manage profitability and the investment in and utilization of assets. In other words, ROA can be driven by increasing margins and/or increasing asset turnover or "turns," depending on the strategy of the company. Excellence in both of these areas should result in an excellent ROA result. Therefore, the DuPont managers decomposed ROA in this way:

$$\text{ROA} = \frac{\text{Net Income}}{\text{Average Total Assets}} = \frac{\text{Net Income}}{\text{Sales}} \times \frac{\text{Sales}}{\text{Average Total Assets}}$$

Profit margin or net profit margin is the term used to describe Net Income/Sales. In its simplest terms it describes how many cents are left out of a dollar of sales after all expenses have been covered.

Total asset turnover or **asset turn** is the term used to describe Sales/Average Total Assets. It says how many dollars of sales can be generated from a dollar invested in the assets a firm uses in its business. As discussed in Topic 2, when a ratio involves one account that measures something over a period of time and another account that measures something at a point in time, the latter account value should be represented by the average of latter account's values at the beginning and end of the period. This is especially important for firms that are growing or shrinking rapidly. People taking the CMA exam are expected to average beginning and ending values of such accounts.

Many analysts offer variations on the above definitions. Some advocate omitting investments in assets that are not being used in the business. Some advocate using original cost of plant, property, and equipment rather than book value. Some may even advocate using replacement values.

Return on Equity and Return on Common Equity

Return on Equity (ROE) measures the return to shareholders. Its definition is:

$$\text{ROE} = \frac{\text{Net Income}}{\text{Average Stockholders' Equity}}$$

However, a special case occurs when a firm uses preferred stock in its capital structure. Two metrics are appropriate in this case. ROE (as defined in the previous key box) is still meaningful. It measures the book return to shareholders—both preferred and common. The second metric is Return on Common Equity (ROCE). It measures the book return to common shareholders. Its definition is:

$$\frac{\left(\text{Net Income} - \text{Preferred Dividends}\right)}{\left(\text{Average Equity} - \text{Average Preferred Equity}\right)}$$

"Preferred Equity" is the amount expected to be paid to preferred shareholders in the event of the firm's liquidation. It includes both the par value of outstanding preferred shares and any premium to be paid in liquidation. Note that par value of the preferred shares excludes any additional paid-in capital arising from preferred stock issued at a price above par value.

ROCE may be meaningfully compared to both ROA and ROE. Use of preferred stock in the capital structure is really a different form of leverage. If leverage is working as intended, then ROCE>ROA and ROCE>ROE.

The DuPont model expands the ROE equation as follows:

$$\text{ROE} = \frac{\text{Net Income}}{\text{Average Assets}} \times \frac{\text{Average Assets}}{\text{Average Equity}} = \text{ROA} \times \text{Financial Leverage Ratio}$$

Average Assets/Average Equity is the definition of the **financial leverage ratio**, which is also frequently referred to as the **equity multiplier**.

$$\text{Financial Leverage Ratio} = \frac{\text{Average Assets}}{\text{Average Equity}}$$

The CMA Exam Ratio Definitions document excludes the word "average" in both numerator and denominator. We recommend that candidates use the information provided in the exam question. If the exam data set permits using average figures then use them.

Illustrations of DuPont Model for ROA and ROE

Some hypothetical financial statements and ratios in Figure 2A-5 illustrate how DuPont analysis might be used as a starting point for analyzing results and diagnosing possible problems. Note that the DuPont model may also be useful in high-level planning. The year headings are explained in detail at the end of this figure.

The base case in the illustration is Alpha Co. for Year 1. Assume that Alpha is a retailing company, an industry with which many people are familiar. As you can see from the balance sheet, Alpha chooses to leverage its capital structure; this is evidenced by Notes Payable in the balance sheet and by Interest Expense in the income statement. Also, the balance sheet for Year 0 and Year 1 are identical. Assume that Alpha is not growing. Therefore, it can afford to pay out 100% of its net income in dividends to its shareholders. DuPont analysis shows a profit margin of 4.5% and an asset turnover of 2.0, resulting in an ROA of 9%. These results could be compared to other companies in the industry, and the comparisons may be valid or they may not be. For example, some of the comparisons to a retailer that chooses not to leverage its capital structure may be flawed. Or another retailer that does not have its own credit program would not provide a good comparative. Next, we can see that the equity multiplier has a value of 1.667, and the resulting ROE is 15%.

Figure 2A-5 DuPont Analysis—3 Companies Contrasted

	Alpha Co.				Beta Co.		Gamma Co.	
	Yr. 0	Yr. 1	Yr. 2a	Yr. 2b	Yr. 0	Yr. 1	Yr. 0	Yr. 1
Cash	$50	$50	$50	$50	$50	$50	$50	$50
A/R	200	200	200	240	200	200	200	200
Inventory	150	150	150	150	150	150	150	150
Net PP&E	100	100	100	100	100	100	100	100
Assets	$500	$500	$500	$540	$500	$500	$500	$500
A/P	$100	$100	$100	$100	$100	$100	$100	$100
Accr. Rent							100	100
N/P	100	100	100	110			75	75
Liabilities	$200	$200	$200	$210	$100	$100	$275	$275
Comm. Stk.	$100	$100	$100	$100	$200	$200	$100	$100
Ret. Earnings	200	200	200	230	200	200	125	125
Equity	$300	$300	$300	$330	$400	$400	$225	$225
Total	$500	$500	$500	$540	$500	$500	$500	$500
Sales		$1,000.00	$1,000.00	$1,000.00		$1,000.00		$1,000.00
COGS		600.00	600.00	600.00		600.00		600.00
Gross Profit		$400.00	$400.00	$400.00		$400.00		$400.00
SG&A		314.00	319.00	314.00		314.00		314.00
Operating Inc.		$86.00	$81.00	$86.00		$86.00		$86.00
Interest Exp.		11.00	11.00	11.55				8.25
Inc. before Tax		$75.00	$70.00	$74.45		$86.00		$77.75
Inc. Tax Expense		30.00	28.00	29.78		34.40		31.10
Net Income		$45.00	$42.00	$44.67		$51.60		$46.65
Ratios								
Profit Margin		4.50%	4.20%	4.47%		5.16%		4.67%
Asset Turnover		2.000	2.000	1.923		2.000		2.000
Return on Assets		9.00%	8.40%	8.59%		10.32%		9.33%
Equity Multiplier		1.667	1.667	1.651		1.250		2.222
Return on Equity		15.00%	14.00%	14.18%		12.90%		20.73%

LOS §2.A.3.b

Now let's compare Year 2a to the first year's results. In the second year, assume the increase in operating expenses is to increase the number of salespeople on the floor. This would be signaled immediately by the decrease in the profit margin from 4.5% to 4.2%.

Next, we'd be likely to compare the gross profit percentage and see that it had not changed. That finding rules out a decrease in pricing power or increased costs from suppliers that could not be passed along to customers.

The gross profit margin percentage is a measurement of gross profit (sales minus cost of sales) as a percentage of sales:

> Gross Profit = Sales − Cost of Sales
> Gross Profit Margin = Gross Profit/Sales

Possible reasons for changes in the gross profit margin percentage include:

- Sales prices not changing at the same rate as unit costs
- Sales prices increasing/decreasing due to the intensity of competition
- Mix of products sold shifting to products with lower or higher margins
- Changes in inventory shrinkage (disappearance of inventory)

Next, the operating profit margin would be examined. The **operating profit margin** is the ratio of operating profit (EBIT, as noted) to sales.

$$\text{Operating Profit Margin Percentage} = \frac{\text{Operating Income}}{\text{Sales}}$$

In this case, the operating profit margin has declined from 8.6% to 8.1%; additional vertical income statement analysis would show the change to be in the relationship of sales salaries to sales. And, of course, there is no evidence of any increase in sales, which suggests that the strategy of trying to provide an improved shopping experience for the customer has not produced the hoped-for increase in sales. Any differences in the behavior of the operating profit margin percentage and the net profit percentage would, of course, be due either to interest expense and/or to income tax expense. In this case, the erosion of the profit margin is due entirely to the change in the relationship between sales salaries and sales and the related impact on income taxes. Also, there is no change in the equity multiplier, so the decrease in ROE from 15% to 14% is completely attributable to the decreased profit margin coming from the increase in sales salaries.

$$\text{Net Profit Margin Percentage} = \frac{\text{Net Income}}{\text{Sales}}$$

Next, let's turn to Year 2b, and assume those were the results for the second year. In that version of the second year, the profit margin remained nearly constant. However, there was a decrease in the asset turnover. Using ratios such as days of sales outstanding, inventory turnover, and fixed asset turnover, it's easy to ascertain that the problem is a significant increase in accounts receivable at year-end without a corresponding increase in the level of sales. Almost all of the decrease in

ROA from 9% to about 8.6% was attributable to a decrease in accounts receivable collections. Again, there was hardly any change in the equity multiplier. Therefore, the decrease in ROE from 15% to about 14.2% was the consequence of the receivables collection problem.

Now let's do a comparison of Alpha's first year in relation to that of a competitor, Beta. At first blush, Beta may appear to be the better of the two companies, because it has the higher profit margin (almost 5.2% compared to 4.5% for Alpha). However, checking the gross profit margin percentages and the operating margin percentages shows the two companies to be operating identically. The real difference is in how the two managements choose to finance their companies. Alpha has used leverage, and Beta has not. Therefore, Alpha has interest expense in its income statement and Beta does not. That is the real difference in the profit margins of the two companies and in their ROAs. Asset turnovers are identical. Beta, of course, must maintain additional equity in its balance sheet to make up for the absence of borrowed money. However, when we direct our attention to the ROEs, the tables are turned. Beta has the smaller equity multiplier and the smaller ROE (12.9% versus 15%). While both companies have been illustrated as having the same level of sales and assets, the ratio comparisons of companies of different scale is valid; ratios make them comparable by removing the effect of scale differences. The illustrations use companies of the same sales levels simply to make it easier to immediately identify the source of the problem. It should also be pointed out that the weighted average cost of capital (WACC) for Alpha is likely lower than that for Beta. Prudent use of debt in the capital structure usually reduces the cost of capital due to the tax deductibility of interest expense. In some sense, you can think of the U.S. Government subsidizing a firm's borrowings. However, remember that the party that holds that debt is being taxed on its interest income. The lower cost of capital makes it likely that Alpha does a better job of creating shareholder value.

Finally, consider one other competitor of Alpha, Gamma Co. Gamma's profit margin is a tiny bit better than Alpha's. With the same value of the asset turnover, Gamma's ROA is also a tiny bit better than Alpha's. However, the real difference comes from the equity multiplier (2.222 for Gamma versus 1.667 for Alpha). That results in a 20.7% versus 15% ROE advantage for Gamma over Alpha. What accounts for this large difference? There is an item called "Accrued Rent Payable" on Gamma's balance sheet that does not appear on Alpha's. Gamma has negotiated lower front-end rent payments and higher back-end rent payments to its landlords for stores leased under operating leases. The ASC requires that uneven rental payments in an operating lease should be recognized on a straight-line basis unless some other basis is more appropriate. Gamma needs to accrue rental expense in excess of its lower front-end rental payments in order to even out the payments on a straight-line basis. When the lower payment provision expires and higher rents are required, the accrued rent payable amounts will be released as an offset to the higher latter-year lease payments. This has exactly the same effect as accounts payable (A/P). Every dollar of either A/P or accrued rent payable is a dollar of "free" financing; it will reduce the amount of "expensive" financing the company would have to get from either creditors or shareholders.

To summarize the discussion to this point, when Alpha uses DuPont analysis to analyze its results over time, the analysis seems to work well. However, when a firm uses DuPont analysis to make comparisons against other firms in the industry, the analysis may not be as revealing and may even be misleading.

> **NOTE:** The IMA's CMA LOS and Ratio Definitions documents do not directly address the information that follows. However we feel that this information is important in understanding this variation in DuPont analysis.

Is there a way to remedy some of the deficiencies of DuPont analysis? Yes! One useful ratio to measure profitability is the NOPAT margin. NOPAT stands for *net operating profit after tax*. It can be calculated most simply as Operating Income (1 − Tax Rate). It calculates how much income would remain after income taxes if the company were taxed on all its operating income. Next, NOPAT should be divided by sales to turn it into a margin (%). By this measure, all three companies—Alpha, Beta, and Gamma—would have the same measure of profitability in Year 1: 5.16%. In other words, this measure of operating profitability is not affected by differences in how the companies choose to finance themselves.

Another helpful ratio is called invested capital turnover. Invested capital can be defined as either (assets less operating liabilities) or (stockholders' equity plus interest-bearing liabilities). The former is the net resources financed by expensive sources of capital, and the latter is the sources of financing for those resources. They must produce the same value, given that the balance sheet must balance. If you divide average invested capital into sales, you have determined the value of the invested capital turnover. In the earlier illustrations, Alpha and Beta had invested capital turnover values of 2.5; Gamma had a much higher value of 3.33 due to its advantageous lease payment arrangements with its landlords.

Finally, the product of the NOPAT margin and the invested capital turnover is the return on invested capital (ROIC). This ratio has an important attribute. If a firm's ROIC is greater than the firm's WACC, the firm should be creating shareholder value; conversely, a firm earning a ROIC that is lower than its WACC is likely to be destroying shareholder value. (A quick calculation of ROIC demonstrates that Gamma's ROIC is significantly higher than Alpha's or Beta's ROIC.) This one attribute could make the ROIC ratio the most important of all; it is the primary responsibility of for-profit business organizations to create shareholder value. Please note that the ROA does not have such a "standard" to be compared to.

Sustainable Growth Rate

The sustainable growth rate discussed in this section might be confused with the sustainability movement that has evolved in recent years. In fact there exists the

Sustainability Accounting Standards Board that has issued a number of sustainability standards that have already found their way into U.S. SEC disclosure requirements. As you read the following information on sustainable growth rate, remind yourself that this rate has little to do with the environmentally charged sustainability movement.

A reason for believing the ROE is an important ratio is that a firm's maximum sustainable growth rate is a function of the firm's ROE.

Sustainable Growth Rate = (1 − Dividend Payout Ratio) × ROE

To see why this is true, another illustration may be helpful. In this instance, we have chosen not to use the average value of equity but the beginning-of-the-year value for the sake of simplicity.

Figure 2A-6 Illustration of Sustainable Growth

	Year 0	Year 1 10% Incr.	Year 2 13% Incr.
Cash	$55.00	$60.50	$68.37
A/R	220.00	242.00	273.46
Inventory	165.00	181.50	205.10
Net PP&E	110.00	121.00	136.73
	$550.00	$605.00	$683.65
A/P	$110.00	$121.00	$136.73
N/P	110.00	121.00	136.73
Liabilities	$220.00	$242.00	$273.46
Comm. Stock	100.00	100.00	100.00
Ret. Earnings	230.00	263.00	300.29
Equity	$330.00	$363.00	$400.29
Total	$550.00	$605.00	$673.75
Capital shortfall			$9.90
Sales		$1,100.00	$1,243.00
COGS		660.00	745.80
Gross Profit		$440.00	$497.20
SG&A		345.40	390.30
Operating Inc.		$94.60	$106.90
Interest Exp.		12.10	13.67
Inc. before Tax		$82.50	$93.22
Inc. Tax Expense		33.00	37.29
Net Income		$49.50	$55.93

The firm in Figure 2A-6 earns a 15% return on equity and pays out one-third of its income as dividends, retaining two-thirds. This means the firm will increase its stockholders' equity by 10% year over year. It can "afford" to grow its debt by 10% as well, because the ratio of debt to equity will be 1:3 at the end of the year, just as it was at the beginning of the year. This enables all assets (cash, accounts receivable, inventory, and fixed assets) to grow by 10% and assumes that A/P, an operating liability or a spontaneous liability, also grows by 10%. As you can see, the cash flows work out just fine, and retained earnings is increased by two-thirds of the net income.

Now consider that the firm has market opportunities that would permit its sales to grow by 13% in the next year (and remain equally profitable). All of the asset accounts must grow by 13% to support the increased sales. A/P will also grow by 13%. Assume also that we allow notes payable to increase by 13%. Common stock will not increase because the firm's management does not want to issue new shares of common stock. In fact, not issuing new shares is a part of the definition of the sustainable growth rate. The increase in retained earnings would simply be two-thirds of net income, because one-third was to be paid in dividends. There is obviously a capital shortage, given all the above assumptions. How can the capital shortage be solved? There are three methods:

1. *Borrow additional money.* Such borrowing would increase the principal amount of the note payable, which in turn would increase interest expense. However, the ratio of debt to equity would also increase; likely that could cause an increase in the interest rate, which would be another reason for interest expense to increase. The increase in interest expense needs to "feed back" into the income statement, which would cause net income to fall and, in turn, cause both the dividend to fall and the amount available for reinvestment to fall. This would necessitate another round of changes to both the balance sheet and the income statement.
2. *Issue additional shares of common stock.* However, many firms are reluctant to do this, either because of the high costs of floating new common stock or because their managements fear that doing so sends a negative signal to the capital markets.
3. *Cut the dividend.* This solution is very obvious from the formula for sustainable growth.

Try this simulation with other growth rates, and you'll become convinced that the product of ROE and the complement of the payout ratio (known as the retention ratio) is the highest rate at which sales can grow while

1. Not changing the capital structure
2. Not issuing new common stock
3. Given that profitability (as measured by the NOPAT margin) doesn't improve
4. Given that asset intensity (as measured by the earlier mentioned invested capital turnover) doesn't improve

Because firms that are creating shareholder value will want to grow as rapidly as possible, ROE is a very important performance metric.

Revenue Analysis

Revenue is an indicator of resources generated by a business from its customers through its operations. Fundamentally, a company exists to provide goods or services to a customer and generate more resources than it expends in providing the good or service. Lenders and owners provide capital to the business because they believe in the business model that the firm would be able to, in the long run, provide some good/service to customers at a price higher than what is required to provide that service. Accountants must be careful to accurately recognize revenue as it is one of the fundamental measures in the financial statement. Remember that revenue is used as the base for common-sizing the income statement.

The FASB and IASB have already issued new revenue recognition standards with effective dates of 2018. The new revenue recognition standards will be tested beginning with the January 2019 exam.

While many revenue transactions are recognized on a point-of-sale basis without complications, the current revenue recognition standards impose additional requirements on the timing and amount of revenue recognition. These requirements are examined on the current CMA exams.

Under current revenue recognition guidance enhanced by the US SEC, revenue should not be recognized until it is realized or realizable and earned. The two conditions (being realized or realizable and being earned) are usually met by the time product or merchandise is delivered or services are rendered to customers, and revenues from manufacturing and selling activities and gains and losses from sales of other assets are commonly recognized at time of sale (usually meaning delivery.) If services are rendered or rights to use assets extend continuously over time (for example, interest or rent), reliable measures based on contractual prices established in advance are commonly available, and revenues may be recognized as earned as time passes. Revenue generally is realized or realizable and earned when all of the following criteria are met: persuasive evidence of an arrangement exists; delivery has occurred or services have been rendered; the seller's price to the buyer is fixed or determinable; and collectibility is reasonably assured.

An analyst must evaluate carefully whether the timing of revenue recognition is appropriate, given the nature of the business. Early recognition of revenue would lead to higher reported income and better profitability as well as liquidity ratios. In order to ascertain whether revenue recognition policies are acceptable, the analysis must consider how the company "earns" revenue—that is, what constitutes the "earnings" process. The definition will vary across firms depending on their business models.

Revenue Trends and Stability

Analysts, investors, and creditors all need to determine whether revenue represents the stable trend of a growing business or an unusual or one-time event. Sales indexes of various product lines can be correlated and compared to composite industry figures or to product sales trends of specific competitors. Important considerations bearing on the quality and stability of the sales and revenues trend include those listed next.

- Elasticity of demand for products (how consumers respond to a change in the price of a product)
- Ability of the business to anticipate demand trends by the introduction of new products and services
- Level of competition
- Degree of customer concentration and dependence on a single industry or a single customer, such as for government contractors
- Degree of dependence on relatively few leading sales associates
- Degree of geographical diversification of markets

Interrelationships Among Revenue, Inventory, and Receivables

Noncash revenue (sales) is recorded as accounts receivable. Thus, the implicit assumption behind accounts receivable is that revenue must have been earned to be recognized. If a company inappropriately recognizes revenue early, net income is overstated and current assets on the balance sheet are overstated. Inappropriately recognizing revenues after they are earned will understate net income and current assets. Further, an increase in receivables without a corresponding increase in sales may signal problems with collections from customers.

Because merchandising and manufacturing primarily earn revenue through sales of merchandise, the increase in revenue should correspond to an increase in inventory. However, an increase in inventory balance without a corresponding increase in sales may signal problems with inventory management. Again, the application of ratios (such as inventory turnover) may highlight potential problems.

Income Measurement Analysis

There is no absolute measure of "real earnings." The income and expenses presented in the income statement are subject to a variety of judgments and accounting methods.

The FASB holds that the entities should prepare general purpose financial statements for external users. This requirement is necessary to keep the burden of financial reporting costs approximately in line with costs of producing the information those reports contain. Furthermore, financial accounting and reporting contains considerable need for estimations. Of course, estimations can change. Additionally companies in some circumstances may appropriately wish to change between two or more acceptable accounting and reporting methods for a particular type of transaction. Also the FASB from time to time issues new accounting and reporting requirements to be integrated into the ASC (the new revenue standards, for example). Where there is a change in accounting the usual method of presenting the new information is via retrospective application net of income taxes. Finally, financial reporting includes not only the four basic financial statements but myriads of required disclosures that further explain accounting policies and complex transactions. For all of these reasons, income measurement is complicated.

These factors need to be considered in measuring income:

- Estimates
- Accounting methods
- Disclosure
- Different needs of users

Estimates

The determination of income depends on estimates regarding future events and their outcomes. For publicly traded companies, management makes the estimates, which the auditors verify for reasonableness. The estimates and assumptions could affect the measurement of income significantly. For example, the estimate of useful life for depreciable assets affects the depreciation expense and thereby the reported income. A generous estimate of longer useful life reduces depreciation expense, thereby increasing income.

Accounting Methods

It is important to understand and assess the implications that the use of one accounting principle as opposed to another (such as straight-line versus accelerated depreciation) has on the firm's measurement of income as well as how it compares to other businesses. The accounting methods are chosen at the discretion of management, and the auditor's role is to ensure that the method selected is one of the many generally accepted accounting methods and that its use has been consistent over years. Auditors are responsible for understanding the effect of these methods on reported income and other financial statement measures, including how they affect the computation of ratios.

For example, two commonly used methods of inventory valuation are first-in, first-out (FIFO) and last-in, first-out (LIFO). For the same underlying economic event, use of LIFO, under certain assumptions of increasing inventory units and prices, yields lower income than the FIFO inventory valuation method. Thus, a firm using LIFO would report lower income and lower inventory value than a similar firm using FIFO inventory valuation method. Lower income and lower assets both affect the computation of the return of asset ratio. An analyst is required to consider such effects of accounting policy choices on various financial ratios. The CMA exam tests the ability to evaluate and deduce the effects of various accounting choices on common ratios.

Disclosure

The ASC includes requirements for specific disclosures. The SEC often adds disclosure requirements for issuers. In practice it is not unusual for companies, including issuers, to draft disclosures that only nominally meet the ASC requirements.

In other instances companies have been known to draft disclosures that are so dense and detailed that readers of the financial statements may be unable to determine exactly what has been said in the disclosure.

The degree of informative disclosure about the results of operations and the asset base of segments of a business can vary widely. Full disclosure would call for providing detailed income statements for each significant segment. This is rarely found in practice because of the difficulty of obtaining such breakdowns internally and management's reluctance to divulge information that could harm the business's competitive position.

The more relevant information a company discloses, the better its position will be understood, and as a result, the stock price will more correctly reflect its fair value. However, because it is not always in the best interest of management to disclose information that might be used by competitors, the level of disclosure may be tempered, even at the expense of undervaluation in the equity market.

Different Needs of Users

Users of financial statement analysis often have different needs. For example, the investing public is interested in analysis of the financial position of the business and its ability to earn future profits. Investors use an analysis of past trends and the current position to project the future prospects of the business.

Creditors obtain limited return from extending credit and tend to judge conservatively. Creditors risk loss of capital loaned and so look for the firm's ability to repay both short- and long-term debt. Suppliers extend credit and must weigh their risk of loss of income if not paid for merchandise. If, for example, a supplier sells a product with a 10% markup, it would need to sell ten of the product items to make up for the loss on one not paid for.

Management analyzes data from the viewpoints of both investors and creditors. Management is concerned about the current position to meet obligations and future earnings prospects. Union representatives analyze financial statements for the firm's ability to grant increases in wages and fringe benefits. Government is interested in financial statements and the health of businesses for tax and regulatory purposes.

Knowledge Check: Profitability Analysis

The following questions are intended to help you check your understanding and recall of the material presented in this topic. They do not represent the type of questions that appear on the CMA exam.

Directions: Answer each question in the space provided. Correct answers and section references follow these questions.

1. Which of the following statements is false?

   ☐ a. Unproductive assets are assets that currently are not being utilized.

   ☐ b. Depreciable assets result in lower ROI.

   ☐ c. Current liabilities are not included in total liabilities for purposes of defining invested capital.

   ☐ d. Preferred shareholders' book value usually is excluded from shareholders' book value.

Use the following financial statements for XYC Company to answer questions 2 and 3.

XYC Company Balance Sheet		
	December 31, Y2	December 31, Y1
ASSETS		
Current assets:		
Cash and short-term investments	$24,628	$36,125
Trade receivables, net of $30K allowance	429,949	385,273
Other receivables	18,941	15,210
Note receivable—related party	80,532	
Inventory	252,567	215,619
Prepaid insurance	7,500	7,500
Total current assets	**$814,117**	**$659,727**
Fixed assets:		
Property and equipment	209,330	209,300
Less accumulated depreciation	(75,332)	(63,402)
Net fixed assets	**133,998**	**145,898**
TOTAL ASSETS	**$948,115**	**$805,625**
LIABILITIES AND EQUITY		
Current liabilities:		
Accounts payable	$175,321	$165,200
Accrued expenses	2,500	1,200
Current portion of long-term debt	36,000	36,000
Line of credit	145,000	111,993

Total current liabilities	$358,821	$314,393
Long-term debt:	117,343	120,000
Total current and long-term liabilities	$476,164	$434,393
Shareholders' equity:		
Common stock, $1 par value	$100,000	$100,000
Additional paid-in capital	50,000	50,000
Retained earnings	321,951	221,232
Total shareholders' equity	$471,951	$371,232
TOTAL LIABILITIES AND SHAREHOLDERS' EQUITY	**$948,115**	**$805,625**

Note: Y1 and Y2 dividends per share $1 paid $.25 per quarter; 100,000 shares of common stock outstanding.

XYC Company Income Statement

	YTD Actual	
	December 31, Y2	December 31, Y1
INCOME		
SALES, NET	$1,986,456	$1,822,326
Less:		
Cost of goods sold	1,187,652	1,020,503
GROSS PROFIT	**$798,804**	**$801,823**
Operating expenses:		
Operating expenses, combined	$556,732	$546,698
Total operating expenses	$556,732	$546,698
Operating income (loss)	$242,072	$255,125
Other income (expense):		
Interest expense	($16,453)	($16,523)
Other income (expense)	(2,600)	(1,900)
Income taxes	(22,300)	(23,646)
Total other income (expense)	(41,353)	(42,069)
NET INCOME (LOSS)	**$200,719**	**$213,056**

2. What is XYC Company's ROA for Y2 and Y1? (Use year-end assets for calculations.) _____

3. What is XYC Company's ROE for Y2 and Y1? _____

4. All of the following are possible needs of users of financial statements **except**:

   ☐ **a.** The investing public needs to know what the company will make in the next fiscal year.

   ☐ **b.** Credit grantors need assurances about the company's ability to repay obligations.

- c. Suppliers need assurances that the company will pay for products or materials the supplier sells it on credit.
- d. Management needs to know about the company's ability to pay obligations and the prospects for future earnings.

5. Which of the following statements is true?
   - a. Revenue is sales minus cost of sales.
   - b. A company that discloses more in its financial statements will provide investors with more information to assess the fair value of the stock's price.
   - c. Revenue can be recognized when a business sells inventory to a subsidiary with a buy-back guarantee contract.
   - d. An increase in receivables with a corresponding increase in sales indicates trouble with collections.

6. Which of the following statements is true?
   - a. Depreciation expenses are write-offs of already purchased fixed assets and do not affect the bottom line.
   - b. After a year of negative income, a company should use percentages in variation analysis, because this helps clarify the trend of income.
   - c. The operating cash flow to income ratio requires information from the statements of shareholders' equity to be calculated.
   - d. Trend analysis or variation analysis help analysts compare performance from year to year.

Use the following information to answer Questions 7–10.

Breeze Eastern Annual Income Statement (values in 000's)			
	3/31/Y3	3/31/Y2	3/31/Y1
Period Ending:			
Total Revenue	89,782	85,933	79,956
Cost of Revenue	54,918	54,802	47,143
Gross Profit	34,864	31,131	32,813
Operating Expenses			
Research and Development	6,607	8,162	9,377
Sales, General and Admin.	15,352	13,880	15,246
Operating Income	12,905	9,089	8,190
Add'l income/expense items	1,611	(89)	(93)
Earnings Before Interest and Tax	14,516	9,000	8,097

Interest Expense	32	49	227
Earnings Before Tax	14,484	8,951	7,870
Income Tax	(423)	3,310	3,794
Net Income-Cont. Operations	14,907	5,641	4,076
Net Income	14,907	5,641	4,076

Breeze Eastern Balance Sheets (values in 000's)

	3/31/Y3	3/31/Y2	3/31/Y1
Period Ending:			
Current Assets			
Cash and Cash Equivalents	$22,806	$6,021	$6,688
Short-Term Investments	$0	$0	$0
Net Receivables	$30,827	$28,799	$22,712
Inventory	$19,427	$18,909	$17,790
Other Current Assets	$1,681	$1,868	$1,506
Total Current Assets	$74,741	$55,597	$48,696
Long-Term Assets			
Long-Term Investments	$0	$0	$0
Fixed Assets	$9,498	$10,132	$10,486
Goodwill	$402	$402	$402
Intangible Assets	$0	$0	$0
Other Assets	$8,516	$9,465	$9,540
Deferred Asset Charges	$3,821	$4,197	$4,289
Total Assets	$96,978	$79,793	$73,413
Current Liabilities:			
Accounts Payable	$12,329	$10,675	$9,592
Short-Term Debt and Current Maturities	$0	$0	$0
Other Current Liabilities	$5,938	$5,214	$5,070
Total Current Liabilities	$18,267	$15,889	$14,662
Long-Term Debt	$0	$0	$0
Other Liabilities	$11,596	$13,420	$15,679
Total Liabilities	$29,863	$29,309	$30,341
Stockholders' Equity			
Common Stocks	$102	$101	$100
Capital Surplus	$100,454	$98,707	$97,113
Retained Earnings	($26,437)	($41,344)	($46,985)
Treasury Stock	($7,041)	($6,983)	($6,972)

Other Equity	$37	$3	($184)
Total Equity	$67,115	$50,484	$43,072
Total Liabilities & Equity	$96,978	$79,793	$73,413

7. Assume that Breeze entered into a contract to manufacture and deliver an order to one of its largest customers. For manufacturing scheduling reasons Breeze decided to complete the manufacturing of the order during the third week of March Y3. Delivery was requested by the customer to occur during the second week of April Y3. Is Breeze permitted to recognize the revenue for this order in March Y3, considering the fact that the order is already finished and set aside for delivery to the customer?

8. Breeze-Eastern's revenue increased from Y1 to Y2 and again from Y2 to Y3. Breeze's accounts receivable also increased during these periods. Is the company's increase in receivables approximately consistent with its increase in revenues for the same periods?

9. Breeze shows a decreasing deficit in retained earnings for each of the three years presented and shows profits for the same three years. What is a plausible explanation for the retained earnings deficit?

10. Compute the following ratios for 3/13/Y3 and 3/31/Y2

    Return on assets _____ _____
    Return on equity _____ _____
    Asset turnover   _____ _____

 **Knowledge Check Answers: Profitability Analysis**

1. Which of the following statements is false? [See *Return on Assets*.]

    ☐ a. Unproductive assets are assets that currently are not being utilized.
    ☒ b. Depreciable assets result in lower ROI.
    ☐ c. Current liabilities are not included in total liabilities for purposes of defining invested capital.
    ☐ d. Preferred shareholders' book value usually is excluded from shareholders' book value.

2. The ROA for Y2 is .212 ($200,719 / $948,115); the ROA for Y1 is .265 ($213,056 / $805,625). [See *Return on Assets*.]

3. The ROE for Y2 is .425 ($200,719 / $471,951); the ROE for Y1 is .574 ($213,056 / $371,232). [See *Return on Equity and Return on Common Equity*.]

4. All of the following are possible needs of users of financial statements except: [See *Limitations of Ratio Analysis*.]

    ☒ a. The investing public needs to know what the company will make in the next fiscal year.
    ☐ b. Credit grantors need assurances about the company's ability to repay obligations.
    ☐ c. Suppliers need assurances that the company will pay for products or materials the supplier sells it on credit.
    ☐ d. Management needs to know about the company's ability to pay obligations and the prospects for future earnings.

    Financial statements cannot tell investors what the profits will be in the next year.

5. Which of the following statements is true? [See *Disclosure Incentives*.]

    ☐ a. Revenue is sales minus cost of sales.
    ☒ b. A company that discloses more in its financial statements will provide investors with more information to assess the fair value of the stock's price.
    ☐ c. Revenue can be recognized when a business sells inventory to a subsidiary with a buy-back guarantee contract.
    ☐ d. An increase in receivables with a corresponding increase in sales indicates trouble with collections.

6. Which of the following statements is true? [See *Limitations of Ratio Analysis*.]

    ☐ a. Depreciation expenses are write-offs of already purchased fixed assets and do not affect the bottom line.

    ☐ b. After a year of negative income, a company should use percentages in variation analysis, because this helps clarify the trend of income.

    ☐ c. The operating cash flow to income ratio requires information from the statements of shareholders' equity to be calculated.

    ☑ d. Trend analysis or variation analysis help analysts compare performance from year to year.

7. Assume that Breeze entered into a contract to manufacture and deliver an order to one of its largest customers. For manufacturing scheduling reasons Breeze decided to complete the manufacturing of the order during the third week of March Y3. Delivery was requested by the customer to occur during the second week of April Y3. Is Breeze permitted to recognize the revenue for this order in March Y3, considering the fact that the order is already finished and set aside for delivery to the customer? [See *Revenue Analysis*.]

    Not based on this information alone. If the customer requested that Breeze bill the order in March and hold the order for delivery in April for business reasons, then it might be acceptable to recognize the revenue in March.

8. Breeze-Eastern's revenue increased from Y1 to Y2 and again from Y2 to Y3. Breeze's accounts receivable also increased during these periods. Is the company's increase in receivables approximately consistent with its increase in revenues for the same periods? [See *Revenue Analysis*.]

    Breeze's revenue increased by approximately 6% from FY 1–2 and 25% from FY 2–3. Accounts receivable increased 25% and 7% respectively. The 25% increase in receivables appears to be inconsistent with the FY 1–2 increase in revenues.

9. Breeze shows a decreasing deficit in retained earnings for each of the three years presented and shows profits for the same three years. What is a plausible explanation for the retained earnings deficit? [See *Revenue Analysis*.]

    It is likely that Breeze had earlier losses, possibly from startup operations and is now profitable.

10. Breeze Eastern Annual Income Statement (values in 000's)

Period Ending:	3/31/Y3	3/31/Y2	3/31/Y1
Total Revenue	89,782	85,933	79,956
Cost of Revenue	54,918	54,802	47,143
Gross Profit	34,864	31,131	32,813
Operating Expenses			
Research and Development	6,607	8,162	9,377
Sales, General and Admin.	15,352	13,880	15,246
Operating Income	12,905	9,089	8,190
Add'l income/expense items	1,611	(89)	(93)
Earnings Before Interest and Tax	14,516	9,000	8,097
Interest Expense	32	49	227
Earnings Before Tax	14,484	8,951	7,870
Income Tax	(423)	3,310	3,794
Net Income-Cont. Operations	14,907	5,641	4,076
Net Income	14,907	5,641	4,076

Breeze Eastern Balance Sheets (values in 000's)

Period Ending:	3/31/Y3	3/31/Y2	3/31/Y1
Current Assets			
Cash and Cash Equivalents	$22,806	$6,021	$6,688
Short-Term Investments	$0	$0	$0
Net Receivables	$30,827	$28,799	$22,712
Inventory	$19,427	$18,909	$17,790
Other Current Assets	$1,681	$1,868	$1,506
Total Current Assets	$74,741	$55,597	$48,696
Long-Term Assets			
Long-Term Investments	$0	$0	$0
Fixed Assets	$9,498	$10,132	$10,486
Goodwill	$402	$402	$402
Intangible Assets	$0	$0	$0
Other Assets	$8,516	$9,465	$9,540
Deferred Asset Charges	$3,821	$4,197	$4,289
Total Assets	$96,978	$79,793	$73,413

Current Liabilities			
Accounts Payable	$12,329	$10,675	$9,592
Short-Term Debt and Current Maturities	$0	$0	$0
Other Current Liabilities	$5,938	$5,214	$5,070
Total Current Liabilities	$18,267	$15,889	$14,662
Long-Term Debt	$0	$0	$0
Other Liabilities	$11,596	$13,420	$15,679
Total Liabilities	$29,863	$29,309	$30,341
Stockholders' Equity			
Common Stocks	$102	$101	$100
Capital Surplus	$100,454	$98,707	$97,113
Retained Earnings	($26,437)	($41,344)	($46,985)
Treasury Stock	($7,041)	($6,983)	($6,972)
Other Equity	$37	$3	($184)
Total Equity	$67,115	$50,484	$43,072
Total Liabilities & Equity	$96,978	$79,793	$73,413

Compute the following ratios for 3/13/Y3 and 3/31/Y2 [**See *Financial Ratio Analysis*.**]

Return on assets	**16.9%**	**7.4%**
Return on equity	**25.4%**	**12.1%**
Asset turnover	**1.02**	**1.12**

TOPIC 4

Special Issues

THIS TOPIC PRESENTS SEVERAL THEORETICAL and contemporary issues affecting accounting practice. Fundamentally, accounting income purports to measure economic profitability; however, there are differences in measurement, and it is important for the management accountant or financial analyst to understand those differences. Such differences in accounting measurement lead to a divergence in the accounting value and the economic value of the firm as measured through share prices. Furthermore, economic complexities, such as inflation and foreign currency transactions, affect financial reporting and are discussed in this topic.

International Financial Reporting Standards (IFRS) issued by the International Accounting Standards Board (IASB) have been adopted by nearly all countries of the world. The United States is the most visible country that has not adopted IFRS. Nonetheless IFRS cannot be ignored in the U.S. simply because there are a significant number of U.S. entities that have IFRS reporting subsidiaries, foreign investors reporting under IFRS with U.S. subsidiaries, and an even larger number of U.S. entities that either buy from or sell products or services to IFRS reporting entities. The U.S. SEC since 2008 has allowed foreign registrants to provide their IFRS financial statements to the SEC without reconciliation. The FASB and IASB continue to work together and have significant joint standard-setting projects underway including heavyweight projects on leases, revenue recognition, and a joint conceptual framework for financial reporting.

READ the Learning Outcome Statements (LOS) for this topic as found in Appendix B and then study the concepts and calculations presented here to be sure you understand the content you could be tested on in the CMA exam.

Economic Profit and Accounting Profit

Economic profit and accounting profit are two different measures that can be used to assess a company's performance. The measurement of accounting profit is based on accrual accounting, as measured by generally accepted accounting principles (GAAP).

Accounting Profit = Accounting Revenues − Accounting Costs

The measurement of economic profit considers opportunity costs (implicit costs) in addition to accounting costs (explicit costs). Opportunity costs can be defined as benefits that are given up by choosing one alternative over another.

$$\text{Economic Profit} = \text{Accounting Revenues} - \text{Accounting Costs} - \text{Opportunity Costs}$$

The concept of economic profit can be useful for decision making, as illustrated in the following example: Suppose you are self-employed and earn revenues of $100,000 and incur accounting costs of $70,000. Your accounting profit would be $30,000 ($100,000 − $70,000). If, however, you could have worked as an employee of another company and earned $50,000, then your economic profit would have been a $20,000 loss ($100,000 − $70,000 − $50,000). Even though you earned $30,000 of accounting profits in your business, you could have earned $20,000 more as an employee in another business, so you essentially lost $20,000 choosing to be self-employed.

The concept documents explicitly state the objectives of financial reporting as follows: "The objective of general purpose financial reporting is to provide financial information about the reporting entity that is useful to existing and potential investors, lenders, and other creditors in making decisions about providing resources to the entity. Those decisions involve buying, selling, or holding equity and debt instruments and providing or settling loans and other forms of credit."

The previous example illustrates that it is possible to have a positive accounting profit and a negative economic profit. This means you should have chosen a different alternative. A positive economic profit means you have chosen the better alternative. The existence of positive economic profit implies that the opportunity costs discussed above can be negative.

Accounting Changes and Error Corrections

Financial statements must reflect the results of:

- Changes in accounting principle
- Changes in estimates
- Changes in reporting entities
- Error corrections

Changes in accounting principle occur as a result of new guidance in the Accounting Standards Codification, which is the sole authoritative source for U.S. GAAP or because management has elected to change from one generally accepted accounting principle (GAAP) method to another GAAP method, where a choice is allowed. An example would be a company changing from the weighted average cost method for valuing inventory to the first in, first out (FIFO) method. Note that changing from a cash-based method to a GAAP method is not considered a change in accounting principle as the cash-based method is not GAAP. This type of change would be considered an *error correction* (further discussed below) and would be treated as such. Further note that a change in depreciation method (e.g., changing from the straight-line method to the double-declining balance method) is not considered a change in accounting principle. Instead, it is considered a *change in accounting estimate* effected by a change in principle.

Changes in accounting principle require retrospective application. This approach requires an adjustment of prior period financial statements to incorporate the effect of the new principle "as if" that principle had been used in prior periods. The cumulative effect of the change will be reflected in the carrying values of assets and liabilities of the earliest period presented. It is not appropriate to record the cumulative effects of the change on prior periods in current net income. Instead, beginning retained earnings of the earliest period presented will be adjusted to reflect the effect of this change on all prior periods not presented.

Changes in estimate involve the change in an estimated financial statement amount based on new information or experience. This might include, for instance, changing the bad debt percentage of sales estimate from 2% to 3% or changing the useful life of an asset from five to seven years. Changes in estimate require prospective application, meaning that the financial statements are not restated or retrospectively applied to prior periods; rather, the change is reported in the current period and in future periods only.

Changes in reporting entities include changes that result in the financial statements representing a different entity. Some examples include presenting consolidated statements in place of individual statements, a change in subsidiaries, or a change in the use of the equity method for an investment. Changes in reporting entities also require retrospective application similar to changes in accounting principle. Prior-period financial statements are reflected to show the financial information for the new reporting entity as if the entity had existed in that form all along. Cumulative earnings differences are reported through beginning retained earnings as of the beginning of the first period presented.

A correction of an error occurs when a material error is made in a prior period's financial statements and requires an adjustment to restate the financial statements so that, cumulatively, they reflect an accurate retained earnings balance. Errors made that affect the income or loss reporting in prior periods are corrected by adjusting the beginning balance of retained earnings. When financial statements of prior years are being reported on a comparative basis, they are restated to correct amounts. The effect of the error on earlier periods is presented as an adjustment of beginning retained earnings net of income tax effects for the earliest period presented.

Earnings Quality

Reported business income, as measured by the accounting process, is not an absolute truth but is a result of many assumptions used and the accounting principles applied. Changing the assumptions or changing the accounting principle employed could change the reported income drastically. Investors, as a result, are very much interested in earnings quality.

Earnings quality pertains to the validity and veracity of the reported information. Quality earnings are those that both reflect current-period performance and help users to assess future performance. Analysis of earnings quality identifies the results of management choices on financial statements and judges management's motivations, propensities, and attitudes. The basic factors of earnings quality are:

- Selection of accounting principles
- Off–balance sheet financing and its effect on the financials
- Provision for maintenance of assets and future earnings power
- Effect of economic forces on earnings

Selection of Accounting Principles

Management has discretion in choosing from among accepted accounting principles. A company can tend to be liberal or conservative in its accounting methods. Conservative accounting is less likely to overstate earnings, so the quality of earnings is higher. The last-in, first-out (LIFO) inventory valuation method is considered conservative during times of rising prices (earnings are lower and assets are valued lower). However, excessive conservatism may result in lack of reporting integrity over the long run and is not desirable. The analyst can examine the selection of accounting principles to determine their effects on the financial health and reporting of the company.

Off–Balance Sheet Financing and Its Effect on the Financials

The term **off–balance sheet financing** is used to denote various types of transactions through which a firm can use a resource without showing either the asset or the corresponding liability on the balance sheet. For example, a company might structure a lease in such a way that it would be classified as an operating lease rather than a capital lease. With an operating lease, the leased asset is not capitalized, and the lease liability is not carried on the books. The company simply recognizes the lease payments as rent expense. In contrast, leases structured as capital leases would result in the leased asset being carried on the balance sheet, along with the corresponding liability. Interest expense would be recognized over the life of the lease as principal payments are made on the lease liability. The leased asset is depreciated by the lessee as if the asset were owned by the lessee.

Other forms of off–balance sheet financing involve the use special-purpose entities, the transfer of receivables, and the participation in joint ventures. Special-purpose entities (SPEs) are, as their name suggests, entities created for a particular purpose. For example, an SPE might be formed for the purpose of financing the construction of a large asset. The SPE would construct the asset and then, once the asset is operational, sell its output to the organization that controls the SPE. The asset and the related liability appear on the books of the SPE rather than on the books of the controlling company. A particular form of SPE is a Variable Interest Entity (VIE). VIEs were introduced in Topic 2. If an entity qualifies as a VIE then an assessment must be made to determine if another entity is the primary beneficiary. If an entity is the primary beneficiary of the VIE, then the VIE must be consolidated with the primary beneficiary. Consolidation eliminates many of the off–balance sheet issues related to VIEs.

Another form of off-balance sheet financing involves choosing to transfer accounts receivables to a third party rather than obtain a loan. With this method, the company is able to obtain cash while removing the accounts receivable from the books and avoiding debt. This type of financing could also be achieved through an SPE.

Joint ventures with other companies also can be utilized as a form of off-balance sheet financing. Participants can invest together in a joint venture with none of the investors having a controlling interest in the venture. As such, the venture's financial statements will not be consolidated with the financial statements of any of the participants. Only the investment in the venture will appear on the participants' balance sheet, and this amount will subsequently be increased by the company's percentage share of net income reported by the venture and decreased by any dividends paid by the venture to the company. The venture company can take out loans (guaranteed by the investors), but those loans will not show up on the participants' balance sheets.

Firms might structure transactions such as those mentioned above to improve the appearance of the balance sheet by improving such ratios as return on assets, the debt-to-equity ratio, and the debt-to-total assets ratio, among others. Although some of these methods are within the permissible domain under FASB standards, some may get eliminated under the International Financial Reporting Standards (IFRS).

Provision for Maintenance of Assets and Future Earnings Power

Management can put off discretionary expenses, such as repairs and maintenance, to show higher earnings. However, if necessary maintenance and repairs are neglected for the short-term reason of showing higher profits, premature deterioration of assets may have a negative effect on earnings in the long run.

Other discretionary expenses, which have little effect in the short run if put off but great effect in the long run, include advertising and research and development (R&D) costs. It should be noted, however, that R&D costs must be examined carefully, as they do not always produce results that increase corporate profits.

Effect of Economic Forces on Earnings

The effects of cyclical and other economic forces on earnings are not a primary result of management decisions. However, skillful management can minimize the effects of business cycles on the stability of sources and variability of earnings.

Earnings Persistence

Earnings persistence is a measure of how well current earnings predict future earnings. The trend of income is important. Earnings that fluctuate up and down with business cycles are less desirable than earnings that display a larger degree of stability, or persistence, over the business cycle. Earnings that display a steady growth trend are most desirable.

Earnings may show fluctuations from year to year that are due not to income from operations but to other unusual income and expenses. In order to isolate the effect of extraordinary income or expenses, financial analysts often recast and adjust income statements to show persistent earnings over a number of years for a company.

Book Value per Share

Book value is the amount of money that would be available to shareholders if an organization's assets were sold at their balance sheet value and all liabilities were paid. Book value per share is calculated by subtracting all liabilities from all assets, then dividing it by the total number of outstanding shares (or equivalents). If an organization's calculated book value per share is higher than the current stock price, the organization may be undervalued; if an organization's stock price is substantially higher than the book value per share, the organization may be overvalued and prone to corrections. A major limitation with book value is that it may be difficult to value assets accurately. However, book value is an accounting construct. Book value is not intended to represent market or fair value. A variety of legitimate accounting techniques for measuring assets may result in different valuations. Further, it may be unrealistic to assume that the value of an asset on the balance sheet equals the value an organization would receive if the asset were sold.

In determining book value per share, the par value of the preferred shareholders' equity (or its call value if the shares are callable) is deducted from total equity because preferred shareholders have priority in liquidation; thus, the par value of preferred stock would not be available to holders of common stock. When calculating book value per share, total stockholders' equity is reduced by any preferred stock dividends in arrears.

$$\text{Book Value per Share} = \frac{\text{Total Stockholders' Equity} - (\text{Preferred Stock} + \text{Dividends in Arrears})}{\text{Number of Common Shares Outstanding}}$$

For example: Company Q with $10,000,000 in shareholders' equity, $500,000 par value of preferred stock, and 9 million shares of common stock outstanding would compute the book value per share in this way:

$$\text{Book Value per Share} = \frac{\$10,000,000 - \$500,000}{9,000,000} = \frac{\$9,500,000}{9,000,000} = \$1.06$$

This measure is used in conjunction with the market value of the shares to determine the premium the market places on the future potential of the company.

Market to Book Value Ratio

The financial market considers additional information beyond the numbers found in the balance sheet and income statement. As a result, book value and market value typically differ. The **market to book value** ratio compares the current book value of each share of common stock to its current market value.

$$\text{Market to Book Ratio} = \text{Current Stock Price} / \text{Book Value per Share}$$

Price/Earnings P/E Ratio

The price/earnings (P/E) ratio compares the market price of the stock to earnings per share (EPS):

Price Earnings Ratio = Market Price per Share / Earnings per Share

The P/E ratio is expressed as a multiple of EPS. Investors consider the P/E ratio when choosing an acceptable investment; P/E ratios vary by industry. Businesses in high-growth industries generally have high P/E ratios. Managers like to see a high P/E ratio because it indicates strong market confidence.

Earnings Yield

The earnings yield is the inverse of the P/E ratio. It represents the income-producing power of $1 invested in common stock (at its current price):

Earnings Yield = EPS / Current Market Price per Common Share

Analysis also can be made regarding the percentage of earnings retained for future growth and the percentage of earnings paid out as dividends to common shareholders.

Effects of Changing Prices and Inflation

Inflation, or an increase in prices over time, is an important consideration in analyzing financial statements. Financial statements are based on historical costs (usually) and are not adjusted for the effects of increasing prices. If a company's sales revenue increases over the year, that does not necessarily mean that the company's business is growing in real terms. For example, an increase in total sales from $200,000 in one year to $210,000 the next year could be due to increase in the sales volume or an increase in the sales price. If it is the latter, and the company raised the selling price by 5% when the economy-wide inflation was 8%, it is a bad sign. In fact, it signifies a drop in the "real" economic price and did not even result in a higher sales volume.

Fortunately, inflation has been relatively subdued in the United States in the past several years. Thus, the factors and concerns just mentioned are not that important in the United States or in most western European countries. However, these concerns could be of significant importance to highly inflationary economies, such as in Latin America. Through horizontal (or trend) analysis, the effects of inflation could be considered by calculating the rates in terms of a base-year dollar value. That is, if the inflation is, say, 10%, the sales amount in successive years is divided by a factor of 1.1, 1.21, and so on.

For example: Assume the base year to be 2014, and sales were $300,000. In successive years 2015 and 2016, sales were $320,000 and $350,000. Thus, the sales growth in absolute dollars was 6.67% ($20,000 / $300,000) in 2015 and 9.375% ($30,000 / $320,000) in 2016. However, in terms of base-year dollars, these sales would be recast as $290,909 ($320,000 / 1.1) and $289,256 ($350,000 / 1.21), which actually reflects a decline in sales over the two years.

Fair Value Standards

FASB Accounting Standards Codification (ASC) Topic 820, *Fair Value Measurements and Disclosures* (formerly FAS No. 157, *Fair Value Measurements*), defines the term *fair value* and establishes a framework for measuring fair value uniformly for various accounts and accounting treatments. A fair value measurement assumes that the asset or liability is exchanged in an orderly transaction between market participants on the measurement date. When a principal market exists, the price at that market is the fair value. However, in situations where a principal market does not exist, the price at the "most advantageous" market would be used to determine the fair value if there are multiple markets for the asset or the liability. Additionally, a fair value measurement assumes the highest and best use of the asset by market participants. In broad terms, the phrase *highest and best use* refers to use of an asset that would maximize the value of the asset. Best use is determined based on the use of the asset by market participants even if the intended use is different. For example, if a land in prime residential neighborhood is acquired to build a warehouse, the fair value of the land would be the value if it were used for residential purposes.

In order to determine fair value, three approaches are suggested: market approach, income approach, and cost approach. The **market approach** uses prices generated by transactions involving identical or comparable assets. The **income approach** uses valuation techniques to convert future amounts to a single discounted present amount. The **cost approach** is based on the replacement value of the asset.

To increase consistency and comparability in fair value measurements, a fair value hierarchy is created to prioritize the inputs to valuation techniques to determine the fair value. This hierarchy gives the highest priority to quoted prices in active markets (Level 1) and lowest priority to unobservable inputs (Level 3). In the intermediate term, the input could be determined indirectly from the values of related assets, which have quoted prices in active markets (Level 2). The disclosure in the financial statement has to include the classification of assets into these three categories.

Using fair value in financial reporting, as opposed to cost-based reporting, provides more current information about the valuation of assets in comparison to using historical cost.

Many financial institutions and investors rely on fair values to make decisions that involve financial assets and liabilities. In many cases, fair value represents the market's expectations about expected future cash flows that may be derived from such assets or liabilities. Fair value makes it possible to compare financial instruments (assets or liabilities) that embody the same economic characteristics, regardless of when they were issued or purchased, when making decisions to buy, hold, or sell those financial instruments. The disadvantages of using fair value include increased volatility in the value of the asset and uncertainty as to the reliability of estimates related to the flexibility in the estimate of the fair value of those instruments.

In May 2011, the IASB issued IFRS No. 13, *Fair Value Measurement*. IFRS No. 13 defines fair value and replaces the requirement contained in individual standards. This new guidance establishes a single-source framework for fair value measurement, as well as required fair value measurement disclosures. IFRS 13 is very similar to FAS 157. With limited exceptions this makes a comparison between IFRS and the ASC on fair value measurement a little easier.

Accounting for Foreign Currency Transactions and Financial Statements

The exposure of U.S. corporations to foreign currency (FC) has rapidly expanded, and currently U.S. companies' purchases and sales abroad amount to approximately $4 trillion per year. For some companies, almost 70% of their revenues are realized abroad, in FC. Conducting business abroad poses multiple accounting challenges; primary problems include these seven:

1. Accounting for sales made abroad and denominated in FC
2. Accounting for purchases made abroad and denominated in FC
3. Accounting for assets held abroad, the value of which is denominated in FC
4. Accounting for liabilities held abroad, the value of which is denominated in FC
5. Accounting for a foreign subsidiary that must be consolidated in a U.S. corporation's financial statements
6. Accounting for intercompany transactions with a foreign subsidiary
7. Hedging in foreign currency to mitigate exposure to fluctuations in foreign currency

Of these concepts, the ones relevant for the CMA exam are the first five, which are covered in this section.

When U.S. corporations conduct business abroad (buying or selling of goods), these transactions usually are denominated in the currency of the place where the transaction takes place. For example, prices at McDonald's in New York City are denominated in U.S. dollars (USD), but prices at McDonald's in Mexico City are denominated in pesos and those in London are denominated in British pounds. Thus, a business may have multiple transactions in various FCs during the course of a year. However, when preparing the financial statements, all of those transactions must be converted to USD.

Similarly, assets and liabilities of the company may be denominated in FC and ultimately would get settled in that currency. However, for reporting purposes, the equivalent amount has to be shown in USD.

This illustration uses FC as the foreign currency. An **exchange rate** is the purchase price of one unit of a currency in terms of the other. Exchange rates are quoted either directly (the number of units of the domestic currency [i.e., the USD] that can be converted into one unit of foreign currency [i.e., the FC]) or indirectly (the number of foreign currency units [i.e., FC] that one unit of the domestic currency [i.e, USD] can be converted into). For example, a direct quote of USD for one FC of $1.40 (presented as $1.40 = FC1), means that $1.40 could be exchanged (purchased or sold) for one FC. This quote can also be stated indirectly as $1 = FC0.714286, meaning that one USD can be exchanged (purchased or sold) for .714286 FC. Note that an exchange rate quoted "indirectly" is simply the reciprocal of the direct exchange quote (1 / $1.40 = FC0.714286).

The exchange rates may be fixed by a government or allowed to fluctuate based on demand and supply of a particular currency. The terminology related to these fluctuations is called weakening or strengthening of the currency. A currency falls, or weakens, relative to another currency if it takes more of that currency to purchase one unit of the other currency. A currency rises, or strengthens, if it takes fewer units of that currency to purchase one unit of the other currency.

The most common types of FC transactions are imports and exports of goods and services. An export of goods by a U.S. company to a German customer would be considered an FC transaction if the sale is denominated in the foreign currency (i.e., FC). This transaction will have to be translated into USD using the FC/USD exchange rate on a specified date. Similarly, an import of goods from a Canadian company by a U.S. business would be considered an FC transaction if the purchase was denominated in Canadian dollars. ASC Topic 830, *Foreign Currency Matters*, stipulates two requirements for foreign currency transactions:

1. At the date of a foreign currency transaction, each asset, liability, revenue, expense, gain, or loss arising from the transaction shall be measured and recorded in the functional currency (usually the reporting currency) using the exchange rate in effect on that date.
2. At each balance sheet date, recorded balances (receivables and/or payables) shall be adjusted to reflect the exchange rate on the balance sheet date. Any gain or loss resulting from a change in the exchange rate would appear in the income statement during the period of the change. Recorded balances (receivables and/or payables) may also require further adjustment on the payment date, if the exchange rate has changed from the balance sheet date to the payment date.

Sales Denominated in Foreign Currency

Example: Suppose on December 16, Trading Company sold merchandise to a foreign company for FC20,000, when the (indirect) spot rate for FC was $0.660. The balance sheet was prepared on December 31, when the indirect spot rate was $0.665. Trading Company collected the amount (in FC) on January 31, when the indirect spot rate was $0.6725. The journal entries that would be recorded on each of these dates are:

December 16:
Accounts Receivable	30,303	
Revenue		30,303

Calculation: (FC 20,000/$0.660 = $30,303)

Note: The indirect exchange rate can be converted into a direct exchange rate by dividing the $0.660 into 1. The resulting quotient (i.e., 1.515152) can then be multiplied by the FC20,000 to derive the same USD equivalent.

December 31:
Exchange Loss	228	
Accounts Receivable		228

Calculation: [(1/$0.665) − (1/$0.660)] × (FC20,000) = ($228)

January 31:
Cash	29,740	
Exchange Loss	335	
Accounts Receivable		30,075

Calculations: [(FC20,000 × (1/$0.6725) = $29,740) (USD received on January 31)]; ($29,740 − $30,075 (USD A/R balance at December 31)) = ($335)

In the December 31 financial statements, the transaction would result in the following balances:

Revenue	$30,303
Accounts Receivable	30,075
Exchange Loss	($228)

Purchases in Foreign Currency

Example: Assume that a U.S.-domiciled company purchases inventory from a foreign supplier for 10,000 FC. The spot rate (quoted directly) in effect on the date of purchase is $0.70 = FC1. The U.S. company records the transaction as shown:

Inventory	7,000	
Account Payable		7,000

Calculation: (FC10,000 × 0.70 = $7,000)

If the account payable has not been settled on December 31 (the balance sheet date), when the spot rate is $0.69, the following adjustment would be made:

Accounts Payable	100	
Exchange Gain		100

Calculation: [(0.70−0.69)(FC10,000)] = $100

Effects on Financial Ratios

When sales are denominated in FC, it results in accounts receivables denominated in FC. If the dollar subsequently weakens with respect to the FC, an exchange gain is recorded on the balance sheet date and the A/R balance becomes larger, thus favorably affecting the short-term liquidity ratios. If the dollar strengthens with respect to the FC, an exchange loss is recorded on the balance sheet date and the A/R balance becomes smaller, thus unfavorably affecting short-term liquidity ratios.

Similarly, when a purchase is denominated in FC, it results in accounts payable (A/P) denominated in FC. If the dollar subsequently weakens with respect to the FC, an exchange loss is recorded on the balance sheet date and the A/P balance becomes larger, thus unfavorably affecting short-term liquidity ratios. If the dollar strengthens with respect to the FC, an exchange gain is recorded on the balance sheet date and the A/P balance becomes smaller, thus favorably affecting short-term liquidity ratios.

Exchange rate volatility can cause volatility in earnings. Investors would certainly be concerned with the risk that companies face with regard to FC changes. To mitigate the effects of fluctuations in FC, management sometimes hedges the company's exposure through purchase of forward contracts or options. Such hedges are called cash flow hedges for accounting purposes.

Accounting for Financial Statements of Foreign Subsidiaries

When a foreign subsidiary does not keep its records in the parent's currency (also known as the reporting currency), the subsidiary's financial statements must be translated into the parent's reporting currency prior to consolidation.

Functional Currency

Choosing the appropriate method for translating subsidiaries' foreign currency financial statements depends on what an entity's functional currency is. ASC Topic 830, *Foreign Currency Matters* (formerly addressed in FASB Statement No. 52), defines the **functional currency** as the currency of the primary economic environment in which the subsidiary operates. The subsidiary's local currency would be its functional currency if its operations are relatively self-contained and integrated within a particular country. In contrast, the parent's currency would be the functional currency if the operations of the branch or subsidiary are essentially an extension of the parent company's operations.

Determining which currency is the functional currency would depend on factors such as where the subsidiary's sales market is, how its sales prices are determined, where its expenses are incurred, its sources of financing, and the extent of intercompany transactions. Self-contained operations typically have their sales, purchases, and financing denominated in their local currency and have few intercompany transactions. Integral operations, in contrast, typically have their sales, purchases, and financing denominated in the parent's currency and have a number of intercompany transactions.

If a subsidiary operates in a hyperinflationary environment (one with inflation of 100% or more over a three-year period), the parent's currency is always the functional currency.

Currency Translation Methods

ASC Topic 830 identifies two different methods for converting the financial statements of foreign subsidiaries into USD, based on the foreign subsidiary's functional currency. The method used depends on whether the foreign subsidiary's functional currency is the local currency or the U.S. dollar.

When the subsidiary's currency is not the functional currency, its financial statements are remeasured into the parent's currency using the historical rate/temporal method. However, when the subsidiary's local currency is the functional currency, the statements are translated using the current rate method. When the subsidiary maintains its books in the local currency but this currency is not the functional currency or the parent's reporting currency, the statements must first be remeasured to the functional currency using the historical rate/temporal method and then translated to the parent's reporting currency.

Typically, there are three steps in consolidating a foreign subsidiary:

1. Modify the foreign financials so they conform to U.S. GAAP. *Doing this may require numerous modifications.*
2. Remeasure the trial balance into the functional currency. *This step is needed only when the currency used to maintain the financial records is not the functional currency.*
3. Translate the financials from the functional currency into the reporting currency.

Thus, the conversion process may apply either the temporal method or the current-rate method individually, or it may apply the temporal method followed by the current-rate method. As stated above the method used is not optional; rather, the method used is determined by the subsidiary's functional currency.

Remeasurement Using the Temporal Method

Under the historical rate/temporal method, nonmonetary balances (all balance sheet items other than cash, claims to cash, and cash obligations) are translated using historical exchange rates, and the expenses associated with them should be translated at the historical exchange rate in effect when the item was recorded originally.

Nonmonetary accounts include marketable securities carried at cost including:

a. Marketable securities carried at cost
b. Inventories carried at cost and cost of goods sold
c. Prepaid expenses such as insurance, advertising, and rent
d. Property, plant, and equipment and depreciation expense

e. Accumulated depreciation on property, plant, and equipment
f. Patents, trademarks, licenses, and formulas and amortization expense
g. Goodwill
h. Other intangible assets
i. Deferred charges and credits, except policy acquisition costs for life insurance companies
j. Deferred income
k. Common stock
l. Preferred stock carried at issuance price
m. Revenues and expenses related to nonmonetary items

(From FASB Accounting Standards Codification 830-10-45-18.)

Monetary assets and liabilities (cash, receivables, and payables) and other assets and liabilities measured at current values (market values or discounted cash flows) are translated at the current exchange rate on the balance sheet date. Income statement accounts other than those just mentioned are translated using the

Figure 2A-7 Remeasurement Using the Temporal Method

Bounce Sporting Goods Company
Remeasurement of European Branch Trial Balance to U.S. Dollars
December 31, Year 1

	Balance (FC) debit (credit)	Exchange Rates	Balance (U.S. dollars) debit (credit)
Cash	FC19,950	$0.24*	$4,788
Trade accounts receivable	352,800	0.24*	84,672
Inventories	157,500	0.21†	33,075
Home office	(432,250)		(78,400)
Sales	(700,000)	0.225‡	(157,500)
Cost of goods sold	472,500	0.21†	99,225
Operating expenses	129,500	0.225‡	29,138
Subtotals	FC0		$14,998
Transaction gain	0		(14,998)
Totals	FC0		$0

*Current rate (on December 31, Year 1) = .24.
†Applicable historical rate.
‡Average exchange rate for the year.

weighted-average exchange rate for the current period for simplicity. In the temporal method, translation gains and losses are reported in income.

The example in Figure 2A-7 shows a remeasurement from FC to U.S. dollars, the branch's functional currency. As indicated, accounts have been translated using the current rate on the balance sheet date, the historical exchange rate, or the weighted-average rate for the year. The home office account, which represents equity, is not remeasured; rather, the beginning balance in dollars is carried forward.

Translation Using the Current Rate Method

In the current rate method, all assets and liabilities are translated using the current exchange rate on the balance sheet date. Paid-in capital accounts are translated using the historic rate. Translation of income statement accounts is based on

Figure 2A-8 Translation Using the Current Rate Method (Subsidiary Financial Statements) to Reporting Currency from Functional Currency

Bounce International Germany
Translation of Financial Statements to U.S. Dollars
for Year Ended August 31, Year 2

	Foreign Currency	Exchange Rate	U.S. Dollars
Income Statement			
Net sales	FC206,400	$0.515*	$106,296
Other revenue	51,600	0.515*	26,574
Total revenue	FC258,000		$132,870
Cost of goods sold	FC154,800	0.515*	$79,722
Operating expenses and income taxes	82,560	0.515*	42,518
Total costs and expenses	FC237,360		$122,240
Net income	FC20,640		$10,630
Balance Sheet			
Cash	FC8,600	$0.49†	$4,214
Trade accounts receivable (net)	34,400	0.49†	16,856
Inventories	154,800	0.49†	75,852
Short-term prepayments	3,440	0.49†	1,686
Plant assets (net)	275,200	0.49†	134,848
Intangible assets (net)	17,200	0.49†	8,428
Total assets	FC493,640		$241,884
Notes payable	FC17,200	$0.49†	$8,428
Trade accounts payable	25,800	0.49†	12,642
Common stock	430,000	0.54‡	232,200
Retained earnings	20,640		11,146
Cumulative translation adjustments			(22,532)
Total liabilities and stockholders' equity	FC493,640		$241,884

*Average for year ended December 31, Year 2.

†Current rate (on December 31, Year 2).

‡Historical rate (on December 31, Year 1, date of X Corporation's investment).

the weighted-average rate for the current period. Translation gains and losses are not shown in net income but are reported as a component of other comprehensive income.

An example of a translation worksheet from FC to U.S. dollars appears in Figure 2A-8. Use of the current, average, or historical exchange rate is indicated. The ending retained earnings balance is not translated; rather, the dollar amount of beginning translated retained earnings from the prior year would be carried forward, and ending retained earnings would be the sum of this beginning balance, plus the translated income amount, less any dividends declared during the year.

Financial Statement Presentation and Disclosure Requirements for Foreign Currency

The income statement or notes should list the aggregate gains or losses from foreign entities over the accounting period. Changes in cumulative translation adjustments for the period also must be disclosed in a separate statement, a note, or the statement of stockholders' equity. Details of translation adjustments include the beginning and ending amounts of cumulative translation adjustments, aggregate adjustments, hedges of net investments, long-term intercompany transactions, income taxes allocated to translation adjustments, and decreases from liquidating a foreign investment.

After the financials have been converted into the parent's reporting currency (USD), the parent company prepares the worksheet eliminations to consolidate the foreign subsidiary and the parent company.

Knowledge Check: Special Issues

The following questions are intended to help you check your understanding and recall of the material presented in this topic. They do not represent the type of questions that appear on the CMA exam.

Directions: Answer each question in the space provided. Correct answers and section references follow these questions.

1. To consolidate a German subsidiary of a U.S. company for which the functional currency is euro, the process includes:
   - ☐ a. translation of the financials.
   - ☐ b. remeasurement of the financials.
   - ☐ c. first remeasurement, then translation of the financials.
   - ☐ d. first translation, then remeasurement of the financials.

2. Fair value standards require measurement of fair value of an asset by using
   - ☐ a. the commonly available price in the primary use of the asset.
   - ☐ b. the average of the prices in all available markets for the asset.
   - ☐ c. the price in the most advantageous market.
   - ☐ d. the price in the most conservative market (worst use).

3. Lester Company's comparative balance sheets showed total assets to be $1,500,000 and total liabilities of $900,000 on December 31, 2012. It has 250,000 shares outstanding. The shares are trading at $12 per share. What is the market to book value for Lester?
   - ☐ a. 0.2
   - ☐ b. 2
   - ☐ c. 5
   - ☐ d. Cannot be determined.

4. Name some of the variables affecting the quality of earnings.
   - a. _____
   - b. _____
   - c. _____
   - d. _____
   - e. _____

Knowledge Check Answers: Special Issues

1. To consolidate a German subsidiary of a U.S. company for which the functional currency is euro, the process includes: *[See Accounting for Foreign Subsidiaries.]*
   - ☑ a. translation of the financials.
   - ☐ b. remeasurement of the financials.
   - ☐ c. first remeasurement, then translation of the financials.
   - ☐ d. first translation, then remeasurement of the financials.

2. Fair value standards require measurement of fair value of an asset by using: *[See Fair Value Standards.]*
   - ☐ a. the commonly available price in the primary use of the asset.
   - ☐ b. the average of the prices in all available markets for the asset.
   - ☑ c. the price in the most advantageous market.
   - ☐ d. the price in the most conservative market (worst use).

3. Lester Company's comparative balance sheets showed total assets to be $1,500,000 and total liability of $900,000 on December 31, 2012. It has 250,000 shares outstanding. The shares are trading at $12 per share. What is the market to book value for Lester? *[See Market to Book Value Ratio.]*
   - ☐ a. 0.2
   - ☐ b. 2
   - ☑ c. 5
   - ☐ d. Cannot be determined.

   Equity or Book value = $600,000

   Market value = 250,000 × 12

4. Name some of the variables affecting the quality of earnings. *[See Earnings Quality.]*
   - a. Choice of accounting methods
   - b. Accounting estimates
   - c. Effects of inflation
   - d. Off–balance sheet financing
   - e. Maintenance of assets and future earning

Practice Questions: Financial Statement Analysis

Directions: This sampling of questions is designed to emulate actual exam questions. Read each question and write your response on another sheet of paper. See the "Answers to Section Practice Questions" section at the end of this book to assess your response. Validate or improve the answer you wrote. For a more robust selection of practice questions, access the **Online Test Bank** at www.wileycma.com.

Question 2A1-AT01

Topic: Basic Financial Statement Analysis

Gordon has had the following financial results for the last four years:

	Year 1	Year 2	Year 3	Year 4
Sales	$1,250,000	$1,300,000	$1,359,000	$1,400,000
Cost of goods sold	750,000	785,000	825,000	850,000
Gross profit	$ 500,000	$ 515,000	$ 534,000	$ 550,000
Inflation factor	1.00	1.03	1.07	1.10

Gordon has analyzed these results using vertical common-size analysis to determine trends. The performance of Gordon can **best** be characterized by which one of the following statements?

- ☐ a. The common-size gross profit percentage has decreased as a result of an increasing common-size trend in cost of goods sold.
- ☐ b. The common-size trend in sales is increasing and is resulting in an increasing trend in the common-size gross profit margin.
- ☐ c. The common-size trend in cost of goods sold is decreasing, which is resulting in an increasing trend in the common-size gross profit margin.
- ☐ d. The increased trend in the common-size gross profit percentage is the result of both the increasing trend in sales and the decreasing trend in cost of goods sold.

Question 2A1-AT02

Topic: Basic Financial Statement Analysis

In assessing the financial prospects for a firm, financial analysts use various techniques. An example of vertical, common-size analysis is

- ☐ a. an assessment of the relative stability of a firm's level of vertical integration.
- ☐ b. a comparison in financial ratio form between two or more firms in the same industry.

- c. advertising expense is 2% of sales.
- d. comparison in financial form between two or more firms in different industries.

Question 2A1-AT03

Topic: Basic Financial Statement Analysis

When preparing common-size statements, items on the balance sheet are generally stated as a percentage of _____ and items on the income statement are generally stated as a percentage of _____.

- a. total assets; net sales
- b. total shareholders' equity; net income
- c. total assets; net income
- d. total shareholders' equity; net sales

Question 2A1-LS01

Topic: Basic Financial Statement Analysis

Which of the following statements is **true** regarding common-size statements?

- a. Common-size statements can be used to compare companies of different sizes.
- b. Common-size statements indexed over two years for two companies, with both showing a 10% increase in profits, show that both companies would make equally attractive investments.
- c. Horizontal common-size statements can be made only for companies with at least ten years of operational data.
- d. All of the above.

Question 2A1-LS02

Topic: Basic Financial Statement Analysis

A common-size statement is helpful

- a. for figuring out how assets are allocated.
- b. for determining the next investment the company should make.
- c. for considering whether to buy or sell assets.
- d. in comparing companies of different sizes.

Question 2A2-CQ01
Topic: Financial Ratios

Broomall Corporation has decided to include certain financial ratios in its year-end annual report to shareholders. Selected information relating to its most recent fiscal year is provided next.

Cash	$10,000
Accounts receivable	20,000
Prepaid expenses	8,000
Inventory	30,000
Available-for-sale securities	
At cost	9,000
Fair value at year-end	12,000
Accounts payable	15,000
Notes payable (due in 90 days)	25,000
Bonds payable (due in 10 years)	35,000
Net credit sales for year	220,000
Cost of goods sold	140,000

Broomall's working capital at year-end is

- a. $40,000
- b. $37,000
- c. $28,000
- d. $10,000

Question 2A2-CQ02
Topic: Financial Ratios

Birch Products Inc. has the following current assets:

Cash	$ 250,000
Marketable securities	100,000
Accounts receivable	800,000
Inventories	1,450,000
Total current assets	$2,600,000

If Birch's current liabilities are $1,300,000, the firm's

- a. current ratio will decrease if a payment of $100,000 cash is used to pay $100,000 of accounts payable.
- b. current ratio will not change if a payment of $100,000 cash is used to pay $100,000 of accounts payable.
- c. quick ratio will decrease if a payment of $100,000 cash is used to purchase inventory.

☐ d. quick ratio will not change if a payment of $100,000 cash is used to purchase inventory.

Question 2A2-CQ08

Topic: Financial Ratios

Lowell Corporation has decided to include certain financial ratios in its year-end annual report to shareholders. Selected information relating to its most recent fiscal year is provided next.

Cash	$ 10,000
Accounts receivable (end of year)	20,000
Accounts receivable (beginning of year)	24,000
Inventory (end of year)	30,000
Inventory (beginning of year)	26,000
Notes payable (due in 90 days)	25,000
Bonds payable (due in 10 years)	35,000
Net credit sales for year	220,000
Cost of goods sold	140,000

Using a 365-day year, compute Lowell's accounts receivable turnover in days.

☐ a. 26.1 days
☐ b. 33.2 days
☐ c. 36.5 days
☐ d. 39.8 days

Question 2A2-CQ14

Topic: Financial Ratios

Cornwall Corporation's net accounts receivable were $68,000 and $47,000 at the beginning and end of the year, respectively. Cornwall's condensed income statement is shown next.

Sales	$900,000
Cost of goods sold	527,000
Operating expenses	175,000
Operating income	198,000
Income tax	79,000
Net income	$119,000

Cornwall's average number of days' sales in accounts receivable (using a 365-day year) is

☐ a. 8 days
☐ b. 13 days

☐ c. 19 days
☐ d. 23 days

Question 2A2-CQ21
Topic: Financial Ratios

Marble Savings Bank has received loan applications from three companies in the auto parts manufacturing business and currently has the funds to grant only one of these requests. Specific data, shown next, have been selected from these applications for review and comparison with industry averages.

	Bailey	Nutron	Sonex	Industry
Total sales (millions)	$4.27	$3.91	$4.86	$4.30
Net profit margin	9.55%	9.85%	10.05%	9.65%
Current ratio	1.82	2.02	1.96	1.95
Return on assets	12.0%	12.6%	11.4%	12.4%
Debt/equity ratio	52.5%	44.6%	49.6%	48.3%
Financial leverage	1.30	1.02	1.56	1.33

Based on this information, select the strategy that should be the **most** beneficial to Marble Savings.

☐ a. Marble Savings Bank should not grant any loans as none of these companies represents a good credit risk.

☐ b. Grant the loan to Bailey as all the company's data approximate the industry average.

☐ c. Grant the loan to Nutron as both the debt to equity ratio and degree of financial leverage are below the industry average.

☐ d. Grant the loan to Sonex as the company has the highest net profit margin and degree of financial leverage.

Question 2A2-CQ29
Topic: Financial Ratios

The following information concerning Arnold Company's common stock was included in the company's financial reports for the last two years.

	Year 2	Year 1
Market price per share on December 31	$60	$50
Par value per share	10	10
Earnings per share	3	3
Dividends per share	1	1
Book value per share on December 31	36	34

Based on the price/earnings information, investors would **most likely** consider Arnold's common stock to

- a. be overvalued at the end of year 2.
- b. indicate inferior investment decisions by management in year 2.
- c. show a positive trend in growth opportunities in year 2 compared to year 1.
- d. show a decline in growth opportunities in year 2 compared to year 1.

Question 2A2-CQ30

Topic: Financial Ratios

Devlin Inc. has 250,000 shares of $10 par value common stock outstanding. For the current year, Devlin paid a cash dividend of $3.50 per share and had earnings per share of $4.80. The market price of Devlin's stock is $34 per share. Devlin's price/earnings ratio is

- a. 2.08
- b. 2.85
- c. 7.08
- d. 9.71

Question 2A3-CQ01

Topic: Profitability Analysis

For the year just ended, Beechwood Corporation had income from operations of $198,000 and net income of $96,000. Additional financial information is given next.

	January 1	December 31
7% bonds payable	$95,000	$77,000
Common stock ($10 par value)	300,000	300,000
Reserve for bond retirement	12,000	28,000
Retained earnings	155,000	206,000

Beechwood has no other equity issues outstanding. Beechwood's return on shareholders' equity for the year just ended is

- a. 19.2%
- b. 19.9%
- c. 32.0%
- d. 39.5%

Question 2A3-AT01
Topic: Profitability Analysis

For a given level of sales and holding all other financial statement items, including liabilities, constant, a company's return on equity (ROE) will

- ☐ a. decrease as its total assets increase.
- ☐ b. increase as its debt ratio decreases.
- ☐ c. decrease as its cost of goods sold as a percentage of sales decrease.
- ☐ d. increase as its equity increases.

Question 2A3-LS01
Topic: Profitability Analysis

BDU Company has net income of $500,000 and average assets of $2,000,000 for the current year. If its asset turnover is 1.25 times, what is its profit margin?

- ☐ a. 0.25
- ☐ b. 0.31
- ☐ c. 0.36
- ☐ d. 0.2

Question 2A3-LS05
Topic: Profitability Analysis

Which of the following must be considered in measuring income?

I. Estimates regarding future events

II. Accounting methods used by the company

III. The degree of informative disclosure about results of operations

IV. Different needs of users

- ☐ a. I and II only
- ☐ b. II and III only
- ☐ c. I, II, III, and IV
- ☐ d. I, II, and IV only

Question 2A3-LS09
Topic: Profitability Analysis

In the last fiscal year, LMO Company had net sales of $7,000,000, a gross profit margin of 40%, and a net profit margin of 10%. What is its cost of goods sold?

- ☐ a. $4,200,000
- ☐ b. $6,300,000

- ☐ c. $2,800,000
- ☐ d. $700,000

Question 2A3-LS10

Topic: Profitability Analysis

An increase in the gross profit margin for a merchandising firm indicates that the firm

- ☐ a. is increasing its revenues.
- ☐ b. is decreasing its fixed costs.
- ☐ c. is doing a better job of managing cost of sales.
- ☐ d. has been managing its quality control better, which results in fewer returns.

Question 2A4-LS01

Topic: Special Issues

Which of the following are elements of earnings quality?

I. Management's discretion in choosing from among accepted accounting principles

II. Management compensation in relation to net earnings

III. The degree to which assets are maintained

IV. The effect of cyclical and other economic forces on the stability of earnings

- ☐ a. I, III, and IV only
- ☐ b. I and III only
- ☐ c. II and IV only
- ☐ d. I, II, III, and IV

Question 2A4-LS02

Topic: Special Issues

Which of the following statements is true?

- ☐ a. Economic profits are accounting profits minus explicit costs.
- ☐ b. Economic profits are accounting profits minus implicit costs.
- ☐ c. Accounting profits are economic profits minus implicit costs.
- ☐ d. Accounting profits are economic profits minus explicit costs.

Question 2A4-LS03
Topic: Special Issues

Which of the following statements is true?

- ☐ a. Financial statements need not make adjustments for inflation, as earnings automatically reflect the higher prices.
- ☐ b. Financial statements generally make adjustments for inflation, so earnings may be clearly represented over time.
- ☐ c. Financial statements make adjustments for inflation every year and state the inflation rate for the year in the footnotes of the annual report.
- ☐ d. Financial statements generally do not make adjustments for inflation, so earnings may be significantly compounded over time.

Question 2A4-LS04
Topic: Special Issues

A European company provides annual reports for U.S. investors purchasing American depositary receipts (ADRs) of the company's stock in the United States. The company reports €1,500,000 net income. The exchange rate between the euro and the U.S. dollar is €1.19/$1. Which of the following statements is true?

- ☐ a. Annual statements sent to U.S. investors will show net income as €1,500,000.
- ☐ b. Annual statements sent to U.S. investors will show net income as $1,260,504.
- ☐ c. Annual statements sent to U.S. investors will show net income as $1,785,000.
- ☐ d. Annual statements sent to U.S. investors will show net income as $1,500,000.

To further assess your understanding of the concepts and calculations covered in Part 2, Section A: Financial Statement Analysis, practice with the **Online Test Bank** for this section. **REMINDER:** See the "Answers to Section Practice Questions" section at the end of this book.

SECTION B

Corporate Finance

Corporate finance is a cornerstone in advancing core business goals and achieving strategic objectives. For-profit businesses, not-for-profit institutions, and public entities all must make expenditures to cover a wide variety of costs. All investments—both short and long term—must support organizational core competencies. Simply stated, corporate finances must support organizational strategies and ensure that any short-term obstacles do not disrupt long-term strategies.

Organizations may choose from several types of financial instruments. Management accountants often are called on to evaluate the appropriateness of the instruments for an organization. To do so, they need to understand the general uses of the different instruments and the economic risks and benefits of owning or issuing them. They also must ensure that the organization can earn a sufficient rate of return from the investments chosen to cover the costs of generating funds.

Prudent investment decisions help to ensure the financial soundness of any firm. For publicly traded corporations in particular, financial stability and value creation induce investors to purchase the firm's stocks, bonds, and other securities.

This section examines key concepts in corporate finance, ranging from basic risk and return concepts to international finance issues. The section covers these topics:

- Risk and return
- Long-term financial management
- Raising capital
- Working capital management
- Corporate restructuring
- International finance

Management accountants provide valuable assistance in all of these areas.

TOPIC 1

Risk and Return

MANAGING THE FINANCES OF AN ORGANIZATION or making investments requires an understanding of risks and returns and their relationships. Since risk is variability in expected returns, this section begins with a discussion of rates of return.

This topic looks at risk and return relationships, portfolio theory, systematic and unsystematic risk, and the capital asset pricing model.

READ the Learning Outcome Statements (LOS) for this topic as found in Appendix B and then study the concepts and calculations presented here to be sure you understand the content you could be tested on in the CMA exam.

Risk

In corporate finance, **risk** is the variability of returns from those that are expected. Risk implies a degree of uncertainty. Risk is measured by variability in returns; the greater the potential variability of returns, the riskier an investment. A one-year U.S. Treasury bill (T-bill) that provides a "guaranteed" rate of return on investment would be considered risk-free. The annual returns on shares of a stock or some other variable investment instrument are inherently riskier; the return may be much less than expected or even negative.

There are many types of risk, including:

- *Credit risk/Default risk.* An investor's risk that the borrower will not pay the interest and/or principal when they come due
- *Foreign exchange risk.* The risk that there will be a change in the exchange rate of one currency in relation to another (also called currency risk)
- *Interest rate risk.* The risk that the market rate of interest will vary, affecting the value of an interest-bearing asset
- *Market risk.* The risk that a portfolio's value will decrease due to changes in market risk factors, including stock prices, interest rates, foreign exchange rates, and commodity prices

- *Industry risk.* The combined set of risks particular to an industry
- *Political risk.* The risk that political decisions may complicate the operations and profitability of business

Calculating Rates of Return

Companies and investors assume risks to earn investment returns commensurate with the risks. A **return** (or **rate of return**) is the amount received on an investment from holding that investment for a period of time relative to the amount of the initial investment. Of course, not all returns end up as financial gains. The owner of a financial investment or asset may experience a loss over a given period of time. Returns reflect any change in market prices for the investment as well as interest or dividends received from the investment and usually are expressed as a percentage of the beginning market price of the investment.

At the simplest level, a return is calculated as the change in market price, plus any cash payments received in the form of dividends or interest, divided by the beginning price of the security.

For example, the rate of return, also called the **holding period return (HPR)** for common stock over one period is:

$$R = \frac{(P_t - P_{t-1}) + D_t}{P_{t-1}}$$

where:

R = rate of return (holding period return)
P_t = stock price at the end of the period
t = time period
P_{t-1} = stock price at the beginning of the period
D_t = cash dividend at the end of the time period

For example: Assume that an investor buys a share of common stock for $20 exactly one year ago and the stock price rises to $22. During the period, the company pays a $2 cash dividend per share. What is the one-year rate of return for this stock?

- P_t (current stock price) = $22
- P_{t-1} (previous stock price) = $20
- D_t (cash dividend) = $2

$$R = \frac{(\$22 - \$20) + \$2}{\$20} = \frac{\$4}{\$20} = 0.20 \text{ or } 20\%$$

The time period (*t*) can be any length of time. In this case, *t* represents the holding period for the common stock of one year. Thus, the rate of return on common stock is 20%.

Risk and Return Relationship

Risk is an important consideration in making financial decisions. Under rational market conditions, those investments with greater expected risk should provide a higher expected rate of return than investments with lower risk.

Numerous studies of capital market history support the idea that returns to investors typically are a reflection of the risks they take. As an example, the following generalizations can be made about U.S. investment instruments. These are based on historical performance over long periods of time—typically several decades—so average rates of returns are not distorted by fluctuations of unusually high or low returns.

Risk and Returns from Treasury Bills

U.S. T-bills are U.S. government securities that mature in less than one year and are very safe securities. There is no risk of default. Because of the short maturity period, the prices are relatively stable, even though they are subject to inflation. T-bills offer the most conservative rate of return.

Risk and Returns from Bonds

U.S. government bonds and corporate bonds have longer maturity periods than T-bills. They also have an additional dimension: Prices fluctuate as interest rates vary. Historically, bond prices rise when interest rates fall and fall when interest rates rise relative to the bond's stated rate of interest.

Thus, there is an inverse relation between the movement of bond prices and interest rates.

Similar to U.S. T-bills, government bonds have no risk of default. Corporate bonds do have a default risk. Historically, bond rates of return are higher than those of T-bills. In addition, corporate bonds have slightly higher returns than government bonds in general.

Risk and Returns from Stocks

Stocks provide investments signifying an ownership position, or equity position, in a corporation. A stock investor also has a direct share in the risks of the enterprise.

On average, stock returns are significantly higher than the safe rates of return from T-bills or bonds. Stock investments in small U.S. firms historically outperform the returns from large U.S. firms. In addition, returns on common stocks are higher than returns on preferred stocks.

Risk and Return Attitudes

Evaluating the trade-offs between risk and return is a major component in the maximization of shareholder wealth.

Shareholder wealth is the market value of a company's common stock. It is also called the **market capitalization**. Shareholder wealth is calculated as the number of common shares outstanding times the market price per share (the price at which the firm's common stock trades for in the marketplace, such as the New York Stock Exchange).

Shareholder wealth maximization (SWM) is based on the premise that wealth improves as the market price per share increases. It is calculated as the market price per share times the number of common shares outstanding. SWM is a long-term goal of financial management and is based on cash flows. It is used instead of profit maximization, which is a short-term goal because it focuses on profits in the current year. Achieving the largest profit is most often done at the expense of long-term goals and future profits.

Certainty equivalent (CE) is a concept that describes the amount of cash an investor would have to receive to be indifferent between the payoff and a given risk. It answers the question: What is the smallest certain payoff an investor would accept in exchange for a risky cash flow? A CE factor is used to convert a projected cash flow into a certain cash flow. General principles correlating the relationship of an investor's CE and the expected monetary value are summarized in Figure 2B-1.

Figure 2B-1 Certainty Equivalent and Attitudes Toward Risk

When the certainty equivalent is:	Then:
Less than expected value	→ Risk aversion (a risk-adverse position) is present.
Equal to expected value	→ Risk indifference (a risk-indifferent or neutral position) is present.
Greater than expected value	→ Risk preference (a risk-seeking position) is present.

The term **risk aversion** refers to an investor's dislike of risk and need for a higher rate of return as an inducement to take on riskier investments. Thus, high-risk investments should offer an investor a higher expected return than that offered by low-risk investments. In other words, the greater the risk an investment poses, the higher the expected return needed to compensate an investor for buying and holding the investment. Conversely, an investor expects to earn lower expected returns for low-risk investments. Generally speaking, most investors are risk averse and seek higher returns for increasing risks.

There is no true or single measure of certainty in discussing investment returns.

Probability Distributions and Risk and Return

With the exception of risk-free Treasury securities, the actual rate of return often is described as a random variable subject to probability distribution. A **probability distribution** is a set of possible values that a random variable (e.g., an investment return) can take and the likelihood that each will occur.

Three major descriptive statistical measures in a probability distribution are expected return, standard deviation, and coefficient of variation.

1. Expected Return

Expected return is the weighted average of the possible returns where the weights represent the probabilities of occurrence. It is a measure of central tendency of a probability distribution. The formula for expected return is:

$$\bar{R} = \sum_{i=1}^{n}(R_i)(P_i)$$

where:
 $\bar{R}$ = expected return
 n = total number of possibilities
 R_i = return for the ith possibility
 P_i = probability of that return occurring

2. Standard Deviation

Standard deviation is a statistical measure of the variation or dispersion around the most likely *expected return* on an investment. It measures the variability of a distribution around the mean (average) and is computed as the square root of the variance.

The formula for standard deviation (σ) is:

$$\sigma = \sqrt{\sum_{i=1}^{n}(R_i - \bar{R})^2(P_i)}$$

In the equation, the deviations from the mean $(R_i - \bar{R})$ are squared and then weighted by the probabilities of the returns occurring. Typically, the higher the standard deviation, the greater the variability of returns and the greater the total risk.

For example: Here is how an expected return and standard deviation of return would be computed given the probability distributions shown:

 σ = standard deviation
 n = total number of possibilities
 R_i = return for the ith possibility
 P_i = probability of that return occurring

Possible Return, R_i	Probability of Occurrence, P_i	Expected Return, $\bar{R}$ Calculation $(R_i)(P_i)$	Variance, σ Calculation $(R_i - \bar{R})^2 (P_i)$
−0.02	0.10	−0.002	$(-0.02 - 0.10)^2(0.10) = 0.00144$
0.05	0.20	0.010	$(0.05 - 0.10)^2(0.20) = 0.00050$
0.10	0.40	0.040	$(0.10 - 0.10)^2(0.40) = 0.00000$
0.15	0.20	0.030	$(0.15 - 0.10)^2(0.20) = 0.00050$
0.22	0.10	0.022	$(0.22 - 0.10)^2(0.10) = 0.00144$
	$\Sigma = 1.00$	$\Sigma = 0.10 = \bar{R}$	$\Sigma = 0.00388 = \sigma^2$

Standard deviation $= \sqrt{0.00388} = 0.06229$, or 6.229%

In this example:

- Distribution's variance $= 0.00388$
- Distribution's standard deviation $= \sqrt{0.00388}$
- Distribution's standard deviation $= 0.06229$, or 6.229%

3. Coefficient of Variation

Standard deviation can be misleading when comparing the risk or uncertainty of different investments if those investments are of different sizes. Calculating the coefficient of variation helps to adjust for such size or scale differences.

Coefficient of variation (CV) provides a measure of relative risk. The CV is calculated by dividing the standard deviation by the mean of expected return.

$$CV = \frac{\sigma}{\bar{R}}$$

For example: Investment A and Investment B with normal probability distributions have these characteristics:

	Investment A	Investment B
Expected return, $\bar{R}$	0.06	0.18
Standard deviation, σ	0.04	0.06

Based on a comparison of the standard deviations for both investments, the larger of the two is Investment B (0.06), appearing to make it riskier than Investment A. However, Investment A has greater variation relative to the size of the expected return. To adjust for these differences, the CV provides a measure of risk per unit of expected return.

	Investment A	Investment B
CV	$0.04/0.06 = 0.67$	$0.06/0.18 = 0.33$

Using a measure of relative risk, Investment A with a CV of 0.67 is riskier than Investment B with a CV of 0.33. A higher CV indicates higher relative risk.

Risk and Return in a Portfolio Context

Investors rarely hold a single type of investment. Instead, they combine multiple investments in a portfolio. Simply defined, a **portfolio** is a mix of two or more assets. A portfolio may include any combination of cash, bonds, stocks, mutual funds, or other investments. The purpose of having a portfolio of investments rather than a single investment is to reduce risk.

Portfolio Risk

Up to now, this topic has focused on individual security risk. Risk and return in a portfolio differs from the risk and return concepts for a single investment. Calculations used to assess the risk of a portfolio are more complicated than the standard deviation and the variance of a single investment.

Covariance and correlation are useful portfolio measures. They are both statistical measures showing the degree to which two random variables (such as two investment returns in a portfolio) move together. Given one of these measures, along with the standard deviations of the individual investments, allows for the calculation of the other.

1. Covariance

Where variance measures how a single random variable moves with itself, **covariance** extends the concept. Covariance shows the way two different assets in a portfolio are expected to vary together—the way returns move relative to one another—rather than independently.

For example:

- If the expected returns of two stocks move in opposite directions, they will have a negative covariance.
- If the expected returns for two stocks move in the same direction, they will have a positive covariance.
- If the expected return of two investments are unrelated, they would have zero covariance.

As the number of assets in a portfolio grows, the covariance between various securities that have been paired becomes more important. The more different the movement between assets, the lower the portfolio risk.

The basic notation for covariance between random variables, x and y, is:

$$\text{Cov}_{x,y}$$

Simplified, this formula becomes:

$$\text{Correlation Coefficient } \sigma_1 \times \sigma_2$$

Using the standard deviations of Investment A of .04 and Investment B of .06 and assuming a correlation coefficient of +.80, results in a covariance of:

$$.80 \times .04 \times .06 = +.00192$$

Given the positive sign of the covariance, the returns on the two investments move in the same direction. Therefore, the covariance calculation for a portfolio depends on the variance of individual securities and the correlations between all of the pairs.

2. Correlation

Correlation and covariance are related to each other as shown in the following formulas:

$$\text{Corr}_{1,2} = \frac{\text{Cov}_{1,2}}{\sigma_1 \sigma_2}, \text{ which implies } \text{Cov}_{1,2} = \text{Corr}_{1,2}\, \sigma_1 \sigma_2$$

where:

σ_1 and σ_2 = standard deviations of a probability distribution of possible returns for the portfolio, security 1, and security 2, respectively

Key characteristics to understand about the correlation of the two random variables, in this case two investments, are:

- Correlation measures the strength of the linear relationship between two random variables.
- The correlation coefficient always lies in a range from −1.0 to +1.0. This is represented as:

$$-1 \leq \text{Corr}_{1,2} \leq +1$$

- A **positive correlation** means the two securities' returns generally move in the same direction. A +1 correlation means the random variables have perfect positive correlation. This means that a movement in one security return results in an exact measurable positive movement in the other. This is represented as:

$$\text{Corr}_{1,2} = +1$$

- A **negative correlation** implies the securities' returns generally move in the opposite direction. A −1.0 correlation means the random variables have perfect negative correlation. This means that a movement in one security return results in an exact measurable negative movement in the other. This is represented as:

$$\text{Corr}_{1,2} = -1$$

- A **0 correlation** means there is no linear relationship between the variables, indicating that prediction of R_1 cannot be made on the basis of R_2 using linear methods. This is represented as:

$$Corr_{1,2} = 0$$

Risk-adverse investors generally would want to diversify holdings in a portfolio to include securities that have less-than-perfect positive correlation. The standard deviation of the portfolio decreases as the correlation coefficient goes from +1 to 0 to −1.

Portfolio Return

A portfolio rate of return is the weighted average of the expected returns of all the investments that make up that portfolio. The weights represent the proportions of each item in the portfolio; the sum of the weights must be equal to 100%.

The general formula for the expected rate of return for a portfolio is:

$$\overline{R}_p = \sum_{i=1}^{n} W_i \overline{R}_i$$

where:
$\overline{R}_p$ = expected return of a portfolio
n = number of different securities in the portfolio
W_i = proportion or weight of the total funds invested in security i
$\overline{R}_i$ = expected return for security i

A typical portfolio investment strategy is to construct an efficient portfolio (or optimal portfolio) that maximizes the rate of return for a given level of risk or minimizes risk for a given level of return.

For example: A two-asset portfolio with 40% in Asset A with an expected return of 12% and 60% in Asset B with an expected return of 18%. The rate of return on this portfolio would be:

$$\overline{R}_p = 0.40(12\%) + 0.60(18\%) = 4.8\% + 10.8\% = 15.6\%$$

Diversification

Diversification refers to holding a wide range of different investments in a portfolio. The primary goal of diversification is to reduce the variability (or risk) of a portfolio.

Diversification reduces portfolio risk as long as the different investments are unlikely to all move in the same direction in perfect tandem. Meaning, they are not perfectly positively correlated. For example, having ten stocks in a portfolio all from the same industry tends to result in highly correlated returns. Thus, the performance of these companies typically would move up and down in value in a similar manner. Having fewer stocks in a portfolio representing different industries is more likely to show low correlation and low portfolio return variability. That is, the probability that individual stocks in different industries move up and down in value at the same time or at the same rate is low.

Figure 2B-2 is a conceptual illustration of the offsetting variability that portfolio diversification can provide. Equal dollar amounts are placed in both investments to create the portfolio.

Figure 2B-2 Diversification and Portfolio Risk

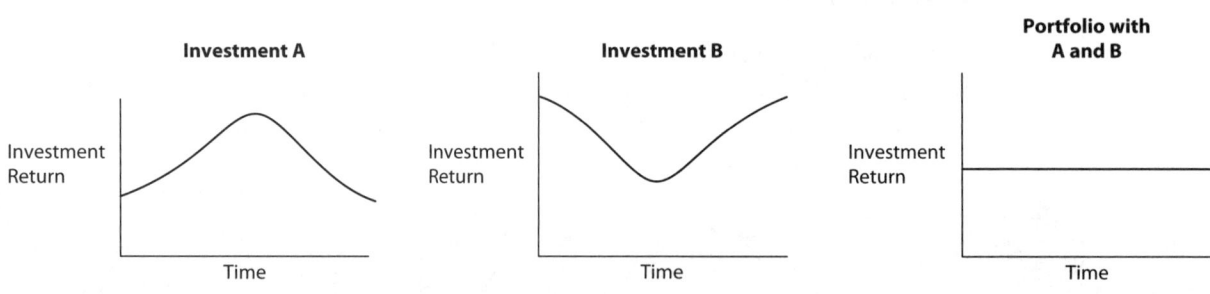

Well-conceived diversification reduces both the upside and downside potential in a portfolio and allows for more consistent performance under a wide range of economic conditions.

Systematic and Unsystematic Portfolio Risk

Extensive market research has examined the effect of diversification on portfolio risk when randomly selected investments are combined in equally weighted portfolios. In smaller portfolios, diversification can cut variability dramatically, but the improvement is much less significant as the portfolio grows in size with numerous investment holdings (typically 15 to 20 different investments).

A portfolio's total risk, as measured by its standard deviation, consists of two specific types of risk: systematic risk and unsystematic risk.

Systematic Risk

Systematic risk (also known as market risk, nondiversifiable risk, or unavoidable risk) is associated with changes in return based on the market as a whole. Systematic risk is common to an entire class of investments because of unavoidable national or global economic changes or other events that threaten the vast majority of (or all) businesses and impact large portions of the market. The value of investments usually declines across the board when investors are exposed to systematic market uncertainties. This is why, for example, stocks tend to move together in response to economy-wide or global perils.

Unsystematic Risk

Unsystematic risk (also known as unique risk, diversifiable risk, or avoidable risk) is independent of economic, political, or other factors or general market movements. It is associated with a specific company or industry.

By most estimates, approximately 60% to 75% of an individual stock's total risk (standard deviation) results from unsystematic risks. For example, a new product entry in an industry could make a company's product obsolete. Labor–management issues or a strike could negatively affect a company or an entire industry.

Most variability resulting from unsystematic risk is avoidable through diversification. For this reason, unsystematic risk sometimes is called diversifiable risk. That is, holding a diversified portfolio reduces unsystematic risk because different portions of the market tend to perform differently at different times.

Figure 2B-3 shows how diversification can minimize unsystematic risk but cannot eliminate systematic risk.

Figure 2B-3 Systematic and Unsystematic Risk in a Portfolio

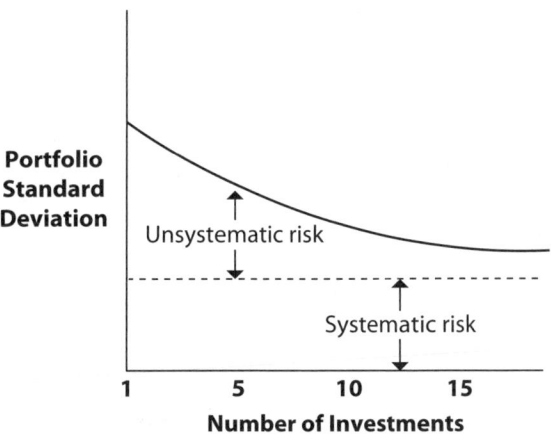

Unsystematic risk is extremely important when a portfolio has a limited number of investments. For a reasonable, well-diversified portfolio, systematic risk assumes much greater importance. That is why, for example, market changes (up or down) carry portfolios with them.

Let's use a coin toss game as a way to explain portfolio risk. You have $1,000 to invest in a game where two coins are flipped. For each **head** you get your initial investment **plus 15%**. For each **tail** you get your initial investment **minus 5%**. The four equally likely outcomes are:

1. Head and Head is a gain of 30%.
2. Head and Tail is a gain of 10%.
3. Tail and Head is a gain of 10%.
4. Tail and Tail is a loss of 10%.

For each outcome there is a 1 in 4 chance, or 25% chance, it will occur. The expected return, based on the weighted average of the possible outcomes, is:

$$\text{Expected Return} = (.30 \times .25) + (.10 \times .50) + (-10 \times .25) = +10\%$$

Further calculations would show that the variance of the returns is 200. The standard deviation is the square root of 200, or 14. Therefore, the game's variability is 14%. The standard deviation and the variance are the appropriate measures of risk, given normally distributed returns. So, the interpretation is that the higher the standard deviation, the higher the risk.

Market Risk and Beta

Because most knowledgeable investors diversify, risk is best judged in a portfolio context. An individual investment's contribution to the risk of a portfolio is a function of how that investment is most likely to be affected by a general market movement.

Beta (β) describes an investment's sensitivity to market movements. It is a quantitative measure (or index) of the volatility of a given investment relative to the overall market.

Specifically, beta indicates the degree to which an investment's return is expected to change with changes in the market's return.

- U.S. T-bills have a beta of 0; the return is unaffected by market changes.
- The average beta of all stocks is 1.0.
- Stocks with a beta greater than 1.0 are more sensitive than average to market movements; they are said to amplify overall market movements.
- Stocks with a beta less than 1.0 are less sensitive than average to market movements. They tend to move in the same direction as the market but not as far.

Another way of describing beta is that a beta above 1.0 is more volatile than the overall market; a beta below 1.0 is less volatile. A stock with a negative beta would move counter to the overall market.

Where systematic (market) risk is the primary determinant of risk in a well-diversified portfolio, the beta of an individual investment in that portfolio reflects its sensitivity to market fluctuations. In other words, the systematic risk of a well-diversified portfolio is proportional to its beta. A diversified portfolio with a beta of 1.0 has half the systematic risk of a portfolio with a beta of 2.0.

Capital Asset Pricing Model

The **capital asset pricing model (CAPM)** is an economic model for valuing a portfolio by relating risk and expected return. The idea behind the CAPM is that investors demand an additional expected return (also known as risk premium) when asked to accept additional risk above that found in a risk-free investment (e.g., T-bills). In other words, the risk premium is the difference between the required rate of return on an investment and the risk-free rate.

The basic premise underlying the CAPM is that the risk premium varies in direct proportion to the beta in a competitive market. The expected risk premium for each investment in a portfolio should increase in proportion to its beta. This means that all investments in a portfolio should plot along a sloping line, known as the security market line.

The security market line (SML) is a graphical representation of the CAPM. The SML provides a benchmark for evaluating the relative merits of different portfolio items. The SML begins at the risk-free T-bills (which have a beta of 0) and slopes upward to the right. Substituting different values of beta into the CAPM equation provides different points on the SML.

The CAPM concepts of risk premium, beta, and SML are shown in Figure 2B-4.

Figure 2B-4 Risk Premium, Beta, and SML

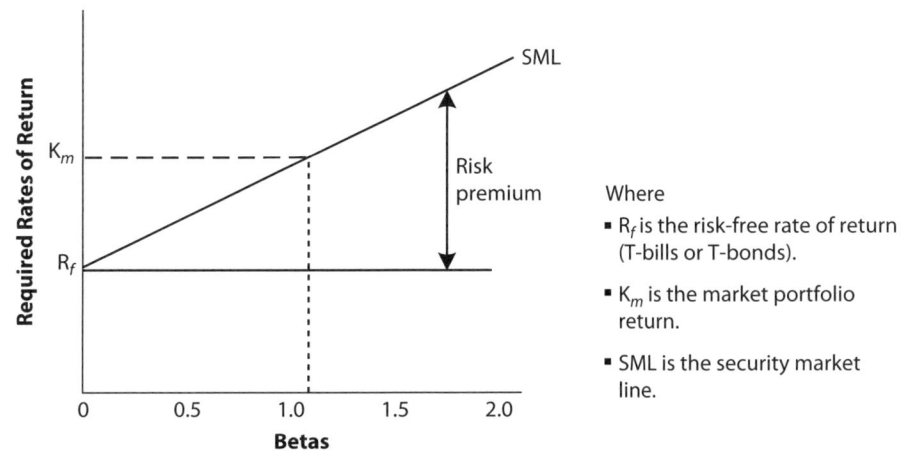

Where
- R_f is the risk-free rate of return (T-bills or T-bonds).
- K_m is the market portfolio return.
- SML is the security market line.

If the aim is to keep portfolio risk low, investments having low betas should be included. Conversely, if a higher return is desired, investments with high betas should be added to the portfolio.

The CAPM calculation can be used to find the required rate of return on a stock or portfolio when the return on a risk-free investment, the beta of the stock or portfolio, and the return on the market portfolio are known.

The formula for CAPM is:

$$K_e = R_f + \beta(K_m - R_f)$$

where:
  K_e = required rate of return
  R_f = risk-free rate (such as the return on U.S. T-bill or T-bonds)
  β = beta coefficient for the company
  K_m = expected return on the market portfolio

Considerable debate exists on whether to use T-bills or T-bonds as the risk-free rate with the CAPM. Evidence shows that for capital budgeting decisions, managers tend to use T-bonds more often as a proxy for the risk-free rate than they do T-bills.

For example: Here is how CAPM would be used to find the required rate of return on a stock, assuming:

R_f = 8% (risk-free rate on a U.S. Treasury security)
β = 1.50 (beta coefficient for the company)
K_m = 12% (estimated return on the market portfolio)

$$K_e = R_f + \beta(K_m - R_f)$$
$$K_e = 0.08 + 1.50(0.12 - 0.08) = 14.0\%$$

The CAPM is considered a single-factor model. It establishes a positive relationship between systematic risk (beta) and expected returns, using the market as a common point of reference. Although the model sometimes is criticized for oversimplification, it does provide one perspective of the implications of risk and the risk premium necessary to compensate investors for bearing risk.

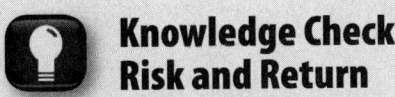

Knowledge Check: Risk and Return

The following questions are intended to help you check your understanding and recall of the material presented in this topic. They do not represent the type of questions that appear on the CMA exam.

Directions: Answer each question in the space provided. Correct answers and section references appear after the knowledge check questions.

1. Suppose an investor buys a stock for $50 and sells it for $45 one year later. Assuming the stock pays a $4 dividend to the buyer, what is the holding period return on the stock?
   - a. −10%
   - b. +8%
   - c. −2%
   - d. −2.2%

2. The standard deviation of a stock investment is best described as the
   - a. variability of expected returns.
   - b. sensitivity to market movements.
   - c. trade-off between risk and return.
   - d. variation around the mean return.

For questions 3 through 5, match the following terms with their appropriate description.

   a. The amount of cash that would make an investor indifferent to a risky return at a point in time

   b. A benchmark for evaluating the relative merits of different portfolio items

   c. The degree to which two stock returns move together in a portfolio

3. _____ Correlation

4. _____ Security market line

5. _____ Certainty equivalent

6. A major benefit of portfolio diversification is
   - a. reduced exposure to foreign exchange rates.
   - b. minimization of unsystematic risk.
   - c. reduction of systematic risk.
   - d. a more favorable borrowing position.

7. Using the CAPM formula, calculate the required rate of return on a stock, assuming:

    R_f = 7% (the risk-free rate on a U.S. Treasury security)

    β = 0.75 (the beta coefficient for the company)

    K_m = 13% (the estimated return on the market portfolio)

    ☐ a. 13%

    ☐ b. 11.5%

    ☐ c. 9.5%

    ☐ d. 9%

Knowledge Check Answers: Risk and Return

1. Suppose an investor buys a stock for $50 and sells it for $45 one year later. Assuming the stock pays a $4 dividend to the buyer, what is the holding period return on the stock? [See *Risk and Return Relationship*.]
   - ☐ a.   −10%
   - ☐ b.   +8%
   - ☑ c.   −2%
   - ☐ d.   −2.2%

   (($45 − $50) + $4)/$50 = −2%

2. The standard deviation of a stock investment is best described as the [See *Standard Deviation*.]
   - ☐ a.   variability of expected returns.
   - ☐ b.   sensitivity to market movements.
   - ☐ c.   trade-off between risk and return.
   - ☑ d.   variation around the mean return.

For questions 3 through 5, match the following terms with their appropriate description.

   - a.   The amount of cash that would make an investor indifferent to a risky return at a point in time
   - b.   A benchmark for evaluating the relative merits of different portfolio items
   - c.   The degree to which two stock returns move together in a portfolio

3. __c__ Correlation
4. __b__ Security market line
5. __a__ Certainty equivalent

6. A major benefit of portfolio diversification is [See *Unsystematic Risk*.]
   - ☐ a.   reduced exposure to foreign exchange rates.
   - ☑ b.   minimization of unsystematic risk.
   - ☐ c.   reduction of systematic risk.
   - ☐ d.   a more favorable borrowing position.

7. Using the CAPM formula, calculate the required rate of return on a stock, assuming: [See *Capital Asset Pricing Model*.]

    $R_f = 7\%$ (risk-free rate on a U.S. Treasury security)
    $\beta = 0.75$ (beta coefficient for the company)
    $K_m = 13\%$ (estimated return on the market portfolio)

    ☐ a. 13%
    ☑ b. 11.5%
    ☐ c. 9.5%
    ☐ d. 9.0%

    $K_e = R_f + \beta (K_m - R_f)$
    $K_e = 7\% + 0.75 (13\% - 7\%)$
    $K_e = 7\% + 0.75 (6\%)$
    $K_e = 7\% + 4.5\%$
    $K_e = 11.5\%$

TOPIC 2

Long-Term Financial Management

A FINANCIAL INSTRUMENT IS EVIDENCE OF a monetary transaction between two parties. For one party in the transaction, the financial instrument represents an investment; for the second party, the instrument is an obligation or liability.

This section covers risks and returns in investment and financing decisions, the various types of financial instruments (such as stocks, bonds, and derivatives), and the valuation of financial instruments.

In addition, this topic focuses on the details of the cost of capital, including the weighted average cost of capital, the cost of individual capital components, calculating the cost of capital, and the marginal cost of capital.

READ the Learning Outcome Statements (LOS) for this topic as found in Appendix B and then study the concepts and calculations presented here to be sure you understand the content you could be tested on in the CMA exam.

Risks and Returns in Investment and Financing Decisions

Individuals and organizations make decisions regarding investments in financial assets (e.g., stocks and bonds), tangible assets (e.g., plant and equipment), and intangible assets (e.g., patents and copyrights). The investment decisions discussed next relate to financial assets. Investment decisions related to other assets are discussed in Section E: Investment Decisions.

Organizations make investments in financial assets for different reasons including to:

- Ensure liquidity—to cover day-to-day cash obligations in a timely manner.
- Generate interest income for cash on hand for which there is no immediate use.

Financing involves obtaining the funding for an organization's assets. It allows a corporation to pursue long-term objectives by obtaining debt or equity capital.

Debt financing implies a legal liability or obligation of an organization to repay a creditor for borrowed funds, usually by a specified date.

Equity financing represents selling an ownership claim in a company. Both debt and equity involve risk and return trade-offs:

- The cost of debt is represented by an interest rate; the interest paid is a tax-deductible expense.
- The value of equity is represented by a stock price or the net value of the company's assets. Dividends paid on equity are not tax-deductible.
- Whether a company finances assets through debt (e.g., types of loan agreements) or equity (preferred or common stock) is a key corporate financial issue.

Every company should have an investment and financing strategy in place. Figure 2B-5 summarizes basic aspects that investment and financing strategies should address.

Figure 2B-5 Basic Investing and Financing Considerations

Investment	Financing
• Corporate goals	• Debt versus equity financing
• Policies and guidelines	• Short- versus long-term financing
• Investment instrument selection and portfolio configuration	• Fixed versus floating-rate interest payments
• Roles, responsibilities, and authority for investment activities	• Secured versus unsecured debt
• Financial controls	• On- versus off–balance sheet financing
• Performance measurement	• Tax considerations

An investment policy reflects an organization's tolerance for risk. The mix of debt and equity in borrowing determines a company's leverage and is closely linked to the firm's capital structure.

In financing, the financing mix is not meant to maximize firm value as measured by the company's common stock price multiplied by the number of common stock shares outstanding. Instead, it should minimize of the firm's weighted average cost of capital (WACC). One method to reduce risk is matching the cash inflows of the assets being financed with the cash outflows used to finance the assets.

A company can reorganize the capital structure by issuing additional debt, refinancing current debt at lower interest rates, buying back already issued debt or stock, and/or issuing stock.

LOS §2.B.2.g

Impact of Income Taxes on Financing Decisions

Many financing decisions rely heavily on tax effects. Generally speaking, debt has tax advantages at the corporate level because interest payments reduce the firm's taxable income, shielding it from federal and state taxes. Dividends and share repurchases do not. Interest tax shields associated with this financing approach tend to support increased leverage, provided a firm balances the tax benefits of debt against the costs of financial distress.

According to trade-off theory, optimal capital structure involves a trade-off between the benefit of debt due to the interest tax shelter and the costs of debt due to financial distress and agency costs. An **agency cost** is a direct or indirect expense that the principal bears as a result of having delegated authority to an agent. An **agent** is the person authorized to act on behalf of another (the principal) to perform some duty or service. Management can be thought of as agents of the owners (the common shareholders or principals). **Financial distress** refers to any general weakening in a company's financial condition caused by issuing too much debt. Bankruptcy is the extreme case of financial distress. Various economic theories challenge this trade-off theory. At issue with this proposition is whether the tax deductibility of the interest payments associated with the borrowing affects the value of the firm.

Valuation

Valuation is the process that links risk and return to estimate the worth of an asset or a company. Understanding the concept of valuation requires a baseline understanding of value and related value concepts.

The term *value* has many different meanings, depending on whether it is applied to an asset or a company. An asset generally is thought of as a financial asset—a monetary claim on an issuer, typically a paper asset such as a bond, common stock, or preferred stock.

Related value concepts are listed next.

- Going-concern value
- Liquidation value
- Liquidation value per share
- Book value
- Book value per share of common stock
- Market value
- Intrinsic value

Going-concern value refers to the value of a company as an operating entity. This value depends on the ability to generate future cash flows rather than balance sheet assets. It is sometimes referred to as value in use.

Liquidation value is the net amount of money that could be realized by selling the entity's assets after paying off the liabilities (debt). It is of utmost concern when an organization is facing bankruptcy.

Liquidation value per share is the actual amount per share of common stock that stockholders would receive if the entity sells all assets, pays all liabilities and preferred stockholders, then divides the remaining money among the common stockholders.

Book value is the value at which an asset is carried on a balance sheet. It is the accounting value of an asset, which is the cost of a fixed asset less its accumulated depreciation. The book value of a liability is its carrying value; for example, a bond is carried at face value plus the premium or minus the discount.

The book value of the firm is equal to the dollar difference between the firm's total assets and its total liabilities (including preferred stock, if any) as listed on its balance sheet. Thus, the book value of the firm is equivalent to the firm's common shareholder equity.

Book value per share of common stock refers to the ratio of stockholder equity to the number of common shares outstanding. Book value per share may have little relation to the liquidation value per share or the market value per share.

Market value is the market price at which investors buy or sell an asset at a given time. The key determinant of market value is supply and demand. The market value of a publicly traded security is its market price.

Intrinsic value is a measure of the theoretical value of an asset. Although not indicative of actual value, intrinsic value provides a basis for determining whether to buy or sell a financial asset when compared to its market value or price. Intrinsic value is also called **fundamental value**.

An asset's value is determined by the amounts and timing of the cash flows expected to be generated by the asset and the rate of return required by investors in the asset. The required rate of return is a function of the risk associated with the projected cash flows.

Measures of cash flow for security investments are:

- Annual dividends from common stock and preferred stock investments.
- Interest received from debt investments.
- Cash received upon the liquidation of investments.

Increased cash flows raise the price of an asset. If cash flows become more uncertain, the price of the asset will decline. In financial management, basic goals are to maintain or increase cash flows and to decrease risk. Attaining these goals supports the maximization of shareholder wealth.

Risk is challenging to estimate. Future cash flows must be discounted back to the present value of the cash flows at an appropriate rate of return to reflect risk. This is because the value of an asset (the price of an asset) is the present value (PV) of its future cash flows determined at the appropriate rate of return.

The following information on this topic examines characteristics of various debt and equity instruments and their valuation.

Bonds

A **bond** is a debt instrument (a loan) issued for a period of more than one year. The investor acquiring a bond earns interest by lending money, while the borrower (the issuer) gets needed capital (cash).

Bonds may be bought on a short-, medium-, and long-term basis. Although these distinctions may vary slightly, the general parameters are listed next:

- Short-term bonds: 2 to 5 years
- Medium-term (intermediate) bonds: 5 to 10 years
- Long-term bonds: 10 to 30 years

The relationship between an interest rate and the time to maturity is called the "yield curve" or the "term structure of interest rates." Investors expect increased returns with increased risks. In general, the longer the time to maturity, the greater the risk of fluctuation in the market value of the security. Thus, the shape of a normal yield curve is upward sloping, and longer-term bonds normally pay returns (yields) higher than those of short-term bonds. Investor expectations concerning economic growth and inflation affect the shape of the yield curve.

Issuers and Types of Bonds

There are many types of bonds, issued by several different sources. Common ones are listed in Figure 2B-6.

Figure 2B-6 Common Types of Bonds

Type	Description
Corporate bonds	Issued by large and small U.S. companies
	Used to finance growth, expansion, and other activities
Government bonds	Backed by the full faith and credit of the U.S. government
	Used to sustain government operations and pay interest on national debt
	Examples include U.S. Treasury bonds, Treasury notes, and savings bonds
Municipal bonds	Issued by various cities and states
	Used to pay for construction projects and other activities
Agency bonds	Issued by various federal, state, and local government agencies
	Examples include bonds issued by mortgage lenders (e.g., Ginnie Mae, Fannie Mae, and Freddie Mac) as well as other agency bonds issued to finance operations and raise money for special projects
International bonds	Marketed simultaneously in several countries, usually by London branches of international banks and security dealers

Bond Agreements

The written legal agreement among all parties involved in a bond issue is called an **indenture** (or deed of trust). An indenture defines the details of the bond issue, including:

- Terms and conditions of the bond issue
- The stated interest rate (also called the coupon rate)
- Maturity date
- Protective covenants (restrictions placed on the issuer such as maintaining certain financial ratios)
- Conditions defining default
- Subordination

- Sinking fund terms—payments made by the borrower to a separate custodial account; used to repay the debt at maturity—or periodically—and assure creditors that adequate funds are available
- Callability
- Conversion features
- Collateral property to be pledged, if any
- Designation and duties of the trustee

Covenants

Protective covenants set limits or restrictions on certain actions the company might be taking during the term of the agreement. They are a particularly important feature in a bond indenture.

There are two types of covenants: negative and positive.

1. **Negative covenants** limit or prohibit the borrower from certain actions. Paying too much in dividends, pledging assets to other lenders, selling major assets, merging with another firm, and acquiring more long-term debt are all examples of actions that a negative covenant may require.
2. **Positive (affirmative) covenants** specify actions that the borrower promises to perform. Examples of positive covenants include maintaining certain ratios, preserving collateral in good condition, and making timely interest and principal payments. A failure to abide by positive covenants could place the bond issuer in default.

Bond Administration

Bonds are administered by a qualified trustee. The trustee is a third party chosen by the bond issuer to serve as the official representative of the bondholder. Individuals or institutions may serve as trustees, while banks often administer bonds.

Trustee responsibilities include:

- Authenticating the bond issue's legality
- Ensuring that all contractual obligations are carried out
- Ensuring that sinking fund and interest payments are properly paid and applied
- Initiating appropriate actions if the borrower does not meet obligations
- Representing the bondholder in legal proceedings
- Administering redemption

The issuer of the bond compensates the trustee. The trustee's compensation is included in the costs of borrowing.

Bond Terminology

Generally speaking, a bond is a promise to pay a specified amount of interest over time and to repay principal at maturity.

Bond Principal

Principal (also known as par value, par, or face value) represents the dollar amount of the bond and is the amount the lender is repaid when the bond matures. Most bonds are denominated in increments of $1,000.

Bond Interest

The interest rate stated on a bond is referred to as the coupon rate. A bond's **coupon rate** generally is comparable to what other bonds being issued at that time are paying.

Three common forms of coupon interest on bonds are:

1. *Fixed coupon rate.* Interest is paid consistently at the same rate.
2. *Floating coupon rate.* Interest varies based on economic changes.
3. *Zero coupon rate.* There are no ongoing interest payments because the bond is sold at a deep discount and redeemed at full value as compound interest accrues up to the par value.

Bonds are classified as fixed income securities if the coupon rate and the amount of bond payments are fixed at the time the bond is offered for sale. Traditionally, most bonds are sold with fixed coupon rates. This is the primary reason bonds generally are considered conservative investments and less risky than stocks and other types of investments with highly variable return rates.

After the initial issue (the sale of a bond), bonds are bought and sold through brokers in the **secondary market** similar to the way stocks are traded. In the secondary market, a bond's price fluctuates with market interest rates. If market interest rates fall, the bond price will rise. If market interest rates rise, the bond price will fall.

A bond's coupon rate is expressed as a percentage of the par value. In the United States, interest usually is paid semiannually (every six months). For example, if a semiannual bond has a 7% coupon, the issuer pays bondholders $35 (3.5%) every six months for every $1,000 par value bond that they hold.

A zero coupon bond is an exception. As the name implies, zero coupon bonds pay no interest. The face (par) value is paid at maturity.

The term *coupon* originated because bondholders traditionally received certificates specifying the terms of the bond with attached coupons that had to be physically detached and redeemed when it was time to collect the interest on the bond. The vast majority of newer bonds are issued electronically, similar to stock purchases and the interest is paid automatically to the bondholder. However, many coupon certificates still exist, as they have not yet reached maturity.

Bond Maturity

Bonds typically have a stated maturity. This is the date on which the bond debt becomes due for payment and the obligation is settled. **Face** or **par value** is the value of a bond at maturity and the amount that is paid to the bondholders.

A bond often is bought and sold during its lifetime. At maturity, the bondholder receives the par value of the bond. A $1,000 bond is worth $1,000 at maturity.

Provisions for Redeeming (Retiring) Bonds

Bonds can be redeemed (retired or repaid) in a number of ways. For example, bonds could simply be retired at final maturity by making a single payment of principal plus the last interest payment. Many bonds carry a **sinking fund** provision that requires the company to make periodic cash payments to a bond issue's trustee in order to retire bonds at maturity or on a periodic basis. If the bond has a **call provision,** the issuer can repurchase the bond at a specified price (or series of set prices) before maturity.

Conversion Provisions

Some bonds can be converted at the option of the holder into a specified number of shares of common stock of the same company. Such bonds give the holder interest payments from the bond plus an **option** on the common stock. Because this option has value, the company can sell the convertible bond at a lower yield than a similar bond without this option feature.

Bond Ratings

A bond rating allows an investor to assess the general risks of buying a bond before making the actual purchase.

Bond issues often are rated by credit agencies based on numerous factors including:

- Current financial status of the issuer
- Future financial prospects
- Collateral (if any) securing the bond

Moody's Investors Service and Standard & Poor's are two well-known credit rating services. A summary of their ratings and very general characteristics is provided in Figure 2B-7.

Figure 2B-7 Moody's and Standard & Poor's Bond Rating

Moody's	Standard & Poor's	
Aaa	**AAA**	
Aa	**AA**	
A	**A**	Generally considered high-quality bonds
Baa	**BBB**	
Ba	**BB**	Somewhat questionable; lack some of the high-quality characteristics
B	**B**	
Caa	**CCC**	Poor quality; danger of default
Ca	**CC**	
C	**C**	Junk bonds (highly speculative bonds with a greater-than-average chance of default)
—	**D**	

Some key points to understand about bond ratings are listed next.

- Bond ratings apply to the bond issue, not the company.
- U.S. Treasury bonds are rated AAA, because they are backed by the full faith and credit of the U.S. government.
- Ratings may be adjusted either up or down during the lifetime of a bond; a downgraded rating means that future issues will need to offer higher interest rates to attract buyers.
- Bonds with Aaa and AAA ratings have the lowest rates of interest.
- Because of the default risk associated with junk bonds, they are higher-yield bonds.
- Junk bonds have a greater chance of default, but in some circumstances they also may be an emerging entity and provide a highly profitable return.

Bond Yields

A bond's coupon rate never changes, but inflation and changes in market interest rates do affect the value of a bond.

Yields and Return

Current yield is the annual rate of return expressed as a percentage of the annual interest payment relative to the current price of the bond. A ten-year $1,000 bond paying 5% interest per annum earns $50 per year for ten years. If the current price of the bond is $1,250, the current yield would be about 4% ($50/$1,250).

Yield to maturity is the actual return earned on a bond from the time it is purchased to maturity. Yield to maturity considers:

- Interest earned over the life of the bond.
- Purchase price in relation to par value, meaning it sells at a premium or discount.

Inflation and Bond Real Returns

Inflation eats into the return of a bond. If a bond's return is more than the inflation rate, the bond produces a positive return. If the bond's return is less than the inflation rate, the bond produces a negative return. Consider the next examples.

- If a bond's return is 6% and inflation is 4%, the bond produces a 2% real return.
- If a bond's return is 6% and inflation is 8%, the bond produces a –2% real return.

Bond Duration

Bonds are subject to inflation. If interest rates fall, the interest payments and principal that bond investors receive will have to be reinvested at lower rates. Thus, bond investors face reinvestment risk when interest rates fall.

Duration gives an approximate sensitivity of bond/portfolio values to changes in yield to maturity. Thus, **bond duration** considers how the price of a bond changes in response to yield changes. The best interpretation of duration is the approximate percentage price changes for a 1% change in yield to maturity. Duration is an approximation of the price yield relation because the relation follows a curve, not a straight line.

Convexity is a measure of the curvature of how the price of a bond changes as the interest rate changes. Price changes in response to rising rates are smaller than price changes in response to falling rates.

A bond price-yield curve is shown in Figure 2B-8. Bond prices go up faster than they go down.

Figure 2B-8 Bond Price–Yield Curve

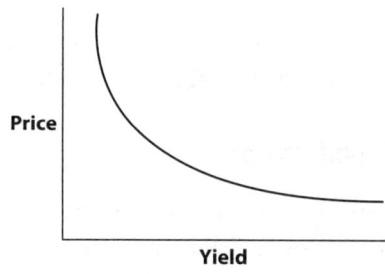

Bond duration is determined by a ratio of the percentage change in price to the change in yield.

$$\text{Effective Duration} = \frac{\text{(Bond Price when Yields Fall} - \text{Bond Price when Yields Rise)}}{2 \times \text{(Current Price)} \times \text{(Change in Yield in Decimal Form)}}$$

This is often expressed as:

$$\text{Duration} = \frac{V_- - V_+}{2V_0 (\Delta y)}$$

where:
    V_- = bond value if the yield decreases by Δy
    V_+ = bond value if the yield increases by Δy
    V_0 = current bond price
    Δy = the change in yield. It is used to get V_- and V_+, expressed in decimal form

Effective duration shows the average percentage price change for a 1% change in yield.

For example: Consider a ten-year, semiannual-interest-paying bond with a 9% coupon that is currently priced at $1,067.95 to yield 8%. If the yield declines by 50 basis points (100 basis points = 1%) to 7.5%, the price of this bond will rise to $1,104.22. If the yield increases by 50 basis points to 8.5%, the price will fall to $1,033.24. Using the formula previously given, the effective duration of this bond would be:

$$\text{Effective Duration} = \frac{\$1,104.22 - \$1,033.24}{2\,(\$1067.95)\,(0.005)} = \frac{\$70.98}{10.6795} = 6.65$$

An effective duration of 6.65 means that a 1% change in yield produces an approximate change in the price of this bond of 6.65%.

Why is bond duration important? Understanding how much a bond price will move in response to changing interest rates allows investors to buy, sell, or hold bonds according to how they think they will perform. Investors can use duration to compare bonds with different issue and maturity dates, coupon rates, and yields to maturity.

Some relationships involving bond duration are shown next. Holding other characteristics constant:

- A higher (lower) coupon means a lower (higher) duration.
- A longer (shorter) maturity means higher (lower) duration.
- A higher (lower) market yield means lower (higher) duration.

Bond Security

Bonds may be issued on a secured (asset-backed) or unsecured basis.

A **secured bond** is one that is backed by the collateral of a specific asset (e.g., inventories, real estate, or fixed assets) or revenues created from a specific project. A secured bond provides the investor with a lien (or creditor claim) against an asset in the event of default.

An **unsecured bond** (or **debenture**) is backed only by the good faith, integrity, and credit of the borrower and offers no specific collateral. When holding an unsecured bond, an investor has only a general claim against the assets. Because unsecured bonds have greater risk than secured bonds, they usually pay higher yields. Debentures may be subordinated (i.e., it ranks after other debts) or unsubordinated.

Bond Ranking and Liquidation

Bonds may be classified as equal, senior, or subordinated in relation to other debt obligations. These rankings affect priority in liquidation. If a bond issuer in default has both secured and unsecured bonds:

- Secured bondholders are paid off first.

- Unsubordinated debenture holders become general creditors and are paid off after the secured debt holders are paid.
- Subordinated debenture holders are paid off after the general creditors.

Bond Valuation

The value of a bond is the sum of its discounted cash flows. The discount rate used is the market rate of interest. The market rate is also called the effective rate, the yield rate, or the required rate of return. The steps to determine the value of a bond are:

- Calculate the PV of interest payments at the market rate.
- Calculate the PV of the face value at the market rate.
- Add the two PVs.

The next formula can be used to determine the value of a bond.

$$V_b = I(\text{PVIFA}_{k,n}) + F(\text{PVIF}_{k,n})$$

where:
V_b = value of the bond
I = interest in each time period (calculated at the coupon rate of interest, assuming interest is paid annually)
PVIFA = PV interest factor of an annuity
k = discount rate (market rate of interest)
n = number of periods
F = principal or face value of the bond
PVIF = PV interest factor

For example: A company issued a 15-year annual pay bond that has five years before maturity. At issuance, the bond had a 10% coupon and a face value of $1,000. Investors require an 8% return on bonds of similar risk. The value of the bond is calculated as shown:

- Determine the annual interest (10% × $1,000 = $100).
- Use the PV annuity table in Appendix A to discount the annual interest of $100 at the required rate of 8% for five years. The discount factor is 3.993.
- Use the PV tables in Appendix A to discount the face value of $1,000 at the required rate of 8% for five periods (years). The discount factor is 0.681.
- Add the two PVs.

$$V_b = I(\text{PVIFA}_{k,n}) + F(\text{PVIF}_{k,n})$$
$$= \$100(3.993) + \$1{,}000(0.681)$$
$$= \$399.30 + \$681.00 = \$1{,}080.30$$

The value of the bond is $1,080.30 and represents the price an investor would pay for the bond. In this example, the bond value is above the face value. Because the discount rate is lower than the coupon rate, the bond sells at a premium. If the required rate was higher than the coupon rate, the bond would sell at a discount. If the required rate was equal to the coupon rate, the bond would sell at par or its face value.

If the bond had paid interest semiannually versus annually, changes to the computation would need to be made, as follows:

- The interest paid in each time period would be equal to $50 ($100/2).
- The interest would be discounted at a rate of 4% (8%/2) for 10 periods. There would be 10 interest payments made over the 5 years.
- The $1,000 face value would be discounted at a rate of 4% for 10 periods.

Bond Refinancing

When a company issues bonds, the bonds' coupon rate reflects current market interest rates and the company's credit rating. If market interest rates drop and/or a company's credit rating improves, the company may want to consider refinancing its debt by replacing an old debt issue with a new one.

Stocks

A **stock** is an equity investment instrument that signifies an ownership position (equity) in a corporation. Stockholders (or shareholders) who buy stock (shares) in a corporation have a claim on the corporation's assets and profits based on the proportional shares of stock owned. Their claims, however, are subordinate to all debt holders. In addition, common stockholders' claims are subordinate to preferred stockholders' claims. The differences between common and preferred stocks are discussed later in this section under "Common Stock" and "Preferred Stock."

The level of equity ownership takes into consideration the number of shares outstanding. The term **outstanding shares** refers to the number of shares of a corporation's stock held by shareholders.

Ownership is calculated by dividing the number of shares an investor owns by the total number of shares outstanding. For example, if a company has 10,000 shares of stock outstanding and an investor owns 200 of them, that investor owns 2% of the company.

Market Value of a Stock

A stock's **market value**, the last reported sale price for outstanding shares, determines the firm's **market capitalization**. Market capitalization (or **market cap**) is determined by multiplying the current common stock market price per share by the number of outstanding common stock shares. A public corporation with 30 million shares outstanding that trade at $30 each has a market capitalization of $900 million.

Market capitalization is one of many methods used to categorize types of stocks. Figure 2B-9 shows stock classifications based on market capitalization. Corporations usually are classified as large cap, medium cap (mid cap), small cap, or micro cap, depending on their market capitalization.

Figure 2B-9 Categories of Stocks Based on Capitalization

Large cap	$15 billion and over
Mid cap	Between $2 billion and $15 billion
Small cap	Between $300 million and $2 billion
Micro cap	Below $300 million

Large-cap stocks frequently offer regular dividends, and the underlying company's size generally lessens the risk of company failure.

A mid-cap stock is a stock with a market capitalization that is between that of large- and small-cap stocks. Similar to large-cap stocks, mid-cap stocks also have a large volume of shares to trade, but the companies are smaller and less mature than large-cap stocks. Typically, these companies offer a greater potential for growth than larger companies, but the risk is also greater.

Small-cap stocks have the potential for dramatic growth, but they also have the potential for greater volatility, and therefore risk.

Investment returns for the different types of stocks often move in different cycles. Micro-cap stocks are considered to be the riskiest group of all.

Other common stock classifications are listed next.

- *Blue-chip stocks.* Stocks of the largest and most consistently profitable publicly traded corporations
- *Growth stocks.* Stocks of corporations that have strong growth potential, with sales, earnings, and market share growing faster than the overall economy
- *Cyclical stocks.* Stocks of corporations whose earnings are highly dependent on economic conditions (e.g., economic upturns and slowdowns)
- *Defensive stocks.* Conservative stocks that are relatively stable and impervious to most economic conditions
- *Value stocks.* Stocks that appear inexpensive when compared to earnings and other performance measures
- *Income stocks.* Stocks of typically solid performers with good track records that usually generate a steady dividend income stream
- *Speculative stocks.* Stocks that are risky investments in corporations that have yet to prove their true worth

Two additional stock classifications are common stock and preferred stock. Common stock and preferred stock have several distinguishing differences, as well as some similarities. Their distinct features offer corporations and investors a variety of risks and rewards.

The common and preferred stock classifications are the focus of the remaining content on stocks.

Common Stock

Common stock provides equity ownership in a corporation. That is, the owner of a common stock has an interest in the assets of the corporation and a share in the earnings. The interest, as noted earlier, is subordinate to all debt holders and to holders of preferred stock. Common stock equity sometimes is referred to as residual equity. Collectively, however, common stockholders own the corporation. Common stock has no maturity date, but shareholders may liquidate their investments by selling their shares in the secondary market.

With common stock, there is no guarantee that an investor will make money. The equity position in a common stock means that the owner shares in the corporation's fortunes and misfortunes.

The common stock **market value per share** is the current trading price per share of the stock. If the stock increases in value, shareholders benefit from capital appreciation of their investment and the potential to receive a dividend. A dividend represents a share in the profits.

Voting Rights

Ownership of common stock gives shareholders the right to vote on important company matters, such as:

- Election of members of the corporate board of directors
- Policies and changes in corporate bylaws
- Approval of stock option plans
- Mergers and acquisitions
- Appointment of auditors

Shareholders typically get one vote for each share of stock owned. Companies administer voting rights in one of two methods: traditional or cumulative.

Traditional Voting

Traditional voting (also known as majority voting, majority-rule voting, or statutory voting) is a corporate voting system in which shareholders voting for the board of directors are limited to one vote per share for any single nominee. The total number of votes for each stockholder equals the number of shares owned times the number of positions open. For example, in an election in which five director candidates are running for open board positions, a shareholder owning 500 shares could cast 500 votes for each candidate, for a total of 2,500 votes.

This traditional majority method of voting precludes minority interests from electing any of their own (minority) candidates.

Cumulative Voting

A **cumulative voting** system allows shareholders to cast different numbers of votes for different candidates. Continuing with the five-director-position example, the shareholder owning 500 shares could distribute the votes equally to the five candidates, distribute the votes among some combination of the candidates, or cast all 2,500 votes for a single candidate.

Cumulative voting attempts to give minority shareholders more voice in corporate governance by increasing their chances to elect a certain number of directors.

Some corporations issue different classes of stocks with different voting rights. In situations in which a class of shareholders is allowed extra voting rights, a small group of individuals could control the direction of the corporation while owning less than a majority of shares.

Shareholders can cast their votes by mail using a proxy statement, in person at the corporation's annual meeting, over the Internet, or by telephone.

A **proxy statement** is a legal document that is mailed out to all shareholders shortly before the annual meeting. The proxy statement lists the business concerns to be addressed at the annual meeting and includes a ballot for voting on company initiatives and electing the board members. Submitting a proxy ballot authorizes someone else at the meeting (usually the management team) to vote on the investor's behalf. If the management team receives proxies for over 50% of the shares voted, the team can select the entire board of directors. However, if investors do not return their proxy statements, their votes are not counted. With fewer shares being voted at the meeting, the subsequent number needed to constitute a majority is lowered. In effect, then, any unreturned proxies become votes in favor of whatever the board of directors wants.

Preemptive Rights

Some common stocks have preemptive rights. By definition, **preemptive rights** allow current shareholders to maintain their proportional ownership in the corporation should the company issue additional stock. Shareholders with preemptive rights have the right, but not the obligation, to purchase new shares before anyone else, enabling them to maintain their current level of equity ownership.

Liquidating Value

In the event of default or liquidation, common stock shareholders have the last claim on assets of the corporation. Specifically, they have residual rights to a corporation's assets only after the claims of bondholders, other debt holders, and preferred stockholders are paid in full. But common stock shareholders also have limited liability and are not responsible for the corporation's debts. Their losses are limited to the par or stated value of the stock.

Common Stock Valuation

The return rates for a common stock can vary. As noted previously, dividends do not have to be paid. In other years, dividends paid may be more or less than the previous year, depending on the company's dividend policy, profitability, and availability of funds.

Valuation for a common stock requires careful projection of future growth and future dividends. Such projections are largely determined by annual dividends, dividend growth, and discount rates.

There are three potential valuation scenarios based on dividend payouts. Dividends may remain fixed (zero growth), grow at a constant rate, or grow at an unusual (variable) rate. Investors use valuation models to compare their results to existing prices to determine whether a stock is over-, under-, or properly valued.

Use of the Dividend Discount Model

The **dividend discount model (DDM)** is a method to value common stock where the intrinsic value of the common stock is based on the discounted value or the PV of all expected future dividends.

Dividend discount models are a type of discounted cash flow (DCF) analysis. There are several different DCF models and, in turn, different DDMs, that an investor can use. There is no one best method. The method used should take into consideration:

- *Measure of cash flow.* The dividends and free cash flows to equity
- *Expected holding period.* Whether the expected period is finite (limited) or infinite
- *Pattern of expected dividends.* Zero growth (no growth), growth, stable (constant) growth, or supernormal growth

The most common models used for valuing common stock are these:

- Basic dividend discount model
- Zero dividend growth model
- Constant dividend growth model
- Variable dividend growth model

Each is described with an example.

Basic Dividend Discount Model

The basic dividend discount model is represented by this formula:

$$V_s = \sum_{t=1}^{\infty} \frac{D_t}{(1+k_s)}$$

where:

V_s = intrinsic value of a share of common stock
D_t = expected dividends per share on the common stock in period t
k_s = investor's required rate of return on the common stock (cost of equity)

This basic dividend discount model assumes that an investor buys a common stock and plans to hold it indefinitely. For this reason, it is sometimes referred to as an infinite period valuation model.

Zero Dividend Growth Model

The next formula can be used for zero growth valuation.

$$V_0 = \frac{D_1}{(1+k_s)^1} + \frac{D_2}{(1+k_s)^2} + \frac{D_3}{(1+k_s)^3} + \cdots + \frac{D_\infty}{(1+k_s)^\infty}$$

where:

V_0 = common stock price to be estimated
$D_1 = D_2 = \ldots = D_n = D_\infty$ a constant annual dividend per share on the common stock
k_s = investor's required rate of return on the common stock (cost of equity)

The required rate of return depends on the risk associated with the common stock. Investors expect a high rate of return if an investment is risky. In other words, a higher payoff must be offered to entice investors to invest their money.

The formula is simplified to:

$$V_0 = \frac{D}{k_s}$$

For example: A company pays an annual cash dividend of $5 per share at the end of each year. Analysts expect no change in the policy. With a required rate of return of 12%, the value of the common stock would be:

$$V_0 = \frac{D}{k_s} = \frac{\$5}{0.12} = \$41.67$$

The zero growth model is a special case of the constant dividend growth model that is also called **Gordon's model**.

Constant Dividend Growth Model

The constant growth dividend discount model is a valuation approach that assumes dividends per share grow at a constant rate each period that is not expected to change. The model represents a single-stage growth pattern. Substituting $D_0 (1 + g)^t$ for D_t in the basic model results in the next formula.

$$V_s = \sum_{t=1}^{\infty} \frac{D_0 (1+g)^t}{(1+k_s)^t}$$

where:
 D_0 = dividends per share on the common stock in the current period
 g = constant dividend growth rate
 k_s = investor's required rate of return on the common stock (cost of equity)
 t = time period

If k_s is greater than g, the formula can be simplified to what is commonly known as the Gordon constant growth model:

$$V_0 = \frac{D_1}{k_s - g}$$

where:
 V_0 = estimated value of common stock
 D_1 = expected dividends per share on the common stock in year 1
 k_s = required rate of return on the common stock
 g = constant (annual) dividend growth rate

For example: A company just paid a $3 dividend per share last year. Analysts expect dividends to grow at a constant rate of 6% per year. If investors expect to receive a 12% return, what is the intrinsic value of the stock?

In this example:

D_1 = $3.00 (1.06) = $3.18
k_s = 0.12
g = 0.06

$$V_0 = \frac{D_1}{k_s - g} = \frac{\$3.18}{0.12 - 0.06} = \frac{\$3.18}{0.06} = \$53.00$$

Key points about the relationship between the required rate of return (k_s) and the growth rate (g) are summarized in Figure 2B-10.

Figure 2B-10 Gordon Model Key Points

If...	Then:
The difference between k_s and g *widens*	The stock value falls.
The difference between k_s and g *narrows*	The stock value rises.
The difference between k_s and g *shows small changes*	Large changes in the stock's value can result.

Variable Dividend Growth Model

This method estimates the stock price when dividends grow at a different rate for two or more periods of time. When a common stock has varying growth rates of dividends:

- Future dividends must be projected separately.
- Projected dividends must be discounted back to the present using PV interest tables.

- The PV of the terminal at the end of the growth period must be calculated.
- All PVs are added together.

For example: Company J paid an annual cash dividend of $5 per share last year. Analysts expect dividends will grow at an annual rate of 20% for the next three years and then level to a normal growth rate of 5%. With a required rate of return of 12%, here is how to determine the price of the common stock today.

$$P_3 = \frac{D_3(1+g)}{k_s - g}$$

First calculate the value of D_3:

$(D_3 = \$5(1.20))^3 = \$8.64$

$$= \frac{\$8.64(1.05)}{0.12 - 0.05} = \frac{\$9.07}{0.07} = \$129.57$$

where:

D_1, D_2, D_3 = dividends in years 1, 2, 3, respectively
P_3 = common stock price in year 3
k_s = required rate of return on the common stock
g = constant (annual) dividend growth rate

Year	Income			PVIF* at 12%		PV of Income
1	$D_1 = \$5(1.20)$	$= \$6.00$	×	0.893	=	$5.36
2	$D_2 = \$6.00(1.20)$	$= 7.20$	×	0.797	=	5.74
3	$D_3 = \$7.20(1.20)$	$= 8.64$	×	0.712	=	6.15
	$P_3 = 129.57$		×	0.712	=	92.25
					Total PV	$109.50

* PVIF = PV interest factor.

In this example, the price of the common stock at the end of year 3 is $129.57. When the discounted values are summed, the estimated stock price is $109.50.

Use of Relative (or Comparable) Valuation Models

Relative valuation is another valuation approach that defines the term *comparable* and chooses a standardized measure of value to compare companies. Value typically is some form of multiple of earnings, book value of equity, or sales. Assets may be cheap based on intrinsic value but expensive based on relative valuation and how the market currently prices the assets.

Essentially the same variables considered in DCF valuation models (e.g., required rate of return, expected growth rate, etc.) are used in relative valuation estimates.

The major difference between the two valuation approaches is that the assumptions underlying DCF valuation are explicit, meaning they are clearly defined or formulated. The assumptions underlying the relative valuation models are implicit, meaning the assumptions provide conditions that they satisfy.

Choosing comparable firms is fundamental to relative valuation. A comparable firm is one having similar business and industry characteristics to the individual firm being valued.

In relative valuation, an analyst:

- Attempts to control/minimize differences across firms (such as size).
- Computes the multiple for each comparable firm and then averages them.
- Computes the multiple for the individual firm to be valued.
- Compares the multiple for the individual firm to the average.
- Evaluates any differences between the two multiples based on characteristics of the individual firm, such as growth or risk.

For example, looking at the price/earnings (P/E) ratios, where the comparable firms' average P/E equals 18 and the individual firm's P/E equals 10, an analyst might consider the individual firm's stock as cheap or undervalued because the multiple is less than average. Conversely, if the multiple were higher than average, the stock would be considered expensive or overvalued.

Three common relative valuation models are price/earnings (P/E) ratios, price-to-book (P/B) ratios, and price-to-sales (P/S) ratios.

Price/Earnings Ratios

The **price/earnings (P/E) ratio** is the most common multiple used to estimate the value of common stock. Earnings power, as measured by earnings per share (EPS), is the primary determinant of investment value. There are two versions of the P/E ratio. The difference between the two is due to how earnings are calculated in the denominator.

The **trailing P/E** ratio uses earnings over the most recent 12 months. This P/E ratio is common in the popular financial press.

$$\text{Trailing P/E} = \frac{\text{Market Price per Share}}{\text{EPS over Previous 12 Months}}$$

The **leading P/E** ratio uses next year's expected earnings (either expected earnings for the next fiscal year or the next four quarters).

$$\text{Leading P/E} = \frac{\text{Market Price per Share}}{\text{Forecasted EPS over Next 12 Months}}$$

For example: A company reports $10 million in earnings in the previous fiscal year. An analyst forecasts a $1.00 EPS over the next 12 months. The company has 15 million shares outstanding at a market price of $15 per share. Given this information, here is how to determine the trailing and leading P/E ratios:

$$\text{Previous year EPS} = \frac{\$10{,}000{,}000}{\$15{,}000{,}000} = \$0.67$$

$$\text{Trailing P/E} = \frac{\$15.00}{\$0.67} = 22.39$$

$$\text{Leading P/E} = \frac{\$15.00}{\$1.00} = 15.0$$

The **advantages** of using P/E ratios are:

- They are commonly used in the investment community.
- Research shows a significant relationship between P/E differences and long-run average stock returns.

Some of the **disadvantages** of using P/E ratios are:

- If earnings are negative, the resulting P/E ratio is meaningless.
- Volatility in earnings can make the interpretation of P/E ratios difficult.
- Management discretion, that is within allowable accounting practices, can distort earnings.

Price-to-Book Ratios

A **price-to-book (P/B) ratio** (or **price-to-book value ratio**) shows how much the market is willing to pay for equity. Book value, also known as common shareholders' equity, as found on the balance sheet, typically is a positive value, even if a company reports a loss and has a negative EPS. The P/B ratio is represented as:

$$\text{P/B Ratio} = \frac{\text{Market Value of Equity}}{\text{Book Value of Equity}} = \frac{\text{Market Price per Share}}{\text{Book Value per Share}}$$

where:

$$\begin{aligned}\text{Book Value of Equity} &= \text{Common Shareholders' Equity} \\ &= (\text{Total Assets} - \text{Total Liabilities}) - \text{Preferred Stock}\end{aligned}$$

For example: The next equation uses some of the information shown in the table to calculate the P/B ratio for a company. In this example, no preferred stock has been issued. The book value of equity and the shares outstanding are for common stock.

Book Value of Equity in Year 1 (millions)	Sales Year 1 (millions)	Shares Outstanding Year 1 (millions)	Price 15 May, Year 1
$14,015	$9,450	3,400	$9.50

$$\text{Book Value per Share} = \frac{\text{Total Stockholders' Equity} - \text{Preferred Equity}}{\text{Number of Common Shares Outstanding}}$$

$$= \frac{\$14,015}{3,400} = \$4.12$$

$$\text{P/B Ratio} = \frac{\text{Market Price per Share}}{\text{Book Value per Share}} = \frac{\$9.50}{\$4.12} = \$2.31$$

The **advantages** of using P/B ratios are:

- Even when EPS is negative, book value is usually a positive value.
- A book value measure is more stable than EPS, so it may be more useful than a P/E ratio when EPS is high, low, or volatile.
- Book value provides an appropriate measure of net asset value for firms holding largely liquid assets (e.g., finance, investment, insurance, and banking).
- P/B ratios can be used to value a company that is expected to go out of business.
- Research shows that P/B ratios help explain differences in long-run average returns.

The **disadvantages** of using P/B ratios are:

- P/B ratios ignore the value of nonphysical assets (e.g., customer goodwill or human capital).
- P/B ratios can be misleading when there are substantial differences in the size of the assets in the firms being compared.
- The true investment made by shareholders can be obscured by different accounting conventions.
- Technological change and inflation can result in substantial differences between the book and market value of assets.

Price-to-Sales Ratios

A **price-to-sales (P/S) ratio** shows how much the market is willing to pay for a dollar of sales. The use of this ratio is based on the belief that sales are the basic component of profits.

The P/S ratio is represented as:

$$\text{P/S Ratio} = \frac{\text{Market Value of Equity}}{\text{Total Sales}} = \frac{\text{Market Price per Share}}{\text{Sales per Share}}$$

For example: The next equation uses some of the information shown in the table to calculate the P/S ratio for a company.

Book Value of Equity in Year 1 (millions)	Sales Year 1 (millions)	Shares Outstanding Year 1 (millions)	Price 15 May, Year 1
$14,015	$9,450	3,400	$9.50

$$\text{Sales per Share} = \frac{\text{Sales}}{\text{Number of Shares Outstanding}}$$

$$= \frac{\$9,450}{3,400} = \$2.78$$

$$\text{P/S Ratio} = \frac{\text{Market Price per Share}}{\text{Sales per Share}} = \frac{\$9.50}{\$2.78} = 3.42$$

The **advantages** of P/S ratios are:

- The ratio provides meaningful measure even for distressed firms.
- Sales figures tend to be more reliable than EPS and book value because they are not as easy to manipulate or distort as EPS and book value.
- P/S multiples tend to be more stable because they are not as volatile as P/E multiples.
- P/S ratios are useful for valuing a range of stocks from mature or cyclical industries to start-up companies with no record of earnings.
- Research shows significant relationships between differences in P/S ratios and differences in long-term average stock returns.

The **disadvantages** of P/S ratios are:

- High sales are not necessarily indicative of operating profits measured by earnings and cash flow.
- P/S ratios do not capture differences in cost structures across companies.
- Although P/S ratios are less subject to distortion than EPS and book value, revenue recognition practices can distort sales forecasts.

Preferred Stock

Similar to common stock, **preferred stock** also provides partial ownership in a corporation. However, there are some important differences. To a degree, preferred stock is more similar to bonds than to common stock. For that reason, preferred stock often is described as a hybrid form of security having characteristics of both debt and equity. Don't let this confuse you; it is reported in stockholders' equity.

Equity Characteristics

A preferred stock generally offers a fixed dividend; the dividend amount does not fluctuate based on earnings. The term *preferred* also implies that shareholders have a right to receive their specified dividend before common stockholders are paid any dividends.

A fixed dividend reduces investor risk, but it also limits financial rewards. Preferred stock has less volatility when markets fall. But shareholders cannot count on large price gains in rising markets. In fact, the dividend is not guaranteed. The board of directors, which votes on dividend issues, does not have to pay the fixed dividend if it so chooses.

Voting Rights

Preferred stockholders usually do not have the voting rights that common stockholders have. Special voting privileges may be granted if the corporation is unable to pay the fixed dividend or if it defaults on a loan agreement or bond indenture.

Liquidating Value

In the event of default or bankruptcy, preferred stockholders have a claim on the company's assets ahead of common stockholders. Because preferred stock takes precedence over common stock, preferred stockholders have a greater chance of getting some of their investment back if the corporation fails than do common stock shareholders. Should asset liquidation take place, preferred stockholders are paid only after short- and long-term debt holder claims are satisfied.

Unique Features

A corporation cannot deduct the dividends paid to shareholders on its tax return. This is a principal drawback to using preferred stock in corporate financing.

Other important characteristics of preferred stock are described next.

Cumulative Dividends

Unlike a common stock dividend, which a company is not required to pay, a preferred stock dividend is an obligation regardless of the corporation's earnings. When issuing preferred stock, a corporation often commits to offer a fixed annual dividend. However, the payment is discretionary if the company does not have sufficient earnings to pay. In some situations, unpaid dividends for preferred stock may accumulate.

Many preferred stocks have a cumulative dividends feature that requires that all unpaid cumulative dividends on the preferred stock to be paid from future earnings before common stock dividends are paid. It should be noted that if the corporation has no intention of paying out common stock dividends, there is no requirement to pay the cumulative preferred stock dividends in arrears.

Participating Feature

A participating feature allows preferred stockholders to participate in increasing dividends when common stockholders' dividends reach a certain amount. The exact amount of participation varies and is determined by some predetermined formula that relates additional preferred stockholder payouts to increases in common stockholder payouts.

Participating preferred stock gives preferred stockholders a prior claim on income and the opportunity for additional return. Unfortunately for investors, the participating feature is not as common as the cumulative feature; most preferred stock returns are limited to the fixed dividend rate.

Call Provision

Preferred stock issues often have a stated call price or redemption price. A call price is specified at issuance and is set above the original issue price. It may decrease over time.

A call provision grants the preferred stock issuer the right to buy back (or call) all or part of an issue at the call price rather than attempting to retire the issue by more expensive methods. These other methods include purchasing the stock in the open market, offering a preferred stockholder a price over market value, or offering another security in its place.

Convertible Feature

Preferred stock issues sometimes have a convertible feature or conversion feature. Convertible preferred stock can be converted into a specified amount of common stock at the option of the holder. Corporations set a fixed ratio for the number of shares of common stock that can be exchanged for the convertible preferred stock. Once converted, the preferred stock issue is retired.

When preferred stock issues have both call provisions and conversion features, a corporation can force conversion by calling the stock. This is done if the current market price of the preferred stock is significantly higher than the call price. This occurs because of the conversion feature.

As noted, common stock does not have a maturity date. Unless preferred stock has a mandatory redemption, preferred stock has no maturity date. The call provision and the convertible feature give a corporation flexibility in retiring preferred stock issues that do not have mandatory redemption, rather than potentially having them outstanding in perpetuity.

Preferred Stock Valuation

If a company pays a fixed dividend at the end of each year, the valuation is determined using the zero dividend growth model used for common stock.

The simplified equation is:

$$V_p = \frac{D}{k}$$

Once the information about the dividend and discount rate is available, the value of the preferred stock is a straightforward calculation.

For example: A company issues preferred stock. Par value of the preferred stock is $100, and each share pays an annual cash dividend of $7 per share. The discount rate for similar preferred stock in the market is 8%. Here is how to determine the value of the preferred stock issued by the company.

$$V_p = \frac{D}{k}$$
$$= \frac{\$7}{0.08} = \$87.50$$

Although the annual dividend rate is constant, changes in the discount rate will affect the stock price over time.

- If the market discount rate goes down, the value of the preferred stock will increase.
- If the market discount rate goes up, the value of the preferred stock will decrease.

Cost of Capital

The cost of capital is a composite of the costs of various sources of funds comprising a firm's capital structure. It represents the minimum rate of return that must be earned on new investments so that shareholders' interests won't be diluted.

Cost of Capital, Defined

A corporation's management team is charged with ensuring efficiency and profitability from assets as well as minimizing the cost of the funds that the firm incurs from investments. In fulfilling this fiduciary responsibility, management makes various financing decisions that affect the firm's capital structure.

Corporations raise capital from two sources: lenders and shareholders. The total capital of a firm represents a combination of debt capital and equity capital. These capital components are described next.

- **Debt capital** is that portion of total capital derived from the issuance of interest-bearing instruments such as notes, bonds, or loans.
- **Equity capital** is that portion of total capital derived from permanent investments by shareholders in the form of paid-in-capital or from retained earnings. A firm may issue new shares of common or preferred stock, or it may choose to retain earnings instead of distributing them as dividends.

Every activity a firm does to generate capital—either explicit or implicit—has a cost associated with it. The overall **cost of capital** represents a proportional average of the various components a firm uses for financing.

The cost of capital should be considered in capital structure decisions. Corporations can benefit from using the cost of capital to benchmark investment decisions and to manage working capital (e.g., receivables and inventories) more efficiently. The cost of capital can be valuable to use in measuring and evaluating performance. For example, the actual and expected return on capital or net assets may be compared with the cost of capital associated with each.

Calculating the Cost of Capital

LOS §2.B.2.r

The cost of capital is found by determining costs for the individual types of capital and then multiplying each component cost by its proportion in the firm's total capital structure. Here is the general formula for the cost of capital:

$$k_a = w_1 k_1 + w_2 k_2 + \cdots + w_n k_n$$

where:
k_a = cost of capital (expressed as a percentage)
w = proportion that element comprises of the total capital structure
k = cost of an element in the capital structure
1, 2, n = different types of financing (each with its own cost and proportion in the capital structure)

Cost of Capital Example

Consider a corporation that uses the types of financing shown in Figure 2B-11.

Figure 2B-11 Cost of Capital Example

Type (n)	After-Tax Cost (k)	% of Capital Structure (w)
Debt	4%	30%
Preferred stock	8%	20%
Common equity	18%	50%

$$k_a = w_1 k_1 + w_2 k_2 + \cdots + w_n k_n$$
$$= 0.30(4\%) + 0.20(8\%) + 0.50(18\%) = 1.2 + 1.6 + 9 = 11.8\%$$

The calculation of the cost of capital, using the current or prospective cost of the various capital components is generally more appropriate than relying on historical costs. A primary use of the cost of capital is in deciding how to finance new capital investments in such projects as new products, equipment, or facilities. Therefore, relevant costs are the marginal costs associated with incremental funds the firm plans to raise, not historical costs of capital that the firm had already raised.

Primary considerations in determining the costs of capital are how to determine:

- The cost (k) of each individual capital component.
- The respective weights (w) in the total capital structure of the firm.

Cost of Individual Capital Components

Determining the cost of each component in a firm's capital structure is the first step in calculating the cost of capital. Corporations typically use up to three methods of financing: debt, preferred stock, and common equity.

Cost of Debt

The before tax cost of debt represents the required rate of return that providers of debt capital (e.g., loans and bonds) require. The basic formula for the after-tax cost of debt is:

$$\text{After-Tax Cost of Debt} = k_d(1-t)$$

where:
k_d = before-tax cost of debt
t = firm's marginal tax rate

Considerations in determining the after-tax cost of debt are:

- What interest rate (k_d) should be used?
- How should different types of debt be handled?
- What effect do income taxes have on the interest rate?

This formula does not reflect any flotation costs because most debt is privately placed.

The before-tax cost of debt is greater than the after-tax cost of debt because a firm can deduct interest payments when determining taxable income. The higher the tax rate, the lower the after-tax cost of debt.

For example: Blane Company's debt consists of 6% interest-bearing bonds, which are selling at par. The anticipated tax rate is 35%. The cost of debt would be:

$$\text{After-Tax Cost of Debt} = k_d(1-t)$$
$$= 6\%(1-0.35)$$
$$= 3.9\%$$

The current replacement cost (market value) of debt is used in calculating the cost of capital. But with one or more types of debt involved, a weighted average of yields to maturity should be used to calculate the cost of debt.

The weighted average cost of debt is calculated as shown in Figure 2B-12. In this example the anticipated tax tate is 35%.

Figure 2B-12 Weighted Average Cost of Debt Using Yields to Maturity

1 Debt	2 Market Value (millions)	3 % of Total	4 Yield to Maturity*	5 = (3 × 4) Weighted Average Cost
Issue A	$45	10.0%	11.2%	1.12%
Issue B	125	27.8	12.4%	3.45
Issue C	280	62.2	13.1%	8.15
Total:	$450	100.0%		12.72%

*Yield to maturity on a bond is the rate of discount that equates the present value of all interest and principal payments with the current price of the bond.

Weighted average cost of debt before taxes: 12.72%
Adjustment for income taxes (1 − .35): 0.65
Weighted average cost of debt after income taxes (12.72% × 0.65): 8.27%

Cost of Preferred Stock

The cost associated with preferred stock is a function of the dividend paid to shareholders and flotation costs. The cost of preferred stock needs to reflect flotation costs, as they can be substantial. Flotation costs include direct costs (such as underwriting fee, filing fees, legal fees, and taxes) and indirect costs (such as management time working on the new issue). Flotation costs are deducted from the selling price of the preferred stock to determine net proceeds.

The general formula for the cost of preferred stock is:

$$k_p = \frac{D_p}{P_p - F}$$

where:
k_p = cost of preferred stock
D_p = preferred stock dividend
P_p = the current price per share (current or prospective price)
F = flotation costs per share as a dollar amount

For example: Blane Company's preferred stock pays an $8 dividend per share and sells for $100 per share. If the firm issued new shares of preferred, it would incur underwriting and other fees (flotation costs) of $2 per share. Here is how the cost of preferred stock would be calculated for the company:

$$k_p = \frac{D_p}{P_p - F} = \frac{\$8}{\$100 - \$2} = \frac{\$8}{\$98} = 8.16\%$$

In this example, the cost of the preferred stock is shown based on an annual dividend payment. If the dividend payment was quarterly, the same formula could be used. The quarterly rate would be multiplied by 4 to get the nominal annual rate.

Flotation costs sometimes are given as a percentage of the issue. In the last example, the flotation costs were 2%. Thus, the denominator of the cost of preferred stock would become $P_p (1 - F\%)$, where F is a percentage, not a dollar amount.

Because preferred stock dividends are not tax deductible, they represent an outflow of after-tax funds. A preferred stock with a par value of $100 and an 11% dividend costs the firm $11 in after-tax earnings. If the firm has a 35% tax rate, it must earn $1.54 before taxes for each dividend dollar paid. This is calculated as $11 divided by (1 minus the tax rate).

When a corporation has more than one issue of preferred stock outstanding, the weighted average rate on all preferred stock should be used.

Cost of Common Equity

The **cost of common equity** (or **cost of equity**) is the most difficult capital component to calculate. As noted previously, equity consists primarily of common stock issues, paid-in capital, and retained earnings. The cost of equity is the expected, required, or actual rate of return on the firm's common stock, which, if earned, will leave the market value of the stock unchanged. The rate is difficult to estimate because common stock has no fixed contractual payments.

There are various methods, ranging from simple to complex, for estimating the cost of equity. Three of these methods are:

1. Historical rate of return
2. Dividend growth model
3. Capital asset pricing model (CAPM)

Each method has distinct advantages and limitations. Firms may use more than one method to determine a reasonable estimate. The choice of the appropriate method is often a function of the information available for a given situation.

As noted earlier, companies raise equity in one of two ways:

1. Internally, by retaining earnings
2. Externally, by selling new shares of common stock

Mature companies tend to generate most equity internally. Flotation costs make the cost of raising new equity in the market more expensive. Additionally, if the stock is underpriced, losses result from selling stock shares below the correct value. Stated another way, firms generally use lower-cost retained earnings (internal equity) before issuing a new common stock (external equity) because of flotation costs and potential losses from under-pricing.

Estimating the Cost of Internal Equity Using Historical Rate of Return

As the name implies, the historical rate of return method of determining the cost of equity capital involves the historical rate stockholders have earned. It considers the rate of return earned by an investor who bought the stock in the past, held it to the present, and sold it at the current market price.

For example: Consider a situation where common stock shares were issued and sold for $100 per share and sell today for $110 per share. Dividends of $8 were paid annually. Using the historical method, the average rate of return for the investor was 10% a year ($8 dividend plus $2 average annual share price gain/$100). The 10% is then used as the estimate of the current rate of return on the stock and the firm's cost of equity capital.

Using the historical method implies that:

- The firm's performance will not change substantially in the future.
- No significant changes in interest rates will occur.
- Investor attitude toward risk will not change.

Although this historical method is relatively easy to calculate, the limitation is that the future rarely remains the same as the past.

Estimating the Cost of Internal Equity (Retained Earnings) Using the Dividend Growth Model

The dividend growth model reflects a market value approach. The underlying logic of this model is that the market price of a stock equals the cash flow of expected future incomes, from both dividends and market price appreciation, discounted to their present value. This means that when the present value of the future incomes equals the market price, the discount rate equals the cost of equity capital. An underlying assumption is that incomes will grow at a constant compound rate.

The formula for calculating dividend growth is:

$$k_s = \frac{D_1}{P_0} + g$$

where:
    k_s = cost of internal equity capital
    D_1 = dividend per share at time 1
    P_0 = market price per share at the time 0
    g = expected dividend growth rate

For example: If Blane Company's stock is currently selling at $50 per share, the dividend at the end of the first year is expected to be $3.50 per share, and future dividends are expected to grow at 5% per year, the cost of equity capital would be:

$$k_s = \frac{\$3.50}{\$50} + 5\% = 12.00\%$$

Similar to other methods for calculating the cost of equity capital, the dividend growth rate involves an estimate. In this case, the estimate is for the value of *g*. The model is useful only if market expectations are for dividends to grow at that rate. Investors must believe that the past trends of earnings per share will continue. If this is the case, the trend (expressed as a percentage) can be used.

Estimating the Cost of Internal Equity (Retained Earnings) Using the Capital Asset Pricing Model

The CAPM is useful in measuring the cost of equity capital for a firm.

The CAPM implies that the rate of return on any security equals the riskless rate of interest plus a premium for risk. The riskless rate is usually based on the current or anticipated rate on long-term U.S. Treasury bonds or short-term U.S. Treasury bills. The premium for risk is derived from the security's beta.

The formula for applying the CAPM to estimate the cost of equity capital is:

$$k_e = R_f + \beta(k_m - R_f)$$

where:
- k_e = cost of internal equity capital
- R_f = risk-free rate (e.g., the rate on T-bonds or a 30-day T-bill)
- β = stock's beta estimate (obtained from a brokerage firm or investment advisory service, or calculated by the firm)
- k_m = estimate of the return on the market as a whole

The term $(k_m - R_f)$ is called the "market risk premium," which is somewhere in the area of 5% to 7%, depending on the date of the estimate and the data sources used by the analysts. Firms often add 6% to the T-bond rate to obtain the rate of return for the market as a whole.

For example: If the T-bond rate is 8%, a firm's stock beta is 0.9, and the expected rate of return for the market is 14%, Blane Company's cost of equity capital using the CAPM would be:

$$k_e = 8\% + 0.9(14\% - 8\%)$$
$$= 8\% + 5.40\%$$
$$= 13.40\%$$

Using the CAPM involves estimates for each term in the equation. Challenges arise in deciding:

- Whether to use long-term or short-term T-bond rates for R_f.
- Estimating the future beta investors expect.
- Estimating the expected rate of return for the market as a whole.

Estimating the Cost of New Equity (Issuing Additional Common Stock) Using the Dividend Growth Model

Determining the cost of new common stock (k_e) must consider flotation costs and possible under pricing losses. The constant growth dividend discount model (DDM) formula used to calculate the cost of existing equity (k_s) can be adjusted to account for both factors. The formula for calculating the cost of new equity is:

$$k_e = \frac{D_1}{P_0 - (F+U)} + g$$

where:

k_e = cost of external equity capital
D_1 = dividend per share at time 1
g = expected dividend growth rate
P_0 = market price per share at time 0
U = underpricing losses per share
F = flotation costs per share

For example: Suppose Blane Company can issue stock for $50 per share, before $5 from flotation costs and under-pricing losses. The dividend at the end of the first year is expected to be $3.50 per share, and future dividends are expected to grow at 5% per year. The estimated cost of new equity capital would be:

$$k_e = \frac{D_1}{P_0 - (F+U)} + g$$

$$= \frac{\$3.50}{\$50 - \$5} + 0.05 = 12.78\%$$

Comparing the cost of new equity (12.78%) to the cost of internal equity (12%), the difference is the flotation costs and under-pricing losses. These factors make the cost of new equity more costly by almost 1 percentage point.

Estimating the cost of capital, especially when the cost of equity is involved, is not exact. Decision making about inputs and the different models themselves can result in substantial differences in estimates.

Weighted Average Cost of Capital

Once the different capital components have been determined, the final goal is to calculate the relative importance of each source in the total capital structure of the firm. In other words, the individual components must be weighted to show the extent to which each one contributes to the total value of the firm's capital structure.

The **weighted average cost of capital (WACC)** is the firm's overall cost of capital and reflects the risks associated with typical or average projects. Many companies use this WACC formula:

$$\text{WACC} = \sum_{i=1}^{n} w_i k_i$$

where:

n = total number of capital components

w_i = percentage of total permanent capital represented by each capital component

k_i = after-tax cost of each capital component

Because WACC includes all sources of permanent financing in a firm's capital structure, the sum of the weighted components must equal 1.0.

Three weighting schemes commonly are used to calculate WACC: book value weights, market value weights, and target value weights.

1. **Book value weights** measure the proportion of each type of capital based on accounting (book) values shown on the firm's balance sheet.
2. **Market value weights** represent current proportions of each type of capital in the firm's capital structure at current market prices.
3. **Target value weights** represent the weights based on the firm's optimal (target) capital structure.

Book values remain stable because they do not depend on changing market values for debt and equity. They represent historical costs. However, using book values can skew WACC because book values may differ substantially from the market.

Many believe that market value weights are the most accurate way to compute WACC because market weights consider the effects of changing market conditions and the current prices of each security. Some debate exists, however, between the merits of using weights based on the actual market or the target market capital structure. Because target weights represent the best estimate of how the firm will raise money in the future, they make sense if the firm is migrating toward the target structure.

For example: Management considers the current mix as optimal and wants to maintain this target structure in raising future capital. If Blane Company raises new capital in target proportions, here is how to determine the firm's WACC.

Capital Component	Weight	After-Tax Cost	WACC
Long-term debt	0.40	3.90%	1.560%
Preferred stock	0.10	8.16%	0.816%
Common (internal) equity	0.50	11.80%	5.900%
	1.00		8.276%

Using the average cost of the historical rate of return (10.0%), dividend growth model (12.0%), and the CAPM (13.4%), the cost of common (internal) equity (retained earnings) is (10.0% + 12.0% +13.4%) / 3 = 11.8%. If management thought that one method of estimating the cost of retained earnings was better than another, it could use that cost instead of determining an average based on several methods.

Thus, Blane Company's WACC before using external equity would be 8.276% and is calculated as shown:

$$WACC = (0.40)\ (3.9\%) + (0.10)\ (8.16\%) + (0.50)\ (11.8\%)$$
$$WACC = 1.56\% + 0.816\% + 5.9\% = 8.276\%$$

Marginal Cost of Capital

LOS
§2.B.2.s

Companies do not have unlimited sources of funds for investments so they do not have the ability to satisfy all of their potential investment desires.

Market investors evaluate the financial merits of different companies, compare them, and determine reasonable limits for individual companies, beyond which investors will not make funds readily available. Should a firm attempt to extend financing beyond its market-determined limit, those funds are available only at higher costs.

The **marginal cost of capital (MCC)** is the last dollar of new capital that the firm raises. The **weighted marginal cost of capital (WMCC)** is the incremental cost of financing beyond the previous MCC level. The **marginal cost of capital schedule** sets a series of ranges and specifies the incremental costs a firm will incur when financing exceeds the maximum limit in each range.

MCC Schedules

There are five steps to develop an MCC schedule:

1. Determine the appropriate weights of the new financing.
2. Calculate the component cost of capital associated with each amount of capital raised.
3. Calculate the range of total new financing at which the cost of the new components increases.

4. Calculate the MCC for each range of total new financing.
5. Plot an MCC schedule.

Setting MCC Schedule Break Points

Establishing the range of total new financing at which the cost of the new components increases requires setting break points. A **break point (BP)** is defined as the total financing a firm can raise before the cost of capital increases.

The formula for calculating an MCC break point is:

$$BP_{RE} = \frac{TF_i}{w_i}$$

where:
BP_{RE} = break point for capital component i
TF_i = total amount of funds available from capital component i
w_i = percentage of total permanent capital represented by capital component i

Using this formula, a BP can be determined by dividing the total amount of funds available for a particular capital component at a stated cost by its capital structure weight.

An MCC schedule may include several BPs.

For example: Blane Company's expects to have $50 million in earnings available during the next year to pay out cash dividends to common shareholders or to reinvest. The firm expects to have a 40% dividend payout ratio. Thus, the company will have $30 million [($50) (1 − 0.40)] in new retained earnings before having to issue more common stock shares. Given the company's capital structure of 40% debt, 10% preferred, and 50% equity, what is the BP for retained earnings?

$$BP_{RE} = \frac{TF_i}{w_i}$$

$$= \frac{\$30 \text{ million}}{0.50} = \$60 \text{ million}$$

Thus, Blane Company can raise $60 million before having to issue external equity as the equity component of its financing mix. This $60 million will consist of $24 million in debt (0.40 × $60 million), $6 million in preferred stock (0.10 × $60 million), and $30 million in internal equity (Retained Earnings = (0.50 × $60 million)). If the company has a capital budget greater than $60 million, it will need to use more expensive common stock as the equity component. Thus, the company's marginal cost of capital will increase due to the higher cost of common stock compared with retained earnings.

Calculating the MCC

Blane Company wants to calculate its MCC after the retained earnings BP. Based on the DDM, the firm's cost of retained equity is 12% but its cost of new equity is 13% when considering flotation costs and under pricing. Thus, the difference of 1 percentage point represents an estimate of the flotation and under pricing costs. Management decides to add 1 percentage point to the cost of common (internal) equity previously calculated. Thus, the estimated cost of new common stock is 12.8% (i.e., 11.8% + 1.0%).

For example: Here is how to calculate Blane Company's MCC after the retained earnings BP of $60 million.

Capital Component	Weight	After-Tax Cost	WACC
Long-term debt	0.40	3.90%	1.560%
Preferred stock	0.10	8.16%	0.816%
Common (internal) equity	0.50	12.80%	6.400%
	1.00		8.776%

Thus, the MCC after $60 million increases to 8.776%. The MCC schedule is plotted in Figure 2B-13.

Figure 2B-13 MCC Schedule for Blane Company

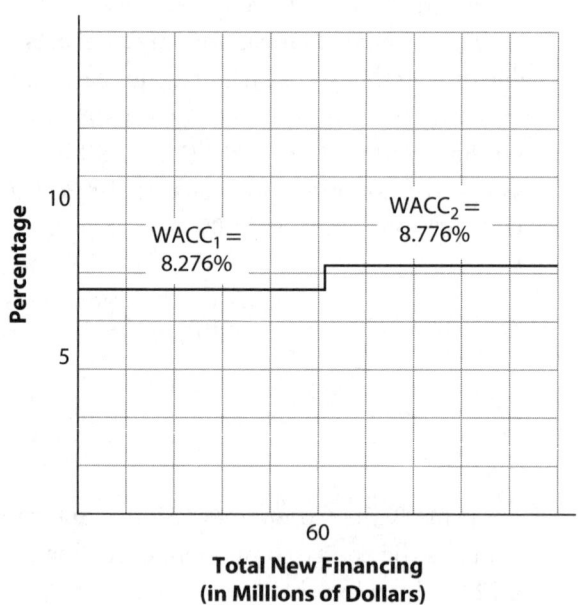

The MCC recognizes the responses of investors to increased financing requirements. The market imposes limits on different levels. Excessive levels lead to successively higher costs of capital.

Income Taxes Impact on Capital Structure and Capital Investment Decisions

Taxes can affect a firm's capital structure in these ways:

- Firms with large taxable income possibly can reduce taxes through more debt financing—which increases the total cash flows distributed to debt and equity holders.
- Firms with volatile operating earnings pose a higher business risk and lower the probability that they will be able to use tax deductions from borrowing during lower-income years. These firms may not want to borrow as much as other firms that have lower business risk.

Use of Cost of Capital in Investment Decisions

Corporations must decide where to invest income to gain the highest possible rate of return within the firm's risk profile. Firms can use the cost of capital as a discount rate of return to evaluate the present value of project cash flows or as a hurdle (threshold) rate to evaluate the internal rate of return.

Cost of capital provides a benchmark for assessing whether the risk and returns on a firm's securities are high or low. These ratings are important for two reasons:

1. High risk means a high cost of capital; low risk is indicative of a low cost of capital.
2. A high cost of capital (discount rate) typically means a low valuation of the firm's securities; a low cost of capital means a high valuation for securities.

The sale of securities provides a corporation with necessary funds for investments. If the value of securities is low, the cost of financing increases. Conversely, financing costs decrease when the value of securities is high.

Ultimately, the solvency of a firm depends on its total risk. Management must consider the impact of various investments on the total risk of the firm.

Derivatives

A **derivative** is a financial instrument whose characteristics and value are derived from the underlying price or value of some other, more basic financial instrument. The underlying asset (also known as an **underlying** or **underlier**) could be a bond, an equity investment, a commodity, or currency.

A derivative involves a contract between two parties. Payment is exchanged between the two parties. The amount of the payment can be either:

- A predetermined amount triggered by a specific event (e.g., the price of the underlying asset exceeding some minimum value); or
- An amount resulting from the change in value of a specified quantity of the underlier. The specified quantity of the underlier is referred to as the **notional amount** (or face amount) of the contract.

Accounting Standards Codification (ASC) Topic 815, *Derivatives and Hedging* (formerly FASB Statement No. 133 and relevant amendments), deals with accounting rules for derivatives. In defining a derivative, ASC Topic 815 notes these points:

- It includes one or more underlying assets.
- It has one or more notional amounts or payment provisions, or both.
- It requires no initial net investment, or it has a smaller investment than other types of contracts that would be expected to have a similar response to changes in market factors.
- The net settlement (contract payment) must be a cash payment, delivery of an asset that can be easily converted to cash, or another derivative.

Inevitably, new derivatives will be developed. In specifying these characteristics (rather than defining a derivative in terms of financial instruments considered to be derivatives), FASB's intent was to ensure that ASC Topic 815 can be applied to new derivatives—as long as their characteristics are similar to those outlined in this topic and relevant authoritative literature.

Corporations do not use derivatives to raise money but buy or sell them to protect against adverse changes in market factors.

Conceptually, there are two basic types of derivatives: **options** and **forward** contracts. Other derivative instruments, such as futures and swaps, are some combination or variation of options and forwards.

Derivatives are complex instruments, which can be risky. The information on derivatives contained in this text is intended to provide an overview.

Much of this content summarizes information from:

- *Accounting for Derivatives and Hedging* by Mark A. Trombley (McGraw-Hill Higher Education, 2002)
- AFP Learning System: *Treasury*

Options

An **option** is a contract between two parties wherein the purchaser of the contract has the right, *but not the obligation*, to buy or sell a given amount of an underlying asset.

Key Characteristics and Terminology

Some of the notable characteristics and terminology associated with option contracts are listed next.

- The party with the option to buy or sell is the owner of the option (also known as the buyer or holder of the option). The other party is the writer or seller of the option.
- The underlying asset may be tangible (such as shares of stock, a commodity, or currency) or intangible (such as an index value or an interest rate).

LOS
§2.B.2.I

- A **call option** is a type of option contract giving the owner the right to buy the underlying asset from the writer at a fixed price during the specified time period.
- A **put option** is a type of option contract giving the owner the right to sell to the writer the underlying asset at a fixed price during the specified time period.
- **Strike price** (or **exercise price**) refers to the fixed price of the contract.
- **Exercise date** (also known as **maturity date** or **expiration date**) is the last day on which the buyer can exercise (buy or sell) the underlying asset.
- The **premium** is the initial purchase price of the option; it is usually stated on a per-unit basis. The writer (seller) of an option contract receives an up-front premium from the buyer (owner) of the contract. This premium obligates the writer to fulfill the contract (sell or buy the underlying asset) if the buyer chooses to exercise the option.
- A **European option** is a contract allowing the owner to exercise the option only on the maturity date.
- An **American option** is a contract allowing the owner to exercise the option at any time during the exercise period.

Payoff Structure

Different payoffs are possible with options.

- An option is referred to as **at-the-money** if the underlying asset price equals the strike price.
- An option that is generally referred to as **in-the-money** requires a payment to the owner if the contract is exercised immediately.
- The option is **out-of-the-money** if there is no incentive for the holder to exercise the option.
- A **call** option is referred to as **out-of-the-money** if the strike price exceeds the price of the underlying asset; it is referred to as **in-the-money** if the price of the underlying asset exceeds the strike price.
- A **put** option is referred to as **in-the-money** if the strike price exceeds the price of the underlying asset; it is referred to as **out-of-the-money** if the price of the underlying asset exceeds the strike price.

Simplified examples of call and put option payoffs are presented next.

Call option example. A 30-day option contract is made between a buyer and a seller for a commodity; the strike price is $50 per unit. The premium is $2 per unit. Two scenarios are possible at maturity:

1. If the market price is equal to or less than the strike price of $50 plus the $2 premium, the owner (buyer) would not exercise the option because they could buy the commodity at the current market value price which is cheaper than the exercise price of the option. The buyer loses $2 for the option premium.
2. If the market price is greater than the strike price plus the option premium ($50 + $2 = $52), the owner (buyer) would exercise the option and make a profit.

Put option example. A 60-day option contract is made between a buyer and a seller for a commodity; the strike price is $30 per unit. The premium is $1 per unit. Two scenarios are possible at maturity:

1. If the market price is equal to or greater than the strike price of $30 plus the $1 premium, the owner would not exercise the option. The owner can make more money by selling the commodity at the current market value price than by exercising the option. The loss is $1 for the option premium.
2. If the market price is less than the strike price minus the option premium ($30 − $1 = $29), the owner makes a profit by exercising the option.

At the time an option contract is set, neither party is required to own the underlying asset. In an option involving shares of stock, for example, the writer of the option does not have to currently own the shares of stock. The writer can offer the buyer the option to buy the stock without actually owning it. However, if the owner exercises the call option, the writer must deliver the stock. If the writer does not already own the stock, the writer must buy the shares specified by the contract on the open market and deliver them to the option owner. If the current market value exceeds the strike price, the option writer receives only the strike price per share as payment. The difference between the strike price and the market value must be taken as a loss by the buyer.

Options have an asymmetric payoff profile. Call option owners have the opportunity for unlimited gain with limited possible losses. If the option is not exercised, it expires. No units are exchanged, and the owner's loss is limited to the premium—the price paid to acquire the option. Call option writers may experience unlimited potential losses unless the contract is covered. This means that the writer already owns the underlier. Put option owners face limited gain and limited losses.

Options typically are used for leverage or protection. Using an option for leverage provides the owner with equity in the underlying asset for the premium payment, which is a fraction of the actual market value. Because options provide the right to acquire the underlying asset at a fixed price for a limited time, they offer protection by guarding against price fluctuations until the maturity date. This limits risk of forfeiture of the option premium, unless the underlier is not already owned.

Price and Value of Options

To a degree, the price or value of an option depends on the expected future value of the underlying asset.

The following factors influence the theoretical value of an option:

- Current price of the underlying asset
- Time until expiration of the option
- Volatility in price of the underlying asset
- Strike price of the option
- The interest rate on risk-free income securities (usually Treasury bills) expiring at the same time as the option contract
- PV of any expected dividends or interest for common stocks or interest-bearing securities

In practice, mathematical formulas are required to calculate theoretical option values. Furthermore, balance sheet accounting requires that a derivative must be shown at fair value on the balance sheet as either an asset or a liability (depending on the specific contract). Accountants must be able to determine the fair value of derivatives.

Financial Accounting Standards Board (FASB) ASC Topic 820, *Fair Value Measurements and Disclosures* (as formerly addressed in FASB Statement No. 157), provides a methodology for determining the fair value of financial instruments (including derivatives) by using a hierarchy of inputs (Level 1, Level 2, Level 3) and requires using valuation techniques consistent with conventional approaches (market, income, and/or cost). This hierarchy and these valuation techniques are further elaborated on and discussed in Part 1 of the CMAexcel Learning System. Several pricing models are used in practice to value option-related derivatives while meeting the requirements of ASC Topic 820. They include the Black-Scholes model, the binomial lattice model, and Monte Carlo simulation.

The Black-Scholes model is best suited for valuing plain-vanilla options (non-complex option derivatives and those with the most standard components—an expiration date and straightforward strike price). Both the binomial lattice model and Monte Carlo simulation are better suited for valuing more complex options such as option-related derivatives.

Forward Contracts

A forward contract is a customized agreement between two parties to buy or sell a specific amount of an asset at a future date for a set price. Forwards are fundamentally different from options because both parties are obligated to perform according to the terms of the contract.

Key Characteristics and Terminology

Some of the notable characteristics and terminology associated with forwards are listed next.

- In a forward contract, one party purchases the contract; the other party is usually referred to as the counterparty.
- The underlying asset may be tangible (such as a commodity or currency) or intangible (such as a stock index or a debt instrument).
- The party who agrees to **buy** the underlying asset on a specified future date assumes a **long position** (or is said to be long a forward contract).
- The party who agrees to **sell** that underlying asset on the specified date assumes a **short position** (or is said to be short a forward contract).
- The delivery price (or contract price) is the purchase/sale price specified in the contract.
- The delivery date (or maturity date) refers to the specified future date of the contract; delivery of the contract takes place at maturity.

- The amount of the underlying asset and the delivery date are set at the time the contract is negotiated; no initial payment (premium) is made.

The counterparty in a forward contract is often a bank, a dealer, or a trader in foreign exchange (FX) markets. The most common application of forwards is with FX payments. In many cases, these entities serve as "market makers" and facilitate private contracts between two parties.

Forward contracts are not traded on organized exchanges. This is a key distinction from futures contracts, which are traded on standardized exchanges.

Payoff Structure

In the absence of a premium payment, the initial value of the contract to both parties is zero. The contract has no value when it is written. The forward price determines the value of the contract. A long position gains value when the underlying asset price rises and loses value when the asset price falls. Conversely, the short position gains value when the underlying asset price falls and loses value when the asset price rises.

Forwards have symmetrical payoffs, meaning the gains and losses for favorable and unfavorable positions are equal. As the value of the underlying asset changes, the value of the long and short positions in a forward contract becomes proportionally positive or negative, depending on the position held.

Forward contract example. A simple scenario illustrating use of a forward contract might be a U.S. importer with a 60-day invoice due in euros. Purchasing a forward contract for euros deliverable in 60 days locks in the exchange rate regardless of the fluctuation that occurs in the currency exchange rate during the 60-day period.

Futures Contracts

A **futures contract** (or futures) is a forward-based contract conceptually similar to a forward contract but different in its execution. The basic difference is that unlike forwards, which are often privately negotiated by an intermediary, futures are standardized contracts traded on organized exchanges.

In the United States, futures are traded on these exchanges:

- New York Mercantile Exchange (e.g., for metals, petroleum, and fiber)
- Chicago Board of Trade (e.g., for livestock, wood, and meat)
- International Money Market wing of the Chicago exchange (e.g., for foreign currency futures)

The exchanges dictate the notional amounts and maturity dates. They also require daily settlements during the contract based on changes in the underlying asset. Gains and losses are marked against a margin account.

Futures usually are closed out before maturity. They rarely are settled by actual delivery. Final settlement generally is accomplished through a cash payment. The payoff profile from a long position and a short position in a futures contract looks exactly the same as the payoff profiles from a forward contract.

Swaps

A **swap** is a private agreement between two parties (called "counterparties") to exchange (or swap) future cash payments. Similar to a forward contract, a swap agreement usually is facilitated by an intermediary. Swaps are characterized by a series of forward contracts and the exchange of payments on specified payment dates.

The most common type of swap is an interest rate swap—where two parties exchange future interest payments on a notional amount. The principal amount is notional because it never changes hands and is used only to calculate the payment amounts.

The simplest type of interest swap, called a "plain vanilla interest rate swap," involves trading fixed interest rate payments for floating-rate payments:

- Party A agrees to pay Party B a series of future payments that are equal to a *predetermined fixed interest rate* multiplied by the notional principal.
- Party B agrees to pay Party A a series of future payments that are equal to a *floating interest rate* multiplied by the same notional principal.

At the initiation of the swap in a single currency, Party A and Party B typically do not swap the notional principal. When payments are due, net interest is paid by the counterparty that owes it. That is, the appropriate counterparty pays the difference between the fixed-rate and variable-rate payments.

The main motivation for using interest rate swaps is to reduce exposure to adverse changes in interest rates. The parties convert a fixed-rate obligation or investment into a floating-rate obligation (or vice versa) that might be desirable to match the fixed or floating character of their assets and liabilities.

A potential risk in using swaps is that either counterparty may default on the agreed-on interest payment stream and thus potentially leave the other party liable for the original payment stream. The use of a third-party intermediary can help to mitigate such risks.

There are other forms of interest swaps as well as many other types of swaps. Some of the more common ones are currency rate swaps, where an obligation in one currency is converted to another currency, and commodity swaps, where a floating price for a commodity is exchanged for a fixed price.

Other Long-Term Financial Instruments

In addition to the instruments described thus far, corporations can use other instruments as sources for long-term financing. Figure 2B-14 summarizes key features about leases, convertible securities, and warrants.

Figure 2B-14 Other Long-Term Financial Instruments

Instrument	Description	Key Characteristics

Lease	Legal contract through which the owner (the lessor) of an asset grants another party (the lessee) the right to use the asset for a certain period of time in return for a specified payment	• Binds the lessee to make payments specified in the lease contract.
		• Can take various forms:
		  • Operating leases: short-term, cancelable leases where the lessor bears the risk of ownership.
		  • Financial lease (also known as full payout or capital lease): usually noncancelable and fully paid out (amortized) over its term and where the lessee bears the risks (i.e., the lessee bears the responsibility for maintenance, insurance, and taxes).

Convertible security	A fixed income security or a preferred stock that includes an option to exchange that security for a stated number of shares of another security	• Typically used to convert the security into a specified number of shares of an equity security. • Allows a corporation to raise funds at a cost of capital lower than a straight bond or common stock issue; when convertibles are exchanged, debt is removed from the balance sheet.
Warrant	Long-term call option to purchase common stock directly from the corporation	• Gives bondholders or preferred stockholders the right to purchase shares of common stock at a given price. • Derives value from the investor's expectation that the stock price will increase beyond the strike price.

Knowledge Check: Long-Term Financial Management

The following questions are intended to help you check your understanding and recall of the material presented in this topic. They do not represent the type of questions that appear on the CMA exam.

Directions: Answer each question in the space provided. Correct answers and section references appear after the knowledge check questions.

1. Which statement accurately describes bond yields?
   - ☐ a. Higher-quality bonds typically pay lower yields than lower-grade bonds.
   - ☐ b. Short-term bonds typically pay higher yields than long-term bonds.
   - ☐ c. Fixed interest rate bonds have a lower "current yield" than zero coupon bonds.
   - ☐ d. Secured bonds typically pay higher yields than unsecured bonds.

2. Which type of bond is **most** attractive to buy on the secondary market when interest rates are low?
   - ☐ a. Aaa- or AAA-rated bond
   - ☐ b. Zero coupon bond
   - ☐ c. Floating-rate bond
   - ☐ d. U.S. Treasury bond

For questions 3 through 8, match the financial instruments with the appropriate description.

   a. An agreement between two parties to buy or sell a specific amount of an asset at a future date for a set price
   b. A private agreement between two parties to exchange future cash payments
   c. Long-term call option to purchase common stock directly from the corporation
   d. An instrument providing a limited ownership interest in a corporation and a fixed dividend
   e. A contract allowing the purchaser the right to buy or sell the underlying asset at a stated price on or before a specific date
   f. An instrument providing equity interest in the assets of the corporation and a share in the earnings

3. _____ Common stock

4. _____ Preferred stock

5. _____ Option

6. _____ Forward contract

7. _____ Warrant

8. _____ Swap

9. The price of a bond
   - [ ] a. increases as market interest rates increase.
   - [ ] b. decreases as market interest rates decrease.
   - [ ] c. is independent of market interest rates.
   - [ ] d. moves inversely to market interest rate changes.

10. Using the constant dividend growth model (Gordon's model), the value of a common stock with a current dividend of $4, a dividend growth rate of 5%, and a required rate of return of 16% would be
    - [ ] a. $25 per share.
    - [ ] b. $36.36 per share.
    - [ ] c. $38.18 per share.
    - [ ] d. $80 per share.

11. The value of a 6%, $50 par, preferred stock with a required rate of return of 8% would be
    - [ ] a. $37.50 per share.
    - [ ] b. $42.86 per share.
    - [ ] c. $50 per share.
    - [ ] d. $53 per share.

12. What is the approximate cost of capital for a firm given the following information?

Type	After-Tax Cost	% of Capital Structure
Debt	8%	34%
Preferred stock	9%	26%
Common equity	10%	40%

    - [ ] a. 8%
    - [ ] b. 9%
    - [ ] c. 10%
    - [ ] d. 27%

13. Which factor makes determining the cost of debt challenging?
    - [ ] a. More than one type of debt may be involved.
    - [ ] b. Retained earnings are subject to dividend payments.

☐ c. Common stock has no fixed contractual payments.

☐ d. The firm's future performance levels are difficult to estimate.

14. An underlying premise in applying the capital asset pricing model to estimate a firm's cost of equity capital is

☐ a. investor attitudes toward risk will not change.

☐ b. dividends are expected to grow at a constant compound rate.

☐ c. individual capital components must be weighted based on their contributions to the firm's capital structure.

☐ d. the return rate equals the riskless rate of return plus a premium for risk.

Match the following terms to their description.

15. _____ Cost of capital	a. The after-tax interest rate a company pays on all of its capital debt (e.g., loans and bonds)
16. _____ Cost of debt	b. Its expected return is normally higher than debt but lower than retained earnings
17. _____ Cost of preferred stock	c. The weighted average of the various components a firm uses for financing its investments
18. _____ Cost of common equity	d. The expected, required, or actual rate of return on the firm's stock that, if earned, will leave the market value of the stock unchanged

19. What is the after-tax cost of a 6% bond with a 5.94% yield to maturity when the effective tax rate is 40%?

☐ a. 3.6%

☐ b. 3.56%

☐ c. 5.94%

☐ d. 6%

20. What is the after-tax cost of a 5% preferred stock with a 2% flotation cost when the effective tax rate is 40%?

☐ a. 5%

☐ b. 3%

☐ c. 5.1%

☐ d. 3.06%

21. What is the after-tax cost of a common stock selling at $40 per share when the dividend expected at the end of the upcoming year is $3 per share and the dividend growth rate is 4%? Assume the effective tax rate is 40%.
    - a. 11.5%
    - b. 7.5%
    - c. 7.8%
    - d. 11.8%

22. What is the after-tax cost of a common stock selling at $40 per share that has a beta coefficient of 1.8? Assume an effective tax rate of 40%, a 90-day Treasury bill rate of 2%, and a required market rate of return of 8%.
    - a. 12.8%
    - b. 7.68%
    - c. 16.4%
    - d. 9.84%

Knowledge Check Answers: Long-Term Financial Management

1. Which statement accurately describes bond yields? [See *Bond Yields*.]
   - ☑ a. Higher-quality bonds typically pay lower yields than lower-grade bonds.
   - ☐ b. Short-term bonds typically pay higher yields than long-term bonds.
   - ☐ c. Fixed interest rate bonds earn more than zero coupon bonds.
   - ☐ d. Secured bonds typically pay higher yields than unsecured bonds.

2. Which type of bond is **most** attractive to buy on the secondary market when interest rates are low? [See *Bond Interest*.]
   - ☐ a. Aaa- or AAA-rated bond
   - ☐ b. Zero coupon bond
   - ☑ c. Floating-rate bond
   - ☐ d. U.S. treasury bond

For questions 3 through 8, match the financial instruments with the appropriate description.

   a. An agreement between two parties to buy or sell a specific amount of an asset at a future date for a set price
   b. A private agreement between two parties to exchange future cash payments
   c. Long-term call option to purchase common stock directly from the corporation
   d. An instrument providing a limited ownership interest in a corporation and a fixed dividend
   e. A contract allowing the purchaser the right to buy or sell the underlying asset at a stated price on or before a specific date
   f. An instrument providing equity interest in the assets of the corporation and a share in the earnings

3. __f__ Common stock
4. __d__ Preferred stock
5. __e__ Option
6. __a__ Forward contract
7. __c__ Warrant

8. __b__ Swap

9. The price of a bond [See **Bond Valuation**.]
   - ☐ a. increases as market interest rates increase.
   - ☐ b. decreases as market interest rates decrease.
   - ☐ c. is independent of market interest rates.
   - ☒ d. moves inversely to market interest rate changes.

10. Using the constant dividend growth model (Gordon's model), the value of a common stock with a current dividend of $4, a dividend growth rate of 5%, and a required rate of return of 16% would be [See **Constant Dividend Growth Model**.]
    - ☐ a. $25 per share.
    - ☐ b. $36.36 per share.
    - ☒ c. $38.18 per share.
    - ☐ d. $80 per share.

11. The value of a 6%, $50 par, preferred stock with a required rate of return of 8% would be [See **Preferred Stock Valuation**.]
    - ☒ a. $37.50 per share.
    - ☐ b. $42.86 per share.
    - ☐ c. $50 per share.
    - ☐ d. $53 per share.

12. What is the approximate cost of capital for a firm given the following information? [See **Calculating the Cost of Capital**.]

Type	After-Tax Cost	% of Capital Structure
Debt	8%	34%
Preferred stock	9%	26%
Common equity	10%	40%

   - ☐ a. 8%
   - ☒ b. 9%
   - ☐ c. 10%
   - ☐ d. 27%

13. Which factor makes determining the cost of debt challenging? [See **Cost of Debt**.]
    - ☒ a. More than one type of debt may be involved.
    - ☐ b. Retained earnings are subject to dividend payments.
    - ☐ c. Common stock has no fixed contractual payments.
    - ☐ d. The firm's future performance levels are difficult to estimate.

14. An underlying premise in applying the capital asset pricing model to estimate a firm's cost of equity capital is [See *Cost of Common Equity*.]
    - ☐ a. investor attitudes toward risk will not change.
    - ☐ b. dividends are expected to grow at a constant compound rate.
    - ☐ c. individual capital components must be weighted based on their contributions to the firm's capital structure.
    - ☒ d. the return rate equals the riskless rate of return plus a premium for risk.

Match the following terms to their description.

15. __c__ Cost of capital	a.	The after-tax interest rate a company pays on all of its capital debt (e.g., loans and bonds)
16. __a__ Cost of debt	b.	Its expected return is normally higher than debt but lower than retained earnings
17. __b__ Cost of preferred stock	c.	The weighted average of the various components a firm uses for financing its investments
18. __d__ Cost of common equity	d.	The expected, required, or actual rate of return on the firm's stock that, if earned, will leave the market value of the stock unchanged

19. What is the after-tax cost of a 6% bond with a 5.94% yield to maturity when the effective tax rate is 40%? [See *Cost of Debt*.]
    - ☐ a. 3.6%
    - ☒ b. 3.56%
    - ☐ c. 5.94%
    - ☐ d. 6%

20. What is the after-tax cost of a 5% preferred stock with a 2% flotation cost when the effective tax rate is 40%? [See *Cost of Preferred Stock*.]
    - ☐ a. 5%
    - ☐ b. 3%
    - ☒ c. 5.1% = .05/.98
    - ☐ d. 3.06%

21. What is the after-tax cost of a common stock selling at $40 per share when the dividend expected at the end of the upcoming year is $3 per share and the dividend growth rate is 4%? Assume the effective tax rate is 40%. [See *Estimating the Cost of New Equity (Issuing Additional Common Stock) Using the Dividend Growth Model.*]

   ☑ a. 11.5% = ($3/$40) + 4%
   ☐ b. 7.5%
   ☐ c. 7.8%
   ☐ d. 11.8%

22. What is the after-tax cost of a common stock selling at $40 per share that has a beta coefficient of 1.8? Assume an effective tax rate of 40%, a 90-day Treasury bill rate of 2%, and a required market rate of return of 8%. [See *Estimating the Cost of Internal Equity (Retained Earnings) Using the Capital Asset Pricing Model.*]

   ☑ a. 12.8% = 2% + 1.8(8% − 2%)
   ☐ b. 7.68%
   ☐ c. 16.4%
   ☐ d. 9.84%

TOPIC 3

Raising Capital

In Topic 2: Long-Term Financial Management of this section, securities, such as common stock and preferred stock and debt (without convertible features), as well as methods for their valuation, were discussed as a means for providing capital to a corporation. This topic addresses other means through which a corporation may raise capital, including approaches that involve intermediate-term (one to ten years) sources and other long-term (over ten years) sources, having convertible features.

The final part of this topic covers other matters relevant to the raising of capital for corporations, such as the capital markets within which the raising of capital occurs; the role of investment banks, underwriters, and credit rating agencies; insider trading; and a corporation's dividend policies and stock repurchase transactions.

 **READ** the Learning Outcome Statements (LOS) for this topic as found in Appendix B and then study the concepts and calculations presented here to be sure you understand the content you could be tested on in the CMA exam.

Intermediate-Term Sources

Intermediate-term sources for raising capital include the following:

- Term loans
- Equipment financing loans
- Operating leases
- Capital (financial) leases

Each of these sources is discussed separately below.

Term Loans

Term loans are debt obligations having one- to ten-year maturities. The primary issuers of term loans are commercial banks, savings and loan associations, insurance companies, pension funds, the U.S. Small Business Administration (SBA), Small Business Investment Companies (SBICs), Industrial Development Authorities (IDAs), and equipment suppliers. Term loans are used most often to finance small additions to facility and equipment. Large additions usually are financed through stock or bond issues or retained earnings. Term loans are used to finance moderate increases in assets under these circumstances:

- The cost of stock or bond issuance is prohibitive.
- The loan will be paid off from intermediate-term earnings.
- The increase in assets is intermediate term rather than permanent.

Most term loans are secured. In addition, lenders will attach other conditions to term loans. Among them are compensating balances on commercial bank loans, various security provisions, protective covenants, and default provisions. Protective covenants may be positive or negative. Security provisions include these five:

1. Assignment of payments due
2. Assignment of portions of inventory or receivables
3. Assignment of cash surrender values of key executive life insurance policies
4. Liens on the borrower's inventory, receivables, property, plant, and equipment
5. Pledges of marketable security investments held by the borrower

Default provisions allow the lender to demand immediate repayment of the term loan when certain conditions occur. Among the conditions are:

- Failure of the borrower to pay interest, principal, or both as specified in the loan agreement
- Discovery by the lender of financial statement misrepresentations made by the borrower
- Failure of the borrower to observe any of the covenants specified in the loan agreement

Since term loans are negotiated privately between the borrower and the lender, they are less costly than public offerings of stock or the issuance of bonds. The interest on term loans is usually a bit higher than the prime bank lending rate. Generally the rates are 0.25 to 2.5 percentage points above the prime rate.

Term loans normally require that the principal be amortized (paid off) over the life of the loan. In other words, a term loan is basically an installment loan. The installments may be monthly, quarterly, semiannually, or annually.

For example: Suppose a company borrows $100,000 at 9% per annum payable in eight equal installments, the first occurring at the end of the first year. Given that the present value (PV) of the annuity of eight payments at 9% equals $100,000, the annual payment (R) is computed as:

$$R = \$100{,}000 / 5.535 = \$18{,}067$$

The 5.535 is the PV of an annuity discount factor for $i = 9\%$ and $n = 8$ periods and can be found in the Present Value of an Annuity Table in Appendix A.

Each payment of $18,067 would consist of principal repayment and interest as shown in Figure 2B-15. Once the annual annuity amount is known, the interest is calculated using the annual interest rate of 9% multiplied by the remaining balance. The principal repayment is the difference between the annual amount and the current interest amount. For n = 1, $100,000 multiplied by 9% results in an interest amount of $9,000. When that amount is subtracted from the $18,067 payment, the result is a repayment of principal in the amount of $9,067.

Figure 2B-15 Amortization Table

End of Year	Annual Annuity Amount	Interest	Principal Repayment	Remaining Balance
0	$0	$0	$0	$100,000
1	18,067	9,000	9,067	90,933
2	18,067	8,183	9,884	81,049
3	18,067	7,294	10,773	70,276
4	18,067	6,324	11,743	58,533
5	18,067	5,267	12,800	45,733
6	18,067	4,116	13,951	31,782
7	18,067	2,860	15,207	16,575
8	18,067	1,492	16,575	$0
Total	$144,536	$44,536	$100,000	

Equipment Financing Loans

Equipment financing loans often use the equipment purchased as collateral for the intermediate-term loan. Such loans are secured either through a conditional sales contract or a chattel mortgage. In a conditional sales contract (sometimes referred to as a purchase money mortgage), the seller holds the title to the equipment until the buyer makes all of the payments stipulated in the loan agreement. Such contracts are used almost exclusively by equipment sellers.

A chattel mortgage is a lien on personal (as opposed to real) property. Real property (real estate) consists of land and buildings. Equipment is personal property. Chattel mortgages occur most commonly when a commercial bank makes a direct equipment financing loan to a borrower.

Mathematically, equipment loans are handled as a term loan, as shown in the previous example.

Leases

Leasing is a way of obtaining the use of an asset for a specified period of time without actually having an ownership interest in the asset. The lessor allows the lessee to use the asset for the specified period. In return, the lessee agrees to make periodic lease payments to the lessor. Leases may be operating, capital (financing), or leveraged. The advantages and disadvantage of leases and the net advantage to leasing are covered next.

Changes in GAAP and/or IFRS are reflected on the CMA exam one year after the effective date. This material addresses required knowledge for the 2017 and 2018 CMA testing window. Users are encouraged to monitor FASB and IFRS updates and effective dates, as well as the ICMA Learning Outcome Statements posted on the IMA website to guide appropriate preparation for the CMA exam.

Operating Leases

An operating lease, sometimes called a service or maintenance lease, provides the lessee with the use of the leased asset on a period-by-period basis. The period of an operating lease usually is considerably shorter than the asset's economic life. An example of an operating lease is the rental of an asset. For example, a company might rent a truck for three months, the duration of its business season. An operating lease is technically a shorter-term financing method.

Capital Leases

A **capital (financing) lease** is essentially an installment purchase. Capital leases are noncancellable and involve the transfer of the rights and obligations of ownership from the lessor to the lessee. Title to the asset, however, remains with the lessor.

When an asset is obtained using a capital lease, the lessee records the asset on its books at cost, just as it would any other fixed asset. The asset would then be depreciated in the normal way. If the straight-line method is used, the total cost minus the salvage value would be divided by the useful life in years to arrive at the annual depreciation expense. The lessee would also record a liability for the total amount of the lease payments to be made over the life of the lease.

From the lessor's point of view, there are two types of capital leases:

1. Sales Type—under this type of lease, the lessor recognizes a profit (or loss) on the sale of the leased asset, along with the interest income over the life of the lease.
2. Direct Financing—under this type of lease, the lessor recognizes the interest income over the life of the lease.

The lessor would determine the amount of the lease payments to be made by the lessee using the criteria of income as defined above.

Leasing Advantages

Leasing offers five advantages.

1. The primary advantage of leasing is flexible financing, because leasing agreements generally have fewer restrictive covenants than loan agreements.
2. Another advantage is in cash flow management. The lessee may be able to make lower payments on a lease as opposed to a term loan because of income tax benefits and/or a lowered interest rate.
3. Some leases provide 100% financing, whereas loans usually require a down payment.

4. A lessee avoids the risk of the asset becoming obsolete.
5. Leasing may be expedient as it often avoids some or all of the time-consuming capital budgeting process.

Leasing Disadvantages

There are two disadvantages of leasing.

1. *Cost.* A company with good credit opportunities may find purchasing to be more cost effective than leasing.
2. *Loss of flexibility.* It is not unusual for a lessor to deny the lessee the right to make changes to a leased asset, and there is often a penalty for the early cancellation of a lease.

Net Advantage of Leasing

Lease evaluation by the lessee is essentially a lease versus borrow and buy decision analysis. It involves the calculation of the **net advantage of leasing (NAL)**. The NAL compares the PV cost of leasing an asset with the PV cost of borrowing to own the asset. If the cost of borrowing to own is greater than the cost of leasing, the NAL is positive and the asset should be leased.

The NAL is calculated as shown:

1. Installed cost of asset
2. Less: PV of the after-tax lease payment at the cost of borrowing
3. Less: PV of the depreciation tax shield at the cost of borrowing
4. Plus: PV of the after-tax operating costs incurred if owned and not leased at the cost of borrowing
5. Less: PV of the after-tax salvage value at the lessee's target rate of return
6. Equals: NAL

The NAL model assumes that the lease is treated as an operating lease for tax purposes by the lessee. This assumption is critical. Both the cost of borrowing and the target rate of return used in the model are after tax.

The installed cost of the asset includes the purchase price less discounts plus freight, installation, and tryout costs. The installed cost is the depreciation base.

Other Long-Term Sources

Other long-term sources for raising capital, such as convertible debt and convertible preferred stock, are discussed next.

Convertible Debt

Convertible debt is normally a debenture (unsecured bond) that is convertible to the debt issuer's common stock at the debt issuer's option. A convertible bond is, in essence, a deferred equity offering. The issuer of the convertible bonds is expecting that these securities will be converted to common stock, which would make it unnecessary to repay the bond principal at a later date. It is important to note that convertible bonds are reported as a liability. When converted, the liability goes away and equity is recorded.

Convertible bonds are exchangeable for common stock at a stated conversion price. For example, suppose the ABC Corporation issues convertible bonds with a conversion price of $25. That means that each $1,000 bond is convertible to 40 ($1,000 / $25) shares of common stock. The conversion ratio is 40.

Normally, the conversion price is set at 15% to 30% above the common stock price at the time of the bond issuance. That would be $19 to $22 in this example. When the market value of the common stock exceeds the conversion price of $25, it would be profitable for bondholders to convert.

Because convertible bonds possess both debt and equity characteristics, their market value is a function of both the common stock value (conversion value) and their value as straight debt. The buyer of the convertible will pay a premium for the equity portion. The equity portion of a convertible bond is the difference between the market price of the convertible and what its value would be as a straight bond. For example, suppose a convertible bond sells for $1,012 per $1,000 bond and its value as a straight bond is $718. The equity portion of the convertible issue would be $294 ($1,012 − $718) per bond.

Convertible Preferred Stock

A convertible preferred stock behaves similarly to a convertible bond. Convertible preferred stock is not commonly issued. It is important to note that prior to any conversion, convertible preferred stock is recorded as preferred until it is converted. At that point, the preferred stock accounts are decreased and the common stock accounts are increased.

Other Capital-Raising Matters

Other matters related to raising capital focus on: the **capital markets** within which long-term financial securities (e.g., bonds and stocks) are bought and sold; the role of investment banks, underwriters, and credit rating agencies in the capital-raising process; insider trading; and a company's dividend policies and stock repurchase transactions.

Capital Markets

The discussion of capital markets that follows encompasses the key factors and contributions in regard to the issuance and trading of long-term debt and equity securities in the capital-raising process.

Primary and Secondary Markets

The migration of a company from private to public ownership often occurs when a private company finds that it needs access to additional funds. The *primary market* and the *secondary market* are terms referring to where securities are created and where they are traded among investors. The initial public offering (IPO) of securities to investors occurs in the primary market. Subsequent trading is facilitated through the secondary market. These markets are further discussed below.

Role of Investment Banks and Underwriters

Investment banks are financial institutions that assist companies and governments in issuing securities. The services of an investment bank include providing advice, selling securities, and underwriting. When an investment bank acts as an underwriter, it bears some or all of the risks of selling and holding the securities in exchange for a premium.

An investment bank may join an underwriting syndicate consisting of the originating house (the investment banker dealing with the issuer) and other investment banking firms selected by the issuer. The originating house is referred to as the syndicate manager or underwriting manager.

The investment bank or syndicate (group of investment banks) normally sets up a best efforts agreement with the IPO issuer. In a best efforts agreement, the investment bank or syndicate agrees to use all reasonable efforts to sell as much of the issue to the public. The investment bank or syndicate can purchase either an entire issue from the issuer or merely the amount of the issue required by the issuer's demand. The investment bankers often use tombstone ads to announce an issue.

An underwriter may place a "tombstone" ad in a financial journal or in the financial pages of a regular newspaper to announce a new security will be issued. The ad gets its name from the bold black border surrounding the information and the stark nature of the information.

As the need for the funding for expansion grows and exceeds the money that can be raised through such sources as investments, trade credit, lines of credit, loans, and venture capital, management goes to investment bankers who agree to underwrite a stock offering. By definition, the **primary market** is the market in which investors have the first opportunity to buy a newly issued security.

Underwriters help the firm prepare a prospectus. A stock prospectus is a formal written offer to sell securities to the public. It is filed with the Securities and Exchange Commission (SEC) and made available to all investors. The prospectus includes details such as how the security is valued, the issue price per unit, size, and goal of the issuing company.

Through the underwriting process, investment banks may buy all the public shares at a set price. The corporation receives that money, which can be used for financing operations. Investment banks earn money from the spread between the offering price of an IPO issued to the public and the price of the IPO issue paid to the issuer.

After the IPO, the stock shares are traded in the secondary market. The corporation does not receive any capital or cash from shares trading in the secondary market. The stock price in the secondary market is determined by how much investors are willing to pay for the stock at the time of purchase.

After a firm goes public, it may continue to issue new stock in the primary market. The only difference is that the stocks are no longer IPOs but seasoned (subsequent or secondary) offerings.

By definition, the **secondary market** is a market in which an investor purchases an asset from another investor rather than from the issuing corporation. This is the defining characteristic of the secondary market—investors trade among themselves. They buy and sell previously issued securities from other investors without the involvement of the issuing companies.

The secondary market is generally synonymous with the stock market and includes the New York Stock Exchange (NYSE), NASDAQ, and all major exchanges around the world.

Role of Credit Rating Agencies

Standard & Poor's, Moody's, and Fitch are the three largest bond credit rating agencies. The purpose of the agencies is to assign a rating to each debt security based on creditworthiness of the company or government issuing the security. This rating is used to determine the market rate of interest on the debt security. When the market interest rate of a debt security is higher than its stated rate, the security will sell at a discount. When the market interest rate equals a debt security's stated rate, it will sell at par (face) value. When the market interest rate is lower than the stated rate, the security will sell at a premium.

Market Efficiency

The U.S. security markets are relatively efficient. The markets quickly reflect information relevant to the value of a security. The idea of market efficiency is called the efficient market hypothesis (theory). The hypothesis has three forms:

1. **Strong form:** The strong form of the theory states that all information (public or private) is incorporated in a security price. Therefore, it is not possible for insiders to earn abnormal profits.
2. **Semistrong form:** The semistrong form states that all publicly available information (no private information) is incorporated in a security price. Therefore, abnormal returns from insider trading are possible.
3. **Weak form:** The weak form of the theory says that security prices reflect all recent price movements only. Therefore, technical analysis will not provide a basis for abnormal returns.

Securities Registration

The Securities and Exchange Commission (SEC) is charged with the regulation of the sale of securities across U.S. state borders. The Securities Act of 1933 regulates the sale of new securities, the initial offerings including initial public offerings (IPOs), i.e., the primary market. The Securities Exchange Act of 1934 regulates the secondary security markets and financial reporting by SEC registrants.

The Securities Act of 1933 requires that investors receive significant information concerning securities being offered for public sale and prohibits deceit and fraud in the sale of securities. In order to accomplish these objectives, companies desiring to issue securities to the public file registration statements that include:

- A description of the company's properties and business
- A description of the security to be offered for sale
- Information about the management of the company
- Financial statements certified by independent accountants

Insider Trading

Insider trading involves the directors and management of a corporation buying or selling the corporation's securities to gain an advantage over investors who are not privy to the information.

The Insider Trading Act of 1984 specifies civil penalties for illegal insider trading of up to three times the profit gained or three times the loss avoided from the illegal trading. The Insider Trading and Securities Fraud Enforcement Act of 1988 stipulates that brokers, dealers, and investment advisors must enact and enforce policies to prevent insider trading and to prevent the firm, its employees, or any associated persons from misusing material nonpublic information.

Dividend Policy

For the firm that has preferred stock outstanding, a dividend of a stipulated constant dollar amount per share is the norm. It is important to note, however, that the dividend is a discretionary rather than a fixed obligation of the firm. Failure to make a preferred dividend payment will not result in a default on the security nor force the firm into insolvency.

Most preferred stocks have a **cumulative dividend feature**, which requires that any unpaid dividends be carried forward until paid. Before a firm can pay a cash dividend on its common stock, any unpaid preferred dividends (i.e., dividends in arrears) must be paid.

In general, dividends are considered an incentive to own common stock. Corporations offering regular dividends generally have progressed beyond the growth phase, tend not to derive much benefit from reinvesting profits, and, therefore, choose to share those profits as dividends. Thus, the stage of a company's life cycle tends to affect its dividend policy.

If corporate earnings decline, a company may decide to reduce or omit its cash dividend, which may signal a decline in the company's future prospects and result in a lower stock price.

The discussion of dividend policy covers the types of dividends a corporation may issue, the impact of stock splits, various types of dividend policies a corporation may employ, and the dividend payout process.

Types of Dividends

With common stock, there is no guarantee that an investor will make money. The equity position in a common stock means that the owner shares in the corporation's fortunes and misfortunes.

Common stock **market value per share** is the current trading price of the stock. If the stock increases in value, shareholders benefit from capital appreciation of their investment and potentially receive a dividend.

A dividend (or payout) represents a share in profits. Corporations are not required to pay dividends unless declared by the board of directors. Payments vary based on earnings and how much the board decides to pay out. Corporations usually pay cash dividends quarterly, but they may also pay dividends in kind or in the form of stock.

- A **cash dividend** is paid in the form of cash, usually a check. Cash dividends typically are taxable to the stockholder.
- **Dividends in kind** involve a dividend paid in assets other than cash. In the past, Wrigley Chewing Gum paid dividends in gum.
- **Stock dividends** are paid as additional shares of stock (rather than cash). They allow a corporation to conserve cash for investment purposes while still rewarding investors. When a corporation issues a stock dividend, there typically are no tax consequences until shareholders sell their shares.
- **Liquidating dividends** are dividends that exceed the corporation's retained earnings. They are not taxable.

Stock Splits

Stock splits involve the issuance of additional shares to stockholders, based on their current ownership. A two-for-one stock split, for example, involves the issuance of one additional share of stock for each share currently owned. The two-for-one split *doubles* authorized, issued, treasury, and outstanding shares and *halves* the par or stated value of the stock.

Corporations typically split stocks to lower the price of a stock, to make the price more appealing to investors, and stimulate trading. The rationale is that when the price of the stock is high, individual investors may be reluctant to buy shares either because the shares cost so much or because of concern that the stock price has peaked in value.

Stocks can be split in various increments: two for one, three for one, three for two, and so on. In a two-for-one split, a stockholder with 100 shares would receive 100 new shares. If the stock is trading at $100 a share, the price drops to about $50 a share. If the stock price drops to exactly $50, the total market value remains the same (200 shares at $50 a share versus the original 100 shares at $100; both equal $10,000). Although the total market value initially remains the same, stockholders may profit if the price eventually goes up.

A stock also may undergo a **reverse split**. In a reverse split, the number of shares decreases, and the price increases accordingly. For example, in a one-for-two reverse split, 100 shares of stock trading at $1 a share become 50 shares worth $2 a share. A reverse split often is used to keep a stock at the stock market's minimum listing price or to increase the stock's general attractiveness to investors who shy away from low-priced stocks. Stock splits and reverse splits do not result in any taxable gain or loss to the stockholder.

Dividend Policies

The issue that corporations face in selecting a dividend policy is how much the corporation should return to the shareholders versus how much it should reinvest in the business. The policy is determined by the board of directors, which generally meets quarterly to declare and approve a quarterly dividend or to approve the decision not to pay a dividend. The determinants of dividend policy are:

- *Shareholder preferences.* Dividend versus corporation growth.
- *Liquidity.* Short-run cash position.
- *Solvency.* The corporation cannot declare a dividend if insolvent
- *Borrowing capacity.* If low, the corporation may wish to reinvest earnings rather than issue dividends.
- *Earnings stability.* Stable earnings correlate with regular, stable dividends.
- *Growth opportunities.* If high, the corporation may wish to reinvest earnings rather than issue dividends.
- *Inflation.* If high, the corporation may need the earnings to reinvest.
- *Capital impairment restrictions.* Legal capital or appropriations (reservations) of retained earnings.
- *Restrictive covenants.* From term loans, bond indentures, or leasing agreements.
- *Taxes.* Dividends are ordinary income to the recipient whereas stock appreciations are treated as capital gains when realized (i.e., when the appreciated stock is sold).

There are four basic dividend policies:

1. Passive residual
2. Stable dollar
3. Constant dividend payout ratio
4. Small regular dividend plus extras

A company following the **passive residual** policy reinvests earnings as long as there are opportunities whose returns exceed the company's required rate of return. Any residual is returned to the shareholders.

A corporation using a **stable dollar** policy pays a regular constant dividend as long as the corporation has the ability to do so. There is evidence that most corporations and shareholders prefer the predictability of stable dividends. Changes in dividends are equated with changes in profitability and, consequently, changes in stock prices.

In contrast, a company using a **constant dividend payout ratio** will have dividends that vary from year to year. This method calculates dividend payments as a constant or fixed percentage of each year's earnings per share.

Historically, dividend payouts in the United States have been between 40% and 60% of earnings. However, because most corporations are reluctant to reduce dividends, dividend payout ratios tend to increase when earnings drop and decrease when earnings rise.

At the option of the investor, some companies provide a dividend reinvestment plan in which the investor does not receive the dividend as cash. Instead, the dividend is used to purchase new shares of the company stock, which allows the investor to have immediate reinvestment of earnings and lowered transaction costs and the company to maintain value and thereby increase stock price.

Many corporations pay a **regular small quarterly dividend plus year-end extras** in high-earnings years. Large companies, such as U.S. Steel and DuPont, often have followed this policy.

Dividend Payout Process

Four dates are relevant to the dividend payout process:

1. Declaration date
2. Ex-dividend date
3. Record date
4. Payment date

A dividend declaration would state that Company X declares a dividend today payable on a set date to shareholders of record on a date between the declaration and payment dates. On the declaration date, the corporation reduces its retained earnings and establishes the dividend payable.

The ex-dividend date is a date set by the stock exchange handling the stock. The date usually is four business days prior to the record date, which allows the exchange time to record ownership changes. For example, suppose the record date is March 3 and the ex-dividend date is February 27; investors who purchase the stock prior to February 27 are eligible for the March 3 dividend while investors purchasing the stock after February 27 are not entitled to the dividend. Investors would expect the stock price to decline by the dividend per share between February 27 and March 3 when it is selling ex-dividend. Research indicates that stock prices decline by slightly less than the dividend per share.

Stock Repurchases

Corporations often repurchase their own stock shares. Repurchased shares may be retired and returned to authorized shares or held in the corporation's treasury as treasury stock.

Shares normally are retired when a corporation is attempting to go private by eliminating nonmanagement shareholders and taking the corporation's stock off the exchange on which it had been trading.

Corporations hold repurchased shares (treasury stock) for use in the future. Potential uses of the shares include:

- Employee stock ownership plans
- Employee retirement plans
- Mergers and acquisitions
- Stock options and warrants

A corporation may also purchase its own shares in order to control the share price, especially when management believes the market price is unreasonably low.

 **Knowledge Check: Raising Capital**

The following questions are intended to help you check your understanding and recall of the material presented in this topic. They do not represent the type of questions that appear on the CMA exam.

Directions: Answer each question in the space provided. Correct answers and section references appear after the knowledge check questions.

1. How much are the annual payments on a 6-year, 8%, $1,000,000 term loan? The present value of annuity factor for 6 years at 8% is 4.623. The PV of a lump-sum factor for 6 years at 8% is .630.
   - ☐ a. $216,310
   - ☐ b. $246,667
   - ☐ c. $80,000 for each of the first 5 years and $1,080,000 at the end of year 6
   - ☐ d. Not determinable given the data

2. What is the first-year interest portion of the annual payment on a $200,000, 5-year, 7% term loan? The first-year principal payment on the term loan is $34,780.
   - ☐ a. $14,000
   - ☐ b. $20,780
   - ☐ c. $12,545
   - ☐ d. $22,232

3. In determining the net advantage of leasing (NAL), the expected after-tax salvage of the asset leased is discounted at what rate?
   - ☐ a. The lessee's target rate of return
   - ☐ b. The lessee's borrowing rate
   - ☐ c. The lessee's after-tax borrowing rate
   - ☐ d. The lessee's after-tax target rate of return

4. The straight debt value of a convertible bond at issue is normally
   - ☐ a. greater than the market value of the bond at issue.
   - ☐ b. less than the market value of the bond at issue.
   - ☐ c. the same as the market value of the bond at issue.
   - ☐ d. equal to its value as an equity instrument.

5. Primary security markets handle
   - ☐ a. only debt security issues.
   - ☐ b. only blue-chip stock issues.
   - ☐ c. debt or equity issues.
   - ☐ d. only equity securities.

6. Which of the following is true regarding the efficient market theory?
   - ☐ a. The semistrong form supports the idea that abnormal returns from insider trading are possible.
   - ☐ b. None of its forms supports the idea that abnormal returns from insider trading are possible.
   - ☐ c. The weak form supports the idea that technical analysis will provide a basis for earning abnormal returns.
   - ☐ d. The strong form supports the idea that private information is not incorporated in a security price.

7. The four dates related to the dividend process are the:
   - I. payment date.
   - II. ex-dividend date.
   - III. declaration date.
   - IV. record date.

   The proper chronological order of these dates is:
   - ☐ a. III, IV, II, I
   - ☐ b. II, III, IV, I
   - ☐ c. II, III, I, IV
   - ☐ d. III, II, IV, I

8. Which of the following is **not** a basic dividend policy?
   - ☐ a. Passive residual
   - ☐ b. Small regular dividend plus extras
   - ☐ c. Variable dividend payout ratio
   - ☐ d. Stable dollar

Knowledge Check Answers: Raising Capital

1. How much are the annual payments on a 6-year, 8%, $1,000,000 term loan? The present value of annuity factor for 6 years at 8% is 4.623. The PV of a lump-factor for 6 years at 8% is 0.630. [See **Term Loans.**]
   - ☒ a. $216,310
   - ☐ b. $246,667
   - ☐ c. $80,000 for each of the first 5 years and $1,080,000 at the end of year 6
   - ☐ d. Not determinable given the data

2. What is the first-year interest portion of the annual payment on a $200,000, 5-year, 7% term loan? The first-year principal payment on the term loan is $34,780. [See **Term Loans.**]
   - ☒ a. $14,000
   - ☐ b. $20,780
   - ☐ c. $12,545
   - ☐ d. $22,232

3. In determining the net advantage of leasing (NAL), the expected after-tax salvage of the asset leased is discounted at what rate? [See **Net Advantage of Leasing.**]
   - ☐ a. The lessee's target rate of return
   - ☐ b. The lessee's borrowing rate
   - ☐ c. The lessee's after-tax borrowing rate
   - ☒ d. The lessee's after-tax target rate of return

4. The straight debt value of a convertible bond at issue is normally [See **Convertible Debt.**]
   - ☐ a. greater than the market value of the bond at issue.
   - ☒ b. less than the market value of the bond at issue.
   - ☐ c. the same as the market value of the bond at issue.
   - ☐ d. equal to its value as an equity instrument.

5. Primary security markets handle [See **Role of Investment Banks and Underwriters.**]
   - ☐ a. only debt security issues.
   - ☐ b. only blue-chip stock issues.
   - ☒ c. debt or equity issues.
   - ☐ d. only equity securities.

6. Which of the following is true regarding the efficient market theory? [See *Market Efficiency.*]
   - ☒ a. The semistrong form supports the idea that abnormal returns from insider trading are possible.
   - ☐ b. None of its forms supports the idea that abnormal returns from insider trading are possible.
   - ☐ c. The weak form supports the idea that technical analysis will provide a basis for earning abnormal returns.
   - ☐ d. The strong form supports the idea that private information is not incorporated in a security price.

7. The four dates related to the dividend process are the:
   I. payment date.
   II. ex-dividend date.
   III. declaration date.
   IV. record date.

   The proper chronological order of these dates is: [See *Dividend Payout Process.*]
   - ☐ a. III, IV, II, I
   - ☐ b. II, III, IV, I
   - ☐ c. II, III, I, IV
   - ☒ d. III, II, IV, I

8. Which of the following is **not** a basic dividend policy? [See *Dividend Policy.*]
   - ☐ a. Passive residual
   - ☐ b. Small regular dividend plus extras
   - ☒ c. Variable dividend payout ratio
   - ☐ d. Stable dollar

TOPIC 4

Working Capital Management

THE BASIC COMPONENTS OF AN ORGANIZATION'S working capital are cash, marketable securities, accounts receivable, and inventory. This topic looks at working capital and the management of each of these components. Upon completing this topic, you should have a good understanding of the many ways to manage working capital, their benefits, and their associated costs.

READ the Learning Outcome Statements (LOS) for this topic as found in Appendix B and then study the concepts and calculations presented here to be sure you understand the content you could be tested on in the CMA exam.

Working Capital Terminology

The term **working capital** (or current capital) generally refers to the firm's investment in its current asset accounts. It is also referred to as **gross working capital**. **Net working capital** refers specifically to the dollar difference between a firm's current assets and its current liabilities. Net working capital provides a measure of the immediate liquidity a firm has available to sustain and build its business. Depending on a firm's level of current liabilities, the number may be positive or negative.

Short-term financial forecasts are essential in planning for the working capital needs of a company. Good forecasts can help the firm avoid holding excess amounts of cash and inventories as well as plan for working capital financing beyond that provided by accounts payable. The **percentage of sales method** of forecasting (see: Part 1, Section B, Topic 6: Top-Level Planning and Analysis) is often used for making short-term working capital forecasts. This method is based on the idea that most balance sheet and income statement items vary with sales. Balance sheet accounts are then forecast as a percentage of updated or currently forecasted sales, based on historical relationships. This method works well in forecasting working capital requirements because the balance sheet items that vary most closely with the amount of sales are cash, accounts receivable, inventory, and accounts payable.

Working capital management refers to decisions made about a firm's current assets and the financing needed to support those assets. Working capital management policies are generally categorized as aggressive, conservative, or moderate.

Management decides on the working capital policy for the firm, beginning with risk tolerance. Figure 2B-16 summarizes the three different policies and is based on an assumption of a defined amount of sales.

Figure 2B-16 Working Capital Management Policies

Strategic Factors:	Working Capital Policy:		
	Aggressive	Conservative	Moderate
Management's risk tolerance is	High	Low	In Between
Level of current assets for a defined amount of sales	Low	High	In Between
Liquidity measures will be	Low	High	In Between
Interest costs will be	Low	High	In Between
Profits will be	High	Low	In Between
These factors result in	Operations could be disrupted due to no contingency plan for unforeseen events	Guarantees smooth functioning of the operating cycle	Reasonable assurance of smooth functioning of the operating cycle

Effective net working capital management is important for all businesses. Firms need to review the complete operations of their working capital management programs to ensure efficiencies in:

- *Cash management.* Managing cash inflows and outflows
- *Marketable securities management.* Managing short-term investment portfolios
- *Accounts receivable management.* Managing cash receivables
- *Inventory management.* Maintaining stock of items at desired levels of raw materials, work in progress, or finished products
- *Short-term credit management.* Using accounts payable and having other short-term credit available such as a line of credit

One goal of net working capital management is to reduce both the operating cycle and the cash cycle.

The operating cycle is the number of days of inventory on hand plus the receivables collection period. The cash cycle is the operating cycle less the accounts payable (A/P) payment cycle. Both cycles are reduced by decreasing the number of days' inventory on hand and the receivables collection period and/or maximizing the A/P payment cycle. Reducing a firm's cash cycle requires close attention by management. Subsequent content in this topic examines each of these working capital components in more detail.

Cash Management

Cash management describes the collective activities by which a corporation administers and invests its cash. The primary goal of cash management is to use cash as efficiently as possible and in a manner that is consistent with the firm's strategic objectives and risk management profile.

Finance and treasury departments are integrally involved in cash management. Working together, they must ensure that the necessary cash resources are available in a timely manner to sustain business operations, starting with the purchase of raw materials and other resources and continuing through to payment for those materials and resources, the sale of goods and services, and the collection of sales receipts.

Factors Influencing Cash Levels

Liquidity requirements and a firm's profitability and risk policies are the primary determinants of its cash levels.

Liquidity Requirements

Liquidity refers to the ability to convert assets into cash quickly without incurring loss. A firm's cash inflows and cash outflows for expenditures are rarely synchronized—which means that they are not for the same amount and do not occur at the same time. A business needs to monitor working capital to cover the imbalances of cash inflows and outflows and ensure sufficient liquidity. Ultimately, an efficient cash management system can increase a firm's overall liquidity. In turn, increased liquidity can lead to increased profitability and reduced risk of insolvency.

Profitability and Risk Policies

Profitability typically varies inversely with liquidity. A firm must determine the optimal levels of investment in current assets as well as the appropriate mix of short- and long-term financing necessary to support liquidity requirements. Such investments must take into account the interrelationship and trade-offs between profitability and risk. For example, offering more liberal credit terms to customers may increase receivables. Thus, the firm may have to sell short-term securities, reduce cash balances, and/or increase short-term funding from banks to generate cash flows. Trying to reduce idle cash in bank accounts may result in increased transaction costs.

The person(s) managing cash and doing the forecasting does NOT manage the various components of changes in cash needs. Hence, this is a very challenging responsibility and requires excellent communications with many others in the organization. The effective management of liquidity, profitability, risk, and cash requires a cash management system that must address the day-to-day management of:

- *Collections.* How to bring funds into the firm from customers or other sources

- *Concentration.* How to concentrate funds where they can be used most effectively by moving cash from deposit banks (field banks) and other banks in the firm's collection system to one primary concentration bank
- *Disbursements.* How to move funds from the concentration bank to the firm's disbursement bank(s) for payments to employees, vendors, investors, and other payees
- *Banking relations.* How to manage relationships with banks and other financial service providers
- *Cash forecasting.* How to forecast future cash flows and predict potential shortages or surpluses
- *Information management.* How to develop and maintain appropriate information systems for collecting and analyzing financial data
- *Investing and borrowing.* How to invest excess cash balances and have available short-term borrowing
- *Compensation.* How to cover wages and other financial benefits to employees

The magnitude of these operations will vary according to the size and nature of the business enterprise. A large international corporation would, of course, have a much more complex cash management system than a small domestic company.

Motives for Holding Cash

Corporations need sufficient financial resources such as cash balances in banks and short-term marketable securities, as well as backup lines of credit and other short-term borrowing arrangements to maintain adequate liquidity. The reasons businesses need to manage liquidity typically are summarized as being driven by transactions, precautionary, or speculative motives.

- The **transactions motive** for holding cash addresses the unsynchronized nature of cash flows. A firm must have sufficient cash reserves or near-cash reserves to meet payments arising from ordinary business operations (e.g., small purchases, employee compensation, taxes, and dividends).
- The **precautionary motive** for holding cash is to provide a buffer for unexpected cash needs. The unpredictable nature of cash inflows and outflows means that a firm must maintain sufficient levels of cash or near-cash balances to cover expenses.
- The **speculative motive** involves the use of surplus liquid reserves to take advantage of short-term investments or other temporary opportunities that may arise. For example, the price of a raw material suddenly may decline and offer a substantial savings if purchased with reserve funds.

Ensuring proper levels of liquidity necessitates continuous measuring, monitoring, and forecasting activities. Excess liquidity and insufficient liquidity both have disadvantages:

- Excess liquidity can translate into a loss of potential earnings because funds are not used profitably.

- Insufficient liquidity can result in a variety of negative costs, such as delayed payments, additional interest from unexpected borrowing, or brokerage and administrative costs if securities must be sold. In the worst-case scenario, excessive liquidity deficits can lead to insolvency and bankruptcy.

Management of Cash Flows

Forecasting data and financial controls contained in a cash budget provides a starting point for cash management. Specifics on building a forecast cash budget are found in Part 1, Section B, Topic 5: Annual Profit Plan and Supporting Schedules. These forecasting techniques can be used to develop updated cash budgets for current weekly, monthly, or quarterly needs. An annual cash budget developed in the prior year will not provide the useful information that is needed. But efficient cash management also involves day-to-day activities pertaining to collection, disbursement, and temporary investments.

These types of cash flows must be managed:

- **Cash inflows.** Funds collected from customers; funds obtained from banks, lenders, and other financial sources; and funds received from investors and other sources
- **Concentration flows.** Internal transfers among a firm's business units and between various bank accounts the firm owns to create liquid reserves
- **Cash outflows.** Funds distributed from the firm's liquid reserves to employees, vendors, shareholders, and other payees of the company

The timing of these cash flows is important to maintain adequate liquidity, optimize cash resources, and manage risk. The challenge in cash flow timing is to be able to meet current and future financial obligations in a timely manner while minimizing idle cash balances, borrowing any necessary funds at an acceptable cost, and controlling the firm's exposure to financial risks.

A firm generally benefits from shortening the timing of cash inflows and lengthening the timing of cash outflows. Speeding up accounts receivable (A/R) collection allows a business access to funds sooner; slowing down A/P payments provides a longer time frame for the firm to use the money it has on hand. Naturally, both must be managed carefully so as not to jeopardize vendor and customer relations and the firm's credit standing with suppliers and lenders.

Businesses can use various techniques to speed up collections and control disbursements.

Methods to Speed Up Cash Collections

LOS §2.B.4.g

A **collection system** is the set of banking arrangements and processing procedures used to process customer payments and gather incoming cash.

A firm's collection system affects the timing of cash inflows. Firms generally attempt to speed up cash collections by reducing collection float. **Collection float** is the time interval between when the payor mails a check and when the funds are available for the receiving firm to use.

Collection float has three components:

1. **Mail float.** The time between when a check is mailed and when it is received by the payee or a processing site
2. **Processing float.** The time between when the payee or processing site receives a check and when it is deposited at a financial institution
3. **Availability float.** The time between when the check is deposited and when the firm's account is credited with the collected funds

Figure 2B-17 presents a simple representation of collection float.

Figure 2B-17 Components of Collection Float

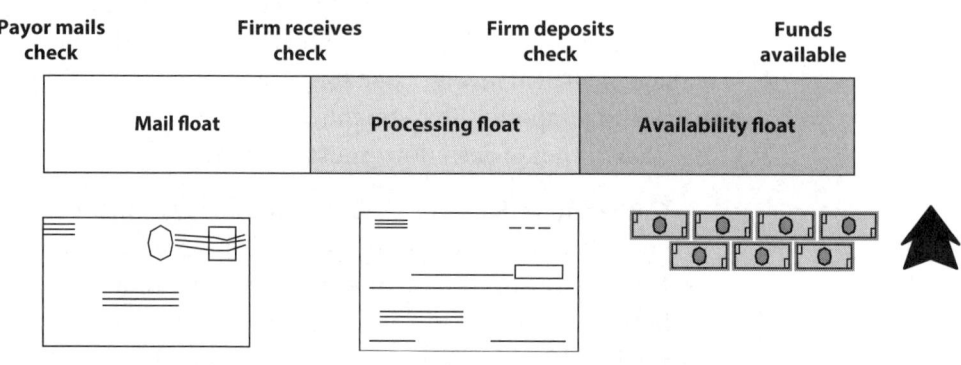

In attempting to reduce collection float, important considerations include the optimal number and location of collection points, whether to use a lockbox system or an electronic payment system, and how to manage the concentration banking system.

Collection Points

Depending on the nature of the business, firms collect payments from customers over the counter, through the mail, and electronically (via home banking, telecommunications, personal computers, and the Internet). Over-the-counter receipts may be cash, checks, or credit card payments. Mail receipts are normally checks or credit card payments. Electronic receipts are usually credit card payments. In general, the more collection points available, the shorter the collection float, especially if collection points are closer to customers or near Federal Reserve banks for faster check-clearing purposes. However, there may be higher operating costs associated with additional collection points.

Lockbox System

A **lockbox system** is an arrangement between a firm and a banking institution in which all deposits are received directly by the bank and immediately deposited into the firm's account.

The arrangement sets up the bank's post office box number for all remittances rather than the firm's address. The lockbox process is invisible to customers because the remittance envelopes and statements show the firm's name, not the bank's name. Some firms have multiple collection locations in the form of a lockbox network.

In setting up a lockbox system, a firm usually requests that the bank photocopy all checks received, attach a photocopy of the check to the remittance, and include the envelope (which often notes an address change) or anything else sent with the payment.

A lockbox system ensures that deposits are made on the day they are received, which dramatically reduces processing float. Depending on the lockbox location(s), mail float and availability float also can be shortened. Once the day's receipts are deposited, the bank forwards a validated deposit slip and other requested documents to the company.

The main drawback of a lockbox system is the cost associated with the additional banking services. Lockboxes have fixed and variable costs.

Fixed lockbox costs may include recurring (e.g., annual or monthly) fees for renting the post office box, preparing deposits, transmitting remittance data, balance reporting, and other account maintenance activities. Typically all fixed costs are bundled into a single lockbox maintenance charge.

Examples of variable lockbox costs include per-item deposit and processing charges, charges for transmitting remittance data, and photocopying and microfilming charges.

To decide whether to use a lockbox system, a firm needs to compare the added costs of the system with the potential income that can be gained from having accelerated funds availability, as shown:

Net Benefit from Lockbox = Reduction in Float Opportunity Cost
+ Reduction in Internal Processing Costs
− Lockbox Processing Costs

Float opportunity cost is a function of:

- Dollar amount of the collected items.
- Total collection time for the items.
- A firm's current investment or borrowing rate.

The lockbox system is profitable if the additional (marginal) income is greater than the additional (marginal) costs.

For example: As illustrated in Figure 2B-18, a company is considering a lockbox proposal. The company has $96 million in annual sales ($8 million per month). The annual volume of checks is 12,000, and the average check size in each batch of checks is $8,000. Internal check processing cost (assuming no lockbox) is $0.20 per item. The annual opportunity cost for the company is 8%. For example, funds freed (released) through the lockbox system might earn an 8% return by being invested in short-term securities or, alternatively, might be used to reduce short-term borrowing at 8%.

Figure 2B-18 Lockbox Example

Without a Lockbox

Batch	Dollar Amount per Month	Collection Float Days	Total Dollars
1	$1,400,000	× 4 =	$5,600,000
2	4,400,000	× 2 =	8,800,000
3	2,200,000	× 6 =	13,200,000
Total Deposits	$8,000,000	Total Dollar-Days of Float per Month	$27,600,000
		Divided by 30 calendar days (Average Daily Float)	$920,000
		Annual opportunity cost of float ($920,000 × 0.08)	$73,600

With a Lockbox

Batch	Dollar Amount per Month	Collection Float Days	Total Dollars
1	$1,400,000	× 3 =	$4,200,000
2	4,400,000	× 1 =	4,400,000
3	2,200,000	× 4 =	8,800,000
Total Deposits	$8,000,000	Total Dollar-Days of Float per Month	$17,400,000
		Divided by 30 calendar days (Average Daily Float)	$580,000
		Annual opportunity cost of float ($580,000 × 0.08)	$46,400
		Annual opportunity cost of float without a lockbox	$73,600
		Annual opportunity cost of float with a lockbox	($46,400)
		Lockbox float savings	$27,200
		Fixed lockbox costs	($8,500)
		Variable lockbox costs (12,000 × $0.45)	($5,400)
		Savings of internal processing costs (12,000 × $0.20)	$2,400
		Net annual dollar benefit of a lockbox	**$15,700**

A lockbox processor proposes to charge $8,500 per year plus a $0.45 processing cost per item.

Based on the cost-benefit analysis that examined the trade-off between the savings from float reduction and the cost of the lockbox, the economic benefit to the company is $15,700 per year.

An **electronic payment system** facilitates a payment or a transfer in an electronic format. Because electronic systems bypass mail and manual processing, they can guarantee fund availability on the payment date. In the United States, two of the primary electronic payment methods are the automated clearing house system and Fedwire.

The **automated clearing house (ACH)** system provides an electronic alternative to checks. Payment information is processed and settled electronically. In the United States, the Federal Reserve is the main operator of ACH. Increased reliability, efficiency, and cost-effectiveness are the primary benefits. ACH also offers the capability to transfer more information about a payment than is possible on a check.

Fedwire is the Federal Reserve's funds transfer system. It provides a real-time method to transfer funds immediately between two financial institutions via their respective Federal Reserve bank accounts. Although reliable and secure, the system is relatively expensive to use.

A **concentration banking system** systematically transfers deposits received from field banks and/or lockbox banks to the firm's disbursement bank to create a centralized inventory of liquid reserves held as cash or for short-term credit or investment transactions.

Some banks require a **compensating balance**, which is a non-interest-bearing deposit maintained in the company's deposit accounts at the bank for account service charges, lines of credit, or investments. The balance requirement can be specified as a percentage of the total commitment, the unused amount of the commitment, or the outstanding borrowings.

In general, cash concentration reduces idle balances in field banks, improves control over a firm's cash inflows and outflows, and facilitates more effective investments. Naturally, there are administrative and control costs associated with a cash concentration system. Cost should be weighed against the expected value of the benefits provided.

Methods to Slow Down Payments

A **disbursement system** is the set of banking arrangements, payment mechanisms, and processing procedures used to disburse funds to employees, vendors, suppliers, tax agencies, and other payees such as shareholders and/or bondholders.

A firm's disbursement system affects the timing of cash outflows and disbursement float. **Disbursement float** is the time between when the paying firm (payor) mails a check and when the funds are deducted from the paying firm's (payor's) account.

Disbursement float has three components. The first two are mail float and processing float, the same two components that are part of collection float. The third component, which is different from the collection float, is called **clearing float**—the time between when the check is deposited by the receiving firm (payee) and when the paying firm's (payor's) account is debited.

A simple representation of disbursement float is shown in Figure 2B-19.

Figure 2B-19 Components of Disbursement Float

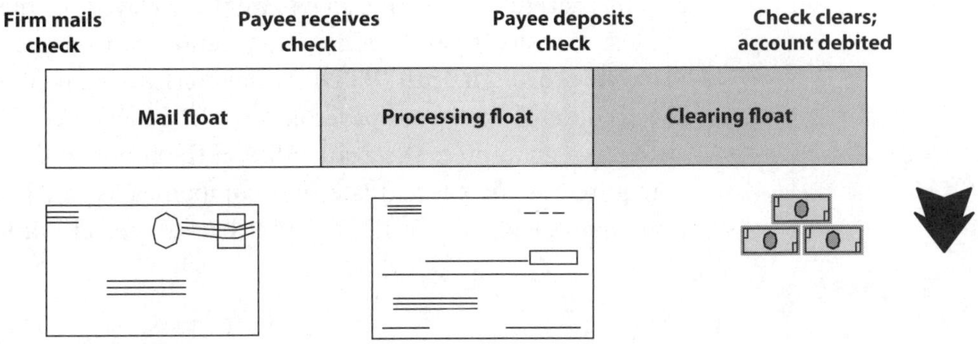

Typical costs associated with disbursement systems are time-value costs, excess balances, transaction costs, payee relations, and information and control costs. Banks and other institutions offer companies a variety of services to help control disbursement system costs. In particular, a zero balance account system is one way a firm can improve management of the disbursement process.

A **zero balance account (ZBA)** is a disbursement account against which a firm can write checks even though the balance is maintained at zero. A transfer from a master account located in the same bank covers any checks debited against the ZBA.

Firms often have several subsidiary ZBAs (e.g., separate ZBAs for payroll, dividends, and other payables) under one master disbursing account. Furthermore, some ZBAs may be used for collections as well as disbursements. Funding is automatic. Credits and debits are posted daily; the bank transfers just enough funds between the master account and the ZBA to keep the balance of the ZBA at zero.

The benefits of a ZBA system include control over account balances and the elimination of idle excess balances in subsidiary accounts. Firms can invest the master account balance in securities more accurately. ZBAs also can facilitate decentralization of payables for firms with multiple locations by providing local check-writing authorization while maintaining funding control at headquarters. However, those individuals in a company with final cash management authority must forecast the timing of check clearing accurately and ensure that the master account has sufficient reserves to cover the associated ZBAs.

Although the overall goal of a disbursement system is to make payments in a timely, accurate, and cost-effective manner, firms sometimes deliberately attempt to slow down the clearing of payments. Centralized payables and the use of payable through drafts are two methods of slowing down payments.

- Having **centralized payables** means payments are made through a single account, usually headquarters or a centralized processing center. Centralizing the payment function provides greater assurance that checks and funds will be disbursed when desired rather than with a decentralized payables system. With a decentralized system the likelihood of excess balances is greater as well as increased transfer, reconciliation, and administrative costs. Concentrations of excess cash can be used for loan repayments or investments. Improved access to cash position information may allow a firm to earn a greater investment return by being able to hold the money longer. However, a centralized payables system requires careful monitoring to ensure that delayed payments do not result in the loss of cash discounts or damage relations with payees.
- A **payable through draft (PTD)** is a payment instrument that is drawn against the account of the issuer/payer at a specific bank. A PTD is a bank-created check that guarantees the availability of the funds to the payee. Sometimes it is required by the payee. Insurance companies use a PTD to pay claims. The potential downside of a PTD is that banks typically impose higher service charges.

Electronic Commerce

From a cash management perspective, **electronic commerce** (or **e-commerce**) refers to the application of information and network technology to facilitate business relationships among trading partners. Many formats and communication protocols are included under the umbrella of e-commerce, including the Internet, internal intranet networks, Web-based commerce, and electronic data interchange (EDI) and the EDI subsets of electronic funds transfer (EFT) and financial EDI (FEDI).

Although many transactions among North American companies are still paper based, e-commerce provides an alternative. The primary benefits of e-commerce include:

- Increased productivity because it basically eliminates manual processing
- Reduced cycle time
- Lower error rates
- Improved cash flow forecasting
- Improved communication capabilities

Hardware and software requirements and their associated costs, security issues, and the education and training of internal personnel and trading partners are the basic considerations in implementing e-commerce. Properly implemented and supported, e-commerce can facilitate stronger ties between a company and its vendors and customers.

Complex or simple, a cash management system should fulfill these objectives:

- Speed cash inflows.
- Slow cash outflows.
- Minimize idle cash.
- Minimize administrative costs connected with cash flows.
- Maintain good relations with customers and suppliers.
- Minimize the costs of providing backup liquidity.
- Maximize the value of financial information provided to management.

Marketable Securities Management

Corporations need cash to meet their ongoing financial obligations. Although some amount of cash reserves is prudent, holding an excessive level results in several costs. Holding too much cash idle in bank accounts not only incurs maintenance costs but also results in a loss of potential interest income. That is why companies hold a short-term investment portfolio of interest-earning marketable securities.

Marketable securities are investments that mature in a year or less. They generally are classified as short-term investments. Balance sheet accounting differentiates securities with original maturities of three months or less as cash equivalents and those maturing in a year or less as short-term investments.

Why Companies Hold Marketable Securities

Specifically, companies invest in marketable securities for three main reasons:

1. *Reserve liquidity.* To provide a source of near cash, or instant cash, to cover any working capital imbalances resulting from insufficient cash inflows or unforeseen cash needs
2. *Controllable outflows.* To earn interest on funds that are being held for predictable downstream cash outflows such as interest payments, taxes, dividends, or insurance premiums
3. *Income generation.* To earn interest on surplus cash for which the company has no immediate use

Variables in Marketable Securities Selection

Careful consideration should be given to the the marketable security before an investment is made. The safety, marketability, yield, maturity, and taxability are characteristics that firms typically evaluate.

Safety

Safety in the preservation of principal is considered to be the guiding principle or most basic test in selecting a security. Although a certain degree of risk is inherent in any investment, a firm must assess the specific risk associated with a security and weigh that risk against the potential for financial returns (or losses). Firms tend to look for short-term instruments that offer both safety and some level of income generation.

Marketability

The marketability of a security refers to the owner's ability to sell the security relatively quickly without a substantial price concession. High marketability is a function of the availability of a large secondary market. A security with less active secondary markets is considered to be less liquid.

Yield

A security's yield (return) is related to its interest rate and/or price appreciation, as in the case of U.S. T-bills. Some securities offer variable interest, others pay a fixed rate, and some, such as U.S. Treasury bills, pay no interest but are sold at a discount and redeemed at face value. For variable-rate securities, the longer the time to maturity, the greater the potential price variation due to interest rate movements. Yield has an inverse relationship with liquidity, meaning the more liquid a security the lower its yield. In turn, yield has a positive relationship to risk. In general, the higher the risk, the higher the expected return. Yields on safe, short-term securities tend to be quite low.

Maturity

The term **maturity** refers to the life of the security and represents the date on which the obligation is settled. Maturity dates vary. Short-term securities often are chosen based on a maturity date that matches when the firm has forecasted a need for cash. Some securities may be designated for quick liquidity while others may be earmarked for less immediate use.

Taxability

A company should evaluate the tax implications of the security. A firm's effective tax rate will determine the advantage of tax-exempt alternatives and the after-tax rate from taxable investments. The interest earned on all securities except municipal notes and bonds is taxable.

Types of Marketable Securities

There are two major markets for debt and equity instruments: the capital market and the money market. Stocks and long-term bonds are bought and sold in the **capital market**. The **money market** is where short-term debt securities that mature in one year or less trade.

Unlike the capital market, which has specific exchanges (e.g., the New York Stock Exchange), the money market is a group of markets. Major issuers of money market securities are the U.S. government, foreign government securities dealers, commercial paper (CP) dealers, bankers' acceptance (BA) dealers, and other money market brokers specializing in short-term instruments.

Figure 2B-20 provides an overview of various types of money market securities.

Figure 2B-20 Types of Marketable Securities

Instrument	Description
U.S. Treasury securities	Direct obligations of the U.S. Treasury; backed by the full faith and credit of the U.S. government.
	Interest rates provide a reference point and market indicator for other securities.
	Considered "safe" investments because they are free of default risk, are actively traded on a large secondary market, and are highly marketable.
	Common types include:
	Treasury bills (or T-bills): do not bear interest; sold at a discount and mature at face value in one year or less.
	Treasury notes (or T-notes): bear interest semiannually; mature within one to ten years.
	Treasury bonds (or T-bonds): similar to T-notes but have maturities longer than ten years; generally not purchased for a short-term portfolio except when the bond is close to maturity.
Federal agency securities (agency securities)	Interest-bearing securities usually offered and redeemed at face value.
	Generally not backed by the full faith and credit of the U.S. government but still considered relatively safe investments with minimal risk of default.
	Typically smaller issues than Treasury securities; not quite as marketable but still highly liquid.
	Limited tax exposure; many are exempt from state/local income taxes but not state franchise taxes.

Repurchase agreements (repos)	Purchase of a security from another party, usually a bank or security dealer who agrees to buy it back at a specified date for a fixed price.
	Commonly involve U.S. Treasury securities as the underlying security to be repurchased at a rate slightly less than the U.S. Treasury securities offer.
	Varying maturity, starting with overnight repurchase agreements.
	Generally considered a relatively safe investment because of the government underlier.
	Often transferred to a third party to ensure that securities are available for sale if the issuer defaults.
Bankers' acceptances (BAs)	Essentially time drafts that result from commercial trade financing; frequently involve international transactions.
	Involve a letter of credit "accepted" by a bank; typically implies the BA is backed by that bank.
	Varying maturities and denominations.
	Liquidity is provided by an active secondary market of dealers.
Commercial paper	Unsecured short-term promissory note (loan) issued by a corporation.
	Negotiable instrument but typically held to maturity because of a weak secondary market; typically higher yield than similar securities because of its low marketability.
	Maturity normally ranges from 1 to 270 days. In the United States, commercial paper must be registered with the Securities and Exchange Commission before it can have a maturity exceeding 270 days.
	May be interest bearing or discounted; usually is discounted.
	Generally rated by credit rating agencies (e.g., Moody's or Standard & Poor's) to help investors assess risk.
Auction rate preferred stock	Equity usually purchased by other corporations that invest in short-term debt instruments.
	Dividend rate is reset regularly (usually every seven weeks) to keep the price from fluctuating.
	Investors usually have the opportunity to sell the stock if they do not want the adjusted rate, unless the auction process fails.
	Desirable because of the 70% dividend exclusion allowance on the dividend income.
Negotiable certificates of deposit (CDs)	Interest-bearing deposits issued by banks or saving and loan institutions that can be traded in money markets; generally sold at face value in denominations of $1 million.
	Most mature between one and three months; some can be for several years.
	Offer fixed and variable interest rates.
	Not guaranteed by the Federal Deposit Insurance Corporation if in excess of $250,000; therefore, issuing bank should be investigated carefully.
	Highly marketable if issued by a large, established bank.
	Common types include:
	Eurodollar (or euro) certificates of deposit (CDs)—dollar-denominated CDs issued by foreign branches of U.S. banks and foreign banks, primarily in London.
	Yankee CDs—CDs issued by U.S. branches of foreign banks.
	Thrift CDs—CDs issued by savings and loan associations, savings banks, and credit unions.
Eurodollar deposits	Typically nonnegotiable dollar-denominated time deposits held by banks outside the United States although not necessarily in Europe; not subject to U.S. banking regulations.
	May be purchased through most large U.S. banks.
	Maturities range from overnight to several years; most are six months or less.
Short-term municipals	State and local government issues.
	Two common types:
	CP instrument with floating interest rate reset weekly.
	Longer-term note with a one- to two-year maturity.
	Short-term municipal has great price stability and better marketability.

Accounts Receivable Management

The term **accounts receivable (A/R)** refers to the money customers owe a company resulting from its decision to sell products and services on a credit basis. An item is classified as an account receivable after it is sold and an invoice is sent. An account receivable is treated as a current asset on the company's balance sheet.

Why Companies Carry Accounts Receivable

Credit is often described as a sales tool. In deciding to extend credit and carry A/R, companies consider these factors:

- General economic conditions
- Target market (e.g., terms necessary to attract new customers and needs of current customers)
- Industry practices (e.g., credit terms competitors offer)
- Potential profit from interest income for credit terms

As with other current assets, A/R have profitability and risk trade-offs. Extending credit may stimulate sales and profits. But a company incurs costs for carrying receivables and runs the risk of potential bad-debt losses. Companies must have efficient and effective policies and procedures in place for managing A/R.

The general factors that influence the management of a company's receivables are:

- Defined credit policies and terms of sale
- Provisions for the evaluation of customer creditworthiness and the determination of customer credit lines
- Prompt A/R billing and collection
- Accurate and up-to-date A/R records
- Provisions for follow-up on overdue accounts and initiation of collection procedures, if necessary

Managing credit and A/R activities at a company involves the sales, accounting, and finance functions. The decision as to whether to grant credit to a customer considers five things called the five C's of credit granting. Listed in the normal order of priority, they are:

1. *C*haracter: the customer's reputation
2. *C*onditions: the customer's financial condition and the state of the economy
3. *C*ash flow: the customer's cash position
4. *C*redit: the customer's credit rating and status
5. *C*ollateral: against the receivable

Credit Terms

Credit terms stipulate the form and timing of payment extended to a customer for the receipt of goods and services as well as the discount terms, if any. The **credit**

period is the net due date (e.g., 20 days, 30 days). **Discount terms** are stated in terms of the credit period and the cash discount given for early payment. The **cash discount** is the percent reduction allowed for early payment. For example, terms of 5/10, net 30 means the buyer can take a 5% discount by paying within 10 days of the invoice date. If not paid by the 10th day the net amount is due 30 days after the invoice date.

Common terms of credit that companies offer are described in Figure 2B-21.

Figure 2B-21 Types of Credit Extension

Form	Description
Open account (open book credit)	Seller's invoice represents the formal obligation between buyer and seller and records the sale as an account receivable.
	Customer receives an invoice for each transaction or a monthly statement showing invoices for the period.
	Full payment is due according to specified credit terms and any discounts; fees generally are charged for late payments.
	Includes periodic review of creditworthiness.
	Most common type of credit.
Installment credit	Requires the customer to make equal monthly payments consisting of principal plus interest.
	May involve a written contract specifying terms of the obligation, credit terms, interest rate, and so on.
	Often used for large-value consumer purchases (e.g., automobiles).
Revolving credit	Provides ongoing credit without requiring approval of individual transactions as long as an account is in good standing, meaning the credit outstanding is below an established limit, and payments are current.
	Assesses an interest charge based on the average amount outstanding for the period if the account is past due.
Letter of credit (L/C)	Involves a letter of credit instrument where a bank guarantees the seller (not the buyer) payment for an agreed-on purchase.
	Buyer typically pays a fee for opening an L/C.
	Commonly used for import/export transactions.

Extending the Credit Period

LOS
§2.B.4.r

Extending the credit period and changing the discount terms can affect both the profitability and the risk associated with A/R. A firm extends a credit period with the expectation of increased profitability from increased sales.

For example: A firm changes credit terms from net 30 to net 60; the credit period is increased from one month to two months. The more liberal credit terms encourage additional sales. But the extended collection period results in additional carrying costs for the firm as customers slow down their payments.

In extending a credit period, the firm must compare the profitability of additional sales with the opportunity costs of the additional receivables. If the increased sales profits exceed the required return on investment for the additional receivables, the change in the credit period is worthwhile.

Changing the Discount Terms

A firm offers a cash discount or varies an existing one in an attempt to speed up the collection of receivables.

For example: A firm's current collection period averages 60 days with no cash discount given. The firm decides to offer the discount terms of 2/10, net 45. The hope is that a large proportion of the firm's customers in dollar volume will start taking advantage of the cash discount.

In changing the discount terms, the firm must determine if the increased speed in collections offsets the cost of offering the discount. If the opportunity costs of accelerated collections are greater than the cost of the discount, the discount is worthwhile; if the savings do not offset the cash discount, the discount is not a good idea.

Default Risk

A receivable is only as good as the probability of it being paid. The term **bad debts** generally refers to the slowness in the collection of receivables and the portion of receivables in default. Default occurs when a customer fails to meet the terms of an obligation. **Default risk** is the risk that a company, or an individual, will not make payments on debt obligations.

To minimize default risk, firms need to set and maintain credit standards for credit extension, billing, and collection. Credit information on an applicant may be gathered from internal and external sources.

Typical sources of internal credit information are:

- A credit application completed by an applicant
- An agreement form completed by an applicant
- A firm's records on past dealings with the applicant (e.g., payment history)

External sources of credit information are:

- *Financial statements.* Review of audited (or unaudited) financial statements and related ratios that can be compared to industry averages
- *Trade references.* Contact with other companies regarding their actual payment experiences with the applicant
- *Banks and other lenders.* For standardized credit information about the applicant's financial condition and available credit
- *Agencies.* Local and national agencies report on the credit history of most companies

Factors Contributing to Optimal Credit/Collection Policies

Credit and collection policies involve an assessment of the creditworthiness of the buyer, the credit terms extended, and the level of collection procedures required. At the very least, the gains derived from credit and collection policies should be equal to the costs associated with them.

To maximize the profitability of credit and collection polices, a firm needs to vary these policies. The optimal solution is reached based on the best possible combination of credit standards, credit terms, and collection expenditures. Typically, the next relationships have been found to exist:

- In the absence of credit standards, sales revenues and contribution margins are maximized but are often offset by large bad-debt losses, collection costs, and high costs from carrying very large receivables.
- With tighter credit standards, sales revenues and contribution margins decline but so do the average collection period, bad-debt losses, and receivable carrying costs.
- The optimal credit policy would be the one that considers the costs and benefits of credit granting and attempts to maximize net benefits.

Inventory Management

Understanding inventory management requires an understanding of these basic inventory control terms:

- **Stock** refers to all the goods a company stores and represents a supply that is kept for future use.
- **Inventory** is a list of all the items held in stock.
- An **item** is a single type of product kept in stock or one entry in the inventory.
- A **unit** is the standard size or quantity of an item.

Given these definitions, the concepts of inventory control and inventory management can be explained.

Inventory control (or **stock control**) refers to the collective activities and procedures that ensure that the right amount of each item is held in stock. Inventory control requires that the organization be able to answer three questions. They are:

1. What do we have?
2. How much do we have?
3. Where is it?

Inventory management refers to the process of determining and maintaining the required level of inventory that will ensure that customer orders are properly filled on time. Inventory management requires that the organization answer three additional questions. They are:

1. What to order (or make)?
2. When to order (or make)?
3. How much to order (or make)?

Why Companies Carry Inventory

Inventories are carried to compensate for the variability between the supply of an item and the demand for it. Inventory control involves balancing conflicting costs—balancing the cost of holding sufficient stock to provide a specified level of customer service with the cost of purchasing the inventory. The point at which those costs intersect provides answers to many inventory control issues, such as what to keep in stock, when orders should be placed, how much should be ordered, and so on.

To some degree, every company holds inventory. But holding inventory is costly because of storage and handling costs, the danger of inventory obsolescence, and the costs associated with tied-up capital. When capital is tied up, businesses must forgo other profitable opportunities for investments. These disadvantages and costs for holding inventory lead to the question: Why do companies carry inventory?

At a simplistic level, inventory provides a buffer between supply and demand. But there are many other reasons for holding inventory, including:

- Coverage for mismatches between supply and demand
- Efficient servicing of customer demands that are larger than expected or at unexpected times
- Coverage for delayed or insufficient supplier deliveries
- Economies in purchasing such as price discounts on large orders or savings on purchases when prices are low and expected to rise
- Economies in production
- Maintenance of consistent levels of operation
- Coverage for emergencies

In general, the level of inventory should be increased only if the benefits outweigh the costs of maintaining the additional inventory.

Economic Order Quantity

Economic order quantity (EOQ) represents the optimum order size—the quantity of a regularly ordered item to be purchased at a point in time that results in minimum total cost (i.e., the sum of ordering costs and carrying costs).

Ordering Costs

Ordering costs include the marginal costs of placing a purchase or production order. They are the marginal cost of computer time to prepare orders and the cost of the supplies used to generate an order. Fixed costs of ordering, such as salaries, are irrelevant.

The more frequently orders are placed, the more costs incurred by the ordering process. The general relationship between ordering cost and order quantity is shown in the first frame of Figure 2B-22. The rationale for ordering larger quantities at one time is to minimize ordering costs.

Carrying Costs

Carrying costs (also called storage costs or holding costs) are the costs of carrying the inventory. They include storage and handling costs, obsolescence and deterioration costs, insurance, taxes, and the cost of the funds invested in inventories. Total carrying costs increase as the order size grows and decrease when items are ordered in smaller amounts. This is true because a smaller space is needed when the quantity stored is smaller.

Figure 2B-22 EOQ and the Relationship Between Carrying Cost, Ordering Cost, and Order Quantity

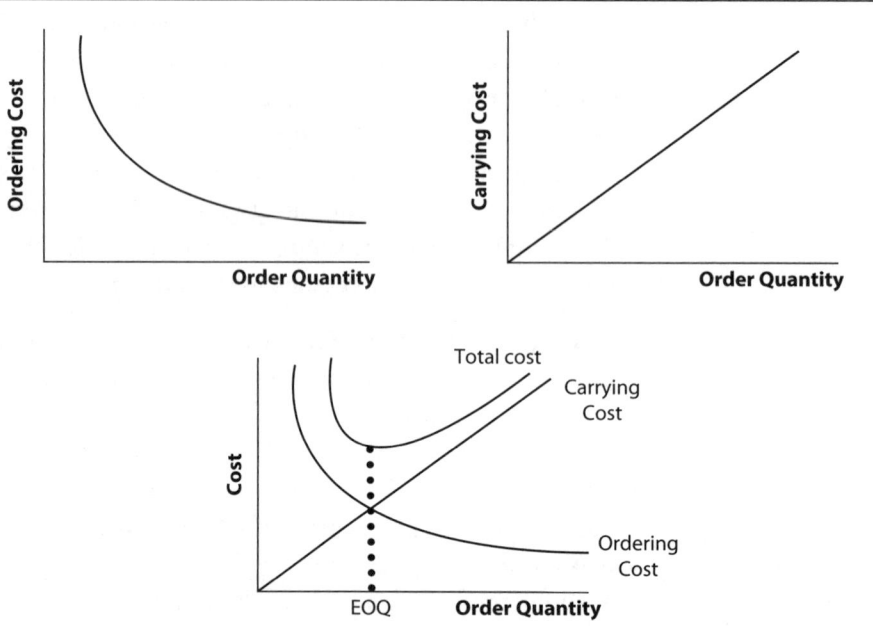

The second frame of Figure 2B-22 depicts this simple relation between carrying cost and order quantity.

EOQ can be determined when ordering and carrying costs are related to demand. The last frame in Figure 2B-22 illustrates EOQ. The costs depicted on the vertical axis in the three frames represent the total dollar costs per year.

The EOQ formula is:

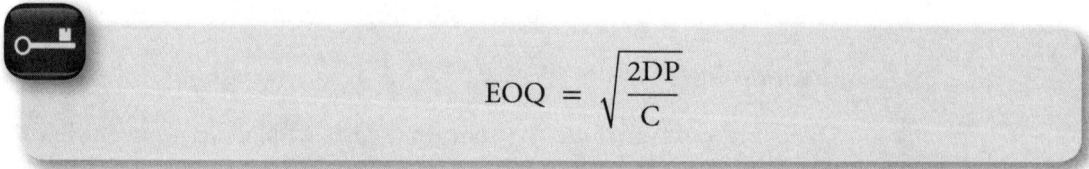

$$EOQ = \sqrt{\frac{2DP}{C}}$$

where:
  D = total inventory units demanded over a planning period (e.g., a year)
  P = fixed cost per purchase order
  C = carrying or holding cost per inventory unit over the planning period

If the carrying costs decrease, the EOQ increases. If total inventory units demanded or fixed cost per order decrease, EOQ also decreases.

EOQ is based on these assumptions:

- Lead time is constant and known.
- Demand occurs at a relatively stable and known rate.
- Operating and storage costs are known.

- Replenishment is instantaneous; there are no stock-outs.
- The demand for the item in question is independent.

EOQ principles also can be applied to the quantities of an item to be manufactured.

For example: Assume that a manufacturer of financial calculators uses 10,000 units of an item annually. Its order cost is $75 per order and the storage cost is $1.50 per unit per year. The EOQ would be:

$$\text{EOQ} = \sqrt{\frac{2(10,000)(\$75)}{\$1.50}} = \sqrt{1,000,000} = 1,000 \text{ units}$$

If the company uses 10,000 units per year and its EOQ is 1,000, the company would reorder 10 times a year (10,000 / 1,000).

Although widely used, EOQ analysis has these weaknesses:

- Assumptions sometimes are unrealistic and inaccurate; situations where all relevant factors (demand, lead time, and costs) are known with complete certainty are rare.
- Calculations are based on estimated costs and forecast demands.
- In manufacturing environments, where setup costs are high, large quantities lead to excess capacity and inventory.
- Too much capacity leaves too much capital tied up in inventory.

Impact of Lead Time and Safety Stock

In practice, replenishment is not instantaneous, and when stock-outs occur, they typically have myriad associated costs. Stock-outs can result in reduced profits from lost sales, loss of goodwill, loss of future sales, and loss of reputation. In manufacturing, disruptions in production can be considerable and costly, ranging from rescheduling issues to employee layoffs and premium prices for emergency orders and special deliveries from suppliers.

Such shortage issues can be minimized or avoided by shortening lead time and having some level of safety stock.

Lead Time

Lead time is the time between placing an order and getting the units in stock and ready for use. Lead time may vary for several reasons. Effective inventory management attempts to keep lead time short by reducing the time for:

- Order preparation: the time to gather order information and prepare the order
- Order delivery to a supplier: the time to get the order to a supplier via electronic transmissions, telecommunications, or mail
- Order processing and fulfillment by the supplier
- Order delivery from the supplier
- Process delivery: getting the items into stock

Safety Stock

Safety stock (or **buffer stock**) generally refers to a quantity of stock held in inventory to protect against fluctuations in supply and demand, as protection against production forecast errors, or short-term changes in backlog.

Where EOQ analysis is based on the theoretical assumption that demand and lead time are known with certainty, safety stock uses a model involving probability. Safety stock analysis attempts to address the uncertainty found in inventory systems, particularly the real-world uncertainty in demand and lead time.

Determining the level of safety stock to maintain involves balancing the probability and cost of a stock-out with the cost of carrying sufficient safety stock to avoid this possibility. Specific calculations, that are beyond the scope of this text, are used. These general concepts apply:

- The greater the uncertainty in forecasted demand, the more safety stock a firm may want to keep.
- The greater the uncertainty in lead time to replenish a stock-out, the more safety stock a firm may want to maintain.

Safety stock analysis considers all costs associated with stock-outs. But the final factor is the cost of carrying additional inventory and loss of interest income from tying up working capital. If not for these costs and loss of interest-earning investments, a firm theoretically could carry sufficient safety stock to prevent stock-outs from ever occurring.

Reorder Points

When to order an item is a function of the lead time for the item, its usage rate, and the safety stock of the item maintained. The item has to be ordered so that the usage of the item over the lead time does not cut into the safety stock of the item. The reorder point (ROP) specifies the level of inventory on hand that would trigger an order. The formula for an ROP is:

$$ROP = UL + \text{Safety Stock}$$

where:
U = usage rate (demand per unit of time [D/t])
L = lead time

For example: Suppose an item has a demand of 10,000 units over 50 weeks, a safety stock of 400 units, and a lead time of three weeks. The ROP would be:

$$ROP = UL + \text{Safety Stock} = [(10{,}000/50)\,(3)] + 400 = [(200)\,(3)] + 400$$
$$= 600 + 400 = 1{,}000$$

An order would be triggered when the inventory on hand reaches 1,000 items.

Just-in-Time Systems and Kanban

Basic principles of just-in-time (JIT) systems and Kanban are covered in Part 1 of the *Wiley CMAexcel Learning System*. These concepts are also appropriate to mention in the context of inventory control.

The underlying objective of JIT systems is to minimize all waste in manufacturing operations by meeting production targets with the minimum number of materials, equipment, operators, and so on. This is accomplished by completing all operations just at the time they are needed. Kanban is the simple manual method of control used in conjunction with JIT to ensure that all materials actually do arrive just as they are needed. The Kanban system is known as a pull system because it pulls the inventory items through the process based on demand in the next step within the process. This is in contrast to a traditional system of pushing inventory through the system based on the budgeted demand for a final product.

Some similarities exist between EOQ and JIT/Kanban systems. For example, both monitor stock levels and place orders for replenishment with fixed quantities. However, a major difference is that with JIT and Kanban, activity reduces stock to its reorder level, which is when the replenishment will occur. The choice of EOQ versus JIT depends on a variety of factors specific to the organization.

JIT and Kanban systems have been described as deceptively simple. Careful evaluation and planning are required for effective implementation. But when JIT and Kanban are well conceived and properly adopted as a means of inventory control, they can reduce stocks of raw materials and work in progress dramatically. In turn, such reductions translate to additional cost savings by:

- Reducing the manufacturing and warehousing space needed
- Lowering property and overhead expenses
- Reducing the investments for stock

In the end, JIT and Kanban can lead to more efficient use of working capital.

Inventory Management Metrics

There are two measures of effective inventory management: inventory turnover and number of days supply in inventory. The inventory turnover is calculated as shown:

$$\text{Inventory Turnover} = \frac{\text{Cost of Goods Sold}}{\text{Average Inventory}}$$

The average inventory often is calculated by adding the beginning and ending balances for the period and dividing by 2.

The days supply in inventory is calculated as shown:

$$\text{Days Supply in Inventory} = \frac{365}{\text{Inventory Turnover}}$$

For example: Suppose a company has a beginning inventory of $24,000 and an ending inventory of $36,000 and cost of goods sold for the year of $240,000. Its inventory turnover would be:

Inventory Turnover = $240,000 / [($24,000 + $36,000) / 2]
= $240,000 / ($60,000 / 2)
= $240,000 / $30,000 = 8 times per year

Its days supply would be:

Days Supply in Inventory = 365 / 8 = 45.6 days

A firm's inventory turnover that is much lower than average for its industry may indicate that the firm's inventory is too large. Increasing this firm's inventory turnover has a number of positive effects. As inventory levels decrease, there is a lowering of costs related to holding inventory (e.g., storage, warehousing, insurance, spoilage). This, in turn, leads to an increase in the firm's gross and net profit as well as a decrease in average total assets. The increase in net profit, coupled with a reduction in average total assets, results in a boost to the firm's profitability as measured by ROA (net profit divided by average total assets).

Types of Short-Term Credit

Businesses usually meet short-term borrowing needs in one of two ways:

1. By raising funds externally through financial intermediaries (e.g., through banks and financial institutions)
2. By issuing commercial paper (CP)

The vast majority of businesses rely on financial intermediaries to perform the lending function.

Several types of short-term credit arrangements are possible, including the use of:

- Accrued expenses
- Trade credit
- Unsecured short-term bank loans (lines of credit and revolving credit)
- Secured short-term loans (collateralized A/R and collateralized inventory)
- Commercial paper
- Bankers' acceptances

A brief description of each is presented next.

Accrued Expenses

Accrued expenses represent the amount a firm owes but has not yet paid for wages, taxes, interest, and dividends. The most common accrued expenses are wages and taxes.

Accrued expenses are considered a spontaneous source of interest-free financing. Businesses can use current funds to fulfill immediate cash needs up to the point the accrued expenses become due for payment. In that respect, accrued expenses must be used with discretion.

Trade Credit

Trade credit is a source of short-term financing created when a supplier grants credit terms to customers on purchases. Trade credit often is the largest source of short-term credit for small firms.

Trade credit represents an indirect loan with these terms:

- A seller supplies goods according to predefined credit terms.
- The credit appears as A/R on the seller's books and A/P on the customer's books.
- The credit represents cash the customer keeps until the specified final payment date.

An open account, where a seller gives the buyer a specified time period to pay for goods or services, is the most common type of trade credit.

Cash Discounts Extended with Trade Credit

Trade credit represents cash a firm can invest up until the specified payment date (e.g., 30, 60, or 90 days). The longer the payment period, the longer the firm can use the funds.

The amount of short-term financing costs the firm saves depends on the number of days of credit. For example, if a firm were to use credit worth $100,000 for 30 days rather than borrowing that amount from another source at a cost of 2%, the firm would save $2,000 ($100,000 × 0.02).

Firms grant trade credit to help facilitate a sale. Discounts are offered as incentives for customers to pay early and reduce the cost of carrying receivables. The customer must weigh the discount against the option of using the trade credit and decide whether it is beneficial to take the discount and pay early. Generally, a firm saves money by taking the discount rather than delaying payment to the net payment date.

The formula for determining the effective annual interest cost of forgoing a cash discount and, therefore, delaying payment beyond the discount period and paying on the final [net] due date is as follows:

$$\text{EID} = \frac{\text{DR}}{1-\text{DR}} \times \frac{365}{\text{N}-\text{DP}}$$

where:
EID = effective annual rate of interest for forgoing the cash discount
DR = discount rate
N = net payment period
DP = discount period

For example: Credit terms are 2/10 net 30. The effective interest rate of forgoing the cash discount and instead paying the full amount on the final (net) due date is:

$$\text{EID} = \frac{0.02}{1 - 0.02} \times \frac{365}{30 - 10}$$
$$= 37.24\%$$

If the firm is short on cash but can borrow funds elsewhere for less than 37.24%, it should do so and take the discount for early payment of the trade credit. However, if borrowing exceeds 37.24%, or funds are not available elsewhere, the firm might want to delay payment until the net due date.

Unsecured Short-Term Bank Loans

An **unsecured short-term bank loan** is a form of bank credit that is not backed by a pledge of specific collateral or assets. Such loans are made based on the financial soundness and creditworthiness of the borrower.

Unsecured short-term bank loans are negotiated between the bank and the business. A loan agreement stipulates the terms of the loan (e.g., interest to be paid, payment terms, maturity date, etc.). The borrower signs a **promissory note** as a formal obligation to repay the loan according to the specified terms.

Unsecured short-term bank loans generally are considered self-liquidating, meaning that the assets the company purchases with the loan will generate sufficient cash flows to pay off the loan. For example, unsecured short-term bank loans are popular instruments to finance seasonal buildups in A/R or inventory.

Lines of credit and revolving credit are two types of unsecured loans that provide quick and ready sources of short-term financing for businesses.

Lines of Credit

A **line of credit** is an agreement allowing a firm to borrow up to a specified limit during a particular time period. The borrower has access to the full credit-line amount but pays interest only on actual borrowings. Borrowing against a line of credit is done through a specific short-term note. A sequence of short-term notes can be issued against the same line of credit. Maturities of the short-term notes vary; generally notes range from overnight to 90 days, although some may be longer. As seen in the topic on effective annual interest rate, a commitment fee could be charged with a line of credit.

Technically, lines of credit are established for a set period (usually a year), but most are renewed on an ongoing basis at maturity. Many lines of credit are kept in force for years.

Revolving Credit

Revolving credit (also known as a revolver) allows a business to borrow, repay, and reborrow up to a specified amount. Credit terms of a revolver are similar to those of a line of credit. Although revolvers often are used for short-term borrowing, many times the term is longer with a range of two to five years.

Secured Short-Term Loans

A **secured short-term loan** (or **asset-based borrowing**) is a form of credit based on the pledging of an asset for collateral. A/R and inventory are the most common assets used in this form of secured lending.

In a **collateralized accounts receivable** type of arrangement, the lender spends time evaluating the borrower's business; the volume of customer purchases, the timeliness of customer payments, delinquency rates, and the number of bad-debt write-offs are all considered. Based on this evaluation, an advance rate is determined, stated as a percentage of the A/R outstanding. The percentage is then applied to the amount of pledged A/R and determines the maximum amount that can be borrowed. When a loan is in force, the borrower's customers typically make payments directly to the lender, who applies them to the outstanding loan balance.

Collateralized inventory is similar to A/R financing. The amount of credit is limited by the advance rate and determined as a percentage of inventory. The advance rate also considers the risk that the borrower may not be able to sell the inventory due to changes in market conditions, fluctuating commodity prices, or inventory obsolescence or spoilage. In general, lenders are more willing to collateralize raw materials and finished goods than work in progress. On occasion, some lenders may calculate different advance rates for different types of inventories. Generally, the advance rate is much less for inventory than for A/R.

Commercial Paper

Commercial paper (CP) is an unsecured short-term promissory note issued by a corporation. CP is sold at a discount from par value and is backed by a promise of the corporation to buy back the paper at maturity by paying par value.

The major credit rating agencies will rate the CP of a specific issuer. CP typically is sold in denominations of $100,000. For public issues, maturities ordinarily range from overnight to 270 days.

CP interest rates vary. The rate is market based and is a function of the issuing company's credit rating, the size of the issue, and the market short-term interest rates.

Most CP is sold through dealers, who are either investment banking institutions or commercial banks. Some companies may sell their CP issues directly to investors.

In general, the use of CP for short-term financing:

- Provides a broad distribution for borrowing, which results in more funds at lower rates than other methods provide.
- Allows the borrower to avoid the expense of maintaining a compensating balance with a commercial bank.
- Promotes the name of the borrower because of the broad market the CP is issued in, the borrower's name becomes more widely known.

Bankers' Acceptances

A **bankers' acceptance (BA)** is a negotiable short-term instrument used primarily to finance the import and export of goods. Some issues may be used for the domestic shipment and storage of readily marketable goods.

A BA is a time draft drawn by a borrower and accepted by the bank on which it is drawn. Accepting the draft implies that the bank assumes the obligation for the payment of the draft at maturity to the investor who purchased it.

BAs are readily marketable and often are discounted in the money market. The borrower receives discounted proceeds and is obligated to pay the full draft amount to the accepting bank at maturity.

Short-Term Credit Management

Different short-term credit options have different costs for the borrower. This section looks specifically at two types of short-term financing costs:

1. The effective annual interest rate associated with unsecured short-term bank loans
2. Factoring costs associated with collateralized secured short-term bank loans

Effective Annual Interest Rate

Banks charge interest for unsecured short-term bank loans. They generally assess a commitment fee and also may require a compensating balance.

Interest Rate

The interest rate charged consists of a premium added to a base rate such as prime, the Intercontinental Exchange Benchmark Administration Limited (ICE) London Interbank Offered Rate (LIBOR), or the Fed rate for T-bills. During the financial crisis of 2007, LIBOR's credibility was questioned. On February 1, 2014, the Intercontinental Exchange Benchmark Administration Limited took over the administration of LIBOR from the British Bankers' Association (BBA). The name is now ICE LIBOR. In determining the interest rate, banks evaluate the customer's ability to repay the loan. The rate charged reflects the bank's assessment of the loan risk. The rate is usually variable and is adjusted according to the changes in the base rate.

Commitment Fee

In addition to interest, banks often charge a commitment fee for holding lines of credit or revolvers available for the borrower. The commitment fee is some percentage of the line or the unused portion of the line.

Compensating Balance

Some banks also may require a compensating balance. The compensating balance designates the percentage of the loan the bank may require the borrower to hold on deposit without earning interest or offsetting other service charges. A compensating balance may be specified as a percentage of the total commitment, the unused portion of the commitment, or the outstanding borrowings.

A commitment fee and a compensating balance effectively reduce the amount of funds the borrower can use. In doing so, they also increase the effective annual interest rate charged for the loan. In other words, the effective annual interest rate is higher than the initial interest rate quoted by the bank.

The formula for effective annual rate of interest, assuming any fees and compensating balance are based on the total commitment, is

$$EI = \left(\frac{PR + CF}{1 - CB}\right)\left(\frac{365}{M}\right)$$

where:
 EI = effective annual rate of interest
 PR = principal interest charge (%)
 CF = commitment fee (%)
 CB = compensating balance (%)
 M = loan length in days

For example: A firm negotiates a one-year loan for $1 million with an interest rate of 12%. The commitment fee is 0.25 % of the total amount, and the compensating balance is 10% of the line.

$$EI = \left(\frac{0.12 + 0.0025}{1 - 0.10}\right)\left(\frac{365}{365}\right) = \left(\frac{0.1225}{0.9}\right) = 13.6\%$$

The quoted rate is 12%, but the effective annual interest rate the firm actually pays is 13.6%.

A more general formula for calculating the effective annual rate of interest (EI) using dollar amounts is

$$EI = \frac{\text{Total Interest Paid} + \text{Total Fees Paid}}{\text{Amount Borrowed} - \text{Compensating Balance}} \times \frac{365}{\text{Loan Length in Days}}$$

Factoring Costs

Factoring is the sale or transfer of A/R in a secured short-term loan to a third party known as a factor. A factor is a finance company or bank that buys receivables from businesses.

Factoring receivables is governed by a contract between the factor and the client. A factor makes credit checks on accounts and charges a percentage commission on the receivables, based on the amount and the quality of the receivables and the overall financial soundness of the client. The factor also charges interest, which usually is variable.

A factor can liquidate collateralized assets in the event the client cannot repay the loan. To protect itself against default risk, the factor typically applies a

haircut to the current value of the receivables. This means that the loan amount will be for substantially less than the face value of the receivables. Applying a haircut provides a buffer for the factor. Should the factor have to sell the assets at distressed prices, the factor still may be able to cover the loan amount in default.

For example: The face value of A/R is $200,000. The haircut is 15%, and the interest charges and commission are $30,000.

The proceeds of the loan to the borrowing firm would be $140,000.

$170,000	Face value of A/R × (1 − the haircut) [$200,000 × (1 − 15%)]
− 30,000	Total charges
$140,000	Loan proceeds

In some cases, factoring arrangements are transparent to the customer, who continues to make payments to the firm, who, in turn, endorses the payments to the factor. In other cases, the customer is notified of the transfer and has to make payments directly to the factor. Most arrangements are without recourse, which means that the selling company would not be liable for any receivables not collected by the factor.

Factoring arrangements also can be set up for inventories. But because inventories are the least liquid of the current assets, the haircut is higher and a trust receipt is required. A **trust receipt** allows the borrower to sell goods out of stock and remit the proceeds to the factor.

Knowledge Check: Working Capital Management

The following questions are intended to help you check your understanding and recall of the material presented in this topic. They do not represent the type of questions that appear on the CMA exam.

Directions: Answer each question in the space provided. Correct answers and section references appear after the knowledge check questions.

1. The transactions motive for holding cash is **best** described as
    - ☐ a. using surplus liquid reserves to take advantage of short-term investments or other temporary situations.
    - ☐ b. synchronizing cash inflows and outflows so that excess cash balances can be invested in short-term instruments.
    - ☐ c. providing a buffer for unexpected cash needs that result from the unpredictable nature of cash inflows and outflows.
    - ☐ d. maintaining sufficient cash or near-cash reserves to meet financial payments arising from ordinary business operations.

2. Which of the following techniques will **not** speed up collections?
    - ☐ a. Lockbox system
    - ☐ b. ACH and Fedwire processing
    - ☐ c. Payable through draft
    - ☐ d. Cash concentration banking system

For questions 3 through 7, match each type of marketable security with its characteristic.

3. ___ Federal agency securities 4. ___ Commercial paper 5. ___ Bankers' acceptances 6. ___ Negotiable certificates of deposit 7. ___ Auction rate preferred stock	a. Interest-bearing deposits issued by banks or saving and loan institutions that can be traded in money markets b. Time drafts that result from commercial trade financing c. Relatively safe investment and many are exempt from state/local income taxes d. Equity usually purchased by other corporations that invest in short-term debt instruments e. Unsecured short-term promissory note issued by a corporation

8. A primary benefit that a firm expects to gain from lengthening a credit period is
   - ☐ a. increased profitability resulting from increased sales.
   - ☐ b. increased revenue from interest charges on past due accounts.
   - ☐ c. fewer collections procedures necessary for past due accounts.
   - ☐ d. improved inventory control resulting from relatively stable demand.

9. Which of the following statements accurately characterizes economic order quantity (EOQ) and safety stock principles?
   - ☐ a. Both models advocate reducing stock to a predetermined reorder level.
   - ☐ b. EOQ analysis assumes demand and lead time are known with certainty; safety stock uses a model involving probability.
   - ☐ c. EOQ analysis and safety stock both assume that demand varies but lead time is known with certainty.
   - ☐ d. Both models are based on the premise that there is no true measure of certainty in inventory control.

For questions 10 through 15, match each short-term credit arrangement with its characteristic.

10. _____ Accrued expenses	a. Negotiated arrangements exemplified by lines of credit and revolvers
11. _____ Trade credit	b. Negotiable short-term instrument used primarily to finance the import and export of goods
12. _____ Unsecured short-term bank loans	
13. _____ Secured short-term loans	c. Lending based on an advance rate; typically stated as a percentage of accounts receivable or inventory
14. _____ Commercial paper	d. An indirect loan between a supplier and customers for purchases
15. _____ Bankers' acceptance	
	e. Spontaneous interest-free financing used to fulfill cash needs up to the point at which they become due for payment
	f. An unsecured promissory note issued by a corporation and sold at a discount from par value

16. What is the effective annual interest rate on a $5 million loan with an interest rate of 8%, a commitment fee of 0.25%, and a compensating balance of 10% (assuming any fees and compensating balance are based on the entire loan amount)?
    - ☐ a. 8%
    - ☐ b. 8.64%
    - ☐ c. 9.17%
    - ☐ d. 11.11%

Knowledge Check Answers: Working Capital Management

1. The transactions motive for holding cash is **best** described as [See *Motives for Holding Cash*.]
   - ☐ a. using surplus liquid reserves to take advantage of short-term investments or other temporary situations.
   - ☐ b. synchronizing cash inflows and outflows so that excess cash balances can be invested in short-term instruments.
   - ☐ c. providing a buffer for unexpected cash needs that result from the unpredictable nature of cash inflows and outflows.
   - ☒ d. maintaining sufficient cash or near-cash reserves to meet financial payments arising from ordinary business operations.

2. Which of the following techniques will **not** speed up collections? [See *Methods to Speed Up Cash Collections*.]
   - ☐ a. Lockbox system
   - ☐ b. ACH and Fedwire processing
   - ☒ c. Payable through draft
   - ☐ d. Cash concentration banking system

For questions 3 through 7, match each type of marketable security with its characteristic.

3. _c_	Federal agency securities	a.	Interest-bearing deposits issued by banks or saving and loan institutions that can be traded in money markets
4. _e_	Commercial paper		
5. _b_	Bankers' acceptances		
6. _a_	Negotiable certificates of deposit	b.	Time drafts that result from commercial trade financing
7. _d_	Auction rate preferred stock	c.	Relatively safe investment and many are exempt from state/local taxes
		d.	Equity usually purchased by other corporations that invest in short-term debt instruments
		e.	Unsecured short-term promissory note issued by a corporation

8. A primary benefit that a firm expects to gain from lengthening a credit period is [See *Credit Terms*.]
   - ☒ a. increased profitability resulting from increased sales.
   - ☐ b. increased revenue from interest charges on past due accounts.

☐ c. fewer collections procedures necessary for past due accounts.

☐ d. improved inventory control resulting from relatively stable demand.

9. Which of the following statements accurately characterizes economic order quantity (EOQ) and safety stock principles? [See *Economic Order Quantity*.]

   ☐ a. Both models advocate reducing stock to a predetermined reorder level.

   ☒ b. EOQ analysis assumes demand and lead time are known with certainty; safety stock uses a model involving probability.

   ☐ c. EOQ analysis and safety stock both assume demand varies but lead time is known with certainty.

   ☐ d. Both models are based on the premise that there is no true measure of certainty in inventory control.

For questions 10 through 15, match each short-term credit arrangement with its characteristic.

10. __e__ Accrued expenses	a. Negotiated arrangements exemplified by lines of credit and revolvers
11. __d__ Trade credit	b. Negotiable short-term instrument used primarily to finance the import and export of goods
12. __a__ Unsecured short-term bank loans	
13. __c__ Secured short-term loans	c. Lending based on an advance rate; typically stated as a percentage of accounts receivable or inventory
14. __f__ Commercial paper	
15. __b__ Bankers' acceptances	d. An indirect loan between a supplier and customers for purchases
	e. Spontaneous interest-free financing used to fulfill cash needs up to the point at which they become due for payment
	f. An unsecured promissory note issued by a corporation and sold at a discount from par value

16. What is the effective annual interest rate on a $5 million loan with an interest rate of 8%, a commitment fee of 0.25%, and a compensating balance of 10% (assuming any fees and compensating balance are based on the entire loan amount)? [See *Effective Annual Interest Rate*.]

    ☐ a. 8%

    ☐ b. 8.64%

    ☒ c. 9.17%

    ☐ d. 11.11%

TOPIC 5

Corporate Restructuring

CORPORATE RESTRUCTURING INVOLVES CHANGES in corporate ownership, asset structure, and/or capital structure. This topic looks at the means by which corporate restructuring can take place (e.g., by mergers, acquisitions, leveraged buyouts, various types of divestitures, and tracking stocks). It also covers various takeover defense tactics, the evaluation of factors for restructuring (e.g., benefits or synergies), valuing a business for merger or acquisition, business failure issues such as bankruptcy, and forced reorganizations.

READ the Learning Outcome Statements (LOS) for this topic as found in Appendix B and then study the concepts and calculations presented here to be sure you understand the content you could be tested on in the CMA exam.

Mergers and Acquisitions

LOS
§2.B.5.a

Businesses often grow by acquiring, or combining with, other businesses. Often the acquisition is facilitated through a merger. A **merger** (acquisition) is a type of business combination in which an acquiring company absorbs a second company, and the second company ceases to exist as a separate legal entity subsequent to the merger. In effect, the second company is merged into the acquiring company, which remains in business as the legal entity of the then-combined two or more companies. For example, Company A purchases Company B. Company A continues with Company B subsumed. Another way of looking at it in equation form is as follows: A + B = A. A merger can be financed through a combination of cash, debt/borrowings, and/or stock (equity securities). Mergers may be horizontal—combining two or more companies in the same industry, vertical—combining a company with its suppliers or customers, or conglomerate—combining of companies not in the same industry and not having buyer–seller relationships. Approval of the shareholders of each company to the merger transaction is required.

A **consolidation** is a type of business combination, similar to a merger, that creates an entirely new company that remains in business and retains legal existence from the merged companies. Again, the acquired companies are merged into the newly formed company and cease to exist as separate legal entities subsequent to the consolidation.

For example, Company A and Company B consolidate to form a new Company C, expressed as A + B = C.

An **acquisition** is the purchase of all of another company's assets or the purchase of a controlling interest in the target company's outstanding voting stock (e.g., common stock). An acquisition transaction in which the target company's assets are purchased requires a vote of the target company's shareholders. In a stock acquisition, a formal vote of the target company stockholders is not required, and the acquisition can be executed even when the target company's management and board of directors are hostile to the proposed acquisition. In such a case, the acquirer company can make a tender offer for a controlling interest of the target company's outstanding voting stock directly to the target company's shareholders. A **tender offer** is a public, open offer or invitation (e.g., takeover bid), announced in a newspaper advertisement, by the acquirer company to the stockholders of a target company, for those stockholders to "tender" their stock for sale at a specified price during a specified time.

Takeover Defense Tactics

Takeovers of a company may be friendly or hostile. In a hostile takeover, the target company often tries to prevent the takeover. To do so, the target company will use a host of different defense tactics in their attempt to ward off the takeover. Those defense tactics, often called shark repellants, include the following:

- **Staggering terms for the board of directors** instead of all of them coming up for election at the same time.
- **Golden parachutes** for key executives providing exorbitant pay and benefits if discharged through a merger.
- **Corporate charter rules** requiring a supermajority (such as 80%) of the shareholders to approve a takeover.
- **Poison pills** are securities that have value only when an unfriendly bidder obtains control of a certain percentage of the target's shares. An example would be a bond having a poison put. A **poison put** allows the bondholders to force the target to redeem the bonds, making the potential takeover less attractive.
- **Fair price provisions**, or shareholders' rights plans, involve warrants issued to shareholders that permit the purchase of the target company's stock at a fraction of the market price in the event of a takeover attempt.
- A **white knight defense** involves the target finding a friendlier buyer to merge with.
- A **"Pacman" defense** is when the target company attempts to buy out the so-called hostile buyer.
- **Litigation** is when the target company challenges one or more aspects of a tender offer in an attempt to delay the takeover.

- **Greenmail** is a targeted repurchase of the target company's stock by the target company after the potential acquirer has purchased a large number of shares of the target company's stock. Essentially, the potential acquirer is offered the opportunity to sell the shares they acquired back to the target company at an amount substantially in excess of the stock's market value.
- **Delisting the public company stock and going private or pursuing a leveraged buyout (LBO).** In an LBO transaction, the management and/or other employees of the target company purchase the company using large amounts of debt, thus preventing the acquirer company from gaining control over the target company.
- **"Lobster traps"** are when the target company issues a charter preventing individuals with more than 10% of convertible securities from converting them to voting stock. This catches the "large lobsters" and lets the small ones escape.
- **Selling off the crown jewels** is a tactic in which the target company sells off or disposes of certain assets that make it a desirable target.
- Other tactics include flip-in and flip-over rights, creating an employee stock ownership plan (ESOP), and a reverse tender offer.

Divestitures

A **divestment** is the opposite of an investment. A divestment, or divestiture, involves the sale of an operating unit or the reduction or elimination of a company's assets. There are a variety of reasons why a company might look to divest an operating unit or reduce or eliminate certain assets. These reasons include raising capital for its core business operations, refocusing on the company's operations, or due to governmental antitrust litigation. Some typical divestiture methods used by companies include spin-offs, equity carve-outs, and split-ups.

Spin-offs

In a **spin-off transaction**, an independent company is created through the sale or distribution of new shares of an existing business or division of a parent company. These shares are distributed on a pro rata basis to existing shareholders of the parent company. In essence, a spin-off is a type of dividend to existing shareholders. A business wishing to streamline its operations may sell unproductive or unrelated subsidiary businesses as spin-offs. For example, a company might spin off one of its mature businesses that is experiencing little growth so that it can focus on high-growth related businesses. The company or business spun off is expected to be worth more as an independent company than as part of the larger business. Recent examples of this include Expedia's spin-off of TripAdvisor in 2011, and Sears Holding Corporation's spin-off of Sears Canada in 2012. The AT&T breakup in 1984 is considered to be one of the most successful spin-offs in history. During the breakup, AT&T gave each of its shareholders one share of stock in each of its seven regional telephone companies for every ten shares of AT&T they owned.

Equity Carve-outs

An **equity carve-out** is also known as a split-off initial public offering (IPO) or a partial spin-off and is a type of corporate reorganization in which a company (parent) creates a new subsidiary and subsequently facilitates an IPO of the new subsidiary without fully spinning it off. The parent company usually offers only a minority share (typically up to 20%) of the newly created subsidiary company to outsiders, thereby retaining management control. Equity carve-outs increase the access to capital markets, enabling the carved-out subsidiary strong growth opportunities and a degree of autonomy, such as its own board of directors, while retaining access to resources at the parent company. Often an equity carve-out ultimately results in the parent company fully spinning off the subsidiary company.

Split-ups

A split-up occurs when a single company splits into two or more separately run companies. Shares of the original company are exchanged for shares in each of the new companies. The exchange ratios are determined by the parent's board of directors and approved by its shareholders prior to the split-up. After the split-up, the original company ceases to exist.

Split-ups are executed either for strategic reasons or because of a government mandate resulting from monopolistic concerns. Strategic split-ups are an attempt to break the original company into separate companies whose overall shareholder value exceeds the shareholder value of the original company.

Evaluating Factors for Restructuring

The overall objective of corporations that enter into restructuring transactions is to maximize shareholder wealth. Mergers and acquisition transactions enable an acquirer company to receive a number of benefits through operating or financial synergies with a target company that the acquirer company may not have been able to realize prior to the merger or acquisition. Some examples include the acquirer company's ability to:

- Obtain another company's assets, skills, or technology.
- Achieve economies of scale.
- Obtain resources, such as through the combination of sales forces, facilities, and outlets.
- Obtain additional distribution channels and global expansion of the products and services.
- Obtain customers.
- Grow faster than internally possible.

- Diversify product and services offerings.
- Utilize net operating loss carryforwards.

Similarly, companies consider divesting existing business units or assets for a host of reasons. Motives include:

- Divesting businesses that are not part of the company's core operations so that it can focus on what it does best.
- To obtain necessary funds.
- To realize greater market value than the company may be able to realize as a whole.
- To create stability in the company's stock price, which may be experiencing fluctuations as a result of volatility of one or more of the company's business units.
- Getting rid of underperforming or failing businesses that may be depressing earning and/or draining cash flows.
- Pressure from regulatory agencies and/or stockholders.

Valuing a Business for Merger or Acquisition

Three major techniques or methods are used to value a target company for merger or acquisition:

1. Discounted cash flow method (DCF)
2. Adjusted book value method
3. Comparative price/earnings (P/E) ratio method

Conceptually, the **DCF method** is the soundest of the three methods. It compares the present value (PV) of the cash flow benefits to be derived from the merger with the PV of the merger costs. The discount rate used in computing the PV of the cash benefits typically would be the acquired company's after-tax required rate of return or cost of capital. This rate best reflects the riskiness of the acquired firm's cash flows. The merger cash flow benefits are the target company's expected future after-tax free cash flows. There are many methods that can be used to calculate after-tax free cash flow. The choice of method is often based on what information is available about a company's financial statements. Examples are the tax rate, depreciation expense, and amortization expense. One of the most basic methods is:

Net Income

+ Depreciation and Amortization Expense

+ Interest Expense

− Changes in working capital from the prior year's current assets and current liabilities to the current year's amounts

− Changes in capital expenditures from the prior year to the current year property, plant, and equipment accounts

− Tax shield on interest expense

= After-Tax Free Cash Flow

The PV of the merger costs is often the purchase price paid by the acquiring company.

For example: Suppose the after-tax free cash flow from a merger is estimated to be $2,000,000 per year and is expected to last for 15 years. Assuming the acquired company's required rate of return is 14%, the PV of the postmerger cash flow benefits would be $2,000,000 × 6.142 = $12,284,000. The 6.142 rate represents the PV of an annuity at 14% for 15 years. Therefore, the price that would be offered by the acquirer company would be less than or equal to the $12,284,000.

The **adjusted book value method** for valuing a business in a merger or acquisition transaction involves determining the market value of the target company's assets and subtracting the value of its liabilities. Because identifying market valuations for the target company's assets and liabilities can be both difficult and costly, this method is not commonly used.

The **comparative P/E ratio method** establishes the exchange of the acquiring company's stock for the target company's stock so as to obtain a desired postmerger P/E ratio. The use of this method is based on the assumption that the acquirer firm should pay a premium over the market value for the target firm due to expected synergistic benefits.

For example: Suppose the ABC Corp. is considering acquiring XYZ Co. in a stock-for-stock exchange. Financial data for the two companies is shown in Figure 2B-23.

If no synergistic benefits are expected, what is the maximum exchange ratio ABC should agree to if it wants *no dilution* in earnings per share (EPS)? For this to occur, the combined EPS would have to be at least $5.00 per share. To maintain a $5.00 EPS, the combined number of common shares outstanding would have to be 8 million shares. This is calculated by taking the $40 million in combined net income divided by the required $5.00 EPS. Therefore, ABC would trade an additional 2 million of its shares for the 4 million XYZ shares, resulting in a 1-for-2 (0.5-for-1) exchange ratio.

Figure 2B-23 Financial Data for ABC Corp. and XYZ Co.

	ABC	XYZ	Combined
Sales (millions)	$600	$75	$675
Net income (millions)	$30	$10	$40
Common shares outstanding (millions)	6	4	?
Earnings per share	$5.00	$2.50	?
Common stock price per share	$50	$20	$50

In addition to the comparative P/E ratio method, other relative (or comparable) valuation methods also rely on simple multiples (or ratios). These methods include:

- Market price-to-book (P/B) ratio
- Market price-to-sales (P/S) ratio

These methods suggest that a target firm's stock price would be some multiple of an item found on the target's financial statements such as book value per share, sales, or earnings. For example, an acquiring firm might use a P/B ratio for a peer firm in the target's industry times the target's book value of equity to value the

Business Failures

An organization is **technically insolvent** when it is unable to meet current obligations even though the value of its assets exceeds its liabilities. Technical insolvency denotes a lack of liquidity. A firm is **legally insolvent** when its liabilities exceed the "fair value" of its assets. It is **bankrupt** when it files a bankruptcy petition in accordance with the U.S. 2005 Bankruptcy Reform Act as amended in 2008. A bankruptcy may be a corporate reorganization filed under Chapter 11 of the Act or a formal bankruptcy resulting in liquidation under Chapter 7 of the Act.

Chapter 11 Reorganization

Chapter 11 provides a debtor company the opportunity to restructure its business. A variety of actions may be used, such as restructuring of existing loans, acquisition of new financing with priority of company earnings, rejection of specific contracts, and the cancellation of certain contracts. A trustee, often the debtor as "debtor in possession," acts as trustee of the business during the reorganization. During the period of reorganization, the automatic stay provision requires all creditors to cease collection attempts. The court must approve the reorganization plan, and may convert the case to a Chapter 7 liquidation if it is in the best interests of the creditors.

Chapter 7 Bankruptcy

Chapter 7 involves a corporate liquidation of assets. In liquidation, a trustee normally is appointed to handle the administrative aspects of the bankruptcy procedure. The trustee arranges a meeting of the creditors. The trustee liquidates the business and pays the creditors according to the priority of claims set forth in Chapter 7.

The priority of claims states that secured claims are satisfied first by the proceeds from the sale of the secured assets. The amount paid each secured claim holder is the lower of the amount of the claim and the amount received from the sale. If the amount of the claim *is less than* the amount of the sale, the secured creditor receives the amount of the claim and the difference becomes available to satisfy the unsecured creditors. If the amount of the claim *exceeds* the amount of the sale, the secured creditor receives the amount of the sale and the difference becomes an amount that is now considered to be an unsecured creditor claim.

The order of priority for unsecured creditors is described next.

1. First-priority creditors are paid in a specific order:
   a. Expenses for the administration of the bankruptcy, including the trustee's fee and attorney fees

b. Creditor claims that arise in the ordinary course of the debtor's business from the time the case starts to the time a trustee is appointed
c. Wages earned by employees within 90 days of the bankruptcy petition, limited to $2,000 per employee
d. Claims for contributions to employee benefit plans for services rendered within 180 days of the bankruptcy petition, not to exceed $2,000 per employee
e. Claims of customers who make cash deposits for goods or services not provided by the debtor, not to exceed $900 per customer
f. Taxes owed

2. Unsubordinated debentures
3. General and unsecured creditors are paid next.
4. If any monies remain, preferred shareholders receive their liquidation values.
5. Common shareholders receive any monies remaining on a pro rata basis.

Other Forms of Corporate Restructuring

There are still some other forms of restructuring that can help a company to meet its primary goal of maximizing shareholder wealth, weathering tough economic times, or simply ensuring its long-term viability.

For example, a company may choose to go private. This can be accomplished by repurchasing outstanding common stock shares and retiring them. In doing so, the stock is delisted and is no longer traded. These types of transactions are often executed through a **leveraged buyout (LBO)**. An LBO, previously introduced in the context of takeover defense tactics, is a type of acquisition by which the management or other employees of a company buy the company using little equity and significant amounts of debt with the company's assets serving as collateral for the debt. A company can benefit from an LBO because of the savings it realizes from a reduction in administrative costs associated with it having been a public company. Additionally, managers/employees, who then become owners in the company, have greater incentives and greater operational flexibility.

Alternatively, a private company can pursue restructuring through an initial public offering (IPO) of its stock and becoming a public company.

A company may also restructure its ownership by setting up an **employee stock ownership plan (ESOP)** whereby the company transfers its ownership to its employees. ESOPs are commonly used to provide a market for the shares of departing owners of successful closely held companies, to motivate and reward employees, or to take advantage of incentives to borrow money for acquiring new assets in pretax dollars. ESOPs also provide major tax benefits, including but not limited to, tax deductibility of contributions of stock and cash contributions to the ESOP. ESOPs were also mentioned previously as a tactic a company can use in defending itself from a potential takeover.

Letter stock, also known as **tracking stock** or targeted stock, is yet another restructuring technique. Tracking stock are specialized equity offerings issued by a parent company that are based on the operations of a specific division or strategic business unit (SBU) of a diversified organization. They are issued for the purpose of tracking the performance of the SBU. All revenues, expenses, income, and cash flows of the SBU being tracked are separated from the parent company and attached to the SBU's tracking stock. The tracking stock is, therefore, separately traded at a price related to the operations of the SBU being tracked. Tracking stock often is used to separate a high-growth SBU from a larger parent that has been experiencing losses. The parent and its shareholders, however, still control the tracked SBU.

Companies can also restructure through changes in their asset or capital structure. This might be facilitated through a liquidation of assets of an underperforming operating unit where the assets of that operating unit are sold piecemeal. An asset restructuring can also be executed through a sale-leaseback transaction. In a sale-leaseback transaction, a company sells certain property or assets and then leases them back from the buyer. Doing so allows the company to free up capital and raise money while retaining possession and use of the property or asset. As it relates to restructuring through changes in its capital structure, a company (as an alternative to bankruptcy) may work with its creditors through a debt restructuring. Debt restructuring is a process that allows a company to reduce and renegotiate its delinquent debts in order to improve or restore liquidity so that it can continue its operations.

Knowledge Check: Corporate Restructuring

The following questions are intended to help you check your understanding and recall of the material presented in this topic. They do not represent the type of questions that appear on the CMA exam.

Directions: Answer each question in the space provided. Correct answers and section references appear after the knowledge check questions.

1. A merger may be any of the following **except**
   - a. horizontal.
   - b. vertical.
   - c. cross-functional.
   - d. conglomerate.

2. Potential defenses against hostile takeovers include
   - a. poison pills.
   - b. white knights.
   - c. Pacman.
   - d. all of the above.

3. Which of the following is **not** a type of divestiture?
   - a. A spin-off
   - b. An equity carve-out
   - c. An equity carve-up
   - d. A split-up

4. Techniques used to value and evaluate potential mergers and acquisitions include:
   - a. adjusted book value.
   - b. discounted cash flow.
   - c. comparative P/E ratios.
   - d. all of the above.

5. Which of the following is **not** a priority unsecured creditor in a bankruptcy proceeding?
   - a. An unsubordinated debenture
   - b. Taxes owed
   - c. Customer deposits subject to limits
   - d. Unpaid wages subject to limits

Knowledge Check Answers: Corporate Restructuring

1. A merger may be any of the following **except** [See *Mergers and Acquisitions*.]
   - ☐ a. horizontal.
   - ☐ b. vertical.
   - ☑ c. cross-functional.
   - ☐ d. conglomerate.

2. Potential defenses against hostile takeovers include [See *Takeover Defense Tactics*.]
   - ☐ a. poison pills.
   - ☐ b. white knights.
   - ☐ c. Pacman.
   - ☑ d. all of the above.

3. Which of the following is **not** a type of divestiture? [See *Divestitures*.]
   - ☐ a. A spin-off
   - ☐ b. An equity carve-out
   - ☑ c. An equity carve-up
   - ☐ d. A split-up

4. Techniques used to value and evaluate potential mergers and acquisitions include: [See *Valuing a Business for Merger or Acquisition*.]
   - ☐ a. adjusted book value.
   - ☐ b. discounted cash flow.
   - ☐ c. comparative P/E ratios.
   - ☑ d. all of the above.

5. Which of the following is **not** a priority unsecured creditor in a bankruptcy proceeding? [See *Chapter 7 Bankruptcy*.]
   - ☑ a. An unsubordinated debenture
   - ☐ b. Taxes owed
   - ☐ c. Customer deposits subject to limits
   - ☐ d. Unpaid wages subject to limits

TOPIC 6

International Finance

AS GOODS ARE TRADED BETWEEN COUNTRIES, they must be paid for. The cost of imported goods to a country depends on the value of its currency in relation to the value of the currency of the exporting country.

In addition to using currency to pay for goods and services, investors purchase and sell currencies as a form of hedge investment. For example, if an investor feels that the American dollar will soon be declining against the Japanese yen, she will trade dollars for yen in order to profit from the future change in rates. If she is correct, later she will be able to purchase more dollars than she sold with the same number of yen.

This topic looks at fixed and flexible or floating exchange rates; means of managing transaction exposure; financing and paying for international trade; transfer pricing; and diversification of international assets.

READ the Learning Outcome Statements (LOS) for this topic as found in Appendix B and then study the concepts and calculations presented here to be sure you understand the content you could be tested on in the CMA exam.

Foreign Currency Exchange

LOS
§2.B.6.a

As any international traveler knows, one currency can be exchanged for another. A U.S. citizen who travels to England, exchanges U.S. dollars (USD) for British pounds (GBP). The same traveler, when crossing the channel to France, may exchange USD or GBP for euros. In effect, the traveler is buying one currency with another currency at a price determined by the rate of exchange.

One difficulty in following currency rates is that many exchange rates are subject to change in the currency marketplace. In other words, like other commodities, currencies can depreciate or appreciate in value in the global marketplace. When tangible objects, such as real estate or works of art, appreciate in value, they simply have a higher price tag. Intangible goods, such as stocks and bonds, also carry higher prices when they appreciate and lower prices when they depreciate in value. The same is true of currencies, although in a less straightforward manner.

When a currency *appreciates* in value, it has *more buying power* in relation to another specific currency. When it *depreciates* in value, it has *less buying power* in relation to other specific currencies. As a result of appreciation, a currency will buy more units of another currency. Therefore, the holder of the currency can buy more goods than before. Travelers experience this when their home currency appreciates against the currency of the country they are visiting, allowing them to purchase better hotel accommodations, eat at better restaurants, and purchase more goods to bring home. If their home currency depreciates against that of the other country, the opposite happens, and they may have to scale back their purchasing or even cancel their visit.

Shortly after World War II, the rate of exchange between USD and British pounds was about $4 to £1. When visiting the United States, Winston Churchill could "buy" $4 with approximately £1, whereas President Truman, when visiting London, would have needed about $4 to purchase £1. As the years passed, the pound gradually depreciated against the USD (or the USD appreciated in relation to the pound) until at one point in the 1990s, the two currencies were very nearly equal in value. The dollar then began depreciating against the pound (the pound appreciated against the dollar) until the pound rose in dollar value to nearly $2 per £1. That was good for British travelers to the United States and not so good for U.S. travelers to Great Britain.

Fluctuations in exchange rates are continuous unless the exchange is fixed, as described later in this topic. These constant changes can be viewed on the Internet at Web sites such as www.xe.com.

The exchange rate quote has a domestic currency component and a foreign currency component. The quoted rate will look different depending on which country's point of view is taken. Either way, the exchange rate results in the same amount of money changing hands.

The exchange rate quote can be either a direct or an indirect quote. In a **direct quote**, the first currency is considered to be the domestic or base currency. The second currency is the foreign or counter currency. It tells you the amount of a domestic currency required to buy or sell one monetary unit of the foreign currency. The currency relationship that is used in Figure 2B-24 means in the direct type of quote, that 1 USD divided by 0.69628 GBP = 1.4433 USD.

The opposite calculation is true for the **indirect** type of quote.

For example: Assume that John is a U.S. citizen planning to tour Britain. He lands at Heathrow Airport in London, and the tour director says he will need

Figure 2B-24 Relationship Between Direct and Indirect Quotes

Type of Quote	Currency Relationship (U.S. Perspective)	Example
Indirect quote	Foreign currency/Domestic currency	USD 1 = 0.6928 GBP
Direct quote	Domestic currency/Foreign currency	1 GBP = 1.4434 USD

500 GBP for his various expenses. A direct quote tells John how many dollars are required to buy 1 GBP. An indirect quote is the inverse amount—the number of pounds John can receive in exchange for 1 USD. In this example, John will pay $721.70 to get the 500 GBP he needs (500 times 1.4434).

Figure 2B-24 illustrates the relationship between direct and indirect quotes.

Although understanding exchange rates is easiest in relation to transactions by John, the U.S. traveler, the impact of exchange rates goes far beyond the purchases of international tourists. International trade is facilitated by the currencies of the trading nations. Purchases of oranges from Mexico will be made in Mexican pesos; purchases of American merchandise will be made in USD. For a consumer in a foreign country to purchase U.S. merchandise, he or she must be able to get USD for the trade to take place. Thus, there is a market for exchange of foreign currencies.

Fixed and Flexible or Floating Currency Exchange Rates

Exchange rates have evolved from fixed rates in the first half of the twentieth century to flexible or floating rates.

Fixed Currency Exchange Rates

In a **fixed exchange rate system**, each country is required to maintain its currency at or near a certain value in relation to other currencies or to another measure, such as the value of gold. In 1944, the United Nations Monetary and Financial Conference (commonly known as the Bretton Woods Conference) was convened to regulate the international monetary and financial situation at the end of World War II. Among other actions, the conference established a system in which world currencies were pegged to the value of the USD, with the dollar set at a certain value in relation to gold. The USD was designated the medium of foreign exchange. The initial value of the dollar, $35 per ounce of gold, was maintained until the 1960s.

In a fixed system, governments can take various actions to offset the changes that normally would result from fluctuations in the supply and demand for the currency. One straightforward method is to intervene in the currency market, using a nation's currency reserves to buy or sell dollars in the marketplace. This increases or decreases the supply and thereby decreases or increases its price in terms of other currencies.

Assume, for example, that under the old fixed rate system, the Swiss franc's value is fixed at 2 francs to 1 dollar. And assume that demand for the franc increases in the world exchange markets to 1.90 francs to 1 dollar. Remember, as the franc strengthens, the dollar weakens, so traders will be able to buy more dollars with fewer francs. To restore the dollar's value against the franc, the U.S. Treasury could dip into its reserves of Swiss francs and use them to buy USD in the marketplace, thus reducing the available supply of dollars and increasing the supply of francs, until the exchange rate settles at 2 francs to 1 dollar.

Instead of intervening in exchange markets to buy or sell currency, the U.S. government might react to a depreciating dollar by other means. For example, if the dollar's decline were a reaction to a trade imbalance, the government might enact trade policies to decrease a trade deficit or increase a trade surplus. This would bring dollars back into the country and increase the demand for dollars to purchase U.S. goods abroad, thus raising the dollar's value in exchange for other currencies.

Nations also can place controls on currency exchange to make a currency easier or more difficult to acquire, or they can make domestic macroeconomic adjustments that decrease or increase the supply of the country's currency in the markets. For instance, if domestic price inflation were reducing the value of the dollar, the Fed might raise interest rates. This would reduce the domestic demand for money by making it more costly to borrow funds, and it also would make dollars more valuable in currency markets by increasing the interest paid on dollar-based bonds. Thus, the supply of dollars would be reduced and the demand increased, raising the currency's value from both the supply and demand sides.

Flexible or Floating Exchange Rates

A **flexible** or **floating exchange rate** is a system wherein the exchange rates for currencies are determined by market supply and demand just as are the prices of other financial assets, such as stocks and bonds. Thus, the value of the currency floats according to market actions. Figure 2B-25 summarizes the features and claimed benefits of fixed and floating exchange rates.

Figure 2B-25 Benefits of Fixed and Floating Exchange Rates

Exchange Rate Type	Essential Features	Claimed Benefits
Fixed	Exchange rates do not vary.	• **Promote monetary discipline** Fixed rate systems (such as the gold standard described earlier) include restrictions on each country's monetary and fiscal policies, thus preventing governments from pursuing policies designed to expand or contract the country's money supply arbitrarily. • **Prevent speculation** Because rates are fixed, there is no incentive to buy or sell currencies in hopes of benefiting from future rate changes. • **Reduce uncertainty** Because rates are fixed, prices remain stable and predictable, removing uncertainty about the value of future payments received for exports.
Floating	Exchange rates fluctuate with supply and demand.	• **Allow monetary autonomy** When rates are allowed to float with supply and demand, government monetary policy is not restricted by the demands of exchange rate agreements, such as a requirement to buy or sell currency to maintain a set rate. • **Allow trade balance adjustment** Floating rates allow a country to adjust automatically to changes in international trade, whereas fixed rate structures make such adaptation difficult—and usually too late.

With floating exchange rates, the short-run rates are a function of the interest rate differentials between countries. In the medium range, exchange rates are a function of trade imbalances. In the long run, exchange rates move toward **purchasing power parity (PPP)** between the countries. PPP is the idea that a basket of standardized goods should sell at the same price in two countries, after exchange rates are taken into account.

In a **managed floating exchange rate system**, the currency rate normally fluctuates according to supply and demand but is also supported by currency interventions by central banks in order to stabilize or alter rates. Monetary intervention by central banks is based on recognition that changing economic conditions may require changes in exchange rates to avoid persistent payment deficits and surpluses. A managed floating exchange rate system allows for more volatility in exchange rates than did the fixed rates under the Bretton Woods agreement.

Changes in foreign currency exchange rates can be disruptive to an economy and discourage the flow of trading. Speculators in foreign currency exchange add to the problem by purchasing and selling currencies as commodities. As a result, the usual intervention in the managed float system is for a central bank to manage or stabilize the exchange rate in a way similar to the monetary controls used by the Federal Reserve Board in the United States—purchasing or selling the currency in order to control supply and demand.

Floating exchange rate systems have both advantages and disadvantages. Trade growth has not been found to diminish under the floating exchange rate system. Proponents believe that managed float has enabled nations and the world to prevent severe economic turmoil. Floating exchange rates facilitate international adjustments to negative or dangerous economic developments, and proponents believe that such events would put unbearable pressures on a fixed rate system.

Opponents of managed floating exchange rate systems believe that managed float results in excessively volatile exchange rates. Volatility has occurred even when the underlying economic and financial conditions of a particular nation have been stable. Opponents believe that managed float has not resolved balance of payments imbalances as flexible rates were presumed to do.

Opponents of managed systems feel that managed float lacks clear rules and guidelines to make the system viable in the long run. Nations inevitably will be tempted to intervene, not merely to smooth out short-term or speculative fluctuations but to prop up their currency if it is chronically weak and to manipulate the value of the currency to achieve domestic stabilization goals. Some fear that the future will bring more managing and less floating.

Currency Fluctuations

Currencies float in relation to each other, meaning they are relative. If one currency goes down in value, other currencies will be relatively higher in value. The exchange rate is determined as a trading relationship between two currencies. The following factors are not mutually exclusive and, in fact, have impacts on each other. Six factors affect exchange rates:

1. *Differences in inflation rates:* in general, consistently lower inflation rates will raise currency value and therefore purchasing power
2. *Differences in interest rates:* central banks manipulate interest rates which influences both inflation and exchange rates
3. *Current-account deficits:* the balance of trade between one country and its trading partners
4. *Level of public debt:* a large level of debt increases inflation
5. *Ratio of exports to imports:* also known as the terms of trade: is a ratio that compares export prices to import prices
6. *Political and economic stability:* stable countries attract foreign investors which shows confidence in a currency

Determinants of exchange rates are changes in consumer tastes, income changes, changes in relative price (to be discussed shortly), speculation by investors in foreign currencies which increase demand (buying) or supply (selling), and interest rates. If interest rates are high in one country relative to another, they will attract foreign investments into that country. As a result, the demand on the currency of that country will increase the currency's exchange rate.

Changes in a foreign currency will affect the cost of importing that country's goods. If the foreign currency is down relative to the currency of the importing country, its currency and products will be cheaper for the importing country. If the foreign currency is up relative to the importing country's currency, currency and products will be more expensive for importers.

Companies that denominate transactions in foreign currencies are responsible for managing exchange rate risks. Currency futures, currency options, and currency swaps are tools used to manage those risks. **Currency futures**, also called FX futures and foreign exchange futures, are transferrable contracts to exchange a number of foreign currency units for another, at a specific date, for a specific price (exchange rate). These contracts allow the company to exit the obligation to buy/sell the currency before the contract exchange date. Currency futures are used to hedge against foreign exchange risk. **Currency options** give the holder the right, but not the obligation, to buy (call) or sell (put) a specific amount of foreign currency at a specific price, during a specific time period. This enables a firm to hedge against adverse exchange rate movements. The benefit of the currency option is that the option does not need to be exercised unless it is beneficial. In a **currency swap**, two parties agree to exchange the interest and sometimes the principal of a loan in one currency for the equivalent interest and principal of another loan in a different currency. Currency swaps closely resemble interest rate swaps, except that they may include the exchange of principal.

The difference in the cost of imports is called the **relative price**. For example, suppose that Italy is exporting product A to the United States for €50 and the United States is exporting product B to Italy for $50. The exchange rate determines what the relative cost will be to consumers in the United States importing Italian goods and to consumers in Italy importing American goods.

If the exchange rate ($/€) is 1.25 or €1 = 1.25 USD:

- The relative price of product A for U.S. consumers is 1.25($/€) × €50 = $62.50.

Figure 2B-26 Equilibrium for USD and Euro Exchange Rate

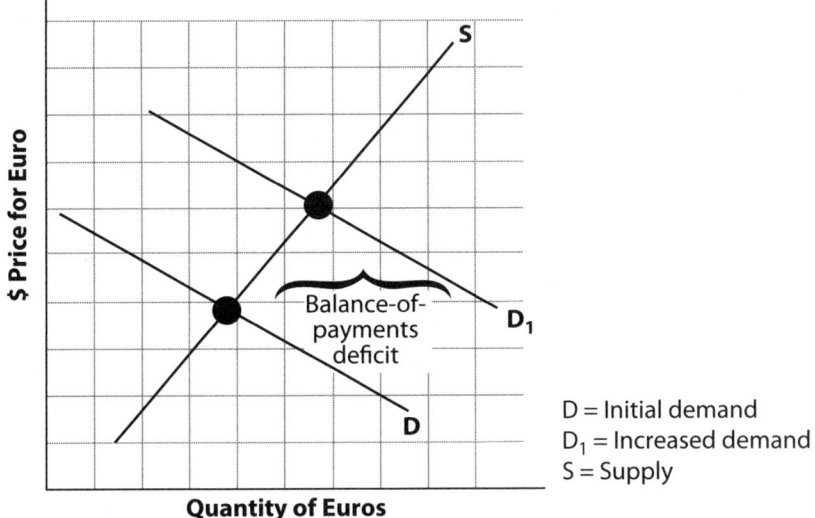

- The relative price of product B for Italian consumers is € (1/1.25) = .8 (€/$) × $50 = €40.

If, two months later, the price of product A is still €50 in Italy but has fallen to $60 (from $62.50) in the United States, we can conclude that the dollar has risen in value (appreciated) relative to the euro. Correspondingly, the euro has fallen relative to the dollar. Product B, still at $50 in the United States, will now cost a European buyer €41.67. We can calculate the exchange rate based on the real versus relative price as shown:

$$\$60 \ / \ €50 = 1.2 \ (\$/€)$$
$$€41.67 \ / \ \$50 = .8334 \ (€/\$)$$

Another way to show the fluctuation in exchange rates is on a graph. Figure 2B-26 demonstrates an increase in the value of the euro relative to the USD.

Figure 2B-26 shows an increasing demand for the euro from demand line D to demand line D_1. This occurs in the case of a balance-of-payments deficit resulting from increased exports, increased income for Europeans, and increased demand on the euro. Notice that, for the quantity of euros supplied, it would cost more in USD to purchase euros as the demand increases.

Types of Exchange Risk Exposure

A fundamental risk results from changes in currency exchange rates. Three specific types of exchange rate risks are translation, transactions, and economic.

1. **Translation exposure**, also called accounting exposure, occurs when a company has a foreign subsidiary that denominates its financial statements in a foreign currency. At the time of consolidation for financial reporting, the

foreign subsidiary's financial statements are translated into U.S. dollars at the current exchange rate. When consolidated, this results in an exchange rate gain or loss that is reported in the financial statements.

2. **Transactions exposure** is the gain or loss that occurs when settling a specific foreign transaction, such as the purchase or sale of a foreign product or the settlement of open-credit terms.

   Assume that a U.S. business purchases inventory on credit from a Canadian supplier for 10,000 Canadian dollars (C$). The exchange rate at the time is 0.70 Canadian dollars to 1 USD. Payment is not due for two months. When the account is settled, the exchange rate is 0.69 Canadian dollars to 1 USD. At the time of purchase, the payment is valued at C$10,000 / 0.70 = $14,285.71. When payment is made it is C$10,000 / 0.69 = $14,492.75. This results in a transaction loss of $207.40 ($14,492.75 − $14,285.71). If the Canadian dollar were to have weakened to 0.71, there would have been a transactions gain.

3. **Economic exposure**, also known as operating exposure, is the change in a firm's future cash flows due to *unanticipated* exchange rate fluctuations. Translation and transaction exposure are different because these are based on *anticipated* currency fluctuations. This makes economic exposure difficult to hedge. The most effective method is the currency swap.

   An example is of a U.S. company basing their operating forecasts on a 1% per annum gradual increase in the U.S. dollar against a major foreign currency. An economic exposure would result if the U.S. dollar declined instead.

   Economic exposure impacts large multinational companies the most. However, small domestic firms will be impacted to some extent as well.

Various hedging (risk management) techniques can be used for managing exchange rate risk exposure. For example, currency hedges, through forward contracts, futures contracts, currency options, and currency swaps, can all be utilized.

For example, to see how a company might use a forward contract to hedge exchange rate risk, consider U.S. Blivet Company selling blivets to a wholesaler in Switzerland. The purchase price for a shipment of blivets is 50,000 Swiss francs (Fr) with terms of net 90 days. Upon payment in 90 days, U.S. Blivet will convert Swiss francs to U.S. dollars. The present (spot) rate for francs per dollar is 1.17, and the 90-day forward rate is 1.70. To hedge exchange rate risk, U.S. Blivet decides to sell francs forward 90 days. Upon delivery of Fr50,000 in 90 days, it would receive Fr50,000 / 1.70 = $29,412. Had U.S. Blivet received Fr50,000 today and exchanged them for U.S. dollars, it would have received Fr50,000 / 1.71 = $29,240.

Risk and Rate of Return for Foreign Investment

One of the risks of holding any financial asset is that it may prove to be unfavorable and decline in value. International investment that spans a number of countries is seen as a way of diversifying that risk.

Consider the example of investors in Country A and Country B, both of which grow coffee. In international trade, residents of each country purchase 50% ownership in the farm cooperatives of the other. When climate and economic conditions are good in Country A and Country B experiences a drought, each investor earns the same on their portfolio. If, for example, Country A harvests 75 tons of coffee and Country B harvests only 25 tons, each country earns a return of 50 tons. In this instance, the investor in Country B benefits from diversification. In another year, when Country B produces 100 tons of coffee and Country A produces 50 tons, each will recognize a return of 75 tons. In this case, Country A benefits from diversification.

Similar diversification will aid investors in the case of adverse interest rate changes in one country; diversification of portfolio assets in other countries will minimize the impact of the adverse change.

When considering an international investment, a company naturally wants to consider the potential rate of return of its new foreign investments. But it also should consider the impact on the risk of its overall portfolio.

An investment in a developing country, for example, may promise a higher rate of return than domestic operations. But higher rates of return tend to be correlated with higher risk. In this case, risk means variability.

For example: Assume that Luxury Luggage, Inc., a domestic U.S. company, starts an operation overseas that returns 45% one year followed by a return of –5% the next. That may be a mean rate of return of 20% ([45% + –5%] / 2 = 40% / 2 = 20%. However, if Luxury Luggage has a conservative outlook on risk, it is likely to prefer an investment with more predictable returns, such as 20% followed by 18% followed by 19%. That is only a 19% return, but the risk profile is more consistent with a conservative outlook. Investors in the company will not be subjected to those nerve-wracking quarters when returns drop abruptly, causing the risk averse to sell their investments. Lenders are more amenable to providing funds for investments with stable rates of return, because fluctuating returns means lean quarters that may jeopardize the ability to cover loan obligations.

Investing overseas, however, is a form of diversification. And diversification actually tends to reduce risk as the investor—Luxury Luggage, in this case—multiplies the number of investments in its portfolio. For risk reduction to work, diversification requires more than mere multiplication of investments. If all the investments have the same characteristics, they will not alter the risk profile of the portfolio.

If, for example, Luxury Luggage maintains assembly plants in ten locations, each of which earns a 20% return in year 1, an 18% return in year 2, and a 22% return in year 3, it has done nothing to alter the risk–return relationship of maintaining only one of those operations.

Diversification evens out variability if the earnings in one location tend to be up when earnings elsewhere are down. This is a simple way of saying that a company considering an overseas investment must look at the expected rate of return, plus the variability of the return (the standard deviation) but must do so in light of the correlation of those good and not-so-good years.

For example: Assume that Luxury Luggage is considering two new locations for assembly plants. Its financial department concludes that the two locations offer the potential returns and risk shown in Figure 2B-27.

Figure 2B-27 Rate of Return and Risk in Countries A and B

Country	Mean Return Rate	Standard Deviation
A	18%	8%
B	22%	13%

If Luxury Luggage is currently making a 16% return from its U.S. operation, with a standard deviation of 10%, and it ships half of its business to the new location, the resulting rate of return is easy to calculate because it is a simple average. For the combined operations in the United States and Country A, the mean rate of return will be 17% (16% + 18% / 2 = 17%). And for Country B, the mean return will be 19% (16% + 22% / 2).

If the rate of return were the only consideration, Country B would be the easy choice for the new location. But Country B, with its standard deviation of 13%, involves greater risk. Luxury Luggage cannot determine how much risk is involved by simply averaging the standard deviations. Instead, it will have its financial experts put their computer programs to work to determine the correlation coefficients and come up with standard deviations for the two potential combinations of domestic and overseas operations.

It is quite possible that Country B, although riskier when considered alone, may counterbalance Luxury Luggage's weak domestic quarters with its own stronger quarters, so that the two operations together have a lower standard deviation than either one separately.

There always will be political risk in international investments. In the event of political upheaval, adverse changes may result for the foreign investor, including nationalization of assets and seizing of the assets from that investor. The political risk of investing in another country is tied to the possibility of financial upheaval in the country, which ultimately can be tied to politics.

Other risks associated with international projects include currency fluctuations and inflation risks.

Multinational Budgeting and Financing

Comparative advantage is the ability of a firm or individual to produce goods and/or services at a lower opportunity cost than other firms or individuals. Each country can benefit by focusing on production of goods or services that provide an advantage when compared with other goods or services that could be produced within that country. Assuming the free flow of capital across borders, multinationals also can consider investing in goods or services according to the absolute advantage offered, no matter where production might take place.

Like domestic capital budgeting, investing in capital projects across borders focuses on analysis of long-term cash flows. This is true whether the project involves setting up new operations similar to one's domestic businesses (e.g., opening a new chain of stores) or acquiring existing businesses. However, the next issues, among others, arise in addition to those involved in budgeting for domestic capital investment.

Returns and Risks

Expected returns may have to be adjusted in light of political and economic risks. Doing business in foreign countries may involve more risk than doing business domestically. The opposite may be true, depending on the countries involved. Investors will shy away from putting money into unstable, unpredictable situations unless expected returns justify the added risk. One method of providing more attractive returns is offering a higher rate of return.

Overall Cash Flows versus Local Cash Flows

The parent company's cash flows must be considered separately from the foreign operation's cash flows. From the foreign operation's point of view, cash flows are looked at and evaluated at the local level.

For example: If a division in Vietnam generates an acceptable return, the manager on site will be satisfied. Management at the headquarters in the United States, however, has to balance cash flows in Vietnam as well as the cash flows in the firm's other divisions, say in the Philippines and the Dominican Republic, as well as in the United States. Headquarters is interested in maximizing total cash flows. So if the cash flows in Vietnam are earned by diverting business from operations elsewhere, headquarters would most likely change its overall strategy.

Currency Considerations

Because of currency exchange rate fluctuations, future investment returns may be reduced in value when translated from the local currency back into dollars. Those returns also may be enhanced in value by currency fluctuations. To analyze the impact of currency fluctuations, budgets can be projected with several different assumptions about future exchange rates to judge the impact each might have on the returns from the investment. The method of doing this is called sensitivity analysis, which is covered in Part 1, Section B: Planning, Budgeting, and Forecasting. Risk also can be hedged by various currency investment strategies.

Effects of Inflation

Different long-term rates of inflation in the foreign and domestic countries can affect an overseas capital project in several ways. Inflation will affect the local market by its impact on the price of resources and the price of the product or service produced. It also may affect demand for the product, depending on price elasticity. Currency exchange rates also respond to inflation; high inflation rates correlate with depreciating currency, and low inflation correlates with a strengthened currency. Finally, potential sources of borrowed funds will be more or less attractive depending on the rate of inflation. Inflation generally favors the borrower and penalizes the lender; inflated currency makes the initial amount, as well as fixed payments, easier to repay. These various effects of inflation—on prices, currency exchange rates, and financing—must be considered together; some may be favorable and some harmful.

Taxation

Tax rates can vary considerably among countries, and they must be taken into account when determining where to make capital investments. If a multinational company has divisions that buy and sell among themselves, it can benefit from differential tax rates in the various countries by the way it sets transfer prices. Divisions in high-tax countries generally should record the lowest profits on such transfers, while divisions in low-tax jurisdictions should record the highest profits.

Different Accounting Standards

Accounting standards may be different between the country of the parent company and the division or subsidiary. This creates added cost and complexity when analyzing returns according to the different systems. The International Accounting Standards Board (IASB) continues to work to minimize these differences through the issuance of International Financial Reporting Standards (IFRS).

Financing and Paying for International Trade

Forms of Payment in International Trade

If Company A in Europe ships products to Company B in the United States, how and when does money change hands? A number of instruments are used to do this.

The import-export business involves a degree of payment risk when money changes hands across borders. Like any seller, an exporter of goods risks nonpayment, and like any buyer, an importer risks paying for items that never appear or show up damaged or defective. Importers and exporters handle these risks through a number of different methods of payment.

- A **letter of credit** is a letter sent by a lender to an exporter on behalf of an importer stating that the bank will accept a draft (bill of exchange) with appropriate accompanying documentation and will back the obligation of the importer. A confirmed letter of credit also includes the guarantee of a bank in the exporter's country.
- A **sight draft** is a bill for imports that is payable immediately. This is similar to a cash on demand (COD) order, where the importer pays for the goods when they arrive with proper documentation. A sight draft is also called a demand draft.
- A **time draft** is a bill that must be paid at a specified time in the future or upon completion of specified requirements by the exporter.
- A **consignment** is when the exporter sends goods to the importer to be sold. The importer sends money to the exporter once the goods are sold.

- An **open account** occurs when the exporter mails documents to the importer (buyer) before there is any obligation on the part of the importer. At this point, the importer has no obligation. This arrangement can be risky for the exporter, as it runs the risk of default by the buyer. An open account is most likely between two companies that have conducted business together successfully in the past.
- Importers sometimes **prepay** for goods or services. This subjects the importer to the maximum amount of risk and therefore is suitable only for transactions between counterparties with sound reasons to trust one another, such as units of the same multinational company.

Methods of Financing Foreign Trade

Import-export transactions also can be financed in several different ways.

Bankers' Acceptance

Bankers' acceptances (BAs) are forms of time drafts drawn to finance the export, import, domestic shipment, or storage of goods. A BA is accepted when a bank writes on the draft its agreement to pay it at maturity. A bank will accept the draft from either the drawer of the BA or the holder of the instrument.

BAs are traded at discounts from face value in the secondary market. For example, if Company A ships from Country A to Company B in Country B, Company B will arrange with the bank to pay the costs of the imported goods at a specified time in the future. The BA will be sent to the exporter, who can sell the BA in the market at a discount rate in order to finance export expenses. The holder of the BA at the time of its maturity presents it to the guaranteeing bank for payment at face value.

Denominating Transactions in a Foreign Currency

A company may transact business (buying inventory or selling products) in the local currency (USD) or in a foreign currency. If the company decides to transact in the foreign currency, also called denominating the transaction in the foreign currency, there is the risk that the foreign currency will appreciate or depreciate relative to the local currency, creating a gain or loss. For example, suppose a U.S. company denominated the sale of merchandise for €1,000 when the euro had a spot exchange rate of $1.40 with terms of net 30 (due in full in 30 days). If the euro has appreciated in value to $1.45 by the date of receipt, the company receives the €1,000, which are now worth $1,450 instead of the original $1,400, creating a gain of $50. Alternatively, if a company was the buyer in this transaction, a $50 loss would be created because $1,450 would be required to satisfy the €1,000 payment. The buyer could hedge this transaction using a forward contract to lock in the current spot rate of $1.40. Many companies choose to transfer the risk of changing currency rates with currency swaps, currency options, currency futures, or other techniques, such as countertrading, forfaiting, or cross-border factoring.

Countertrade

The term **countertrade** is a generic term for forms of trade that involve exchanging goods or services with other goods or services (in whole or in part) rather than with money. Countertrade covers a wide range of commercial mechanisms for reciprocal trade. It involves the exchange of goods or services to finance purchases rather than using cash. Barter is probably the oldest and best-known example of this. Other methods of countertrade have evolved to meet the requirements of a more sophisticated world economy. In its various forms, countertrade represents 10% to 15% of world trade.

Countertrade facilitates trade flows and investments into countries that have difficulty externalizing hard currency or that impose certain **counterpurchases** (or offset obligations) on sellers of products, projects, and technologies. It focuses on ways to create financing and investment solutions to mitigate political and commercial risk.

On the downside, countertrade exposes participants to several risks, such as pricing risk, the risk of handling unfamiliar goods, and the risk of receiving goods in poor condition. Pricing risk results from the fluctuation of exchange rates. Over a long-term countertrade contract, the value of the goods received may vary considerably in world currencies. Perhaps the most common problem experienced by countertraders is having to handle goods with which they are not familiar, leading to expense and liability involved in handling or reselling the goods. Countertraders also risk receiving goods in poor condition or of substandard quality—a risk shared by those who purchase goods and services.

Forfaiting

Forfaiting is a form of factoring that refers to the purchase of a receivable for capital goods, commodities, or a large project from an exporter in order for the exporter to obtain immediate cash. Forfaiting is typically without recourse, meaning that the forfaiter does not have the ability to go back to the exporter in the event of nonpayment.

A typical forfaiting transaction is for a credit period of at least 180 days, but can be up to seven years. Payment is most often guaranteed by the importer's bank because it is based on a debt instrument. These debt instruments, such as a promissory note, can be sold on the secondary market.

A forfaiter is a commercial bank or financing firm in a foreign country.

Cross-Border Factoring

A **factor** is a financial institution that buys a firm's short-term accounts receivable that result from the export of goods and services and collects on the accounts. Cross-border factoring is facilitated when there is a network of factors across borders. The exporter's domestic factor may contact factors in other countries to handle the collection of accounts receivables.

In both forfaiting and cross-border factoring, the amount received by the exporter is reduced by both a fixed and variable fee charged by the forfaiter or factor.

Foreign Currency Loans

Companies may borrow foreign currencies when financing transactions or operations in another country. The methods of handling foreign currency transactions are varied and complicated, but one aspect of such borrowing is important to know: the impact of exchange rate changes on the cost of borrowing.

The effective interest rate on a currency loan (the actual cost of borrowing) combines the nominal interest with the effects of changing exchange rates. If the borrowed currency depreciates during the term of the loan, the interest rate effectively decreases, because the amount owed will be less in terms of the weaker currency. The opposite happens when the foreign currency appreciates, making the loan effectively more costly.

Assume, for example, a U.S. company with operations in Germany wants to borrow euros when the USD is trading at par with the euro—1 USD purchases 1 euro. On day one of the loan's term, the €1,000,000 is equal to $1,000,000. So the U.S. company takes out a one year loan for €1,000,000 from a German bank at 5% per annum.

At the time the loan is made, the repayment amount in one year is calculated as follows:

Interest on Euro Loan

$1{,}000{,}000 \times (0.05) = €50{,}000$

Debt Repayment in Euros

$$\begin{aligned} \text{Principal} &= 1{,}000{,}000 \\ \text{Interest} &= 50{,}000 \\ \text{Total Repayment} &= 1{,}050{,}000 \end{aligned}$$

If the euro has appreciated against the USD to 1 USD/1.0526 euros (more USD are required to purchase 1 euro) after one year when the repayment of principal and interest is due, then the repayment amount will be:

Principal and Interest Repayment at $1.0526

€1,050,000 × 1.0526 = $1,105,230

The effective interest rate combines the interest expense with the currency fluctuation required to repay the loan.

Effective Interest Rate on Euro Loan

105,230 / 1,000,000 = 10.52%

The net loss on this transaction, for accounting purposes, is $55,230 ($1,050,000 − $1,105,230).

If the euro had depreciated in value, the effective interest rate would have been less than the nominal 5% rate making the repayment amount less than $1,050,000.

Transfer Pricing

Transfer pricing is the pricing of a product when transferring inventory from one subsidiary of a company to another. When the subsidiaries are in different countries, one objective of transfer pricing is to minimize the company's effective worldwide income tax obligations. To accomplish this, a company sets a higher transfer price (perhaps based on the market price) on goods shipped to the buying division in a country with a relatively higher tax rate. The company would set a lower transfer price (perhaps based on direct costs) on goods shipped to the buying division in a country with a relatively lower tax rate.

For example: If the income tax rate in the United States is 30% and the income tax rate in a foreign country is 40%, the company will use a higher transfer price when selling from the United States to the foreign country in order to tax the profit at the 30% rate. The higher cost to the foreign division will yield a lower profit and, therefore, decrease the taxable income at the 40% rate.

Other objectives take into consideration:

- U.S. tax laws limiting the amount of profit that can be transferred from the U.S. subsidiary to the foreign one
- Tariffs charged by foreign countries

The transfer prices used by a company are usually scrutinized by the taxing authorities in the countries involved in the transactions.

Transfer pricing has become an important component in global tax minimization. Creative transfer pricing approaches, applied in the context of acquisitions, divestitures, plant relocations, research and development activities, and global restructuring transactions, assist in the management and minimization of global tax rates.

Legal and Social Issues in Global Business

There are many legal challenges in international business, including disparities between international law and the laws of individual nations; continuing debate about free trade versus protectionism, particularly in regard to developing countries; and differing customs between countries.

Disparities Between International and Domestic Law

Different countries have different laws for how to conduct business. Some businesses may choose to do business in nations in which they can conduct certain activities not allowed in their own countries. For example, some firms have moved their businesses to Caribbean island nations that do not charge taxes, simply to avoid U.S. taxes.

The **U.S. Foreign Corrupt Practices Act (FCPA)** forbids an American company doing business overseas to pay bribes to a foreign government official for obtaining contracts or business. This can pose an ethical dilemma because it places the American company at a disadvantage in a country where bribes to government officials are the standard mode of doing business.

Free Trade versus Protectionism

Although the governments of most nations generally believe that free trade and open markets are avenues toward greater world wealth, the controversy over free trade versus protectionism continues within and between nations.

Many people in developed countries fear the loss of jobs as businesses move their production operations overseas to countries that have lower wage levels and fewer costly environmental and worker protection laws. Those in developing countries disagree with protectionist acts, such as agricultural subsidies. Some resent that they have been required, as developing nations, to be completely open to free trade while tariffs and subsidies still exist in developed nations, such as the United States and the European nations.

Among leaders of international organizations as well as heads of nations, there is disagreement about the pace of opening markets and privatizing businesses in emerging markets. Some leaders want to push developing nations to rapidly privatize businesses (private ownership as opposed to government ownership of the business) and to open markets to free trade. However, some believe that opening a market too soon or privatizing businesses in a country too quickly results in a lack of stability. They believe that businesses in a developing country need time to develop stable business practices before tariffs are removed.

Differing Customs

Businesses managing international offices also must deal with the customs, practices, and attitudes in the workplace that can differ greatly between countries. Common areas of disparity are vacation time, work schedule, benefits, employee supervision, and social position.

Threat of Expropriation

One significant risk of operating a business in a foreign country is the threat of expropriation. Certain countries may expropriate private company assets and, usually, expel the U.S. workers and managers. **Expropriation** is forceful confiscation and redistribution of private property outside of common laws, such as those of eminent domain. An international company should consider the potential risk of expropriation before operating in a foreign country.

Diversification of International Assets

Diversification means reducing risk by investing in a variety of assets. A diversified portfolio is one in which values do not move up and down in perfect synchrony. Thus, the diversified portfolio is less risky than the weighted average risk of total assets. More risk-averse companies seek to diversify to a greater extent in order to limit unexpected foreign currency gains and losses.

Knowledge Check: International Finance

The following questions are intended to help you check your understanding and recall of the material presented in this topic. They do not represent the type of questions that appear on the CMA exam.

Directions: Answer each question in the space provided. Correct answers and section references appear after the knowledge check questions.

1. Last year, import of a European product that cost €100 in Europe cost $125. This year, the same import, which has not changed price in euros, costs $140. Which of the following is true?
   - ☐ a. The exchange rate of USD for euros has increased from 0.80 to .71.
   - ☐ b. The exchange rate of USD for euros has decreased from 1.25 to 1.40.
   - ☐ c. The exchange rate of USD for euros has decreased from 0.71 to 0.80.
   - ☐ d. The exchange rate of USD for euros has increased from 1.25 to 1.40.

2. All of the following are risks specific to foreign investment **except**
   - ☐ a. political risk.
   - ☐ b. foreign currency fluctuation risk.
   - ☐ c. interest rate risk.
   - ☐ d. potential nationalization of businesses by the foreign country.

3. An American firm that sells products from all over the world wishes to import a collection of Chinese art. The Chinese art dealer needs cash in order to finance the shipment, but the American art dealer does not wish to pay for the imported art before it arrives. What can the American importer use to meet both her needs and those of the exporter?
   - ☐ a. Consignment agreement
   - ☐ b. Bankers' acceptance
   - ☐ c. Sight draft
   - ☐ d. Letter of credit

4. An American company has three foreign subsidiaries: X, Y, and Z. The corporate income tax is 45% in X's country, 35% in Y's country, and 40% in Z's country. How can the American company use transfer pricing to improve its combined after-tax earnings?
   - ☐ a. By increasing the price that X charges Y
   - ☐ b. By decreasing the price that Y charges Z
   - ☐ c. By reducing the price that X charges Y
   - ☐ d. No combination of increases or reductions in transfer prices

Knowledge Check Answers: International Finance

1. Last year, import of a European product that cost €100 in Europe cost $125. This year, the same import, which has not changed price in euros, costs $140. Which of the following is true? [See **Currency Fluctuations**.]
   - ☐ a. The exchange rate of USD for euros has increased from 0.80 to .71.
   - ☐ b. The exchange rate of USD for euros has decreased from 1.25 to 1.40.
   - ☐ c. The exchange rate of USD for euros has decreased from 0.71 to 0.80.
   - ☒ d. The exchange rate of USD for euros has increased from 1.25 to 1.40.

2. All of the following are risks specific to foreign investment **except** [See **Risk and Rate of Return for Foreign Investment**.]
   - ☐ a. political risk.
   - ☐ b. foreign currency fluctuation risk.
   - ☒ c. interest rate risk.
   - ☐ d. potential nationalization of businesses by the foreign country.

   Interest rate risks are not unique to foreign investments. In fact, diversification in different countries can minimize interest rate risk.

3. An American firm that sells products from all over the world wishes to import a collection of Chinese art. The Chinese art dealer needs cash in order to finance the shipment, but the American art dealer does not wish to pay for the imported art before it arrives. What can the American importer use to meet both her needs and those of the exporter? [See **Financing and Paying for International Trade**.]
   - ☐ a. Consignment agreement
   - ☒ b. Bankers' acceptance
   - ☐ c. Sight draft
   - ☐ d. Letter of credit

4. An American company has three foreign subsidiaries: X, Y, and Z. The corporate income tax is 45% in X's country, 35% in Y's country, and 40% in Z's country. How can the American company use transfer pricing to improve its combined after-tax earnings? [See **Methods of Financing Foreign Trade**.]
   - ☐ a. By increasing the price that X charges Y
   - ☐ b. By decreasing the price that Y charges Z
   - ☒ c. By reducing the price that X charges Y
   - ☐ d. No combination of increases or reductions in transfer prices

Practice Questions: Corporate Finance

Directions: This sampling of questions is designed to emulate actual exam questions. Read each question and write your response on another sheet of paper. See the "Answers to Section Practice Questions" section at the end of this book to assess your response. Validate or improve the answer you wrote. For a more robust selection of practice questions, access the **Online Test Bank** at www.wileycma.com.

Question 2B1-AT05
Topic: Risk and Return

Using the capital asset pricing model (CAPM), the required rate of return for a firm with a beta of 1.25 when the market return is 14% and the risk-free rate is 6% is

- a. 7.5%
- b. 14.0%
- c. 16.0%
- d. 17.5%

Question 2B1-AT06
Topic: Risk and Return

The expected rate of return for the stock of Cornhusker Enterprises is 20%, with a standard deviation of 15%. The expected rate of return for the stock of Mustang Associates is 10%, with a standard deviation of 9%. The stock that would be considered riskier is

- a. Mustang, because the coefficient of variation is higher.
- b. Cornhusker, because the standard deviation is higher.
- c. Cornhusker, because the coefficient of variation is lower.
- d. Mustang, because the return is lower.

Question 2B2-LS04
Topic: Long-Term Financial Management

Which of the following statements about correlation and return variability **best** describes a portfolio with a limited number of stocks representing different industries?

- a. Low correlation and low portfolio return variability
- b. Low correlation and high portfolio return variability
- c. High correlation and high portfolio return variability
- d. High correlation and low portfolio return variability

Question 2B2-LS05

Topic: Long-Term Financial Management

If a firm's goal is to keep portfolio risk low, the **best** strategy would be to include

- ☐ a. investments with low betas and highly correlated returns.
- ☐ b. investments with high betas and low correlated returns.
- ☐ c. diversified investments with high betas.
- ☐ d. diversified investments with low betas.

Question 2B2-CQ06

Topic: Long-Term Financial Management

Cox Company has sold 1,000 shares of $100 par, 8% preferred stock at an issue price of $92 per share. Stock issue costs were $5 per share. Cox pays taxes at the rate of 40%. What is Cox's cost of preferred stock capital?

- ☐ a. 8.00%
- ☐ b. 8.25%
- ☐ c. 8.70%
- ☐ d. 9.20%

Question 2B2-CQ07

Topic: Long-Term Financial Management

Bull & Bear Investment Banking is working with the management of Clark Inc. in order to take the company public in an initial public offering. Selected financial information for Clark is as shown next.

Long-term debt (8% interest rate)	$10,000,000
Common equity: Par value ($1 per share)	3,000,000
Additional paid-in capital	24,000,000
Retained earnings	6,000,000
Total assets	55,000,000
Net income	3,750,000
Dividend (annual)	1,500,000

If public companies in Clark's industry are trading at 12 times earnings, what is the estimated value per share of Clark?

- ☐ a. $9.00
- ☐ b. $12.00
- ☐ c. $15.00
- ☐ d. $24.00

Question 2B2-LS13

Topic: Long-Term Financial Management

A long-term call option to buy common stock directly from a corporation is a

- ☐ a. forward contract.
- ☐ b. warrant.
- ☐ c. convertible security.
- ☐ d. futures contract.

Question 2B2-LS15

Topic: Long-Term Financial Management

An analyst observes a 15-year, 7% option-free bond with semiannual coupons. The required yield on this bond was 7%, but suddenly it drops to 6.5%. The price of this bond

- ☐ a. will increase.
- ☐ b. will decrease.
- ☐ c. will stay the same.
- ☐ d. cannot be determined without additional information.

Question 2B2-LS23

Topic: Long-Term Financial Management

What is the after-tax cost of debt for a 6% interest-bearing bond at an anticipated tax rate of 38%?

- ☐ a. 3.80%
- ☐ b. 3.72%
- ☐ c. 4.40%
- ☐ d. 6.00%

Question 2B2-CQ09

Topic: Long-Term Financial Management

The Hatch Sausage Company is projecting an annual dividend growth rate for the foreseeable future of 9%. The most recent dividend paid was $3.00 per share. New common stock can be issued at $36 per share. Using the constant growth model, what is the approximate cost of capital for retained earnings?

- ☐ a. 9.08%
- ☐ b. 17.33%
- ☐ c. 18.08%
- ☐ d. 19.88%

Question 2B2-CQ10
Topic: Long-Term Financial Management

Angela Company's capital structure consists entirely of long-term debt and common equity. The cost of capital for each component is shown next.

Long-term debt	8% before tax
Common equity	15%

Angela pays taxes at a rate of 40%. If Angela's weighted average cost of capital is 10.41%, what proportion of the company's capital structure is in the form of long-term debt?

- ☐ a. 34%
- ☐ b. 45%
- ☐ c. 55%
- ☐ d. 66%

Question 2B2-CQ15
Topic: Long-Term Financial Management

Thomas Company's capital structure consists of 30% long-term debt, 25% preferred stock, and 45% common equity. The cost of capital for each component is shown next.

Long-term debt	8% before tax
Preferred stock	11%
Common equity	15%

If Thomas pays taxes at the rate of 40%, what is the company's after-tax weighted average cost of capital?

- ☐ a. 7.14%
- ☐ b. 9.84%
- ☐ c. 10.94%
- ☐ d. 11.90%

Question 2B3-AT13
Topic: Raising Capital

Arch Inc. has 200,000 shares of common stock outstanding. Net income for the recently ended fiscal year was $500,000, and the stock has a price/earnings ratio of 8. The board of directors has just declared a three-for-two stock split. For an investor who owns 100 shares of stock before the split, the approximate value (rounded to the nearest dollar) of the investment in Arch stock immediately after the split is

- ☐ a. $2,000
- ☐ b. $1,333
- ☐ c. $3,000
- ☐ d. $4,000

Question 2B4-CQ08

Topic: Working Capital Management

Shown next are selected data from Fortune Company's most recent financial statements.

Marketable securities	$10,000
Accounts receivable	60,000
Inventory	25,000
Supplies	5,000
Accounts payable	40,000
Short-term debt payable	10,000
Accruals	5,000

What is Fortune's net working capital?

- ☐ a. $35,000
- ☐ b. $45,000
- ☐ c. $50,000
- ☐ d. $80,000

Question 2B4-CQ10

Topic: Working Capital Management

The Rolling Stone Corporation, an entertainment ticketing service, is considering the following means of managing cash flow for the corporation:

Lockbox system. A lockbox system would cost $25 per month for each of its 170 banks and would result in interest savings of $5,240 per month.

Drafts. Drafts would be used to pay for ticket refunds based on 4,000 refunds per month at a cost of $2.00 per draft, which would result in gross interest savings of $6,500 per month.

Electronic transfer. Items over $25,000 would be transferred electronically; it is estimated that 700 items of this type would be made each month at a cost of $18 each, which would result in increased interest earnings of $14,000 per month.

Which of these methods of speeding cash flow should Rolling Stone Corporation adopt?

- ☐ a. Lockbox and electronic transfer only
- ☐ b. Electronic transfer only
- ☐ c. Lockbox, drafts, and electronic transfer
- ☐ d. Lockbox only

Question 2B6-AT14

Topic: International Finance

A U.S.-based infant clothing company, Tiny Tot, is interested in importing fabric from China. Which of the following should Tiny Tot arrange first for the Chinese company to ship the merchandise?

- ☐ a. Bill of lading
- ☐ b. Time draft
- ☐ c. Letter of credit
- ☐ d. Sight draft

Question 2B6-AT18

Topic: International Finance

An appreciation of the U.S. dollar against the Japanese yen would

- ☐ a. make U.S. goods more expensive to Japanese consumers.
- ☐ b. increase the translated earnings of U.S. subsidiaries domiciled in Japan.
- ☐ c. increase the cost of buying supplies for U.S. firms.
- ☐ d. make travel in Japan more expensive for U.S. citizens.

Question 2B6-AT19

Topic: International Finance

Technocrat Inc., located in Belgium, currently manufactures products at its domestic plant and exports them to the United States, since production is less expensive at home. The company is considering the possibility of setting up a plant in the United States. All of the following factors would encourage the company to consider direct foreign investment in the U.S. **except** the

- ☐ a. expectation of more stringent trade restrictions by the United States.
- ☐ b. depreciation of the U.S. dollar against Belgium's currency.
- ☐ c. changing demand for the company's exports to the United States due to exchange rate fluctuations.
- ☐ d. widening of the gap in production costs between locations in the United States and Belgium.

To further assess your understanding of the concepts and calculations covered in Part 2, Section B: Corporate Finance, practice with the **Online Test Bank** for this section. **REMINDER:** See the "Answers to Section Practice Questions" section at the end of this book.

SECTION C

Decision Analysis

Decision making is a key activity in every organization. In any business, a wide variety of decisions have to be made on a daily basis. Decisions may range from small to large scale in scope and can be individual decisions or group decisions. Furthermore, a given decision can have short- and/or long-term consequences in regard to the resources involved in reaching the decision as well as the financial impact.

Management accountants often are called on to provide critical data used in the decision-making process. This section reviews fundamental information that management accountants need to know about the decision-making process, the importance of relevant cost and revenue data, the use of cost/volume/profit, and marginal analyses.

Management decision making also involves the setting of prices for goods and services. The current competitive, global environment demands careful setting and managing of output prices. Management accountants assist price setters by providing cost information for short-run and long-run pricing, market-based pricing, cost-based pricing, target pricing, target costing, and target rate of return pricing. Management accountants also help price setters apply the laws of supply and demand to pricing decisions.

Risk management is a required component of decision making and pricing. The objective of risk management is to reduce risk to an acceptable level. The management accountant often is involved in the assessment and management of risk. In particular, management accountants help identify threats to the organization and their probabilities, controls against the threats and their effectiveness, and the losses incurred by not preventing or detecting threats prior to their occurrence.

TOPIC 1

Cost/Volume/Profit Analysis

COST/VOLUME/PROFIT (CVP) ANALYSIS is a method for analyzing the interrelationships among total cost, volume, and profits in an organization. CVP analysis examines the interactions among the:

- Selling prices of products and services
- Sales volume (the level of activity)
- Per-unit variable costs
- Total fixed costs
- Mix of products and services sold

Managers can apply CVP analysis data in a wide variety of decision-making situations, such as:

- Raising or lowering prices for existing products and services
- Introducing a new product or service
- Setting prices for new products and services
- Expanding product and service markets
- Deciding whether to replace an existing piece of equipment
- Deciding whether to make or buy a product or service

READ the Learning Outcome Statements (LOS) for this topic as found in Appendix B and then study the concepts and calculations presented here to be sure you understand the content you could be tested on in the CMA exam.

CVP Terminology and Assumptions

Cost/volume/profit analysis uses certain terms in specific ways:

Cost generally refers to a resource expended to achieve a specific objective.

A **cost driver** is any factor that affects costs. A change in a cost driver will result in a change in the total cost of a related cost object. Examples of cost drivers are

275

the number of units manufactured or the number of packages shipped. In CVP analysis, the cost driver normally used is units produced or sold.

A **cost object** is anything for which cost data is accumulated. Products, product lines, customers, jobs, and organizational business units are examples.

A **fixed cost** is a cost that remains constant, in total, regardless of changes in the level of activity within a relevant range. In other words, fixed costs are a function of time rather than activity. Fixed costs have to be changed by management action. Fixed costs either are committed, facility-related costs, such as rent and depreciation resulting from prior management decisions, or discretionary (managed or budgeted) fixed costs, such as advertising, indirect labor or selling, and administrative salaries set by management during the annual budgeting process.

A **variable cost** is a cost that varies, in total, in direct proportion to changes in the level of activity within a relevant range. In other words, variable costs are a function of activity. Variable costs include: direct materials; direct labor; variable overhead, such as utilities and supplies; variable selling costs, such as shipping and sales commissions; and variable administrative costs, such as royalties paid for the use of a patent.

The **relevant range** is the range of activity within which the variable and fixed cost functions remain valid.

Revenues are inflows of assets received in exchange for products or services. Revenues are the sum of the price multiplied by the number of units sold for each product.

A **revenue driver** is a factor that affects revenue, such as advertising and promotion costs, the selling prices of units, or the number of units sold.

Total costs (or total expenses) are made up of total variable costs and total fixed costs. Total variable costs are the sum of unit variable cost multiplied by the number of units sold for each product. Total costs are represented as:

Total Costs = Total Variable Costs + Total Fixed Costs

Operating income is total revenues from operations less total costs from operations. This excludes interest expense and income taxes. Operating income generally is represented as:

Operating Income = Total Operating Revenues − Total Operating Costs

Companies generally exclude financing costs from operating income for analytical purposes, because such costs are not related to operations (i.e., nonoperating).

Net operating income is the after-tax operating income for a period. Net operating income is represented as:

Net Operating Income = Operating Income − Operating Income Taxes

Operating income taxes are calculated by taking the relevant tax rate and multiplying it by operating income. Therefore, net operating income is also calculated as:

Net Operating Income = (1 − Relevant Tax Rate) (Operating Income)

Activity level (also known as output level, measure of output, or output) refers to the number of units produced or sold during a period. Activity level nomenclature can vary across industries. For example, instead of units, airlines use passenger miles, hospitals may use patient days or beds occupied, hotels use rooms occupied, and colleges and universities use student credit hours.

Four assumptions underlie CVP analysis. They are:

1. *Linearity.* Revenue and cost functions are linear over the relevant range.
2. *Certainty.* The parameters (prices, unit variable costs, and fixed costs) are known or can be reasonably estimated.
3. *A single product or a defined product mix.* A defined product mix allows the analyst to look at a hypothetical weighted average product.
4. *Production is equal to sales.* This is the critical limiting assumption. The assumption is that there is no change to the finished goods inventory account. The use of variable costing and a contribution margin approach to operating income determination relieves the need for this assumption.

Fixed and Variable Cost Behavior

Cost behavior generally refers to how a cost will react to changes in business activity levels. As the business output changes, a given cost may rise, fall, or remain constant.

A key assumption in CVP analysis is that costs can be classified as either fixed or variable with respect to activity level—the amount of goods produced or services provided by a company. Figure 2C-1 summarizes how fixed and variable costs behave in total and on a per-unit basis within the relevant range. Note in the figure how fixed and variable costs behave differently if they are viewed as total costs or on a per-unit basis.

Figure 2C-1 Fixed and Variable Cost Behavior Within Relevant Range

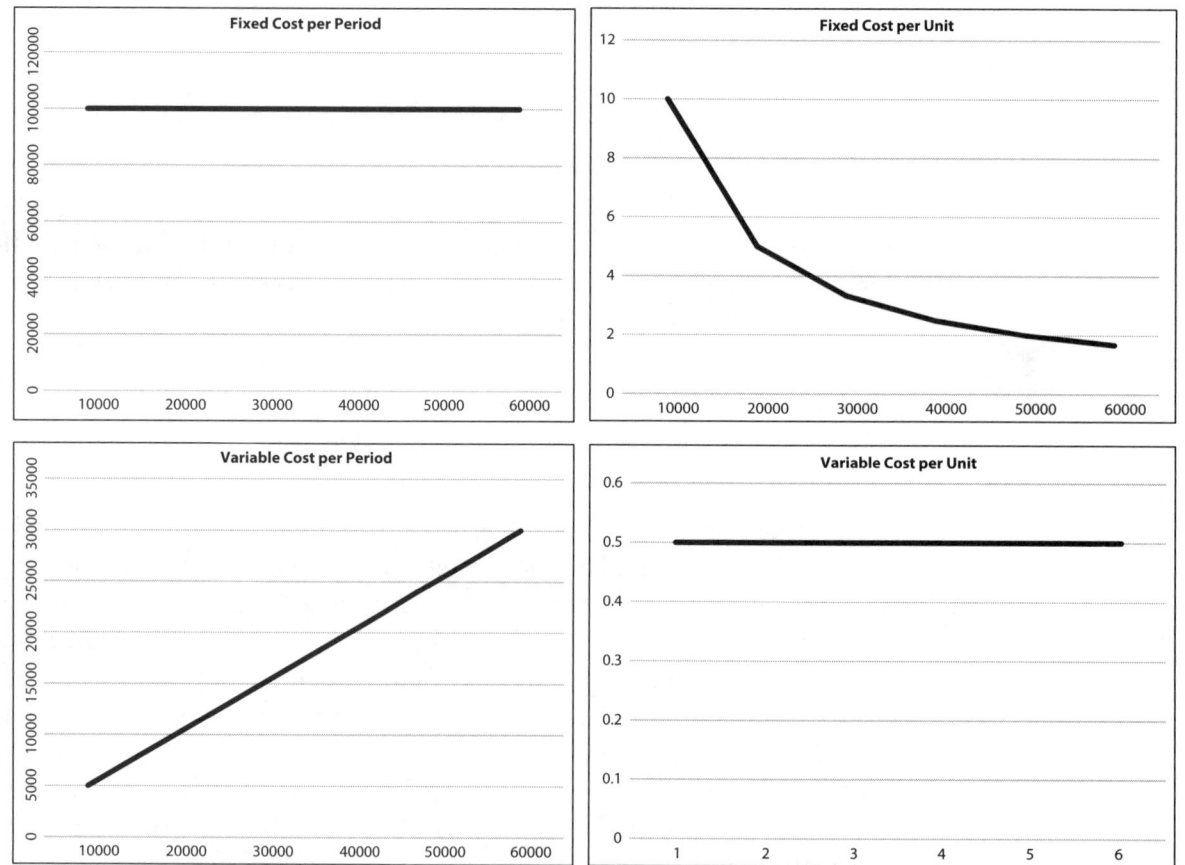

Examples of costs that are fixed irrespective of the environment in which they are incurred (e.g., manufacturing, retail, or service) include insurance premiums, rental charges, property taxes, salaries, and advertising.

In manufacturing environments, variable costs include direct materials, direct labor, variable overhead, sales commissions, shipping costs, and royalties. For a merchandising business, variable costs include costs of goods sold, sales commissions, and some billing costs. In a service environment such as a hospital, variable costs include the cost of prescription drugs, hospital supplies, and patient meals.

Fixed and Variable Classifications Over Time

The classifications of costs as fixed and variable can be affected by the time horizon being considered. In other words, some variable costs may be reclassified as fixed. Given an extended period of time, a fixed cost, although it is not variable, may change.

Generally, these principles apply to fixed and variable cost classifications over time:

- The shorter the time period, the higher the percentage of total costs that can be viewed as fixed.
- The longer the time horizon, the more costs that can be viewed as variable.

- Overall, whether a cost is fixed or variable is often a function of:
  - Relevant range
  - Time frame
  - The given decision situation

The example in Figure 2C-2 further illustrates fixed and variable cost behavior.

Figure 2C-2 Fixed and Variable Cost Behavior

	Total Cost at 10,000 Units	Cost per Unit	Total Cost at 25,000 Units	Cost per Unit	Total Cost at 50,000 Units	Cost per Unit
Direct materials	$16,000	$1.60	$40,000	$1.60	$80,000	$1.60
Direct labor	25,000	2.50	62,500	2.50	125,000	2.50
Distribution	13,000	1.30	32,500	1.30	65,000	1.30
Depreciation	50,000	5.00	50,000	2.00	80,000	1.60
Rent	25,000	2.50	25,000	1.00	40,000	0.80

The per-unit costs for materials and labor are fixed over the relevant range. Total costs for depreciation and rent are fixed whether the company produces one unit or 25,000 units. However, when sales increase beyond the plant's capacity of 25,000 units, the company would need to add on to its production line. Total and per unit costs would increase as additional equipment and space would be required.

The following set of facts illustrates the key points in this topic.

Company Special K sells a single product for a price of $200/unit. Currently, Special K sells 75 units per month. Here is the cost structure: The variable costs are $150/unit, and the fixed costs are $2,000/month.

This set of facts can be represented in an income statement. Special K chooses to cast its income statement in a contribution format. This format subtracts all variable expenses from revenue and calls the difference the contribution margin. Then all fixed costs, whether manufacturing, selling, general, or administrative, are treated as period costs and subtracted from the contribution margin to determine the operating income. See Figure 2C-3.

Figure 2C-3 Special K Contribution Income Statement at 75 Units

Sales	$15,000	$200
Variable costs	11,250	150
Contribution margin	$3,750	$ 50
Fixed costs	2,000	
Operating income	$1,750	

CVP (Break-Even) Graph

Another way this set of data could be represented is in a cost/value/profit (CVP) graph of total revenues, total costs, and output levels, as shown in Figure 2C-4. This

Figure 2C-4 CVP Graph of Total Revenues, Total Costs, and Units Sold

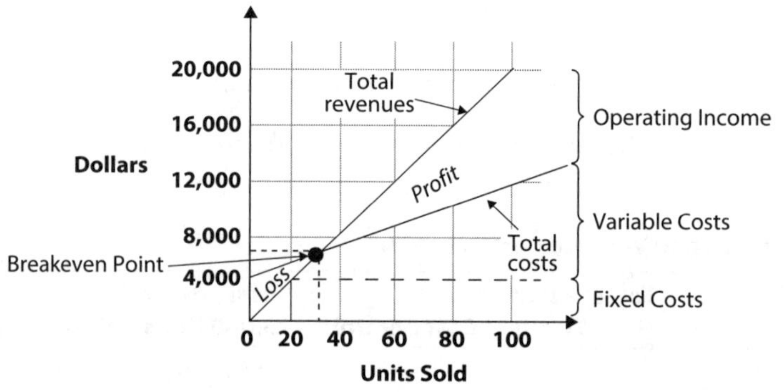

is more frequently referred to as a break-even graph. Revenue is plotted on the graph as a function of the number of units sold. Due to the linearity assumption discussed earlier, the revenue line is a straight line that starts from the origin. Next there is a total cost line, which represents the sum of both variable and fixed costs. Most frequently, fixed costs are at the bottom of the stack, and variable costs are stacked on top of the fixed expenses. If the graph is drawn carefully to scale, answers to a number of useful questions can be determined directly. The value on the horizontal axis at which the revenue and total cost lines intersect is known as the *break-even point*, because, if revenue and total cost are equal, operating income must be zero. To the right of the break-even level of units sold is the profit wedge; to the left of the break-even level of units sold is the loss wedge.

Essentially, the income statement and the CVP graph convey the same information to the reader at the current level of activity. However, the CVP graph conveys operating income information at other levels of units sold.

The Single-Product Firm

Next a set of symbols is used to convey these relationships in equation form.

Two variables are expressed in dollars per period. They are:

F = fixed costs
I = income (operating)

Two variables are expressed in dollars per unit. They are:

P = price per unit
V = variable cost per unit

One variable is expressed in units per period. That is:

Q = quantity

Income is the difference between revenue and total cost. Total cost is composed of variable cost and fixed costs. Because both revenue and variable cost are functions of quantity sold, then it must be true that:

$$I = [(P - V) \times Q] - F$$

This equation is helpful in predicting operating income given values for all of the other variables. But the equation also can be useful in determining the quantity, selling price, or variable cost per unit that will satisfy a given set of conditions. Some what-if questions that may be of interest are discussed next.

Companies often want to determine how many items they need to sell in order to realize some specific profit objective. Turning the previous expression around to solve for Q results in:

$$Q = \frac{(I + F)}{(P - V)}$$

Assume that the target operating income level is $2,000 per month. Substituting the values results in the conclusion that 80 units per month would need to be sold to achieve that operating income level. The difference between the selling price and the variable cost per unit is used so frequently that it is given the name *contribution margin per unit* or *unit contribution margin*. Simply dividing the sum of the fixed cost and the target operating income by the contribution margin per unit provides the answer to the question: 80 units per month. Another way to think of this result is that each additional unit sold contributes an additional $50 to the contribution margin and to the bottom line. Since it is already known that the operating income level at 75 units sold per month is $1,750 per month, it can be reasoned that an additional $250 of operating income per month is needed to reach the $2,000-per-month operating income level. That additional $250 per month can be achieved by selling 5 additional units per month. Therefore, the original 75 plus the additional 5 confirms that 80 units per month will generate the target operating income goal.

Companies may also want to know how many units they must sell in order to break even. Breaking even, of course, means simply that operating income is zero. To determine the answer, set income, I, to zero; the equation simplifies to $Q_{BE} = F / (P - V)$. The result is 40 units per month, given the set of facts. Q_{BE} is the break-even quantity or break-even point.

Rarely is the management of a business satisfied to simply break even. The goal is to earn a profit and, frequently, to try to maximize the level of profit within the constraints of the firm's capacity and the demand for the product. Therefore, the more general expression for quantity, Q, given in the previous key formula is the more useful expression.

Another question of interest is the price that will achieve a desired result. Turning the original expression around to solve for price per unit, P, produces this result:

$$P = V + \frac{F+1}{Q}$$

This result makes intuitive sense. The price needs to recover the variable cost to make and sell the item and, additionally, to recover the fixed costs and target operating income spread over the number of units expected to be sold.

Multiple Products and Units Are Not Meaningful

There are many environments where a firm sells more than one product. A retailer can have tens of thousands of different products, or stockkeeping units (SKUs). For example, a hardware store sells items as small as screws and as large as snowblowers. In cases such as this, the sum of the number of units sold is not very meaningful, but the break-even concept is still important. Management still needs to know what level of sales dollars are needed to break even or to hit a target operating income level. To determine this, we need to know the contribution margin ratio for the business. The **contribution margin ratio** is determined by dividing the contribution margin dollars by the sales dollars or by knowing and manipulating the markup rule by which the business establishes its selling prices based on the cost of its merchandise. The data in the income statement (Figure 2C-3) show the contribution margin ratio is .25, or 25% ($3,750/$15,000). Alternatively, adding one-third of the purchase cost (as markup) to the purchase cost of an item results in a 25% contribution margin ratio,

Again, a little bit of algebraic manipulation of the definition of Income in an earlier key box provides the generic result that

$$R = \frac{(F+I)}{CMR}$$

where
R = revenue dollars per period
CMR = contribution margin ratio

and the special case result that

$$R_{BE} = \frac{F}{CMR}$$

where

R_{BE} = revenue dollars per period to break even

Assume the retail store has fixed cost of $2,000 per month and a 25% contribution margin ratio. If the goal is to generate $2,000 of operating income per month, then the required sales level must be $16,000 per month. The level of sales for break-even must be $8,000 per month. Note that any of the calculated results could be put into a contribution format income statement in order to prove that the solution in fact works. This finding provides good general advice for the CMA exam itself; if time permits, subject your answers to quick double-checks.

The Effect of Income Taxes

So far in these examples a real-world reality has been omitted—income taxes. If some of the complexities of the Internal Revenue Code, such as tax credits and progressive tax rates, are ignored, the effect of taxes can be incorporated into the model fairly simply. A profit objective is logically expressed on an after-tax basis. Earlier it was shown that net operating profit is simply: Operating Profit × (1 − Tax Rate). Now turn that expression around:

$$\text{Operating Profit} = \frac{\text{Net Operating Profit}}{(1 - \text{Tax Rate})}$$

The existence of income taxes should not change the break-even point for a firm. A zero operating profit before tax should always be the equivalent of a zero operating profit after tax. The easiest way to deal with a nonzero target for net operating profit is simply to determine the equivalent before-tax operating profit and then determine the sales quantity that would satisfy that objective.

In the original example, Special K has a 40% tax rate. The after-tax profit objective is to earn $1,500 after tax. Using the relationship in the immediately preceding key box, the objective should be satisfied by before-tax operating profit of $2,500 ($1,500/.60 = $2,500). The units that must be sold to produce operating income of $2,500 is 90. Prove this result by creating a contribution margin income statement. Contribution margin should be $4,500, and operating profit should be $2,500. Now two more lines are added to the income statement: The first is for income taxes, and the calculation is $2,500 × .4 = $1,000. The second line is for net operating profit, which is $2,500 − $1,000 = $1,500, which is indeed the goal.

Multiple Products and Units Are Meaningful

The next example concerns CVP analysis in a firm with multiple products and aggregated units sold are meaningful. We assume the product mix remains unchanged to simplify the analysis. Consider the income statement shown in

Figure 2C-5 Special K Multi-Product Contribution Margin Statement

	Product KA			Product KB			Total		
	Units	Per Unit	Amount	Units	Per Unit	Amount	Units	Per Unit	Amount
Sales	45	$180	$8,100	30	$230	$6,900	75		$15,000
Variable cost		128	5,760		183	5,490			11,250
Contrib. margin		$52	$2,340		$47	$1,410		$50	$3,750

Figure 2C-3. But now, assume that Special K sells two products, KA with a unit contribution margin of $52 and KB with a unit contribution margin of $47. The mix of the sales of the two products is 60% KA and 40% KB.

Figure 2C-5 shows that the weighted average unit contribution margin is $50. This, of course, could have been calculated simply as

$$(0.6 \times \$52) + (0.4 \times \$47) = \$50$$

The unit contribution margin of each product is multiplied by its sales mix weight, and all of those results are summed to determine the weighted average unit contribution margin.

This calculation makes it possible to determine the quantity to hit a given target income or to determine the quantity to break even. Once this quantity is known, the quantity of each product to be sold is determined by the total quantity multiplied by the product's sales mix weight.

LOS
§2.C.1.h

Multiple Products and Income Taxes

We now consider two concepts in a single example. Special K anticipates no change in its sales mix. It still has a 40% tax rate, and it desires to earn an operating profit of $1,800 a month after tax. The company needs to determine the quantity it must sell of Product KA and of Product KB, and the total quantity of both Products it must sell to achieve net operating profit of $1,800.

The first step is to determine the level of pretax operating profit that must be achieved.

$$\text{Operating profit} = \$1,800 / (1 - .40) = \$3,000$$

The next step is to determine the quantity that needs to be sold to earn an operating profit of $3,000 from the relationship.

Q = (F + I) / Unit Contribution Margin = ($2,000/Month + $3,000/Month)/$50 of CM/Unit = 100 Units/Month

Sixty percent of those units (60) must be Product KA, and 40% (40) must be Product KB. Time permitting on the CMA exam, you could construct the income statement to demonstrate that this formula, indeed, works. See Figure 2C-6.

Figure 2C-6 Special K Multi-Product Income Statement

	Product KA		Product KB		Total	
	Units	Amount	Units	Amount	Units	Amount
Sales	60	$10,800	40	$9,200	100	$20,000
Variable cost		7,680		7,320		15,000
Contrib. margin		$3,120		$1,880		$5,000
Fixed cost						2,000
Operating income						$3,000
Income taxes						1,200
Net operating income						$1,800

Margin of Safety

The **margin of safety** defines how far the firm is beyond its break-even point at the current volume level. The margin of safety can be calculated and expressed in sales units, sales dollars, or as a percentage. Using the original data for Special K, the company is operating at the level of 75 units per month or $15,000 of sales per month. The margin of safety expressed in units is 35 units per month (75 less 40). The margin of safety expressed in sales dollars is $7,000 per month ($15,000 less $8,000). Finally, the margin of safety ratio is 46.7% of current sales.

The following two key formulas are important for the CMA examination.

$$\text{Margin of Safety (Dollars)} = \text{Planned Sales} - \text{Break-Even Sales}$$

$$\text{Margin of Safety Ratio (or Percentage)} = \frac{\text{Margin of Safety}}{\text{Planned Sales}}$$

Sensitivity Analysis and CVP

Sensitivity analysis involves asking "what if?" regarding one or more changes in values of the key variables of price, quantity, unit variable cost, and fixed costs to determine the effect on operating profit. Frequently, sensitivity analysis involves changing the value of a single variable while holding the values for all other variables constant and observing the effect on operating profit. After this has been done for each of the variables, the analyst gets a sense as to which variables are the most important ones. Those important variables are then the ones deserving of getting the greatest attention in refining the estimates of their values in the future. Sensitivity analysis can greatly benefit capital budgeting.

However, in CVP analysis, it is likely that all four of the variables will prove to be important and worthy of management's best efforts in estimating their future values: price, variable cost per unit, sales quantity, and fixed costs.

The next topic will demonstrate how CVP analysis can be effectively applied to situations that are frequently encountered in the business world.

Knowledge Check:
Cost/Volume/Profit Analysis

The following questions are intended to help you check your understanding and recall of the material presented in this topic. They do not represent the type of questions that appear on the CMA exam.

Directions: Answer each question in the space provided. Correct answers and section references appear after the knowledge check questions.

1. In the CVP model, total revenues and total costs
   - ☐ a. remain constant within a limited range of output.
   - ☐ b. increase and decrease inversely to changes in activity level.
   - ☐ c. increase and decrease proportionately to changes in activity level.
   - ☐ d. increase at a linear rate within a relevant range of activity.

2. All of the following statements accurately describe a break-even point **except**
   - ☐ a. operating income is zero.
   - ☐ b. total revenues and total costs are equal.
   - ☐ c. above break-even signifies profits; below break-even signifies loss.
   - ☐ d. below break-even signifies profits; above break-even signifies loss.

Match the following terms with their description.

3. _____ Relevant range	a.	How a cost will react to changes in business activity levels
4. _____ Activity level	b.	The activity range over which the variable and fixed cost functions remain valid
5. _____ Cost behavior		
6. _____ Contribution margin	c.	Relative proportions of products or services sold
7. _____ Sales mix	d.	Number of units produced and sold
	e.	Amount remaining from sales revenue after variable expenses are deducted

8. Given fixed costs of $8,000, variable costs of $100, and a unit contribution margin of $200, how many units must be sold to reach a target operating income of $34,000?

   ☐ a. 130
   ☐ b. 140
   ☐ c. 210
   ☐ d. 260

Questions 9 and 10 refer to these data:

Sale revenues (20,000 units)	$1,200,000
Less variable costs	900,000
Contribution margin	300,000
Less fixed costs	240,000
Operating income	$60,000

9. Calculate the company's contribution margin ratio and its complement, the variable cost ratio.

10. Compute the company's break-even point in both unit and sales dollars.

Knowledge Check Answers: Cost/Volume/Profit Analysis

1. In the CVP model, total revenues and total costs [See *CVP Terminology and Assumptions*.]
   - ☐ a. remain constant within a limited range of output.
   - ☐ b. increase and decrease inversely to changes in activity level.
   - ☐ c. increase and decrease proportionately to changes in activity level.
   - ☒ d. increase at a linear rate within a relevant range of activity.

2. All of the following statements accurately describe a break-even point **except** [See *The Single-Product Firm*.]
   - ☐ a. operating income is zero.
   - ☐ b. total revenues and total costs are equal.
   - ☐ c. above break-even signifies profits; below break-even signifies loss.
   - ☒ d. below break-even signifies profits; above break-even signifies loss.

Match the following terms with their description.

3. __b__ Relevant range	a.	How a cost will react to changes in business activity levels
4. __d__ Activity level	b.	The activity range over which the variable and fixed cost functions remain valid
5. __a__ Cost behavior		
6. __e__ Contribution margin	c.	Relative proportions of products or services sold
7. __c__ Sales mix	d.	Number of units produced and sold
	e.	Amount remaining from sales revenue after variable expenses are deducted

8. Given fixed costs of $8,000, variable costs of $100, and a unit contribution margin of $200, how many units must be sold to reach a target operating income of $34,000? [See *The Single-Product Firm*.]

- ☐ a. 130
- ☐ b. 140
- ☑ c. 210
- ☐ d. 260

To calculate the number of units needed to achieve a target profit, use this formula:

$Q = (F + I)/(P - V)$

$Q = (\$8,000 + \$34,000) / \$200 = 210$ units

Questions 9 and 10 refer to these data:

Sale revenues (20,000 units)	$1,200,000
Less variable costs	900,000
Contribution margin	300,000
Less fixed costs	240,000
Operating income	$60,000

9. Calculate the company's contribution margin ratio and variable cost ratio. [See *Multiple Products and Units Are Meaningful*.]

   Contribution Margin Ratio = Contribution Margin / Sales

   Contribution Margin Ratio = $300,000 / $1,200,000 = 25%

   Variable Cost Ratio = Variable Costs / Sales

   Variable Cost Ratio = $900,000 / $1,200,000 = 75%

10. Compute the company's break-even point in both unit and sales dollars. [See *The Single-Product Firm*.]

    Break-Even Point in Units = Fixed Costs / Unit Contribution Margin

    Fixed Costs = $240,000

    Unit Contribution Margin = Total Contribution Margin / Number of Units

    Unit Contribution Margin = $300,000 / 20,000 Units = $15

    Break-Even Point in Units = $240,000 / $15 = 16,000 Units

    Break-Even Point in Dollars = Fixed Costs / Contribution Margin Ratio

    Fixed Costs = $240,000

    Contribution Margin Ratio = Contribution Margin / Sales

    Contribution Margin Ratio = $300,000 / $1,200,000 = 0.25

    Break-Even Point in Dollars = $240,000 / 0.25 = $960,000

TOPIC 2

Marginal Analysis

DECISION MAKING INVOLVES A CHOICE between at least two alternatives. In some situations, there are several alternatives to consider. But other decisions may require choosing between only two alternatives, one of which may be the status quo. Regardless of the number or types of options, the costs and benefits of the various alternatives need to be evaluated during the decision process.

Marginal analysis (also known as incremental or differential analysis) is a method of analyzing short-term decisions. It emphasizes incremental cost increases or decreases rather than total costs and benefits associated with an action or set of alternative actions. The short term is defined as the lesser of the time frame over which capacity is fixed, or one year. Marginal analysis is generally applied to these types of decisions:

- Special orders and pricing
- Make or buy
- Sell or process further
- Add or drop a segment
- Maximize contribution per unit of the limiting factor

LOS §2.C.2.a

LOS §2.C.2.b

The key factor in applying marginal analysis is deciding which information is relevant to the decision. Relevant costs and relevant revenues are those that differ among options and are future oriented. Costs and revenues that already have been incurred or committed are sunk and are irrelevant in decision making. Stated another way, any costs, including allocated costs, that do not differ between alternatives should be ignored in marginal decision analyses. Historical costs are irrelevant.

This topic takes a closer look at the application of marginal analysis in organizational decision making.

READ the Learning Outcome Statements (LOS) for this topic as found in Appendix B and then study the concepts and calculations presented here to be sure you understand the content you could be tested on in the CMA exam.

Special Orders and Pricing

A special-order pricing decision involves a situation in which a firm has a one-time and short-term opportunity to accept or reject a special order for a specified quantity of its product or service. Making a determination about whether to accept or decline a special order request involves an assessment of profitability (based on relevant revenues, costs, and opportunity costs) as well as consideration of capacity utilization. If the relevant revenue exceeds the relevant costs (including opportunity costs), the special order will be profitable.

If there is excess capacity—more than enough to cover the order—the firm needs to identify variable costs associated with the special order (unit variable costs multiplied by the number of units) and any additional fixed costs (avoidable fixed costs) that might be caused by accepting the order. Such costs are relevant costs and determine the minimum acceptable (break-even) price. If the price offered for the special order times the number of units involved is greater than the unit variable costs plus the avoidable fixed costs, the order is profitable and should be accepted.

However, it is important to consider whether sales to current customers at current prices might be disrupted were those customers to hear about the special order. If the company were to lose some of that current sales volume or were to have to make some pricing concessions to current customers, that needs to be factored into the analysis. If the special-order customer is a competitor of any current customers, the firm will not want to be seen as aiding a newcomer in a fight with current, loyal customers. It is easy to frame stories in textbooks where special-order customers operate in markets totally insulated from those in which regular customers operate, but in the real world, those separate watertight markets may not exist often.

If the firm is operating at or near capacity, the minimum acceptable price is the normal sale price. When there is no excess capacity, a special order should be taken only if the price offered exceeds the normal price. In the case of full capacity, a firm also must consider whether accepting the order could result in the loss of other more profitable sales. The opportunity costs resulting from lost sales that have a higher contribution margin should be evaluated.

Special-Order Cost Analysis

Consider this scenario:

> The unit selling price for a product is $4.
> The average variable cost per unit is $2.75.
> The average fixed cost per unit is $1.
> The total cost per unit is $3.75.
> Normal production is 500,000 units.
> Fixed costs are $500,000.
> A special order for 50,000 units is offered at a selling price of $3.50 per unit.

You must be cautious whenever a fixed cost is expressed in dollars per unit. The analyst who sees this should immediately seek to establish the value of the number of units from which this fixed cost per unit was calculated, because the value of the fixed cost per period must be established. In this instance, the analyst does not need look very far. The fixed costs are given as $500,000 per period, and the number of units divided into that value was 500,000 units per period. This is important; absent any words that suggest the need to incur any incremental fixed costs, the $500,000 level of fixed costs should remain exactly at that level. In other words, fixed costs should be irrelevant, because they should not change as a result of changes in activity level.

Excess Capacity

In the case of excess capacity, the correct analysis for the decision is to compare the relevant costs to the special-order price. Relevant costs include the cost to produce a unit ($2.75) and the special-order price offered per unit ($3.50). The total fixed cost ($500,000 per period) remains the same whether the order is accepted or not; it is not relevant. There is a $0.75 ($3.50 − $2.75) contribution to income for each unit sold, or a total contribution of $37,500 (50,000 units × $0.75). The order is profitable and should be accepted.

A common error in evaluating a special-order decision is to focus on the total cost per unit. If the total cost per unit is used as the comparison figure, the order probably would be rejected because the unit cost ($3.75) exceeds the special-order price ($3.50).

At or Near Full Capacity

Assuming that the firm is operating at or near full capacity, the proper decision analysis should consider the opportunity cost arising from any lost sales. For example, if the special order would result in the loss of other sales that have a higher contribution margin ($1), the opportunity cost of lost sales is $50,000 (50,000 × $1). The net contribution loss for the order is $12,500 ($50,000 − $37,500). Accepting the special order would reduce total profits by $12,500, so the order should be rejected.

In relevant-cost analysis scenarios, fixed costs are irrelevant unless they are avoidable. For example, a special order might require additional indirect labor, such as inspectors or material handlers to fulfill it; this would increase manufacturing costs and make the added (avoidable) fixed costs relevant for the decision.

As the term *special order* implies, special orders are unexpected and infrequent. They are short term and are accepted in those infrequent situations when they can increase total contribution. Accepting special-order pricing on a regular (long-term) basis can erode profits.

Make versus Buy

Make versus buy, as used here, refers to short-term outsourcing. *Outsourcing* describes a company's decision to purchase a product or service from an outside supplier rather than producing it in-house. The definition of *short term* implies that the organization has the capacity to produce the product in question. Reaching a decision about whether to make or buy involves a comparison of the relevant costs to make the item internally with the cost to purchase externally. In some situations, opportunity costs and qualitative factors also need to be considered.

Relevant costs represent the short-term costs to make the item in-house. They are the incremental or differential costs, which include the variable costs to manufacture the product as well as any avoidable fixed costs related to manufacturing the product and any forgone contributions caused by manufacturing the product. Relevant costs are those that can be avoided or eliminated by buying externally.

Irrelevant costs are those unavoidable costs that will not change regardless of whether the firm makes or buys the item. They are the sunk costs or future costs that will remain in place even if the item is bought externally. Typically, these are fixed overhead costs.

If the relevant costs are less than the purchase price, the decision should be to keep production inside. If the outside purchase price is less than these avoidable costs, the logical decision is to outsource.

Make-versus-Buy Cost Analysis

Consider this scenario: AAPartCo manufactures 5,000 units of a part each year. The cost of manufacturing one unit of the part at this volume is shown in Figure 2C-7:

Figure 2C-7 AAPartCo Manufacturing Cost

Direct materials	$2.50
Direct labor	3.50
Variable overhead	1.50
Fixed overhead	1.00
Total cost per unit	$8.50

The company can buy unlimited quantities of the part from an outside supplier at a unit cost of $7.75. Because the relevant costs to make are $7.50, the only costs that could be avoided if purchased, the part should not be outsourced. At the 5,000-unit level, this translates to an additional $1,250 (5,000 × $0.25) in favor of continuing to make the item internally.

Note that there is no discussion about revenue when discussing make-buy decisions. The same quantity of items will be sold to the same customers at the same prices. Thus, revenue would not be expected to change, and, therefore, revenue is not relevant. In fact, the company would hope that its customers are oblivious to the fact that the company is purchasing the item or a component from a vendor should the change be made.

Consideration of Avoidable Fixed Costs and Other Opportunity Costs

Avoidable fixed costs and other opportunity costs should be considered in a make-or-buy decision. A common make-or-buy opportunity cost is whether some part of the fixed overhead could be avoided by outsourcing. For example, perhaps an inspector could be eliminated. Another common opportunity cost is whether some part of the space being used during internal production could be used for another purpose, such as the manufacture of some alternative product or renting it to another organization.

If the space now being used to produce an item internally has no alternative use and would remain idle, the opportunity cost is zero. But if the space could be used for some other purpose, that opportunity cost should be considered when evaluating an outsourcing offer.

Returning to the AAPartCo example, if the company could eliminate 50% of the fixed costs per unit and also recoup $6,000 a year by leasing the space to another company, the economic benefits from outsourcing change the decision. In this situation, the $6,000 is an avoidable fixed cost and the opportunity cost per unit from renting out the space is $1.20 ($6,000 / 5,000 units). The relevant cost to make is now $9.20. This is calculated as $7.50 original relevant cost from before plus $0.50 of fixed cost that could be avoided if the firm outsources (i.e., opportunity cost #1) plus $1.20 of lost rent (i.e., opportunity cost #2). The relevant cost to buy is $7.75. Comparing the two, the potential savings from outsourcing is now $1.45 per unit, or $7,250 in total ($1.45 × 5,000 units) in favor of buying externally.

Consideration of Qualitative Factors

LOS §2.C.2.i

The make-or-buy marginal analysis of relevant costs has a key role in the decision to outsource. But there is more to successful outsourcing than the potential profit margins. In addition to the profit alternatives in make-or-buy decisions, firms also need to evaluate the qualitative factors of dealing with an external supplier. Examples of such qualitative factors include the need to tap an external supplier's unique knowledge, unusually skilled labor, or access to rare materials.

The desire to control quality traditionally has been the driving factor in the decision to make rather than buy. Increasingly, buying and selling organizations are forming quasi-partnerships and alliances to collaborate on improving products and services. Buying companies now often temper the make-or-buy decision with the potential for mutually advantageous supplier relationships. If the buying organization can be assured that established quality and service levels will be consistent with its needs and that the supplier's practices will be improved continuously, lower prices can result. The flip side is that erratic order-giving to suppliers (making parts during slack times and buying them during prosperous times) can backfire and potentially create problems in securing parts when sales demand is high but there are shortages of material and workers.

For example, if the part being outsourced requires a special die, there could well be considerable hassle in shipping the die to the supplier for outsourcing, and then getting the die back when the company resumes making the part in-house.

Also, will the lead time for obtaining the item be longer as a consequence of outsourcing? If so, safety stocks will need to be increased. Increasing safety stocks should be viewed as an additional relevant cost of outsourcing.

The final decision to outsource to an external supplier should not ignore the supplier's reputation for dependability and quality in:

- Ensuring on-time delivery and a smooth flow of parts and materials.
- Maintaining acceptable quality control.
- The strategic aspects of retaining control over core competencies are also important. Any outsourcing of an internal capability essential to maintaining competitive position requires careful consideration.
- Some suppliers and/or their home country may not respect intellectual property rights. The company must determine if it is willing to take the risk of exposing its intellectual property to misappropriation.

Sell or Process Further

Sell or process further concerns the decision to sell a product or service before an intermediate processing step or to add further processing and then sell the product or service for a higher price. Common examples of sell or process further include decisions to:

- Add features to a product to enhance functionality.
- Improve the flexibility or quality of a service.
- Repair defective products so they can be sold in the usual manner (rather than selling them for a discount in a defective state).

Sell-or-process-further decisions require analysis of relevant costs. In many situations, such decisions also involve consideration of joint products or services. A key point in this type of sell-or-process-further decision is that all costs that have already been incurred, such as joint costs, are irrelevant.

Joint products or **joint services** involve situations in which two or more products or services are produced from a single common input. For example, gasoline, diesel fuel, and heating oil are three joint products that are prepared (refined) from crude oil. The split-off point is the point in the production process at which the joint products can be recognized as separate products. **Joint costs** describe the costs incurred up to the split-off point.

The reason joint costs are irrelevant is that they are common costs that must be incurred to get the product or service to the split-off point. Because joint costs are not directly attributable to any of the intermediate products or services or the end products or services, they are irrelevant in deciding what to do from the split-off point forward.

For sell-or-process-further decisions, continuing to process a product or service is profitable as long as the incremental revenue received (the revenue attributable to the added processing) exceeds the incremental processing costs incurred. This rule also applies to processing beyond the split-off point in the case of joint products and services. Figure 2C-8 summarizes the steps in a sell-or-process-further decision.

Figure 2C-8 Sell-or-Process-Further Decision-Making Steps

Step 1	Determine the selling price for a product or service, or determine the selling price of each product or service in a joint production process at the split-off point.
Step 2	Determine the selling price of each product or service if it were processed further.
Step 3	Calculate the incremental revenue from processing further; subtract the Step 1 amount from the Step 2 amount.
Step 4	Calculate the incremental costs.
Step 5	Compare the incremental revenue to the incremental costs by subtracting the cost of processing further (or the separable costs of processing each product or service beyond the split-off point; Step 4) from the incremental revenue (Step 3). A positive net value supports processing further, and a negative result indicates selling before processing further (or at the split-off point).

Sell-or-Process-Further Cost Analysis

Example

Consider this scenario involving joint products:

> A company processes raw material A into joint products B and C.
>
> Each 100 units of raw material A yield 60 units of product B and 40 units of product C.
>
> Raw material A costs $5 per unit.
>
> Processing 100 units of raw material A into joint products B and C costs $100.
>
> Product C can be sold immediately for $5 per unit, or it can be processed further, causing a 25% loss of units, and sold for $15 per unit. Additional processing costs are $4 per unit started.

Given this information, there is a net benefit of $6 per unit to process product C further:

> The incremental revenue for processing further is $6.25 [$15 × (1 − .25) − $5] which is the selling price for product C after further processing minus the selling price for product C at the split-off point).
>
> The incremental cost for processing further is $4.
>
> The net benefit of $2.25 is the incremental revenue minus the incremental cost ($6.25 − $4).
>
> The raw material A cost ($5) and the $100 to process raw material A into products B and C are joint costs incurred up to the split-off point; they are irrelevant costs.

Add or Drop a Segment

A short-run decision to keep or drop an existing product or a service or whether to add a new one is largely determined through relevant cost analysis and the impact the decision will have on net operating income. Avoidable and other opportunity costs must be determined. Only those costs that are avoidable are relevant to consider in the decision analysis.

For example, given a product line made up of five different products, deciding to drop one of those products from the sales mix solely on the basis of its recent net operating loss may prove to be unwise. Instead, there should be an analysis to distinguish between traceable fixed costs and common fixed costs for the product. The traceable fixed costs are potentially avoidable costs if the product is dropped. The common fixed costs are unavoidable costs and will remain whether the product is dropped or kept. Common fixed costs are irrelevant.

Once the contribution margin and avoidable fixed costs are identified, the decision to add, drop, or keep a segment can be made with greater assurance.

If the avoidable fixed costs saved are less than the contribution margin amount that will be lost, the decision should be to keep the segment.

If the avoidable fixed costs saved are greater than the contribution margin amount lost, the decision should be to eliminate the segment because overall net operating income should improve.

If there are other opportunity costs, such as the forgone contribution from an alternative product or the ability to rent out the space released by not producing the product, these costs need to be added to the avoidable fixed costs in the add-or-drop decision process. In considering whether to drop a product, it is important to be mindful of its effect on related products, such as complementary products or impulse purchase products.

Add-or-Drop-a-Segment Cost Analysis

Example

Consider the income statement in Figure 2C-9 for a product segment reporting losses.

Figure 2C-9 Income Statement

Sales		$500,000
Variable expenses		200,000
Contribution margin		300,000
Fixed expenses:		
General factory overhead*	$60,000	
Salary of product manager	90,000	
Depreciation of equipment†	50,000	
Product advertising	100,000	
Rent for factory space‡	70,000	
General administrative expenses*	30,000	400,000
Net loss		$(100,000)

*Represents allocated common costs that would be redistributed to other product lines if the product is dropped.

† For equipment that has no resale value and does not wear out through use.

‡ For space owned by the company.

LOS §2.C.2.g

Based on evaluation of this income statement, as shown in Figure 2C-10, the company should keep the product.

Allocated common costs (*) are unavoidable and would still be incurred.

The equipment depreciation (†) is an unavoidable expense.

The factory space (‡) rental cannot be eliminated.

Figure 2C-10 Cost Analysis

Lost contribution margin	($300,000)
Savings from avoided fixed costs:	
Salary of product manager	90,000
Product advertising	100,000
Net loss from dropping the line	($110,000)

The fixed costs that can be saved by dropping the product are less than the contribution margin, so the company is better off in the short run keeping the product line.

The wisdom of keeping the product is demonstrated in the income statement shown in Figure 2C-11; company profit without the segment would become a loss.

Figure 2C-11 Income Statement

	Segment A	Company	Company without Segment A
Sales	$500,000	$4,000,000	$3,500,000
Variable expenses	200,000	2,000,000	1,800,000
Contribution margin	300,000	2,000,000	1,700,000
Fixed expenses:			
General factory overhead*	$60,000	$600,000	600,000
Salary of product manager	90,000	400,000	310,000
Depreciation of equipment†	50,000	300,000	300,000
Product advertising	100,000	300,000	200,000
Rent for factory space‡	70,000	200,000	200,000
General administrative expenses*	30,000	100,000	100,000
Net loss	$(100,000)	$100,000	$(10,000)

*Represents allocated common costs that would be redistributed to other product lines if the product is dropped.

†For equipment that has no resale value and does not wear out through use.

‡ For space owned by the company.

As the schedule of operating data shows, in this case, the company should keep Segment A. Overall net income is greater with the segment. Avoidable fixed costs saved from discontinuing Segment A are not as much as the contribution margin amount that will be lost.

Maximize Contribution per Unit of the Limiting Factor

When the firm's ability to meet customer demand is constrained by one factor that determines capacity, the firm's goal becomes maximizing contribution margin per unit of capacity (the limiting factor).

For example: Barlow Company manufactures three products: A, B, and C. The selling price, variable costs, and contribution margin for one unit of each product are shown in Figure 2C-12.

Figure 2C-12 Barlow Company Products

	Product A	Product B	Product C
Selling price	$180	$270	$240
Less variable expenses:			
Direct materials	24	72	32
Other variable expenses	102	90	148
Total variable expenses	126	162	180
Contribution margin	$54	$108	$60
Contribution margin ratio	30%	40%	25%

The same raw material is used in all three products. Barlow Company has only 5,000 pounds of raw material on hand and will not be able to obtain any more for several weeks due to a strike at its supplier's plant. Management is trying to decide which product(s) to concentrate on next week in filling its backlog of orders. The material costs $8 per pound. The next process can be used to determine which products the company should work on next week.

First, the company needs to determine each product's contribution per pound of material, and identify the product that maximizes contribution per pound, as shown in Figure 2C-13.

Figure 2C-13 Barlow Products Contribution Margin per Pound of Material

	A	B	C
(1) Contribution margin per unit	$54	$108	$60
(2) Direct material cost per unit	$24	$72	$32
(3) Direct material cost per pound	$8	$8	$8
(4) Pounds of material required per unit (2) ÷ (3)	3	9	4
(5) Contribution margin per pound (1) ÷ (4)	$18	$12	$15

LOS
§2.C.2.g

The company should concentrate its available material on product A, as shown in Figure 2C-14.

Figure 2C-14 Total Contribution Margin

	A	B	C
Contribution margin per pound (from Figure 2C-13)	$18	$12	$15
Pounds of material available	× 5,000	× 5,000	× 5,000
Total contribution margin	$90,000	$60,000	$75,000

Although product A has the lowest contribution margin per unit and the second lowest contribution margin ratio, it is preferred over the other two products because it has the greatest amount of contribution margin per pound of material, and material is the company's constrained resource.

The prior example indicates how a decision might be made when there is one constraining resource and many products. But what about the case when there are many constraining resources and many products?

Linear programming is the answer to the question posed. Consider the case of an oil refinery, where management has to deal with a large number of variables. The refinery may be capable of refining several types of crude oil. For each type of crude, different amounts are available for purchase at known prices. Each type of crude is expected to produce a different (but relatively predictable) mix of refined products. Each refined product has an expected sale price within the supply chain. And the production rate at which each type of crude is refined differs among the types. Refinery management relies on linear programming for its profit-maximizing decisions.

A special case of linear programming is two products and many constraining resources. It is special because it can be graphed; since it can be visualized, it is more easily understood.

Consider Santa's Workshop, which makes and sells two specialty Christmas ornaments—a Partridge in a Pear Tree and Five Gold Rings. Both ornaments have intaglio designs. However, the latter also has five rings embedded in the glass. Three processes are involved in creating the product: ring making, molding, and packaging. Each process is handled by one elf. Elf Adelaide does the ring making and works 4.5 hours per day. Elf Beatrice does the molding and works 11 hours per day. Elf Contessa does the packaging and works 5 hours per day. Each is a talented craftswoman, and Santa does not want to lose any of them. It takes .25 hours to make the rings for one Rings ornament; .25 hours to mold one Rings ornament; and .25 hours to package one Rings ornament. The Partridge in a Pear Tree ornament requires .5 hours to mold, but 6 ornaments can be packaged in 1 hour. The Partridge in a Pear Tree ornament sells for $47.50 and has a variable cost of $17.50. The Five Gold Rings ornament sells for $37.50 and has a variable cost of $12.50. What daily output of each ornament will maximize Santa's profit?

Santa knows next to nothing about linear programming. He takes a piece of graph paper and puts Five Gold Rings on the vertical axis with a maximum value of 50 per day and Partridge in a Pear Tree on the horizontal axis with a maximum value of 30 per day. He next draws a horizontal line at y = 18, because he knows the maximum ring sets that Adelaide can make in her 4.5 hours is 18 per day. All feasible solutions must lie on or below this line. The molding constraint is a little more of a challenge. He knows that, if there were no Partridge ornaments to be made, Beatrice could produce 44 Five Gold Rings ornaments in a day. So, he puts a dot at $x = 0$, $y = 44$. Then he figures that 22 Partridge ornaments could be produced if there were no Five Gold Rings ornaments to be produced. So he puts another dot at $x = 22$, $y = 0$ and connects the two points with a straight line. Again, any feasible solution must be either on or to the left of and below this line. Finally, using the same thought process, he puts dots at $x = 0, y = 20$ and $x = 30, y = 0$ and connects the two dots. This represents the packaging constraint. Then he shades the area inside the boundaries of this polygon. Any pair of values in the shaded area represents a feasible solution.

Santa reasons that, since both products have positive contribution margins, he wants his production schedule to be as far to the right as possible and as far up as possible; in other words, the best solution must lie on a border. Finally, he reasons that the best solution must lie at one of the corners.

Santa has constructed his graph very carefully. He is certain that one of the corners is ($x = 3, y = 18$) and his CM $ at this point must be (3 × $30) + (18 × $25) = $540 per day. But he isn't quite so confident of the coordinates of the next corner.

So, he constructs equations for the molding and packaging constraints, then calculates the x and y values where the two equations intersect. Those coordinates turn out to be $x = 18, y = 8$. Santa's CM $ at this point must be (18 × $30) + (8 × $25) = $740 per day. The last corner to evaluate is $x = 22, y = 0$ and the daily CM $ would be $660. Clearly, Santa's best production plan is to produce 18 Partridges in a Pear Tree and 8 Five Gold Rings.

But, after a few moments, his creative juices stir again. He thinks:

- Beatrice and Contessa are the bottlenecks. Is there any way he can make each elf more productive? Some automation, perhaps?
- Given that those two elves are the bottlenecks, is there any way he could induce each elf to work more hours? However, Santa is already worried about Beatrice's 11 hours per day.
- And then there is Adelaide, who has a pretty cushy job. Given his contribution margin level, Santa is clearly OK with paying her 4.5 hours of wages for only 2.0 hours of real work. But he wonders if Adelaide can be taught to do the work of each of the other two elves? Would she be able to do the work at the same high-quality level established by the other two elves? And how would Beatrice and Contessa feel about having "their" work done by someone else? So far they had functioned very well as a team. And, outside of work, they appeared to be the best of friends.

Income Taxes and Marginal Analysis

As the previous topic described, in a simple tax world with no tax credits, when pretax operating income is maximized, after-tax operating income (NOPAT) also is maximized. Therefore, income taxes are typically irrelevant in marginal analysis.

The decision-making process requires identifying the various types of relevant costs. A relevant cost may be variable or fixed. Typically, most variable costs are relevant because they are different for each alternative and have not been committed; the majority of fixed costs are irrelevant because they usually are the same for all options. The only relevant fixed costs are those that are avoidable.

One erroneous assumption is classifying depreciation expenses as relevant costs. The depreciation of facilities or equipment is a portion of a committed cost. The purchase cost is allocated over the life of the asset. For this reason, depreciation expenses are sunk costs and usually irrelevant in decision analysis.

Economic versus Accounting Concepts of Marginal Revenue and Marginal Costs

The economic concept of costs includes both explicit costs—such as direct labor; direct material; overhead; and selling, general, and administrative costs—as well as implicit costs not included in accounting records or in the determination of accounting income. Implicit costs include the opportunity cost of capital provided to the firm by its owners. Accounting costs include only explicit costs; implicit costs are excluded.

Cost analysis performed by management accountants can be similar to analysis done by economists but may have subtle differences. For example, the economic definition of marginal cost is the cost of the next unit produced. In performing marginal analysis, management accountants use unit variable costs (UVCs) as a surrogate for marginal costs. Likewise, the economic definition of marginal revenue is the revenue derived from the sale of the next unit. Management accountants use unit selling price (USP) as a surrogate for marginal revenue.

Total costs (TC), as noted earlier, are calculated by adding together all variable costs (VC) plus all fixed costs (FC). Using Q as production volume, average variable costs would then equal variable cost divided by production volume, or (AVC) = VC/Q, and average fixed costs would equal fixed costs divided by production volume, or (AFC) = FC/Q. Therefore, average total costs would be calculated by adding together average variable costs plus average fixed costs, or (ATC) = AVC + AFC.

Conclusion

All six of the decisions illustrated in this topic—including one each of Special Order, Make-Buy, Sell or Process Further, and Add or Drop and two of Constrained Resources—have a number of points in common with one another:

- The analysis requires a good understanding of cost behavior. The separation of costs into fixed and variable is absolutely critical.
- The decisions are based on the effect on operating income. Since the decisions are exactly the same even if they are based on after-tax income, it may be safely said that income taxes are not relevant.
- There are no changes in assets or liabilities. If this were not true, then net present value analysis would be the appropriate decision-making tool.
- Although opportunity costs are not recorded in accounting records, they are relevant to these decisions.

Knowledge Check:
Marginal Analysis

The following questions are intended to help you check your understanding and recall of the material presented in this topic. They do not represent the type of questions that appear on the CMA exam.

Directions: Answer each question in the space provided. Correct answers and section references appear after the knowledge check questions.

1. For a firm that has excess capacity, a special order pricing decision should
   - a. consider the opportunity costs from potential lost sales.
   - b. compare relevant costs to the special order price.
   - c. compare the total cost per unit and the special order price.
   - d. evaluate any joint costs incurred up to the split-off point.

2. A make-or-buy cost analysis involves all of these factors **except**
   - a. comparison of relevant internal costs with the cost to purchase externally.
   - b. consideration of opportunity costs.
   - c. evaluation of an external supplier.
   - d. comparison of incremental revenue with incremental costs.

3. What is the profit or loss of a decision to sell or process a product further given the following information?
   - The unit production cost for the product is $10,000.
   - The unit selling price for the product is $6,000.
   - The incremental processing cost per unit is $1,000.
   - The new unit selling price is $6,650.
   - a. −$350
   - b. −$650
   - c. +$350
   - d. +$650

4. When making an add/drop product decision, common corporate costs should be
   - a. considered to be avoidable.
   - b. ignored.
   - c. allocated based on sales.
   - d. allocated based on relative contribution margins.

5. Given the information shown for the four products produced by Huron Machining, which product should Huron produce first? There is unlimited demand for each product.

   Product A: Price = $100; Unit Contribution = $40; Contribution per Machine Hour = $10

   Product B: Price = $80; Unit Contribution = $50; Contribution per Machine Hour = $8

   Product C: Price = $75; Unit Contribution = $35; and Contribution per Machine Hour = $12

   Product D: Price = $110; Unit Contribution = $55; Contribution per Machine Hour = $11

   ☐ a. Product A
   ☐ b. Product B
   ☐ c. Product C
   ☐ d. Product D

Knowledge Check Answers: Marginal Analysis

1. For a firm that has excess capacity, a special order pricing decision should [See *Special Orders and Pricing*.]
    - ☐ a. consider the opportunity costs from potential lost sales.
    - ☒ b. compare relevant costs to the special order price.
    - ☐ c. compare the total cost per unit and the special order price.
    - ☐ d. evaluate any joint costs incurred up to the split-off point.

2. A make-or-buy cost analysis involves all of the following factors except [See *Make-versus-Buy Cost Analysis*.]
    - ☐ a. comparison of relevant internal costs with the cost to purchase externally.
    - ☐ b. consideration of opportunity costs.
    - ☐ c. evaluation of an external supplier.
    - ☒ d. comparison of incremental revenue with incremental costs.

3. What is the profit or loss of a decision to sell or process a product further given the following information? [See *Sell-or-Process-Further Cost Analysis*.]

    The unit production cost for the product is $10,000.

    The unit selling price for the product is $6,000.

    The incremental processing cost per unit is $1,000.

    The new unit selling price is $6,650.
    - ☒ a. −$350
    - ☐ b. −$650
    - ☐ c. +$350
    - ☐ d. +$650

    New Unit Selling Price − Unit Selling Price Before Further Processing − Cost of Further Processing = Profit/(Loss) of Product That Is Processed Further

    $6,650 − $6,000 − $1,000 = − $350

4. When making an add/drop product decision, common corporate costs should be [See *Add or Drop a Segment*.]
    - ☐ a. considered to be avoidable.
    - ☒ b. ignored.
    - ☐ c. allocated based on sales.
    - ☐ d. allocated based on relative contribution margins.

5. Given the information shown for the four products produced by Huron Machining, which product should Huron produce first? There is unlimited demand for each product. **[See *Maximize Contribution per Unit of the Limiting Factor.*]**

   Product A: Price = $100; Unit Contribution = $40; Contribution per Machine Hour = $10

   Product B: Price = $80; Unit Contribution = $50; Contribution per Machine Hour = $8

   Product C: Price = $75; Unit Contribution = $35; and Contribution per Machine Hour = $12

   Product D: Price = $110; Unit Contribution = $55; Contribution per Machine Hour = $11

   - ☐ a. Product A
   - ☐ b. Product B
   - ☒ c. Product C
   - ☐ d. Product D

   Huron should select the product with the highest contribution margin per machine hour.

TOPIC 3

Pricing

To survive in today's competitive environment, a company must manage both costs and prices carefully. Long-term financial success depends on whether prices charged for products and services exceed costs and provide sufficient reserves to fund growth, finance reinvestment, and deliver a satisfactory return to investors. Management accountants have a key role in collecting, analyzing, measuring, and reporting information crucial to cost and pricing decisions.

 READ the Learning Outcome Statements (LOS) for this topic as found in Appendix B and then study the concepts and calculations presented here to be sure you understand the content you could be tested on in the CMA exam.

Setting Prices

Pricing decisions generally refers to the collective decisions a company makes about what to charge for its products and services. There is no universally accepted method of setting prices, although pricing decisions can be critical in the success or failure of a business. Prices set too high tend to discourage sales, and prices set too low may not cover costs.

Relevant product and service costs are an important part of pricing decisions. Earlier sections introduced the concepts of cost-behavior patterns, cost traceability, cost drivers, and cost relevance. Contemporary cost system elements include:

- Use activities and operations as intermediate cost objects to trace costs to final cost objects.
- Assign costs to final cost objects based on cost drivers.
- Provide multiple views of costs (by resources consumed, activities consumed, and drivers consumed).
- Facilitate cost management of a product or a service by making the various causal relationships visible to managers.

A well-designed cost management system increases the likelihood of good pricing decisions and helps an organization to meet its strategic objectives. Other factors, such as supply and demand and the time horizon for a product or service, also influence decisions.

Supply and Demand Considerations

The traditional pricing practice in situations in which there are few competitors and demand exceeds supply is to mark up product or service costs to yield a sufficient profit. As long as demand remains strong and the competition is limited, any increases in costs can be offset with price increases.

The primary pitfall of pricing based on supply and demand in this manner is that it provides little incentive for cost management. Many companies in various industries have priced their products and services out of the market by perpetually increasing prices to cover costs. Furthermore, unless there are strong barriers to market entry (such as technological superiority or large capital investment requirements), such pricing creates the opportunity for competitors to enter the marketplace. As competition increases and supply exceeds demand, the ability to survive by marking up costs to yield good profits becomes problematic.

Demand-based pricing uses customer demand and customers' perceived value of the product as the primary pricing basis. Demand-based pricing includes price skimming, penetration pricing, yield management, price points, psychological pricing, bundle pricing, value-based pricing, and premium pricing.

Time Horizons

Pricing decisions are often categorized as short run or long run.

Short-run pricing decisions have implications for a year or less with many examples being for a period of six months or less. Short-run decisions apply to one-time and short-run special product purchase orders or responses to competitive market conditions that require more immediate product line and output volume adjustments.

Long-run pricing decisions have a time horizon greater than one year. Long-run decisions generally focus on a product or service in a major market.

The time horizon, either short run or long run, ultimately dictates which product or service costs are relevant to pricing. Some pricing decisions may have both short- and long-run implications.

Short-Run Costing and Pricing

Consider this scenario illustrating costing and pricing for a one-time special order. Company K has decided to bid on a one-time opportunity with a quick turnaround. Excess manufacturing capacity is available, so the order will have no effect on existing sales. Current variable and fixed costs per unit for a normal production run of 100,000 units are shown in Figure 2C-15.

Figure 2C-15 Fixed and Variable Costs for Company K

	Variable Cost per Unit	Fixed Cost per Unit	Variable and Fixed Costs per Unit
Manufacturing			
Direct materials	$10	—	$10
Packaging	5	—	5
Direct labor	6	—	6
Manufacturing overhead	8	$10	18
Total manufacturing costs	29	10	39
Advertising and commissions	4	12	16
Distribution	7	5	12
Total costs	$40	$27	$67

The variable manufacturing overhead ($8) represents utility costs. At the normal production run of 100,000 units, details of the total fixed manufacturing overhead costs and the fixed manufacturing overhead costs per unit are shown in Figure 2C-16.

Figure 2C-16 Fixed Manufacturing Overhead Unit Costs

	Total Fixed Manufacturing Overhead Costs	Fixed Manufacturing Overhead Cost per Unit
Depreciation	$300,000	$3
Materials procurement	100,000	1
Salaries	200,000	2
Engineering	400,000	4
Total fixed manufacturing overhead costs	$1,000,000	$10

The one-time special order is for 10,000 units. If the company decides to bid on the order, the current fixed manufacturing costs ($1,000,000) will continue to be incurred. The only additional expenditures the company would incur are for materials procurement ($10,000) and engineering setups ($25,000).

The firm requesting the bid has indicated that any offer in excess of $35 per unit would be noncompetitive. The company must determine what short-term price to bid for this special offer.

Relevant costs must be analyzed, and in this example, only the additional materials procurement and engineering manufacturing costs are relevant. Advertising and distribution costs are irrelevant to the pricing decision. Existing fixed manufacturing costs are also irrelevant because they will remain whether Company K accepts the special order or not. Relevant costs are summarized in Figure 2C-17.

Figure 2C-17 Relevant Cost Data

Direct materials (10,000 units × $10)		$100,000
Packaging (10,000 units × $5)		50,000
Direct labor (10,000 units × $6)		60,000
Variable manufacturing overhead (10,000 units × $8)		80,000
Fixed manufacturing overhead		
Materials procurement	$10,000	
Engineering	25,000	
Total fixed manufacturing overhead costs		35,000
Total relevant costs		$325,000

Based on this relevant cost data, per-unit relevant costs are $32.50 ($325,000 / 10,000 units). This is below the $35 price deemed competitive. Any bid above the cost per unit ($32.50) and below $35 will contribute to the company's operating income. For example, a short-term price of $34 would result in a profit of $15,000 [10,000 × ($34.00 − $32.50)].

As noted in the discussion of special-order pricing in Section C, Topic 2: Marginal Analysis, making a price decision based on the total cost per unit would be misleading and probably would result in not bidding on the business. In this example, if the total cost per unit is used as the comparison figure, the order would be rejected because the company's unit cost ($67) exceeds the bid ceiling price ($35). Even if only the variable cost per unit was used in the analysis, the order would have been rejected ($40 compared to the bid ceiling of $35).

Long-Run Costing and Pricing

Accurate cost information is essential in the decisions a company makes about what to charge for a product or service and how to best compete in the marketplace. Analysis methods make assumptions regarding costs and prices. To the extent that these constraints are stable, the analyses have a greater probability of accuracy.

Given an extended time horizon, stable and predictable costs are much preferred for pricing decisions. Stable, long-run costs lead to greater price consistency and reduce the need for continuous monitoring of suppliers' prices and other relevant cost data. Stable, long-run costs also improve other planning decisions and foster stronger, longer-term buyer and seller relationships. Forecasting becomes easier and customer relations become stronger.

In the previous example, the company must cover all costs (including fixed overhead) in the long run. With excess capacity, no additional fixed overhead costs are incurred as production increases; therefore, the more units produced, the lower the total unit cost.

Market-Based Pricing

Companies must often compete in markets in which products and services have little differentiation. Market-based pricing generally prevails in such product or service parity situations, whereby the market prices of identical and substitutable products determine the market price.

Two market methods help determine prices: demand-based pricing and competition-based pricing. If the demand for the product is high, the price will be set high. If demand is low and/or there are numerous substitutes for the product, the price will be set low. Under competition-based pricing, the selling price is set according to the price offered by competitors for identical and/or substitutable products.

In market-based pricing circumstances:

- Market forces strongly influence the price set for a product or service.
- Customers are reluctant to pay more than the prevailing market price.
- Companies typically charge the prevailing market rate.
- Companies consider what customers expect, want, and value.
- Companies determine the intensity of competitive rivalries.
- Companies anticipate how customers and competitors will react to its pricing.

Because the selling price cannot be changed easily, a company using this strategy should determine a cost/benefit analysis using the market price. If the cost to produce and sell a product will not result in an acceptable level of profit, the company will typically make the decision not to remain in the market for that product.

In market-based pricing, companies make decisions about product and service features as well as pricing decisions based on anticipated customer and competitor reactions. The general goal is to avoid setting prices that could lead to costly market destabilizing or competitive price warfare. As such, the market-based approach is a logical pricing approach in highly competitive and commodity-type markets such as airlines, oil, gas, minerals, and many farm products.

Cost-Based Pricing

The **cost-based pricing** (or **cost-plus pricing**) approach looks at the costs to develop a product or service and sets a price to recoup those costs and make a desired profit. Cost-based pricing is appropriate when some level of product or service differentiation exists and a company can exercise modest discretion in setting prices. Where market-based pricing is fairly restricted by market conditions, cost-based pricing considers market reactions as one factor in setting prices.

Under cost-based pricing, a firm:

- Determines the costs to produce and sell a product at a certain volume level.
- Identifies a reasonable return (markup).

- Adds the markup to the cost.
- Adjusts the markup as necessary in response to market forces.

With cost-based pricing, the markup typically is expressed as a percentage of cost. A predetermined markup is applied to the cost base to determine a target selling price.

> Selling Price = Unit Cost + (Markup % on Unit Cost × Unit Cost)

For example, consider a product with these variable costs:

Direct materials	$50
Direct labor	40
Variable factory overhead	20
Total	$110

Total fixed overhead costs are $100,000 ($100 per unit at the 1,000-unit level).

Selling and administrative (S&A) expenses are $500,000 ($500 per unit at the 1,000-unit level).

The challenges of cost-based pricing are determining what costs to use and what the final markup should be. There are three cost-plus methods to determine the selling price of a product:

1. Variable cost
2. Product cost
3. Total cost

In this example, variable costs are $110, product costs are $210, and the total costs are $710 per unit ($110 + $500 S&A Expenses per Unit + $100 Fixed Overhead per Unit).

The formula for the selling price in these three methods requires computing the markup and adding it to the costs. The markup is different under all three methods. For the variable cost markup, the computation is:

$$\text{Markup Percentage} = \frac{\text{Desired Profit} + \text{Total Fixed Costs} + \text{Expenses}}{\text{Total Variable Costs}}$$

At a level of 1,000 units in the example, with a desired profit of $200,000, the markup percentage is computed to be [$200,000 + $100,000 + $500,000] /$110,000 = 727% at the 1,000-unit level. The selling price will be:

$$\text{Selling Price} = \text{Markup per Unit} + \text{Costs per Unit}$$

So in this case, selling price = [(727% ×$110) + $110] = $910.

The product cost markup is computed as:

$$\text{Product Cost Markup Percentage} = \frac{\text{Desired Profit} + \text{Expenses}}{\text{Total Product Costs}}$$

The total cost markup is computed as:

$$\text{Total Cost Markup Percentage} = \frac{\text{Desired Profit}}{\text{Total Costs}}$$

Under all three cases, the selling price will remain $910.

In the end, the desired markup is evaluated and may be modified based on the prices competitors charge for similar products and the anticipated reactions of customers to alternative prices.

Target Pricing

The traditional pricing approaches discussed thus far are all based on the idea that:

$$\text{Price} = \text{Unit Cost} + \text{Unit Profit}$$

This equation presumes that a product or service has been developed, costs have been or can be identified, and the item is ready to be marketed once a price is set.

Target costing offers a fundamentally different way to look at the relationship of price and costs. The underlying concept of target costing is:

$$\text{Cost} = \text{Competitive Price} - \text{Unit Profit}$$

The cost for the product or service is computed by starting with the anticipated selling price and deducting the desired profit.

Keep in mind that both unit cost and unit profit are functions of volume. Increased volumes lower unit costs and raise unit profits while decreased volumes raise unit costs and lower unit profits.

Target Costing Process

Just as there is no universal definition for target costing, no definitive list of steps exists for target costing. Target costing practices in any company tend to evolve based on specific business circumstances. However, *Statement on Management*

Accounting (SMA) "Implementing Target Costing," notes that the steps shown in Figure 2C-18 are common to most target costing applications.

Figure 2C-18 Target Costing Steps

Establish a target price in the context of market needs and competition.
Establish the target profit margin.
Determine the allowable cost that must be achieved.
Calculate the probable cost of current products and processes.
Establish the target cost—the amount by which costs must be reduced.
Establish the cross-functional team to be involved in the implementation process from the earliest design stages.
Use tools such as concurrent engineering, value engineering, and quality function deployment in the design process.
Implement cost reductions (through life-cycle costing) once production is under way.

Target Costing

Various definitions of target costing exist and *SMA* "Implementing Target Costing" lists these characteristics as common to most definitions:

- A competitive market environment
- A situation in which market prices drive cost (and investment) decisions
- Implementation of cost planning, cost management, and cost reduction early in product or service design and development
- Cross-functional team involvement, including management accounting

Essentially, **target costing** is a comprehensive cost management process that determines a target cost for a product or service and then develops a prototype for that product or service that can be made profitably for the identified amount. It is a proactive methodology whereby product and service costs are managed early on during the design and development processes rather than in the later stages of product development and production.

The fundamental objective of target costing is to enable businesses to manage operations in a competitive market. As such, the foundation for target costing is the determination of market- and price-based costs. The cross-functional participation of research and design, engineering, production, marketing, and accounting is necessary to ensure that the proposed product or service, when sold, generates the desired profit margin. Stated another way, the cross-functional team is given the responsibility to design and develop the product or service so that it can be made for the target cost.

Target Cost

In defining **target cost**, *SMA* "Implementing Target Costing" indicates that the term means different things to different companies. For some, target cost is the same as allowable cost. Other definitions describe target cost as the difference between the allowable cost and the current cost—the amount by which costs must be reduced to achieve the allowable costs.

Allowable Cost

Allowable cost is the difference between the target price (set by market forces) and the target profit (set by management). In effect, the allowable cost represents the maximum unit cost, given an expected volume that a firm can commit to a product to achieve the company's profit objective. Target operating income per unit and target cost per unit are required in order to calculate allowable cost. Remember that both targets are functions of target volume.

- Target operating income per unit is the operating income a company strives for on each unit of product or service sold at the target volume.
- Target cost per unit is the estimated long-run product or service cost per unit at the target volume.

Target cost per unit is determined by subtracting target operating income per unit from the target price. When a unit is produced for the target cost and sold at the target price, a company will be able to achieve its target operating income.

Consider the next scenario illustrating target operating income per unit and target cost per unit. Due to increasing market competition, a firm needs to reduce its per-unit selling price from $100 to $75. At this lower price, the firm expects to increase annual sales from 10,000 units to 12,000. Management wants to earn a 15% target operating income on sales revenues. Total current cost per unit at 12,000 units would be $80. Figure 2C-19 shows target revenues and cost.

Figure 2C-19 Target Revenues and Cost

Total Target Sales Revenues	=	12,000 Units × $75 = $900,000
Total Target Operating Income	=	15% × $900,000 = $135,000
Target Operating Income per Unit	=	$135,000 / 12,000 = $11.25
Target Cost per Unit	=	Target Price − Target Operating Income per Unit
	=	$75.00 − $11.25 = $63.75

In target pricing, the market price of a product is taken as a given. The target cost per unit usually is lower than the full product or service cost per unit. This is the case in the example just presented, where the target cost per unit is $63.75 and the current (full) cost per unit is $80. But in order to make money, a company must recover all of its costs. Thus, all costs—both fixed and variable—are relevant in target cost calculations. Under these circumstances, businesses constantly are challenged in target costing to improve a product or service and the associated production processes throughout the entire life cycle of the item.

Target Price

In target costing, the **target price** represents the maximum allowable price that can be charged for the product or service. It is an estimate of the amount that potential customers would be willing to pay based on their value perceptions—their needs and expectations for products and services, quality, timeliness, and price. A target price also reflects the firm's understanding of the market competition—its capabilities and probable responses. In the final outcome, a target price should result in an acceptable price to customers as well as an acceptable price to the organization.

Designing a Proposed New Product or Service under Target Costing

Figure 2C-20 summarizes basic techniques (as identified in *SMA* "Implementing Target Costing") that firms use to design a proposed new product or service and establish its target price and target margin.

Figure 2C-20 Target Costing Process Techniques

Technique	Description
Market assessment tools	Any of several methods to assess the market and customers' wants and needs in regard to a proposed product or service including surveys, focus groups, interviews, and customer comment cards with current, prospective, or former customers.
Reverse engineering (teardown analysis)	The acquisition and disassembly of competitors' products to investigate their design, material(s), likely manufacturing processes, attributes, quality, and costs.
Industry and competitive analysis	Analysis techniques used to develop an understanding of competitors and how to best position a firm and its products and services to a competitive advantage. This may include any variety of strategies (such as Michael E. Porter's strategies) for conducting comprehensive industry and competitive analysis.
Financial planning and analysis	Detailed financial planning and statement analysis to examine the relationships between process, volume, and revenue. This approach also looks at cost and investments in the aggregate and for specific segment lines and individual products (or services); it allows a comparison to the proposed product or service.
Internal cost analysis	Determination of product and service costs and related investments for current offerings in order to estimate the costs of the proposed new product or service under existing and proposed product/service and process characteristics. This technique often involves activity-based management (ABM) and activity-based costing (ABC) to identify costs associated with specific cost-incurring activities.
Cost tables	Maintenance and use of detailed databases of cost information based on various manufacturing variables; facilitate cost projections for the proposed new product or service, assuming the use of different designs, materials, manufacturing processes, and end user functions. This technique helps managers determine in advance the effect of alternative choices.

Industry and competitive analysis used in combination with market assessment and reverse engineering data help to facilitate setting of the target price. Financial planning and analysis facilitates the determination of the target profit margin. Internal cost analysis and cost tables facilitate the comparison of allowable and current costs and the determination of the target cost.

Once the target cost is identified, the challenge of achieving it ensues. The emphasis on cross-functional teams promotes a high degree of interdependence among all functions in the organization. Companies will try to adapt different approaches to arrive at a product/service and process design that achieves the target cost. Most firms use some elements of concurrent engineering, value engineering, quality function deployment, and life-cycle costing.

Concurrent Engineering

Concurrent engineering is a process in which an organization designs a product or service using input and evaluations from all business units and functions early in the process, anticipating problems and balancing the needs of all parties. The emphasis is on maintaining customer requirements and incorporating upstream prevention rather than downstream correction.

Value Engineering

Value engineering is a principal technique in closing the gap between current cost and allowable cost. It is the systematic analysis of a product or service design, materials, specifications, and production processes in the context of customer requirements.

A differentiation is made between value-added costs and non-value-added costs. **Value-added costs** are those costs that convert resources into products or services consistent with customer requirements. They are costs that customers perceive as adding value or utility to a product or service. Conversely, non-value-added costs are not critical to customer preferences. In a manufacturing environment, examples of value-added costs might be costs associated with design, assembly, tools, and machinery. Examples of non-value-added costs could be special delivery charges, rework costs, or the cost of obsolete inventory.

In practice, the distinction between value-added and non-value-added costs can be somewhat difficult to assess. Some costs may fall in both categories, given specific circumstances. In manufacturing, testing costs or ordering costs often are difficult to differentiate between value-added and non-value-added.

The objective in value engineering is to balance overall costs and benefits and increase the ultimate value of the product. The process is best achieved using cross-functional teams, as trade-offs among design, development, production, and cost are involved. Management accountants are often called on to assess the potential savings resulting from the elimination of non-value-added activities and associated costs.

For the most part, the terms *value engineering* and *value analysis* are used interchangeably. Some firms use *analysis* for the design and development stages and *engineering* for the postdevelopment stage.

Quality Function Deployment

Quality function deployment (QFD) is a structured method in which customer requirements for a product or service are translated into appropriate technical requirements at each stage of development and production. The QFD process is often referred to as "listening to the voice of the customer."

Product Life-Cycle Costing and Life-Cycle Costing

Target costing assumes that the price of a product or service is stable or decreasing over time because of market conditions—due to competition on price, quality, and functionality. Companies must respond to these competitive pressures through a product's or service's life cycle.

Products and services pass through stages of existence. The product-life-cycle concept assumes that products:

- Have a limited life.
- Pass through phases, each of which has different opportunities and threats to sales.
- Require different marketing strategies in different life-cycle phases.

There are four phases in the life of a product or service:

1. *Market introduction.* High costs, slow sales volume, low competition, a need to create demand, and little profit.
2. *Growth.* Decreased costs due to economies of scale, increased sales volume, increased competition, increased profitability but sometimes with lowered sales prices.
3. *Maturity.* Costs are lowered, sales are at their peak, competition is high, prices tend to drop, and differentiation is needed to maintain market share.
4. *Saturation and decline.* Sales volume decreases, profits decrease, and sales prices decrease.

Target costing is designed to reduce the overall costs of a product or service over its entire life cycle. In applying target costing principles, firms must periodically redesign products and services to reduce price and improve value simultaneously.

Life-cycle costing tracks and accumulates all actual costs associated with a product or service throughout its life cycle. Capturing all costs provides important information for a variety of planning decisions to minimize overall costs.

Cost-Plus Target Rate of Return Pricing

Earlier discussions of cost-based pricing described the general formula of setting a price as adding a markup percentage to the cost base. A cost-plus target rate of return is one method of determining the markup based on the target rate of return on investment.

The **target rate of return on investment** is the target operating income a firm must earn divided by its invested capital. Companies often specify a target rate of return on investment.

Consider the next scenario illustrating cost-plus target rate of return pricing:

Full costs per unit for a product are $1,000.

The number of units expected to be sold is 10,000.

The pretax target rate of return is 20%.

Invested capital (long-term or fixed assets plus current assets) is $10,000,000.

Total target operating income is 20% × $10,000,000, or $2,000,000.

Target operating income per unit is $2,000,000 / 10,000 units, or $200.

Based on this information, the desired target operating income per unit is $200. Given the full product costs per unit of $1,000, the markup percentage that this translates to is:

$$\$200/\$1,000 = 20\%$$

The 20% markup represents operating income per unit as a percentage of full product cost per unit.

Peak Load Pricing Considerations

Thus far, all the pricing methods discussed have been based on costs in some manner. In some circumstances, non-cost factors must be considered in setting a price. Peak load pricing is such a situation.

Peak load pricing is the practice of charging more or less for a product or service based on demand and physical capacity limits. With peak load pricing, prices differ among market segments even though there is no significant difference in the outlay costs.

Prices may go up or down with peak load pricing:

- When demand approaches capacity limits, prices go up.
- When slack or excess capacity is available, prices go down.

Peak load pricing is found in a variety of industries, such as airlines, hotels, car rental, electric utilities, and telecommunications.

LOS §2.C.3.d

Laws of Supply and Demand

Pricing decisions must consider the relationship of supply and demand. Demand is inversely related to price, and supply is directly related to price. As prices increase, all other things being equal, demand will decrease. As prices decrease, all other things being equal, demand will increase. As prices increase, all other things being equal, supply will increase. As prices decrease, all other things being equal, supply will decrease.

A market is not merely the corner store with predetermined prices; it is any situation in which buyers and sellers come together (physically or electronically) to exchange goods and services. Buyers create a demand for products or services that sellers create and supply. The demand is the amount of a product or service consumers are willing and able to buy. The supply is the amount producers of goods or services are willing and able to make available for sale.

We examine the relationship between supply and demand in the context of the soybean market.

Demand

A demand schedule is a table of potential demand, with each price matched to its corresponding demand. Figure 2C-21 is a demand schedule for soybeans that Farmer J has constructed.

Figure 2C-21 Demand Schedule for Soybeans

Price of Soybeans per Bushel	Quantity Demanded (per Week)
$6	20
$5	30
$4	40
$3	60

To be meaningful, a demand schedule must indicate a time period. The quantity of soybeans demanded in Figure 2C-21 is for a period of one week. If Farmer J prices soybeans at $6 per bushel, he will be able to sell 20 bushels in the week (making $120). If he prices his soybeans at $4 per bushel, he will be able to sell twice as much, or 40 bushels per week (making $160).

Farmer J must determine which route he will take: produce fewer soybeans and sell less at a higher price, or produce more soybeans and sell more at a lower price.

The demand curve in Figure 2C-22 corresponds to the demand schedule in Figure 2C-21, with the curve showing the quantity demanded at each given price. The demand curve slopes downward, indicating that quantity demanded increases as the price falls and decreases as the price rises.

Figure 2C-22 Demand Curve for Soybeans

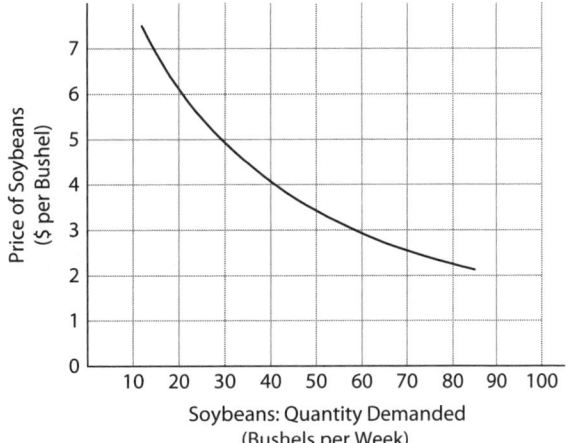

Change in Quantity Demanded

A change in quantity demanded is a movement along the demand curve. If the price of soybeans increases, the quantity demanded will decrease.

Several factors can cause a change in the quantity demanded:

- Part of the law of diminishing marginal utility states that consumers will buy more only if the price is lowered.
- There is an **income effect**; that is, consumer incomes are relatively higher if the price is lowered and consumers are, therefore, able to purchase more.
- The **substitution effect** is the tendency for consumers to purchase more of a product when its price falls, thus in effect substituting that product for others they were buying before (assuming the same amount of income to spend). For instance, if the price of restaurant meals declines, people may eat out more often and at home less often. As the price of one item falls, the price of competitive items, in effect, rises, making consumers less likely to keep buying them. The substitution effect applies more generally. For instance, when the cost of labor rises, employers will tend to use less of it, and if the same work can be automated, employers will tend to substitute machine processes for human labor.

Change in Demand

A change in demand itself is a shift of the entire demand curve. For example, if buyers learn in a news article about the health benefits of soybeans, the demand for soybeans may increase.

This increased demand is shown in Figures 2C-23 and 2C-24.

Figure 2C-23 Increased Demand Schedule for Soybeans

Price of Soybeans per Bushel	Quantity Demanded (per Week)
$6	30
$5	40
$4	50
$3	80

Figure 2C-24 Shift of Demand Curve for Soybeans

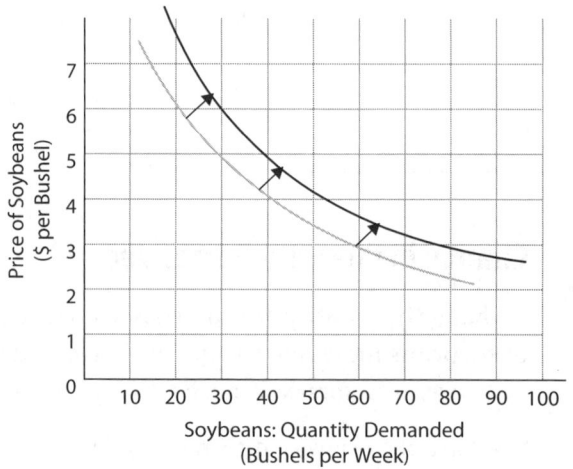

Demand is affected by a number of factors:

- **Personal taste.** Different consumers like different goods, and those tastes change over time. Personal taste has an effect on demand based on the number of consumers in the market. As the population increases, decreases, or shifts, buyers enter or leave the market, increasing or decreasing demand.
- **Income.** As income rises, consumers purchase more of most types of goods and services. Such goods are normal goods. The demand for inferior goods decreases as incomes rise. Steak is a normal good while hamburger is an inferior good. The concept of normal versus inferior relates to consumer incomes, not to quality or the perception of quality.
- **Price of related goods.** Substitutes can affect demand for a product or service, as can complements (items that normally are purchased together; e.g., golf clubs and golf bags). If the price of one product drops (golf clubs), there will be an increase in demand for the complementary product (golf bags).
- **Expectations of buyers.** Buyers may anticipate a weak or strong economy and reduce or increase spending, or they may expect price increases and buy products before the increases occur.

Supply

Now that Farmer J has studied the demand for soybeans, he must determine how much he is willing to supply at given prices.

After calculating his production costs and other factors, Farmer J creates his supply schedule (a table of potential supply and corresponding prices), as shown in Figure 2C-25.

Figure 2C-25 Supply Schedule for Soybeans

Price of Soybeans per Bushel	Quantity Supplied (per Week)
$6	100
$5	90
$4	80
$3	65

Farmer J uses the numbers from his supply schedule to graph the supply curve shown in Figure 2C-26. Note that the supply curve slopes upward, indicating that supply will increase as the price rises and decrease as the price falls.

Figure 2C-26 Supply Curve for Soybeans

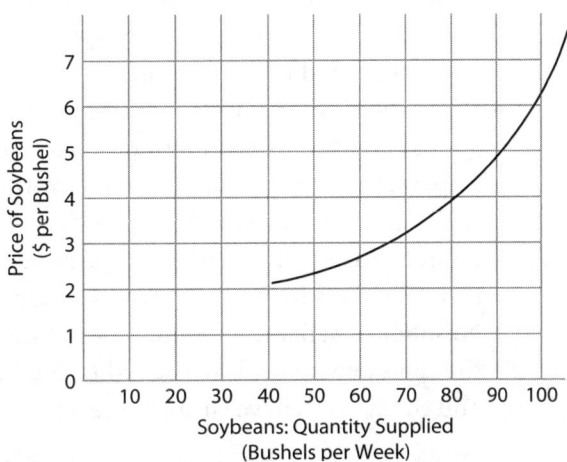

A change in quantity supplied is movement from one point to another on the supply curve. If the price of soybeans drops from $4 to $3, Farmer J will be willing to supply only 65 bushels per week instead of the 80 he is willing to supply at $4 per bushel.

A change in supply itself is represented by a shift of the entire supply curve. Figure 2C-27 shows a change in supply.

Figure 2C-27 Shift in Supply Curve for Soybeans

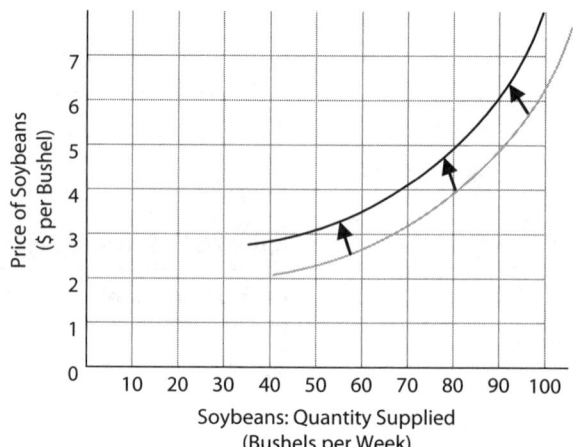

Changes in supply are caused by:

- **Resource prices.** Resource prices affect the cost of production and, therefore, the quantity a business is willing to supply at a given price.
- **Technology.** Technological advances or increased use of technology can lower production costs, thereby enabling an increase in supply at a given price.
- **Taxes and subsidies.** Changes in taxes can affect costs and thus affect the quantity a producer is willing to supply at various prices. Government subsidies lower costs and increase supply.
- **Prices of similar goods.** The price of similar, substitute, or complementary goods can affect the amount producers are willing to supply.
- **Expectations.** Expectations about the future of a product can affect the industry's willingness to supply the product. For example, after September 11, 2001, manufacturers of American flags added workers to increase production and supply of flags to meet an increased demand.
- **Number of sellers.** As more sellers enter the market, supply is increased, and the supply curve shifts to the right. As sellers leave the market, supply decreases, and the supply curve shifts to the left.

Ultimately, it is the interaction of aggregate supply and aggregate demand that determines prices. Excess supply (a surplus) decreases prices in the face of unchanged demand. Supply shortage, against unchanged demand, results in price increases. Increasing demand for limited resources results in increasing prices.

Market Equilibrium

Equilibrium is the price at which quantity supplied equals quantity demanded. Market equilibrium differs depending on the level of competition in the market. In a market with monopolistic competition, where there are products that may be differentiated but are not identical and, therefore, not substitutable, firms behave like monopolies in the short run. Pricing in the short run typically ignores the impact of other firms, increasing marginal net revenues. However, in the long run, firms in monopolistic competition become more like purely competitive firms. In a monopoly, firms typically sell fewer products at higher prices, resulting in higher net marginal revenue, unless they are legally required to do otherwise. In an oligopoly, marginal net revenues are higher than in pure competition, unless and until laws prohibit the lack of competition.

Note that when we discuss equilibrium in the next examples, we are dealing with multiple buyers and sellers (pure competition). The quantities in these examples are now in thousands of bushels, because many more buyers and sellers are included in the determination of market supply and demand.

Equilibrium price and equilibrium quantity are the price and quantity demanded (or supplied) at equilibrium. Market clearing price is another term for equilibrium price. Equilibrium tends to be a rationing function of prices: a price where selling and buying decisions are synchronized, or coordinated. Figure 2C-28 shows equilibrium for soybeans.

Figure 2C-28 Market Equilibrium

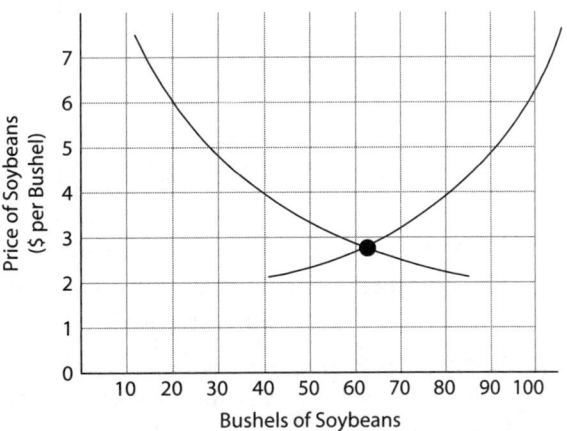

The equilibrium point is the point on the graph of market equilibrium at which the supply curve and the demand curve intersect. The equilibrium price in this example is $2.75 per bushel for soybeans; the equilibrium quantity is 62,000 bushels per week.

Disequilibrium is lack of equilibrium—any price at which quantity supplied and quantity demanded are not equal. A price above equilibrium results in excess supply; a price below equilibrium results in a shortage of supply or excess demand. Disequilibrium can be temporary, such as that which occurs during the growth of one industry and the decline of another (the move from the VHS video format to DVD).

There is a direct relationship between a shift in the demand curve and the equilibrium price and equilibrium quantity. When demand increases, the equilibrium price increases.

There is an inverse relationship between a shift in the supply curve and the equilibrium price, but a direct relationship with the equilibrium quantity. When supply increases, the equilibrium price decreases.

These rules are based on the assumption that all other things, such as income and economic conditions, are equal.

Figure 2C-29 shows the relationships among supply, demand, and equilibrium.

Figure 2C-29 Effects on Equilibrium of Changes in Supply and Demand

		Demand	
		Increase	**Decrease**
Supply	**Increase**	Effect on equilibrium **price** cannot be predicted. Equilibrium **quantity** will increase.	Equilibrium **price** decreases. Effect on equilibrium **quantity** cannot be predicted.
	Decrease	Equilibrium **price** increases. Effect on equilibrium **quantity** cannot be predicted.	Effect on equilibrium **price** cannot be predicted. Equilibrium **quantity** will decrease.

Price Elasticity of Demand

The law of demand states that consumers respond to price changes by buying more or less of a product. However, consumer responsiveness to a price change can vary considerably from product to product and between different price ranges for the same product.

Price elasticity of demand is the degree to which consumers will respond to a price change. Similar to the elasticity of a rubber band, the question for the supplier is: How far can I stretch this without breaking it? For products that have elastic or relatively elastic demand curves (two degrees of the same measure), consumers will be very responsive to a change in price. For example, when the price of travel increases, statistics show that travel decreases at a faster rate. If a product is inelastic or relatively inelastic (two measures, again, along the same scale), such as basic foods, consumers are not as responsive to price changes.

A perfectly inelastic demand indicates that a change in price will result in no corresponding change in demand. A perfectly elastic demand indicates that a small decrease in price will result in consumers demanding as much of the product as they can get or a small increase in price will result in demand falling to zero. Perfectly elastic demand happens only in a purely competitive market.

Figure 2C-30 shows perfectly inelastic and perfectly elastic demand curves on a graph.

Figure 2C-30 Perfectly Inelastic and Perfectly Elastic Demand

The formula for price elasticity of demand (a midpoint average) is:

$$\text{Price Elasticity of Demand } (E_d) = \frac{[\text{Change in Quantity}/(\text{Average of Quantities})]}{[\text{Change in Price}/(\text{Average of Prices})]}$$

LOS §2.C.3.m

This formula calculates elasticity of demand as a percentage of price. This is important because a change in price of $1 is different for a car than it is for one bushel of soybeans. Elasticity of demand normally varies over a range of prices. In addition, the percentage of change is calculated based on an average of the starting price and the new price. Although some economists favor using the initial value as the basis of the calculations rather than the average of the initial and ending values, the CMA exam only tests the approach that uses the averages. This approach is called the "midpoint formula" approach.

As an example of the calculation using the midpoint formula approach, consider a change in quantity demanded between prices on the demand curve for soybeans. Assume that at $5 per bushel, the demand is 30,000 bushels, and at $4 per bushel, the demand increases to 40,000 bushels. Note when substituting the values into the formula that the percentage change is calculated by using the midpoints formula—that is, the dollar change is divided by the average of the beginning and ending values to determine the percentage change [(30,000 + 40,000 / 2) and ($5 + $4 / 2)]. The next computations are made to arrive at the elasticity of demand for soybeans.

$$\% \text{ Change in Quantity Demanded} = \frac{\text{Change in Quantity Demanded}}{\text{Average Quantity Demanded}} = \frac{10{,}000}{(30{,}000 + 40{,}000)/2} = 0.2857$$

$$\% \text{ Change in Price} = \frac{\text{Price Change}}{\text{Average Price}} = \frac{\$1}{(\$5 + \$4)/2} = 0.22$$

$$\text{Elasticity of Demand } (E_d) \text{ for Soybeans} = \frac{\% \text{ Change in Quantity Demanded of Product X}}{\% \text{ Change in Price of Product X}} = \frac{0.2857}{0.22} = 1.30$$

When using the averages of the beginning and ending values, one gets the same answer regardless of whether the values change upward or downward; for example, ($5 + $4) / 2 is the same as ($4 + $5) / 2. When interpreting the price elasticity of demand, the negative sign usually is ignored.

Conclusions can be reached about price elasticity of demand based on a product's elasticity value:

- A price elasticity of demand value greater than 1 is considered elastic or relatively elastic. A percentage change in price results in a larger percentage change in quantity demanded.
- A price elasticity of demand value less than 1 is considered inelastic or relatively inelastic. A percentage change in price results in a smaller percentage change in quantity demanded.
- **Unit elastic demand** is the term used to describe the price range at which a percentage change in price results in an equal percentage change in quantity demanded.

Although it is common to refer simply to price elasticity of demand, one also may see references to price elasticity coefficient or price elasticity coefficient of value. All these terms have the same meaning.

A business uses information about elasticity of demand to determine the selling price that will maximize revenues. Farmer J can create a table of soybean demand based on demand schedules, adding consideration for the elasticity coefficient of price changes of soybeans, as shown in Figure 2C-31. As the unit price drops from $10, at first revenues climb; additional demand is sufficient to offset the decreasing per-unit price. At a price of either $5 or $6 per unit—the unit elastic price—a $1 change in price has no effect on total revenue, which is 150 at either price. As unit price drops to $4 and below, however, the elasticity coefficient becomes negative; revenue actually drops even though demand keeps rising.

Figure 2C-31 Price Elasticity of Demand, Elasticity Coefficient, and Total Revenue

Quantity Demanded (per Week)	Unit Price	Elasticity Coefficient	Total Revenue (Quantity × Price)	Total Revenue Test
5	$10		$50	
		6.33		Elastic
10	9		90	
		3.40		Elastic
15	8		120	
		2.14		Elastic
20	7		140	
		1.44		Elastic
25	6		150	
		1		Unit elastic
30	5		150	
		.692		Inelastic
35	4		140	
		.467		Inelastic
40	3		120	
		.294		Inelastic
45	2		90	
		.158		Inelastic
50	1		50	

Figure 2C-32 shows the elasticity of demand of Product X on the demand curve.

Figure 2C-32 Elasticity of Demand of Product X

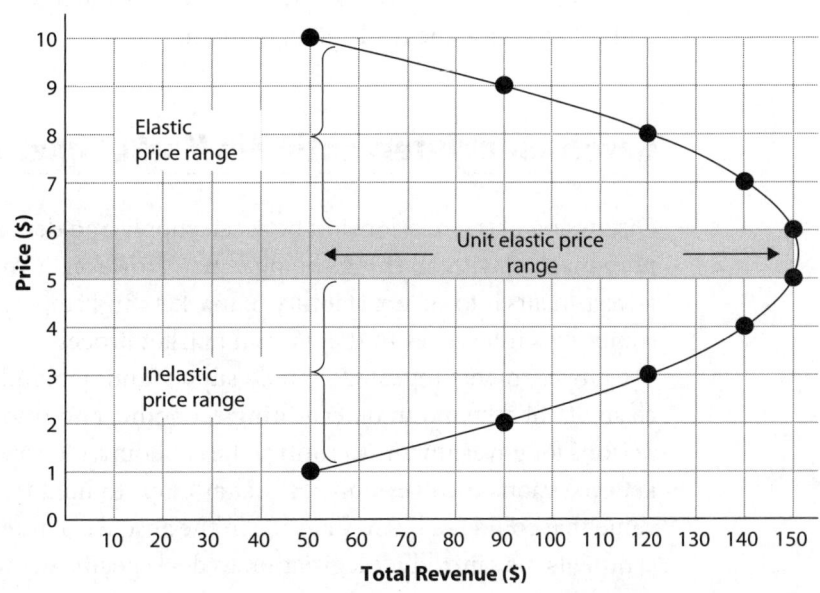

Figure 2C-33 graphs elasticity of demand and total revenues based on the numbers in Figure 2C-31. Note that total revenues are maximized between prices of $5 and $6, where total revenues equal $150. Prices above $6 and below $5 will reduce total revenues.

Figure 2C-33 Total Revenue Curve of Product X

Note that elasticity of demand differs between ranges of prices, with the price more elastic at lower quantities and less elastic at lower prices and higher quantities. In the graph on the right in Figure 2C-34 (a less detailed version of Figure 2C-33), you can see that revenue increases when prices increase, as price goes up in the inelastic portion of the graph, but revenue decreases in the elastic portion.

Figure 2C-34 Impact of Price Elasticity of Demand in Terms of Quantity and Total Revenue

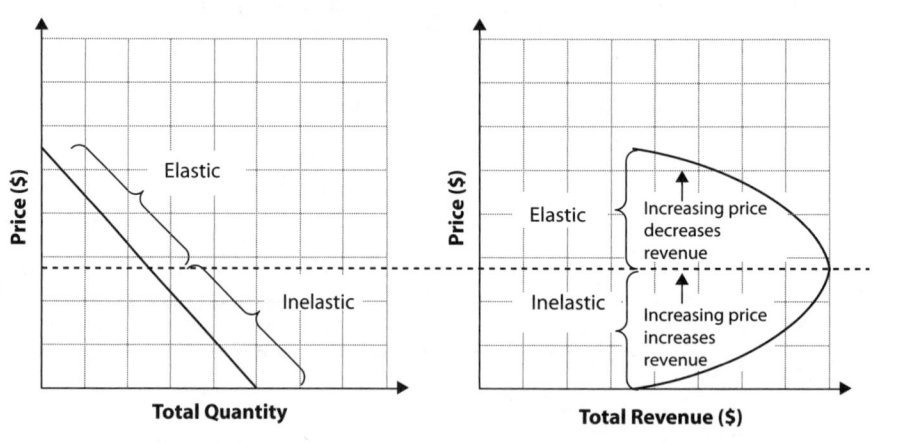

In competitive markets, firms should seek to price their products with regard to elasticity of demand in order to set a price that increases revenues. When a firm faces an elastic demand curve, it can increase its revenue by lowering prices and thereby increasing the (elastic) demand. When a firm faces an inelastic demand curve, however, it can increase revenues by raising prices—because the higher price will not decrease the (inflexible) demand.

Government Intervention in Market Operations

Discussion of the relationship between supply and demand thus far has assumed a pure market, with all things being equal. However, a large focus of many national governments is to ensure stability in markets and employment, and the government sometimes intervenes in the natural market process.

Governments repeatedly apply supply and demand analysis and measures of elasticity of demand in determining economic and trade policies. There are many reasons for governments to control the economy. Government intervention in market operations involves policies that attempt to hold the price at a disequilibrium value that could not be maintained in the absence of intervention. In addition, governments may introduce legislation to deal specifically with pricing and maintaining market competitiveness.

Impact of Cartels on Pricing

A cartel is a formal agreement among competitors to fix prices, marketing, and/or production. Cartels usually occur where there are a small number of sellers (an oligopoly) and usually are in industries with homogenous products. Generally, cartels are designed to increase profits and to decrease competition. Cartels can be categorized as private or public. A public cartel involves a government or governmental agency and generally is protected from legal actions concerning cartel activities. Private cartels, however, are subject to antitrust laws in most nations and generally are prohibited because of the impact of decreased competition and increased pricing.

Knowledge Check: Pricing

The following questions are intended to help you check your understanding and recall of the material presented in this topic. They do not represent the type of questions that appear on the CMA exam.

Directions: Answer each question in the space provided. Correct answers and section references appear after the knowledge check questions.

1. What characteristics differentiate the traditional pricing approach from target pricing?

   ☐ a. Traditional pricing is based on the premise that price equals cost plus the profit margin; target costing implies that cost equals the competitive price minus the profit margin.

   ☐ b. Traditional pricing is based on the premise that cost equals the competitive price minus the profit margin; target costing implies that price equals cost plus the profit margin.

   ☐ c. Traditional pricing marks up prices as a percentage of costs; target costing marks up prices in response to competitors.

   ☐ d. Traditional pricing marks up prices in response to competitors; target costing marks up prices as a percentage of costs.

Match each pricing approach with the appropriate characteristic.

2. _____ Market-based price	a. Generally used when some level of product or service differentiation exists and a company can exercise modest discretion in setting prices
3. _____ Cost-based price	b. Generally used in a competitive environment to enable businesses to manage operations profitably
4. _____ Target price	c. Generally used in product or service parity situations and when a company has little latitude in setting prices

5. Which practice would be **most** useful in a firm's attempt to close the gap between current cost and allowable cost during the design process?

   ☐ a. Reverse engineering
   ☐ b. Product life-cycle costing
   ☐ c. Value engineering
   ☐ d. Quality function deployment

6. What is a primary benefit of involving cross-functional teams in the target costing process?
   - ☐ a. Improved analysis of how to gain and sustain competitive advantage
   - ☐ b. More accurate input and maintenance of cost table databases
   - ☐ c. More realistic market assessment of customer wants and needs
   - ☐ d. Better assurance that the proposed product or service generates the desired profit margin

7. Which of the following statements about supply and demand is (are) true?
   I. There is a direct relationship between shifts in the demand curve and the equilibrium price and equilibrium quantity.
   II. An increase in supply with an increase in demand will result in an increase in equilibrium price and quantity.
   III. A perfectly elastic demand would be shown in a graph as a vertical line, while a perfectly inelastic demand is shown as a horizontal line.
   IV. A price elasticity of demand value greater than 1 is considered elastic or relatively elastic.
   - ☐ a. I
   - ☐ b. I and II
   - ☐ c. I and IV
   - ☐ d. I, II, III, and IV

8. Which of the following statements about supply and demand are true?
   I. When demand increases, the price of complementary products will increase.
   II. The substitution effect states that when the price of a product decreases, consumers will buy a substitute product.
   III. The law of diminishing marginal utility states that consumers will buy more of a product only if the price decreases.
   IV. An increase in the quantity supplied without a change in demand will result in a decrease in price.
   - ☐ a. I and II
   - ☐ b. I, II, and III
   - ☐ c. I, III, and IV
   - ☐ d. I, II, III, and IV

Knowledge Check Answers: Pricing

1. What characteristics differentiate the traditional pricing approach from target pricing? [See *Target Pricing*.]
   - ☑ **a.** Traditional pricing is based on the premise that price equals cost plus the profit margin; target costing implies that cost equals the competitive price minus the profit margin.
   - ☐ **b.** Traditional pricing is based on the premise that cost equals the competitive price minus the profit margin; target costing implies that price equals cost plus the profit margin.
   - ☐ **c.** Traditional pricing marks up prices as a percentage of costs; target costing marks up prices in response to competitors.
   - ☐ **d.** Traditional pricing marks up prices in response to competitors; target costing marks up prices as a percentage of costs.

Match each pricing approach with the appropriate characteristic.

2. __c__ Market-based price	**a.**	Generally used when some level of product or service differentiation exists and a company can exercise modest discretion in setting prices
3. __a__ Cost-based price	**b.**	Generally used in a competitive environment to enable businesses to manage operations profitably
4. __b__ Target price	**c.**	Generally used in product or service parity situations and when a company has little latitude in setting prices

5. Which practice would be **most** useful in a firm's attempt to close the gap between current cost and allowable cost during the design process? [See *Allowable Cost*.]
   - ☐ **a.** Reverse engineering
   - ☐ **b.** Product life-cycle costing
   - ☑ **c.** Value engineering
   - ☐ **d.** Quality function deployment

6. What is a primary benefit of involving cross-functional teams in the target costing process? [See *Designing a Proposed New Product or Service under Target Costing.*]
   - ☐ a. Improved analysis of how to gain and sustain competitive advantage
   - ☐ b. More accurate input and maintenance of cost table databases
   - ☐ c. More realistic market assessment of customer wants and needs
   - ☑ d. Better assurance that the proposed product or service generates the desired profit margin

7. Which of the following statements about supply and demand is (are) true? [See *Laws of Supply and Demand* and *Price Elasticity of Demand.*]
   - I. There is a direct relationship between shifts in the demand curve and the equilibrium price and equilibrium quantity.
   - II. An increase in supply with an increase in demand will result in an increase in equilibrium price and quantity.
   - III. A perfectly elastic demand would be shown in a graph as a vertical line, while a perfectly inelastic demand is shown as a horizontal line.
   - IV. A price elasticity of demand value greater than 1 is considered elastic or relatively elastic.
   - ☐ a. I
   - ☐ b. I and II
   - ☑ c. I and IV
   - ☐ d. I, II, III, and IV

8. Which of the following statements about supply and demand are true? [See *Laws of Supply and Demand.*]
   - I. When demand increases, the price of complementary products will increase.
   - II. The substitution effect states that when the price of a product decreases, consumers will buy a substitute product.
   - III. The law of diminishing marginal utility states that consumers will buy more of a product only if the price decreases.
   - IV. An increase in the quantity supplied without a change in demand will result in a decrease in price.
   - ☐ a. I and II
   - ☐ b. I, II, and III
   - ☑ c. I, III, and IV
   - ☐ d. I, II, III, and IV

Practice Questions: Decision Analysis

Directions: This sampling of questions is designed to emulate actual exam questions. Read each question and write your response on another sheet of paper. See the "Answers to Section Practice Questions" section at the end of this book to assess your response. Validate or improve the answer you wrote. For a more robust selection of practice questions, access the **Online Test Bank** at www.wileycma.com.

Question 2C1-CQ01

Topic: Cost/Volume/Profit Analysis

Following are the operating results of the two segments of Parklin Corporation.

	Segment A	Segment B	Total
Sales	$10,000	$15,000	$25,000
Variable costs of goods sold	4,000	8,500	12,500
Fixed costs of goods sold	1,500	2,500	4,000
Gross margin	4,500	4,000	8,500
Variable selling and administrative	2,000	3,000	5,000
Fixed selling and administrative	1,500	1,500	3,000
Operating income (loss)	$1,000	$(500)	$500

Variable costs of goods sold are directly related to the operating segments. Fixed costs of goods sold are allocated to each segment based on the number of employees. Fixed selling and administrative expenses are allocated equally. If Segment B is eliminated, $1,500 of fixed costs of goods sold would be eliminated. Assuming Segment B is closed, the effect on operating income would be

- ☐ **a.** an increase of $500.
- ☐ **b.** an increase of $2,000.
- ☐ **c.** a decrease of $2,000.
- ☐ **d.** a decrease of $2,500.

Question 2C1-CQ02

Topic: Cost/Volume/Profit Analysis

Edwards Products has just developed a new product with a variable manufacturing cost of $30 per unit. The marketing director has identified three marketing approaches for this new product.

Approach X	Set a selling price of $36 and have the firm's sales staff sell the product at a 10% commission with no advertising program. Estimated annual sales would be 10,000 units.
Approach Y	Set a selling price of $38, have the firm's sales staff sell the product at a 10% commission, and back them up with a $30,000 advertising program. Estimated annual sales would be 12,000 units.
Approach Z	Rely on wholesalers to handle the product. Edwards would sell the new product to the wholesalers at $32 per unit and incur no selling expenses. Estimated annual sales would be 14,000 units.

Rank the three alternatives in order of net contribution, from highest to lowest.

- a. X, Y, Z
- b. Y, Z, X
- c. Z, X, Y
- d. Z, Y, X

Question 2C1-CQ04

Topic: Cost/Volume/Profit Analysis

Elgers Company produces valves for the plumbing industry. Elgers' per-unit sales price and variable costs are as shown.

Sales price	$12
Variable costs	8

Elgers' practical plant capacity is 40,000 units. Its total fixed costs aggregate $48,000, and it has a 40% effective tax rate.

The maximum net profit that Elger can earn is

- a. $48,000.
- b. $67,200.
- c. $96,000.
- d. $112,000.

Question 2C1-CQ09

Topic: Cost/Volume/Profit Analysis

Cervine Corporation makes two types of motors for use in various products. Operating data and unit cost information for its products are presented next.

	Product A	Product B
Annual unit capacity	10,000	20,000
Annual unit demand	10,000	20,000

Selling price	$100	$80
Variable manufacturing cost	53	45
Fixed manufacturing cost	10	10
Variable selling and administrative	10	11
Fixed selling and administrative	5	4
Fixed other administrative	2	0
Unit operating profit	$ 20	$10
Machine hours per unit	2.0	1.5

Cervine has 40,000 productive machine hours available. The relevant contribution margins, per machine hour for each product, to be utilized in making a decision on product priorities for the coming year, are

	Product A	Product B
a.	$17.00	$14.00
b.	$18.50	$16.00
c.	$20.00	$10.00
d.	$37.00	$24.00

Question 2C1-CQ10

Topic: Cost/Volume/Profit Analysis

Allred Company sells its single product for $30 per unit. The contribution margin ratio is 45%, and fixed costs are $10,000 per month. Allred has an effective income tax rate of 40%. If Allred sells 1,000 units in the current month, Allred's variable expenses would be

- ☐ a. $9,900.
- ☐ b. $12,000.
- ☐ c. $13,500.
- ☐ d. $16,500.

Question 2C1-CQ11

Topic: Cost/Volume/Profit Analysis

Phillips & Company produces educational software. Its unit cost structure, based on an anticipated production volume of 150,000 units, is:

Sales price	$160
Variable costs	60
Fixed costs	55

The marketing department has estimated sales for the coming year at 175,000 units, which is within the relevant range of Phillips' cost structure. Phillips' break-even volume (in units) and anticipated operating income for the coming year would amount to

- ☐ a. 82,500 units and $7,875,000 of operating income.
- ☐ b. 82,500 units and $9,250,000 of operating income.
- ☐ c. 96,250 units and $3,543,750 of operating income.
- ☐ d. 96,250 units and $7,875,000 of operating income.

Question 2C1-CQ15

Topic: Cost/Volume/Profit Analysis

For the year just ended, Silverstone Company's sales revenue was $450,000. Silverstone's fixed costs were $120,000, and its variable costs amounted to $270,000. For the current year, sales are forecasted at $500,000. If the fixed costs do not change, Silverstone's operating profits this year will be

- ☐ a. $60,000.
- ☐ b. $80,000.
- ☐ c. $110,000.
- ☐ d. $200,000.

Question 2C2-CQ01

Topic: Marginal Analysis

Williams makes $35,000 a year as an accounting clerk. He decides to quit his job to enter a one-year MBA program full-time. Assume Williams doesn't work in the summer or hold any part-time jobs. His tuition, books, living expenses, and fees total $25,000 a year. Given this information, the annual total economic cost of Williams's MBA studies is

- ☐ a. $10,000.
- ☐ b. $35,000.
- ☐ c. $25,000.
- ☐ d. $60,000.

Question 2C2-CQ03

Topic: Marginal Analysis

Daily costs for Kelso Manufacturing include $1,000 of fixed costs and total variable costs, as shown:

Unit Output	10	11	12	13	14	15
Cost	$125	$250	$400	$525	$700	$825

The average total cost at an output level of 11 units is

- a. $113.64
- b. $125.00
- c. $215.91
- d. $250.00

Question 2C2-CQ04
Topic: Marginal Analysis

Harper Products' cost information for the normal range of output in a month is shown next.

Output in Units	Total Cost
20,000	$3,000,000
22,500	3,325,000
25,000	3,650,000

What is Harper's short-run marginal cost?

- a. $26
- b. $130
- c. $146
- d. $150

Question 2C2-CQ11
Topic: Marginal Analysis

Refrigerator Company manufactures ice makers for installation in refrigerators. The costs per unit, for 20,000 units of ice makers, are:

Direct materials	$ 7
Direct labor	12
Variable overhead	5
Fixed overhead	10
Total costs	$34

Cool Compartments Inc. has offered to sell 20,000 icemakers to Refrigerator Company for $28 per unit. If Refrigerator accepts Cool Compartments' offer, the plant would be idled and fixed overhead amounting to $6 per unit could be eliminated. The total relevant costs associated with the manufacture of ice makers amount to

- a. $480,000.
- b. $560,000.
- c. $600,000.
- d. $680,000.

Question 2C2-CQ14
Topic: Marginal Analysis

Capital Company has decided to discontinue a product produced on a machine purchased four years ago at a cost of $70,000. The machine has a current book value of $30,000. Due to technologically improved machinery now available in the marketplace, the existing machine has no current salvage value. The company is reviewing the various aspects involved in the production of a new product. The engineering staff advised that the existing machine can be used to produce the new product. Other costs involved in the production of the new product will be materials of $20,000 and labor priced at $5,000.

Ignoring income taxes, the costs relevant to the decision to produce or not to produce the new product would be

- a. $25,000.
- b. $30,000.
- c. $55,000.
- d. $95,000.

Question 2C2-CQ15
Topic: Marginal Analysis

Current business segment operations for Whitman, a mass retailer, are presented next.

	Merchandise	Automotive	Restaurant	Total
Sales	$500,000	$400,000	$100,000	$1,000,000
Variable costs	300,000	200,000	70,000	570,000
Fixed costs	100,000	100,000	50,000	250,000
Operating income (loss)	$100,000	$100,000	$(20,000)	$ 180,000

Management is contemplating the discontinuance of the Restaurant segment since "it is losing money." If this segment is discontinued, $30,000 of its fixed costs will be eliminated. In addition, Merchandise and Automotive sales will decrease 5% from their current levels. What will Whitman's total contribution margin be if the Restaurant segment is discontinued?

- a. $160,000
- b. $220,000
- c. $367,650
- d. $380,000

Question 2C2-CQ16
Topic: Marginal Analysis

Aril Industries is a multiproduct company that currently manufactures 30,000 units of Part 730 each month for use in production. The facilities being used to produce Part 730 have fixed monthly overhead costs of $150,000 and a theoretical capacity to produce 60,000 units per month. If Aril were to buy Part 730 from an outside supplier, the facilities would be idle and 40% of fixed costs would continue to be incurred. There are no alternative uses for the facilities. The variable production costs of Part 730 are $11 per unit. Fixed overhead is allocated based on planned production levels.

If Aril Industries continues to use 30,000 units of Part 730 each month, it would realize a net benefit by purchasing Part 730 from an outside supplier only if the supplier's unit price is less than

- a. $12.00.
- b. $12.50.
- c. $13.00.
- d. $14.00.

Question 2C3-CQ01
Topic: Pricing

A market research analyst determined the next market data for a commodity.

Price	Quantity Supplied	Quantity Demanded
$ 25	250	750
50	500	500
75	750	250
100	1,000	0

Based on this information, which one of the following statements is **correct**?

- a. At a price of $30, there will be excess demand.
- b. A market clearing price cannot be determined.
- c. At a price of $80, there will be insufficient supply.
- d. A market price of $50 cannot exist for very long.

Question 2C3-CQ03
Topic: Pricing

An economic research firm performed extensive studies on the market for large-screen televisions (LSTs). Portions of the results are shown next.

Household Income	LST Sales (units)
$50,000	20,000
60,000	28,000
72,000	39,200
Price of LSTs	**LST Sales (units)**
$1,000	100,000
900	115,000
810	132,250

The income elasticity of demand for LSTs is

- a. 0.4
- b. 1.5
- c. 1.8
- d. 2.5

Question 2C3-CQ04

Topic: Pricing

Jones Enterprises manufactures three products, A, B, and C. During the month of May, Jones's production, costs, and sales data were as shown.

	A	B	C	Totals
Units of production	30,000	20,000	70,000	120,000
Joint production costs to split-off point				$480,000
Further processing costs	$-	$60,000	$140,000	
Unit sales price				
At split-off	3.75	5.50	10.25	
After further processing	-	8.00	12.50	

Based on this information, which one of the following alternatives should be recommended to Jones's management?

- a. Sell both Product B and Product C at the split-off point.
- b. Process Product B further but sell Product C at the split-off point.
- c. Process Product C further but sell Product B at the split-off point.
- d. Process both Products B and C further.

Question 2C3-CQ05

Topic: Pricing

Synergy Inc. produces a component that is popular in many refrigeration systems. Data on three of the five different models of this component are shown next.

	Model		
	A	B	C
Volume needed (units)	5,000	6,000	3,000
Manufacturing costs			
Variable direct costs	$10	$24	$20
Variable overhead	5	10	15
Fixed overhead	11	20	17
Total manufacturing costs	$26	$54	$52
Cost if purchased	$21	$42	$39

Synergy applies variable overhead on the basis of machine hours at the rate of $2.50 per hour. Models A and B are manufactured in the Freezer Department, which has a capacity of 28,000 machine processing hours. Which one of the following options should be recommended to Synergy's management?

- ☐ a. Purchase all three products in the quantities required.
- ☐ b. Manufacture all three products in the quantities required.
- ☐ c. The Freezer Department's manufacturing plan should include 5,000 units of Model A and 4,500 units of Model B.
- ☐ d. The Freezer Department's manufacturing plan should include 2,000 units of Model A and 6,000 units of Model B.

Question 2C3-CQ06

Topic: Pricing

Leader Industries is planning to introduce a new product, DMA. It is expected that 10,000 units of DMA will be sold. The full product cost per unit is $300. Invested capital for this product amounts to $20 million. Leader's target rate of return on investment is 20%. The markup percentage for this product, based on operating income as a percentage of full product cost, will be

- ☐ a. 42.9%.
- ☐ b. 57.1%.
- ☐ c. 133.3%.
- ☐ d. 233.7%.

Question 2C3-CQ08

Topic: Pricing

Almelo Manpower Inc. provides contracted bookkeeping services. Almelo has annual fixed costs of $100,000 and variable costs of $6 per hour. This year the company budgeted 50,000 hours of bookkeeping services. Almelo prices its services at full cost and uses a cost-plus pricing approach. The company developed a billing price of $9 per hour. The company's markup level would be

☐ a. 12.5%.
☐ b. 33.3%.
☐ c. 50.0%.
☐ d. 66.6%.

Question 2C3-CQ09

Topic: Pricing

Fennel Products is using cost-based pricing to determine the selling price for its new product based on the next information.

Annual volume	25,000 units
Fixed costs	$700,000 per year
Variable costs	$200 per unit
Plant investment	$3,000,000
Working capital	$1,000,000
Effective tax rate	40%

The target price that Fennell needs to set for the new product to achieve a 15% after-tax return on investment (ROI) would be

☐ a. $228.
☐ b. $238.
☐ c. $258.
☐ d. $268.

To further assess your understanding of the concepts and calculations covered in Part 2, Section C: Decision Analysis, practice with the **Online Test Bank** for this section. **REMINDER:** See the "Answers to Section Practice Questions" section at the end of this book.

SECTION D

Risk Management

Risk is the level of uncertainty about future events. Organization managers need to identify, assess, and respond to risks in order for the organization to achieve its goals and objectives and its vision. Risks must be managed to an acceptable level to adequately protect organizational assets and to mitigate losses. Even though risks are difficult to determine and quantify, management should make a best effort to identify, assess, and respond to them. This section focuses on the enterprise risk management (ERM) model. ERM provides a comprehensive approach to risk identification, assessment, and response.

TOPIC 1

Enterprise Risk

Risk is a condition that may prevent one from achieving an objective. Organizations need to identify, assess, and manage risks to achieve their objectives, including the objective to protect the organization's assets and avoid unexpected losses. Although risks often are difficult to determine and quantify, management should make a best effort to identify risks and their probabilities of occurrence.

Several organizations provide guidance to assist with the design and implementation of an effective enterprise-wide risk management approach. The latter part of this topic focuses on the most widely used and accepted enterprise risk management framework, the *COSO Enterprise Risk Management Integrated Framework*, which is a comprehensive approach to assessing an organization's risk.

> **READ** the Learning Outcome Statements (LOS) for this topic as found in Appendix B and then study the concepts and calculations presented here to be sure you understand the content you could be tested on in the CMA exam.

Risk and Expected Loss

LOS
§2.D.1.g

In a business context, *risk* is defined as the level of exposure to a chance of loss. For example, if a company determines that a particular risk could result in a loss of up to $50,000, the company would be willing to spend at the most $50,000 to mitigate the risk. The amount of the loss calculated by the company represents the maximum possible loss (extreme or catastrophic loss). This loss often is referred to as the value at risk (VaR). VaR includes cash flow at risk, earnings at risk, and distribution of losses arising from cash flow or earnings risks. Normal risk models cannot deal with totally unexpected losses such as an atomic attack.

Value at Risk

LOS
§2.D.1.s

In managing risk, organizations should not rely solely on historical data. Those managing risk should know about risks at the time those risks are being taken. Historical performance over long periods of time provides an estimate of average rates of return and high and low returns. But as the name implies, *historical* provides a retrospective indication of risk. When reviewing a portfolio, historical volatility illustrates how risky the portfolio was over a previous period of time. It provides no indication about the current market risk of the portfolio. VaR gives organizations the ability to assess current risk to the extent that losses from those risks are distributed normally.

VaR is the maximum loss within a given period of time and at a given specified probability level (level of confidence). Unlike retrospective risk metrics that measure historical volatility, VaR is prospective. It quantifies market risk while it is being taken.

Figure 2D-1 overviews key VaR concepts.

Figure 2D-1 Value at Risk Characteristics

Application	VaR can be applied to any portfolio that can reasonably be marked to market performance on a regular basis. VaR is not applicable to illiquid assets such as real estate.
Time frame/horizon	VaR evaluates a portfolio's performance over a specific period of time, such as a trading day, week, or a month.
Base currency	VaR measures risk in a currency. Any currency can be used.
VaR measurement	A resulting VaR measure summarizes a portfolio's market risk with a single number.

VaR can be calculated using any of these methods: historical method, variance-covariance method, or Monte Carlo simulation.

Historical Method

The historical method estimates risk based on actual historical returns for a time period by putting them in order from worst to best. The historical method assumes that history will repeat itself, from a risk perspective. A histogram plot correlates frequency of returns with losses. The results indicate the confidence level related to the occurrence of a worst-case daily loss. (For example, if we invest $1,000, we are 95% confident that our worst daily loss will not exceed $40 ($1,000 × 4%).)

Variance-Covariance Method

The variance-covariance method assumes that stock returns are normally distributed. Expected (or average) return and a standard deviation are estimated and a normal distribution curve is plotted. By reviewing the normal curve, one can see exactly where the worst percentages lie on the curve.

Monte Carlo Simulation

A Monte Carlo simulation refers to any method that randomly generates trials. This method involves developing a model for future returns and running multiple hypothetical trials through the model. It enables the calculation of the expected loss and the variance related to the losses, and thus the probabilities related to the maximum loss.

The CMA candidate is expected to be able to identify and explain VaR but not perform calculations.

Types of Risk

Risks can be any of these types:

- Hazards
- Financial
- Operational
- Strategic
- Capital adequacy

Hazard risks relate to natural disasters such as storms, floods, hurricanes, blizzards, earthquakes, and volcanoes.

Financial risks are caused by debt/equity decisions related to financing the business. They include liquidity (short-term bill paying) and solvency (long-term bill paying) risks usually controlled through adequate financial and capital reserves.

Operational risk relates to the composition and mix of fixed and variable costs in an organization's cost structure. An organization is deemed to be exposed to more risk when a greater percentage of the cost structure is comprised of fixed costs. Operational risks also arise from:

- Internal process failures
- System failures
- Personnel
- Legal and compliance
- Political

Legal and compliance risks relate to the organization's compliance with laws, relevant regulations, and contractual obligations. Political risk is the risk of loss on an investment due to instability or changes in the political environment in a country, such as changes in taxes, passage of laws that prevent the movement of capital, or expropriation of assets.

Capital adequacy applies to all business entities. The following discussion and formula relates specifically to financial institutions, which are not specifically addressed in the LOS.

Capital adequacy measures how well a financial institution protects its depositors and protects the financial systems around the world. The measure of capital adequacy is called the capital adequacy ratio (CAR):

$$\text{CAR} = \frac{\text{Tier 1 Capital} + \text{Tier 2 Capital}}{\text{Risk} - \text{Weighted Assets}}$$

Tier 1 capital is the capital of a financial institution that can absorb losses without being required to cease business. Tier 2 capital is capital that can absorb losses in the event of winding up the business, so it provides a lesser degree of protection to depositors than does tier 1 capital. Winding up is a process that entails selling all the assets of a business entity, paying off creditors, distributing any remaining assets to the principals, and then dissolving the business. The computation of risk-weighted assets requires an evaluation of each of the financial institution's assets in terms of riskiness. The CAR is an important factor in determining the riskiness of a financial institution in relation to solvency, liquidity, reserves, and sufficient capital.

Risks are a function of volatility (variability) and time. Increased volatility, such as variability in expected returns, translates into increased risk. The longer the time frame, the more the uncertainty and, consequently, the higher the risk. Shorter time frames imply lower risk.

Risks should be considered on an entity-wide or portfolio perspective. A portfolio view can be useful for allocating resources across company divisions or changing strategic direction. The remainder of this topic covers risk identification, risk assessment, and risk management, with the enterprise risk management (ERM) model.

Risk Identification

Risk identification seeks to identify as many threats as possible. Risk identification will naturally drive the process to include as many individuals from the organization as possible, especially those with specific detailed information about the particular risk area being considered. For example, a strategic risk assessment would involve senior management, senior finance people, and the strategic planning area. An operational risk assessment would include those from the operating units because they have the insight into how the business processes actually work and, specifically, what threats would interrupt the accomplishment of operational objectives.

A risk framework can be helpful to facilitate the risk identification process. The framework provides guidance to the risk assessment participants and helps them organize the identified threats. The framework can organize risks by categories and by structural element (e.g., strategy, people, process, technology, data) or by business process (e.g., revenue cycle, disbursement cycle, cash management and treasury, financial reporting, operations).

The risk framework should consider both internal and external factors. Risk assessment participants should be tasked and encouraged to identify threats from both factors. Examples of internal and external risk factors are listed next.

Internal Risk Factors

- Communication methods
- Risk assessment activities
- Appropriateness of internal control activities
- Labor relations
- Training and capability of the employees
- Degree of supervision of employees
- Operational risks
- Financial risks
- Strategic risks

External Risk Factors

- Regulatory changes
- Industry competition
- Relationships with key suppliers
- Relationships with customers
- Recruiting and hiring activities
- International risk
- Hazard risks

Tools, diagnostics, and processes that may be used to support risk identification include:

- Checklists
- Flowcharts
- Scenario analysis
- Value chain analysis
- Business process analysis
- Systems engineering
- Process mapping
- Computed cash flow at risk
- Projected earnings at risk
- Projected earnings distributions
- Projected EPS distributions

Once risks are identified, they can be prioritized by risk ranking or risk mapping. A risk map graphically illustrates the impact of risks.

It is useful for management to periodically perform a hindsight evaluation to identify events that were not identified in the prior risk assessment. This allows management to refine and improve the risk assessment process.

Risk Assessment

Risk assessment is the process of analyzing the potential effects of identified risks. Risks are analyzed, considering likelihood and impact, as a basis for determining how they should be managed.

1. *Impact.* The effect the risk occurrence would have on the organization's objective if it were to actually occur. For example, what loss would occur if a particular risk factor occurred and was not detected and corrected?
2. *Likelihood.* The probability or chance that the risk actually will occur.

Risk assessment is a function of the organization's risk appetite as well as the estimate of potential risk. **Risk appetite** is the level of risk the organization is willing to accept given its mission and business model. The organization's risk appetite determines how management will manage risks. For example, the more risk averse an organization is, the more management will be willing to spend on mitigating the risk.

Probabilistic or nonprobabilistic models may be used to quantify risk. Management uses qualitative techniques to assess risk when risks do not lend themselves to quantification or when sufficient reliable data is not available to use a quantitative model. Nonprobabilistic models use subjective assumptions to estimate the impact of events without quantifying an associated likelihood. Examples of nonprobabilistic models include sensitivity measures and stress tests. Probabilistic models associate a range of events and the resulting impact with the likelihood of those events based on certain assumptions. Examples of probabilistic models include VaR and the development of credit and operational loss distributions. Scenario analysis may be applied on a nonprobabilistic or probabilistic basis. As described previously, scenario analysis involves identifying possible future outcomes, attaching probabilities to the outcomes, and mitigating the risks that exceed the organization's risk appetite. For example, consider a manufacturer that contracts with a sole supplier for a particular product. Management might consider a scenario in which the supplier's processes are disrupted by a natural disaster. Management might decide to mitigate this risk by contracting with multiple suppliers.

Ideally, risk assessment activities are performed on a continuous basis by all employees within the organization. However, the process must be driven by those responsible for organization governance: the board of directors and the audit committee. Their commitment and involvement and attitude toward risk must be communicated down through the entire organization. As risks are identified, they are assigned to the appropriate level of management for consideration. The resulting risk assessment culture becomes an integral part of the organization's control environment. In most instances, and typically for strategic risks, the risk assessment process is conducted at regular intervals, usually once a year.

Management should assess both the inherent risk and the residual risk for an event. **Inherent risk** is the risk to the organization if management does nothing to alter its likelihood or impact. **Residual risk** is the risk of the event after considering management's response, including internal control.

Assessing risk generally involves the use of probabilities. For example, if there is a 40% chance that a company will suffer a $1,000,000 loss and a 60% chance that the company will suffer a $300,000 loss, the expected loss can be estimated as $580,000 [(.4 × $1,000,000) + (.6 × $300,000)]. Determining the estimated amounts and their probabilities involves experience, information, and judgment.

Risk response involves reducing risks to an acceptable level by employing the following tactics:

- *Avoidance.* This response involves exiting the activity that gives rise to the risk.
- *Reduction.* This response involves taking action to reduce risk likelihood or impact, or both. For example, this might involve managing the risk or adding additional controls to processes.
- *Acceptance.* This response involves either self-insuring any loss or exploiting the risk for some other benefit.
- *Transfer.* This response involves transferring risk using techniques such as purchasing property and casualty insurance and may also include hedging the risk or outsourcing the activity to which the risk relates.

Note that the IMA's professional partner, Association of Chartered Certified Accountants (ACCA), uses an acronym to aid candidates in remembering these four responses to assessed risk:

T Transfer

A Avoid

R Reduce

A Accept

Operational risks may be lessened by shifting the organization's costs from fixed to variable. For example, a company can outsource parts or activities rather than producing or performing them internally.

Financial risks may be lessened by adjusting the organization's capital structure to minimize the cost of capital. The cost of capital is a function of the mixture of debt, preferred stock, retained earnings, and common stock issued in the organization's capital structure. The proper mix will reduce bankruptcy risk and agency costs to an acceptable level.

It is important to perform a cost–benefit analysis on all risk responses. As an example, establishing controls costing $10,000 per year to mitigate a low risk of $50,000 would probably not be a good business decision.

Risk Management

Given the potential ramifications of mismanaging risk, companies should implement a risk management process that will enable them to avoid risks, reduce the negative effects of risks, prepare to accept some risks, and/or transfer risks to another party (typically by purchasing insurance). As an example, an organization may purchase hazard insurance to transfer the loss from major catastrophes. Although the formality and specifics of the process will vary across different organizations, the general steps of a risk management process are summarized in Figure 2D-2.

Figure 2D-2 Steps in the Risk Management Process

Step 1	**Determine the company's tolerance for risk.**
	This step identifies the organizational attitude toward risk. Will the company accept significant financial risks? Does the company want to take on only selective risk exposures? Must the firm eliminate all risks?
Step 2	**Evaluate the risk exposure.**
	During this step, the specific nature of the exposure must be identified (e.g., what is the primary risk factor?). Then the exposure must be quantified so that a decision can be made as to whether the level of risk is acceptable to the organization.
Step 3	**Implement an appropriate risk management strategy.**
	A risk management strategy identifies what actions (if any) must be taken to manage the risk exposure. A wide variety of strategies is possible.
Step 4	**Monitor the risk exposure and the strategy.**
	Periodic monitoring assesses the status quo or any unexpected changes in the risk exposure (as a result of market volatility, etc.). This step also considers whether the risk management strategy selected is effective. Strategy adjustments may be necessary.

In addition to setting forth specific objectives and strategies with respect to risk management, organizations typically identify the roles and responsibilities of key individuals and establish a hierarchy for decision making. Consideration also is given to how performance results will be measured and reported. *Statement on Management Accounting Enterprise Risk Management: Frameworks, Elements, and Integration* (2014) includes Exhibit 5 A Continuous Risk Management Process. This exhibit illustrates a slightly different approach that CMA candidates may find useful to understanding as we progress to the next subtopic, Enterprise Risk Management: set strategy/objectives, identify risks, assess risks, treat risks, control risks, communicate and monitor.

Enterprise Risk Management

Enterprise risk management (ERM) is the comprehensive analysis and management of all risks facing the organization, including financial, operational, and compliance risk. A variety of software vendors offer ERM packages with the analytics needed to accomplish an effective ERM. IMA's *Statements on Management Accounting, Enterprise Risk Management: Frameworks, Elements, and Integration*, states that the goal of ERM is "to create, protect, and enhance shareholder value by managing the uncertainties that could either negatively or positively influence achievement of the organization's objectives. Stronger internal controls, more effective corporate governance, and implementation of ERM can lead to improved stability, reaction time, and increased shareholder value. Instead of managing risk in many individual silos, ERM takes an integrated and holistic perspective on risks facing an organization."

In September 2004, the Committee of Sponsoring Organizations of the Treadway Commission (COSO) introduced the *Enterprise Risk Management—Integrated Framework (ERM Framework)*, which expands on the COSO's 1992 *Internal Control—Integrated Framework* model. The two frameworks are intended to be complementary, and neither supersedes the other. As such, the *ERM Framework* notes that internal control is a part of ERM.

The *ERM Framework* includes this definition:

Enterprise risk management is a process, effected by an entity's board of directors, management and other personnel, applied in strategy setting and across the enterprise, designed to identify potential events that may affect the entity, and manage risk to be within its risk appetite, to provide reasonable assurance regarding the achievement of entity objectives.

This definition recognizes that ERM is an ongoing, fluid process involving the entire organization. Just as the COSO model of control is intended to be a unifying theory of internal control, the COSO *ERM Framework* is intended to be a unifying and comprehensive analysis of risk. The framework includes eight interrelated components:

1. *Internal environment.* The internal environment refers to the organization's risk management philosophy and risk appetite, integrity and ethical values, and the environment in which it operates.

2. *Objective setting.* Management should establish a process for setting objectives so it can better identify events that may either aid in the organization's success or threaten to impede it. The objectives should be in line with the overall mission of the organization and consistent with its appetite for risk.
3. *Event identification.* This is the process for identifying internal and external events that are relevant to achievement of an entity's objectives. The organization needs established criteria for distinguishing between risks and opportunities and methods for responding to the former and capitalizing on the latter.
4. *Risk assessment.* Risk assessment involves determining the probabilities and importance of risks. Management assesses both inherent risk and residual risk for an event. Inherent risk is the risk to the organization if management does nothing to alter its likelihood or impact. Residual risk is the risk of the event after considering management's response, including internal control.
5. *Risk response.* Risks are analyzed, considering likelihood and impact, as a basis for determining how they should be managed. Responses to inherent risks are developed first. After completing that task, management develops a residual risk profile that identifies the risks that will remain even after inherent risks have been dealt with. Management then must seek ways to manage acceptable risks and transfer unacceptable risks (perhaps with insurance from outside companies).
6. *Control activities.* Policies and procedures are established and implemented to help ensure that the risk responses are effectively carried out. The COSO model lists six control activities:

    a. The assignment of authority and responsibility (job descriptions)
    b. A system of transaction authorizations
    c. Adequate documentation and records
    d. Security of assets
    e. Independent verifications
    f. Adequate separation of duties

7. *Information and communication.* The COSO model recognizes that relevant information must be identified, captured, and communicated in a form and time frame that enables people to do their jobs successfully. This model assumes that the data communicated are secure and accurate.
8. *Monitoring.* All aspects of internal controls are monitored, and modifications made as necessary. Monitoring is accomplished through ongoing management activities, separate evaluations, or both. Internal auditors, the audit committee, and the disclosure committee as well as management all may be involved in monitoring controls.

The eight components of the COSO *ERM Framework* stretch across the strategic, operational, reporting, and compliance functions of an organization and also are relevant across all of the various reporting units of an organization.

According to the COSO model, ERM provides the following advantages:

- *Aligning risk appetite and strategy.* Management considers the entity's risk appetite in evaluating strategic alternatives, setting related objectives, and developing mechanisms to manage related risks. Note that risk appetite is an entity-wide concept while risk tolerance is applied at levels subordinate to the entity as a whole, such as operating units.

- *Enhancing risk response decisions.* ERM provides the rigor to identify and select among alternative risk responses: risk avoidance, reduction, sharing, and acceptance.
- *Reducing operational surprises and losses.* Entities gain enhanced capability to identify potential events and establish responses, reducing surprises and associated costs or losses.
- *Identifying and managing multiple and cross-enterprise risks.* Every enterprise faces a myriad of risks affecting different parts of the organization. ERM facilitates effective response to the interrelated impacts and integrated responses to multiple risks.
- *Seizing opportunities.* By considering a full range of potential events, management is positioned to identify and proactively realize opportunities.
- *Improving deployment of capital.* Obtaining robust risk information allows management to effectively assess overall capital needs and enhance capital allocation.

Source: *Enterprise Risk Management Integrated Framework, Executive Summary*, Copyright © 2004, Committee of Sponsoring Organizations of the Treadway Commission

The capabilities inherent in ERM help management achieve the entity's performance and profitability targets and prevent loss of resources. As noted in the COSO framework, ERM helps ensure effective reporting and compliance with laws and regulations and helps avoid damage to the entity's reputation and associated consequences. In sum, ERM helps an entity get to where it wants to go and avoid pitfalls and surprises along the way. As with any new program, each company should perform a cost–benefit analysis of the ERM before implementation.

ERM involves corporate governance, risk analytics, and portfolio management. The organization must be managed and governed properly, management must assess risks, and it must develop an appropriate portfolio of investments. The portfolio of investments includes current assets (cash, trading securities, receivables, inventories, and prepayments) and noncurrent assets (property, plant, and equipment; long-term investments; natural resources; and intangibles). Management attempts to put together a diversified portfolio balanced to hedge risks in a way that properly addresses the organization's risk appetite.

Knowledge Check: Enterprise Risk

The following questions are intended to help you check your understanding and recall of the material presented in this topic. They do not represent the type of questions that appear on the CMA exam.

Directions: Answer each question in the space provided. Correct answers and section references appear after the knowledge check questions.

1. Controls should be implemented to reduce risk to
   - a. zero.
   - b. the level at which management believes the risk benefit is less than its cost.
   - c. the level of materiality specified by the external auditors.
   - d. the level of materiality specified by the audit committee.

2. The enterprise risk management model looks at
   - a. financial risk.
   - b. operating risk.
   - c. compliance risk.
   - d. all of the above.

3. Enterprise risk management is
   - a. unrelated to internal controls.
   - b. an element of the COSO *Integrated Framework*.
   - c. a unified and comprehensive risk analysis model.
   - d. all of the above.

4. Risks include all of the following **except**:
   - a. hazard risks.
   - b. financial risks.
   - c. personal risks.
   - d. operational risks.

5. Financial risks
   - a. decrease with time.
   - b. are independent of time.
   - c. cannot be controlled.
   - d. are a function of variability.

6. Risk assessment looks at
   - a. the likelihood of threats.
   - b. the impact of threats.
   - c. neither a nor b.
   - d. both a and b.

7. The risk identification framework considers
   - a. only external threats.
   - b. both external and internal threats.
   - c. only internal threats.
   - d. risk priorities.

8. Which of the following risks is usually managed by purchasing an appropriate insurance policy?
   - a. financial risk
   - b. hazard risk
   - c. operational risk
   - d. compliance risk

Knowledge Check Answers: Enterprise Risk

1. Controls should be implemented to reduce risk to [See **Risk Assessment**.]
   - ☐ a. zero.
   - ☑ b. the level at which management believes the risk benefit is less than its cost.
   - ☐ c. the level of materiality specified by the external auditors.
   - ☐ d. the level of materiality specified by the audit committee.

2. The enterprise risk management model looks at [See **Enterprise Risk Management**.]
   - ☐ a. financial risk.
   - ☐ b. operating risk.
   - ☐ c. compliance risk.
   - ☑ d. all of the above.

3. Enterprise risk management is [See **Enterprise Risk Management**.]
   - ☐ a. unrelated to internal controls.
   - ☐ b. an element of the COSO *Integrated Framework*.
   - ☑ c. a unified and comprehensive risk analysis model.
   - ☐ d. all of the above.

4. Risks include all of the following **except**: [See **Types of Risk**.]
   - ☐ a. hazard risks.
   - ☐ b. financial risks.
   - ☑ c. personal risks.
   - ☐ d. operational risks.

5. Financial risks [See **Risk Assessment**.]
   - ☐ a. decrease with time.
   - ☐ b. are independent of time.
   - ☐ c. cannot be controlled.
   - ☑ d. are a function of variability.

6. Risk assessment looks at [See **Risk Assessment**]
   - ☐ a. the likelihood of threats.
   - ☐ b. the impact of threats.
   - ☐ c. neither a nor b.
   - ☑ d. both a and b.

7. The risk identification framework considers [See *Risk Identification*.]
   - ☐ a. only external threats.
   - ☒ b. both external and internal threats.
   - ☐ c. only internal threats.
   - ☐ d. risk priorities.

8. Which of the following risks is usually managed by purchasing an appropriate insurance policy? [See *Risk Response*.]
   - ☐ a. financial risk
   - ☒ b. hazard risk
   - ☐ c. operational risk
   - ☐ d. compliance risk

Practice Questions: Risk Management

Directions: This sampling of questions is designed to emulate actual exam questions. Read each question and write your response on another sheet of paper. See the "Answers to Section Practice Questions" section at the end of this book to assess your response. Validate or improve the answer you wrote. For a more robust selection of practice questions, access the **Online Test Bank** at www.wileycma.com.

Question 2D1-AT16

Topic: Enterprise Risk

Which of the following is **not** an example of a form of political risk associated with foreign direct investment?

- a. Uncontrolled inflation
- b. Nationalization of factories
- c. Change in government regime
- d. Civil war

Question 2D1-AT17

Topic: Enterprise Risk

All of the following are valid reasons for expansion of international business by U.S. multinational corporations, **except** to

- a. secure new sources for raw materials.
- b. find additional areas where their products can be marketed successfully.
- c. protect their domestic market from competition from foreign manufacturers.
- d. minimize their costs of production.

Question 2D1-AT18

Topic: Enterprise Risk

Risk assessment is a process

- a. designed to identify potential events that may affect the entity.
- b. that establishes policies and procedures to accomplish internal control objectives.
- c. that identifies risk but does not include management's response to risk.
- d. that assesses the quality of internal controls throughout the year.

Question 2D1-AT19

Topic: Enterprise Risk

Within a financial risk management context, the term *value at risk* (VaR) is defined as the

- ☐ a. maximum value a company can lose.
- ☐ b. worst possible outcome given the distribution of outcomes.
- ☐ c. most likely negative outcome.
- ☐ d. maximum loss within a certain time period at a given level of confidence.

To further assess your understanding of the concepts and calculations covered in Part 2, Section D: Risk Management, practice with the **Online Test Bank** for this section. **REMINDER:** See the "Answers to Section Practice Questions" section at the end of this book.

SECTION E

Investment Decisions

Capital can refer to assets and/or the financing used to acquire assets—debt and/or equity, in particular. Even the most stable of firms can only borrow up to a certain level or issue a limited amount of shares of common stock to raise capital.

Organizations have limited capital resources and every firm must evaluate investment projects carefully. Management accountants often have a key role in deciding whether an investment is worth undertaking. Content in this section begins with an overview of the capital budgeting process and then reviews the fundamental principles that can facilitate intelligent choices between two or more investment alternatives.

TOPIC 1

Capital Budgeting Process

CAPITAL BUDGETING is the process of making long-term investment decisions that enables a firm to evaluate the viability of a long-term project and whether it is worth undertaking.

READ the Learning Outcome Statements (LOS) for this topic as found in Appendix B and then study the concepts and calculations presented here to be sure you understand the content you could be tested on in the CMA exam.

Capital Budgeting

In financial accounting and reporting we generally think of investments as being long-lived. Long-lived investments are usually in the form of some physical asset such as land, buildings, or equipment, or in some cases in the form of identifiable intangible assets such as patents, copyrights, and other revenue-generating rights. Long-lived investments may also be in the form of equity investments in other entities.

In this topic we devote most of our time to capital budgeting. That is planning for capital expenditures (sometimes referred to as CAPEX).

Current investments (or **current expenditures**) are short term in nature because they are investments that can be expensed in the same year that the costs occur. Wages, salaries, many administrative expenses, and expenditures for raw materials in manufacturing are all examples of current investments.

An **operating budget** (or **current budget**) is a plan for the operating expenses and revenues associated with activities for the current time period.

Capital investments (or **capital expenditures**) are long term in nature because they are investments that require a current cash outlay today with the expectation of future benefits. For tax reporting, the value of the initial cash outlay (for a qualified investment) is gradually reduced (amortized) for tax purposes over a period of years according to Internal Revenue Service (IRS) regulations. Examples of capital investments include expenditures for new or replacement equipment, buildings, and land as well as investments made in research and design (R&D) and the development of new products and services. Although R&D costs are long-term investments for budgeting purposes, annual R&D costs also are expensed in the current period per the requirements of the Accounting Standards Codification [ASC].

A **capital budget** is a plan of proposed outlays for acquiring or constructing long-term assets and includes the means for financing the acquisition.

A firm's stability and future success often depends on its capital investments. Thus, firms need a sound capital budgeting process to analyze and control long-term capital investments. Firms often have great difficulty recovering money tied up in bad capital investments, and bad capital investments reduce the firm's value.

Capital Budgeting Applications

Capital budget proposals can come from a variety of sources. For the process of decision analysis, a capital investment is often placed into one of the following categories:

- *Expansion projects.* New assets (machines, buildings, etc.) bought with the purpose of expanding business operations
- *Replacement projects.* Replacement of existing machines and equipment
- *Mandatory (compliance) projects.* Required by law to maintain safety in the workplace, safety of consumers, or to protect the environment
- *Other projects.* Allocations for R&D for new products and/or the expansion of existing products as well as various other long-term investments for buildings, land, patents, and the like

Alternate capital investment classifications exist, such as:

- Operating efficiency and/or revenue generation
- Competitive effectiveness
- Regulatory, safety, health, and environmental requirements

Whatever classification scheme a company uses, organizational strategies and objectives will influence the evaluation criteria and decision procedures in making a capital investment. It is important to consider qualitative factors in evaluating capital budgeting projects, such as the impact on employee morale, the support of the company's mission statement, and the company's reputation.

Project and Time Dimensions in Capital Budgeting

Two important aspects of capital budgeting are the project dimension and the time dimension.

Project Dimension

Where operational budgeting decisions focus on income determination, planning, and control of activities for the current time period, capital budgeting decisions look at projects that span multiple accounting periods. A capital budgeting project related to the development of a new product, for example, might span several years from R&D through product fulfillment and customer service.

Life-cycle costing must be used to accumulate capital budgeting costs and revenues on a project-by-project basis and track income over the entire project. For the new product development example just given, costs must be accumulated for all business functions in the value chain over many accounting periods.

Time Dimension

Typically, a capital budgeting decision lowers reported income for the current period but has the potential to generate high cash inflows in the future. Therefore, capital budgeting decisions cannot be based solely on the current accounting period's income statement.

Certainly income for any given period is important. For publicly traded companies, income reported in a given period can affect the firm's stock price and can affect management bonuses. But excessive focus on short-term accounting can result in investment decisions that forgo long-term profitability.

The concept of the time value of money is basic to capital budgeting. The time value of money states that:

- A dollar (or any other monetary unit) is worth more today than a dollar received tomorrow because that dollar can be invested today to earn a return.
- A dollar tomorrow is worth less than a dollar today because of the interest forgone.

A $10,000 investment made today with the potential for a 15% annual rate of return would be worth $11,500 at the end of the year. But according to the time value of money, had the investment not been made, the opportunity cost is the $1,500 forgone. Of course the investor would still have the $10,000 available for some other investment purposes, presumably of greater value than its cost.

Stages of Capital Budgeting

LOS
§2.E.1.a

A capital budgeting project consists of a logical progression of activities. The specific names for the stages or steps vary across firms. In general, firms address all of the stages or steps shown in Figure 2E-1.

Figure 2E-1 Stages of Capital Budgeting

Stage 1	**Identification**
	Identify which types of capital budget expenditures are necessary and consistent with organizational goals, objectives, and strategies.
Stage 2	**Search**
	Thoroughly investigate the initial capital investment proposals and explore alternative investments.
Stage 3	**Evaluation**
	Project revenues, financial and nonfinancial benefits, costs, and cash flows for each alternative and compare them for the project's entire life cycle. Management must assess how the project will affect the organization's resources and whether the firm can absorb the costs.

(Continued)

Figure 2E-1 (Continued)

Stage 4	**Selection**
	Choose projects for implementation, which typically means selecting those in which the predicted financial benefits exceed costs (after adjusting for time and risk). Consideration also should be given to the nonfinancial (qualitative) outcomes. For example a company's customer service after the sale is very important to its long-term reputation (and revenue-generating capacity). A decision to invest in an internal customer service activity as opposed to outsourcing that customer service activity can have significant impact on the reputation of the company even though both options have explicit costs.
Stage 5	**Financing**
	Secure project financing either internally (retaining earnings) or externally by selling debt and/or equity in the capital market.
Stage 6	**Implementation and control**
	Implement the capital project and then initiate the monitoring and evaluation tools necessary to keep the project within the capital budget. Adjustments may need to be made to obtain optimal results throughout the project life cycle. **Post-audits** should compare estimates used at the time the project was selected with actual results. A key element of a post-audit is to provide feedback to relevant personnel so that future decision making can be improved.

Incremental Cash Flows

Competent managers and knowledgeable investors always give special attention to the firm's cash position, which is also described as the firm's operating cash flow—hence the saying "Cash is king."

Estimating future cash flows is one of the most important tasks in capital budgeting. A firm must be able to evaluate the difference between its cash flows with and without an investment project—where all relevant costs and benefits are those which have an effect during the project.

Key points in evaluating capital investment cash flows are:

- Income statement items that do not affect cash, such as depreciation expense, amortization expense, gains, and losses, are ignored in cash flow analysis problems (except for any effects they may have on taxes). Additionally, expenses and revenues are adjusted to remove deferrals and accruals, such as unearned revenues, prepaid expenses, accrued revenues, and accrued expenses.
- All items affecting cash flows must be examined regardless of whether they are revenues or expenses for the accounting period.
- Sunk costs are ignored because they are unrecoverable historical costs that are not relevant to the current investment decision.
- Opportunity costs must be included and typically are treated as the equivalent of a cash outlay at the onset of the project.
- Investments in net working capital are treated as cash outflows at the time they occur and as cash inflows when they are released.

- The anticipated effects of inflation must be taken into account in both the relevant cash flows and the required rate of return. Cash flows related to revenues, wages, and material costs are all subject to inflation. To be consistent with inflation-adjusted cash flows, the required rate of return should also contain a premium for inflation (and properly calculated, it does).
- Depreciation expenses are relevant in capital budgeting only to the extent that they affect the firm's tax obligation. Depreciation provides the firm with non-cash expenses that are tax deductible.

Capital investment projects generally begin the same way, with a cash outflow as a payment, incurrence of a liability, or commitment of funds. However, during the life of the investment, different cash flow outcomes are possible. The return on the initial cash outflow may decrease cash expenditures and/or generate additional cash inflows. Furthermore, based on information provided by the project's monitoring and control activities, funds for additional capital investments may be needed.

Relevant incremental cash flows during a capital investment project are categorized based on the timing of when they occur during the capital investment project: at the start of the project, during the course of the project, or at the end. Figure 2E-2 summarizes characteristics of these capital project cash flow categories.

Figure 2E-2 Cash Inflows and Outflows During a Capital Budgeting Project

Category	Description	Cash Flow Activities
Initiation	Initial cash investment	Outflows to fund the investment and initiate the project
		Commitments for net working capital (i.e., current assets minus current liabilities that are non-interest bearing)
		Inflows or outflows if there is an asset being replaced
Operation	Interim incremental net cash flows	Outflows for operating expenditures
		Outflows for additional capital investments (if necessary)
		Commitments for additional net working capital (i.e., current assets minus current liabilities that are non-interest bearing) for operations
		Inflows generated by the investment (e.g., revenues and cash savings) and cash released from net working capital no longer needed for operations
Disposal	Incremental net cash flow for the final year	Inflows or outflows related to the investment's disposal
		Cash inflows from the release of net working capital (i.e., current assets minus current liabilities that are non-interest bearing) no longer committed to the investment

Cash inflows increase the cash available to the business; cash outflows or cash commitments decrease the cash available to the business. Committing funds to working capital makes those funds unavailable for other uses. Working capital is the excess of current assets over current liabilities and is considered the amount of additional funds available to meet operational requirements.

Understanding the next concepts is important before examining each of these relevant cash flow categories further.

- **Direct effect** is the immediate effect that a cash inflow, outflow, or commitment has on cash flows.
- **Tax effect** (or indirect effect) is the change in a firm's tax payments caused by the taxability of revenues and the deductibility of expenses.
- **Net effect** (or total effect) is the total of the direct effect and the indirect tax effect.

Incremental Cash Flow Example

Consider this example of incremental cash flow determination involving the purchase of a new machine in a manufacturing operation:

- The cost for the new machine is $80,000.
- Shipping and installation charges for the machine are $20,000.
- The estimated salvage value for the machine after a useful life of four years is $33,000.
- No additional working capital is required.
- The machine will be installed in an area that has no alternative use so there are no opportunity costs.
- The firm's tax rate is 40%.
- The machine is in the 3-year property class for tax purposes.

Incremental cash flows at the initiation of the project can be summarized as in Figure 2E-3.

Figure 2E-3 Incremental Cash Flows at Initiation

Direct effect for the cost of the new asset	($80,000)
Additional capitalized expenditures (shipping and installation)	(20,000)
Initiation cash flow	($100,000)

Projections for net operating revenue (before depreciation and taxes) after the project begins are shown in Figure 2E-4.

Figure 2E-4 Projections for Net Operating Revenue

	Year-End			
	1	2	3	4
Net cash flows	$40,000	$42,000	$50,000	$38,000

Incremental (future) cash flows during operations and at disposal are shown in Figure 2E-5.

Figure 2E-5 Incremental Cash Flows from Operations and Disposal

	Year-End			
Operation cash flows (years 1 to 4)	1	2	3	4
Net change in operating revenue, excluding depreciation	$40,000	$42,000	$50,000	$38,000
Net increase in tax depreciation charges*	(33,330)	(44,450)	(14,810)	(7,410)
Net change in income before taxes	$6,670	($2,450)**	$35,190	$30,590
Net increase or decrease in taxes at 40% tax rate	(2,668)	980	(14,076)	(12,236)
Net effect after taxes	$4,002	$(1,470)	$21,114	$18,354
Net increase in tax depreciation charges	33,330	44,450	14,810	7,410
Incremental cash flow for years 1 to 4	$37,332	$42,980	$35,924	$25,764
Disposal cash flows (year 4)				
Salvage value of any sold or disposed assets†				$33,000
Net tax effect (taxes due) on the sale or disposal of assets				(13,200)
Disposal cash flow				$19,800

*According to the Modified Accelerated Cost Recovery System (MACRS) depreciation schedule for a three-year asset with a depreciable basis of $100,000, the depreciation rates are year 1 = 33.33%, year 2 = 44.45%, year 3 = 14.81%, and year 4 = 7.41%.

**Assumes that the tax loss shields other income of the firm.

†Assumes salvage value is recapture of depreciation and taxed at the ordinary income rate of 40%.

The expected incremental cash flows determined above are summarized in Figure 2E-6. Note that in capital budgeting, the year when the initial cash outflows begin is referred to as year 0. Note that the concept illustrated and discussed here is similar to the TVM concept. The starting point is time zero. However in this table the figures are not discounted. This concept is similar to what is found in the Accounting Standards Codification where assets are tested for impairment based on undiscounted cash flows; but then, if an impairment is indicated, the cash flows are discounted, assuming that DCF is being used as a substitute for fair value.

Figure 2E-6 Expected Incremental Cash Flows

	Year-End				
	0	1	2	3	4
Net cash flows	($100,000)	$37,332	$42,980	35,924	$45,564*

* Year 4 includes operational cash flows of $25,764 and disposal cash flows of $19,800.

This incremental cash flow data provides the relevant information necessary to judge the financial attractiveness of the project. Management would need to assess how the project will affect the organization's resources, and comparisons should be made to other mutually exclusive alternatives (if any).

A firm then would need to examine the expected cash inflows and outflows of the capital investment project further using various methods. These methods are explained in detail in the next two topics of this section:

- Discounted cash flow (DCF) analysis
- Payback method

The DCF methods adjust cash flows by incorporating the time value of money. For this reason, they are used widely in assessing long-run investment decisions. An important element of DCF is the determination of the hurdle rate to be used. DCF measures the time value of money. The difference between the present value and the future value is interest cost which is reflected in the determination of risk inherent in the investment. If inflation is a factor then inflation should be taken separately into the project evaluation.

Income Tax Considerations

Cash flows resulting from capital investments have various tax effects. Under some circumstances, taxes can either increase or decrease net cash flows from a project and influence their desirability. For example, Congress has been known to offer generous tax credits or depreciation in excess of asset cost for certain types of investments.

Most tax rules set forth for preparing financial statements under GAAP apply to cash flows from capital investment projects. But there are also special tax rules related to capital investments. In particular, tax rules pertaining to depreciation differ in these ways:

- Depreciation amount allowable
- Depreciation time period
- Depreciation pattern
- Investment tax credits

The tax treatment of a depreciable asset can be complex. Whenever a firm invests in an income-producing asset, the productive life of that asset is estimated. The value of any capital asset decreases as its useful life is expended. For accounting purposes, the asset is depreciated over this period.

However, depreciation may not reflect the true value of a capital asset during its useful life because obsolescence may occur at any time. For example, a superior machine is developed that renders an existing one obsolete even though it is not worn out. Furthermore, the depreciation method a firm chooses may be more of a function of the effect on taxes rather than the ability to make a project's book value reflect its true resale value. Modified Accelerated Cost Recovery System (MACRS) is not optional for tax purposes. The depreciation method choices referred to here relate to depreciation for financial reporting purposes. As pointed out earlier, depreciation is a noncash expense; thus the only impact for capital depreciation purposes would be tax savings from using MACRS tax depreciation for income tax purposes.

In practice, a variety of factors can complicate depreciation. Thorough investigation of the current and applicable tax code and/or consultation with a tax specialist is advisable.

Depreciation Amount Allowable

While it is important for CMA candidates to understand how depreciation is calculated, candidates are not expected to calculate depreciation amounts on the CMA exam. Depreciation amounts related to capital budgeting decisions will be provided in exam problems. The "Depreciation Pattern" section later in this topic provides an overview of several depreciation methods, so that candidates gain an understanding of the effect that the various methods may have on evaluating a potential investment.

Computing the depreciation amount allowable for an asset requires a determination of the asset's depreciable basis. In tax accounting, **depreciable basis** (or fully installed cost) is the amount that can be written off for tax purposes over a period of years.

Typically, the amount allowable is the original cost of the asset. This includes other capitalized expenditures that are necessary to prepare the asset for use (such as shipping and installation charges). Capitalized expenditures are treated as depreciable cash outlays and not as expenses of the period in which they are incurred.

In some situations, the amount allowable can be greater or less than the original investment costs. For example in some situations Congress offers investment tax credits for certain capital expenditures and also allows the full cost of the asset to be depreciated. In other instances Congress may allow an asset to be depreciated beyond its actual cost. Tax credits, for example, can reduce the amount allowable below the original cost, and some tax laws permit companies to claim depreciation amounts for specific assets in excess of the investment made.

Depreciation Time Period

There are three main techniques for determining the depreciation time period for capital investments:

1. The taxpayer estimates the useful life.
2. Tax authorities estimate the useful life.
3. Tax law specifies the allowable life through a series of tax tables, such as the Modified Accelerated Cost Recovery System (MACRS), pronounced "makers." (NOTE: Under MACRS, the asset's original cost is NOT reduced by the estimated salvage value of the asset in determining the amount that can be written off for tax purposes.)

Generally, the shorter the allowable life of the asset, the fewer periods over which the depreciation of the asset can be claimed. This shorter allowable life results in a higher depreciable amount per year, higher tax deductions, and greater tax savings in the early years. Of course in most instances the total depreciation is the same no matter which method is used to calculate depreciation.

Depreciation Pattern

Tax authorities allow different depreciation patterns based on the time periods. A variety of depreciation methods are possible. An overview of a few of the more common methods follows.

Straight-Line Depreciation

Straight-line (SL) depreciation allocates expenses equally over the depreciable life of the asset. An equal depreciation amount is taken each year.

The general formula for straight-line depreciation is:

$$\text{Straight-Line Depreciation} = \frac{\text{Cost} - \text{Salvage Value}}{\text{Estimated Useful Life}}$$

For example: An asset costs $10,000 with an estimated useful life of 5 years and a salvage value of $2,000. Using the straight-line depreciation method results in equal depreciation expenses each year over the equipment's 5-year life of:

$$\text{Straight-Line Depreciation} = \frac{\$10,000 - \$2,000}{5} = \$1,600 \text{ each full year}$$

Accelerated Depreciation

Accelerated depreciation refers to any method that writes off a capital investment faster than under straight-line depreciation. More of the depreciable amount is written off in the early years of the investment than with the straight-line method. Sum-of-the-years' and declining-balance depreciation are examples of accelerated depreciation methods.

Sum-of-the-years' digits (SYD) is one method to reduce the book value of a capital investment rapidly in the early years and at a lower rate in the later years of the asset's life. The SYD method takes into consideration the estimated salvage value in the same manner as the SL method.

For example: Use the same $10,000 asset with a 5-year life and a $2,000 estimated salvage value to determine the amount of depreciation during the first year using the SYD method. Because this asset has an estimated useful life of 5 years, the sum of the numbers is 15 (as 1 + 2 + 3 + 4 + 5 = 15). Each factor shown here assumes the depreciation is for a full year. This becomes messy when SYD is used with a partial first-year depreciation amount.

The asset is depreciated in this manner:

- 33.33% (5/15) in the first year.
- 26.67% (4/15) in the second year.

- 20.00% (3/15) in the third year.
- 13.33% (2/15) in the four year.
- 6.67% (1/15) in the fifth year.

Thus, the depreciation for the first year is $2,667 ($8,000 × 0.3333) using the SYD method versus $1,600 using the SL method. During the fifth year, the SYD depreciation is $536 ($8,000 × 0.067) versus $1,600 using the SL method. Compared with depreciation using the SL method, depreciation using the SYD method is higher during the early years but lower in the latter years of an asset's life.

Declining-balance (DB) depreciation decreases the asset's book value by a constant percentage each year. Unlike the SL and SYD methods, the DB method does not explicitly use the salvage value in its calculations. However, depreciation expense will be halted when the cost less salvage value has been depreciated. The general formula for the DB method to determine the depreciation charge in any period is:

$$(1/n) \text{ Book Value}$$

where:

n = depreciable life of the asset
NBV = asset's net book value at the start of the year
(cost − accumulated depreciation)

For example: For a $10,000 asset with a 5-year life, the depreciation in the first year would be $2,000. The 1/5 determines the fixed percentage, or 20%, that is applied against the declining book value each year. The net book value for the second year would be $8,000 (the acquisition cost minus accumulated depreciation). Thus, the depreciation charge for year 2 would be:

$$(0.20) \$8,000 = \$1,600$$

Depreciation ceases when book value is reduced to equal salvage value. The asset should never be reduced below the estimated salvage value.

MACRS tables categorize all business assets into classes (e.g., computers and peripheral equipment, office machinery, office furniture, nonresidential real estate, etc.) and then specify the time period over which the assets can be written off in each class (e.g., 3-year property, 5-year property, 7-year property, etc.). Depending on the class of an asset, different conventions can be used to adjust the first-year depreciation depending on the placed-in-service date.

Candidates are reminded that for companies whose operations are based outside the U.S., many countries have tax-specific depreciation guidance that differs from ASC accounting and reporting. For example, in the United Kingdom (UK), there is no depreciation for income tax determination purposes. In place of depreciation the UK provides capital allowances each year that reduce the income tax liability. Consult with the local tax authorities for the appropriate tax guidance. The IRS provides special tables to determine the percentage of the item's tax basis that can be depreciated each year. The asset's tax basis does not change over the years, only the percentage used as a multiplier changes.

For example: Assume that the $10,000 asset previously discussed is classified as 5-year asset life category. The depreciation rates as a percentage shown in Figure 2E-7 apply to the original basis ($10,000), not the depreciable basis ($10,000 − $2,000).

Figure 2E-7 5-Year Asset Life Category

Year	% (rounded)
1	20.00
2	32.00
3	19.20
4	11.52
5	11.52
6	5.76

This table is based on the DDB method, which switches to straight-line depreciation. Year 1 is the year in which the asset is placed in service. This table uses the midyear convention, which assumes that the asset is placed in service at midyear. Thus, the company can expense only half of the normal amount of depreciation during year 1. And, in the sixth year—because of the midyear convention—the company can expense at only half of the year 5 rate (i.e., 11.52%/2 = 5.76%). The company may have a different policy for financial reporting purposes for acquisitions other than at the beginning or ending of the year. The mid-year convention embedded in the MACRS tables is one of the possible financial accounting policy choices the company could use.

For the $10,000 asset with an estimated salvage value of $2,000, the depreciation expense for year 1 is 0.20 ($10,000) = $2,000.

Although a full discussion of how income taxes specifically can affect cash inflows and outflows for capital investments is beyond the scope of this text, the next general points can be made about depreciation and tax considerations in profitable companies:

- Depreciation deductions are not cash payments; they are non-cash costs that reduce taxable income and taxes.
- A depreciation expense has an effect on the amount of income taxes a firm must pay for a given period.
- Because depreciation reduces taxable income and reduces the tax outflow, depreciation effectively results in a cash inflow. Using the example above of a

MACRS 5-year life asset with a depreciable cost of $10,000 with an estimated salvage value of $2,000, the depreciation expense for year 1 is 0.20 ($10,000) = $2,000. If the company's marginal tax rate is 30%, the $2,000 depreciation expense will reduce the tax liability by $600, in effect creating a cash inflow or a reduced cash outflow.
- The decrease in the tax liability due to the depreciation charge is referred to as a **depreciation tax shield**.
- This tax shield is equal to the depreciation amount multiplied by the tax rate.

Companies may favor accelerated depreciation patterns for certain high technology assets because those assets tend to become obsolete sooner than other depreciable assets. One side issue is that if depreciation charges do not accurately relate to declining use of the asset, then the company may be faced with impairment charges later. Compared to the SL method, however, accelerated methods result in lower earnings per share (EPS) during the early years but higher EPS during the later years, holding other factors constant.

Qualitative Considerations in Capital Investments

There are a variety of quantitative methods available for evaluating capital budgeting projects. Most of the techniques discussed have distinct strengths and weaknesses. As a result, managers should, and often do, use multiple criteria for evaluating investment projects. Collectively, multiple methods mitigate the potential for estimation errors and/or incorrect decisions that are not in the best interests of the firm or shareholders.

In addition to quantitative methods, a firm also should recognize these important qualitative factors that can influence investment decisions:

- Management may not have the necessary information to make capital budgeting decisions (e.g., type of information or frequency).
- Loan provisions may limit borrowing.
- The firm may have self-imposed capital rationing limits.
- Decision makers may be risk averse.
- Conflict may exist between decisions to take on a project and performance evaluation of managers (a manager might be concerned about how a project will affect a bonus plan based on reported annual accrual accounting numbers).
- A firm may not have sufficient or qualified personnel to implement capital projects successfully.
- Management may assess whether the investment can increase customer loyalty and retention.

Capital investments often are strategic in nature and are based partly on qualitative factors that are important to consider but difficult to estimate. When companies reject what may seem to be intuitively obvious superior investments in favor of less quantitatively endowed investments, the qualitative factors may have influenced the decision. For example, in 1987 the Australian tycoon and America Cup champion Alan Bond decided that he simply had to purchase the G. Heileman Brewing Company. All analytic data related to the share price that Bond offered Heileman's shareholders pointed to overwhelming evidence that the offered price would render Heileman insolvent within a few years because the entire hostile takeover price was debt financed. The interest expense alone exceeded Heileman's highest yearly earnings ever. Bond proceeded with the hostile takeover anyway. And sure enough, Heileman was forced into bankruptcy in 1991.

Knowledge Check: Capital Budgeting Process

The following questions are intended to help you check your understanding and recall of the material presented in this topic. They do not represent the type of questions that appear on the CMA exam.

Directions: Answer each question in the space provided. Correct answers and section references appear after the knowledge check questions.

1. Capital budgeting is **best** described as
   - ☐ a. decision making related to current expenditures.
   - ☐ b. the process of making long-term investment decisions.
   - ☐ c. the process of planning for short-term investments.
   - ☐ d. decision making to support operating efficiency.

2. Which of the following items is **not** an example of a capital expenditure?
   - ☐ a. Heating, ventilation, and air-conditioning system upgrade for Environmental Protection Agency compliance
   - ☐ b. Purchase of a new assembly machine that will cut labor and maintenance costs
   - ☐ c. Purchase of a new computer server for the research and development group
   - ☐ d. Project bonuses paid to salaried employees

3. As it relates to relevant cash flow categories, *direct effect* refers to the
   - ☐ a. immediate effect that a cash inflow, outflow, or commitment has on cash flows.
   - ☐ b. change in a firm's tax obligations.
   - ☐ c. net increase or decrease in tax depreciation charges.
   - ☐ d. total of the indirect effect and the tax effect.

Knowledge Check Answers: Capital Process

1. Capital budgeting is **best** described as [See *Capital Budgeting*.]
   - ☐ a. decision making related to current expenditures.
   - ☑ b. the process of making long-term investment decisions.
   - ☐ c. the process of planning for short-term investments.
   - ☐ d. decision making to support operating efficiency.

2. Which of the following items is **not** an example of a capital expenditure? [See *Capital Budgeting*.]
   - ☐ a. Heating, ventilation, and air-conditioning system upgrade for Environmental Protection Agency compliance
   - ☐ b. Purchase of a new assembly machine that will cut labor and maintenance costs
   - ☐ c. Purchase of a new computer server for the research and development group
   - ☑ d. Project bonuses paid to salaried employees

3. As it relates to relevant cash flow categories, *direct effect* refers to the [See *Initiation Cash Flows*.]
   - ☑ a. immediate effect that a cash inflow, outflow, or commitment has on cash flows.
   - ☐ b. change in a firm's tax obligations.
   - ☐ c. net increase or decrease in tax depreciation charges.
   - ☐ d. total of the indirect effect and the tax effect.

TOPIC 2

Discounted Cash Flow Analysis

VARIOUS TECHNIQUES ARE AVAILABLE to evaluate capital investment projects. This topic discusses one of the more technically correct techniques: **discounted cash flow (DCF)** analysis. DCF analysis adjusts cash flows over time for the time value of money. DCF methods are used to evaluate a capital investment by comparing the present value of all future net cash flows against the initial investment. The payback and discounted payback methods, for example, will be covered in the next topic.

Two popular DCF methods are covered:

1. Net present value (NPV) uses a specified discount rate to bring all subsequent net cash flows after the initial investment to their present values at the time of the initial investment, sums them, then subtracts the investment's initial cash outlay. NPV emphasizes the dollar amount of value added to the firm at the time of the investment. The NPV method is the preferred method for evaluating capital budgeting projects. It is consistent with the objective of maximizing shareholder wealth. Shareholder wealth is the NPV of the firm's future cash flows at its weighted average cost of capital (WACC).

2. Internal rate of return (IRR) estimates the discount rate at which the present value of all the subsequent net cash flows after the initial investment equal the initial cash outlay(s) of the investment. (NOTE: IRR can also be viewed as the discount rate that gives a capital investment project an NPV equal to zero.) IRR uses the discount rate as a point of comparison. There are two limitations to using the IRR method:
   a. First, the method implicitly assumes that the firm reinvests cash inflows earned from a capital budgeting project at the IRR, which may not always be correct.
   b. Second, if any of the cash flows other than the initial investment are negative, the project might have multiple IRRs.

READ the Learning Outcome Statements (LOS) for this topic as found in Appendix B and then study the concepts and calculations presented here to be sure you understand the content you could be tested on in the CMA exam.

Required Rate of Return

Although each discounted cash flow (DCF) method takes a different approach, net present value (NPV) and internal rate of return (IRR) both use these criteria to evaluate a capital investment:

- Total initial cash flow for the investment
- Expected future cash inflows and outflows from the investment
- Firm's required rate of return for the investment

The capital budgeting process, discussed in Topic 1 of this section, covered initial cash investment and incremental cash flows. The next step in the capital budgeting process is to determine if the anticipated cash flows meet the required rate of return and the WACC requirements established by the company.

The **required rate of return** represents the minimum return the firm will accept in choosing an investment. Stated another way, it is the return that a firm could expect to receive elsewhere for a capital investment of comparable risk. The required rate of return also is referred to as the desired rate of return, the **hurdle rate**, the threshold, or the (opportunity) cost of capital. Opportunity cost was discussed in an earlier topic.

From a practical standpoint, determining the desired rate of return for all potential investments is challenging as well as time consuming. Firms tend to use two alternative discount rates to expedite the process: a minimum rate of return or the firm's weighted average cost of capital (WACC). WACC is the conceptually correct discount rate.

Minimum Rate of Return

Firms typically have a minimum rate of return figure that they use to evaluate investments. This rate usually is based on the firm's strategic objectives, industry averages, and common investment opportunities. When a firm uses a minimum rate of return as an investment benchmark, capital investment projects must meet this rate.

Cost of Capital

The WACC is a weighted average of the various components a firm uses for long-term financing. WACC is found by determining the cost of each individual capital component (e.g., issues of preferred or common stock; borrowing through various forms of debt, such as loans and bonds; or retained earnings) and then multiplying the cost of each by its proportion in the firm's total capital structure. As an example of WACC, GlaxoSmithKline plc reports that its WACC for 2015 is 7%, but the discount rate is adjusted where appropriate for the company's foreign operations in specific country or currency risks. By comparison, Rio Tinto plc reports that its discount rate was 9.2% in 2014 but adds a comment: "The discount rate applied is based upon the Company's weighted average cost of capital, with appropriate adjustment for the risks associated with the relevant unit."

Recall the general formula for the cost of capital:

$$k_a = w_1 k_1 + w_2 k_2 \ldots + w_n k_n$$

where:
- k_a = cost of capital (expressed as a percentage)
- w = weight that component comprises of the total capital structure
- k = cost of a component in the capital structure
- 1, 2, and n = different types of financing (each with its own cost and proportion in the capital structure)

Section B: Corporate Finance covers the specific formulas for determining the cost of each component in a firm's capital structure. It also examines how the WACC is used to calculate the relative importance of each source in the total capital structure of the firm once the individual capital components have been determined.

Recall the formula for the WACC:

$$\text{Weighted Average Cost of Capital} = w_d k_{dt} + w_e k_e$$

where:
- w_d = percentage of debt
- k_{dt} = after-tax cost of debt
- w_e = percentage of equity
- k_e = cost of equity

Firms often use WACC to evaluate the cost of capital investments that have risk profiles consistent with the firm's overall risk profile (i.e., projects of average riskiness for the firm).

Thus, in making capital investment decisions, the cost of capital can be applied as the discount rate to evaluate the present value (PV) of project cash flows. It may also provide the basis for the required rate of return and the point of comparison for a capital investment project's internal rate of return.

Net Present Value

Net present value (NPV) is the PV of a project's future cash flows less the initial investment in the project. It discounts all expected future cash inflows and outflows to the present.

In order to calculate NPV, the PV first must be determined.

Present Value Calculation

Present value (PV) is the equivalent dollar value today of future net cash flows. It is determined by applying appropriate discount rate factors (based on the required rate of return) to the future cash flows. Discount rate factors can be derived in two ways: by using an algebraic formula or by applying a discount rate factor from a table. The discount rate factor tables simply list the discount rates that are calculated by using the algebraic formula. Some CMA candidates may prefer to use a financial calculator to complete these problems; the financial calculator will calculate the discount factor based on the data that is input by the user.

As stated in the CMA Handbook on page 11 under the "Calculator Policy" heading: "Small battery or solar powered electronic calculators restricted to a maximum of six functions—addition, subtraction, multiplication, division, square root, and percentage are allowed. The calculator must not be programmable and must not use any type of tape. Candidates can also use the Texas Instruments BA II Plus, Hewlett-Packard 10BII, HP 12c, or HP 12c Platinum calculators when taking the exams. Candidates will not be allowed to use calculators that do not comply with these restrictions."

Many of the time-value-of-money calculations illustrated in the Investment Decisions section include the keystrokes and variables from the Texas Instruments BA II Plus calculator. You may wish to set your BA II Plus calculator to at least three decimal places to minimize differences that might arise from rounding. The TVM tables that are provided are set to three decimal places.

The TVM table factors are provided in the examples and questions here, as well as on the CMA exams to facilitate TVM calculations.

The next formulas can be used to calculate PV amounts using the algebraic approach or the discount rate factor tables.

$$\text{Present Value (PV)} = \frac{\text{Amount of Cash Flow}}{(1+r)^n}$$

where:
  r = discount rate
  n = number of periods

or

$$\text{Present Value (PV)} = \text{Amount of Cash Flow} \times \text{Discount Rate Factor}$$

Using the algebraic formula, the PV of $20,000, to be received in one year, with a 10% required rate of return would be calculated as shown:

$$\text{Present Value (PV)} = \frac{\text{Amount of Cash Flow}}{(1+r)^n}$$

$$PV = \$20{,}000 / (1 + 0.10)^1$$

$$PV = \$20{,}000 / 1.1$$

$$PV = \$18{,}182$$

The PV of $20,000, to be received in one year, with a 10% required rate of return also can be determined by using the PV of $1 factor table listed in Figure 2E-8. Refer to the figure to locate the appropriate discount rate.

Figure 2E-8 Partial Present Value of $1 Interest Factor Table

(n) Periods	10%	11%	12%
1	**0.909**	0.901	0.893
2	0.826	0.812	0.797
3	0.751	0.731	0.712
4	0.683	0.659	0.636
5	0.621	0.593	0.567
6	0.564	0.535	0.507
7	0.513	0.482	0.452
8	0.467	0.434	0.404
9	0.424	0.391	0.361
10	0.386	0.352	0.322

The discount rate (0.909) taken from the PV interest factor table is the discount factor for 10% in one period.

Present Value (PV) = Amount of Cash Flow × Discount Rate
  PV = $20,000 × 0.909
  PV = $18,180

Note that the PV is $2 different from the amount calculated using the algebraic formula. This is simply due to rounding of the PV interest factor in the table.

Proof of this calculation can be found by determining the cash investment one year from now as shown:

Present value of cash now	=	$18,180
Interest for one year ($18,180 × 10%)	=	1,818
Total cash in one year from now	=	$19,998

In other words, $18,180 is the PV equivalent of a $20,000 cash inflow that will be received one year from now.

Using the BA II Plus TVM Calculator on the CMA Exams

The third row of the BA II Plus is used for TVM problems. It is a good idea to press 2nd clear TVM keys before starting. If an annuity problem is being solved make sure to set the calculator to BGN or END for annuity due or ordinary annuity situations. 2nd BGN 2nd SET flips back and forth between annuity due and ordinary annuity. If the calculator is set for annuity due, BGN will appear in the upper right corner of the screen. If BGN does not appear then the calculator is set for ordinary annuity.

Identify the variables you will be using. Most problems use four variables, one of which is unknown and to be solved. If the problem is one that includes both periodic annuity payments and a future or present value, then there will be five variables used, one of which is unknown and is to be solved. The five variables are as listed below and coincide with the BA II Plus third row except that I is I/Y on the BA II Plus. The BA II Plus usually comes from the factory with I/Y being 12, which stands for interest per month. It is a good idea to change this so that I/Y is 1. To make this change, press 2nd P/Y. If it says 1 no change is necessary. If it says 12, press 1 enter then 2nd SET.

N
I
PV
PMT
FV

As stated in the above example, we want to compute the PV of $20,000, to be received in one year, with a 10% required rate of return. There are four variables, of which we know three and one is unknown and must be solved.

N = 1
I = 10
PV = compute this after entering the three other variables;
FV = 20000

Note that PMT is not used because this is not an annuity problem. Also note that 20000 is the amount we want in one year. That amount is a cash inflow at the end of one year so it is entered as a plus, but the plus sign is implied by showing no sign. Then press CPT PV. The answer is –18,181.181. The minus sign indicates that 18181.181 must be deposited today to grow to 20000 at the end of one year at 10% discount rate. The number of decimal places can be set in the calculator as you wish.

Net Present Value Calculation

NPV is the amount in dollars today that an investment is worth over cost.

The six steps in determining the NPV for a capital project are listed next.

1. Determine net cash flows for each year.
2. Identify the required rate of return.

3. Determine the discount for each year using the appropriate table factor or a Texas Instrument BA II Plus calculator for the required rate of return in Step 2.
4. Determine the PVs for the net cash flows; multiply the amount for Step 1 by the amount for Step 3.
5. Total the amounts in Step 4 for all years of the investment.
6. Subtract the initial investment amount.

NPV can be used to evaluate investments with both uniform net cash flows and with uneven cash flows. Step-by-step examples of both types of calculations are shown next.

Uniform Net Cash Flows Example

Uniform cash flows also is described as an **annuity investment**. An annuity provides a series of equal cash flows over a specified number of periods and requires the use of the PV interest factor annuity table to determine the discount factor. The discount factor varies based on the number of years and the desired rate of return.

For example: Consider this scenario:

- The minimum desired rate of return for an investment over three years is 10%.
- Net cash flows for each year of the investment are $125,000 with each cash flow occurring at the end of the year, hence ordinary annuity.

Refer to Figure 2E-9 to locate the appropriate discount rate.

Figure 2E-9 Partial Present Value Interest Factor Annuity Table

(n) Periods	10%	11%	12%	13%
1	0.909	0.901	0.893	0.885
2	1.736	1.713	1.690	1.668
3	**2.487**	2.444	2.402	2.361
4	3.170	3.102	3.037	2.974
5	3.791	3.696	3.605	3.517
6	4.355	4.231	4.111	3.998
7	4.868	4.712	4.564	4.423
8	5.335	5.146	4.968	4.799
9	5.759	5.537	5.328	5.132
10	6.145	5.889	5.650	5.426

The discount rate of 2.487 is found using the PV interest factor annuity table for three years at 10%. The PV of the net cash inflows can then be calculated as shown:

$$\text{PV of Net Cash Inflows} = \$125{,}000 \times 2.487 = \$310{,}875$$

This problem can also be solved with the BA II Plus calculator as follows:

The four variables used are

N = 3
I = 10

PV = compute = −310857: note the rounding difference. If the table factor was rounded to four decimal places the result would be −310,857, the same as computed with the BA II Plus.

PMT 125000

Note: FV is not used in this problem so make sure it is zero in the calculator.

If an initial cash investment of $300,000 is required, then the PV of the investment is determined by subtracting the initial investment from the PV of the net cash inflow as shown:

$$NPV = \$310{,}875 - \$300{,}000 = \$10{,}875$$

The NPV calculation in this example indicates that the initial investment of $300,000 is worth $10,875 (over cost) given a discount rate of 10%.

Uneven Cash Flows Example

A project with uneven cash flow projections over its life starts with the net cash inflows generated each year and then discounts them using the PV interest factor table. The discount factor will vary for each year of the investment.

For example: Consider this scenario:

- The total initial investment is $90,000.
- The minimum required rate of return over four years is 10%.
- Annual net cash inflows over the life of the investment are $60,000, $40,000, $30,000, and $20,000.

Refer to the Present Value of $1 Table in Appendix A and locate the appropriate values for the four periods. If you are using the BA II Plus, the keystroke sequence using CF and NPV functions appears at the end of this section.

Figure 2E-10 shows how the cash flows are discounted using the PV interest factor table excerpt to determine the PV for each year.

Figure 2E-10 Using Net Present Value to Evaluate a Project

Year	Cash Inflows		Discount Factor at 10%		Present Value
1	$60,000	×	0.909	=	$54,540
2	40,000	×	0.826	=	33,040
3	30,000	×	0.751	=	22,530
4	20,000	×	0.683	=	13,660
Total present value of net cash inflows					$123,770
Less initial investment					(90,000)
NPV					$33,770

The NPV calculation indicates that the initial investment of $90,000 is worth $33,770, over cost.

Notice how Figure 2E-10 provides a useful worksheet for evaluating the effect of each of the various factors. A 10% decrease in cash inflows or an increase in the discount factor to 11% could be done and would result in a different PV amount. The worksheet also could be useful for doing a comparison of DCFs for a selection of projects. This type of analysis is often part of the risk analysis that is done when evaluating projects.

Using the BA II Plus we need to use the cash flow function when cash flows are in uneven amounts. Press CF key. The calculator requests CFo. This is the initial investment of −90000. Key −90000 Enter. Press down arrow. Input first cash flow C01 60000. Press Enter. Press down arrow. Input the frequency of cash flow C01, which is 1. Enter. Press down arrow and input the second cash flow 40000, Enter, press down arrow, press 1 for F02. Press down arrow, 30000 Enter, down arrow, 1 Enter. Press down arrow, 20000 Enter, down arrow, 1 Enter. Press NPV. Calculator requests discount rate. 10 Enter. Press down arrow. Press CPT. NPV = 33803, which once again is the rounding difference that could be resolved with tables using more decimal places. Note that in this problem you did not use the third row of the calculator but rather the CF function and the NPV function.

Net Present Value Interpretation

NPV may be interpreted in this way:

- An NPV of zero means that the investment earns the same rate of return as the required rate of return.
- A positive NPV indicates that the investment earns a higher rate of return than the required rate; the present value of future cash flows is greater than the initial investment cost.
- A negative NPV means that future cash flows will earn a return less than the required rate.

Projects with NPV of zero are accepted if no higher NPV project is available. This is true because an NPV of zero indicates that the project data produces an NPV equal to the required rate of return. Projects with a positive NPV are acceptable because they add value to the firm. Projects with a negative NPV indicate that the firm would earn less than required in a PV sense. However, a positive NPV does not mean that the project is the best possible investment alternative for a firm. A positive NPV simply means that the investment will earn a higher rate of return than the firm's required rate. Alternative investment opportunities may offer even better returns. This fact is important when faced with mutually exclusive investment opportunities (i.e., the acceptance of one project precludes the acceptance of other alternative projects).

Internal Rate of Return

The **internal rate of return (IRR)** estimates the discount rate that makes the PV of net cash inflows equal to the initial investment. Stated another way, IRR is a discount rate that will make the NPV of an investment zero (if the rate is used as the required rate of return to compute NPV). Further, the IRR represents the discount rate where the PV of future net cash flows equals the initial investment.

Internal Rate of Return Interpretation

The IRR method evaluates a capital investment by comparing the estimated IRR to a predetermined criterion. This criterion is based on whatever rate the firm uses to evaluate investments, such as its minimum required rate of return, the rate from another desirable alternate investment, or an industry average. The criterion rate serves as a cutoff point. Projects below this cutoff rate are rejected unless they are mandatory projects.

Internal Rate of Return Calculation

If you are performing the IRR calculation manually, the IRR method has two fundamental steps:

1. Determine the rate of return that makes the PV of net cash inflows equal the investment's initial dollar investment.
2. Compare the estimated rate of return with the firm's required rate of return (the criterion cutoff) to assess the investment's desirability.

If you are performing the IRR calculation with a BA II Plus please follow the keystroke instructions at the end of each of the following examples. Similar to NPV, IRR may be used to evaluate investments with uniform net cash flows and with uneven cash flows. Examples of both types of calculations follow.

Uniform Net Cash Flows Example

The steps in determining IRR for a capital project with uniform net cash flows are:

1. Determine the total initial investment for the project (total initial cash outflows and commitments).
2. Identify the predetermined criterion cutoff rate of return (the minimum required rate of return).
3. Determine net cash inflows for each year.
4. Divide the initial investment (Step 1) by the annual cash flow (Step 3) to obtain the IRR factor, which is basically the present value interest factor for an annuity (PVIFA).
5. Refer to the PV annuity table in Appendix A to locate a discount rate at the specified number of years that matches the IRR factor (or the one closest to it).
6. Compare the IRR rate (Step 5) to the chosen criterion cutoff rate (Step 2).

If the calculated IRR exceeds the criterion cutoff rate, which serves as the minimum desired rate of return, the project is a desirable investment.

For example: Consider this scenario:

- The total initial investment is $35,000.
- The predetermined criterion required rate is 10%.
- Net cash inflows for each of the next three years are $15,000 each.

The IRR factor can then be calculated as shown:

$$\text{IRR factor} = \$35{,}000 / \$15{,}000 = 2.33$$

Refer to the Present Value of an Annuity Table in Appendix A to locate the IRR value.

In this example, IRR equals 13% (using the annuity table for three periods and interpolating to the nearest table value, 2.361).

Because the criterion cutoff rate (serving as the required rate of return) is 10% and the IRR value for the project is very close to 13%, the project is a desirable investment. If the desired rate of return had been 14%, the project should be rejected.

The BA II Plus can be used for both even and uneven IRR calculations. Use the CF function to input the investment variables. Press CF, press –35000, down arrow, press 15000 Enter, down arrow, press 3 Enter. If any earlier CF problem data is still in the calculator it needs to be deleted. The F0 frequencies should be 1 for any deleted CF. Press IRR. Press CPT. The IRR is approximately 13.7%.

Uneven Cash Flows Example

For a project with uneven cash flow projections, the IRR calculation becomes trial and error and interpolation. Cash flows must be discounted at various rates until a rate is found that makes the PV of the future cash flows equal to the initial investment.

In practice, computer spreadsheet programs and financial calculators make determining the IRRs of changing cash flows fairly easy. The next numerical example helps to illustrate the concepts behind the procedures.

For example: Consider this scenario:

- The total initial investment is $10,675.
- The criterion cutoff rate is 10%.
- The predicted annual net cash inflows over the life of the investment are $6,000, $4,000, and $3,000, occurring at the ends of years 1, 2, and 3, respectively.

Refer to Figure 2E-11 and locate the appropriate table factors for the three periods.

Figure 2E-11 Partial Present Value Interest Factor Table

(n) Periods	10%	11%	12%
1	0.909	0.901	0.893
2	0.826	0.812	0.797
3	0.751	0.731	0.712
4	0.683	0.659	0.636
5	0.621	0.593	0.567
6	0.564	0.535	0.507
7	0.513	0.482	0.452
8	0.467	0.434	0.404
9	0.424	0.391	0.361
10	0.386	0.352	0.322

Figure 2E-12 shows how the cash flows are discounted using the PV interest factor table to determine the PV for each year.

Figure 2E-12 Total Present Value of Net Cash Inflows at 10%

Year	Cash Inflows		Discount Factor at 10%		Present Value
1	$6,000	×	0.909	=	$5,454
2	4,000	×	0.826	=	3,304
3	3,000	×	0.751	=	2,253
Total present value of net cash inflows					$11,011
Total initial investment (cash outflow)					(10,675)
Net present value					$ 336

The NPV for the three years is $336. A positive NPV means that the project is expected to yield a return higher than the one applied (in this case, 10%). Therefore, the next step is to use a higher rate. Figure 2E-13 computes the NPV at a discount rate of 12%. Refer to the Present Value of $1 Table in Appendix A and locate the appropriate values for the three periods at 12%.

These are uneven cash flow amounts. Use the CF function on the the BA II Plus to input the investment variables. Press CF. Press –10675, down arrow, press 6000 Enter, down arrow, press 1 Enter. Press 4000 Enter, down arrow, press 1 Enter. Press 3000 Enter, down arrow, press 1 Enter. If any earlier CF problem data is still in the calculator it needs to be deleted. The F0 frequencies should be 1 for any deleted CF. Press IRR. Press CPT. The IRR is approximately 12.04%.

Figure 2E-13 Total Present Value of Net Cash Inflows at 12%

Year	Cash Inflows		Discount Factor at 12%		Present Value
1	$6,000	×	0.893	=	$ 5,358
2	4,000	×	0.797	=	3,188
3	3,000	×	0.712	=	2,136
Total present value of net cash inflows					$10,682
Total initial investment (cash outflow)					(10,675)
Net present value					$ 7

At a 12% discount rate, the NPV is $7, which implies that the project is expected to yield slightly above 12%. Because the criterion cutoff rate is 10%, the project is acceptable. When NPV is negative, the rate of return is below the computed rate. As an example, Figure 2E-14 computes the NPV at a 14% discount rate. Therefore, the IRR of the project is between 12% and 14%, but much closer to 12%.

Section E, Topic 2—Discounted Cash Flow Analysis

Figure 2E-14 Total Present Value of Net Cash Inflows at 14%

Year	Cash Inflows		Discount Factor at 14%		Present Value
1	$6,000	×	0.877	=	$ 5,262
2	4,000	×	0.769	=	3,076
3	3,000	×	0.675	=	2,025
Total present value of net cash inflows					$10,363
Total initial investment (cash outflow)					(10,675)
Net present value					$ (312)

Do not clear the BA II Plus after the operations performed above. Press CF. The original data should be there: −10675, +6000, +4000, +3000 each with frequency of 1. Press down arrow until the last amount +3000 and frequency 1. Press NPV. Press 12, Enter as the discount rate. Press down arrow, press CPT. The NPV is approximately 6.26.

At a 12% discount rate, the PV for the net cash flows for the three years is $10,682, which is close to the total initial investment of $10,675. Because the criterion cutoff rate is 10%, the project should be accepted.

Do not clear the BA II Plus after the operations performed above. Press CF. The original data should be there: −10675, +6000, +4000, +3000 each with frequency of 1. Press down arrow until the last amount +3000 and frequency 1. Press NPV. Press 14 Enter. Press down arrow, press CPT. The NPV is approximately −309, so it is negative. This indicates that at 14% the project does not meet the minimum return required and should be rejected. However in Figure 2E-14 the calculations are only to show a comparison of 14% with 12% in Figure 2E-13.

Comparison of NPV and IRR

The same basic assumptions of risk or uncertainty underlie both the NPV and IRR methods and are based on estimates, some of which are difficult to predict. The more accurate the estimates, the more accurate will be the NPV or IRR. The advantages of DCF methods are that both NPV and IRR consider:

- The time value of money.
- The initial cash investment.
- All cash flows after the initial investment.

A major difference is that the end result of NPV is a dollar figure whereas the final computation for IRR is a percentage. This is because the IRR percentage cannot be appropriately compared with different relative dollar amounts of cash flows. The NPV amounts can be summed because both are money amounts.

Another advantage of the NPV method is its usefulness in evaluating a project in which the required rate of return varies over the life of the project. The total PV of the cash inflows can be determined and compared with the total initial investment to evaluate the attractiveness of a project. Again, using the IRR method, it is not possible to infer if the project is unattractive. Different required returns for each year means that there is no single rate of return or a single IRR value that can be referenced. Different required returns for each year can result in a difference in ranking available capital budgeting projects.

NPV is also more reliable than IRR when there are several alternating periods of net cash inflows and net cash outflows, because it can lead to maximizing shareholder wealth.

Both methods have some reliability cautions:

- NPV is only as reliable as the discount rate that is selected. An unrealistic discount rate can result in an erroneous decision to accept or reject a project. Of course this is true of any TVM situation if either the discount rate is unrealistic or the CF are inaccurate. The calculation in any case will only be as reliable as the variable inputs.
- A capital investment project should not be accepted solely on the basis of a high IRR value. A high IRR result must be looked at further to assess whether an opportunity to invest cash flows at such a high IRR is realistic.
- NPV and IRR have different reinvestment rate assumptions. NPV implicitly assumes that the firm can reinvest all cash inflows at the required rate of return. By contrast, IRR implicitly assumes that the firm can reinvest all cash inflows at the IRR. The reinvestment rate underlying NPV generally is considered to be the more appropriate, conservative assumption.

However, among the various methods available for analyzing capital investments, the DCF methods are theoretically the most reliable. The NPV and IRR methods typically yield similar results as long as there are no differences in:

- Project size (the amount of the initial investment);
- Net cash flow pattern;
- Life of the project; or
- Cost of capital over the life of the project.

If any of the cash flows in the analysis, other than the initial investment, are negative, the IRR might yield multiple answers, which will all be correct and absurd. In such situations, only NPV should be used.

Knowledge Check:
Discounted Cash Flow Analysis

The following questions are intended to help you check your understanding and recall of the material presented in this topic. They do not represent the type of questions that appear on the CMA exam.

Directions: Answer each question in the space provided. Correct answers and section references appear after the knowledge check questions.

Match each term with its application.

1. _____ Present value	a. Proportional average of the various capital components a firm uses for financing
2. _____ Net present value	b. Estimates the discount rate that makes the present value of net cash inflows equal to the initial investment
3. _____ Internal rate of return	c. The equivalent dollar value today of future net cash flows less the initial investment
4. _____ Required rate of return	d. Minimum rate of return the firm will accept in choosing an investment
5. _____ Weighted average cost of capital	e. The equivalent dollar value today of future net cash flows

6. What is the importance of the criterion rate in internal rate of return calculations?
   - ☐ a. Projects below this rate are rejected.
   - ☐ b. Projects above this rate are rejected.
   - ☐ c. The rate is used to find the discount rate in a present value annuity table.
   - ☐ d. The rate is used to find the discount rate in a present value interest factor table.

Note: Use the following two figures duplicated from Figures 2E-8 and 2E-9 or your BA II Plus calculator to solve questions 7–9.

Figure 2E-8 Partial Present Value Interest Factor Table

(n) Periods	10%	11%	12%
1	0.909	0.901	0.893
2	0.826	0.812	0.797
3	0.751	0.731	0.712
4	0.683	0.659	0.636
5	0.621	0.593	0.567
6	0.564	0.535	0.507
7	0.513	0.482	0.452
8	0.467	0.434	0.404
9	0.424	0.391	0.361
10	0.386	0.352	0.322

Figure 2E-9 Partial Present Value Interest Factor Annuity Table

(n) Periods	10%	11%	12%	13%
1	0.909	0.901	0.893	0.885
2	1.736	1.713	1.690	1.668
3	2.487	2.444	2.402	2.361
4	3.170	3.102	3.037	2.974
5	3.791	3.696	3.605	3.517
6	4.355	4.231	4.111	3.998
7	4.868	4.712	4.564	4.423
8	5.335	5.146	4.968	4.799
9	5.759	5.537	5.328	5.132
10	6.145	5.889	5.650	5.426

7. As part of its investment analysis, Zulu Company estimates the disposal value of equipment acquired for $75,000 at the commencement of the investment project. The disposal proceeds for this equipment at the end of its investment life are estimated to be $12,000. The project is expected to generate cash flows evenly during the project's seven-year life. The required rate of return for this project is 11%. Calculate the present value of the equipment disposal proceeds.

8. As part of its investment analysis, Zulu Company estimates the net cash flows from the investment. Net cash flows for each year of the investment are estimated to be $14,000. The project is expected to generate cash flows evenly during the project's seven-year life. The required rate of return for this project is 12%. Calculate the present value of the net cash flows generated during the project's life.

9. As part of its investment analysis, Zulu Company estimates the net cash flows from the investment to be $15,000 per year and the disposal value of equipment acquired for $75,000 at the commencement of the investment project. The company expects the equipment will have zero disposal proceeds at the end of the investment project. The project is expected to generate cash flows evenly during the project's eight-year life. The required rate of return for this project is 10%. Calculate the net present value and IRR of this investment project.

Knowledge Check Answers: Discounted Cash Flow Analysis

Match each term with its application.

1. __e__ Present value		a.	Proportional average of the various capital components a firm uses for financing
2. __c__ Net present value		b.	Estimates the discount rate that makes the present value of net cash inflows equal to the initial investment
3. __b__ Internal rate of return		c.	The equivalent dollar value today of future net cash flows less the initial investment
4. __d__ Required rate of return		d.	Minimum rate of return the firm will accept in choosing an investment
5. __a__ Weighted average cost of capital		e.	The equivalent dollar value today of future net cash flows

6. What is the importance of the criterion rate in internal rate of return calculations? [See *Internal Rate of Return Calculation*.]

   ☑ a. Projects below this rate are rejected.
   ☐ b. Projects above this rate are rejected.
   ☐ c. The rate is used to find the discount rate in a present value annuity table.
   ☐ d. The rate is used to find the discount rate in a present value interest factor table.

Note: Use the following two figures duplicated from Figures 2E-8 and 2E-9 or your BA II Plus calculator to solve questions 7–9.

Figure 2E-8 Partial Present Value Interest Factor Table

(n) Periods	10%	11%	12%
1	0.909	0.901	0.893
2	0.826	0.812	0.797
3	0.751	0.731	0.712
4	0.683	0.659	0.636
5	0.621	0.593	0.567
6	0.564	0.535	0.507
7	0.513	0.482	0.452
8	0.467	0.434	0.404
9	0.424	0.391	0.361
10	0.386	0.352	0.322

Figure 2E-9 Partial Present Value Interest Factor Table

(n) Periods	10%	11%	12%	13%
1	0.909	0.901	0.893	0.885
2	1.736	1.713	1.690	1.668
3	2.487	2.444	2.402	2.361
4	3.170	3.102	3.037	2.974
5	3.791	3.696	3.605	3.517
6	4.355	4.231	4.111	3.998
7	4.868	4.712	4.564	4.423
8	5.335	5.146	4.968	4.799
9	5.759	5.537	5.328	5.132
10	6.145	5.889	5.650	5.426

7. As part of its investment analysis, Zulu Company estimates the disposal value of equipment acquired for $75,000 at the commencement of the investment project. The disposal proceeds for this equipment at the end of its investment life are estimated to be $12,000. The project is expected to generate cash flows evenly during the project's seven-year life. The required rate of return for this project is 11%. [See *Net Present Value Calculation*.]

   Calculate the present value of the equipment disposal proceeds.

   Using Figures: 12000 × .482 = 5784

   Using BA II Plus: N = 7, I = 11, PV = compute 5780, PMT not used, FV = 12000

   The difference is due to figures rounded to three decimal places. [See *Net Present Value Calculation*.]

8. As part of its investment analysis, Zulu Company estimates the net cash flows from the investment. Net cash flows for each year of the investment are estimated to be $14,000. The project is expected to generate cash flows evenly during the project's seven-year life. The required rate of return for this project is 12%. Calculate the present value of the net cash flows generated during the project's life. [See *Net Present Value Calculation*.]

   Using Figures: 14000 × 4.564 = 63896

   Using BA II Plus: N = 7, I = 12, PV = compute 63893, PMT = 14000, FV = not used

   The difference is due to figures rounded to three decimal places. [See *Net Present Value Calculation*.]

9. As part of its investment analysis, Zulu Company estimates the net cash flows from the investment to be $15,000 per year and the disposal value of equipment acquired for $75,000 at the commencement of the investment project. The company expects the equipment will have zero disposal proceeds at the end of the investment project. The project is expected to

generate cash flows evenly during the project's eight-year life. The required rate of return for this project is 10%. Calculate the net present value and IRR of this investment project. [See *Comparison of NPV and IRR*.]

NPV

Using Figures: (15000 × 5.335) − 75000 = 80025 − 75000 = 5025

Using BA II Plus: N = 8, I = 10, PV = compute 80024, PMT = 15000, FV = not used; 80024 − 75000 = 5024

Difference is due to figures rounded to three decimal places.

IRR

Using Figures: IRR factor = $75,000/$15,000 = 5.00 from Figure 2E-9 for eight years between 11 and 12%

Using BA II Plus: CF out −75000, CF in evenly over 8 periods 15000, 1 − 10 NPV = 10155 IRR 11.8% [See *Internal Rate of Return Calculation*.]

TOPIC 3

Payback and Discounted Payback

THE PAYBACK METHOD IN CAPITAL BUDGETING DETERMINES THE number of years needed to recoup the net initial investment in a capital budgeting project. In other words, the payback represents the break-even point in terms of cash flows for the investment. The payback method also can be modified to incorporate discounted cash flows to evaluate an investment. This method is referred to as the discounted payback method.

READ the Learning Outcome Statements (LOS) for this topic as found in Appendix B and then study the concepts and calculations presented here to be sure you understand the content you could be tested on in the CMA exam.

Uses of the Payback Method

Similar to the net present value (NPV) and internal rate of return (IRR) techniques, the payback period (PP) does not distinguish between types of cash inflows (whether the cash inflow is the result of operations, the disposal of a piece of equipment, the restoration of working capital, etc.). As a simple measure of cash inflows, the PP also can be used to evaluate capital investments having uniform net cash flows or uneven cash flows.

Uniform Net Cash Flows Example

The next calculation determines the payback period of a capital investment assuming uniform cash flows (i.e., an annuity) are expected:

$$\text{Payback Period} = \frac{\text{Total Initial Investment}}{\text{Expected Annual Net Cash Flow}}$$

For example: Consider this scenario:

- The total initial investment is $600,000.
- The expected annual net cash flow is $175,000.

In this case, the calculation would be:

$$\text{Payback Period} = \frac{\$600,000}{\$175,000} = 3.43 \text{ Years}$$

Uneven Cash Flows Example

In situations in which the annual cash inflows are uneven, determining payback becomes a cumulative calculation. The net cash inflows are accumulated until the initial investment is recovered. Straight-line interpolation is used if the payback amount falls within a year.

The formula for the payback period is:

$$\text{Payback Period} = \text{Years Until Full Recovery} + \frac{\text{Unrecovered Cost at the Beginning of the Last Year}}{\text{Cash Flow During the Last Year}}$$

The formula is not entirely useful in this situation as Figure 2E-15 clearly shows. Figure 2E-15 is constructed with the cash flow information provided above. The figure shows that payback is achieved during the third year. It is not necessary to use the formula above to construct this figure. During the examination it probably would be most efficient to prepare a payback figure similar to Figure 2E-15 rather than to risk a logic error while using the formula.

For example: Consider this scenario:

- The total initial investment is $30,000.
- The predicted annual net cash inflows over the life of the investment are $10,000, $12,000, $16,000, and $14,000 for years 1, 2, and 3, respectively.

Figure 2E-15 shows the figures.

Figure 2E-15 Payback and Uneven Cash Flows

Year	Net Cash Flow	Cumulative Net Cash Flow
0	− $30,000	− $30,000
1	10,000	− 20,000
2	12,000	− 8,000
3	16,000	8,000
4	14,000	22,000

After 2 years, the project requires another $8,000 to pay for itself. In year 3, the project is expected to generate $16,000 in net cash inflows. This means that for this investment, payback will occur sometime between year 2 and year 3. Therefore, dividing the unrecovered cost at the beginning of the last year by the cash flow during the last year ($8,000 / $16,000) results in 0.5 years, yielding a total payback period for the project of 2.5 years.

$$\text{Payback Period} = 2 + \frac{\$8,000}{\$16,000} = 2.5 \text{ Years}$$

Payback Method Interpretation

When using the payback method, firms typically choose a target payback period (or maximum cutoff period) for a project. The target payback period represents what the firm considers to be the maximum acceptable length of time for a project. Projects with a payback shorter than the target payback period are accepted; those with a payback longer than the target payback period are rejected. In the previous example, if the firm had set the maximum acceptable target payback for the $30,000 investment as 3 years, the investment should be accepted because the actual payback is achieved in 2.5 years.

Typically, the higher the risk of a project, the shorter the target payback period should be because it is desirable to recover riskier investments more quickly. When comparing two or more investment projects, those with shorter payback periods are generally preferable.

Advantages and Disadvantages of the Payback Method

The payback method has distinct advantages and disadvantages as listed in Figure 2E-16.

Figure 2E-16 Advantages and Disadvantages of the Payback Method

Advantages	Disadvantages
Uses a simple calculation	Ignores the time value of money; adds cash flows without regard to timing
Produces results that are easy to understand	
	Ignores cash flows occurring after the payback period
Provides a rough measure of liquidity and risk	Provides no measure of profitability
	Promotes the acceptance of short-term projects if the target payback period is short

In some situations, the quick measures of liquidity and risk are beneficial to indicate the risk of losing a capital investment in a high-risk situation. In a rough sense, projects with shorter payback periods are less risky. Projects with shorter paybacks also tend to provide an organization with greater flexibility because the investment funds become available sooner for other projects.

Because of its basic limitations, the payback method can provide only a partial picture of whether an investment is worthwhile. Therefore, it is best used in conjunction with other capital budgeting techniques.

Discounted Payback

The **discounted payback method** addresses one of the shortfalls of the payback period calculation, namely, ignoring the time value of money. Discounted payback uses the PVs of net cash inflows rather than the undiscounted dollar amounts of net cash inflows to determine a payback period.

Similar to the NPV method, the PV of net cash inflows are estimated using the firm's desired minimum rate of return. The time period necessary for the cumulative NPVs of net cash flows to equal the initial project investment is the present value payback period.

Figure 2E-17 Discounted Payback and Even Net Cash Flow

Year	Net Cash Inflows		Discount Factor at 10%		Present Value of Net Cash Flows	Cumulative Present Value of Net Cash Flows
0	− $16,000		0		− $16,000	− $16,000
1	6,000	×	0.909	=	5,454	− 10,546
2	6,000	×	0.826	=	4,956	− 5,590
3	6,000	×	0.751	=	4,506	− 1,084
4	6,000	×	0.683	=	4,098	3,014

A project is shown in Figure 2E-17. The project will recover its initial investment between year 3 and year 4. The amount needed in year 4 to reach PV payback is $1,084. The discounted payback period is then determined as:

$$\text{Discounted Payback} = 3 + \frac{\$1,084}{\$4,098} = 3.27 \text{ Years}$$

This is in contrast to the simple payback method:

$$\text{Payback Period} = \frac{\$16,000}{\$6,000} = 2.67 \text{ Years}$$

Knowledge Check:
Payback and Discounted Payback

The following questions are intended to help you check your understanding and recall of the material presented in this topic. They do not represent the type of questions that appear on the CMA exam.

Directions: Answer each question in the space provided. Correct answers and section references appear after the knowledge check questions.

1. Which of the following statements about using the payback method in capital budgeting is **false**?

   The payback method:

   - a. represents the break-even point for an investment.
   - b. provides a rough measure of project liquidity.
   - c. takes into account the time value of money.
   - d. provides a rough measure of project risk.

2. What is the payback period for a capital budgeting project in which the total initial capital investment is $900,000 and the expected annual net cash flow is $150,000 each year for 8 years?

   - a. 3 years
   - b. 5 years
   - c. 6 years
   - d. 7 years

3. Which of the following statements accurately compares the discounted payback and payback methods?

   - a. Both methods provide simple measures of project profitability.
   - b. Discounted payback uses the present values of net cash inflows; payback does not.
   - c. Discounted payback ignores cash flows after the payback period expiration; payback does not.
   - d. Both methods distinguish between types of cash inflows.

Knowledge Check Answers: Payback and Discounted Payback

1. Which of the following statements about using the payback method in capital budgeting is **false**?

   The payback method: [See *Advantages and Disadvantages of the Payback Method.*]
   - ☐ a. represents the break-even point for an investment.
   - ☐ b. provides a rough measure of project liquidity.
   - ☑ c. takes into account the time value of money.
   - ☐ d. provides a rough measure of project risk.

2. What is the payback period for a capital budgeting project in which the total initial capital investment is $900,000 and the expected annual net cash flow is $150,000 each year for 8 years? [See *Payback Method Interpretation.*]
   - ☐ a. 3 years
   - ☐ b. 5 years
   - ☑ c. 6 years
   - ☐ d. 7 years

3. Which of the following statements accurately compares the discounted payback and payback methods? [See *Discounted Payback.*]
   - ☐ a. Both methods provide simple measures of project profitability.
   - ☑ b. Discounted payback uses the present values of net cash inflows; payback does not.
   - ☐ c. Discounted payback ignores cash flows after the payback period expiration; payback does not.
   - ☐ d. Both methods distinguish between types of cash inflows.

TOPIC 4

Risk Analysis in Capital Investment

Risks are significant conditions, events, circumstances, actions, or inactions that could adversely affect one from achieving one's objectives. For CMA examination purposes risks usually relate to a business, including its owners and creditors. Risks are also related to individuals and businesses within an ethics context on the CMA examinations.

When discussing risk it is also customary to identify specific types of risks, just to keep the discussion and the analysis manageable. Once risks are identified, those risks should be managed. To properly manage risks one must be aware that the risk is present. If a manager is aware of a present risk the manager normally will determine a probability that the risk will occur and assign a value to the risk.

Uncertainty is a condition in which the manager is not aware of all possible risks or the manager cannot reliably value the risks the manager is aware of. While risk and uncertainty are separate and distinct conditions, risk and uncertainty are rarely considered without reference to both.

In several areas of Section B: Corporate Finance, risk was discussed extensively as it relates to long-term financial management. In capital budgeting, risk has different implications.

There are no risk-free capital investments. Consider just a few reasons why that is true:

- Capital budgeting is based on estimates, assumptions, and variables both internal and external to the company. Estimations are subject to change. The assumptions and variables underlying those estimations can change. Future cash inflows and outflows can vary unexpectedly throughout the life of a project.
- The rate of return used in calculations may not be accurate for the life of the project.
- The cost of financing may increase during the life of a project.
- New mandatory regulatory factors can require additional investments at any given point in time.
- The life of the related product or service could be significantly shorter or longer than anticipated.

- Inflationary or recessionary economic conditions may impact the value of cash flows.
- Domestic or global political events may impact project cash flows or the viability of the project as a whole.

Because of all these types of risk associated with capital budgeting, selecting capital investment projects is always a challenge. This topic looks at some of the ways to minimize the uncertainty using various techniques, such as sensitivity analysis, certainty equivalents, the capital asset pricing model, simulations, and specifically adjusted rates.

> **READ** the Learning Outcome Statements (LOS) for this topic as found in Appendix B and then study the concepts and calculations presented here to be sure you understand the content you could be tested on in the CMA exam.

Sensitivity Analysis

Sensitivity analysis not only is performed in evaluating capital investments but is also a required analysis in the notes to the company's financial statements both under the ASC and under IFRS. Of course the exact nature of the sensitivity analysis will be different when applied to capital investments. We focus in this topic only on the impact on capital investments.

Sensitivity analysis, as it pertains to capital investments, is a "what-if" technique evaluating how net present value (NPV), internal rate of return (IRR), and other indicators of the profitability of a project change if the discount rate, labor or materials costs, sales, or some other factor varies from one case to another. The purpose is to assess how sensitive the NPV, the IRR, or another specified profitability measure is to a change.

Sensitivity analysis can be used to answer questions such as these:

- What happens to NPV if cash flow increases or decreases by 10% for each year of the project?
- Will NPV remain positive throughout a project if there is no cash inflow in the second year of a three-year project?
- What will happen to NPV if the discount rate increases from 8% to 10% or decreases from 8% to 7%?
- What would happen to the NPV if a major redesign of the product, requiring additional capital investments, is necessary in year 3 in order to address competitive new products?
- What would be the impact on NPV if the project is extended for three years, with decreasing cash flows and increased maintenance costs in the extended years?

To further understand how sensitivity analysis can be used to answer such what-ifs, consider the next scenario.

- Annual net cash inflows over the life of investment A are $2,000 in year 1 (Y1) and $3,000 in year 2 (Y2).

- Annual net cash inflows over the life of investment B are $3,600 in Y1 and $1,400 in Y2.
- The total initial investment for each project is $3,200.

Given this information, what happens to each project if the discount rate changes from 10% to 12%? Refer to Figure 2E-18.

As previously stated, from the CMA Handbook on page 11 under the "Calculator Policy" heading: "Small battery or solar powered electronic calculators restricted to a maximum of six functions—addition, subtraction, multiplication, division, square root, and percentage are allowed. The calculator must not be programmable and must not use any type of tape. <u>Candidates can also use the Texas Instruments BA II Plus</u>, Hewlett-Packard 10BII, HP 12c, or HP 12c Platinum calculators when taking the exams. <u>Candidates will not be allowed to use calculators that do not comply with these restrictions</u>."

Many of the time-value-of-money calculations illustrated in the Investment Decisions section include the keystrokes and variables from the Texas Instruments BA II Plus calculator. You may wish to set your BA II Plus calculator to at least three decimal places to minimize differences that might arise from rounding. The TVM tables that are provided are set to three decimal places.

The TVM table factors are provided in the examples and questions here and on the CMA exam to facilitate TVM calculations.

Figure 2E-18 Changes in Discount Rate

	Project A at 10%				
Year	Cash Inflows		Discount Factor at 10%		PV
1	$2,000.00	×	0.909	=	$1,818.00
2	3,000.00	×	0.826	=	2,478.00
Total PV of net cash flows					4,296.00
Less initial investment					(3,200.00)
NPV					$1,096.00

BA II Plus keystrokes as follows:
Uneven cash flows; use CF and NPV functions
press CF
CF0 −3200 enter, down arrow
C01 +2000 enter, down arrow
F01 1 enter, down arrow
C02 +3000 enter, down arrow
F02 1 enter, down arrow
press NPV
10 enter, down arrow
press CPT
NPV = 1097.52

	Project A at 12%				
Year	Cash Inflows		Discount Factor at 12%		PV
1	$2,000.00	×	0.893	=	$1,786.00
2	3,000.00	×	0.797	=	2,391.00
Total PV of net cash flows					4,177.00
Less initial investment					(3,200.00)
NPV					$977.00

BA II Plus keystrokes as follows:
Uneven cash flows; use CF and NPV functions
press CF
CF0 −3200 enter, down arrow
CO1 +2000 enter, down arrow
FO1 1 enter, down arrow
CO2 +3000 enter, down arrow
FO2 1 enter, down arrow
press NPV
12 enter, down arrow
press CPT
NPV = 977.30

	Project B at 10%				
Year	Cash Inflows		Discount Factor at 10%		PV
1	$3,600.00	×	0.909	=	$3,272.40
2	1,400.00	×	0.826	=	1,156.40
Total PV of net cash flows					4,428.80
Less initial investment					(3,200.00)
NPV					$1,228.80

BA II Plus keystrokes as follows:
Uneven cash flows; use CF and NPV functions
press CF
CF0 −3200 enter, down arrow
CO1 +3600 enter, down arrow
FO1 1 enter, down arrow
CO2 +1400 enter, down arrow
FO2 1 enter, down arrow
press NPV
10 enter, down arrow
press CPT
NPV = 1230

Project B at 12%

Year	Cash Inflows		Discount Factor at 12%		PV
1	$3,600.00	×	0.893	=	$3,214.80
2	1,400.00	×	0.797	=	1,115.80
Total PV of net cash flows					4,330.60
Less initial investment					(3,200.00)
NPV					$1,130.60

BA II Plus keystrokes as follows:
Uneven cash flows; use CF and NPV functions
press CF
CF0 −3200 enter, down arrow
CO1 +3600 enter, down arrow
FO1 1 enter, down arrow
CO2 +1400 enter, down arrow
FO2 1 enter, down arrow
press NPV
12 enter, down arrow
press CPT
NPV = 1130

Comparison of Projects A and B

Project	NPV at 10%	NPV at 12%	Dollar Change	NPV % Change
A	$1,096.00	$977.00	($119.00)	−10.86%
B	$1,228.80	$1,130.60	($98.20)	−7.99%

These amounts are best computed manually.

The NPV of each project declines when the discount rate increases from 10% to 12%. The percentage change in the NPV for project A is −10.9%, whereas the change for project B is −8.0%. Thus, project A is more sensitive to changes in the discount rate than project B and poses a higher risk if the discount rate changes. Other changes, such as increasing cash inflows, receiving cash inflows earlier, decreasing cash outflows, and paying cash outflows later, will mathematically increase NPV for a project. Conversely, the opposites—decreasing cash inflows, receiving cash inflows later, increasing cash outflows, and paying cash outflows earlier—effectively decrease NPV.

Consider how the quality of the sensitivity analysis becomes a value-adding feature of the project. If company managers see that a project has been planned carefully so as to accommodate variances in discount rates, cash flows, and the like, they will be encouraged to support the project knowing that it has been designed or scaled to accommodate these and other potential challenges. Likewise, investors will have more confidence in a company that has a demonstrated capability of project planning and budgeting. This confidence will result in a higher sustained price for the company's stock even when the inevitable project challenges occur.

Another type of sensitivity analysis is real options valuation (ROV). ROV is in direct contrast to discounted cash flow (DCF) analysis such as NPV and IRR, although the computations often involve these techniques in providing inputs of the model. When using DCF analysis, the most likely outcomes are modeled and management flexibility is ignored, implicitly assuming that management is passive with regard to the capital project once it is committed. The uncertainty in DCF techniques is accounted for by adjusting the discount rate. By contrast, ROV assumes that management can actively modify the project throughout its life by responding to each outcome (in other words, options are exercised), and the possibility of a large negative outcome is reduced or eliminated. Some possible project options available to management include the option to expand or contract, slow down or postpone, and discontinue or abandon. The ROV value of a project can be viewed as the project's traditionally calculated NPV plus the value of any flexibility option(s) available to management. Real options have the highest value when only the company in question can exercise the real options. The model itself parallels financial options in that there is a strike price, options (such as option to contract, option to abandon, and option to expand), and option terms, which are more fully explained throughout Section B.

Simulations

Simulations allow testing of a capital investment project before it is accepted. Because the actual future values for cash flows and discount rates for investment projects are not known, hypothetical cash flows and discount rates are assumed and can be studied using a simulation model.

In capital budgeting, simulations can be used to approximate:

- Expected NPV and IRR.
- Dispersion about an expected value.

When attempting to evaluate more than one risky investment, the NPV or IRR for each project can be simulated several times, and average NPVs, IRRs, and standard deviations can be computed and ranked. Repeating the process many times also allows values to be plotted on a frequency distribution graph to show the distribution of the NPVs and IRRs. The distribution curves enable one to make a reasonable assessment of the risk level of a project.

Many simulation software programs are available. These programs are useful because they can create many more scenarios than can be done by hand. Some of these programs also can draw graphs of the results. One of the best-known computer simulation models in capital budgeting is the Monte Carlo simulation tool, which uses repeated random sampling and computational algorithms to calculate a range of most likely outcomes for the project.

Scenario Analysis

The scenario approach to evaluating risk uses single-point estimates where each possibility is assigned a best-guess estimate. Scenarios (such as best, worst, or most likely case) for each input variable are chosen, and the results are reported. For example, a comparison of a spreadsheet cost construction model is prepared using traditional what-if scenarios. By contrast, Monte Carlo simulations sample probability distribution for each variable to produce hundreds or thousands of possible outcomes, and the results are analyzed to get probabilities of different outcomes occurring.

Monte Carlo Analysis

Monte Carlo analysis is based on the use of computational algorithms that rely on random sampling in order to compute results. The Monte Carlo method uses computerized simulations, which are a class of computational algorithms that rely on repeated random sampling to compute their results. Monte Carlo methods often are used in simulating physical and mathematical systems. These methods are most suited to calculation by a computer when it is not feasible to compute an exact result with a deterministic algorithm, such as to model phenomena with significant uncertainty in inputs (as in the calculation of risk in business).

Expected Values as Replacement for Certainty Equivalents

Expected Cash Flows

The expected cash flow approach to selecting projects attempts to separate the timing of cash flows from their risk. Under this approach, undiscounted cash flows are estimated independently from the risk associated with the cash flows. There may be several different cash flow estimates for the same project. The undiscounted estimated cash flows are weighted in accordance with the probability of their occurrence. The results are discounted using a risk-free rate, usually related to U.S. Treasury bills.

Eight steps are used to determine the expected value of each cash flow scenario within the project:

1. Estimate the future cash flow or series of future cash flows the project is expected to generate.
2. Establish expectations about the variability in those cash flows.
3. Assign a probability factor (0–1) that the cash flows will occur for each amount.
4. Determine the risk-free rate of return to be used, usually made on U.S. Treasury bills.
5. Adjust the risk-free rate of return to reflect inherent uncertainty in this project.
6. Apply time value of money principles using the adjusted current market risk-free rate of interest.

7. Calculate the NPV of the project by subtracting the initial investment from the PV of the certain cash flows.
8. Evaluate the NPV of the project; a zero or positive value is acceptable, and a negative value should be rejected.

Consider the next project evaluation scenario using the expected present value approach:

- Annual net cash inflows over the life of a five-year investment are $10,000, $8,000, $7,000, $6,000, and $5,000. In practice we would have multiple cash flow scenarios. In this example we have only one scenario.
- Probability of occurrence factors are estimated over the life of the investment at .900, .850, .700, .600, and .450.
- The total initial investment for the project is $18,000.
- The risk-free rate of return is 3%. For this purpose assume that there is no inherent risk to the project other than the expected cash flows, probability of their occurrence, and discount rate.

Given this information and applying the expected value approach, an evaluation of what the project looks like is shown in Figure 2E-19.

Figure 2E-19 Project Evaluation and Certainty Equivalent Factors

Year	Expected Cash Inflows		Probability of Occurrence		Certain Cash Flow
1	10,000.00	×	0.900	=	$9,000.00
2	8,000.00	×	0.850	=	6,800.00
3	7,000.00	×	0.700	=	4,900.00
4	6,000.00	×	0.600	=	3,600.00
5	5,000.00	×	0.450	=	2,250.00

Year	Expected Cash Flows		Adjusted Discount Factor at 3%		Present Value of Certain Cash Flow
1	$9,000.00	×	0.971	=	$8,739.00
2	6,800.00	×	0.943	=	6,412.40
3	4,900.00	×	0.915	=	4,483.50
4	3,600.00	×	0.888	=	3,196.80
5	2,250.00	×	0.863	=	1,941.75
Total PV of net cash inflows					$24,773.45
Less initial investment					(18,000.00)
NPV					$6,773.45

The positive NPV value indicates that the project is acceptable.

Capital Asset Pricing Model

The capital asset pricing model (CAPM) was discussed in Section B: Corporate Finance, as it relates to finding the required rate of return on a stock or portfolio. The CAPM also has application in capital budgeting. The formula for the CAPM in capital budgeting is:

$$E(R_a) = R_f + \beta [E(R_m) - R_f]$$

where:
- $E(R_a)$ = required rate of return on an asset (project) being evaluated
- R_f = risk-free rate
- β = beta of an asset (project)
- $E(R_m)$ = return on a market portfolio

The premise behind using the CAPM in capital budgeting is treating a project in the same manner as a share of stock. The rationale is that the return from a project is linked to the return on the firm's total assets or to the return in an industry, just as a stock or market portfolio. With this assumption, the beta of the company is used as the beta for the project. In the event a project is not a typical investment for a company, an average industry beta can be substituted. Comparing betas among similar companies in similar industries is called the pure play approach.

Once the project's required rate of return is identified, NPV can be calculated. Expected cash flows are discounted using the required rate of return, and the total NPV of cash flows is subtracted from the total initial project investment. A zero or positive NPV means that the project can be accepted as it will preserve the required rate of return.

Technically, this basic CAPM approach assumes that projects will be financed entirely by equity, that the firm is entirely equity-financed, and that all beta information pertains to all-equity situations. If some debt financing is employed, however, we would need to determine a weighted-average required return. In that case, the weighting system is the same as that utilized earlier for the firm's WACC.

Use of Specifically Adjusted Rates

Under most circumstances, risky capital projects are less desirable than less risky investments. Firms typically demand a higher rate of return for riskier projects, or they use conservative estimates for cash flows.

Many firms use their company cost of capital as the yardstick to discount cash flows on all new investments. In situations where new projects are more or less risky than is normal for the firm, using the company rate can create problems.

The firm's cost of capital is an appropriate discount rate when capital projects have the same average risk as the firm's existing business. However, care and discretion must be used in determining what exactly constitutes similar risk.

Using the firm's cost of capital rate arbitrarily for all new projects can lead to accepting or rejecting a project regardless of its risk only because it offers a higher rate of return than the company's cost of capital. The problem is twofold:

1. Good low-risk projects may be rejected.
2. Poor high-risk projects may be accepted.

When in doubt, analysts should assess the relative risks of projects on an individual basis and use a new rate specifically adjusted for the project risk. By doing this, every project has its own opportunity cost of capital.

Knowledge Check: Risk Analysis in Capital Investment

The following questions are intended to help you check your understanding and recall of the material presented in this topic. They do not represent the type of questions that appear on the CMA exam.

Directions: Answer each question in the space provided. Correct answers and section references appear after the knowledge check questions.

For questions 1 through 4, match the different approaches to dealing with risk with the appropriate description.

1.	_____ Sensitivity analysis	a.	The use of a hypothetical situation (similar to the real one) to help make a decision
2.	_____ Expected value approach	b.	A measure of the extent to which one factor varies when another factor changes
3.	_____ Capital asset pricing model	c.	The conversion of projected cash flows into certain (risk-less) equivalent cash flows
4.	_____ Simulations	d.	The use of a firm's beta or an industry beta in an assessment of project risk

5. Which method is **best** suited to comparing the net present values for two mutually exclusive capital investment projects when the cash flows vary?
   - ☐ a. Sensitivity analysis
   - ☐ b. Expected value approach
   - ☐ c. Capital asset pricing model
   - ☐ d. Computer simulation

Knowledge Check Answers: Risk Analysis in Capital Investment

For questions 1 through 4, match the different approaches to dealing with risk with the appropriate description.

1. __b__ Sensitivity analysis	a. The use of a hypothetical situation (similar to the real one) to help make a decision
2. __c__ Expected value approach	b. A measure of the extent to which one factor varies when another factor changes
3. __d__ Capital asset pricing model	c. The conversion of projected cash flows into certain (risk-less) equivalent cash flows
4. __a__ Simulations	d. The use of a firm's beta or an industry beta in an assessment of project risk

5. Which method is **best** suited to comparing the net present values for two mutually exclusive capital investment projects when the cash flows vary? [See *Sensitivity Analysis*.]
   - ☑ a. Sensitivity analysis
   - ☐ b. Expected value approach
   - ☐ c. Capital asset pricing model
   - ☐ d. Computer simulation

Practice Questions: Investment Decisions

Directions: This sampling of questions is designed to emulate actual exam questions. Read each question and write your response on another sheet of paper. See the "Answers to Section Practice Questions" section at the end of this book to assess your response. Validate or improve the answer you wrote. For a more robust selection of practice questions, access the **Online Test Bank** at www.wiley.cma.com.

Question 2E1-AT06
Topic: Capital Budgeting Process

In order to increase production capacity, Gunning Industries is considering replacing an existing production machine with a new technologically improved machine effective January 1. This information is being considered:

- The new machine would be purchased for $160,000 in cash. Shipping, installation, and testing would cost an additional $30,000.
- The new machine is expected to increase annual sales by 20,000 units at a sales price of $40 per unit. Incremental operating costs are comprised of $30 per unit in variable costs and total fixed costs of $40,000 per year.
- The investment in the new machine will require an immediate increase in working capital of $35,000.
- Gunning uses straight-line depreciation for financial reporting and tax reporting purposes. The new machine has an estimated useful life of 5 years and zero salvage value.
- Gunning is subject to a 40% corporate income tax rate.

Gunning Industries' initial net cash outflow in a capital budgeting decision would be

- ☐ a. $160,000.
- ☐ b. $190,000.
- ☐ c. $225,000.
- ☐ d. $195,000.

Question 2E1-AT07

Topic: Capital Budgeting Process

In order to increase production capacity, Gunning Industries is considering replacing an existing production machine with a new technologically improved machine effective January 1. Gunning Industries is considering this information:

- The new machine would be purchased for $160,000 in cash. Shipping, installation, and testing would cost an additional $30,000.
- The new machine is expected to increase annual sales by 20,000 units at a sales price of $40 per unit. Incremental operating costs are comprised of $30 per unit in variable costs and total fixed costs of $40,000 per year.
- The investment in the new machine will require an immediate increase in working capital of $35,000.
- Gunning uses straight-line depreciation for financial reporting and tax reporting purposes. The new machine has an estimated useful life of 5 years and zero salvage value.
- Gunning is subject to a 40% corporate income tax rate.

Gunning uses the net present value method to analyze investments and will employ these factors and rates:

Period	Present Value of $1 at 10%	Present Value of an Ordinary Annuity of $1 at 10%
1	0.909	0.909
2	0.826	1.736
3	0.751	2.487
4	0.683	3.170
5	0.621	3.791

Gunning Industries' discounted annual depreciation tax shield for the first year of operation would be:

- ☐ a. $13,817.
- ☐ b. $15,200.
- ☐ c. $20,725.
- ☐ d. $22,800.

Question 2E1-AT08

Topic: Capital Budgeting Process

Which one of the following is **most** relevant to a manufacturing equipment replacement decision?

- ☐ a. Gain or loss on the disposal of the old equipment
- ☐ b. Original cost less depreciation of the old equipment

- [ ] c. A lump-sum write-off amount from the disposal of the old equipment
- [ ] d. Disposal price of the old equipment

Question 2E2-CQ01

Topic: Discounted Cash Flow Analysis

Calvin Inc. is considering the purchase of a new state-of-art machine to replace its hand-operated machine. Calvin's effective tax rate is 40%, and its cost of capital is 12%. Data regarding the existing and new machines are presented next.

	Existing Machine	New Machine
Original cost	$50,000	$90,000
Installation costs	0	4,000
Freight and insurance	0	6,000
Expected end salvage value	0	0
Depreciation method	straight line	straight line
Expected useful life	10 years	5 years

The existing machine has been in service for seven years and could be sold currently for $25,000. Calvin expects to realize a before-tax annual reduction in labor costs of $30,000 if the new machine is purchased and placed in service.

If the new machine is purchased, the cash flows for the fifth year would amount to

- [ ] a. $18,000.
- [ ] b. $24,000.
- [ ] c. $26,000.
- [ ] d. $30,000.

Question 2E2-CQ11

Topic: Discounted Cash Flow Analysis

For each of the next six years, Atlantic Motors anticipates net income of $10,000, straight-line tax depreciation of $20,000, a 40% tax rate, a discount rate of 10%, and cash sales of $100,000. The depreciable assets are all being acquired at the beginning of year 1 and will have a salvage value of zero at the end of 6 years.

The present value (PV) of the total depreciation tax savings would be:

- [ ] a. $8,000.
- [ ] b. $27,072.
- [ ] c. $34,840.
- [ ] d. $87,100.

Question 2E2-CQ14
Topic: Discounted Cash Flow Analysis

Fuller Industries is considering a $1 million investment in stamping equipment to produce a new product. The equipment is expected to last 9 years, produce revenue of $700,000 per year, and have related cash expenses of $450,000 per year. At the end of the 9th year, the equipment is expected to have a salvage value of $100,000 and cost $50,000 to remove. The Internal Revenue Service categorizes this as 5-year Modified Accelerated Cost Recovery System (MACRS) property subject to the next depreciation rates.

Year	Rate
1	20.00%
2	32.00%
3	19.20%
4	11.52%
5	11.52%
6	5.76%

Fuller's effective income tax rate is 40% and Fuller expects, on an overall company basis, to continue to be profitable and have significant taxable income. If Fuller uses the net present value method to analyze investments, what is the expected net tax impact on cash flow in Year 2 before discounting? Assume that a positive impact decreases the income tax liability while a negative impact increases the income tax liability.

- ☐ a. Positive $28,000 impact
- ☐ b. $0 impact
- ☐ c. Negative $100,000 impact
- ☐ d. Negative $128,000 impact

Question 2E2-CQ16
Topic: Discounted Cash Flow Analysis

AGC Company is considering an equipment upgrade. AGC uses discounted cash flow (DCF) analysis in evaluating capital investments and has an effective tax rate of 40%. Selected data developed by AGC are shown next.

	Existing Equipment	New Equipment
Original cost	$50,000	$95,000
Accumulated depreciation	45,000	–
Current market value	3,000	95,000
Accounts receivable	6,000	8,000
Accounts payable	2,100	2,500

Based on this information, what is the initial investment for a DCF analysis of this proposed upgrade?

- ☐ a. $92,400
- ☐ b. $92,800
- ☐ c. $95,800
- ☐ d. $96,200

Question 2E3-CQ01
Topic: Payback and Discounted Payback

Hobart Corporation evaluates capital projects using a variety of performance screens, including a hurdle rate of 16% and payback period of 3 years or less. Management is completing review of a project on the basis of these projections:

Capital investment	$200,000
Annual cash flows (after-tax)	$74,000
Straight-line depreciation	5 years
Terminal value (after-tax)	$20,000

The projected internal rate of return is 20%. Which one of the following alternatives reflects the appropriate conclusions for the indicated evaluative measures?

	Internal Rate of Return	Payback
a.	Accept	Reject
b.	Reject	Reject
c.	Accept	Accept
d.	Reject	Accept

Question 2E3-CQ02
Topic: Payback and Discounted Payback

Quint Company uses the payback method as part of its analysis of capital investments. One of its projects requires a $140,000 investment and has these projected before-tax cash flows:

Year 1	$60,000
Year 2	60,000
Year 3	60,000
Year 4	80,000
Year 5	80,000

Quint has an effective 40% tax rate. Based on these data, the after-tax payback period is

- ☐ a. 1.5.
- ☐ b. 2.3.
- ☐ c. 3.4.
- ☐ d. 3.7.

Question 2E3-CQ03

Topic: Payback and Discounted Payback

Foster Manufacturing is analyzing a capital investment project that is forecasted to produce the following cash flows and net income.

Year	After-Tax Cash Flow	Net Income
0	($20,000)	$ 0
1	6,000	2,000
2	6,000	2,000
3	8,000	2,000
4	8,000	2,000

The payback period of this project will be

- ☐ a. 2.5 years.
- ☐ b. 2.6 years.
- ☐ c. 3.0 years.
- ☐ d. 3.3 years.

Question 2E3-LS02

Topic: Payback and Discounted Payback

Which of the following statements is **not** true of using the payback method in capital budgeting? The payback method

- ☐ a. provides a rough measure of project risk.
- ☐ b. takes into account the time value of money.
- ☐ c. does not distinguish between types of cash inflows.
- ☐ d. represents the break-even point for an investment.

Question 2E4-CQ01

Topic: Risk Analysis in Capital Investment

Long Inc. is analyzing a $1 million investment in new equipment to produce a product with a $5 per unit margin. The equipment will last 5 years, be depreciated on a straight-line basis for tax purposes, and have no value at the end of its life. A study of unit sales produced these data:

Annual Unit Sales	Probability
80,000	0.10
85,000	0.20
90,000	0.30
95,000	0.20
100,000	0.10
110,000	0.10

If Long utilizes a 12% hurdle rate and is subject to a 40% effective income tax rate, the expected net present value of the project would be

- a. $261,750.
- b. $283,380.
- c. $297,800.
- d. $427,580.

Question 2E4-CQ02
Topic: Risk Analysis in Capital Investment

Parker Industries is analyzing a $200,000 equipment investment to produce a new product for the next 5 years. A study of expected annual after-tax cash flows from the project produced these data:

Annual After-Tax Cash Flow	Probability
$45,000	0.10
50,000	0.20
55,000	0.30
60,000	0.20
65,000	0.10
70,000	0.10

If Parker utilizes a 14% hurdle rate, the probability of achieving a positive net present value is best found by utilizing

- a. sensitivity analysis.
- b. scenario analysis.
- c. simulation analysis.
- d. certainty equivalents.

Question 2E4-LS03

Topic: Risk Analysis in Capital Investment

What is a primary caution when using a company's cost of capital as the discount rate to evaluate a capital project?

- a. Evaluation typically rejects high-risk projects.
- b. The cost of capital may need to be risk adjusted.
- c. Low-risk projects are favored.
- d. Opportunity costs can be distorted.

Question 2E4-LS04

Topic: Risk Analysis in Capital Investment

Which type of real option would a firm be **most** likely to choose if there is a high probability that competitors can enter a market and capture profitable future cash flows?

Note that this discussion refers to competitors entering, exiting, or otherwise changing the markets. The earlier discussion concerning whether our firm has exclusive right to exercise its real options (including all four of these choices) is not the same as responding to a competitive action in the marketplace.

- a. Adapt
- b. Abandon
- c. Postpone
- d. Expand

To further assess your understanding of the concepts and calculations covered in Part 2, Section E: Investment Decisions, practice with the **Online Test Bank** for this section. **REMINDER:** See the "Answers to Section Practice Questions" section at the end of this book.

SECTION F

Professional Ethics

This section covers ethics for both management accountants and financial managers, as well as organizations. Management accountants and financial managers confront unique ethical challenges arising from their particular organizational responsibilities. To help accountants in these roles assess the specific ethical demands of their situations, the Institute of Management Accountants updated the *IMA Statement of Ethical Professional Practice* in July 2017. This statement, which is available from IMA's Web site in Statement on Management Accounting (SMA) and is reproduced here, is the basis for this section.

The IMA *SMA*, "Values and Ethics: From Inception to Practice," addresses the needs and rewards for organizations that take a proactive stance in creating and maintaining an ethical culture. The SMA states: "All accounting professionals [should be] aware of their responsibility to act as change agents within their organizations, supporting the maintenance of effective controls and ensuring that their organizations have considered, adopted, and fully implemented a company-wide ethics and compliance program, including a code of ethics and a confidential hot/helpline." This SMA, which appears on IMA's Web site, is the basis of this section of the CMA exam.

There are five primary categories for management to focus on in order to effectively maintain the desired ethical atmosphere:

1. Defining values
2. Leadership by example
3. Ethics and internal controls
4. Practical application
5. Measuring and improving ethical compliance

In addition, no company operates in a vacuum. Therefore, it is essential to understand the difference between acts that are legal and those that are ethical.

Note to students: The Ethics section of the CMA exam addresses the subject from the perspective of individual behavior and in particular how individuals use the *IMA Statement of Ethical Professional Practice*. It also addresses the subject from the perspective of the organization. Students should be aware of and focused on the different perspectives being covered. Be sure to carefully review the Learning Outcome Statements related to ethics.

IMA STATEMENT OF ETHICAL PROFESSIONAL PRACTICE

Members of IMA shall behave ethically. A commitment to ethical professional practice includes overarching principles that express our values and standards that guide our conduct.

PRINCIPLES

IMA's overarching ethical principles include: Honesty, Fairness, Objectivity, and Responsibility. Members shall act in accordance with these principles and shall encourage others within their organizations to adhere to them.

STANDARDS

IMA members have a responsibility to comply with and uphold the standards of Competence, Confidentiality, Integrity, and Credibility. Failure to comply may result in disciplinary action.

I. COMPETENCE

1. Maintain an appropriate level of professional leadership and expertise by enhancing knowledge and skills.
2. Perform professional duties in accordance with relevant laws, regulations, and technical standards.
3. Provide decision support information and recommendations that are accurate, clear, concise, and timely. Recognize and help manage risk.

II. CONFIDENTIALITY

1. Keep information confidential except when disclosure is authorized or legally required.
2. Inform all relevant parties regarding appropriate use of confidential information. Monitor to ensure compliance.
3. Refrain from using confidential information for unethical or illegal advantage.

III. INTEGRITY

1. Mitigate actual conflicts of interest. Regularly communicate with business associates to avoid apparent conflicts of interest. Advise all parties of any potential conflicts of interest.
2. Refrain from engaging in any conduct that would prejudice carrying out duties ethically.
3. Abstain from engaging in or supporting any activity that might discredit the profession.
4. Contribute to a positive ethical culture and place integrity of the profession above personal interests.

IV. CREDIBILITY

1. Communicate information fairly and objectively.
2. Provide all relevant information that could reasonably be expected to influence an intended user's understanding of the reports, analyses, or recommendations.
3. Report delays or deficiencies in information, timeliness, processing, or internal controls in conformance with organization policy and/or applicable law.
4. Communicate professional limitations or other constraints that would preclude responsible judgment or successful performance of an activity.

RESOLVING ETHICAL ISSUES

In applying the Standards of Ethical Professional Practice, the member may encounter unethical issues or behavior. In these situations, the member should not ignore them, but rather should actively seek resolution of the issue. In determining which steps to follow, the member should consider all risks involved and whether protections exist against retaliation.

When faced with unethical issues, the member should follow the established policies of his or her organization, including use of an anonymous reporting system if available.

If the organization does not have established policies, the member should consider the following courses of action:

- The resolution process could include a discussion with the member's immediate supervisor. If the supervisor appears to be involved, the issue could be presented to the next level of management.
- IMA offers an anonymous helpline that the member may call to request how key elements of the ***IMA Statement of Ethical Professional Practice*** could be applied to the ethical issue.
- The member should consider consulting his or her own attorney to learn of any legal obligations, rights, and risks concerning the issue.

If resolution efforts are not successful, the member may wish to consider disassociating from the organization.

TOPIC 1

Ethical Considerations for Management Accounting and Financial Management Professionals

ETHICAL CHALLENGES CAN DERAIL THE career of a management accountant or financial management professional. Therefore, these individuals have an obligation to the public, their profession, the organizations they serve, and themselves to maintain the highest standards of ethical conduct.

The IMA has issued an updated version of *IMA Statement of Ethical Practice* that became effective on July 1, 2017. It is also issued as part of the IMA Statement on Management Accounting (SMA). This new *Statement* continues to focus on ethical values and principles. However, it is a more succinct document with the "IMA's overarching ethical principles include: Honesty, Fairness, Objectivity, and Responsibility" at its core.

The first sentence, "Members of IMA shall behave ethically" says it all. In summary we might say that ethics is guided in each of us by our own moral beliefs, principles, standards, and, where available and appropriate, additional guidance from employers and professional societies, such as the IMA in the *IMA Statement of Ethical Professional Practice*.

READ the Learning Outcome Statements (LOS) for this topic as found in Appendix B and then study the concepts presented here to be sure you understand the content you could be tested on in the CMA exam.

Introduction

Ethics is the intellectual discipline that attempts to distinguish right from wrong in human conduct. It is also a practical endeavor that proposes standards of model behavior as points of comparison when individuals choose among various courses of action. Applying model standards in an imperfect world is rarely easy or straightforward.

Consider the following ethically challenging scenario. It begins with a "normal" situation.

Consider this example taken from everyday accounting work. Mary has been assigned work on the company's inventory. The inventory is presently recorded at historical cost. Mary is well aware that inventory is to be reported at lower of cost or market. This requirement acknowledges that when the utility of inventory declines, usually due to physical deterioration or technical obsolescence, the historical cost principle is no longer relevant. Mary has prepared a schedule listing inventory items that likely should be written down from historical cost. The total amount of the write-down is material to the financial statements. Elizabeth, Mary's supervisor, reviews Mary's list and tells Mary that there is no justification for the proposed write-down. Elizabeth further asks Mary to dispose of the schedule listing inventory items to be written down and to proceed to her next project.

In this scenario involving Mary and Elizabeth, Mary is faced with an ethical dilemma. Mary is obliged to follow her supervisor's instructions. Following her supervisor's instructions would probably result in a violation of the *IMA Statement of Ethical Professional Practice*. One principle that probably would be violated is that of honesty. At least one standard probably would also be violated—integrity. Mary cannot comply with her employment contract (requiring her to perform work that is assigned to her) and at the same time satisfy the IMA's ethical principles and standards (which require her to perform her duties honestly and with integrity). Ethics, then, consists of making morally defensible choices within the sometimes ethically ambiguous, perhaps even threatening, conditions of real life.

Two good questions Mary should ask herself before she takes her next step: "Have I gathered all the information and insight I need to take responsible and objective action?" In this instance, is Mary confident that her assumptions and computations leading to the preparation of her list of inventory items that should be written down to lower of cost or market are supported and accurate? And "Would I, Mary, be pleased to read on her social media page on the Internet about my decision with respect to Elizabeth's instructions to ignore the inventory write-down list and to destroy it?"

IMA Statement of Ethical Professional Practice

Much of this section is excerpted directly from the *IMA Statement of Ethical Professional Practice* that was issued in July 2017. It is recommended that candidates study this statement thoroughly and commit the principles, standards, and resolution of ethical conflict to memory.

Ethical Behavior for Practitioners of Management Accounting and Financial Management

Practitioners of management accounting and financial management, as well as members of IMA, shall not commit acts contrary to these standards nor shall they condone the commission of such acts by others within their organizations.

IMA Statement of Ethical Professional Practice

Members of IMA shall behave ethically. A commitment to ethical professional practice includes overarching principles that express our values and standards that guide member conduct.

Principles

IMA's overarching ethical principles are: Honesty, Fairness, Objectivity, and Responsibility. Members shall act in accordance with these principles and shall encourage others within their organizations to adhere to them.

The fourth principle, responsibility, is directly linked to each of the four standards that follow the four principles. For example, the first standard, Competence, lists the member's responsibilities with respect to competence:

IMA members have a responsibility to:

1. Maintain an appropriate level of professional leadership and expertise by enhancing knowledge and skills.
2. Perform professional duties in accordance with relevant laws, regulations, and technical standards.
3. Provide decision support information and recommendations that are accurate, clear, concise, and timely. Recognize and help manage risk.

The other three standards adhere to the same pattern to clearly state what the member's responsibilities are with respect to that standard.

Honesty

The first principle, honesty, requires conscientious application to the task at hand and truthfulness in all analyses and communications. Honesty is one of the key attributes people look for in an accountant or financial professional: "If you can't trust your accountant, who can you trust?" Examples of honesty include: disclosing all necessary and relevant information to outside auditors; refusing to record information that is anything less than accurate; and providing factual information to others so that they can make informed decisions.

Fairness

Fairness requires empathetic and just consideration of the needs of others involved in a particular situation and full disclosure of all necessary contextual information. The organization deserves adequate and full disclosure in context so that appropriate actions can be taken within a reasonable time frame. To be fair, that context should be fully spelled out. Examples of fairness include: providing information and feedback objectively; identifying and fixing mistakes; and selecting vendors without bias, prejudice, or favoritism.

Objectivity

Objectivity requires impartial and dispassionate evaluation of conflicting points of view before arriving at a conclusion. For many years, organizations have depended on the objectivity of internal and external financial professionals to support them in making critical business decisions. "Let's ask our accountants" is often the course of action when businesspeople want to determine a reasoned, thorough, dispassionate, legally defensible course of action. Examples of objectivity are stating relevant financial and legal guidelines, maintaining standards for documenting information, and making recommendations on existing data despite pressures to favor one course over another.

Responsibility

In the principle of responsibility, the IMA is reminding accounting and financial professionals what, exactly, their responsibilities are. Each of the four standards that follow begin with the phrase *IMA members have a responsibility to*: which then states the member's responsibility within the context of that standard. Examples of responsibility include conveying information at the appropriate time, ensuring information on reports and statements is accurate, and gathering enough information to make an informed decision.

Standards

The *IMA Statement of Ethical Professional Practice* effective July 2017 states that IMA members have a responsibility to comply with and uphold the standards of Competence, Confidentiality, Integrity, and Credibility. Failure to comply may result in disciplinary action.

I. Competence

IMA members have a responsibility to:

1. Maintain an appropriate level of professional leadership and expertise by enhancing knowledge and skills.
2. Perform professional duties in accordance with relevant laws, regulations, and technical standards.
3. Provide decision support information and recommendations that are accurate, clear, concise, and timely. Recognize and help manage risk.

The rules and principles that guide financial accounting and reporting are included in the Accounting Standards Codification (ASC). The rules and principles in the ASC are as diverse as they are dynamic. Keeping up to date with changes in regulations and the adoption of new laws and standards in the industry is essential. Failing to do so may unknowingly lead to unethical behavior.

II. Confidentiality

IMA members have a responsibility to:

1. Keep information confidential except when disclosure is authorized or legally required.

2. Inform all relevant parties regarding appropriate use of confidential information. Monitor to ensure compliance.
3. Refrain from using confidential information for unethical or illegal advantage.

While the confidentiality standard is fairly straightforward, today's technological advances actually may hinder management accountants from following it as diligently as they must. Not only should paper and electronic documents be properly secured, but all conversations, especially those on mobile phones, should be conducted only in a private setting. Technology is advancing rapidly. Today, people carry out activities with mobile phones and devices that just a few years ago required full-blown computers. Internet usage with mobile devices places accounting and finance professionals at risk. The potential for unwittingly disclosing confidential information is high. Accounting and finance professionals must find ways to conduct business on mobile devices without breaching confidentiality. This is a matter of extreme importance.

III. Integrity

IMA members have a responsibility to:

1. Mitigate actual conflicts of interest. Regularly communicate with business associates to avoid apparent conflicts of interest. Advise all parties of any potential conflicts of interest.
2. Refrain from engaging in any conduct that would prejudice carrying out duties ethically.
3. Abstain from engaging in or supporting any activity that might discredit the profession.
4. Contribute to a positive ethical culture and place integrity of the profession above personal interests.

Integrity includes the responsibility to communicate both the good and the bad, whether it is news, analysis, judgment, or professional opinion.

IV. Credibility

IMA members have a responsibility to:

1. Communicate information fairly and objectively.
2. Provide all relevant information that could reasonably be expected to influence an intended user's understanding of the reports, analyses, or recommendations.
3. Report any delays or deficiencies in information, timeliness, processing, or internal controls in conformance with organization policy and/or applicable law.
4. Communicate professional limitations or other constraints that would preclude responsible judgment or successful performance of an activity.

Credibility ties in closely with the competence standard. In order to be credible, an individual must be competent. Underlying credibility is the management accountant's duty to plan ahead and assess potential risks, gather enough information to be fully informed about all relevant facts, and communicate new information promptly, whether the information is favorable or unfavorable.

Resolving Ethical Issues

As can be seen in the scenario concerning Mary and Elizabeth, resolving an ethical conflict can be a difficult and often stressful task. Unfortunately, there is no magic formula that will result in the right decision. Each situation is different, and the circumstances are often complex. The *IMA Statement of Ethical Professional Practice* advises:

> In applying the Standards of Ethical Professional Practice, the member may encounter unethical issues or behavior. In these situations, the member should not ignore them, but rather should actively seek resolution of the issue. In determining which steps to follow, the member should consider all risks involved and whether protections exist against retaliation.

When faced with unethical issues, the member should follow the established policies of his or her organization, including use of an anonymous reporting system if available.

If the organization does not have established policies, the member should consider the following courses of action:

- The resolution process could include a discussion with the member's immediate supervisor. If the supervisor appears to be involved, the issue could be presented to the next level of management.
- IMA offers an anonymous helpline that the member may call to request how key elements of the *IMA Statement of Ethical Professional Practice* could be applied to the ethical issue.
- The member should consider consulting his or her own attorney to learn of any legal obligations, rights, and risks concerning the issue.

If resolution efforts are not successful, the member may wish to consider disassociating from the organization.

Addressing any ethical conflict requires careful consideration and an examination of all the facts before proceeding. This may require:

- Checking data and source material
- Obtaining additional information to either refute or confirm speculative rumors
- Asking more detailed questions
- Probing other people for more information
- Maintain a neutral and open-minded attitude
- Disregarding preconceived ideas

Any of these steps must be done with regard to ethical responsibilities for confidentiality in accordance with the Standards of Ethical Professional Practice. When seeking more corroborative information, extreme care must be taken not to inadvertently disclose confidential information.

The next question to consider when faced with an ethical conflict is "What are the alternatives?" Defining the alternatives will provide a framework within which to examine the merits and drawbacks of each option. Attempting to clearly define the choices may reveal a new option.

Now let's consider Scott London's situation—it probably started some time in the past. London and Bryan Shaw have been friends for many years. London is senior audit partner with one of the Big Four global audit and consulting firms. Shaw is a jewelry store owner and amateur stock trader. London and Shaw usually play golf, weather permitting, about once a week. They talk about all sorts of things while playing golf: what's in the news, how's the family, where's the next holiday destination, and what mutual acquaintances are doing these days.

Many of London's clients have publicly traded securities. Information about which of the Big Four firms are auditors for publicly traded entities is readily available in the clients' annual reports and in the media. Herbal Life had been in the news recently and this fact enters into the friends' conversation. And so the conversation wanders from general chit-chat to some pretty specific matters related to London's clients, in particular Herbal Life. At the conclusion of the golf match on this particular day, Shaw surprises London by giving him four tickets to a highly anticipated NBA game. London initially thinks nothing of Shaw's friendly, generous gesture.

One could argue that, at some point, it may have occurred to Scott London that the friendly chit-chat could go into client confidential information. Once he realized this, one alternative would be for Scott to end his relationship with Bryan. Unless Scott was concerned about Byran's motives, ending their relationship would not be a beneficial alternative. One beneficial alternative would be for Scott to avoid ANY chit-chat about ANY of his clients.

Consider any rules, laws, or regulations that may apply. What do the rules say? How do they apply to each of the alternatives? Depending on the situation, many different rules and regulations may need to be examined, including the company's code of conduct; local, state, and federal laws; generally accepted accounting principles and Financial Accounting Standards Board (FASB) standards, and the *IMA Statement of Ethical Professional Practice*.

The company's policies provide a starting point. The IMA Ethics Helpline (1-800-245-1383) is available for members and can offer an outside perspective. It may be necessary to consult with the company's legal or compliance department and, if necessary, a personal attorney regarding interpretation of laws and regulations as well as the management accountant's legal obligations and rights. The *IMA Statement of Ethical Professional Practice* encompasses one page of guidance. Best practice may be achieved by reference to, in Scott London's scenario, reviewing his employer's (KPMG's) policies regarding confidentiality, which are probably much more detailed than the IMA *Statement*. Also, as a CPA in public practice, London is bound to the AICPA Code of Professional Conduct. The AICPA Code is more detailed than the IMA *Statement* because CPAs have a direct responsibility to the public interest.

When someone feels pressured in a particular direction, the human factor of an ethical conflict comes into play. Individuals may feel pressured by professional obligations and personal values, which, in some cases, may conflict. A person's morals, background, experiences, social and economic circumstances, and the ethical culture of the organization all may contribute to an ethical conflict. Professional obligations related to customer expectations, investor goals, departmental quotas, delivery schedules, and many internal and external factors also may compel an individual to choose one option over another. Personal and professional factors differ, so each individual is likely to respond differently to pressure. One strategy is to try to pinpoint the reasons the decision is difficult to make, considering each side.

Finally, the consequences of each alternative need to be considered carefully, including who else will be affected and how they will be affected.

The Fraud Triangle

Often some aspect of fraud underlies ethical situations that a management or financial accounting professional faces. Fraud is simply an act of deceit or trickery or breach of confidence perpetrated for profit or to gain some unfair or dishonest advantage. There are various types of fraud. Fraud against a company, or occupational fraud, can be committed either internally, by employees, managers, officers, or owners of a company, or externally, by customers, vendors, or other parties. Other schemes defraud individuals rather than organizations. Accounting and finance professionals need to understand how fraud can occur. AU 316 describes the auditor's responsibility with respect to fraud. While AU 316 is not necessarily applicable to accounting and finance professionals who are not engaged in independent audits, this standard provides much useful information. For example, one can learn about potential fraud by discussing the matter with other members of your firm. A normal step in audit planning is for the audit team to engage in brainstorming to consider objectively where and how fraud could be perpetrated. When a fraud scheme is reported in the media, it is useful to read how the scheme occurred. While Enron and WorldCom have become synonymous with fraud, there are many examples both big and small that can provide useful information about how fraud schemes can be perpetrated. Some examples from the past few years include the Koss Corporation, Peregrine Financial Group, City of Dixon Illinois, and the San Diego Community Bible Church. This knowledge can provide the management and financial accounting professional with the ability to recognize the potential for fraud and take proactive steps to mitigate its occurrence.

A widely recognized model for explaining the factors that cause someone to commit occupational fraud is the fraud triangle. The fraud triangle consists of three components: pressure, opportunity, and rationalization.

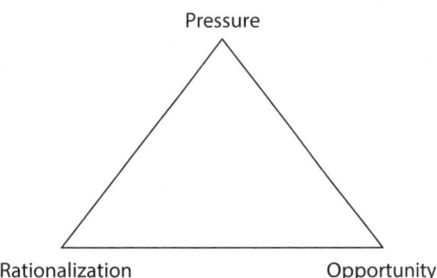

AU 316.7 states that three conditions generally are present when fraud occurs. While the CMA LOS does not specifically mention a fourth condition, some authors expand on *opportunity* by adding *capability*. The reasoning behind this addition is that if the potential fraudster lacks the capability to execute and cover the scheme even if the opportunity to commit fraud is present, the fraudster will not proceed with the scheme. **Pressure**, such as a financial need, may often provide a motive for committing the fraud. Examples of pressure that commonly lead to fraud include the need to meet earnings expectations to sustain investor confidence, the need to meet productivity targets at work, or simply the inability to pay one's bills. **Opportunity**, or perceived opportunity, defines the method by which the crime can be committed. The individual fraudster must see some way he or she can use (abuse) his or her position of trust to solve the financial problem with a low perceived risk of getting caught. For instance, an individual committing a fraud (stealing monies) sees an internal control weakness and, believing no one will notice if funds are taken, begins the fraud with a small amount of money. If no one notices, the amount taken usually grows.

For example, a bank fraud was executed over approximately 20 years in a bank in Sheldon, Iowa. The perpetrator was Bernice Geiger, the daughter of the bank president. On January 22, 1961, a bank examiner unexpectedly arrived at the bank. Bernice was not present at that moment, but when she arrived and saw the examiner, she immediately confessed to embezzling more than $2,000,000 from the bank. This was the largest reported U.S. bank embezzlement in history, at that time.

Finally, **rationalization** involves the individual fraudster justifying the crime to him- or herself in a way that makes it an acceptable or justifiable act. Common rationalizations an individual may use include: "I was underpaid; my employer cheated me" or "I was entitled to the money" or "I was only borrowing the money."

To illustrate forms of rationalization, consider two scenarios. The first scenario involves a notorious fraudster, church minister Barry Minkow, who is presently serving two sentences in federal prison. In the first sentence he is currently serving Minkow pled guilty to a single charge of securities fraud committed against the Lennar Corporation. When asked why he perpetrated this securities fraud, he explained that his work as a minister and the work he performed as a fraud consultant for the FBI did not pay enough. He felt he needed to earn more money so he used privileged insider information to write a false fraud investigative report and then he entered a short-sale position on Lennar, the company he was investigating. One point to remember is that once a person becomes determined to commit fraud, audacious outcomes can result.

The second scenario is far less dramatic on the surface. A Wisconsin bank teller embezzled approximately $40,000 from her bank employer. The scheme unraveled during an independent audit. The bank employee took a vacation. During her absence, her temporary replacement noticed that there were more than 100 empty coin boxes on the floor. The empty boxes were surrounded by full boxes. It turned out that the teller had been experiencing personal financial difficulties. She had started her scheme by taking a few rolls of quarters with the intention of replacing them before her embezzlement could be detected. But she never replaced the embezzled quarters, instead stealing more and more. The final tally of her theft was over $40,000 in quarters—more than 160,000 quarters! One should never underestimate the determination of a fraudster. The teller was convicted of embezzlement.

Now we return to Barry Minkow and why he is serving two consecutive terms in federal prison (this time). As previously mentioned, Minkow was a church minister. He grew a small congregation into a large one. He steadfastly refused to have anything to do with the church's finances because of his earlier incarceration on 57 counts of securities fraud. Minkow had decided to clean up his act as a minister. Unfortunately, even though he distanced himself from the church's money, he decided one day to begin an off-book fundraiser for a children's cancer hospital. He set up a bank account and solicited money from his parishioners. The money never made it to the children's hospital fund. All in all, Minkow relieved church members of about $3,000,000. He argued unsuccessfully at his trial that he was addicted to pain medications that clouded his judgment.

Investors, employees, customers, and vendors will find ways to retaliate against behavior deemed unethical as they define it, and *not as the industry's management teams would choose to define it*. Industry leaders saying that a particular activity is okay does not make it so, no matter how many firms agree.

It is critical that management or financial accounting professionals understand the fraud triangle and its components and be cognizant of employee behavioral issues and changes that might heighten the likelihood of potential fraud. Additionally, management or financial accounting professionals need to be aware of any internal control weaknesses that might create opportunities for fraud.

During the period of January 18–24, 2008, the board of directors of Société Générale confronted a problem of staggering proportions. An internal investigation during the preceding two weeks had revealed that Jerome Kerviel, a derivatives trader employed by the bank, had entered into unauthorized and in some cases fraudulent trades involving derivative financial instruments, exposing the bank to losses totalling €6–7 billion in a plunging securities market. The bank's internal control system had failed to detect more than 1,000 unauthorized or fraudulent transactions entered into over a period of more than three years.

Kerviel had begun working for the bank in 2000. He learned a great deal about administration and control over securities trading. The evidence in his case suggests that Kerviel was well acquainted with both the strengths and weaknesses of the trading control systems. Kerviel's early experience with the bank set the stage for his later work as a trader where his capabilities blossomed. His understanding of the trading control system and in particular his keen awareness of control weaknesses caused by high turnover in trading supervisors, coupled opportunity with capability. Once his fraud unraveled, he stood trial in France. The trial spent considerable time trying to determine his motives (we can substitute the words *pressure* and *rationalization* for the legal term *motive*) to enter into and maintain 1,071 fraudulent or unauthorized transactions without being detected by the internal control system.

During Kerviel's trial, he repeatedly but quietly asserted that his trades were never questioned when he was turning large profits for the bank and that he hadn't actually taken any money from the bank from his trades except for his compensation.

Conducting an organizational fraud risk assessment can assist with managing the risk of fraud. Such an assessment involves identifying and evaluating fraud risk factors (the establishment of unrealistic earnings expectations); identifying possible fraud risk, schemes, and scenarios (intentional overstatement of sales to meet unrealistic earnings expectations); prioritizing identified fraud risks and assessing their likelihood; evaluating internal controls to mitigate fraudulent activity; and documenting and continually monitoring and updating the fraud risk assessment.

The Committee on Sponsoring Organizations (COSO) is a joint initiative of five private-sector organizations and is dedicated to providing thought leadership through the development of frameworks and guidance on enterprise risk management (ERM), internal control, and fraud deterrence. COSO's supporting organizations are the Institute of Internal Auditors (IIA), the American Accounting Association (AAA), the American Institute of Certified Public Accountants (AICPA), Financial Executives International (FEI), and the Institute of Management Accountants (IMA). In 2013 COSO issued the Internal Control—Integrated Framework.

In 2015 COSO and the Institute of Internal Auditors issued *Leveraging COSO Across the Three Lines of Defense* by the Institute of Internal Auditors 2015.

The COSO Internal Control—Integrated Framework (the Framework) outlines the components, principles, and factors necessary for an organization to effectively manage its risks through the implementation of internal control. The Three Lines of Defense (the model) addresses how specific duties related to risk and control could be assigned and coordinated within an organization, regardless of its size or complexity.

Practice Ethical Scenario

The board of directors of Arivan Corporation recently learned that some members of the senior management team had circumvented the company's internal controls for personal gain. The board appointed a special task force of external auditors and outside legal counsel to investigate the situation.

After extensive review, the task force concluded that for a period of several years, the expenses of the company's chief executive officer, president, and vice president for public relations were charged to an account called the Limited Expenditure Account (LEA). The account was established five years before and was not subject to the company's normal approval and authorization process. Approximately $2,000,000 of requests for reimbursement were routinely processed and charged to LEA. Accounting personnel were advised by the controller to process such requests based on the individual approval of the three executives, even when the requests were not adequately documented.

The vice president for public relations and his department were in charge of political fundraising activities. The task force determined, however, that only a small portion of the $1,000,000 raised in the previous year actually was used for political purposes. In addition, departmental resources were used for personal projects of the three identified executives. The task force also uncovered an additional $4,000,000 of expenditures that were poorly documented so that even the amounts for proper business purposes could not be identified.

The task force noted that these payment practices, as well as LEA, were never disclosed in the internal audit department's audit reports, even though company disbursements were tested annually. References to these practices and LEA were included on two occasions in recent years' work papers. The director of internal audit, who reports to the controller, advised that he reviewed these findings with the controller who, in turn, advised that he mentioned these findings to the president. The president recommended that they not be included in the internal audit reports. The task force also noted that the company did not have a formal, published ethics policy.

1. Discuss whether the controller has acted unethically. Reference the relevant standards of ethical practice in your answer.
2. If you were one of the accounting personnel directed to process these transactions, what steps would you take to resolve the ethical conflict?

To help prepare you for essay-type questions on the CMA exams, think about how you would apply the **IMA Statement of Ethical Professional Practice** *to answer these questions. Prepare at least an outline response to both questions, then compare your answer or outline to the proposed solutions below.*

Solution: Question 1

Based on the *IMA Statement of Ethical Professional Practice,* the controller has acted unethically. Even though the company does not have an ethics policy, members must act in accordance with the principles of honesty, fairness, objectivity, and responsibility. The controller also should encourage others in the organization to adhere to these same principles. Furthermore, the controller has violated specific standards of ethical conduct by advising accounting personnel to process payments with individual authorizations, even when the transactions were not adequately documented, and by advising the director of the internal audit department not to include any references to these improprieties in the audit reports. The specific standards violated are discussed next.

Competence

Perform professional duties in accordance with relevant laws, regulations, and technical standards.

Integrity

- Mitigate actual conflicts of interest. Regularly communicate with business associates to avoid apparent conflicts of interest. Advise all parties of any potential conflicts.
- Refrain from engaging in any activity that would prejudice their ability to carry out their duties ethically.
- Refrain from engaging in or supporting any activity that would discredit the profession.

Credibility

Communicate information fairly and objectively.

Confidentiality

The issue of confidentiality arises in this scenario because at a minimum there appear to be violations federal laws. The accountants are obliged in that case to seek outside counsel as an exception to the normal confidentiality requirement.

Solution: Question 2

Given that the company does not have a formal ethics policy, Arivan most likely does not have an established policy for resolving ethical conflicts. However, if a policy does exist, a management accountant should follow the company's procedures. In the absence of an established ethics policy, or if the procedures fail to resolve the ethical conflict, the management accountant should consider these actions:

- Because the accountant's superior appears to be the cause of this ethical dilemma, the accountant should present the issue to the next highest-level manager in the organization and then proceed to successively higher levels (audit committee, board of directors, etc.), until the matter is satisfactorily resolved.

- Political fundraising is regulated by federal law and also by some state laws. For that reason the accountant is both permitted and may be obliged to report apparent violations of federal or state laws concerning political fundraising and funds raised for political purposes.
- The accountant should clarify the ethical issues with an impartial advisor to obtain a better understanding of possible courses of action.
- The accountant should consult his or her own attorney about personal legal obligations and rights concerning this situation.

Resolving an ethical conflict can be a challenging and often stressful task. This scenario becomes more complicated because the accountants have determined that the detected irregularities involved several high levels of management. To whom should the accountants report their findings if all higher levels are involved in the scheme? This situation may force the accountant to consult with outside authorities.

Knowledge Check: Professional Ethics

The following questions are intended to help you check your understanding and recall of the material presented in this topic. They do not represent the type of questions that appear on the CMA exam.

Directions: Answer each question in the space provided. Correct answers and section references appear after the knowledge check questions.

1. The *IMA Statement of Ethical Professional Practice* includes four overarching ethical principles. Name the four principles.

    a. _____

    b. _____

    c. _____

    d. _____

2. The *IMA Statement of Ethical Professional Practice* includes four overarching ethical principles and four standards. Which of the following most accurately describes the relationship between the IMA principles and the IMA standards?

    a. Each standard aligns perfectly with one and only one principle.

    b. One standard may align with two or more principles.

    c. The standards are completely separate from the principles.

    d. The standards guide our conduct while the principles express our values.

    For questions 3 through 7, match the following rules to the IMA standards of ethical responsibility. More than one standard may apply.

    a. Competence

    b. Integrity

    c. Confidentiality

    d. Credibility

3. _____ Refuse any gift that might influence your actions in your capacity as an accountant.

4. _____ Prepare complete and clear reports.

5. _____ Disclose fully all relevant information that could influence a user's understanding of a report.

6. _____ Communicate unfavorable as well as favorable information.

7. _____ Perform your duties in accordance with applicable laws, regulations, and standards.

8. If an accountant's immediate supervisor instructs the accountant to withhold essential but unfavorable information in a management report, the accountant should:

   ☐ a. do as the supervisor asks and tell no one.
   ☐ b. refuse to do as the supervisor asks and alert an investigative reporter to the problem.
   ☐ c. take the matter to the supervisor's immediate supervisor.
   ☐ d. take the matter directly to the corporate legal department.

Knowledge Check Answers: Professional Ethics

1. The *IMA Statement of Ethical Professional Practice* includes four overarching ethical principles. Name the four principles. [**See IMA Statement of Ethical Professional Practice—*Principles*.**]
    a. **Honesty**
    b. **Fairness**
    c. **Objectivity**
    d. **Responsibility**

2. The *IMA Statement of Ethical Professional Practice* includes four overarching ethical principles and four standards. Which of the following most accurately describes the relationship between the IMA principles and the IMA standards? [**See IMA Statement of Ethical Professional Practice—*Standards*.**]
    a. Each standard aligns perfectly with one and only one principle.
    b. One standard may align with two or more principles.
    c. The standards are completely separate from the principles.
    d. The standards guide our conduct while the principles express our values.

    Answer d is correct. See the *IMA Statement of Ethical Professional Practice*.

    For questions 3 through 7, match the following rules to the IMA standards of ethical responsibility. More than one standard may apply.
    a. Competence
    b. Integrity
    c. Confidentiality
    d. Credibility

3. **b** Refuse any gift that might influence your actions in your capacity as an accountant.

4. **a and d** Prepare complete and clear reports.

5. **d** Disclose fully all relevant information that could influence a user's understanding of a report.

6. **b and d** Communicate unfavorable as well as favorable information.

7. **a** Perform your duties in accordance with applicable laws, regulations, and standards.

8. If an accountant's immediate supervisor instructs the accountant to withhold essential but unfavorable information in a management report, the accountant should: [See *Resolution of Ethical Conflict.*]
   - ☐ a. do as the supervisor asks and tell no one.
   - ☐ b. refuse to do as the supervisor asks and alert an investigative reporter to the problem.
   - ☒ c. take the matter to the supervisor's immediate supervisor.
   - ☐ d. take the matter directly to the corporate legal department.

TOPIC 2

Ethical Considerations for the Organization

ETHICS IS ABOUT THE INTEGRITY OF THE DECISION MAKING PROCESS that is used to resolve any number of issues," according to Institute of Management Accountants' *Statement on Management Accounting (SMA)* titled "Values and Ethics: From Inception to Practice."

The IMA's principles and standards work together to guide individuals in determining what it means to "behave ethically." Ethics is guided in each of us by our own moral beliefs, principles, standards, and, where appropriate additional guidance from employers and professional societies, such as the IMA in the *IMA Statement of Ethical Professional Practice*.

In this topic we carry forward the principles and standards that guide ethical behavior of management accountants. Companies are obliged to establish their own standards including much more detailed guidance than one finds in the IMA *Statement*. The company's standards should be unique to the entity. Since each company develops its own ethical standards, those standards and the examples that are often found in the company's code of ethical conduct should be written in such a way as to be directly relevant to that company, as opposed to standards and examples designed by others and simply plugged into the company's code of ethical conduct.

READ the Learning Outcome Statements (LOS) for this topic as found in Appendix B and then study the concepts presented here to be sure you understand the content you could be tested on in the CMA exam.

LOS
§2.F.2.d

Corporate Responsibility for Ethical Conduct

Before turning the ethics focus to the organization itself, it is useful to consider that no matter how pure and clean an organization appears to be on the surface, if corruption exists at the top of the organization, awful things can happen. The following scenario is from a 2013 news report by CNBC correspondent Scott Cohn. Regulators in charge of monitoring the bankrupt futures brokerage

Peregrine Financial Group missed warning signs as far back as 1994, according to an independent report released on same day Peregrine's founder was sentenced to 50 years in prison.

The National Futures Association, an industry organization that was PFG's primary regulator, commissioned the report soon after the firm collapsed in July.

PFG founder and CEO Russell Wasendorf, Sr., admitted stealing some $215 million in customer funds by falsifying the firm's bank statements and lying to the NFA and the Commodity Futures Trading Commission. But the report, authored by former SEC Inspector General David Kotz of Berkeley Research Group, found regulators missed multiple opportunities to catch the fraud.

"Some NFA auditors did not always exhibit sufficient professional skepticism in assessing and evaluating fraud risks," the report said. While the investigation focused on the NFA, it notes that the CFTC—which did not launch an investigation of its own—missed warning signs as well.

The earliest warning sign came in 1994 (almost 20 years before PFG's collapse) when, according to the report, a CFTC employee personally visited a branch of U.S. Bank—where PFG's customer funds were held—asking for a signed confirmation of the firm's accounts. The bank declined to provide the confirmation, but the CFTC did not follow up, according to the report.

Wasendorf, 64, confessed to creating fake bank statements with inflated balances and submitting them to the NFA for years. But in 2011, more than a year before the fraud was exposed, the NFA received an actual bank statement from U.S. Bank showing a balance of just $7 million—a $211 million discrepancy from the balance Wasendorf had reported. What happened next at NFA is in dispute. An NFA auditor claims to have alerted a field supervisor about the discrepancy, according to the report, but the supervisor claims she was not alerted.

Wasendorf, meanwhile, told investigators, "I am in shock—I'm caught," according to the report. But he did not need to worry. He simply claimed the real statement was a mistake, forged a "corrected" statement, sent it to the NFA, and the fraud continued for another year.

"We found no evidence that NFA auditors questioned the new version of the confirmation purportedly from (the bank)," the report said. "Instead, the NFA auditors accepted the new version, despite the vast difference between the numbers provided in the two versions of the confirmation, and did not extend their audit procedures."

The report, which includes nearly two dozen recommendations for reforms, faults the NFA for inexperienced staffers who were easily intimidated by Wasendorf and his director of compliance, Susan O'Meara, who hasn't been accused of wrongdoing.

The report said NFA employees missed other warning signs, including the fact that PFG's audit firm was a one-person operation based in suburban Chicago. The NFA also failed to question some $60 million in capital contributions from Wasendorf himself, which the report said should have been a sign of potential shortfalls. And the report said the regulator did not pay enough attention to warnings signs elsewhere in the industry.

As you read the remainder of this topic, remind yourself of some of the assumptions that are made about the "tone at the top" and what the presumed watchdogs are doing to keep those at the top of the organization from resorting to unethical and/or illegal activities.

In recent years, top executives accused of unethical behavior have stated that they are innocent of any wrongdoing. Despite the fact that a company may have thousands of employees, it still has a responsibility to ensure, to the best of its ability, that all of those employees are behaving in an ethical manner. To achieve control, the organization defines the principles of behavior by identifying and documenting the organizational values, creating a code of ethics and conduct, and implementing internal controls. All of these documents work together to guide daily decision making and behavioral choices. This guidance, according to the *SMA* titled "Values and Ethics: From Inception to Practice," is a "critical element in the creation of a framework for ethical management." Ultimately, these documents create and maintain an ethical culture that actively supports the behavior that the organization desires.

The scope and detail of a company's ethical policies will be determined in part by the size of the organization. In general, larger companies will require a more detailed and comprehensive statement of ethics and conduct, whereas smaller companies may achieve the same ethical culture though the personal example of the firm's operating owner and senior managers. However, as smaller companies grow and the founder becomes less and less accessible, there is a danger that the culture will be diluted. Therefore, it is important for even small companies to document their values and behavioral expectations of employees.

LOS §2.F.2.e
Fortunately, making such an effort will provide many benefits to the organization. It can take years for an organization to build up a reputation for quality or reliability. Yet the behavior of a few or even a single employee can destroy an organization's reputation very quickly. Therefore, companies that take corporate ethical responsibility seriously usually experience improvement in share value, client retention, and attraction of new clients, investors, and employees. In addition, they experience a lowered risk of compliance violations.

Sapienza and Zingales (2013) in their study of which dimensions of corporate culture are related to a firm's performance and why, found that proclaimed values appear irrelevant. Yet, when employees perceive top managers as trustworthy and ethical, the firm's performance is stronger. The authors also studied how different governance structures impact the ability to sustain integrity as a corporate value. Their findings are that publicly traded firms are less able to sustain integrity. Traditional measures of corporate governance do not seem to have much of an impact.

LOS §2.F.2.f
From this study we may conclude that the concept of "tone at the top" of the organization is more influential than what is written in the organization's code of conduct. Improvements like higher levels of productivity, improved interpersonal dynamics, and lower risks of fraud all result in better financial performance for the organization. According to the *SMA* "Values and Ethics: From Inception to Practice":

Organizations that succeed in a broad-based deployment of a code of ethics will create a base for enhanced risk assessment, greater transparency for those responsible for organizational governance, and an increased probability that commitments made in words are truly being fulfilled in practice. As a result, CEOs [chief executive officers] and CFOs [chief financial officers] who are required to sign commitments of compliance will do so with a greater degree of knowledge and certainty that their words and the actions of the organization are aligned. [This requirement is part of the Sarbanes Oxley Act, Section 302.]

Because working within the letter of the law does not guarantee that individuals are behaving ethically, ethical behavior goes beyond the idea of following legally acceptable procedures. Individuals and organizations behave ethically when their actions are aligned with a set of core values. The challenge for most organizations is that each employee comes into the company with his or her own predefined set of values. To present a unified presence to customers, shareholders, vendors, the community, and all other stakeholders, it is essential for the organization to define its core values as they relate to the business in which it is involved. In this manner, all employees are provided with the unifying guidance they require to make ethical choices aligned with corporate values.

Research at DePaul University in Chicago by Frigo and Litman found a pattern of strategic activities of high-performance companies that includes ethical business conduct (*DRIVEN: Business Strategy, Human Actions and the Creation of Wealth* [2008]). Their research involved screening the financial performance of more than 15,000 public companies using 30 years of financial data. They identified about 100 high-performance companies that demonstrated a strong commitment to creating long-term shareholder value by focusing on sustainable return on investment while adhering to ethical business conduct. Such firms included Johnson & Johnson, which is famous for its Credo as a foundation for ethical business conduct at the company. (Even though one study could list Johnson & Johnson at the top of most ethical companies, a subsequent lapse of ethics could still taint the company.)

Ethics Starts at the Top

Ideally everyone in an organization, from the board of directors to the CEO to the front-line worker, will be able to answer the following questions in a similar manner:

- What values does this organization believe in?
- What principles drive this organization's decision making?
- What is the ethical culture of the organization?
- What principles/beliefs do managers and leaders demonstrate?

These questions are the basis for articulating a cohesive code of conduct. Once the company's values are defined, they are applied to different areas of the organization to provide daily guidance on what individuals are expected to do and what they are expected not to do. These principles and standards then provide a framework for ethical management and leadership.

Because they are broadly written, these short statements may be interpreted differently by individuals. Therefore, the next step is for senior management to expand each principle into a more specific behavioral profile. The expanded statement includes examples of what type of behavior exemplifies this principle as well as what type of behavior is inconsistent with it. The goal is to create a concrete foundation that can be used to guide operational decisions on an ongoing basis.

For these principles to become a part of the organizational culture, it is imperative that senior management fully understand the implications that will arise as they are implemented. If the principles cannot be implemented consistently, or if they inadvertently create an environment that is untenable, the end result will be confusion and conflict.

In the absence of a defined code of conduct or ethics, employees will either follow their own beliefs and values or look for guidance from leadership to determine the expected course of action. Therefore, it is essential that management hold itself to a higher standard of conduct than expected from those who are supervised. To be effective, managers will set a good example, follow documented values, keep all promises and commitments, and establish an atmosphere conducive to helping others to adhere to the existing ethics standards.

Applying Ethics in a Corporate Setting

While the code of ethics is important, ultimately it is only a document. What gives the code life and expression of its inherent benefits are the people who live that code. A company's employees are truly its most important asset when creating an ethical culture.

In addition to an unimpeachable ethical tone at the top, if the organization wants to create a climate where doing the right thing is the norm, it is important to hire the right people, provide them with adequate training, and then practice consistent values-based leadership.

The process begins with hiring employees. During the interview process, potential candidates should be screened for personal values and expected workplace behaviors as well as skills and aptitudes. Although values are amorphous and difficult to measure, they can be inferred by asking about personal values, using open-ended interview questions about how they would respond to specific circumstances, or inquiring whether certain actions would be considered ethical. Because of the importance of bringing in only the right people, and the potential cost of hiring and then firing those who behave unethically, the *SMA* states that "management accountants should ensure that part of the HR [human resources] budget is allocated for conducting thorough behavioral analysis and that in-depth assessment is mandatory in the case of sensitive positions."

Once the right employees have been hired, training is the next priority. Orientation should contain information specific to the organization's values and any existing codes of conduct or ethics. Ongoing training should be provided to all staff, on a regular basis, to reaffirm these beliefs. Training programs should be comprehensive, relate to real-world situations faced by employees, and provide a consistent message.

Employee training is a key part of maintaining an ethical organizational culture. In addition to having each employee read and understand the code of ethics, training should explain the concepts that lie behind the code. The training also should translate the high-level corporate-wide ethics statement into expected behavior for specific positions. This makes the code of ethics easier to understand, more memorable, and more likely to be lived.

The *SMA* specifies that ongoing training should include these expectations:

- General employee behavior and personal conduct
- How ethics are built into work management methods
- How ethics affects specific jobs, processes, activities, and relationships
- How the organization monitors compliance with code
- What routes are open to employees who have compliance issues
- What action is taken when a complaint or issue is identified
- The actions and penalties once noncompliance is proven

Consistent, values-based leadership not only models the desired behaviors for staff, it also translates high-level ethical statements into operational examples that can be applied in day-to-day responsibilities. For example, the statement "We believe that all people have the right to be treated with dignity and respect" conveys a principle. To apply this principle, the management accountant would discuss with his or her staff how it applies when they are performing tasks like requesting documentation, collecting receivables, and educating nonfinancial staff members about financial issues. General ethics training is valuable in creating overall awareness, but most employees are more interested in learning about behavioral issues specific to their position and responsibilities.

An organization's culture is made up of the accumulated behavioral actions of all of its employees over time. A culture that is in alignment with the organization's core values and code of ethics will tend to strengthen and reproduce the desired ongoing behaviors. A Booz Allen 2005 survey found that 81% of survey respondents believe their management practices encourage ethical behavior among staff; most companies believe values influence two important strategic areas—relationships and reputation—but do not see the direct link to growth; and, with respect to return on values (ROV), fewer than half say they have the ability to measure a direct link to revenue and earnings growth.

Measuring and Improving Ethical Compliance

As stated in the *SMA* "Values and Ethics: From Inception to Practice," "One of the greatest problems in achieving ethical compliance is the ability of any organization to actually be aware of what is happening on a day-to-day basis and making ethical compliance a core element of its mainstream governance and accountability framework."

While management is responsible for instituting internal controls and for supporting operational transparency, it must also comply with legal and regulatory mandates that serve as a further deterrent to unethical behavior. For example, under the Sarbanes-Oxley Act (SOX), CEOs and CFOs must certify that an organization's internal controls are adequate as part of the organization's ethical compliance framework.

Internal controls provide a framework for identifying and controlling the risks that exist within an organization. They also can be used to assess the amount of risk to which an organization is exposed. Internal controls and an ethical culture are closely related. Internal controls that are in alignment with company values serve to strengthen the culture. At the same time, a vibrant ethical culture provides a strong foundation that compels employees to follow internal controls. Therefore, an effective internal control system becomes an integral part of the organizational culture.

Various tools are available to measure and improve compliance with ethical values; they include the human performance feedback loop, survey tools, and a whistleblowing framework.

Human Performance Feedback Loop

To improve compliance, performance review systems must be aligned with organizational values and ethics statements. Employee job descriptions, required competencies, and performance objectives should include ethical expectations.

Employee reviews, conducted annually (or more frequently), should evaluate the individual's compliance with ethical expectations along with operational goals. For example, an evaluation might rate not only accuracy and timeliness of an employee's reports; it also could rate his performance in treating all others with dignity and respect. Ideally, the feedback used to make this evaluation would include both internal and external responses and a comparison of self-evaluation with the results of evaluations by others.

The human performance feedback loop also should measure the number of employees completing ethics training and their score on any required testing.

Survey Tools

Another useful way to measure ethical performance is the use of surveys. Using the organization's code of ethics as a source, surveys could have employees rate how well the organization is doing.

For example, employees may be asked the degree to which they agree with statements such as: "This organization respects the dignity of all individuals." The results of surveys will indicate the degree of compliance and provide a method to stimulate an ongoing dialogue with employees.

Whistleblowing Framework

A whistleblowing framework provides employees who identify ethically questionable behavior by others with a confidential way to seek advice and report ethical violations.

Research has shown that employee hotlines are a valuable reporting mechanism for discovering fraud within an organization. If the hotline is truly anonymous and also can be used by employees to access advice on ethical situations, employees can raise issues more freely without fear of retaliation.

A further benefit of implementing a whistleblowing framework is the ability to collect, analyze, and summarize existing and potential ethical problems. This information is essential for identifying opportunities to improve training and internal controls. As stated in the *SMA* "Values and Ethics: From Inception to Practice," "Management accountants need to ensure that such processes are in place, that they operate on a fully confidential basis, and that they are capable of generating statistical or event-based reporting through which insight into ethical practice can be created."

Governmental and International Implications for Organizational Ethics

As mentioned earlier, ethical behavior results from actions that are aligned with a core set of values. Governments attempt to legislate broad sets of values by creating laws and regulations that individuals and organizations are required to follow. Although working within the letter of the law does not guarantee that individuals are behaving ethically, understanding and applying applicable laws are a key part of organizational ethics.

The U.S. Foreign Corrupt Practices Act (FCPA) is a good example of this. The FCPA was passed in 1977 as a result of Securities and Exchange Commission (SEC) investigations in the mid-1970s that revealed that hundreds of companies admitted making questionable or illegal payments to foreign government officials to secure favorable action. Among other requirements, the FCPA forbids an American company doing business in another country to pay bribes to a foreign government to obtain contracts or secure business.

The cultural values of the United States were the impetus for the creation of the FCPA; however, not all governments in all parts of the world agree with these values. The challenge for the global organization becomes how to get work done in countries where the expectation of a "commission" (in effect, a payment to local government officials) is commonplace.

Ethically, a key question is: When do commissions become bribes? On an organizational level, senior management must ensure that the code of ethics is being applied consistently across all of the business cultures in which it operates. Specifically, managers should investigate how the code of ethics may conflict with existing practices in other countries. It is essential for employees to see that the code of ethics is applied consistently across the entire organization. Doing this may mean bypassing potential business opportunities when they require the organization to act in a manner that is inconsistent with stated ethical values.

Other important legal and ethical issues for international business involve cultural differences and disparities between international law and the laws of individual countries.

Different countries may have different laws for how to conduct business. Some businesses may choose to do business in nations in which they can conduct certain activities not allowed in their own countries. For example, to avoid U.S. taxes, some firms have moved their businesses to Caribbean island nations that do not charge taxes.

Global corporations based in the United States also have to comply with SOX. Section 406 of SOX requires companies to adopt (or explain why they have not adopted) a code of ethics for senior financial officers. The code applies to the firm's principal financial officer and comptroller or principal accounting officer as well as to the principal executive officer.

Section 406 also includes instructions for the timely reporting of "any change in or waiver of the code of ethics" for these officers. The SEC has defined the term *waiver* as company approval for an officer to make a material departure from the code of ethics. An implicit waiver involves the organization's failure to take action within a reasonable period of time after it becomes aware of a material departure from the code of ethics.

SOX Section 406 also defines a code of ethics as such standards as are reasonably necessary to promote:

1. honest and ethical conduct, including the ethical handling of actual or apparent conflicts of interest between personal and professional relationships;
2. full, fair, accurate, timely, and understandable disclosure in the periodic reports, required to be filed by the issuer; and
3. compliance with applicable governmental rules and regulations.

The SEC recognizes that a code of ethics needs to be applicable to the specific situation and culture of each company. Therefore, the SEC does not offer any specific wording or provisions that should be included in a code of ethics. However, the SEC did add that a code of ethics should also promote prompt reporting of violations of the code of ethics as well as accountability for adhering to the code.

The next scenario illustrates how these concepts and principles might apply to the operations of an organization.

Practice Ethical Scenarios

A. Magneto Industries (MI) recently appointed George Parker as CEO following the retirement of the previous CEO. After spending a few weeks reviewing operations and financial results, George is concerned about how MI is doing business. MI reported record earnings over the last several years, with 15% growth per year—unprecedented in the industry.

When George interviewed Bob Gartner, the chief operating officer, Bob shared with George that the equipment used in production is in bad shape. Despite the fact that the equipment is only five years old, it has begun to break down at unexpected times due to lack of preventive maintenance.

Sam Donato, the head of maintenance, explained that the maintenance budget has been reduced by 10% to 15% every year for the last three years. Despite his pleas to the previous CEO to increase the budget and memos explaining the consequences of not properly maintaining the production equipment, he has had to limit his activities to repairs only. Further, he has had to literally glue some of the equipment back together to keep it running. What should have been a temporary fix became permanent when his purchase requests for replacement parts were returned to him unapproved.

One day while George was walking through the plant, he was astonished to see Tom Haskins, the production supervisor, take chewing gum out of his mouth and place it in a piece of machinery. When George asked what he was doing, Tom explained that there was a piece on the machinery that regularly vibrated loose. Tom had noticed that Sam's staff were getting irritated with having to repeatedly come out and glue it in place, so he had started to fix it himself to save time.

While in the plant, George also spoke to a few production employees. The general message that these people communicated was that they were just earning a paycheck while looking for a better job. MI was known for doing as little as possible to maintain its equipment and its workforce.

When he reviews the current-year financials, George is not surprised to see that revenue and production have slipped substantially on a year-to-date basis as compared to the previous year.

1. What values does this organization believe in, and how do they explain what George has witnessed?
2. How has leadership by example impacted the attitude and actions of Tom Haskins?
3. What steps should George take to create a more ethical and values-based culture at MI?
4. What are some of the potential benefits that MI may realize by making these changes?

Solution

1. MI's most important priority is growing the bottom line, no matter what it needs to do to accomplish this task. This value resulted in utilizing short-term strategies with long-term consequences. For example, expensive and valuable equipment has been allowed to deteriorate, and employee turnover in the production area is very high.
2. Tom Haskins's attitude and actions are direct results of watching the organization prioritize short-term growth over long-term growth. He has watched the maintenance department glue equipment back together regularly and decided that his contribution to cutting costs is to patch the equipment together himself in the most expedient manner.
3. As CEO, George needs to set the tone at the top and let everyone know that past practices are no longer acceptable. If they don't already exist, George should identify and document MI's values and code of ethics.

This should be followed by staff training, which should not only cover the values and code of conduct but also include examples of behaviors that are expected and those that are not acceptable. Examples should be specific to the position being trained. Annual reviews should be modified to include measures of the behavior covered in the training.

All leaders in the organization, such as Bob Gartner and Sam Donato, should be held to a higher level of conduct than those below to set the tone at the top.

Further, budgets should be set that are sufficient for staff to follow these values. For example, the maintenance budget should be looked at closely to determine what is needed to repair the existing equipment properly and to institute a preventive maintenance plan.

On an organizational level, MI should implement a whistleblowing framework that employees can use to report unethical behavior. In addition, employees should be educated and encouraged to use this system as a confidential method for gaining advice in ethically challenging situations.

To measure results, George could do a baseline survey of employees to identify current adherence to values. By repeating the same survey at a later date, George will be able to measure whether the implemented practices resulted in the expected behavioral changes.

4. In the short run, MI will most likely experience a downturn in growth since unsustainable practices were used to create it. In the long run, MI will experience:
   - Sustainable growth as a result of increased production from well-maintained equipment.
   - Improved organizational culture.
   - Improved reputation for quality and reliability.
   - Improved interpersonal dynamics.
   - Lower risk of fraud.

B. Tyco International was founded in 1960 as a research laboratory to conduct experimental work for the U.S. government. From the time of his graduation from Seton Hall University in 1968 to 1975, Dennis Kozlowski worked in finance and accounting, moving up the ranks quickly to become director of audit and analysis. Kozlowski joined Tyco in 1975, becoming CEO in 1992.

Joseph S. Gaziano was the Tyco CEO who hired Kozlowski. Gaziano was described as a jumbo size, profane, MIT-educated engineer. Gaziano had a taste for the high life, with a prize collection of perks including a jet, a helicopter, and three luxury apartments. Kozlowski was entranced by Gaziano's persona and his lifestyle.

Upon Gaziano's death in 1982, John F. Fort became CEO. Fort was also an MIT alum. Unlike Gaziano, Fort was anything but extravagant. He was not into the high life and had no taste for himself or his employees for premium travel or luxury accommodations. His main concern in all business decisions was profitable growth of the company. He is quoted as saying, "The reason we were put on earth is to increase earnings per share." He delivered on this assertion and investors loved him for this. Fort resigned as CEO in 1992 and as chairman a few months later but agreed to remain on the board after he and Kozlowski engaged in a business strategy battle in which Kozlowski prevailed. In spite of this battle, Kozlowski and Fort remained allies until Kozlowski's downfall in 2002.

Kozlowski's finance, accounting, and auditing savvy coupled with his adoption of key traits of both Gaziano (taste for the high life and a shaved head) and Fort (all business decisions based on EPS effects) seemed to set the stage for what followed from about 1995 to 2002. It was during this time that Kozlowski and his company colleague, Mark Swartz, a Big Four alum, formed a quasi-partnership, by which they managed to relieve Tyco of at least $100 million (this in addition to Kozlowski becoming one of the top corporate salary and benefit earners in the country) through various schemes labeled as illegal or unethical or both, depending on which source one wants to reference.

According to information contained in the 2002 State of New York indictment, around 1995 Kozlowski and Swartz, "having knowledge of the existence of a criminal enterprise (hereinafter called the "Top Executives Criminal Enterprise" or "TEXCE") and the nature of its activities, and being employed by and associated with that enterprise, intentionally conducted and participated in the affairs of such enterprise by participating in a pattern of criminal activity." Some evidence indicated that TEXCE existed prior to Kozlowski's appointment as CEO and Chairman of the Board of Tyco.

Information about a Tyco code of conduct prior to 2002 appears to be unavailable. Tyco's financial reports reflect excellent profitability throughout Kozlowski's reign and since that reign ended. The current Tyco website contains the following summarized information about Tyco's values.

> Every day, the company's 57,000 employees come to work with a passion for protecting what matters most. They take great pride in knowing that they make a difference in the world: their work helps protect and safeguard people and property.
>
> Tyco's culture is built on a foundation of four key values. These values shape how our employees interact with every stakeholder and with one another. Together, they drive our company forward.
>
> A Commitment to Doing the Right Thing
>
> As a global industry leader, Tyco is committed to doing the right thing in the workplace and within the communities in which we operate. Our vital values, Integrity, Accountability, Teamwork and Excellence, are central to our role as an ethical and responsible corporate citizen.
>
> Integrity—We demand of ourselves, and each other, the highest standards of individual and corporate integrity.
> Excellence—We continually challenge each other to improve our products, our processes and ourselves.

Teamwork—We foster an environment that encourages innovation and creativity, and delivers results through collaboration.

Accountability—We honor the commitments we make and take personal responsibility for all actions and results.

It is equally essential that we foster an environment where all stakeholders feel comfortable and are encouraged to confidentially speak up about an action or situation that does not feel "right." *To raise an ethical or compliance related concern, click here.*

The following are examples of activities Kozlowski and Swartz engaged in according to the 2002 State of New York indictment:

Kozlowski was the boss of the criminal enterprise, called TME, and set its policies. He decided what bonuses would be paid, to whom, and when, without regard for the restrictions that the Board had put on executive officers' compensation. He entered into private deals with executive officers and directors of Tyco, which he sought to keep secret even when they were required to be disclosed. He caused Internal Audit to report to the Board through himself, and ensured that they would not audit TME. Kozlowski established a system of internal controls in which his assistant's authorization was sufficient to warrant expenditures of many millions of dollars.

Swartz was chief of operations of TEXCE; he was the second-in-command to defendant Kozlowski. Swartz exercised control over the transfer of funds, the booking of accounting entries, and the operations of those portions of Tyco's Human Resources department dealing with certain compensation, bonuses, and loans.

Swartz established a system by which the Finance Department, and not the Tyco Legal Department, controlled the data going into Tyco's filings with the United State Securities and Exchange Commission and caused Tyco's filings to be false and deceptive.

Defendant Swartz deceived investors and the Board by misallocating substantial personnel costs resulting in falsely enhanced operating performance. Because they were the two highest-ranking officers of Tyco, the defendants as members of TEXCE were able to recruit others to join TEXCE, and were also able to use others at Tyco as unwitting agents of the criminal enterprise.

Consider the following questions with respect to Tyco International:

1. While the events leading to Kozlowski and Swartz's indictments in 2002 are more than 14 years in the past, and given that Tyco is traded on the New York Stock Exchange, is it likely that Tyco's stated values are significantly different now than during the period 1995–2002?
2. How has leadership by example (also referred to as tone at the top), which is often cited as a key behavior expected of top corporate executive, been demonstrated or absent in Tyco?
3. As an accounting or financial professional working for Tyco during the period in this scenario, what signs would you have expected to find in

your work that would likely raise a red flag that top management was possibly involved in illegal or unethical activities?
4. As an accounting or financial professional working for Tyco during the period in this scenario, what action would you have taken if you detected evidence that top management was possibly involved in illegal or unethical activities? Specifically, who or what level would you feel most comfortable raising your concerns with?
5. The current Tyco website includes information posted in this scenario. The website states: "To raise an ethical or compliance related concern, click here." What word would you use to describe a concern that a person would enter into this link?

Solution:

1. Certainly there are more laws in effect now than then, such as Sarbanes Oxley. However, it is likely that Tyco had similar stated values to which it subscribed from 1995 to 2002. It would be difficult to determine now whether such values were taken seriously by the company at that time.
2. It appears that leadership by example at Tyco was pretty much the opposite of what we would want to find in a publicly traded company.
3. Much would depend on the specific type of work you were doing for the company. Bear in mind that this is and was a large multinational operation. If you were not part of top management's scheme, it is likely that you would not have access to evidence that would raise red flags of management wrongdoing.
4. In the event that you did encounter evidence that top management was engaged in illegal or unethical activities, you would need to consult with the IMA hotline. If you were not comfortable with that, then you would have had to consult with your personal legal counsel.
5. This appears to be a whistleblower mechanism. Many companies have such mechanisms in place. However, if top management is apparently involved in illegal or unethical activities, then one might question how reliable the whistleblower mechanism really is.

Knowledge Check: Ethical Considerations for the Organization

The following questions are intended to help you check your understanding and recall of the material presented in this topic. They do not represent the type of questions that appear on the CMA exam.

Directions: Answer each question in the space provided. Correct answers and section references appear following these questions.

1. Corporate management is responsible for creating an ethical culture by doing all of the following **except**
   - ☐ a. identifying and documenting organizational values.
   - ☐ b. defining principles of behavior.
   - ☐ c. implementing a whistleblowing mechanism.
   - ☐ d. creating a code of ethics or conduct.

2. The **most** important reason for creating an ethical culture is:
   - ☐ a. decreasing risk in the organization.
   - ☐ b. creating alignment between what an organization believes in and what its employees do.
   - ☐ c. ensuring compliance with SOX.
   - ☐ d. increasing net income.

3. For ethics training to be effective, it should contain all of the following elements **except**
   - ☐ a. Be part of orientation as well as ongoing training.
   - ☐ b. Relate to real-world situations faced by employees.
   - ☐ c. Provide a consistent message.
   - ☐ d. Include a test to evaluate learning.

4. What are three tools available to measure and improve compliance?
   - a. _____
   - b. _____
   - c. _____

5. Which of the following is an example of a metric that an annual review may include to measure compliance with corporate ethical expectations?
   - ☐ a. Ability to complete work accurately
   - ☐ b. Has signed off on having received and read the corporate code of ethics

- [ ] c. Ability to reach a decision when faced with a problem
- [ ] d. Ability to model behavior consistent with the corporate values statement

6. The U.S. Foreign Corrupt Practices Act
   - [ ] a. forbids an American company doing business overseas to pay bribes.
   - [ ] b. requires foreign companies doing business in the United States to comply with SOX.
   - [ ] c. requires foreign companies that want to sell stock in U.S. exchanges to register with the Securities and Exchange Commission.
   - [ ] d. forbids companies that do business in the United States from paying bribes.

7. Section 406 of the Sarbanes-Oxley Act requires
   - [ ] a. senior financial officers to have and follow a code of ethics.
   - [ ] b. organizations to use specific wording in their code of ethics.
   - [ ] c. senior financial officers to sign off on the annual tax return.
   - [ ] d. changes to the code of ethics to be reported on a Form 8-K.

Knowledge Check Answers: Ethical Considerations for the Organization

1. Corporate management is responsible for creating an ethical culture by doing all of the following **except** [See *Ethics Starts at the Top*.]
   - ☐ a. identifying and documenting organizational values.
   - ☐ b. defining principles of behavior.
   - ☒ c. implementing a whistleblowing mechanism.
   - ☐ d. creating a code of ethics or conduct.

   A whistleblower framework does not create an ethical culture.

2. The **most** important reason for creating an ethical culture is [See *Applying Ethics in a Corporate Setting*.]
   - ☐ a. decreasing risk in the organization.
   - ☒ b. creating alignment between what an organization believes in and what its employees do.
   - ☐ c. ensuring compliance with SOX.
   - ☐ d. increasing net income.

   The other three answers are likely outcomes but not the defining reason.

3. For ethics training to be effective, it should contain all of the following elements **except** [See *Applying Ethics in a Corporate Setting*.]
   - ☐ a. Be part of orientation as well as ongoing training.
   - ☐ b. Relate to real-world situations faced by employees.
   - ☐ c. Provide a consistent message.
   - ☒ d. Include a test to evaluate learning.

4. What are three tools available to measure and improve compliance? [See *Measuring and Improving Ethical Compliance*.]
   - a. **Human performance feedback loop**
   - b. **Survey tools**
   - c. **Whistleblowing framework**

5. Which of the following is an example of a metric that an annual review may include to measure compliance with corporate ethical expectations? [See *Measuring and Improving Ethical Compliance*.]
   - ☐ a. Ability to complete work accurately
   - ☐ b. Has signed off on having received and read the corporate code of ethics

- c. Ability to reach a decision when faced with a problem
- ☒ d. Ability to model behavior consistent with the corporate values statement

6. The U.S. Foreign Corrupt Practices Act [See *Governmental and International Implications for Organizational Ethics.*]
    - ☒ a. forbids an American company doing business overseas to pay bribes.
    - ☐ b. requires foreign companies doing business in the United States to comply with SOX.
    - ☐ c. requires foreign companies that want to sell stock in U.S. exchanges to register with the Securities and Exchange Commission.
    - ☐ d. forbids companies that do business in the United States from paying bribes.

7. Section 406 of the Sarbanes-Oxley Act requires [See *Governmental and International Implications for Organizational Ethics.*]
    - ☒ a. senior financial officers to have and follow a code of ethics.
    - ☐ b. organizations to use specific wording in their code of ethics.
    - ☐ c. senior financial officers to sign off on the annual tax return.
    - ☐ d. changes to the code of ethics to be reported on a Form 8-K.

Practice Questions: Professional Ethics

Directions: This sampling of questions is designed to emulate actual exam questions. Read each question and write your response on another sheet of paper. See the "Answers to Section Practice Questions" section at the end of this book to assess your response. Validate or improve the answer you wrote. For a more robust selection of practice questions, access the **Online Test Bank** at www.wileycma.com.

Question 2F1-AT01

Topic: Ethical Considerations for Management Accounting and Financial Management

As management accountants progress in the profession, they often have the responsibility to supervise the work of less experienced workers. Which of the following is an ethical responsibility of the supervisor?

- ☐ **a.** Hire new workers who will fit in socially with existing staff.
- ☐ **b.** Maximize the profit or minimize the cost of the department.
- ☐ **c.** Ensure that workers handle confidential information appropriately.
- ☐ **d.** Encourage the workers to develop relations with customers.

Question 2F1-AT02

Topic: Ethical Considerations for Management Accounting and Financial Management

Sam Smith has been offered a pair of tickets to the pro football team if Smith purchases a computerized inventory control system from a specific vendor. Which of the following steps should Smith take?

- ☐ **a.** Refuse any further conversations with the vendor.
- ☐ **b.** Review his company's policies on gifts from vendors.
- ☐ **c.** Sign the contract for the system if the price of the ticket is less than $50.
- ☐ **d.** Consult with the audit committee of the board of directors.

Question 2F1-AT03

Topic: Ethical Considerations for Management Accounting and Financial Management

John Moore was recently hired as assistant controller of a manufacturing company. The company controller, Nancy Kay, has forecasted a 16% increase in annual earnings. However, during the last quarter of the year, John estimates that the company will report only a 12% increase in earnings. When he reports this to Nancy, she tells him that meeting the numbers won't be a problem. She explains that there are several jobs in production that will finish after the end of the fiscal year, and she will record the associated revenue in the accounting system for the current year.

What is the first step that John Moore should take at this time?

- ☐ a. Notify the audit committee of the issue.
- ☐ b. Contact his lawyer to determine his rights.
- ☐ c. Discuss the issue with the chief financial officer of another company, who does not know any employees at John's company.
- ☐ d. Follow his organization's established policies regarding the resolution of this type of conflict.

Question 2F2-AT01

Topic: Ethical Considerations for the Organization

The Foreign Corrupt Practices Act is a U.S. law that prohibits U.S. companies from

- ☐ a. making "corrupt" payments to foreign officials for the purpose of obtaining or retaining business.
- ☐ b. making products in overseas markets that do not comply with the same safety and environmental regulations as for domestically produced products.
- ☐ c. exporting to countries that do not comply with U.S. human rights regulations.
- ☐ d. selling products for corrupt, unethical, or illegal purposes.

Question 2F2-AT02

Topic: Ethical Considerations for the Organization

Which of the following actions will most likely result in a successful foreign business venture in Islamic countries?

- ☐ a. Employ Islamic people.
- ☐ b. Behave in a manner that is consistent with Islamic ethics.
- ☐ c. Have property in an Islamic nation.
- ☐ d. Adhere to Islamic beliefs.

To further assess your understanding of the concepts and calculations covered in Part 2, Section F: Professional Ethics, practice with the **Online Test Bank** for this section. **REMINDER:** See the "Answers to Section Practice Questions" section at the end of this book.

Essay Exam Support Materials

Writing an effective answer to an essay exam question is a special challenge. It tests your written communication skills in addition to your knowledge of the content. Essay questions also test your understanding of how specific pieces of information relate to one another, and your ability to apply your knowledge to real-life situations. The next information is included to help you learn more about how to respond to the exam part content in written essay form.

Preparing for the Essay Portion of the Exam

The essay portion of the CMA exam can draw from any of the LOS and content from Part 2: Financial Decision Making. It requires understanding the content and being prepared to evaluate the issues presented as well as making recommendations for the resolution of specific situations.

Your study plan should help you learn the content, learn how to respond to the content in multiple-choice questions, and learn to respond to essay questions presented on the content. This is a significant part of the challenge of the CMA exams. One way to meet this challenge is to break it down into smaller challenges—learn the content first, then practice multiple-choice exam-type questions, then learn how to respond to essay questions.

How to Write Essay Answers

The CMA exam essay questions require you to discuss the main points of a specific topic and then examine their implications. When developing your responses, you must support your answers with evidence of your thinking in order to demonstrate your knowledge and comprehension of a topic and your ability to apply that knowledge via thoughtful analysis.

You will be expected to present written answers that:

- Directly respond to the questions asked.
- Are presented in a logical manner.
- Demonstrate an appropriate understanding of the subject matter.

Clues within the questions can be used to help you formulate and organize your responses. Verbs such as *analyze, apply, explore, interpret,* and *examine* can help delineate the requirements of the question. Using the same verbs within your answer will help ensure that you are responding directly and completely to the specific questions being asked.

Candidates are expected to have a working knowledge of using word processing and electronic spreadsheets. They are also expected to have an understanding of basic financial statements, time value of money concepts, and elementary statistics. The essay portion of the exam is computer driven. Answers are entered using a text editor similar to Microsoft Notepad. Some questions may require a spreadsheet similar to, but not exactly the same as, Microsoft Excel.

Writing Skills

The essay section of the CMA exam is a way to assess your ability to analyze, evaluate, and effectively communicate about business situations. Written communication is an important skill required in today's business environment.

The Institute of Certified Management Accountants (ICMA) assesses your writing skills in the essay portion of the CMA exam. The assessment is based on these criteria:

- Use of standard English
- Organization
- Clarity

Use of Standard English

The use of standard English is an integral part of expressing ideas in a business environment. Assessment of the use of clear and concise terminology as is standard to the English language will be administered on the essay portion of the exam.

Organization

When answering essay questions, organizing your answers in a logical manner is important to effective business writing skills. As you read through the question, order your thoughts in a manner that exercises your process of thinking. Make sure that your answer has a clear beginning, outlining what you will be answering, followed by the answer, backed up by CMA content-specific facts, and a summary of what you just described.

Clarity

Being clear in your response is as important as the use of standard English and organization of your response on the CMA exam. Assessors of the essay portion of the CMA exam will look at the answer and critique based on whether the answer is clearly expressed and that the answer is supported by CMA content-specific rationale. When answering, read your answer thoroughly to make sure that your response is clear and that the reader will understand how you are attempting to answer the questions.

Using Standard English, Organization, and Clarity in Your Responses to the Essays

When reading through the essay examples, work through the problems as if you were actually answering the questions on the actual CMA exam. When working through the essays, pay close attention to the key words in the question, organize your response, and start writing the answer to the question. When answering, make sure that you are answering the question in a clear and concise manner and make sure that you use standard English. Once complete, compare your answer to the answer provided in the textbook. Pay close attention to the way the answer is organized, the key words that are used, and way the answer is presented. Compare the textbook answer to your answer to see how you did.

Essay Exam Study Tips

ON THE ACTUAL FOUR-HOUR CMA EXAM, the essay portion of the exam will begin once you complete the multiple-choice section or after three hours, whichever comes first. This means you will have at least one hour to complete the two essay questions presented.

To make the best use of your time to complete the essay portion:
- Prior to taking the exam, take the online tutorial to become familiar with the testing screens. The tutorial is not part of your testing time and may be repeated. However, total tutorial time is limited to 20 minutes.
- Briefly skim through both essay questions and get an idea what each question is asking you to do (i.e., describe, analyze, calculate, etc.).
- You have one hour to complete the full essay exam (more if you have finished the multiple-choice section earlier than the three-hour limit). Determine how much time you will dedicate to each essay question.
- Start with the question you know best. Begin by writing key words, thoughts, facts, figures, and anything else that can be used to answer the question.
- As you answer one question, issues related to the other may occur to you. Write that information next to the appropriate question. This will build your confidence and give you a starting place when you begin to answer the second question.

To answer each question:
- Read the entire question for requirements.
- Be aware of the verb clues that delineate what is being asked. This will help you formulate and organize your answer. Note that you may have more than one task—for example, define abc and interpret its applicability to xyz.
- Write the basic requirements in the answer space so that you are sure to address them.
- Begin your answer with one or two sentences that directly answer the question. If possible, rephrase the question's essential terms in a statement that directly answers the question.
- Use bullet points to show main ideas, and support each point with sufficient detail to show that you understand all the issues relevant to the question.
- Make it as easy as possible for graders to give you points. The goal in grading is to award you points, so show your thinking clearly and effectively. Do not write too little or too much.

- Finish your essay with one or two sentences that summarize your main point(s).
- Proofread your answer for logic, thoroughness, and clarity.
- Keep track of time. Do not spend too much time on one question.
- If you do not have enough time to write a full essay, write an outline of your main points to show what you know in order to get partial credit.

Examples of Essay Question Answers

EACH ESSAY QUESTION ACTUALLY CONSISTS of several related questions based on one scenario. The question as a whole is worth a set number of points and is graded against a scorecard to ensure consistent grading. The scorecard lists appropriate terms, topics, and ideas that address the answer. Presented here are two essay questions drawn from previous exams. The first essay question is followed by an example of an answer that would be awarded maximum points—a "best" answer. How these points are awarded is shown on a scorecard similar to ones used by the Institute of Certified Management Accountants (ICMA).

Following the second essay question are two answers that were awarded fewer points because they do not address all the issues. The "good" answer meets some but not all of the criteria. The "better" answer covers more of the requested information, as shown on the scorecard, and receives more points.

As you will see, the goal of the graders is to give test takers points rather than take them away. If test takers earn more credits than the maximum allowable points, they can be awarded only the maximum allowable number of points.

There are two types of essay questions: questions that ask for a **written response** and questions that ask for a **series of calculations, tables, or charts for a response**.

Note: The questions, answers, and scorecards used in these examples were provided by the ICMA and are used with their permission unless otherwise indicated.

Example Question 1: Amur Company

Amur Company manufactures three lawn care component parts: fuel systems, transmission assemblies, and electrical systems. For the past five years, manufacturing overhead has been applied to products on standard direct labor hours for the units actually produced. The standard cost information is shown next.

Exhibit A shows standard cost information.

Exhibit A Standard Cost Information

	Fuel Systems	Transmission Assemblies	Electrical Systems
Units produced and sold	10,000	20,000	30,000
Standard labor hours	2.0	1.5	1.0
Standard direct material cost per unit	$25.00	$36.00	$30.00
Budgeted and actual manufacturing overhead		$3,920,000	

The current direct labor rate is $10 per hour. New machinery that highly automates the production process was installed two years ago and greatly reduced the direct labor time to produce the three products. The selling price for each of the three products is 125% of the manufacturing cost.

Amur's segment of the lawn care component industry has become very competitive, and the company's profits have been decreasing. Eric West, Amur's controller, has been asked by the president of the company to analyze the overhead allocations and pricing structure. West thinks that future allocations should be based on machine hours and direct labor hours rather than the current allocation method, which is based on direct labor hours only. West has determined the additional product information shown in Exhibit B.

Exhibit B Additional Product Information

	Fuel Systems	Transmission Assemblies	Electrical Systems
Standard machine hours	2.0	4.0	6.0
Manufacturing overhead:			
Direct labor cost		$560,000	
Machine cost		$3,360,000	

Questions

1. By allocating all of the budgeted overhead based on direct labor hours, calculate the unit manufacturing cost and unit sales price for each of the three products manufactured at Amur Company.
2. Prepare an analysis for Amur Company using the appropriate cost driver(s) determined by Eric West for manufacturing overhead. Calculate the unit manufacturing cost and unit sales price for each of the three products.
3. Based on your calculations in Questions 1 and 2, prepare a recommendation for the president at Amur Company to increase the firm's profitability.

Sample "Best" Answer for Amur Business Scenario

Question 1

The allocation of all of Amur Company's budgeted manufacturing overhead based on direct labor hours results in the unit manufacturing costs and unit sales prices for its three products is calculated as follows:

Fuel systems

    Units: 10,000

    Standard labor hour/unit: 2.0

    Total standard labor hours: 20,000

    Direct material: $25.00

    Direct labor at $10/hour: $20.00

    Overhead at $49/DLH[1]: $98.00

    Total cost: $143.00

    Sales price (125% of cost): $178.75

Transmission Assemblies

    Units: 20,000

    Standard labor hour/unit: 1.5

    Total standard labor hours: 30,000

    Machine hours per unit: 4.0

    Total machine hours: 80,000

    Direct material: $36.00

    Direct labor at $10/hour: $15.00

    Overhead at $49/DLH[1]: $73.50

    Total cost: $124.50

    Sales price (125% of cost): $155.63

Electrical Systems

    Units: 30,000

    Standard labor hour/unit: 1.0

    Total standard labor hours: 30,000

    Direct material: $30.00

    Direct labor at $10/hour: $10.00

    Overhead at $49/DLH[1]: $49.00

    Total cost: $89.00

    Sales price (125% of cost): $111.25

Note:

[1] Total manufacturing overhead of $3,920,000 / 80,000 total direct labor hours = $49.00 per direct labor hour.

Question 2

When the cost drivers identified by Eric West are used to allocate manufacturing overhead, the unit manufacturing costs and unit sales prices for the three products manufactured at Amur Company are calculated as follows:

Fuel systems

    Units: 10,000

    Standard labor hour/unit: 2.0

    Total standard labor hours: 20,000

    Machine hours per unit: 2.0

    Total machine hours: 20,000

    Direct material: $25.00

    Direct labor at $10/hour: $20.00

    Overhead DLH at $7/hr[1]: $14.00

    Overhead Machine hrs at $12/hr[2]: $24.00

    Total cost: $83.00

    Sales price (125% of cost): $103.75

Transmission Assemblies

    Units: 20,000

    Standard labor hour/unit: 1.5

    Total standard labor hours: 30,000

    Machine hours per unit: 4.0

    Total machine hours: 80,000

    Direct material: $36.00

    Direct labor at $10/hour: $15.00

    Overhead DLH at $7/hr[1]: $10.50

    Overhead Machine hrs at $12/hr[2]: $48.00

    Total cost: $109.50

    Sales price (125% of cost): $136.88

Electrical Systems

    Units: 30,000

    Standard labor hour/unit: 1.0

    Total standard labor hours: 30,000

    Machine hours per unit: 6.0

    Total machine hours: 180,000

    Direct material: $30.00

    Direct labor at $10/hour: $10.00

    Overhead DLH at $7/hr[1]: $7.00

Overhead Machine hrs at $12/hr[2]: $72.00

Total cost: $119.00

Sales price (125% of cost): $148.75

Notes:

[1] Direct labor overhead of $560,000 / 80,000 total direct labor hours = $7.00 per direct labor hour.
[2] Machine overhead of $3,360,000 / 280,000 total machine hours = $12.00 per machine hour.

Question 3

The summary of the revised margins for each of Amur Company's three products, assuming the sales prices developed in Question 1 (allocation of all manufacturing overhead based on direct labor hours) is compared to revised costs developed in question 2 (allocation of manufacturing overhead based on cost drivers), is as follows:

Fuel Systems

Current price: $178.75

Revised cost: $83.00

Gross profit (loss): $95.75

Margin: 54%

Transmission Assemblies

Current price: $155.63

Revised cost: $109.50

Gross profit (loss): $46.13

Margin: 30%

Electrical Systems

Current price: $111.25

Revised cost: $119.00

Gross profit (loss): ($7.75)

Margin: NA

Based on this analysis, fuel systems and transmission assemblies are producing a higher return than Amur Company previously thought. Fuel systems are the most profitable (54% gross margin) followed by transmission assemblies; however, electrical systems are losing money on a full-cost basis.

Recommendations for improving profitability include:

- Focus on fuel systems, through actions such as increasing marketing expenditures and reducing the price to increase sales.
- Improve profitability of electrical systems through changes to the manufacturing process to reduce the machine hours required.
- Decrease marketing of this electrical system, and increase the selling price if possible.

Scoring of "Best" Answer for Amur Business Scenario

The Amur question would be graded against a scorecard similar to the one shown next. Note that:

- The scorecard addresses more issues than is required by the question. This is done to accommodate variations between test takers and to provide the greatest opportunity for a maximum score. The goal of the graders is to give test takers points rather than taking them away. If test takers earn more credits than the maximum allowable points, they will be awarded only the maximum allowable points.
- At times, the process is more important than the numeric answers. Test takers should show all work/calculations to earn the maximum allowable points.
- Explanations add points.
- Formatting is not judged. You will be using simple text editing, such as Microsoft Notepad, so you may not be able to make charts and should use dashes for bullets.

Amur Scorecard

Amur—Total allowable points 17

Question 1: Maximum allowable points = 5
Issues to address

Unit manufacturing cost and price (DLH allocation) =

Total labor hrs = Standard Hr / Unit × Units for each product

Totals all product labor hrs / (80,000)

Overhead of $3,920,000 / 80,000 DLH = Overhead rate

Includes unit direct materials cost in product cost

Direct labor = $10 × Standard DLH per unit

OH/Unit for each product = OH rate × Standard DLH/Unit

DM + DL + OH = Product cost / ($143($89)) / ($124.5)

Sales price = 125% × Product cost

Question 2: Maximum allowable points = 5

Unit manufacturing cost and price (Cost driver allocation) =

Total machine hours = (Standard hour / Unit) × Units for each product

Totals all product machine hours / (280.000)

Machine OH = $3,360, 000 / 280,000)

DL OH = $560,000 / 80,000 hours / ($7 per DHL)

OH / unit for each product = OH rate × standard MH / unit

OH / unit for each product = OH rate × standard DLH / unit

Includes DM and DLH for each product

Totals all costs / ($83) / ($109.50) / ($119)

Sales price = 125% × Product cost

> **Question 3: Maximum allowable points = 7**
> **Issues to address**
> **Recommendation**
> Increase emphasis on fuel systems
> Margin/profit highest
> Increase emphasis on transmission
> Margin/profit is high
> Increase marketing to generate sales
> Decrease price to stimulate sales
> Other recommendations to leverage profitability
> Decrease emphasis on electrical systems
> Margin is lower/losing money
> Improve manufacturing process
> Raise price if market will bear it
> Other recommendations to deal with electrical systems

Example Question 2: Zylon Corporation

Business Scenario

Jeff Frankie is the chief financial officer of Zylon Corporation, a manufacturer and distributor of electronic security devices primarily suited for residential applications. Frankie is currently in the process of preparing the Y2 annual budget and implementing an incentive plan to reward the performance of key personnel. The final operating plans will then be presented to the board of directors for approval.

Frankie is aware that next year may be very difficult due to announced price increases to major customers. Zylon's president has put pressure on management to achieve the current year's earnings per share amounts. Frankie is, therefore, considering introducing zero-based budgeting in order to bring costs into line with revenue expectations.

Duke Edwards, Zylon's manufacturing director, is attempting to convince Frankie to build budgetary slack into the operating budget. Edwards contends that productivity is burdened by an abnormal amount of product design changes and small lot size production orders that incur costly setup times.

Questions

1. Explain at least three advantages and at least three disadvantages of budgetary slack from the point of view of Zylon Corporation's management group as a whole.
2. Describe how zero-based budgeting could be advantageous to Zylon Corporation's overall budget process.

Sample "Better" Answer for Zylon Business Scenario

Question 1

At least three advantages and three disadvantages of budgetary slack from the point of view of Zylon Corporation's management group as a whole include the following:

Advantages

1. It provides flexibility for operating under unknown circumstances, such as an extra margin for discretionary expenses in case budget assumptions on inflation are incorrect, or adverse circumstances arise.
2. Additional slack may be included to offset the costly setups from design changes and/or small lot size orders.
3. The increased pressure to meet Y1 earnings per share targets may result in postponing expenditures into Y2 or aggressively pulling sales into Y1. Budgetary slack in Y2 may compensate for shifting those earnings from Y2 into Y1.

Disadvantages

1. It decreases the ability to highlight weaknesses and take timely corrective actions on problem areas.
2. It decreases the overall effectiveness of corporate planning. Actions such as pricing changes or reduced promotional spending may be taken from a perceived need to improve earnings, when eliminating the budgetary slack could accomplish the same objective without marketplace changes.
3. It limits the objective evaluation of departmental managers and performance of subordinates by using budgetary information.

Question 2

Zero-based budgeting (ZBB) could be advantageous to Zylon Corporation's overall budget process for the following reasons:

- The ZBB process evaluates all proposed operating and administrative expenses as if they were being initiated for the first time. Each expenditure is justified, ranked, and prioritized according to its order of importance to the overall corporation, not just its role in one department.
- The focus is on evaluation of all activities rather than just incremental changes from the prior year. This allows addressing activities that have been ongoing to determine if they are still useful in the current environment. The objectives, operations, and costs of all activities are evaluated, and alternative means of accomplishing the objectives are more likely to be identified.

Scoring of "Better" Answer for Zylon Business Scenario

The Zylon question would be graded against a scorecard similar to the one shown. Note that:

- The scorecard addresses more issues than is required by the question. This is done to accommodate variations between test takers and to provide the greatest opportunity for a maximum score. The goal of the graders is to give test takers points rather than taking them away. If test takers earn more credits than the maximum allowable points, they can be awarded only the maximum allowable points.
- At times, the process is more important than the numeric answers. Test takers should show all work/calculations to earn the maximum allowable points.
- Explanations add points.
- Formatting is not judged. You will be using simple text editing such as Microsoft Notepad, so you may not be able to make charts and should use dashes for bullets.

Zylon Scorecard
Zylon Total allowable points 12

Question 1: Maximum allowable points = 6
Issues to address
Advantages

Provides flexibility under uncertainty
Extra margin for discretionary expenses
If assumptions wrong or adverse circumstances
Offsets unexpected setup costs
    Design changes
    Small lot sizes
Can compensate for earnings timing shifts
    Pressure to meet EPS
    Postponing expenses or accelerating sales
Other
    Explanation

Disadvantages

Decreases ability to ID weakness and take action
    Expenses are overstated in budget
Decreases effectiveness of overall planning process
Unnecessary actions taken such as
    Price changes or promotional spending cuts
    When eliminating slack would have solved problem
Limits objective evaluation of employees
    Measured against inflated budget
Other
    Explanation

Question 2: Maximum allowable points = 6
Issues to address
Advantages
Each expense is justified and ranked
    Each expense is evaluated as if it were first time

(Continued)

    Unnecessary activities can be eliminated
        All activities are evaluated
        Ongoing activities must be justified
    Slack can be reduced
        Expenses must be grounded in realistic assumptions
    Alternative means can be identified
        Are forced to evaluate processes
    Other
        With explanation

Sample "Good" Answer for Zylon Business Scenario

A good answer would address enough of the identified three issues on the Zylon scorecard to earn a score of 70% or 80% of the maximum allowable points. A good answer for the Zylon scenario is shown next. It addresses the issues but does not go beyond the question to provide explanations and clarification.

Question 1

At least three advantages and three disadvantages of budgetary slack from the point of view of Zylon Corporation's management group as a whole include the following:

Advantages

- It provides operating flexibility.
- Additional slack may be included to offset costs.
- Zylon will need to postpone expenditures.

Disadvantages

- It decreases the ability to highlight weaknesses and take timely corrective actions on problem areas.
- It decreases the overall effectiveness of corporate planning.
- It limits the objective evaluation of departmental managers and performance of subordinates.

Question 2

Zero-based budgeting (ZBB) could be advantageous to Zylon Corporation's overall budget process for these reasons:

- The ZBB process evaluates all proposed operating and administrative expenses as if they were being initiated for the first time.
- The focus is on evaluation of all activities.

Practice Essay Questions and Answers

The next essay questions, and the answers that appear beginning at page 532, were adapted from the *Revised CMA Exam, Questions and Answers: Part 4* (2005 and 2008) books supplied by the Institute of Certified Management Accountants and are used with their permission (unless otherwise indicated).

The focus of the questions will be on the test taker's ability to apply concepts presented in the part being tested to a business scenario.

The answers supplied are meant to serve as samples of answers that address 80% or more of the points listed on the question grading guide. There are generally more points on the grading guide than points that can be awarded (i.e., there may be 110 possible points but only 100 that can be awarded in total), so answers scoring 80% may vary among test takers. Thus, the answers presented here represent one possible answer, not a definitive correct answer.

Part 2 Section A Questions

Question 2A-ES01

The accounting staff of CCB Enterprises has completed the preparation of financial statements for the 2005 calendar year. The statement of income for the current year and the comparative statement of financial position for 2005 and 2004 are reproduced here.

The accounting staff calculates selected financial ratios after the financial statements are prepared. Average balance sheet account balances are used in computing ratios involving income statement accounts. Ending balance sheet account balances are used in computing ratios involving only balance sheet items. The ratios have not been calculated for 2005. Financial ratios that were calculated for 2004 and their respective values are:

- Times interest earned   5.16 times
- Return on total assets   12.5%
- Return on operating assets   20.2%
- Return on common stockholders' equity   29.1%

CCB Enterprises
Statement of Income
Year Ended December 31, 2005
($000 omitted)

Revenue	
Net sales	$800,000
Other	60,000
Total revenue	$860,000
Expenses	
Cost of goods sold	$540,000
Research and development	25,000
Selling and administrative	155,000
Interest	20,000
Total expenses	$740,000
Income before income taxes	120,000
Income taxes (40% tax rate)	48,000
Net income	$72,000

CCB Enterprises Comparative Statement of Financial Position
December 31, 2005 and 2004
($000 omitted)

Assets	2005	2004
Current assets		
Cash and short-term investments	$26,000	$21,000
Receivables, less allowance for doubtful accounts ($1,100 in 2005 and $1,400 in 2004)	48,000	50,000
Inventories, at lower of FIFO cost or market	65,000	62,000
Prepaid items and other current assets	5,000	3,000
Total current assets	$144,000	$136,000
Other assets		
Investments, at cost	$106,000	$106,000
Deposits	10,000	8,000
Total other assets	$116,000	$114,000
Property, plant, and equipment		
Land	$12,000	$12,000
Buildings and equipment, less accumulated depreciation ($126,000 in 2005 and $122,000 in 2004)	268,000	248,000
Total property, plant, and equipment	$280,000	$260,000
Total assets	$540,000	$510,000

Liabilities and Stockholders' Equity		
Current liabilities		
Short-term loans	$22,000	$24,000
Accounts payable	72,000	71,000
Salaries, wages, and other	26,000	27,000
Total current liabilities	$120,000	$122,000
Long-term debt	160,000	171,000
Total liabilities	$280,000	$293,000
Stockholders' equity		
Common stock, at par	$44,000	$42,000
Paid-in capital in excess of par	64,000	61,000
Total paid-in capital	$108,000	$103,000
Retained earnings	152,000	114,000
Total stockholders' equity	$260,000	$217,000
Total liabilities and stockholders' equity	$540,000	$510,000

Questions

A. Explain how the use of financial ratios can be advantageous to management.
B. Calculate the following financial ratios for 2005 for CCB Enterprises (round your answer to three decimal places):
  1. Times interest earned
  2. Return on total assets
  3. Return on operating assets
  4. Return on common stockholders' equity
  5. Total debt ratio
  6. Total debt to equity ratio
  7. Current ratio
  8. Quick (acid-test) ratio

Question 2A-ES02

Renbud Computer Services Co. (RCS) specializes in customized software development for the broadcast and telecommunications industries. The company was started 30 years ago by three people to develop software primarily for a national network to be used in broadcasting national election results. After sustained and manageable growth for many years, the company has grown very fast over the last three years, doubling in size. This growth has placed the company in a challenging financial position for the coming year.

Within 30 days, RCS will need to renew its $300,000 loan, a current liability, with the Third State Bank of San Marcos. Harvey Renbud, president of RCS, is concerned about renewing the loan because of the low amount of cash on hand. The bank has requested RCS's last year's income statement, comparative balance sheets for the last two years, and six ratios relating to operating performance and liquidity.

RCS Financial Statements

Renbud Computer Services Co.
Income Statement
Last Year

Net revenues		$2,500,000
Expenses		
Cost of product services	$1,500,000	
Selling and administration	300,000	
Depreciation and amortization	200,000	
Interest	60,000	
Income taxes	150,000	
Total expenses		$2,210,000
Net income		$ 290,000

Renbud Computer Services Co.
Balance Sheet
Past Two Years

Assets	Last Year	Two Years Ago
Cash	$50,000	$50,000
Accounts receivable, net	350,000	250,000
Operating supplies and other	70,000	60,000
Equipment, net	1,100,000	900,000
Furniture and fixtures, net	120,000	100,000
Other long-term assets	240,000	200,00
Total assets	$1,930,000	$1,560,000
Liabilities and shareholders' equity		
Accounts payable	$150,000	$130,000
Taxes payable	140,000	120,000
Note payable (Third State Bank)	300,000	200,000
Bonds payable (due in 2002)	400,000	400,000
Total liabilities	990,000	850,000
Capital stock (1,000 shares)	100,000	100,000
Retained earnings	840,000	610,000
Total shareholders' equity	710,000	940,000
Total liabilities and shareholders' equity	$1,930,000	$1,560,000

Questions

A. Explain why the Third State Bank of San Marcos would be interested in Renbud's comparative financial statements.
B. Using Computer Services Co.'s comparative financial statements, ratio calculations, and industry ratios, calculate these financial ratios for RCS Co.:
   1. Current ratios for the past two years
   2. Accounts receivable turnover for last year
   3. Total asset turnover for last year
   4. Return on shareholders' equity for last year
   5. Debt to equity ratio for the last two years
   6. Net profit margin percentage (return on sales) for last year
C. Briefly discuss the limitations and difficulties that can be encountered in using ratio analysis.

Question 2A-ES03

In the Statements of Financial Accounting Concepts (SFACs), the Financial Accounting Standards Board (FASB) set forth the fundamentals on which financial accounting and reporting standards are to be based. Specifically, the FASB intends that these concept statements establish objectives and concepts that can be used to develop standards for financial accounting and reporting, and to resolve new and emerging problems. Knowledge of the FASB objectives and concepts should enable those affected by financial accounting standards to better understand the content and limitations of the information provided by financial accounting and reporting. **SFAC No. 8** Chapter 1 discusses the objective of general-purpose financial reporting by a reporting entity, and **SFAC No. 5** recommends the composition of a full set of financial statements.

Question

Identify and describe the major sections of the statement of cash flows.

Question 2A-ES04

Sentech Scientific Inc., a manufacturer of test instruments, is in contract negotiations with the labor union that represents its hourly manufacturing employees. Negotiations have reached an impasse, and it appears that a strike is imminent. The controller has called the general accounting manager into his office to discuss liquidity issues if and when a strike does occur.

The controller asks the accounting manager to recommend measures to assess liquidity if a strike were to occur. Although some of the nonunion employees probably could produce test instruments during a strike, the controller would rather be conservative and assume no shipments during this time frame. Since customers may go to other sources to obtain the products they need during a strike, cash receipts for current outstanding amounts owed by customers may not be paid on a timely basis.

Questions

A. Define *liquidity*, and explain its importance to Sentech.
B. Identify three measures that could be used to assess liquidity, and explain how to calculate these measures.
C. Determine which liquidity measure identified above would **best** fit the controller's requirements, and explain why. Include in your discussion the reasons why the other measures would not be as appropriate.

Question 2A-ES05

Chargrille Inc. is a U.S. firm that manufactures barbecue grills. The majority of the component parts are acquired from a company in Mexico, then shipped to the United States, where the grills are assembled, packaged, and shipped to dealers. Helen Adams, the treasurer, is developing the revision to the cash budget for the second quarter utilizing these forecasted parameters:

Sales Data

	March	April	May	June	July
U.S.—Unit Sales	70,000	80,000	75,000	65,000	65,000
Canada—Unit Sales	50,000	50,000	60,000	45,000	35,000

- Selling price: In U.S. = 50 US dollars (USD); in Canada = 60 Canadian dollars (CAD)
- Variable expenses: U.S. labor = 10 USD per unit

  U.S. materials = 5 USD per unit
  Mexican imported parts = 350 Mexican pesos (MXN) per unit

- Overhead per month = 400,000 USD
- An interest payment on long term-debt of 500,000 USD is due in June.
- An income tax payment of 1,000,000 USD is due in June.
- Collections are assumed to occur in the month following the sale.
- Products are manufactured and the cash is expended one month prior to the sale.
- The cash balance at the end of March is assumed to be 1 million USD.
- Forward exchange rates are assumed to be:

	April	May	June
CAD per USD	1.20	1.19	1.18
MXN per USD	11.3	11.4	11.5

Questions

A. Develop the monthly cash flow budget in U.S. dollars (USD) for April, May, and June, showing the beginning cash balance, cash receipts, cash disbursements, and ending cash balance for each month. (Use the spreadsheet to enter your responses.)

B. Identify and discuss the potential impact of currency fluctuations on receipts and cash disbursements that Chargrille is exposed to based on the calculations you made in Question A.

C. If the spot rate (per 1 USD) on the Canadian dollar is 1.20 and it is 11.00 on the Mexican peso at the time Adams is preparing the budget revision, identify whether the U.S. dollar is expected to appreciate or depreciate during the second quarter relative to the:
   1. Canadian dollar
   2. Mexican peso

D. Identify and discuss two alternatives available to reduce the foreign exchange rate risk to which Chargrille is exposed.

Question 2A-ES06

Giga Industries is a large, publicly held manufacturer of telecommunications equipment. The firm developed the next forecast for the upcoming year.

Balance Sheet (thousands of dollars)		
Current assets		$100,000
Fixed assets	750,000	
Accumulated depreciation	200,000	
Net fixed assets		550,000
TOTAL ASSETS		$650,000
Current liabilities		$50,000
Long-term debt		150,000
Shareholders' equity		
Preferred stock	50,000	
Common—par of $2	100,000	
Common—premium	200,000	
Retained earnings	100,000	
		450,000
TOTAL LIABILITIES and EQUITY		$650,000

Income Statement (thousands of dollars)	
Revenue	$2,000,000
Depreciation expense	50,000
Other expenses	1,775,000
Earnings before interest & taxes	175,000
Interest expense	15,000
Taxes (40% effective rate)	64,000
Net income	96,000
Preferred stock dividends	5,000
Earnings for common stock	$91,000

The product development team has developed a new line of state-of-the-art switching devices and is proposing a major capital investment of $200 million for a new division of the firm that will manufacture and sell the new line. An extensive financial analysis was prepared using estimates for each year of the estimated 10-year product life and presented to the board of directors indicating that the project would result in a positive net present value (NPV) of $60 million and an internal rate of return (IRR) of 25%. A board member commented that the project looked very promising but expressed concern about the impact on earnings. The controller was asked to develop a revised forecast for the coming year, assuming the project was approved.

Questions

A. You are preparing the revised forecast for the controller. For each of the next assumptions, show the balance sheet and/or income statement account that would be affected, the amount of the change, and if the change increases or decreases the account. Assume no flotation costs on all financing.
   1. The $200 million investment in fixed assets will be made on January 1 and will be depreciated on a 10-year straight-line basis for financial statement and income tax purposes.
   2. On January 1, $75 million of 10-year bonds will be issued at par with annual interest of 10% payable December 31 with principal to be repaid at maturity.
   3. On January 1, $25 million of preferred stock will be issued with an annual dividend rate of 14% payable December 31.
   4. On January 1, 4 million new shares of common stock will be issued to net the firm $25 per share. Common stock dividends are expected to be $0.50 payable December 31, as in the original forecast.
   5. During the initial year of operation, the new product is expected to produce cash revenue of $60 million and have cash expenses (other than depreciation) of $30 million.
B. Assume that the tax rate is expected to remain at 40% and that taxes are paid on December 31. Calculate the change in net income resulting from the transactions in question A.
C. Since financial theory indicates that project decisions should be made based on NPV and IRR, why would a large public company be concerned about the effect on earnings in the first year?

Question 2A-ES07

Foyle Inc. has prepared the comparative income statements for the three most recent fiscal years that are shown below. While profitable, Foyle has been losing market share and is concerned about future performance. Also presented are data about Foyle's largest competitor and the industry average.

	Year 1	Year 2	Year 3	Competitor	Industry Average
Revenue	$20,000	$24,000	$30,000	$45,000	$28,000
Cost of goods sold	12,000	12,000	18,000	21,600	14,000
Gross profit	8,000	12,000	12,000	23,400	14,000
Sales and marketing	2,000	2,000	2,000	5,000	3,000
General and administrative	1,500	2,000	3,000	3,150	2,500
Research and development	1,500	2,000	1,000	4,000	1,500
Operating income	$ 3,000	$ 6,000	$ 6,000	$11,250	$ 7,000

Questions

1. Using the three Foyle Inc. statements,
   a. prepare a comparative common-size statement using revenue as the base measure.
   b. prepare a common base-year income statement using year 1 as the base year. Show your calculations.
2. Calculate Foyle's growth rate of both revenue and operating income for year 2 and year 3. Show your calculations.
3. By evaluating Foyle's performance against the performance of Foyle's largest competitor and the industry average, identify and discuss three areas that Foyle should target for further investigation and performance improvement. Support your discussion with data.

Question 2A-ES08

Income statements for Bockman Industries, a retailer, are shown next for the past two years.

	Year 2	Year 1
Revenues	$6,400,000	$6,000,000
Cost of goods sold	3,100,000	2,850,000
Gross margin	3,300,000	3,150,000
Selling expenses	950,000	880,000
Administrative expenses	1,120,000	1,050,000
Loss due to strike	20,000	0
Interest expense	30,000	30,000
Income before taxes	1,180,000	1,190,000
Income tax expense	472,000	476,000
Income from continuing operations	708,000	714,000
Discontinued operations, net	72,000	0
Net income	$ 780,000	$ 714,000
Earnings per share	$2.50	$2.30

Questions

1. Prepare common-size income statements (vertical analysis) for Bockman Industries for the two years presented.
2. Prepare a memo to the controller of Bockman identifying and describing a possible explanation for each of the following.
   a. An increase in sales along with the change in the gross margin percentage
   b. An increase in sales along with the increase in selling expenses
   c. An increase in sales along with the increase in administrative expenses
3. Assume that Bockman has no preferred stock outstanding and that any change in the number of shares of common stock occurred at the beginning of year 2. If the shareholders' equity at the end of year 2 totaled $7,363,200, calculate Bockman's book value per share.

Question 2A-ES09

Knight, Inc. and Day, Ltd. are large firms in the same industry. Each firm has $200 million of assets and produces $50 million of earnings before interest and taxes (EBIT), and both are subject to a 40% income tax rate. Knight finances 30% of its assets with debt at a before-tax cost of 10%. Day finances 60% of its assets with debt at a before-tax cost of 15%.

Questions

1. Develop a summary balance sheet and a summary income statement for each of the two companies based on the information provided. Round dollar amounts to the nearest million.
2. Calculate the return on equity for each company, to the nearest tenth of a percent.
3. Based on the information given, identify which company has the higher level of risk. Explain your answer.
4. Describe and explain four implications (or costs) of financial distress.

Question 2A-ES10

McMullen Industries is planning a major expansion of its facilities in several major markets. The new fixed assets to be acquired are estimated to cost $500 million, and McMullen is discussing financing arrangements with an investment banking firm. The summarized income statement and balance sheet for McMullen are shown next.

McMullen Industries
Income Statement
(millions of dollars)

Sales	$5,500
Cost of goods sold	3,100
Gross profit	2,400
Selling, general, and administrative	1,600
Operating profit	800
Interest expense	100
Pretax income	700
Taxes (40%)	280
Net income	$420
Earnings per share	$7.00

Balance Sheet
(millions of dollars)

Current assets	$ 100
Net fixed assets	3,000
Total assets	3,100
Current liabilities	50
Long-term debt	1,000
Common stock:	
Par value ($2/share)	120
Additional paid-in capital	1,000
Retained earnings	930
Net common equity	2,050
Total liabilities and equity	$3,100

One financing option is the issuance of new shares of common stock. The investment banker estimates that new shares can be issued at a price of $100 per share. McMullen pays an annual dividend of $2 per share every December 31. Another option is to issue $500 million of 20-year mortgage bonds at 6% with principal repayment beginning in year 10. Interest is payable annually on December 31.

Questions

1. Disregarding issue costs and assuming the financing is in place for the full year, develop a pro forma income statement (including earnings per share) and balance sheet by adjusting the income statement and balance sheet above to reflect the acquisition of the new facilities and associated financing for the:
   a. Common stock alternative
   b. Debt alternative
2. Discuss the following financial measures and calculate each for the common stock and debt alternatives:
   a. Financial leverage ratio
   b. Working capital

3. Is the debt issue viable if McMullen has a covenant in one of its prior debt agreements stating that the company must maintain a debt-to-equity ratio below 60%? Show your calculations.
4. Identify and briefly discuss five factors that influence a company's capital structure.

Part 2 Section B Questions

Question 2B-ES01

The Gershenfeld Foundation was established 25 years ago to encourage, promote, and support research in the physical sciences. A wide range of industrial corporations contribute money in support of the foundation's work. The foundation has awarded research grants at a rate commensurate with its contributions and portfolio earnings.

Gershenfeld's contributions have increased significantly the past few months. The results of the foundation's recent fund drive exceeded the expectations of the board of trustees. New research grants are being reviewed and evaluated, but a final decision on which grants to fund and the amount of funding will not be made for at least 60 days. Thus, Gershenfeld has an excess cash position that is expected to continue for two months.

The board of trustees has instructed the foundation's executive director to invest the excess cash during this interim period. The executive director has been instructed to earn the highest possible yield while maintaining marketability and safety of principal. The types of investments that the executive director is considering for the use of $3.5 million of excess cash are (1) certificates of deposit, (2) U.S. Treasury bills, and (3) preferred stock of domestic corporations.

Questions

A. Define each of the next financial instrument characteristics and explain the effect each has on the yield of investments.
   1. Default risk
   2. Marketability
   3. Maturity
B. Evaluate each type of investment being considered by Gershenfeld's executive director in terms of default risk, marketability, and maturity.
C. Discuss the suitability of each type of investment being considered by the executive director for Gershenfeld Foundation's particular situation.

Question 2B-ES02

Atrax Corporation is now a diversified company that was originally founded as a textile and milling company by Adam Traxal. During the 1980s and early 1990s, before any diversification, Atrax's earnings had leveled off to about $2.25 per share. The growth possibilities in this industry were limited so that the demand for expansion funds has been low. There were large internal cash flows during this period, and Atrax regularly paid out 65% of its earnings as cash dividends. By the middle 1990s, this large dividend payout had become a trademark of Atrax's common stock.

The firm began diversifying into high-technology, growth companies in 1994 in an effort to reduce its business risk from its dependence on a single source of sales. Traxal thought such diversification was essential to maintain Atrax's financial health. The diversification program has been successful as far as Traxal is concerned. Atrax is no longer completely dependent on a single source of sales. The earnings have grown moderately to $2.80 per share since 1994 despite the issuance of additional common shares. The price of the Atrax common stock has increased so that the price/earnings (P/E) ratio is slightly higher than it was in 1994. In addition, the 65% cash dividend payout ratio has been maintained during the expansion period.

At first the diversification program was easily financed by the excess funds that were generated internally. Eventually though, the firm began to recognize the need to use external sources—long-term debt and/or additional issues of common stock—to finance its expansion programs. One consequence of the several common stock offerings was to dilute Traxal's control over the firm because he was unable to purchase his pro rata share of the additional offerings due to a shortage of personal funds. The Traxal family holdings amounted to 54% of the firm's stock in 1994, but their ownership has now fallen to around 35%. However, Traxal still is able to maintain effective control over the firm because no other stockholder owns more than 4% of the total stock.

Traxal believes that continued expansion is important for Atrax. Traxal is against any additional issues of common equity because he still cannot generate the personal funds necessary to purchase additional stock to maintain his present equity position. However, further expansion could be greatly hampered if additional issues of common equity are not employed. Traxal has instructed his staff to suggest alternative proposals that would allow him to maintain control of Atrax and still continue the firm's diversification program. Summaries of three proposals are presented next.

Proposal 1

The acquisition program would continue and be financed out of earnings, not paid out as dividends and from long-term debt issues and preferred stock issues. The current 65% cash dividend payout ratio would be maintained, and there would be no additional issues of common stocks. However, there would be an increase in long-term debt and preferred stock issues.

Proposal 2

The acquisition program would continue, and cash dividends would be reduced. The staff estimates that acquisitions could be financed with internally generated funds and a minimum amount of long-term debt. No additional common equity would be required. Atrax probably could distribute cash dividends equal to 10% to 20% of earnings. This proposal would not significantly change Atrax's current debt-to-equity relationship. In an attempt to appease stockholders who face a drop in their cash dividends, a stock dividend would be paid.

Proposal 3

The acquisition program would continue and be financed entirely by internally generated funds by reducing the cash dividend payout rate to zero, if necessary. No additional long-term debt or shares of common stock would be employed.

Questions

A. Adam Traxal finds Proposal 1 interesting but wonders what effect it would have on the rest of the firm and on the market value of Atrax Corporation's common stock. Assuming that the price of a firm's stock is the product of its current earnings per share and its historical price/earnings ratio, indicate the ways in which implementing Proposal 1 would operate to affect the market price of Atrax's common stock.

B. Adam Traxal considers Proposal 3 to be the least attractive because cash dividends might be reduced to zero. Explain what the probable short-term and long-term effects would be on the market price of Atrax's common stock if the acquisition program is dependent on reducing the cash dividend payout ratio to zero.

C. Adam Traxal considers Proposal 2 the most appealing because dividends still would continue to be distributed.
   1. Would Traxal be able to maintain his current equity position of 35% if stock dividends were distributed? Explain your answer.
   2. Explain how, if at all, the market price of Atrax's common stock probably would be affected if this proposal is adopted.
   3. Compare and contrast Proposal 2 with Proposal 3 in terms of the probable effects on the market price of Atrax's common stock.

Question 2B-ES03

Kravel Corporation is a diversified company with several manufacturing plants. Kravel's Dayton plant has been supplying parts to truck manufacturers for over 30 years. The last shipment of truck parts from the Dayton plant will be made December 31, 2006. Kravel's management currently is studying three alternatives relating to its soon-to-be-idle plant and equipment in Dayton.

Alternative 1

Wasson Industries has offered to buy the Dayton plant for $3,000,000 cash on January 1, 2007.

Alternative 2

Harr Enterprises has offered to lease the Dayton facilities for four years beginning on January 1, 2007. Harr's annual lease payments would be $500,000 plus 10% of the gross dollar sales of all items produced in the Dayton plant. Probabilities of Harr's annual gross dollar sales from the Dayton plant are estimated as shown next.

Annual Gross Dollar Sales	Estimated Probability
$2,000,000	0.1
4,000,000	0.4
6,000,000	0.3
8,000,000	0.2

Alternative 3

Kravel is considering the production of souvenir items to be sold in connection with upcoming sporting events. The Dayton plant would be used to produce 70,000 items per month at an annual cash outlay of $2,250,000 during 2007, 2008, and 2009. Linda Yetter, vice president of marketing, has recommended a selling price of $5 per item and believes the items will sell uniformly throughout 2008, 2009, and 2010.

The adjusted basis of the Dayton plant as of the close of business on December 31, 2006, will be $4,200,000. Kravel has used straight-line depreciation for all capital assets at the Dayton plant. If the Dayton plant is not sold, the annual straight-line depreciation charge for the plant and equipment will be $900,000 each year for the next four years. The market value of the plant and equipment on December 31, 2010, is estimated to be $600,000.

Kravel requires an after-tax rate of return of 16% for capital investment decisions and is subject to corporate income tax rates of 40% on operating income and 20% on capital gains.

Questions

A. Calculate the present value (at December 31, 2006) of the expected after-tax cash flows for each of the three alternatives available to Kravel Corporation regarding the Dayton plant. Assume all recurring cash flows take place at the end of the year.

B. Discuss the additional factors, both quantitative and qualitative, Kravel Corporation should consider before a decision is made regarding the disposition or use of the idle plant and equipment at the Dayton plant.

Question 2B-ES04

Langley Industries plans to acquire new assets costing $80 million during the coming year and is in the process of determining how to finance the acquisitions. The business plan for the coming year indicates that retained earnings of $15 million will be available for new investments. As far as external financing is concerned, discussions with investment bankers indicate that market conditions for Langley securities should be as listed next.

- Bonds with a coupon rate of 10% can be sold at par.
- Preferred stock with an annual dividend of 12% can be sold at par.
- Common stock can be sold to yield Langley $58 per share.

The company's current capital structure, which is considered optimal, is shown next.

Long-term debt	$175 million
Preferred stock	50 million
Common equity	275 million

Financial studies performed for Langley indicate that the cost of common equity is 16%. The company has a 40% marginal tax rate. (Ignore floatation costs for all calculations.)

Questions

A. Determine how Langley should finance its $80 million capital expenditure program, considering all sources of funds. Be sure to identify how many new shares of common stock will have to be sold. Show your calculations.

B. Calculate Langley's weighted incremental cost of capital that it could use to assess the viability of investment options.

C. Identify how each of the next events, considered individually, would affect Langley's cost of capital (increase, decrease, no change). No calculations are required.
1. The corporate tax rate is increased.
2. Banks indicate that lending rates will be increasing.
3. Langley's beta value is reduced due to investor perception of risk.
4. The firm decides to significantly increase the percentage of debt in its capital structure since debt is the lowest-cost source of funds.

Question 2B-ES05

Crenshaw Manufacturing has decided to acquire new equipment for its manufacturing facilities and currently is deciding how to finance the acquisition. The equipment has an initial purchase and installation cost of $2 million, will be utilized for five years, and is expected to have a salvage value of $200,000 at the end of the five-year period. The estimated economic life of the equipment is six years. Maintenance cost is expected to be $75,000 per year. Crenshaw has an effective income tax rate of 40%. Crenshaw is considering two options:

1. *Purchase the equipment.* Crenshaw would depreciate the property for financial statement purposes on a straight-line basis over five years and for federal income tax purposes as three-year property using the MACRS general depreciation system and the half-year convention producing tax depreciation rates (rounded) of 33%, 45%, 15%, and 7% for years 1 through 4 respectively. In addition to maintenance costs, Crenshaw would have to pay insurance of $25,000 per year and property taxes of $50,000 per year.
2. *Lease the equipment through Morton Financial, a third-party lessor.* Morton provided a quote of $600,000 per year due at the year-end as the lease payment. Morton would be responsible for insurance and property taxes, but Crenshaw would be responsible for maintenance.

Crenshaw's financial analysis department realizes that the financial community views leasing as a form of debt financing and therefore evaluates the lease versus buy decision as 100% debt financing. Crenshaw could issue debt at a before-tax cost of 10% in today's market.

Questions

A. Should Crenshaw purchase or lease the new equipment? Support your recommendation with calculations that show the net financial advantage.
B. If Crenshaw decides to lease the equipment, should the lease be classified as an operating or a capital lease for financial accounting and reporting purposes? Support your answer.
C. Identify three reasons why firms in general may consider leasing as an alternative to ownership.

Question 2B-ES06

Henderson Inc. needs to raise $15 million for its research and development program. Its investment banker suggested raising the funds through the issuance of original issue discount bonds. The bonds would be outstanding for five years, have a semiannual coupon rate of 6%, and a maturity value of $1,000 each. The current market conditions require a yield of 8%, given Henderson's bond rating. Henderson's marginal income tax rate is 40%. Ignore the issue expense of the bonds and round all calculations to the nearest dollar. Assume the bonds are issued on the first day of the fiscal year.

Questions

A. What is the issue price of each bond? Show your calculations.
B. How many bonds will Henderson have to issue? Show your calculations.
C. Determine the net after-tax cash flows per bond to Henderson relating to the bonds at issuance (time = 0) and for each of the five years they are outstanding. Show your calculations.
D. Assume that at the end of three years, interest rates are 6% for bonds rated the same as Henderson's and maturing at the same time. What would a rational investor be willing to pay for one of Henderson's bonds? Show your calculations.

Question 2B-ES07

Han Electronics Inc. is an electronics retailer with a fitness equipment retailer subsidiary. Han is a mature company with declining sales while the subsidiary is growing and profitable. The management of Han is considering several strategic options for the company as a whole. They considered purchasing additional companies to continue to diversify their product mix or split out some or all of the subsidiary into a separate company so that each company could go in a different direction. Ultimately, the concern is that Han is failing. Management wants to maximize shareholder value, turn the company around, and continue as a going concern.

Questions

1. a. Define mergers and acquisitions.
   b. Does this scenario describe a merger or an acquisition?
   c. Identify three possible synergies or benefits of mergers and acquisitions.
2. a. Identify and describe these two types of divestitures: spin-offs and equity carve-outs.
   b. Identify whether either of these divestiture types is described in the scenario above.
3. a. Define bankruptcy and identify the different types of bankruptcy.
   b. What is the priority of creditors in a bankruptcy proceeding?

Question 2B-ES08

OneCo, Inc. produces a single product. Cost per unit, based on the manufacture and sale of 10,000 units per month at full capacity, is shown next.

Direct materials	$4.00
Direct labor	1.30
Variable overhead	2.50
Fixed overhead	3.40
Sales commission	.90
	12.10

The $0.90 sales commission is paid for every unit sold through regular channels. Market demand is such that OneCo is operating at full capacity, and the firm has found it can sell all it can produce at the market price of $16.50.

Currently, OneCo is considering two separate proposals:

a. Gatsby, Inc. has offered to buy 1,000 units at $14.35 each. Sales commission would be $0.35 on this special order.
b. Zelda Productions, Inc. has offered to produce 1,000 units at a delivered cost to OneCo of $14.50 each.

Questions

1. What would be the effect on OneCo's operating income of each of the following actions?
   a. Acceptance of the proposal from Gatsby but rejection of the proposal from Zelda
   b. Acceptance of the proposal from Zelda but rejection of the proposal from Gatsby
   c. Acceptance of both proposals
2. Assume Gatsby has offered a second proposal to purchase 2,000 units at the market price of $16.50 but has requested product modifications that would increase direct materials cost by $.30 per unit and increase direct labor and variable overhead by 15%. The sales commission would be $.35 per unit.
   a. Should OneCo accept this order? Explain your recommendation.

b. Would your recommendation be different if the company had excess capacity? Explain your answer.
3. Identify and describe at least two factors other than the effect on income that OneCo should consider before making a decision on the proposals.

Part 2 Section C Questions

Question 2C-ES01

Microeconomic theory suggests that the quantity demanded for any good is a function of relative prices, consumer real income, and consumer tastes. If tastes are held constant, changes in the other two independent variables will induce a change in the dependent variable (i.e., the quantity demanded for a particular good). The concept that measures the responsiveness of quantity demanded to changes in the independent variable is called "elasticity of demand."

Questions

A. Define the concept of price elasticity of demand.
B. Explain the significance of the price elasticity of demand concept for a firm's management.

Question 2C-ES02

Candice Company has decided to introduce a new product. The new product can be manufactured by either a capital-intensive method or a labor-intensive method. The manufacturing method will not affect the quality of the product. The estimated manufacturing costs for each of the two methods are shown next.

	Capital Intensive		Labor Intensive	
Raw materials		$5.00		$5.60
Direct labor	.5DLH* @ $12	6.00	.8DLH @ $9	7.20
Variable overhead	.5DLH @ $6	3.00	.8DLH @ $6	4.80
Directly traceable incremental fixed manufacturing costs		$2,440,000		$1,320,000

*DLH = direct labor hour

Candice's market research department has recommended an introductory unit sales price of $30. The incremental selling expenses are estimated to be $500,000 annually plus $2 for each unit sold regardless of the manufacturing method used.

Questions

A. Calculate the estimated break-even point in annual unit sales of the new product if Candice Company uses the

1. capital-intensive manufacturing method.
2. labor-intensive manufacturing method.
B. Determine the annual unit sales volume at which Candice Company would be indifferent between the two manufacturing methods.
C. Candice's management must decide which manufacturing method to employ. One factor it must consider is operating leverage.
   1. Explain operating leverage and the relationship between operating leverage and business risk.
   2. Explain the circumstances under which Candice should employ each of the two manufacturing methods.
D. Identify the business factors other than operating leverage that Candice must consider before selecting the capital-intensive or labor-intensive manufacturing method.

Question 2C-ES03

The City of Blakston owns and operates a community swimming pool. The pool is open each year for 90 days during the summer months of June, July, and August. A daily admission is charged to patrons of the pool. By law, 10% of all recreational and sporting fees must be remitted to a state tourism promotion fund. The city manager has set a goal that pool admission revenue, after subtracting the state fee and variable costs, must be sufficient to cover the fixed costs. Variable costs are assumed to be 15% of gross revenue. Fixed costs for the three-month period total $33,000. The next budget for the pool has been prepared for the current year.

Adult admissions: 30 per day × 90 days × $5.00	$13,500
Student admissions: 120 per day × 90 days × $2.50	27,000
Total revenue	40,500
State tourism fee	4,050
Net revenue	36,450
Variable costs	6,075
Fixed costs	33,000
Expected deficit	$ (2,625)

The city manager is trying to determine what admission mix is necessary to break even and what actions could be taken to eliminate the expected deficit.

Questions

A. Given the anticipated mix of adult and student admissions, how many total admissions must the pool have in order to break even for the season?
B. Regardless of the admissions mix, what is the highest number of admissions that would be necessary to break even for the season?

C. Regardless of the admissions mix, what is the lowest number of admissions that would be necessary to break even for the season?

Question 2C-ES04

Kolobok, Inc., produces premium ice cream in a variety of flavors. Over the past several years, the company has experienced rapid and continuous growth and is planning to increase manufacturing capacity by opening production facilities in new geographic areas. These initiatives have put pressure on management to better understand both their potential markets and associated costs. Kolobok's management identified three aspects of its current operation that could affect the new market expansion decision: (1) a highly competitive ice cream market, (2) the company's current marketing strategy, and (3) the company's current cost structure.

Since the company began operations in 1990, Kolobok has used the markup approach for establishing prices for six-gallon containers of ice cream. The product prices include the cost of materials and labor, a markup for profit and overhead cost (a standard $20), and a market adjustment. The market adjustment is used to appropriately position a variety of products in the market. The goal is to price the products in the middle of comparable ice creams offered by competitors while maintaining high quality and high differentiation. Sales for 2007 based on Kolobok's markup pricing are presented next by product.

Product	Material and Labor	Markup	Market Adjustment	Unit Price	Boxes Sold	Total Materials and Labor	Total Sales
Vanilla	$29.00	$20.00	$1.00	$50.00	10,200	$295,800	$510,000
Chocolate	28.00	20.00	7.00	55.00	12,500	350,000	687,500
Caramel	26.00	20.00	2.00	48.00	12,900	335,400	619,200
Raspberry	27.00	20.00	2.00	49.00	13,600	367,200	666,400
Total					49,200	$1,348,400	$2,483,100

For the year 2007, Kolobok's before-tax return on sales was 7%. The company's overhead expenses were $500,000; selling expenses, $250,000; administrative expenses, $180,000; and interest expenses, $30,000. Kolobok's marginal tax rate is 30%.

Kolobok is considering replacing markup pricing with target costing and has prepared the next table to better compare the methods. Kolobok tries to appeal to the top 30% of the retail sales customers, including restaurants and cafés. In positioning Kolobok's products, three dimensions are considered: price, quality, and product differentiation. Accordingly, there are three main competitors in the market:

Competitor A. Low cost, low quality, high standardization

Competitor B. Average cost, moderate quality, average differentiation

Competitor C. High cost, high quality, high differentiation

Product	Competitor Pricing A	Competitor Pricing B	Competitor Pricing C	Kolobok Target Prices
Vanilla	$49	$55	$55	$53
Chocolate	50	53	56	53
Caramel			51	50
Raspberry		51	52	50

Kolobok also has been reviewing its purchasing, manufacturing, and distribution processes. Assuming that sales volumes will not be affected by the new target prices, the company believes that improvements will yield a $125,000 decrease in labor expense and a 25% reduction in overhead expense.

Questions

A. Describe target costing.
B. Analyze and compare the two alternative pricing methods: markup pricing and target costing.
C. Assuming that the sales volumes will not be affected by the new product pricing based on target costing and that the process improvements will be implemented, calculate Kolobok's before-tax return on sales using the proposed target prices.
D. Recommend which pricing method (markup or target) Kolobok should use in the future and explain why.

Question 2C-ES05

Pearson Foods is the second largest company in the breakfast cereal and fruit juice markets. For the past five years, Pearson's profits have exceeded the industry average, and management has decided to pursue a plan for growth. Two promising opportunities are being evaluated.

1. Enter the high-energy, low-fat cereals market. This project would entail developing new products using new or expanded facilities and would be financed out of earnings and through a series of long-term debt offerings over the next two years. The debt offerings would raise Pearson's debt as a percentage of total capital from 22% to 30% at the end of the two-year period.
2. Acquire Safin Bakery, a long-established and well-known bread and bakery goods company. The acquisition could be completed by the end of the calendar year and would be financed by cash and long-term notes. The debt as a percentage of total capital would rise to 40% by the end of the calendar year. Safin Bakery would be merged into Pearson Foods but operate independently as a separate division for two years. At the end of two years, Pearson would be able to consolidate the administrative, financial, and operating functions.

Both projects meet the investment criteria established by Pearson's management, and the treasurer will be preparing an evaluation of the two projects in terms of financing differences, impact on profitability, and operational and managerial problems.

Questions

A. As part of a risk assessment process, identify the strategic advantages and disadvantages of Pearson Foods' opportunity to use internal expansion by developing new products for the high-energy, low-fat cereals market.

B. As part of a risk assessment process, identify the strategic advantages and disadvantages of Pearson Foods' opportunity to use external expansion by acquiring Safin Bakery.

Question 2C-ES06

David Burns is the manager of the Electrical Division of Madison Inc. The budget for the upcoming year has just been finalized and is summarized next.

Budget Component	Amount
Revenue	$17,050,000
Expenses	
Direct labor (300,000 hours @ $20/hr)	6,000,000
Employee benefits	2,400,000
Tools and equipment	1,800,000
Materials	2,000,000
Material procurement and handling	200,000
Overhead	3,100,000
Pretax profit	$1,550,000

The budget meets the firm's general guideline of a pretax profit equal to 10% of cost. Various components of the budget are described next:

- Direct labor represents the wage costs of employees (craft personnel, job site supervisors, engineers, etc.) who work on specific projects and are directly billable to customer projects. Madison charges this to customers based on the number of hours employees work on the project times the average wage per hour.
- Employee benefits include the cost to Madison of paid time off (vacations, holidays, and sickness), pensions, health and life insurance, and payroll taxes. This is charged to customers as a percentage of direct labor.
- Tools and equipment includes the cost of small tools; larger equipment, such as cranes, backhoes, and generators; and vehicles, including maintenance, fuel, insurance, and so on. This is charged to customers as a percentage of direct labor charged to the job.
- Materials include materials acquired by Madison for use on customer projects, the cost of which is passed directly on to the specific customers.
- Material procurement and handling represents the cost incurred by Madison to purchase, warehouse, and deliver materials (referenced in the preceding bullet point) to job sites. This is charged to customers as a percentage of the material cost.
- Overhead includes the salary and benefit costs of employees not directly chargeable to projects (administrative and corporate staff as well as senior management) and other corporate expenses for facilities and supplies, most of which are relatively fixed. This is charged to customers as a percentage of all other costs incurred on the project.

Questions

A. David Burns received a call from Colby Architects asking for a price quote for a component of electrical work to be done on an office building project. Based on the detailed specifications, Burns estimated that the job would require 10,000 direct labor hours and materials costing $200,000. He decided to develop a cost proposal for other cost elements based on the percentages inherent in the budget, including a pretax profit equal to 10% of cost. Determine the amount of the quote. Show your calculations.

B. Madison measures the performance of its managers, including Burns, based on their ability to achieve budget targets, focusing on pretax profit as a percentage of billable cost for each project completed. Identify three advantages and three disadvantages of a performance measurement and incentive compensation system linked to the budget for a firm such as Madison.

C. Two weeks after submitting his bid, Burns received a call from Colby stating that if Madison could meet the lowest fixed cost bid of $695,000, it would be awarded the contract. Identify the factors that Burns should consider in deciding whether to accept the fixed price of $695,000.

D. If Burns decides to accept the contract for the fixed price of $695,000, identify two reasons that he can use to justify his decision. Explain your answer.

Question 2C-ES07

Charlene Roberts is the controller for PARKCO, a company that owns and operates several parking garages in a large midwestern American city. Recently, the management of PARKCO has been investigating the viability of building a parking garage in an area of the city that has experienced rapid growth. Some years ago, PARKCO acquired the necessary land at a cost of $425,000 and had worthless buildings on the land demolished at a cost of $72,000. Since then, the land has been rented by various construction companies as a temporary storage site for building materials while the construction companies completed projects in the area. PARKCO has averaged revenue of $5,000 per year for this use of the property.

Roberts is currently assembling financial information relating to the proposed garage. In addition to the information already presented, she received from the CFO, John Demming, these projections:

Number of parking spaces in the proposed garage	840
Number of parking spaces rented at the monthly rate	420
Average number of parkers paying the daily rate (for each of the 20 business days per month)	180
Fixed costs to operate the garage per month	$30,000

Roberts estimates that the monthly variable cost of servicing each monthly parker is $12 and that the price of a monthly parking space would be $75. The estimated cost per daily parker is $2, and the daily parking rate is expected to be set at $8. The parking garage would operate 20 business days per month.

Roberts believes, based on PARKCO's past experience with similar garages, that the projected number of monthly and daily parkers was too high. When she questioned Demming, he replied, "This garage is going to be built no matter what your past experiences are. Just use the figures I gave you."

Questions

1. a. Define sunk cost and opportunity cost.
   b. How are these two types of cost recorded in the accounting records?
   c. Identify the sunk costs and opportunity costs, if any, in the PARKCO scenario and show the amount of each.
2. Using the data in the scenario, calculate pretax operating income. Show your calculations.
3. Roberts is uncomfortable with the implications of Demming's statement and has turned to the *IMA Statement of Ethical Professional Practice* for guidance. Based on this guidance,
   a. Identify the ethical principles that should guide the work of a management accountant.
   b. Identify the standards, and describe how they would or would not apply in the circumstances described.
   c. Identify the steps Roberts should take to resolve this situation.

Part 2 Section D Questions

Question 2D-ES01

Upton Industries is a successful manufacturing firm. Until now, Upton has operated exclusively in the United States, but now it wants to expand its production and sales into international markets. Paul Jordan, the CEO of Upton Industries, is concerned about the risks associated with this expansion. He has asked you, as the firm's management accountant, to answer a few questions before he makes the final decision whether to expand the firm internationally.

Questions

A. Discuss the types of financial, operational, and compliance risks that Upton Industries might face if it expands into international markets.
B. To mitigate these risks, Paul Jordan wants to buy an enterprise risk management (ERM) software package. However, before he does, he wants you to explain the benefits that the firm might derive from implementing an ERM system as well as any limitations on these benefits. What would you tell him?
C. Jordan wants the implementation of an ERM to be a success, but he is concerned about how this plan will fit with the corporate culture at Upton Industries. Discuss the key organizational characteristics that would increase the chance that an ERM will be successful.

Question 2D-ES02

EZ-Food runs a fleet of lunch trucks that sell sandwiches, sodas, coffee, and snacks throughout the city. So far, EZ-Food has operated strictly on a cash basis, but now the firm is considering whether to offer weekly credit to its regular customers by allowing them to sign for their food Monday through Thursday and then pay their tabs on Friday. The manager of EZ-Food has developed the risk map shown next. Point A represents the manager's assessment of the impact and likelihood of a few credit customers refusing to pay their bills. Point B shows his assessment of the impact and likelihood of a significant number of customers making late payments. Point C indicates his assessment of a computer virus destroying the records of the amounts that customers owe.

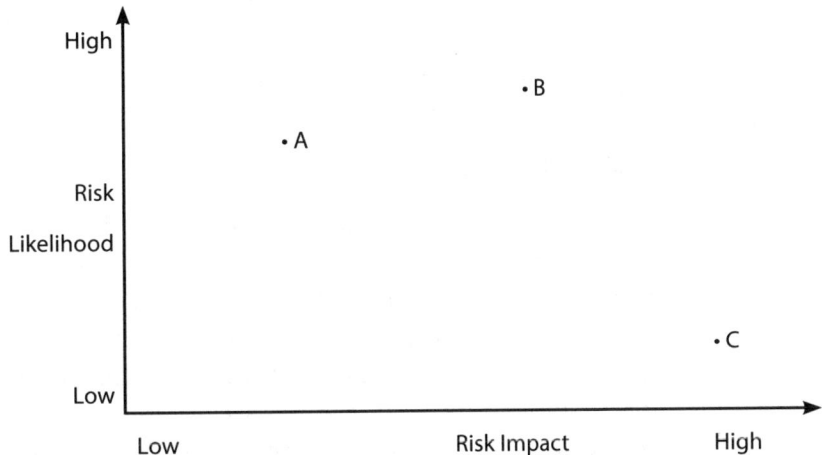

Questions

A. Based on this risk map, which risk should he consider as the highest priority? Explain.
B. Assuming that EZ-Food is unwilling to accept these risks, discuss strategies that the firm could use to avoid, reduce, or transfer each one.
C. The manager of EZ-Food is confused about the difference between inherent risk and residual risk. How would you explain the difference to him?

Question 2D-ES03

Buy-More, Inc. is a chain of retail clothing stores. Recently the firm discovered a serious problem with internal controls over its inventory. Buy-More estimates that there is currently a 5% chance that this problem could result in a $1,000,000 loss. The firm has come up with several possible ways to deal with this problem. Option A: New electronic inventory tags would cost $25,000 and would reduce the chance of the loss to 2%. Option B: Installing $30,000 of surveillance equipment would reduce the chance of the loss to 1%. Option C: If electronic inventory tags and surveillance equipment are both used, the firm estimates there would only be a 0.1% chance of the loss.

Questions

A. Would you consider Option A (electronic inventory tags) and Option B (surveillance equipment) to be controls to prevent inventory theft or controls to detect and correct inventory theft? Explain.
B. What is the expected value of Buy-More's loss if the firm does nothing to fix the problem with the internal controls over its inventory?
C. What is the net benefit (cost) of Option A (electronic inventory tags), Option B (surveillance equipment), and Option C (both electronic inventory tags and surveillance equipment)?
D. Based only on the estimates of benefits and costs, which option should Buy-More implement? Explain.
E. What other factors might be relevant to this decision?

Part 2 Section E Questions

Question 2E-ES01

Miranda Wells joined Sycamore Corporation four months ago as a financial analyst and has been assisting Jake Richter, the controller, in evaluating capital projects. Soon Wells will be making her first presentation to the management committee responsible for selecting capital projects, and she has been working diligently to ensure that her analysis is correct. The management committee will be considering two mutually exclusive projects at this meeting. Both projects require the same initial investment and have the same project lives. Wells has used several capital budgeting methods to evaluate each project and presents the data as a table.

	Project A	Project B
Accounting rate of return	34%	26%
Internal rate of return	16%	19%
Net present value	$2.6 million	$3.5 million
Payback period	4 years	5 years

After completing her analysis, Wells believes Project B is superior to Project A. She intends to recommend Project B to the management committee and Richter agrees.

Questions

A. For each of the four capital budgeting methods used by Miranda Wells to evaluate the two projects at Sycamore Corporation, explain the merits and limitations of each method.
B. Explain why Wells and Richter believe that Project B is superior to Project A.
C. Identify three qualitative considerations that generally should be considered in capital budget evaluations.

Question 2E-ES02

Cambridge Automotive Products (CAP) Inc., a multinational corporation, is a major supplier of a broad range of components to the worldwide automobile and light truck market. CAP is in the process of developing a bid to supply an ignition system module to Korea Auto Corporation (KAC), a South Korean automobile manufacturer, for a new line of automobiles for the next four-year production cycle. The request for proposal issued by KAC specifies a quantity of 200,000 modules in the first year and 250,000 units in years 2 through 4 of the contract. CAP marketing specialists believe that, in order to be competitive, a bid of 100,000 South Korean won (KRW) per unit is appropriate. Other relevant data are shown next.

- Manufacturing specialists estimate that a $12 million (U.S. dollars) investment in equipment (including installation) is required.
- The equipment is expected to last the four-year life of the contract, at which time it would cost $1.4 million to remove the equipment, which would be sold for a scrap value of $900,000.
- Direct labor and material expenses are estimated at $40 per unit.
- The change in indirect cash expenses associated with this contract is expected to be $3 million per year.
- The new product will require additional investment in inventory and accounts receivable balances at the outset, amounting to $1.2 million during the four-year time period. This investment will be recovered at the end of the four-year contract.
- CAP is subject to U.S. income tax at an effective rate of 40%.
- For tax purposes, assume that the initial $12 million cost of the equipment is depreciated evenly over the four-year period.
- The company economist estimates that the exchange rate will average 1,250 KRW per U.S. dollar for the four-year time period.

Questions

A. Calculate the after-tax incremental cash flows in U.S. dollars for these periods:
   1. Period 0
   2. Period 1
   3. Period 4 operating cash flow
B. The assumptions used to develop the cash flows are subject to various degrees of estimation error. For each of three different cash flow variables, identify and discuss one potential risk that could affect the estimates made by CAP.

Question 2E-ES03

Grubstake Mining Ltd. (GML) owns and operates the Dusty Coal Mine, among its other business ventures. The Dusty Coal Mine is a strip mine that has been in operation for a number of years and is expected to operate for another 15 years. Environmental regulations require mine operators to reclaim the land and restore it to its original configuration and vegetation state once mining ceases. GML has been setting aside money for this purpose in an external trust fund managed by a major commercial bank, and currently the balance in the fund is $3 million. Assume that income tax regulations currently allow both the deposits to the trust fund and the earnings on the funds to be exempt from taxation.

GML would like to establish a uniform charge per ton for reclamation costs to be included in contracts with customers for future sales. It is estimated that the reclamation cost in today's dollars is $14 million, and that amount is expected to increase by 4% per year. The trust fund is expected to earn income at a rate of 7% per year on its investments. Annual sales from the mine are expected to be 1,350,000 tons per year over the next 15 years.

Questions

A. Calculate the cost per ton that GML should include in its contracts in order to accumulate a sufficient amount in the trust fund to be able to pay the cost to reclaim the land at the end of the 15-year period.
B. Identify and discuss four uncertainties that GML faces over the 15-year period as far as reclamation is concerned. For each uncertainty, describe what the effect would be on the reclamation cost per ton.
C. Without performing any calculations, discuss the effect on GML if the next changes were to be made in the tax regulations.
   1. Amounts collected for reclamation would be considered taxable income, even if they are deposited in external trust funds.
   2. Currently earnings on the trust funds are taxable.

Question 2E-ES04

Ultra Comp is a large information technology firm with several facilities. The firm's audit committee has determined that management must implement more effective security measures at its facilities. A security improvement team has been formed to formulate a solution. Janet Lynch is the financial analyst assigned to the team. She has determined that a six-year time horizon is appropriate for the analysis and that a 14% cost of capital is applicable. The team is investigating three vendors:

1. Vendor A is a new entrant to the security industry and is in the process of introducing its security system, which utilizes new technology. The system would require an initial investment of $4 million and have a life of six years. A net cash outflow of $500,000 per year for salaries, operation, maintenance, and all costs related to the system also would be required.
2. Vendor B is an established firm in the security industry and has a security system that has been on the market for several years. The system requires an initial investment of $1 million and will have a useful life of three years. At the end of the three-year period, Ultra Comp would have to replace the hardware at an estimated cost of $1,250,000, based on current technology. A net cash outflow of $750,000 per year for salaries, operation, maintenance, and all other related costs would also be required.

3. Vendor C is a nationally recognized firm in the security industry and has proposed to Ultra Comp that it provide a total security solution. Vendor C would provide all hardware and personnel to operate and maintain a security system as called for by the specifications of Ultra Comp for all its locations. Ultra Comp would be required to sign a six-year contract at a cost of $1,400,000 per year.

Questions

A. Ultra Comp utilizes the net present value (NPV) method to quantify the financial aspects of corporate decisions. Calculate the NPV of each of the three alternatives.
B. Based on financial considerations, which of the three alternatives should the team recommend? Explain why.
C. Define *sensitivity analysis*, and discuss how Ultra Comp could use this technique in analyzing the three vendor alternatives.
D. Identify and briefly discuss three nonfinancial considerations that the Ultra Comp team should consider prior to making a recommendation to senior management.

Question 2E-ES05

Dominion Industries is evaluating whether to manufacture and market a new model coffeemaker to broaden its product line. A cross-functional team has analyzed the market and cost structure for the new product, and the analysis has produced these data:

Unit selling price	$110
Variable cost per unit	$45
Fixed costs (excluding depreciation)	$600,000
Capital investment	$3,500,000
Working capital investment	$500,000

The team recognizes that the unit sales level is the most difficult variable to forecast and has conducted market research indicating that the sales distribution could be estimated in this way:

Units per year	Probability
20,000	15%
22,000	20%
25,000	30%
26,000	20%
28,000	15%

The product is expected to have a life of 10 years, the working capital is fully recovered, and there is no salvage expected from the capital investment at the end of its life. For purposes of this analysis, use straight-line depreciation and assume a 30% effective income tax rate. Dominion has a cost of capital of 14%.

Questions

A. What is the expected net present value of the investment in this new product? Show your calculations.
B. What is the probability that this investment will produce a positive net present value? Show your calculations.
C. Corporate financial managers recognize that, in general, new capital investment projects involve a variety of risks, depending on the situation.
   1. Identify three techniques or methods that can be used to quantify and assess risk.
   2. For each technique identified, describe the technique and indicate how it is utilized.

Question 2E-ES06

Right-Way Stores is a chain of home improvement stores with 150 locations. Right-Way has identified an attractive site for a new store, and Jim Smith, director of financial planning, has been asked to prepare an analysis and make a recommendation for or against opening this proposed new store.

In preparing his analysis, Smith has determined that the land at the proposed site will cost $500,000 and the new store will cost $3.5 million to build. The building contractor requires full payment at the start of construction, and it will take one year to build the store. Right-Way will finance the purchase of the land and construction of the new building with a 40-year mortgage. The mortgage payment will be $118,000 payable annually at year-end. Fixtures for the store are estimated to cost $100,000 and will be expensed. Inventory to stock the store is estimated to cost $100,000. Concerned about the possibility of rising prices, the company expects to purchase the fixtures and inventory at the start of construction. Advertising for the grand opening will be $50,000, paid to the advertising agency on retainer at the start of construction. The new store will begin operations one year after the start of construction.

Right-Way will depreciate the building over 20 years on a straight-line basis and is subject to a 35% tax rate. Right-Way uses a 12% hurdle rate to evaluate projects. The company expects to earn after-tax operating income from the new store of $1,200,000 per year.

Questions

A. What is Right-Way's total initial cash outflow? Show your calculations.
B. Calculate the annual expected cash flow from the proposed new store. Show your calculations.
C. Right-Way management evaluates new stores over a five-year horizon as management believes there is too much uncertainty after five years of operation. Calculate the net present value (NPV) for the store for the first five years of operation. Show your calculations.
D. Based solely on your answer to C, would you recommend that Right-Way build this store? Explain your answer.
E. How would you use sensitivity analysis to test your confidence in the recommendation? No calculations are required.

Question 2E-ES07

Bell Company is a large diversified manufacturer organized into profit centers. Division managers are awarded a bonus each year if the division exceeds profit goals. Although division managers are generally given control in operating their division, all capital expenditures over $500,000 must be approved by the home office. Bob Charleson was recently appointed division manager of the Central Division.

Twelve months ago, Charleson's predecessor, who has been fired, was able to convince the home office to invest $700,000 in modern manufacturing equipment with an expected life of 5 years. Included within the $700,000 investment was a special packaging machine at a cost of $200,000. This packaging machine has a 5-year useful life and a zero salvage value. Charleson has just learned of a new packaging process that would save the Central Division $60,000 a year in packaging cost over the 5-year life of the equipment. As a result of the introduction of new technology, the current packaging machine could be sold for $75,000. Acquisition and installation of the new packaging process equipment would cost $210,000. Central Division's cost of capital is 10%, and it has an effective income tax rate of 40%. The new equipment has a zero salvage value and is depreciated over 5 years on a straight-line basis.

Questions

1. Calculate the net present value of acquiring the new packaging process. Show your calculations.
2. From a financial standpoint, should Bell Company invest in the new packaging technology? Explain your answer.
3. Identify and explain three nonfinancial or behavioral factors that could cause Charleson to change the investment decision made in the previous question.
4. a. Identify and explain one problem with a profit-based compensation system such as Bell's.
   b. Recommend an alternative compensation system that would better align managers' behavior with organizational goals. Explain your answer.

Question 2E-ES08

Grandeur Industries is currently in the process of reviewing capital budget submissions from its various divisions. Grandeur uses the capital asset pricing model (CAPM) for a variety of purposes, including the determination of benchmark investment returns. The company's overall cost of capital is 16%, and its beta value is 1.2. The risk-free rate is 4%, and the expected return on the market is 14%. The next projects from different divisions are under consideration, and there is no capital rationing in effect.

Project	Internal Rate of Return	Project Beta
A	16%	1.4
B	18%	1.6
C	12%	0.7
D	17%	1.1

Questions

1. a. Calculate the required return for all four projects. Show your calculations.
   b. Which of the four projects under consideration should Grandeur accept? Support your decision.
2. Define capital rationing.
3. a. Define and explain beta.
   b. Describe four factors that would impact the beta value that is chosen for use in evaluating a project.

Question 2E-ES09

Orion Corp. is a logistics and transportation company. The finance director, John Kochar, is in the process of evaluating a number of proposed capital investment projects. The next information relates to the firm's finances.

- Some years ago the firm issued 10,000 bonds, each with a face value of $1,000 and paying an annual coupon rate of 9.2%. These bonds are now trading at $1,040 per bond. A coupon payment on these bonds was made yesterday, and the bonds mature next year.
- The firm has no other debt or preferred stock outstanding.
- The firm has 2,000,000 shares of common stock outstanding. The stock is currently selling for $14.80 per share, and the firm is expected to pay a dividend of $1.48 per share next year. The dividend is expected to grow at a constant rate of 4% per year in the foreseeable future.
- The firm's corporate tax rate is 30%.

Kochar is reviewing the capital investment projects shown next. All projects are in Orion's usual line of business and are being considered independently of each other. The listed information is available. (Note that the net present values of the projects are estimated using the weighted average cost of capital.)

Project	Initial Outlay	IRR	NPV
A	$450,000	17.0%	$18,800
B	$128,000	19.5%	$2,300
C	$262,000	16.2%	$9,800
D	$180,000	10.5%	−$7,000
E	$240,000	16.5%	$22,500
F	$160,000	11.1%	−$900

The firm is also evaluating another proposed capwital investment, Project X, that is in a completely different line of business from Orion's usual operations. The project is expected to be financed from the existing capital structure and does not fall within any capital rationing restrictions. The next forecasted net after-tax cash flows relate to Project X.

Year 0	Year 1	Year 2	Year 3	Year 4
–$200,000	$60,000	$80,000	$80,000	$80,000

Questions

1. Based on the information provided, calculate Orion's weighted average cost of capital. Show your calculations.
2. Referring to Projects A through F:
    a. Identify which projects should be accepted by Orion. Provide a brief defense of the decision criteria that you have used in arriving at your recommendations.
    b. Assume that the firm faces a capital constraint of $700,000. Identify the project or projects the firm should undertake. Provide a brief explanation for your recommendations.
3. Referring to Project X, state whether the firm should use its weighted average cost of capital to evaluate this project. Explain your answer.
4. Based on an analysis of two firms with operations similar to Project X, Kochar has determined that the project's beta is 1.5. The risk-free rate is 5%, and the market risk premium is 10%.
    a. Calculate the net present value of Project X and provide a recommendation on whether the project should be accepted. Show your calculations.
    b. Calculate the project's profitability index and provide an interpretation of this measure. Show your calculations.
5. In the past, the firm has typically used the payback period method for evaluating risky projects and accepted projects with a payback period less than 3 years.
    a. Calculate the payback period for Project X. Based on the firm's payback period threshold, what decision should the firm make regarding the project?
    b. Provide one reason why using the payback period can result in the firm making a suboptimal decision.

Part 2 Section F Questions

Question 2F-ES01

Borealis Industries has three operating divisions: Sandstone Books, Corus Games, and Sterling Extraction Services. Each division maintains its own accounting system and method of revenue recognition.

Sandstone Books

Sandstone Books sells novels to regional distributors, which then sell to independent bookstores and retail chains in their territory. The distributors are allowed to return up to 25% of their purchases to Sandstone, and the distributors have the same return allowance with the bookstores. The returns from distributors have averaged 20%

over the past five years. During the fiscal year just ended, Sandstone's sales to distributors totaled $15,000,000. At year-end, $6,800,000 of sales are still subject to return privileges over the next six months. The balance of the book sales, $8,200,000, had actual returns of 19%. Sales from the previous fiscal year totaling $5,500,000 were collected in the current fiscal year, with 21% of sales returned. Sandstone records revenue in accordance with the method referred to as revenue recognition when the right of return exists as the company's operations meet all the applicable criteria for use of this method.

Corus Games

Corus Games supplies video arcades with new games and updated versions of standard games. The company works through a network of sales agents in various cities. Orders are received from the sales agents along with down payments; Corus then ships the product directly to the customer, f.o.b. shipping point. The customer is billed for the balance due plus the actual shipping costs. During the fiscal year just ended, Corus received orders for $12,000,000 from the sales agents along with $1,200,000 in down payments. Customers were billed $150,000 in freight costs and $9,180,000 for goods shipped. After an order has been shipped, the sales agent receives a 12% commission on the product price. The goods are warranted for 90 days after sales, and warranty returns have been about 3% of sales. Corus recognizes revenue at the point of sale.

Sterling Extraction Services

Sterling specializes in the extraction of precious metals. During the fiscal year just ended, Sterling entered into contracts worth $36,000,000 and shipped metals worth $32,400,000. One quarter of the shipments was made from inventories on hand at the beginning of the year, and the remaining shipments were made from metals that were mined during the year. Sterling uses the completion-of-production method to recognize revenue, because the operations meet the specified criteria (i.e., reasonably assured sales prices, interchangeable units, and insignificant distribution costs).

Questions

The chief executive officer (CEO) of Sterling Extraction Services has asked the controller, "How do you know which orders were filled from inventory? I want you to take another look at the revenue calculation. At the current level, our incentive payments will be much lower than expected. Besides, I promised the board of directors that this year's revenue would exceed last year's by at least 12%; I don't like not keeping my promises."

The controller is very uncomfortable with the implications of the CEO's statement and has turned to the *IMA Statement of Ethical Professional Practice* for guidance. According to this guidance:

A. Identify the principles that should guide the work of a management accountant.
B. Identify and describe the standards that would be violated if the controller of Sterling were to manipulate the revenue calculation.
C. Identify the steps the controller should take to resolve this situation.

Question 2F-ES02

Alex Raminov is a management accountant at Carroll Mining and Manufacturing Company (CMMC), a large processor of ores and minerals. While working late one night to complete the footnotes for the financial statements, Raminov was looking for a file in his supervisor's office and noticed a report regarding procedures for disposing of plant wastes. According to handwritten notes on the face of the report, CMMC had been using a residential landfill in a nearby township to dump toxic coal cleaning fluid wastes over a considerable period of time. The report stated that locating a new dump site was urgent because the current one was nearing capacity.

Raminov realized that it was possible CMMC had been improperly disposing of highly toxic fluids in a landfill that was restricted to residential refuse. In addition to the obvious hazards to residents of the area, there could be legal problems if and when the authorities were notified. The financial consequences of cleanup actions, as well as the loss of CMMC's generally good environmental reputation, could be catastrophic for the company.

Raminov asked his supervisor how this item was to be included in the footnotes and inquired whether an accrual for cleanup costs was anticipated. His supervisor told him to "forget about this matter" and that he had no intention of mentioning one word about waste disposal in this year's financial statements.

Questions

A. Using the categories outlined in the *IMA Statement of Ethical Professional Practice*, identify the standards that are specifically relevant to Alex Raminov's ethical conflict and explain why the standards are applicable to the situation.
B. According to the *IMA Statement of Ethical Professional Practice*, what further steps, if any, should Raminov take in resolving his ethical dilemma?
C. If he continues to be rebuffed by his employer, should Raminov notify the appropriate authorities? Should he anonymously release the information to the local newspaper? Explain your answers.

Question 2F-ES03

Amy Kimbell was recently hired as an accounting manager for Hi-Quality Productions Inc., a publicly held company producing components for the automotive industry. One division, Alpha, uses a highly automated process that had been outsourced for a number of years because the capital investment required was high and the technology was constantly changing. Two years ago, the company decided to make the necessary capital investment and bring the operation in house. Since all major capital investments must be approved by the board of directors, the budget committee for the Alpha Division recommended the $4 million investment to the board, projecting a significant cost savings.

In her new job as accounting manager, Kimbell is on the budget committee for the Alpha Division. The board has requested from the committee a postaudit review of the actual cost savings. While working on the review, Kimball noted that several of the projections in the original proposal were very aggressive, including an unusually high salvage value and an excessively long useful life. If more realistic projections had been used, Kimbell doubts that the board would have approved the investment.

When Kimbell expressed her concerns at the next meeting of Alpha's budget committee, she was told that it had been the unanimous decision of the committee to recommend the investment because it was thought to be in the best long-term interest of the company. According to the committee members, the postaudit report would not discuss these issues; the committee members believe that certain adjustments to the review are justified to ensure the success of the Alpha division and the company as a whole.

Questions

A. Using the categories outlined in the *IMA Statement of Ethical Professional Practice*, identify the standards that are specifically relevant to Kimbell's ethical conflict and explain why the identified standards are applicable to the situation.

B. According to the *IMA Statement of Ethical Professional Practice*, what specific actions should Kimbell take to resolve her ethical conflict?

Question 2F-ES04

Pro-Kleen specializes in cleaning carpets and upholstery for residences and businesses. Three years ago, the company upgraded its equipment in order to remain competitive and take advantage of new technology. At that time, Pro-Kleen purchased two truck-mounted steam cleaners; the details are shown next.

Purchase date	March 15, 2005
Cost	$200,000
Estimated life	8 years
Salvage value	$20,000

Pro-Kleen takes one-half year's depreciation in both the year of acquisition and the year of disposal and uses the straight-line method for calculating depreciation expense.

Based on recent information, John Morgan, Pro-Kleen's assistant controller, has changed the estimated useful lives of the equipment to five years. The salvage value of the equipment has been reduced to $10,000 due to unexpected obsolescence. These revisions are effective January 1, 2008. After revising the depreciation amounts for the current year's financial reporting, Morgan was told by the controller, Eileen Ryan, that the revision was significant enough to change the small profit projected for the year into a loss. As a result, Ryan has asked Morgan to reduce by half the total depreciation expense for the current year.

Questions

A. Referring to the specific standards outlined in the *IMA Statement of Ethical Professional Practice*, identify and discuss the specific ethical conflicts that Ryan's instruction presents to Morgan.

B. According to the *IMA Statement of Ethical Professional Practice*, identify the steps that Morgan should take to resolve this situation.

Question 2F-ES05

United Forest Products (UFP) is a $1 billion corporation with many large timber and wood processing plants. The company is decentralized into divisions that operate as profit centers. The majority of the centers are evaluated on cost control and the achievement of budgeted output and profits. If target numbers are met, all division employees participate in a profit-sharing plan, and senior management potentially can receive substantial bonuses.

Charlene White is the controller of the Allegheny Division of UFP. Over the past six months, she discussed the division's performance several times with the president of the Allegheny Division, William Jefferson, and it became apparent that the division would not meet its targeted goals unless drastic changes were made. The Allegheny Division is actually a cost center that has been required to use a non-market-based transfer price, but it is evaluated as a profit center. Jefferson realized this problem and told White that the only way to meet budget was "to maximize output and make some serious changes in our cost control." Several weeks later, White noted a dramatic increase in the profitability of the division.

When analyzing the monthly profit and loss details, White noted only a slight increase in output but a significant decrease in the purchase cost of raw timber. She knew her responsibilities required her to understand fully how this sudden change was taking place and began investigating. At the log yard where timber is received and scaled to determine its price, she noticed that a trucker-timber contractor was quite aggravated when he was given the scale report (board feet and quality). When she asked one of the employees what was bothering the contractor, he said, "Are you kidding? You wouldn't believe how much we've been lowering scale measures the last three months!" Further conversations revealed that Jefferson had apparently told the division's mill workers to significantly reduce both the size scale (in inches of log diameter) and quality measures of logs sold to the mill. The impact has been a significant reduction in the price paid to contractors for timber purchased by the division.

White suspects that Jefferson has instructed employees to deliberately give logging contractors arbitrary and inaccurate evaluations of raw material quantity and quality, an unethical business practice.

Questions

A. Identify and discuss Charlene White's ethical conflict, and determine if she has an obligation to act. Be sure to refer to the relevant standards outlined in the *IMA Statement of Ethical Professional Practice* to support your answer.
B. According to the *IMA Statement of Ethical Professional Practice*, what steps should White take to resolve the perceived ethical dilemma?
C. Explain how the performance evaluation system affected behavior at the Allegheny Division, and recommend improvements to the system.

Question 2F-ES06

GRQ Company is a privately held entity that refines a variety of natural raw materials used as primary inputs for the steel industry. The firm has done well over the last several years, and most members of senior management have received bonuses well in excess of 60% of their base salaries. Also, both the chief financial officer and the chief executive officer have earned bonuses in excess of 100% of their base salaries. GRQ has projected this trend of successful earnings and bonuses to continue.

All-American Steel Company (AAS) has tendered a very generous offer to acquire GRQ. At the same time, several top GRQ executives, who own over 40% of GRQ's stock, have learned that the primary supplier of their major raw material will not renew their contract at the end of the current fiscal year. GRQ has no other vendors available within the United States to competitively provide this raw material in the amount needed to support their continued record of profitable operations.

As part of the due diligence process, an analyst with AAS has asked John Spencer, controller of GRQ, if he knows of any material event that would impact earnings over the next several years. Spencer, who also participates in the bonus program, is aware that GRQ's primary supplier will no longer provide raw materials to the firm beyond the end of the current fiscal year. He spoke with Bob Green, the CFO of GRQ, telling him that while the profit projections for the remainder of the current year will match the earnings of prior years, it is obvious that projected earnings for the next year will be greatly reduced. Green informed Spencer that the executive committee had met and decided that only members of top management were to be made aware of the situation with their key supplier. Accordingly, Spencer should not inform AAS of the situation with the supplier.

Questions

A. Referring to the specific standards outlined in the *IMA Statement of Ethical Professional Practice*, identify and discuss Spencer's ethical obligations.
B. According to the *IMA Statement of Ethical Professional Practice*, identify the steps that Spencer should take to resolve the dilemma.

Question 2F-ES07

CenturySound, Inc. produces cutting-edge high-end audio systems that are sold primarily through major retailers. Any production overruns are sold to discount retailers, under CenturySound's private label SoundDynamX. The discount retail segment appears very profitable because the basic operating budget assigns all fixed expenses to production for the major retailers, the only predictable market.

Several years ago, CenturySound implemented a 100% testing program. On average approximately 3% of production is found to be substandard and unacceptable. Of this 3%, approximately two thirds are reworked and the remaining one third are scrapped. However, in a recent analysis of customer complaints, George Wilson, the cost accountant, and Barry Ross, the quality control engineer, have ascertained that normal rework does not bring the audio systems up to standard. Sampling shows that about 25% of the reworked audio systems will fail after extended operation within one year.

Unfortunately, there is no way to determine which reworked audio systems will fail because testing will not detect this problem. CenturySound's marketing analyst has indicated that this problem will have a significant impact on the company's reputation and customer satisfaction if the problem is not corrected. Consequently, the board of directors would interpret this problem as having serious negative implications on the company's profitability.

Wilson has included the audio system failure and rework problem in his written report that has been prepared for the upcoming quarterly meeting of the board of directors. Due to the potential adverse economic impact, Wilson has followed a long standing practice of highlighting this information.

After reviewing the reports to be presented, the plant manager was upset and said to the controller, "We can't trouble the board with this kind of material. Tell Wilson to tone that down. People cannot expect their systems to last forever."

The controller called Wilson into his office and said, "George, you'll have to bury this one. The probable failure of reworks can be referred to briefly in the oral presentation, but it should not be mentioned or highlighted in the advance material mailed to the board."

Wilson feels strongly that the board will be misinformed on a potentially serious loss of income if he follows the controller's orders. Wilson discussed the problem with Ross, the quality control engineer, who simply remarked, "That's your problem, George."

Questions

A. Identify and discuss the ethical considerations that George Wilson should recognize in deciding how to proceed in this matter. Support your answer by referring to the specific standards outlined in the *IMA Statement of Ethical Professional Practice*.

B. According to the *IMA Statement of Ethical Professional Practice*, what are the steps Wilson should take in order to resolve the situation?

Question 2F-ES08

Ambyt Inc., a manufacturer of high-value integrated control devices, became a publicly owned company through an initial public offering less than two years ago. The company had been a privately held firm for over 15 years and has retained its senior management team. The CEO recommended to the CFO that they hire an assistant to prepare the additional reports required of a public company rather than continuing to rely on the outside accounting firm that has been preparing them since the IPO. Wayne Grant, who has experience preparing SEC filings, was hired six months ago to fill this role and reports to the CFO. On July 3, Grant prepared the quarterly reports for the period ending June 30, with information from the Sales and Accounting Departments. Ambyt treats sales and administrative expenses as period expenses; these expenses average about 14% of sales. Parts of the statements are shown next.

Income Statement for Period Ending June 30

Sales	$14,321,000
Less returns and allowances	128,000
Net sales	14,193,000
Cost of goods sold	9,651,000
Gross profit	4,542,000
Selling & administrative expenses	2,024,000
Income from operations	$ 2,518,000

Partial Balance Sheet as of June 30

Current assets	
Cash	$ 269,419
Accounts receivable	2,278,444
Notes receivable	558,000
Inventories	896,000
Short-term investments	532,000
Prepaid expenses	24,222
Supplies	58,798
Total current assets	$4,616,883
Current liabilities	
Accounts payable	$1,639,000
Notes payable	580,000
Accrued wages	421,000
Taxes payable	187,000
Other liabilities	66,000
Total current liabilities	$2,893,000

On July 4, Grant learned from the shipping supervisor that a large order of control devices scheduled to be shipped on June 28 would not be ready until July 6 due to an unauthorized work stoppage by the production machinists. Later the same day, Grant learned that the manager for the Sales Department had included the sale in the June 30 report because the work stoppage was not authorized by the machinist union and therefore was beyond its control. The revenue reported for this sale was $1,250,000 with an associated cost of goods of $715,000.

With this information, Grant determined that he should change the reports he prepared for the period. He discussed this situation with the CFO. The CFO refused to consider the change, explaining that consistent earnings growth is a primary driver of share price. With Amybt shares trading at a P/E of 22, the share price would likely fall even though there was no real problem with production. The CFO stated that although production delays were not common, they had occasionally occurred throughout his years with Amybt and this was not a "big deal."

Questions

1. According to the *IMA Statement of Ethical Professional Practice*, what further steps, if any, should Wayne Grant take in resolving this situation?
2. Should the large shipment originally scheduled for June 28 be included in Ambyt's June 30 Income Statement? Explain your answer.
3. Assuming Grant revises the reports to exclude the sale from the period,
    a. Calculate the revised Income from Operations for the period ending June 30.
    b. Describe the changes that would be made to Ambyt's June 30 Balance Sheet.
    c. Explain how the revisions will impact Ambyt's Cash Flow Statement.
4. Some of Grant's colleagues have been enthusiastic about his new employer's prospects and have been considering the purchase of a large number of shares. Grant is concerned that the share price will fall because of the revised statements and has suggested that they "wait a while" before making the purchase. Discuss Grant's actions with regard to the *IMA Statement of Ethical Professional Practice* by identifying any standards that are specifically relevant and explaining why they are applicable to this situation.

Question 2F-ES09

Global Manufacturing is a Canadian company that processes a wide range of natural resources. Two years ago the company acquired Zeta Manufacturing, a raw material processing firm located in the United States. Over the last year, profits have fallen in the U.S.-based subsidiary. Laura Hammon, the manager of manufacturing accounting for Zeta Manufacturing, has been asked to identify the problems that have impaired the firm's profits.

She has reviewed the monthly production cost reports and discovered that the per unit costs have been consistently increasing over the last year. Since the subsidiary used an actual cost system, Hammon convinced the president and the production manager that a thorough assessment of each product's cost and the implementation of a standard cost system would help to solve the problem.

Within six months, Hammon installed a fully operational standard cost system for the division. After several months of using the new cost system, Hammon is perplexed by unexplainable efficiency and yield variances, which result in material inventory write-downs at the end of each month. The work-in-process account is charged with the actual input costs of direct materials and direct labor, plus a predetermined rate for normal spoilage. At the end of the month, the work-in-process account is relieved by the standard cost per unit multiplied by the number of good units produced. This leaves a balance in the account that should be consistent with the uncompleted units still in process, but when compared to a physical inventory, there is a significant shortage of product in process, resulting in a write-down of inventory.

When Hammon explained her problems to the production manager, he scoffed and said, "It's your crazy standard cost system that is messed up." The production manager says that Hammon's cost system is poorly designed and does not track product costs accurately. Hammon is convinced there is nothing wrong with the design of the standard cost system. She knows that the inventory write-downs have no effect on the production manager's compensation; however, she has heard that his bonus is partially affected by the actual amount of spoilage. She decides to further examine the provision for normal spoilage as well as the actual spoilage reported.

During the following month, she monitored the records of disposal truck traffic that left the plant at night. It would require only one truck nightly to dispose of the spoilage included in her standard cost. The records reflected an average of three disposal trucks leaving the plant each night. This unexplained traffic of disposal vehicles has caused her to be skeptical about the actual spoilage reported by the production manager.

Questions

1. Does Hammon have an ethical responsibility to determine what may explain the unusual inventory write-downs at Zeta Manufacturing? Support your answer by referring to the specific standards outlined in IMA's *Statement of Ethical Professional Practice*.
2. According to the *IMA Statement of Ethical Professional Practice*, what are the steps that Hammon should take in order to resolve the situation?

Question 2F-ES10

The government of a developing country invited several companies to bid on a project to enhance its telecommunications infrastructure. Robert James is vice president of global sales for SouthComm, a large telecommunications company based in the United States. James obtained all of the details required to bid on the project and was able to submit the bid before the deadline. A few weeks after the deadline had passed, he telephoned the deputy minister of the country to find out the status of the project. During that conversation, the deputy minister invited James to a special meeting to present SouthComm's proposal in detail. James spent several days preparing for the meeting and then traveled to the country. During the meeting, James presented the details of SouthComm's proposal for over an hour to the deputy minister and vice deputy. He then answered questions from the men for about 20 minutes. When there were no more questions, James told the deputy and vice deputy that SouthComm was extremely interested in winning the bid for the project and asked if there was anything else he could do to convince them that SouthComm was the best company to select to do the project.

The deputy and vice deputy then spoke between themselves in their native language for several minutes. Finally, the vice deputy told James that SouthComm's bid would be guaranteed to win if a commission of $1 million were paid to the country's government. James knew that this "commission" request was nothing more than a bribe and explained that such a payment would be against U.S. laws as well as SouthComm's corporate policy. The vice deputy then stood up, said good-bye, and shook James's hand.

Questions

A. Why would SouthComm have a corporate policy against these types of payments?
B. James later shared this experience with Rita Lane, who holds a similar position with a large U.S. multinational company. Lane said that such requests are commonplace in global business and that she would do it as long as that practice is acceptable in the foreign country. Do you agree with Lane's opinion?

Question 2-ES11

Morgan Company manufactures engine lubricants. During the manufacturing process, some by-products are produced that have no resale value. The by-products are considered hazardous to the environment and should be disposed of in a very specific manner, following hazardous material protocol. Morgan pays an outside company to come onsite and haul away the hazardous materials. Morgan's sales have been much lower than expected this quarter, and there is a lot of pressure to lower costs.

John Lark has worked in the company's controller's office for ten years and is very familiar with the plant floor processes. While walking the plant floor one day, he sees that one of the workers is putting the by-product in the large trash receptacle instead of placing it in the hazardous material bin. When he inquires about why that is being done, the worker explains he is following a management directive and that disposing of the by-product in the trash would save the company the money that would have to be paid to the hazardous materials company.

Questions

A. Is the management of Morgan Company acting in an ethical manner? What are some of the potential risks that Morgan Company will expose itself to by making decisions like this in order to cut costs?
B. What changes should be made to create a stronger ethical environment? What are some of the potential benefits that Morgan Company could realize by creating a more ethical corporate culture?

Part 2 Section A Answers

Answer to Question 2A-ES01

Answer A:

Among the management accountants' responsibilities are the measurement of economic events and transactions and the communication of information about them to interested parties, including management. Financial ratios are a part of this communication process that includes analysis, interpretation, and evaluation of the financial statements. Ratios display a relationship among various elements of financial data and are used to assist management in interpreting and explaining financial statements. They can be effective tools in evaluating a company's liquidity, debt position, and profitability. Financial ratios are an important part of evaluating a company's past performance and are useful in projecting its financial future.

Answer B:

1. Times interest earned $= \dfrac{\text{Income Before Income Taxes} + \text{Interest Expense}}{\text{Interest Expense}}$

   $= \dfrac{\$120{,}000 + \$20{,}000}{\$20{,}000}$

   $= 7 \text{ times}$

2. Return on total assets $= \dfrac{\text{Net Income} + \text{Interest Expense} - \text{Tax Savings}}{\text{Average Total Assets}}$

   $= \dfrac{\$72{,}000 + \$20{,}000 - (\$20{,}000 \times 0.4)}{(\$540{,}000 + \$510{,}000)/2}$

   $= 0.16 = 16\%$

3. Return on operating assets

   $= \dfrac{\text{Operating Income}}{\text{Average Operating Assets (Total} - \text{Other)}}$

   $= \dfrac{(\text{Income Before Taxes}) - (\text{Other Revenue}) + \text{Interest Expense}}{[(\text{'05 Total Assets} - \text{Other Assets}) + (\text{'04 Total Assets} - \text{Other Assets})]/2}$

   $= \dfrac{\$120{,}000 - \$60{,}000 + \$20{,}000}{[(\$540{,}000 - \$116{,}000) + (\$510{,}000 - \$114{,}000)]/2}$

   $= 0.195 = 19.5\%$

4. Return on common stockholders' equity

   $= \dfrac{\text{Net Income}}{\text{Average Common Stockholders' Equity}}$

   $= \dfrac{\$72{,}000}{(\$260{,}000 + \$217{,}000)/2}$

   $= 0.302 = 30.2\%$

5. Total debt ratio $= \dfrac{\text{Total Liabilities}}{\text{Total Assets}}$

$= \dfrac{\$280{,}000}{\$540{,}000}$

$= 0.519 = 51.9\%$

6. Total debt/equity ratio $= \dfrac{\text{Total Liabilities}}{\text{Total Stockholders' Equity}}$

$= \dfrac{\$280{,}000}{\$260{,}000}$

$= 1.077$

7. Current ratio $= \dfrac{\text{Current Assets}}{\text{Current Liabilities}}$

$= \dfrac{\$144{,}000}{\$120{,}000}$

$= 1.2$

8. Quick (acid-test) ratio $= \dfrac{\text{Cash and Short} - \text{Term Investments} + \text{Net Receivables}}{\text{Current Liabilities}}$

$= \dfrac{\$26{,}000 + \$48{,}000}{\$120{,}000}$

$= 0.617$

Answer to Question 2A-ES02

Answer A:

Third State Bank would be interested in comparative financial statements so that it could analyze trends in data and operating results. Trends are important because they may point to basic changes in the nature of the business.

Ratio analysis would give some indication of the company's short-term solvency and help Third State Bank assess the level of risk involved. The ratios also would be useful in analyzing how RCS is performing compared to industry averages and thus serve as a benchmark for comparison to other companies. Ratios reduce absolute dollar amounts to more meaningful data in order for the bank to compare ratios to prior periods, other companies, and the industry. Ratios can be used to show how well the company is being managed and to highlight areas for further investigation. If the ratios do not appear favorable compared to the company's own past and to other companies in its industry, the bank may consider adjusting the dollar level and/or the interest rate of the note or may even decide not to renew the note.

Answer B:

Calculations of selected financial ratios for Renbud Computer Services Co. are presented next.

1. Current Ratio

$$\text{Current Ratio} = \frac{\text{Current Assets}}{\text{Current Liabilities}} = \frac{\text{Cash} + \text{Net A/R} + \text{Operating Supplies}}{\text{A/P} + \text{Taxes Payable} + \text{Notes Payable}}$$

Last Year: (in '000)
$$= \frac{\$50 + \$350 + \$70}{\$150 + \$140 + \$300} = \frac{\$470}{\$590} = 0.797 \text{ to } 1$$

Two Years Ago: (in '000)
$$= \frac{\$50 + \$250 + \$60}{\$130 + \$120 + \$200} = \frac{\$360}{\$450} = 0.8 \text{ to } 1$$

2. Accounts Receivable Turnover

$$\frac{\text{A/R Turnover}}{\text{(in '000)}} = \frac{\text{Net Sales}}{\text{Average Receivables}} = \frac{\$2,500}{(\$350 + \$250)/2} = \frac{\$2,500}{\$300} = 8.333 \text{ times}$$

3. Asset Turnover

$$\frac{\text{A/R Turnover}}{\text{(in '000)}} = \frac{\text{Net Sales}}{\text{Average Total Assets}} = \frac{\$2,500}{(\$1,930 + \$1,560)/2} = \frac{\$2,500}{\$1,745} = 1.433 \text{ times}$$

4. Return on Shareholders' Equity (SE)

$$\frac{\text{Return on SE}}{\text{(in '000)}} = \frac{\text{Net Income} - \text{Preferred Dividends}}{\text{Average Common Equity}} = \frac{\$290 - \$0}{(\$940 + \$710)/2} = \frac{\$290}{\$825}$$

$$= 0.352 = 35.2\%$$

5. Debt to Equity Ratio

$$\text{D/E Ratio (in '000)} = \frac{\text{Total Current and Long-Term Debt}}{\text{Total Shareholders' Equity}}$$

Last Year: (in '000) $= \dfrac{\$990{,}000}{\$940{,}000} = 1.053 \text{ to } 1$

Two Years ago: (in '000) $= \dfrac{\$850{,}000}{\$710{,}000} = 1.197 \text{ to } 1$

6. Net Profit Margin Percentage (Return on Sales)

$$\text{Net Profit Margin Percentage (in '000)} = \frac{\text{Net Income}}{\text{Net Sales}} = \frac{\$290}{\$2{,}500} = 0.116 = 11.6\%$$

Answer C:

The difficulties and limitations of ratio analysis include these:

1. Although ratios are useful as a starting point in financial analysis, they are not an end in themselves. Ratios can be used as indicators of what to pursue in a more detailed analysis.
2. Difficulties can arise in making industry average comparisons.
   - Different companies could use different accounting methods (e.g., FIFO versus LIFO inventory valuation).
   - Even though two companies are in the same industry, they may not be comparable because they are focused on different aspects of the business. For example, two companies may be in the oil industry, but one may be primarily a marketer of oil and the other may be a refinery.
   - Companies may be conglomerates that operate in many different industries.
3. The ratios are only as good as the data on which they are based. If accounting policies are questionable, the resulting ratios would also be questionable.

Answer to Question 2A-ES03

The major sections of the statement of cash flows describe the cash flows from these areas:

- Operating activities, which involve the cash effects of transactions that enter into the determination of net income, such as cash receipts from sales and cash payments to suppliers and employees
- Investing activities, which include making and collecting loans, and obtaining and disposing of investments and long-term assets

- Financing activities, which include borrowing and repaying cash from creditors (long-term debt) and obtaining funds from owners (investments) while providing a return on their investment (dividends)

Answer to Question 2A-ES04

Answer A:

Liquidity is the ability of an asset to be converted into cash without significant price concessions. Liquidity is important to Sentech because current obligations will continue if there is a strike. Understanding the company's ability to meet its obligations even if normal cash receipts are not forthcoming would give management an indication of whether—and for how long—it could weather a strike. Lack of liquidity can limit a company's financial flexibility, making it unable to take advantage of discounts and other profitable opportunities. Liquidity problems also can lead to financial distress or bankruptcy.

Answer B:

Measures of liquidity include:
- Current ratio: Current Assets / Current Liabilities
- Quick ratio (or acid-test ratio): (Cash + Marketable Securities + Accounts Receivable) / Current Liabilities
    - The quick ratio excludes inventory and prepaid expenses from cash resources.
- Cash ratio: (Cash + Marketable Securities) / Current Liabilities
    - Only cash and securities that are easily convertible into cash are used.
- Net working capital: Current Assets – Current Liabilities
- Net working capital ratio: Net Working Capital / Total Assets
- Sales to working capital: Sales / Average Net Working Capital
- Accounts receivable turnover: Net Sales / Average Gross Receivables
    - This ratio also can be calculated in days.
- Inventory turnover: Cost of Goods Sold / Average Inventory
    - This ratio can also be calculated in days.

Answer C:

Based on the parameters set down by the controller, either the quick ratio or the cash ratio would be best. The reason that these ratios are best is because they focus on the most liquid assets, excluding prepaid expenses and inventories. During a strike, inventories would not be a source of cash. The cash ratio excludes receivables as well and would be the most conservative measure. The cash ratio would reflect the fact that the collection of receivables would be slowed during a strike.

Answer to Question 2A-ES05

Answer A:

Unit Sales	Mar	Apr	May	Jun	Jul
U.S.	70,000	80,000	75,000	65,000	65,000
Canada	50,000	50,000	60,000	45,000	35,000
Total Sales	120,000	130,000	135,000	110,000	100,000

Cash Receipts	Apr	May	Jun	
U.S.				
Units	70,000	80,000	75,000	
Price (USD)	50	50	50	
Collections	3,500,000	4,000,000	3,750,000	
Canada				
Units	50,000	50,000	60,000	
Price (CAD)	60	60	60	
USD/CAD	0.833	0.840	0.847	
Collections (USD)	2,500,000	2,521,008	3,050,847	
TOTAL RECEIPTS (USD)	6,000,000	6,521,008	6,800,847	
Disbursements:				
Labor @ 10 USD/unit	1,350,000	1,100,000	1,000,000	
Overheads	400,000	400,000	400,000	
U.S. Materials @ 5 USD/unit	675,000	550,000	500,000	
Mexican Import @ 350 MXN/unit	47,250,000	38,500,000	35,000,000	
USD/MXN	0.0885	0.0877	0.0870	
Mexican Import in USD	4,181,416	3,377,193	3,043,478	57%
Interest			500,000	
Income Taxes			1,000,000	
TOTAL DISBURSEMENTS (USD)	6,606,416	5,427,193	6,443,478	
Beginning Cash Balance	1,000,000	393,584	1,487,399	
Ending Cash Balance	393,584	1,487,399	1,844,769	

Answer B:

Chargrille is exposed to currency fluctuations in both its receipts and disbursements. Approximately 41% of the unit sales and collections relate to Canadian customers. If exchange rates of Canadian dollars to U.S. dollars were 10% higher than the forecasted amounts, collections for the quarter would be approximately $800,000 USD less. On the disbursement side, approximately 57% of the disbursements for the quarter relate to the imported parts from Mexico. If the exchange rates of Mexican pesos to USDs were 10% lower than the forecasted amounts, disbursements for the quarter would be approximately $1 million USD greater. An unfavorable variance of 10% from the budgeted exchange rates would bring the cash balance at the end of the quarter from $1.8 million USD to approximately zero.

Answer C:

1. If the spot rate (CAD/USD) on the CAD is currently 1.20 and is expected to drop steadily to 1.18 by the end of June, it will take fewer Canadian dollars to buy one U.S. dollar. Therefore, the USD is depreciating relative to the CAD.
2. If the spot rate (MXN/USD) on the Mexican peso is currently 11.0 and is expected to rise steadily to 11.5 by the end of June, it will take more Mexican pesos to buy one U.S. dollar. Therefore, the USD is appreciating relative to the MXN.

Answer D:

Chargrille can buy or sell forward currencies as a means of hedging exchange rate exposure. For example, if Adams forecasts the disbursements in pesos for April, May, and June while she is preparing the budget in March, she could purchase 47 MXN for delivery in 30 days, 38 million MXN for delivery in 60 days, and 35 million MXN for delivery in 90 days at the going forward rates for those periods, thereby locking in the exchange rate and quantifying those disbursements. Of course, during the intervening time periods, the U.S. dollar could appreciate, depreciate, or remain stable relative to the MXN. The cost of the forward market hedge can be thought of as insurance. Another option available would be the currency futures market, which allows firms to purchase or sell futures contracts on an organized exchange. Again, the costs associated with buying and selling futures contracts increase the firm's costs; however, they also can reduce the risk of sharp unexpected fluctuations in exchange rates.

Answer to Question 2A-ES06

Answer A:

1. Using the straight line method, $200 million depreciated over 10 years equals $20 million per year. Depreciation expense increases by $20 million. The purchase will decrease cash and increase gross fixed assets by $200 million. The depreciation expense will increase accumulated depreciation and decrease net fixed assets by $20 million.
2. Long-term debt increases by $75 million. Cash, which is part of current assets, also will increase by $75 million. The annual interest expense is $75 million × 10% = $7.5 million.
3. Preferred stock (part of equity) increases by $25 million. Cash, part of current assets, will increase by $25 million. The preferred dividend will increase by $25 million × 14% = $3.5 million.
4. Common stock, part of equity, will increase by $2 par × 4 million = $8 million. The common stock premium, part of Equity, will increase by $23 × 4 million = $92 million. Cash, part of current assets, will increase by $25 × 4 million = $100 million.
5. Revenues increase by $60 million, operating expenses increase by $30 million, and cash increases by $30 million.

Answer B:

The revised forecast is shown next.

Balance Sheet (thousands of dollars)			
	Original	**Changes**	**Revised**
Current assets	100,000	16,000	116,000
Fixed assets	750,000	200,000	950,000
Accumulated depreciation	200,000	20,000	220,000
Net fixed assets	550,000	180,000	730,000
TOTAL ASSETS	650,000	196,000	846,000
Current liabilities	50,000	0	50,000
Long-term debt	150,000	75,000	225,000
Shareholders' equity			
Preferred stock	50,000	25,000	75,000
Common—par	100,000	8,000	108,000
Common—premium	200,000	92,000	292,000
Retained Earnings	100,000	(4,000)	96,000
	450,000	121,000	571,000
TOTAL LIABILITIES and EQUITY	650,000	196,000	846,000

Income Statement (Thousands of Dollars)			
	Original	**Changes**	**Revised**
Revenue	2,000,000	60,000	2,060,000
Depreciation Expense	50,000	20,000	70,000
Other Expenses	1,775,000	30,000	1,805,000
Earnings Before Interest and Taxes	175,000	10,000	185,000
Interest	15,000	7,500	22,500
Taxes (40% effective rate)	64,000	1,000	65,000
Net Income	96,000	1,500	97,500
Preferred Stock Dividends	5,000	3,500	8,500
Earnings for Common Stock	91,000	(2,000)	89,000

Answer C:

Public companies are concerned about the effect on earnings for several reasons, including:

- Analysts and investors closely follow earnings and are especially concerned when they drop or do not grow as much as expected.
- Earnings growth is a factor in many valuation formulas. The firm is concerned about the market value of the common stock.

- The firm is expecting to raise $200 million to finance the expansion. Reduced earnings forecasts could result in the debt issue having a higher interest rate, the preferred stock to require a higher dividend rate, and the common stock to be issued at a lower market price.
- Estimates of sales volume growth of the new line could be provided. Growth is very important to investors in valuing the stock of a firm.
- The effect on earnings in the initial year is not indicative of the future prospects for the new line.
- The firm is experiencing a high level of certain costs (specify the types of costs as promotion, start-up, etc.) early in the product life cycle, which will be reduced in coming years. Of course, management must believe this to be true.

Answer to Question 2A-ES07

Answer 1:

a.

	Year 1	Year 2	Year 3
Revenue	100%	100%	100%
Cost of goods sold	60%	50%	60%
Gross profit	40%	50%	40%
Sales and marketing	10%	8.3%	6.7%
General and admin.	7.5%	8.3%	10%
Research and dev.	7.5%	8.3%	3.3%
Operating income	15 %	25%	20%

b.

	Year 1	Year 2	Year 3
Revenue	100%	120%	150%
Cost of goods sold	100%	100%	150%
Gross profit	100%	150%	150%
Sales and marketing	100%	100%	100%
General and admin.	100%	133%	200%
Research and dev.	100%	133%	66.7%
Operating income	100%	200%	200%

Answer 2:
Revenue
Year 2: ($24,000 − $20,000)/$20,000 = 20%
Year 3: ($30,000 − $24,000)/$24,000 = 25%

Operating income
Year 2: ($6,000 − $3,000)/$3,000 = 100%
Year 3: ($6,000 − $6,000)/$6,000 = 0%

Answer 3:
Foyle's gross profit margin 50% was comparable in year 2 to competitor 52% and industry average 50%, but Foyle has fallen to 40% in year 3. Foyle's operating income percentage 25% was the same in year 2 to competitor and industry average at 25%, but Foyle has fallen to 20% in year 3.

Foyle in year 3 has lower sales and marketing than competitor and industry average (6.7% versus 11.1% and 10.7%), but higher in general and administration (10% versus 7% and 8.9%). Foyle's research and development is substantially below both competitor and industry average (3.3% versus 8.9% and 5.4%).

Answer to Question 2A-ES08

Answer 1:

	Year 2	Year 1
Revenues	100.0%	100.0%
Cost of Goods Sold	48.4	47.5
Gross Margin	51.6	52.5
Selling Expenses	14.8	14.7
Administrative Expenses	17.5	17.5
Loss Due to Strike	3	
Interest Expense	.5	.5
Income before Taxes	18.4	19.8
Income Tax Expense	7.4	7.9
Income from Continuing Operations	11.1	11.9
Discontinued Operations	1.1	—
Net Income	12.2	11.9

Answer 2:

a. Sales increased but the gross margin percentage decreased. This could be caused by:
   - a change in the product mix.
   - a decrease in the selling price which resulted in selling more units but if the cost per unit did not change or increased, the gross margin percentage would increase.
   - an increase in the cost of goods that was not passed along to customers; sales could have increased because the competition raised its prices.

b. Selling expenses remained fairly constant as a percentage of sales. This could be caused by:
   - nearly all of the selling expenses being variable costs.
   - increased advertising to boost sales.

c. Administrative expenses remained at a constant percentage of sales. Since most of these costs are fixed, when sales rise, the costs as a percentage of sales should decrease. The constant percentage could be caused by:
   - moving outside of the relevant range of year 1's activity, causing step-fixed costs to increase.
   - poor budgeting procedures or poor cost controls that allow administrative spending in proportion to sales.

Answer 3:

Number of shares outstanding = $780,000 / $2.50 = 312,000

Book value = $7,363,200 / 312,000 = $23.60

Answer to Question 2A-ES09

Answer 1:

Knight, Inc. Summary Balance Sheet

Assets	$200 million	Debt	$60 million
		Equity	140 million
		Total Liabilities and Equity	$200 million

Day, Ltd. Summary Balance Sheet

Assets	$200 million	Debt	$120 million
		Equity	80 million
		Total Liabilities and Equity	$200 million

Knight, Inc. Summary Income Statement

EBIT	$50 million
Interest $60m × 10%	6 million
Earnings before tax	44 million
Tax at 40%	17.6 million
Net Income	$26.4 million

Day, Ltd. Summary Income Statement

EBIT	$50 million
Interest $120m × 15%	18 million
Earnings before tax	32 million
Tax at 40%	12.8 million
Net Income	$19.2 million

Answer 2:

Return on Equity

	NI	Equity	ROE
Knight, Inc.	$26.4 million	$140 million	18.86%
Day, Ltd	$19.2 million	$80 million	24.00%

Answer 3:

Day, Ltd. has higher risk, as measured by debt/equity or debt/total assets ratios. Day has higher fixed interest payments. Knight, Inc. is better able to weather a downturn in industry.

Answer 4:

Costs of financial distress include higher interest rates; inaccessibility to debt or equity finance; might have to forgo attractive projects; drop in value of equity; bankruptcy; increased intrusion by creditors; loss of customers, suppliers, employees.

Answer to Question 2A-ES10

Answer 1:

Pro Forma Income Statements and Balance Sheets (millions of dollars)

Income Statement

	Current	Pro Forma Stock (1)	Pro Forma Debt
Sales	$5,500	$5,500	$5,500
COGS	3,100	3,100	3,100
GP	2,400	2,400	2,400
SG&A	1,600	1,600	1,600
Operating Income	800	800	800
Interest Expense	100	100	130
Pretax Income	700	700	670
Income Taxes (40%)	280	280	268
Net Income	$420	$420	$402
Earnings per Share	$7.00	$6.46	$6.70

$500 million @6% = $30 million. Interest Expense for debt is $100 + $30 = $130 million
EPS – Stock: Net Income/Revised # of shares = $420/65 where 65 = 60 (current) + 5 (issued).

Balance Sheet

	Current	Pro Forma Stock (1)	Pro Forma Debt
Current Assets	100	90	82
Net Fixed Assets	3,000	3,500	3,500
Total Assets	**3,100**	**3,590**	**3,582**
Current Liabilities	50	50	50
Long-Term Debt	1,000	1,000	1,000
Common Stock:			
Par Value ($2/share)	120	130	120
Additional Paid-in Capital	1,000	1,490	1,000
Retained Earnings	930	920	912
Net Common Equity	2,050	2,540	2,032
Total Liabilities and Equity	**3,100**	**3,590**	**3,582**

¹To raise $500 million, McMullen must issue 5,000,000 shares at $100 per share. Two dollars per share is recorded in the "Par Value" account and the remaining $98/share is recorded as "Additional Paid-in Capital."

For stock at year end div of $10 million (5,000,000 shares @ $2) paid out of cash so Current Assets are $100 – $10 = $90, $10 million comes out of R/E $930–$10 = $920.

For debt interest after tax requires a payment of $18 million ($500 * 6.00% * (1 – 40%)) so Current Assets are $100 – $18 = $82 and retained earnings are $18 lower.

Answer 2:

a. Financial leverage ratio measures relation between total assets and the common equity capital. The greater the proportion of assets financed by common equity capital, the lower the financial leverage ratio. A higher financial leverage ratio enhances return on equity. The risk inherent in a change in profitability is greater when the financial ratio leverage is higher.

	Pro Forma			
	Common Stock		**Debt**	
Total assets	3,590	141.34%	Debt	3,582	176.28%
Net Common Equity	2,540			2,032	

		Stock		**Debt**
Alternate 1	Debt/	1,050	Debt/	1,550
	Equity	2,540	Equity	2,032
	=	41.34%	=	76.28%
Alternate 2	Debt/	1,050	Debt/	1,550
	Assets	3,590	Assets	3,582
	=	29.25%	=	43.27%

b. Working capital is a measure of liquidity. It is the excess of current assets over current liabilities. Working capital provides a safety cushion to creditors. It measures liquid reserve available to meet contingencies

	Current Assets		Current Liabilities		Working Capital
Common	90	less	50		40
Debt Alt	83	less	50		32

Answer 3:

Debt Covenant Test

LT Debt/Equity	49%	39%	74%
Total Debt to Equity	51%	41%	76%

Debt/equity ratios can be defined in various ways. Whether the ratio is defined as long-term debt to equity or as total debt (short- and long-term) to equity, the result is a ratio greater than 60% if debt is issued. The debt issue is, therefore, not viable.

Answer 4:
- Companies with relatively stable sales are able to take on more debt, and, therefore, more fixed charges than companies in highly cyclical industries or other business situations presenting above normal risks.
- Firms with assets that are suitable as security for loans (i.e. property and equipment) are in a better situation to use debt financing.
- A firm with relatively low operating risk, as measured by the degree of operating leverage or some other measure, is in a better position to have more debt in its capital structure.
- Firms anticipating relatively high growth rates are better able to take on more debt.
- The higher a firm's effective tax rate, the more valuable the tax deductibility (tax shield) of interest payments.
- Those firms having significant amounts of equity controlled by management may be reluctant to issue additional stock since it would dilute control. Debt would be the option if new funds need to be raised.
- Management's attitude toward risk or level of conservatism can have an influence on how much capital structure risk a firm assumes.
- Rating agency assessments of a company can have a definite impact on financial structure. For example, if a rating agency informed management that its bonds would be downgraded if it issued more debt, then the firm would most likely issue common stock if it needed to raise additional capital.
- Market conditions at a specific time have an influence over whether debt or equity is issued. Issues such as whether a firm's stock price is currently depressed or if interest rates were perceived as being either very high or very low, have an influence on the method of financing and, therefore, the capital structure.
- Maintaining financial flexibility, especially for a growth firm, is very important. That means that at any point in time a firm should not be borrowed to capacity, allowing it the option of issuing debt in the event of favorable conditions. Firms that are at their debt limit have little financial flexibility.

Part 2 Section B Answers

Answer to Question 2B-ES01

Answer A:
1. Default risk is the probability of a security issuer being unable to meet its contractual obligations of interest and principal payments. A greater default risk increases the yield because the investor is paid a premium for the default risk.

2. Marketability of a security is the ability to buy and sell the security on a secondary market and relates to the owner's ability to convert it into cash. A lower marketability increases the yield because the investor is paid a premium for the lack of marketability.
3. Maturity is the length of time remaining until a security is redeemed by the original issuer. A longer maturity means an investor has a greater exposure to risk. This risk increases the yield.

Answer B:

Type of Investment	Default Risk	Marketability	Maturity
Certificate of deposit (CD)	Default risk is that of the issuing bank failing, a probability that is low in most cases.	A poor secondary market exists for the negotiable CDs of the large money market banks.	Original maturities are short term and generally range from 30 days to one year.
U.S. Treasury bills	Default risk is negligible because the bills are guaranteed by the U.S. government.	Market activity is excellent, and transaction costs involved in the sale in the secondary market are small.	Treasury bills are auctioned weekly by the U.S. Treasury with short-term maturities of three months, six months, and one year.
Preferred stock of domestic corporations	Not applicable.	Marketability is very good for a listed issue. The realized price dimension of marketability is not as good because of the volatility of preferred stock prices.	Preferred stock has no maturity.

Answer C:

Certificates of deposit (CD) are a suitable investment for Gershenfeld in its situation. The most common denomination is $100,000, so its appeal is mostly to large investors such as Gershenfeld. CDs carry an acceptable default risk and can be purchased with the desired maturity of two months. Yields on CDs are greater than those on U.S. Treasury bills.

U.S. Treasury bills also are a suitable investment for Gershenfeld in its situation. They are the most conservative of the three types of investments being considered, having the lowest default risk and greatest marketability. However, the yield on U.S. Treasury bills would be less than the yield on CDs.

Preferred stock of domestic corporations is not a suitable investment for Gershenfeld in this situation. Such a stock purchase is generally considered a long-term investment.

Answer to Question 2B-ES02

Answer A:

An increase in long-term debt and preferred stock issues would increase Atrax's degree of financial leverage and its debt-to-equity ratio. This action has two primary effects from the stockholders' perspective:

1. The variability of earnings per share (EPS) and return on equity (ROE) will be greater, and EPS and ROE will increase at a faster rate and be at a higher level whenever the firm earns more than its cost of capital. The increased EPS will exert an upward influence on the value of Atrax's common stock.
2. The variability of EPS and ROE increases Atrax's financial risk. This increased risk exposure will exert a downward influence on the common stock value and will be reflected in a lowered price/earnings ratio.

The net effect on the price of Atrax's common stock will depend on which influence is stronger. The price of the stock probably will rise because Atrax is continuing to diversify for the purpose of reducing its business risk exposure. Therefore, investors are likely to accept the increased financial risk as long as stockholders believe that Atrax is not overusing debt and preferred stock (i.e., is not going beyond its optimal capital structure).

Answer B:

The short-term effect probably will be a decrease in the market price of Atrax's common stock. Atrax's high payout ratio coupled with its limited earnings growth means Atrax probably has attracted conservative investors dependent on dividend income. These investors probably will sell their stock due to the change in dividend policy. In addition, investors may interpret the elimination of cash dividends as a decrease in earnings.

The long-term effect probably will be an increase in the market price of the stock. The funds diverted from the payment of cash dividends will be used in the capital expansion and diversification program. This should lead to increased earnings in the future while also decreasing Atrax's business risk. Investors interested in capital gains (rather than dividend income) probably would be attracted to Atrax, which also should result in a positive effect on the market price of the stock.

Answer C:

1. Yes, Traxal would be able to maintain his current equity position of 35% if stock dividends were distributed because all stockholders will receive additional shares of stock in proportion to their current ownership interest in Atrax.
2. The probable short-term effect would be a decrease in the market price of Atrax's stock, because current investors will seek to sell their stock as a consequence of

the change in dividend policy and the implied connotations of reduced earnings. The stock dividends give no substantive value to stockholders who expect a cash dividend. However, the price of the stock may not fall as much as reducing the payout ratio to zero because some current investors may misinterpret the nature of a stock dividend or may accept the reduced cash dividends in the short-term when coupled with the hope for potential capital gains in the long-term.

The probable long-term effect would be an increase in the market price of Atrax's stock because growth-oriented investors should be attracted to Atrax for the capital gain potential. In addition, a nominal dividend payout will act as a downward stabilizer on stock price movements. Furthermore, if Atrax's diversification program is successful, the reduced business risk and increased future earnings should exert a positive influence on the stock price.

3. Proposal 2 is more likely to result in a smaller drop in the stock price than Proposal 3 in the short term due to the higher cash dividends and less negative reaction to an implied earnings decline. The long-term effect on stock prices is less certain. Proposal 3 probably would result in higher stock prices due to increased future earnings growth because all internally generated funds could be reinvested.

Answer to Question 2B-ES03

Answer A:

Alternative 1—Wasson Industries	
Adjusted basis of Dayton Plant	$4,200,000
Less: Proceeds from sale of plant to Wasson	3,000,000
Loss on sale of plant	$1,200,000
Multiply by: Applicable income tax rate[1]	40%
Decrease in income taxes	$480,000

[1] When net losses exceed net gains, the loss is treated as ordinary income for income tax purposes; thus, the 40% tax rate is used.

Determine the after-tax cash flow and apply the discount factor.

Proceeds from sale of plan to Wasson	$3,000,000
Add: Decrease in income taxes	480,000
After-tax cash flow	$3,480,000
Multiply by: Discount factor	1.00
Present value of after-tax cash flows	$3,480,000

[1] The income taxes should be recognized in the years in which the sales occur. The amount of tax is based on sales revenue less costs excluding the depreciation. The depreciation tax shield is shown separately; refer to footnote 2. The income tax charge is $780,000 [($4,200,000 − 2,250,000) × .40].

Alternative 2—Harr Enterprises
Cash flows from annual lease payments

Annual Gross Dollar Sales	Estimated Probability	Expected Value of Sales
$2,000,000	0.1	$200,000
4,000,000	0.4	1,600,000
6,000,000	0.3	1,800,000
8,000,000	0.2	1,600,000

Expected annual gross sales	$5,200,000
Multiply by: Percentage payable to Kravel	.10
Variable portion of lease payment	$520,000
Add: Fixed portion of lease payment	500,000
Before-tax cash flow from lease	$1,020,000
Less: Income tax (40%)	408,000
After-tax cash flow from lease	$612,000
Multiply by: Discount factor	2.798
Present value of after-tax cash flow from lease	$1,712,376

Depreciation tax shield

Annual depreciation	$900,000
Multiply by: Tax rate	.4
Income tax shield from depreciation	$360,000
Multiply by: Discount factor	2.798
Present value of depreciation tax shield	$1,007,280

Sale of Dayton plant (12/31/2010)

Estimated cash value of plant (12/31/2010)	$600,000
Gain or loss computation on sale of plant	
Adjusted basis 12/31/2006	$4,200,000
Less: Depreciation (900,000 × 4)	3,600,000
Adjusted basis 12/31/2006	600,000
Less: Proceeds	600,000
Gain/loss	-0-
After-tax cash flow from sale	$600,000
Multiply by: Discount factor	.552
Present value of sale of Dayton plant	$331,200

Present value of after-tax cash flows

PV of after-tax cash flow from lease	$1,712,376
PV of depreciation tax shield	1,007,280
PV of sale of Dayton plant	331,200
Total present value of after-tax cash flows	$3,050,856

[7]The depreciation charge would be included in the calculation of cost of goods sold. Thus, the recognition of the depreciation charge for income tax purposes in 2007, 2008, and 2009 would be deferred one year. The depreciation tax shield for 2007 and 2008 is $360,000 ($900,000 × .40). The depreciation recognized for income tax purposes in 2010 would be $1,800,000 which consists of the 2009 depreciation charge included in the 2010 cost of goods sold and the 2010 depreciation charge recognized in 2010 when the plant is presumably being used as a warehouse. Thus, the depreciation tax shield in 2010 is $720,000 ($1,800,000 × .40).

Alternative 3—Souvenir Items

	2007	2008	2009	2010
Revenue (70,000 × 12 × $5)	$ -0-	$4,200,000	$4,200,000	$4,200,000
Annual cash outlays	2,250,000	2,250,000	2,250,000	-0-
Annual cash flows	$(2,250,000)	$1,950,000	$1,950,000	$4,200,000
Less income taxes[1]	-0-	780,000	780,000	780,000
After-tax cash flows	$(2,250,000)	$1,170,000	$1,170,000	$3,420,000
Depreciation tax shield[2]	-0-	360,000	360,000	720,000
Salvage[3]				600,000
Net after-tax cash flows	$(2,250,000)	$1,530,000	$1,530,000	$4,740,000
Discount factors	.862	.743	.641	.552
Present value of after-tax cash flows	$(1,939,500)	$1,136,790	$980,730	$2,616,480

[3]There is no gain or loss on the sale of the plant; thus, the cash flow is equivalent to the proceeds (see Alternative 2).

Net present value of after-tax cash flows:

2007	−$1,939,500
2008	1,136,790
2009	980,730
2010	2,616,480
Total	$2,794,500

Answer B:

The additional factors Kravel Corporation should consider before making a decision regarding the disposition or use of the idle plant and equipment at the Dayton Plant include those listed next.

- Kravel should consider the risks involved for each of the alternatives. Alternative 1 is the least risky because it would be completed on January 1, 2007, whereas Alternatives 2 and 3 would involve activities through 2010.

- Kravel should consider the accuracy of the cash flow estimates and discount rates used in the cash flow analysis.
- Kravel should consider the fit between the timing of the cash flows for each alternative and the cash needs of the corporation.
- Kravel should consider the likelihood of an opportunity to resume the production of truck parts at the Dayton plant. Alternative 1 eliminates that possibility, and Alternative 2 precludes it until 2011.

Answer to Question 2B-ES04

Answer A:

Financing Plan (Dollars in Millions)

	Current Structure	Percent of Total	Funds Needed	Retained Earnings	External Sources
Debt	$175	35%	$28		$28
Preferred	50	10%	8		8
Common	275	55%	44	$15	29
Totals	$500	100%	$80	$15	$65

Financing sources will be:

New debt	$28 million
New preferred stock	8 million
Retained earnings	15 million
New common stock[1]	29 million
Total	$80 million

[1] $29 million / $58 per share = 500,000 new common shares

Answer B:

Weighted Incremental Cost of Capital

	% of Capital Structure	Cost	Weighted Cost
Debt	35%	6.00%[1]	2.10%
Preferred	10%	12.00%	1.20%
Common	55%	16.00%	8.80%
Cost of capital			12.10%

[1] Pretax 10% x (1 − Tax Rate) = 6.00%

Answer C:

1. If the corporate tax rate is increased, the after-tax cost of debt would be reduced, thereby reducing the cost of capital. In other words, the tax shield of debt becomes more valuable to the firm.
2. When the banks indicate they are raising rates, the rest of the debt market generally raises rates. The higher cost of debt will increase the overall cost of capital.

3. Beta is a measure of risk. According to the capital asset pricing model, the cost of equity is directly related to risk. As risk is reduced, the cost of equity is reduced, and, correspondingly, the overall cost of capital is reduced.
4. In general, a significant increase in the percentage of debt in the capital structure (especially in this case where the current structure is deemed optimal) results in more risk for the firm. This increases its cost of debt and its cost of equity. The increase in the cost of equity most likely will offset the fact that debt has a lower relative. The result here is that the cost of capital should increase.

Answer to Question 2B-ES05

Answer A:

Ownership Alternative	$t=0$	$t=1$	$t=2$	$t=3$	$t=4$	$t=5$
Purchase Price **(a)**	(2,000)					
Insurance **(b)**		(25)	(25)	(25)	(25)	(25)
Property Taxes **(c)**		(50)	(50)	(50)	(50)	(50)
Tax Depreciation **(d)**		660	900	300	140	
Salvage **(e)**						200
Income Tax Savings **(g)**: 40% × (−b−c+d−e)		294	390	150	86	(50)
Net Cash Flows (a+b+c+e+g)	(2,000)	219	315	75	11	75
Present Value factor @ 6%*	1.000	0.943	0.890	0.840	0.792	0.747
Present value	(2,000)	207	280	63	9	56

NPV = (1,385)

* The discount rate to be used is the after-tax cost of debt (10% × (1 − 0.4))

Lease alternative	$t=0$	$t=1$	$t=2$	$t=3$	$t=4$	$t=5$
Lease payment		(600)	(600)	(600)	(600)	(600)
Tax savings		240	240	240	240	240
Net cash flows		(360)	(360)	(360)	(360)	(360)
PV factor @ 6%*	1.000	0.943	0.890	0.840	0.792	0.747
Present value		(339)	(320)	(302)	(285)	(269)

NPV = (1,516)

*The discount rate to be used is the after-tax cost of debt (10% × (1 − 0.4)).

Conclusion: Ownership is more economic since NPV of ownership ($1,385,000) is less than NPV of leasing ($1,516,000), giving a net advantage to ownership of $131,000 on an NPV basis.

Answer B:

Accounting Standards Topic ASC 840 *Leases* (formerly Statement of Financial Accounting Standards No. 13), establishes standards of financial accounting and reporting for leases by lessees and lessors. The Statement defines a lease as an agreement conveying the right to use property, plant, or equipment (land and/or depreciable assets) usually for a stated period of time.

The criterion for classifying leases is that if at its inception a lease meets one or more of the next four criteria, the lease shall be classified as a capital lease by the lessee. Otherwise, it shall be classified as an operating lease.

a. The lease transfers ownership of the property to the lessee by the end of the lease term.
b. The lease contains a bargain purchase option.
c. The lease term is equal to 75% or more of the estimated economic life of the leased property.
d. The present value at the beginning of the lease term of the minimum lease payments, excluding executory costs such as insurance, maintenance, and taxes to be paid by the lessor, including any profit thereon, equals or exceeds 90% of the excess of the fair value of the leased property to the lessor at the inception of the lease.

In the case of the lease that Crenshaw is evaluating, criteria **a** and **b** are not met since no ownership is transferred at the end and there is no bargain purchase option. Criterion **c** is met since the lease term is equal to the 5 year life of the equipment. Criterion **d** is also met. The lease payment of $600,000 less the executory costs of insurance and property taxes results in a minimum lease payment of $525,000. The present value of this at the Crenshaw's incremental borrowing rate of 10% is $1.99 million, greater than 90% of fair value of the leased property.

The result is that Crenshaw must classify the lease as a capital lease.

Answer C:
- A lessor may be better able to take full advantage of tax benefits, such as accelerated depreciation, than the lessee who may not be a positive taxable income situation. In that case, the lessor may pass those benefits on to the lessee in the lease payment.
- A lessor may be in a better position to realize a high residual value for the equipment. That is often the case where the lessor is a manufacturer of the equipment or a dealer in the equipment as opposed to being a financial institution.
- Certain property, such as general use assets (vehicles, construction equipment, general-purpose buildings, etc.), lend themselves to leasing since the property can be sold or released after the initial term.

Although most financial analysts agree that leasing is basically a form of debt financing, firms may be able to utilize the leverage available from leasing to a greater extent than they could utilize bond financing.

Answer to Question 2B-ES06

Answer A: Issue price of each bond

Maturity value $1,000.00
PV of $1,000 due in 5 years, at 8%, compounded semiannually
= $1,000 × 0.676 = $676.00

PV of $30 paid semiannually for 5 years, compounded semiannually
 = $30 × 8.111 = $243.33
Issue price of bond = $919.33
Discount on bonds payable = $1,000.00 − $919.33 = $80.67

Answer B: How many bonds to issue

Funds needed of $15,000,000 / $919.22 per bond = 16,316 bonds

Answer C: Net after-tax cash flows per bond

	Year 0	Year 1	Year 2	Year 3	Year 4	Year 5
Issue bond	$919					
Cash interest		($60)	($60)	($60)	($60)	($60)
Bond interest		(14)	(15)	(16)	(17)	(19)
Total interest		(74)	(75)	(76)	(77)	(79)
Tax savings		29.60	30	30.40	30.80	31.60
Repay bond						(1,000)
Net cash flow	919	(30.40)	(30)	(29.60)	(29.20)	(1,028)
# of bonds	16,316	16,316	16,316	16,316	16,316	16,316
Total cash flow	$14,999,788	($496,006)	($489,480)	($482,954)	($476,427)	($16,779,374)

Answer D: Rational Investor Calculation

	Amount	PV factor	Present Value
PV of $1,000 due in 2 years @ 6% (4 periods @ 3%)	$1,000	0.888	$888.00
PV of $30 paid semiannually (4 periods @ 3%)	30	3.717	111.51
Market value of bond			$999.51

Note: Would round to $1000 with sufficient numbers in the PV factor.

Answer to Question 2B-ES07

Answer 1:

a. A merger is the combination of two or more companies in which only one firm survives as the legal entity. An acquisition is when one company acquires another as part of its overall business strategy.

b. The scenario describes a potential strategic acquisition as management was hoping to work on product mix.

c. Some of the synergies of a business combination are the economies realized where the performance of the combined firm exceeds that of its previously separate parts. There are economies of scale where the benefits of size cause the average unit cost to falls as volume increases. Acquisitions can increase sales, market share, or help a company gain market dominance. There may be other marketing and strategic benefits, or the acquisition might bring technological advance to the product table, or it may fill a gap in the product line which would enhance sales made throughout the firm. It may be possible for duplicate facilities to be eliminated after a merger or departments like marketing, accounting, purchasing, and other operations can be consolidated. The sales force may be reduced to avoid duplication of effort in a particular territory. The companies may be able to concentrate a greater volume of activity into a given facility and into a given number of people to have a more efficient utilization of resources.

Answer 2:

a. A spinoff is a form of divestiture resulting in a subsidiary or division becoming an independent company. Ordinarily, shares in the new company are distributed to the parent company's shareholders on a pro-rata basis. An equity carve-out is a public sale of stock in a subsidiary in which the parent usually retains majority control. Only the spinoff is described in the scenario above.

b. The spinoff would be if Electronics Inc were to decide to split the subsidiary off into its own separate company.

Answer 3:

a. The main types of bankruptcy are Chapter 7—which is liquidation, or the sale of assets of a firm, and Chapter 11 which is rehabilitation of an enterprise through its reorganization.

b. In distributing the proceeds to creditors, the priority in a bankruptcy proceeding is as follows:
   1. Administrative expenses associated with liquidating the property, including trustees fee and attorney fees.
   2. Creditor claims that arise in the ordinary course of the debtors business from the time the case starts to the time a trustee is appointed.
   3. Wages earned by employees within 90 days of the bankruptcy petition, limited to $2,000 per employee.
   4. Claims for contributions of employee benefit plans for services rendered within 180 days of the bankruptcy petition (limited to $2,000 per employee).
   5. Claims of customers who make cash deposits for goods or services not provided by the debtor (limited to $900 per customer).
   6. Taxes owed.
   7. Unsecured claims either filed on time or tardily filed if the creditor did not know of the bankruptcy.
   8. Unsecured claims filed late by creditors who had knowledge of the bankruptcy.
   9. Fines and punitive damages.
   10. Interest that accrues to claims after the date of the petition.

Answer to Question 2B-ES08

Answer 1:

The cost to produce the units is irrelevant, because OneCo can sell all that it produces at a market price of $16.50. The net realizable value per unit is $15.60 ($16.50 − .90).

a. The first option would decrease net income by $1,600. The net realizable value per unit sold to Gatsby is $14.00 ($14.35 − .35). In order to supply Gatsby, OneCo would be displacing sales in the regular market having a NRV of $15.60. That reduction of $1.60 per unit × 1,000 units would decrease net income by $1,600.

   Alternate solution: Normal profit per unit is $4.40 ($16.50 − $12.10). The profit per unit sold to Gatsby is $2.80 ($14.35 − $11.55). Gatsby cost is $11.55 ($4.00 + $1.30 + $2.50 + $3.40 + .35). The difference of $1.60 per unit ($4.40 − $2.80) × 1,000 units would decrease net income by $1,600.

b. The second option would increase net income by $1,100. The extra units could be sold in the regular market at a NRV of $15.60. The cost is $14.50. Thus, profits would increase by $1.10 per unit, or $1,100 in total.

   Alternate solution: Selling Price $16.50 − Cost to purchase from Zelda $14.50 − Sales commission $.90 = profit per unit $1.10. Increase in net income $1.10 @ 1,000 units = $1,100.

c. The third option would decrease income by $500. Regular business is unaffected. As explained above, the 1,000 units bought cost $14.50 each, and the NRV of the new units sold is $14.00. The net difference is .50 per unit.

   Alternate solution: Action 1 Decrease in Net Income of $1,600 + Action 2 Increase in Net Income of $1,100 = Net Decrease in Net Income of $500.

Answer 2:

a. Direct Material $4.00 + $.30 = $4.30. Direct Labor $1.30 @ 1.15 = $1.495. Variable Overhead $2.50 @ 1.15 = $2.875. Cost $12.42 ($4.30 + $1.495 + $2.875 + $3.40 + .35). Profit per unit $4.08 ($16.5 + 12.42). Market profit $4.40 ($16.50 − $12.10). Decrease in net income ($4.08 − $4.40) = −.32 @ 2,000 = decrease $640. Do not accept proposal.

b. If there is excess capacity, accept the proposal, revenue would contribute to fixed costs.

Answer 3:

Other factors to consider are: the effect on market price/competition, effect on sales force/commissions, quality of Zelda products, and follow-on Gatsby business. There may be other considerations. Some other considerations are: impact on employees; reaction of customers.

Part 2 Section C Answers

Answer to Question 2C-ES01

Answer A: Price elasticity of demand

1. Price elasticity of demand is the percentage change in the quantity demanded of a commodity relative to (divided by) the percentage change in the price of that same commodity.

Answer B:

1. If the price elasticity coefficient of a commodity is greater than 1, the demand for that commodity is classified as elastic. This indicates that the demand for the

commodity is very sensitive to changes in price. If the price elasticity coefficient of a commodity is less than 1, the demand for that commodity is classified as inelastic. This indicates that the demand for the commodity is not sensitive to a change in price. A commodity with a price elasticity of 1 is classified as having unitary elasticity.

2. There is a relationship between changes in total revenue and the price elasticity of demand that would be useful to a firm's management. If demand is elastic, a change in price will cause total revenue to change in the opposite direction. If demand is inelastic, a change in price will cause total revenue to change in the same direction. When unit elasticity exists, an increase or decrease in price will leave total revenue unchanged.

Answer to Question 2C-ES02

Answer A:

	1. Capital Intensive		2. Labor Intensive	
Selling price		$30.00		$30.00
Variable costs:				
Raw materials	$5.00		$5.60	
Direct labor	6.00		7.20	
Variable overhead	3.00		4.80	
Variable selling	2.00	16.00	2.00	19.60
Contribution margin		$14.00		$10.40

Answer B:

Candice Company would be indifferent between the two manufacturing methods at the volume (x) where total costs are equal.

$$\$16x + \$2{,}940{,}000 = \$19.60x + \$1{,}820{,}000$$
$$\$3.60x = \$1{,}120{,}000$$
$$x = 311{,}111 \text{ units}$$

Answer C:

1. Operating leverage is the extent to which a firm's operations employ fixed operating expenses. The greater the proportion of fixed expenses used to produce a product, the greater the degree of operating leverage. Thus, Candice's capital-intensive manufacturing method utilizes a greater degree of operating leverage.

    The greater the degree of operating leverage, the greater the change in operating income (loss) relative to a small fluctuation in sales volume. Thus, there is a higher degree of variability in operating income if operating leverage is high. The greater the operating leverage and the resultant variability in operating income, the greater the degree of business risk.

2. Candice should employ the capital-intensive manufacturing method if annual sales are expected to exceed 311,111 units and the labor-intensive manufacturing method if annual sales are not expected to exceed 311,111 units.

Answer D:

Candice must consider these business factors other than operating leverage before selecting a manufacturing method:

- Variability or uncertainty with respect to demand, both quantity and selling price
- The ability to produce and market the new product quickly
- The ability to discontinue the production and marketing of the new product while incurring the least amount of loss

Answer to Question 2C-ES03

Answer A:

The contribution margin is 75%[1] or $3.75 per adult admission, and $1.875 per student admission. The mix is 20% adult (30/150) and 80% student 120/150. The weighted average contribution margin (WACM) is:

$$WACM = .20\ (\$3.75) + .80\ (\$1.875) = \$2.25$$

The break-even point is fixed cost / WACM, or

$$\$33,000 / \$2.25 = 14,667 \text{ per season.}$$

[1]100% − State Fee of 10% − Variable Cost of 15%

Answer B:

The highest number to break even assumes that all admissions are students:

$$\$33,000 / \$1.875 = 17,600 \text{ per season}$$

Answer C:

The lowest number to break even assumes that all admissions are at the adult rate:

$$\$33,000 / \$3.75 = 8,800 \text{ per season}$$

Answer to Question 2C-ES04

Answer A:

Target costing is focused on market pricing or the prices of a firm's most direct competitors. The process for determining product pricing involves five steps:

1. Determine the market price.
2. Determine the desired profit.
3. Calculate the target cost at market price less the desired profit.

4. Use value engineering to identify ways to reduce product cost.
5. Use continuous improvement and operational controls to further reduce costs and increase profits.

Answer B:

The main difference between the two methods of pricing is a different starting point for determining product price. Markup pricing is based on existing costs and a desired return. The price is then determined by adding the product cost and the desired markup. This method provides little incentive to reduce costs as long as sales are profitable.

Using target costing, product prices are determined by reviewing competitive pricing and setting prices according to market strategies and positioning. Target costing moves from the existing market prices to the process of managing the product costs in order to earn a desired return. Target costing motivates process improvements. The process is intended to increase or maintain sales while increasing product profitability by reducing product costs through the elimination of non-value-added activities.

Answer C:

Calculate earnings before taxes:

Sales*	$2,528,100	
Less material and labor	1,223,400	(1,348,400 − 125,000)
Less overhead	375,000	(500,000 × .75)
Contribution	929,700	
Selling expense	250,000	
Admin expense	180,000	
Interest expense	30,000	
Earnings before taxes	$ 469,700	
*Vanilla	$53 × 10,200	540,600
Chocolate	$53 × 12,500	662,500
Caramel	$50 × 12,900	645,000
Raspberry	$50 × 13,600	680,000
		$2,528,100

Answer D:

The preferable pricing method for Kolobok is target costing as it is projected to significantly increase the return on sales from 7% to 18.6% ($469,700 / $2,528,100) while maintaining the existing sales level. Target costing also will motivate management to improve internal processes to reduce costs to further improve profitability, particularly for any product where the proposed target price is lower than the previous price. This method also will force Kolobok to be continually aware of the actions of its competitors and trends in the marketplace in order to make adjustments when needed.

Answer to Question 2C-ES05

Answer A:

The strategic advantages that Pearson Foods could realize by expanding internally through the development of new products for the low-fat, high-energy food market include these:

- The new products complement the existing product line, creating operational efficiencies and brand loyalty.
- The company would incur less debt than if it purchases another company.
- The company could capitalize on the low-fat diet trend.
- The company has management know-how in the industry.

The strategic disadvantages that Pearson Foods could realize by expanding internally through the development of new products for the low-fat, high-energy food market include these:

- New product development requires large outlays for research, new facilities, test marketing, and so on.
- New product development decreases cash availability.
- The increased debt ratio could increase the firm's risk, and thus its stock price is at risk.
- The company would incur the risk of product failure.
- It takes a long time to develop a new product and realize profits.

Answer B:

The strategic advantages that Pearson Foods could realize by expanding externally through the acquisition of Safin Bakery include these:

- The acquisition would result in immediate, quantifiable earnings and cash flows.
- The company would acquire a complete company with a proven track record and established markets.
- Managerial and technical expertise would be in place already.
- Safin's established distribution channels could provide new markets for Pearson's other products.
- The addition of Safin would diversify Pearson's product base.
- The acquisition could create synergies for both companies, accomplishing together what they could not do alone.
- Safin could create new growth possibilities for Pearson's employees.

The strategic disadvantages that Pearson Foods could realize by expanding externally through the acquisition of Safin Bakery include these:

- In order to make the acquisition, the company would have to incur a large amount of debt, which could impair its financial flexibility, debt rating, and stock price.
- Pearson lacks knowledge and experience with Safin's products.

- Safin would have to be integrated with Pearson in two years—including the computer system, the accounting system, and the culture.
- An independent operation could lead to suboptimal decisions.

Answer to Question 2C-ES06

Answer A:

Colby Quote Based on Budget Proportions

Revenue	Budget $17,050,000	Colby Quote
Direct Labor		
Hours	300,000	10,000
Rate per Hour	20	20
Total Amount	**6,000,000**	200,000
Employee Benefits	2,400,000	
Percent of Direct Labor	40%	40%
Total Amount		80,000
Tools and Equipment	1,800,000	
Percent of Direct Labor	30%	30%
Total Amount		60,000
Materials	2,000,000	200,000
Procurement and Handling	200,000	
Percent of Material Cost	10%	10%
Total Amount		20,000
Subtotal	12,400,000	560,000
Overhead	3,100,000	
Percent of Above Costs	25%	25%
Total Amount		140,000
Total Cost	$15,500,000	700,000
Pretax Profit		
Percent of Total Cost	10%	10%
Total Amount		70,000
Amount of Colby Quote		$770,000

Answer B:

Madison's performance measurement system can be expected to produce these benefits:

- Aligning the performance measurement system with the budget results in everyone working toward the same goals and targets.
- Focusing on earning a profit on each job provides incentives to managers to constantly be cost conscious.
- If the firm is profitable, employees will be able to share in the rewards. When the firm is not profitable, it does not have the expense of bonuses.

Drawbacks to such a system include these:

- If the budget is revised during the year, the firm faces the dilemma of changing the performance measures, which often upsets employees.
- Although the overall target of 10% may be reasonable, a firm such as Madison cannot expect every project to earn 10%. Focusing on all projects completed during the year may be more realistic.
- Utilizing company average percentages for various cost elements may not be appropriate for all projects. For example, some projects may utilize a significant amount of equipment (as a percentage of labor) compared to other projects. A more appropriate way to charge for major equipment may be to have a rate per day (or per hour, as appropriate) for such equipment and charge the customer based on the number of days (or hours) utilized.

Answer C:

Factors that David Burns should consider include:

- The overall workload for the firm. If there are other more profitable projects that could be undertaken, possibly this project should be turned down. If there are no other alternative projects, this one could be advantageous even though it does not show a 10% profit.
- Burns should identify the primary out-of-pocket (incremental, or marginal) costs for the project and compare them to the contract amount. If the out-of-pocket costs exceed the contract amount, the job should be rejected. If the out-of-pocket costs are less than the contract amount, Madison would receive some contribution toward fixed costs. Direct labor ($200,000), benefits ($80,000), and materials ($200,000) are the primary incremental costs in this case and amount to $480,000. This leaves $215,000 ($695,000 less $480,000) to cover other costs, most of which are primarily fixed.
- Burns should assess the importance of a relationship with Colby. If Colby is a critical customer, that would influence the decision. Also, if Colby has not been a customer before, it may be important to take the job for strategic reasons and establish a relationship, even if this first job does not meet the target profit.
- Of course, Burns will be considering the impact on his performance of accepting a project with a less-than-10% profit. However, he should place the interests of his employer above his own in making a decision on whether to accept the contract.

Answer D:

Reasons that Burns can use to justify his decision include:

- Strategic value of having Colby as a customer.
- Other more profitable opportunities were not available.
- This project involved a significant amount of material costs that are a pass-through to the customer. Therefore, the practice of adding 25% for company overhead is not totally appropriate in this case.

Answer to Question 2C-ES07

Answer 1:

a. Sunk cost is cost already incurred, and thus is irrelevant to the decision at hand.
b. Opportunity cost is the profit forgone (given up) by choosing one course of action over another. Only sunk costs are recorded as incurred, because they result from transactions. There is no accounting recording of events that could have happened (opportunity costs), so they are not recorded in the accounting system.
c. The costs to buy and clear the land ($425,000 and $72,000) would be considered sunk costs, as they have already been incurred. The annual rent that from the construction companies (averaging $5000) would be considered opportunity costs going forward, because PARKCO would have to give them up.

Answer 2:

of leases × (monthly rate − monthly cost) = monthly CM

420 × ($75 − $12) = $26,460 monthly CM

# of days × parkers/day × (daily rate − daily cost) = daily CM

20 × 180 × ($8 − $2) = $21,600 daily CM

$26,460 + 21,600 = $48,060 total CM

(30,000) fixed cost

$18,060 pretax operating income

Answer 3:

a. Honesty, Fairness, Objectivity and Responsibility.
b. Under Competence: Prepare complete and clear reports and recommendations after appropriate analysis of relevant and reliable information.
   Under Integrity: Communicate favorable as well as unfavorable information and professional judgment or opinions.

Under Credibility: Disclose fully all information that could reasonably be expected to influence an intended user's understanding of the reports, comments, and recommendations presented.

    c. Identify the steps Roberts should take to resolve this situation.

Part 2 Section D Answers

Answer to Question 2D-ES01

Answer A:

Financial risk depends on the way that Upton finances its international expansion. Financing the expansion through debt reduces the firm's solvency. Debt financing is generally riskier than equity financing because the debt must eventually be paid back. In addition, Upton should consider the effect of its financing choice on the firm's liquidity. If the firm chooses debt financing, the interest on the debt must be paid regularly, which will decrease the cash available to pay other obligations in each period. The best way to mitigate financial risk is to make sure that the firm has adequate capital reserves.

Upton's operational risk comes from the relationship between the firm's fixed and variable costs. If Upton has a high ratio of fixed costs to variable costs, the firm would be riskier because it would have to sell more units just to cover its high fixed costs and break even. By contrast, if the ratio of fixed costs to variable costs is low, Upton would face less operational risk since it would have to sell fewer units to cover its relatively low fixed costs.

Compliance risk is the risk that the firm will fail to follow laws or regulations. This risk would be very high for Upton as it expands into different countries because each country has its own set of rules for contracts, taxes, labor conditions, environmental protection, and the like.

Answer B:

The primary goal of an ERM is to align a firm's risk tolerance with its strategy by helping the firm to identify risks and choose the best ways to deal with them so that it has a better chance of achieve its goals. This process is especially important for firms that face multiple risks and cross-enterprise risks. By using an ERM, the firm should experience fewer operational surprises and losses, should make better use of its capital, and should be in a stronger position to take advantage of opportunities that become available. However, the firm should never spend more on its ERM system than the value of the benefits it expects to receive.

Answer C:

Tone at the top: It is not enough to buy a software package. The board of directors and top managers must demonstrate their commitment to integrating their ERM strategy with their decisions across all areas of the business.

Risk management philosophy and tolerance: Risk-averse, risk-neutral, and risk-seeking firms can all implement successful ERM systems. The key is for decision makers to be clear about the amount of risk that they can tolerate so that they can design an appropriate risk management strategy. Obviously, firms with a low tolerance for risk should plan to invest more energy and resources to their ERM.

Integrity and values: Strong corporate ethics can reduce the risk of agency issues between managers and their supervisors and decrease the chance that managers will try to game the system.

Scope and infrastructure: As firms become more complex and diversified, it becomes increasingly important for them to have ERM systems that integrate their departments and divisions across all aspects of the business.

Answer to Question 2D-ES02

Answer A:

Point B (late payments) should have the highest priority because the manager feels that it is likely to occur and would have a high impact on the firm. Point A (bad debt) is also highly likely, but the manager believes that the impact to the firm is fairly low. Point C (computer virus) would have a serious impact on the firm, but the manager thinks that the likelihood is low.

Answer B:

The risks of bad debt and slow payment could be avoided if the firm simply chooses not to offer credit. These risks can be reduced by running a credit check on customers or at least obtaining employment information about each credit customer, and these risks can be transferred if the firm decides to accept credit cards instead.

The risk of a computer virus destroying records could also be avoided if the firm chooses not to offer credit. The firm can reduce this risk by keeping backup records on paper or an electronic storage medium, or the firm can transfer this risk by outsourcing the record-keeping function to another firm.

Answer C:

Inherent risk is the risk that exists before any steps are taken to reduce it, whereas residual risk is the risk that remains after those steps are taken. For example, if EZ-Food extends credit to its regular customers, there is a certain amount of inherent risk that customers may not pay on time. Choosing to do credit checks on these customers will reduce this risk but will not eliminate it entirely. The risk that remains is called the residual risk.

Answer to Question 2D-ES03

Answer A:

Electronic inventory tags function as preventive controls because their high visibility may discourage thieves. These tags also function as detective/corrective controls because they sound an alarm when merchandise is removed from the store.

Surveillance equipment is designed to identify thieves, so it is primarily for detection and correction of theft. However, if the equipment is installed so that it is visible, it may also serve to prevent theft.

Answer B:

Expected Loss = Risk × Exposure = 0.05 × $1,000,000 = $50,000

Answer C:

Step 1: Expected Loss = Risk × Exposure
Step 2: Loss Reduction = Expected Loss without That Option − Expected Loss with that Option
Step 3: Net Benefit (Cost) = Loss Reduction − Cost of That Option

Option A (electronic inventory tags):
Expected Loss = 0.02 × $1,000,000 = $20,000
Loss Reduction = $50,000 − $20,000 = $30,000
Net Benefit = $30,000 − $25,000 = $5,000 net benefit

Option B (surveillance equipment):
Expected Loss = 0.01 × $1,000,000 = $10,000
Loss Reduction = $50,000 − $10,000 = $40,000
Net Benefit = $40,000 − $30,000 = $10,000 net benefit

Option C (both electronic inventory tags and surveillance equipment):
Expected Loss = 0.001 × $1,000,000 = $1,000
Loss Reduction = $50,000 − $1,000 = $49,000
Net Cost = $49,000 − ($25,000 + $30,000) = ($6,000) net cost

Answer D:

Based only on estimated benefits and costs, Buy-More should implement Option B because its net benefit is greater than for Option A or Option C.

Answer E:

- How reliable are these estimates?
- What is the firm's tolerance for risk?
- How critical is the $1,000,000 loss to Buy-More? If Buy-More is a multibillion-dollar firm, it can base its decision strictly on the estimated costs and benefits.

However, if Buy-More is small, then a $1,000,000 loss could threaten the firm's ability to achieve its goals or even its continued existence.
- If Buy-More has a low tolerance for risk and/or if the potential loss of $1,000,000 would be a severe threat, can the firm buy insurance to reduce the risk of loss even further?

Part 2 Section E Answers

Answer to Question 2E-ES01

Answer A:

Accounting rate of return. The merits of the accounting rate of return (ARR) method are that the method is relatively simple to use and easy to understand. It considers the profitability of the projects under consideration. The limitations of the ARR method include ignoring cash flows and the time value of money.

Internal rate of return. The merits of the internal rate of return (IRR) method are that it considers the time value of money and measures the true economic return of the project and productivity of the capital invested in the project. The limitations of the IRR method are that the answer is stated as a percentage rather than a dollar amount, making it more difficult to understand and explain to management. The IRR method also unrealistically assumes that cash flows are reinvested at the IRR of the project.

Net present value method. The merits of the net present value (NPV) method are that it considers the time value of money and size of the investment. The NPV method measures the true economic return of the project, the productivity of the capital investment, and the change in the organization's shareholders' wealth. The limitations of the NPV method include the assumption that all cash flows are reinvested at the discount (hurdle) rate, and it does not calculate a project's rate of return.

Payback method. The merits of the payback method are that it considers cash flows and provides a measure of the liquidity and risk of the investment. The limitations of the payback method are that it neglects the time value of money and the project's profitability.

Answer B:

Miranda Wells and Jake Richter are basing their judgment on the results of the net present value and internal rate of return calculations. These are both considered better measures because they include cash flows, the time value of money, and the project's profitability. Project B is better than Project A for both of these measures.

Answer C:

At least three qualitative considerations that generally should be considered in capital budget evaluations include:

1. Quicker response to market changes and flexibility in production capacity
2. Strategic fit and long-term competitive improvements from the project, or the negative impact to the company's competitiveness or image if it does not make the investment
3. Risks inherent in the project, business, or country for the investment

Answer to Question 2E-ES02

Answer A:

The analysis shown next yields the next after-tax incremental cash flows:

1. Period 0   ($13,200,000)
2. Period 1   4,200,000

$ Millions

			Year		
Cash Flow Element	0	1	2	3	4
Revenue		$16.0	$20.0	$20.0	$20.0
Equipment	($12.0)				
Equipment Salvage					$0.9
Equipment Removal					($1.4)
Direct Labor and Materials		($8.0)	($10.0)	($10.0)	($10.0)
Indirect Costs		($3.0)	($3.0)	($3.0)	($3.0)
Net Working Capital	($1.2)				$1.2
Total Cash Flow Before Tax	($13.2)	$5.0	$7.0	$7.0	$7.7
Cash Taxes		($0.8)	($1.6)	($1.6)	($1.4)
Net Cash Flow, After Tax	($13.2)	$4.2	$5.4	$5.4	$6.3
Memo: Calculation of Cash Taxes					
Tax Profit Before Tax and Depreciation		$5.0	$7.0	$7.0	$6.5
Tax Depreciation		($3.0)	($3.0)	($3.0)	($3.0)
Tax Profit Before Tax		$2.0	$4.0	$4.0	$3.5

3. The Period 4 operating cash flow is $5,400,000 calculated as shown next.

Revenue	$20,000,000
Direct labor and material	(10,000,000)
Indirect costs	(3,000,000)
Before tax cash flow	7,000,000
Tax effect[1]	(1,600,000)
After tax cash flow	$ 5,400,000

[1]$7,000,000 − $3,000,000 = $4,000,000 × 40% = ($1,600,000)

Answer B:

Cash flow variables with potential risks that could affect the estimates made by CAP include these:

- Volume estimates generally are subject to a high degree of estimation error due to the variety of external factors that impact the volume realized in the future. Competitive forces, consumer acceptance of the new product, and general economic conditions are just a few of the factors that could influence the ultimate demand realized for the new car by KAC, which would impact the demand for ignition system modules from CAP. Since there are a number of fixed costs, including equipment and indirect costs, deviations in volume could have a significant impact on the cash flows and the financial success of the project.
- Exchange rates are another important variable. Since CAP is a U.S. company with a cost structure consisting of U.S. dollar–denominated expenses, there is exchange risk resulting from a revenue stream in the Korean won. The net cash flows from the project in U.S. dollars will be dependent on the exchange rate in effect when each of the KRW denominated payments is received.
- Direct costs are another potential variance, given that the actual productivity of its workforce, the reliability of its manufacturing systems, and unit materials costs could vary substantially from what CAP projects. In a competitive bidding situation, there may be pressure to bid as low as possible to increase the chances for success. If the firm has used best-case assumptions for its cost structure, negative variances in the assumptions for direct costs could decrease the amount of cash flow generated from the project relative to expectations.
- The estimates for the cost of the equipment removal and the salvage value of the equipment could vary significantly as these costs will occur several years in the future and could negatively impact the expected cash flow.

Answer to Question 2E-ES03

Answer A:

The required cost per ton can be calculated as shown:

Required Fund at the End of Year 15

Amount in today's dollars	$14,000,000
Future value factor (15 years, 4%)	1.801
Required fund	$25,214,000

Value of current fund at the end of year 15

Current fund value	$ 3,000,000
Future value factor (15 years, 7%)	2.759
Value in 15 years	$ 8,277,000

Estimated additional amount needed in year 15

Required fund	$ 25,214,000
Value of current fund in 15 years	8,277,000
Additional amount needed	$ 16,937,000

Annual funding required

Additional amount needed	$ 16,937,000
FV of Annuity factor (15 years, 7%)	÷ 25.129
Annual funding required	$ 674,002

Cost per ton

Annual funding required	$ 674,002
Annual output (tons)	÷ 1,350,000
Cost per ton	$ 0.50

Answer B:

Major uncertainties and their effect on the charge per ton could include these:

- *Estimate of the cost in today's dollars for the reclamation.* Since the reclamation will not be done for 15 years, there is considerable uncertainty. The technology could change, resulting in higher or lower cost. The law or associated regulations could also change.
- *Rate of escalation of the reclamation cost.* Future cost increase levels are difficult to project.
- *Estimated earnings level of the fund.* The 15-year horizon is a long period of time. Investment returns from the equities and fixed income markets can fluctuate significantly from year to year.
- *Tax regulation changes.* Changes in tax regulations would affect the annual amount deposited to the fund because earnings could become taxable.
- *Changes in mine output.* Total output could be different and/or the yearly amounts may not be uniform as projected.

Answer C:

Changes in tax regulations could affect the analysis in these ways:

1. If amounts collected for reclamation and deposited in external funds were taxable,
   - GML would have to charge its customers more each year.
   - The charge per ton would initially be adjusted by dividing the amount by (1 − Tax Rate) and offsetting that by an amount equal to the present value of the tax benefit in 15 years when reclamation occurs and a tax benefit is received.

2. If the earnings on the fund were taxable,
   - The charge per ton would have to increase to offset the tax payments.
   - GML may want to communicate to the trustee that it should be more aggressive (i.e., take more risk) so it earns higher pretax returns.
   - GML may want the trustee to invest in tax exempt instruments. This decision should take into account the yields of tax exempt versus taxable instruments.

Answer to Question 2E-ES04

Answer A:

The table shows the net present value of each of the alternatives.

	Time	Amount	14% PV Factor	Present Value
Vendor A				
Initial investment	0	$4,000,000	1.000	$4,000,000
Annual cash outflow	1 – 6	500,000	3.889	1,944,500
NPV				**$5,944,500**
Vendor B				
Initial investment	0	$1,000,000	1.000	$1,000,000
Replacement	3	1,250,000	0.675	843,750
Annual cash outflow	1 – 6	750,000	3.889	2,916.750
NPV				**$4,760,500**
Vendor C				
Annual cash outflow	1 – 6	$1,400,000	3.889	5,444,600
NPV				**$5,444,600**

Answer B:

Ultra Comp should select Vendor B. It is the optimal choice from a financial point of view as it meets the requirements at the lowest cost. Since the decision has already been made to implement a new security system, the issue is to decide on a system that meets the requirements at the lowest cost.

Answer C:

Sensitivity analysis is a tool to test the impact of changing investment assumptions on the resulting net present values. The method helps determine the "sensitivity" of outcomes to changes in the parameters. It shows how the output of the model depends on the input of the model.

Answer D:

Nonfinancial factors that Ultra Comp should consider prior to making a recommendation include these:

- Vendor A technology may be more effective in the long term even though it is the highest-cost solution. However, there is a risk involved in the fact that this is new technology and may not prove effective.

- Vendor B technology is known to be effective and should be satisfactory for the near term. However, there is uncertainty in the long term.
- Since Vendor C is a nationally recognized leader, it may be in a better position to manage the security of Ultra Comp, especially as new developments arise.
- Ultra Comp should review the management capability and the financial stability of each of the vendors.
- Ultra Comp should contact previous clients of each of the vendors to determine their level of satisfaction with the quality and customer service of each vendor.

Answer to Question 2E-ES05

Answer A:

Sales

(a) Units	(b) Probability	(c) Weighted (a) × (b)
20,000	15%	3,000
22,000	20%	4,400
25,000	30%	7,500
26,000	20%	5,200
28,000	15%	4,200
Expected value		**24,300**

Unit selling Price = $110

Revenue = $110 × 24,300 =	$2,673,000
Total Variable Cost $45 × 24,300 =	(1,093,500)
Fixed Costs	(600,000)
Depreciation on New Equipment	(350,000)
Earnings Before Taxes	629,500
Taxes @ 30%	(188,850)
Net Income	440,650
Add back Depreciation	350,000
Annual Cash Flow, Years 1–9	$790,650
PV Annuity Factor (14%, 9 years)	4.946
PV of Annual Cash Flows	$3,910,555
Add Working Capital Recovery, Year 10	1,290,650
PV Factor, 14%, Year 10	0.270
PV of Year 10 Flows	$348,476
Initial Period Costs: Capital Investment	(3,500,000)
Working Capital	(500,000)
NPV	$259,031

Answer B:

NPV for Each Possibility

Unit Sales	20,000	22,000	25,000	26,000	28,000
Revenue @ $110	$2,200k	$2,420k	$2,750k	$2,860k	$3,080k
Variable Cost @ $45	900	990	1,125	1,170	1,260
Fixed Cost	600	600	600	600	600
Pretax Cash Flow	$700k	$830k	$1,025k	$1,090k	$1,220k
Times (1 – 0.3)	490	581	717.5	763	854
Depreciation Shield	105	105	105	105	105
After-Tax Cash Flow	595	686	822.5	868	959
PV Annuity Factor	4.9464	4.9464	4.9464	4.9464	4.9464
PV, Annual Cash Flow, 1 – 9	$2,943k	$3,393k	$4,068k	$4,293k	$4,744k
Year 10 Flow	1,095	1,186	1,322	1,368	1,459
PV Factor	0.2697	0.2697	0.2697	0.2697	0.2697
PV Year 10	295	320	357	369	393
Initial Costs	4,000	4,000	4,000	4,000	4,000
NPV	($762k)	($287k)	$425k	$662k	$1,137k
Result	Neg.	Neg.	Pos.	Pos.	Pos.
Probability	15%	20%	30%	20%	15%

Shortcut method:

PV of Inflows = $3,500k + 500k − 500k × 0.270 = $3,865 for Break-Even

Annual Break-Even Flow $4,000,000 / 5.216 = $740,989

600,000 × .7 = 420,000; 350,000 × .3 = 105,000

$740,989 + $420,000 − $105,000 = $1,055,989 Total After-Tax Break-Even CM

$65 Pretax CM × .7 = $45.50 After-Tax CM

$1,055,989 / $45.50 Unit CM = 23,209 Units

35% Probability of Selling < 22,000 Units, 65% Probability of Selling > 22,200 Units

Answer C:

Techniques or methods that can be used to factor risk into a capital budget analysis are:

Sensitivity Analysis

Sensitivity analysis is a technique used to test the sensitivity of net present value (NPV) to a change in one or more input variable. A variable is changed by specified amounts or percentages, and the resulting NPV is calculated to get a picture of how sensitive NPV is to that variable. This method gives the analyst a feel for the riskiness of a project and points to the sensitive variables that he or she may want to investigate further to obtain more accurate estimates or to hedge the risk in certain cases.

Risk-Adjusted Discount Rates

This method recognizes the fact that there is a relationship between risk and return. Projects with higher-than-average levels of risk should earn higher-than-average returns in order to compensate for the risk. This results in using the company's cost of capital to evaluate projects of average risk to the firm and requiring projects with significantly higher risk to earn higher returns. Those projects determined to be less risky than average can be evaluated using discount (hurdle) rates less than the average cost of capital. Since risk cannot be measured precisely, the incremental adjustments above or below the average cost of capital are in many cases judgmental, but at least an attempt to balance risk and return is made.

Certainty Equivalent

The certainty equivalent method is one that also attempts to reflect the risk return relationship. Using this method, the expected cash flows are adjusted to reflect their risk. In this manner, those cash flow elements that are perceived to be riskier (e.g., unit sales levels in a very competitive market) are adjusted to reflect that risk while other cash flows that are perceived to have minimal risk (e.g., property taxes on a building) have correspondingly different adjustments. Since risk is accounted for by adjusting the cash flows, the resulting certainty equivalent cash flows are discounted at the risk-free rate. With this method, as with others, the adjustments are generally made utilizing judgment.

Break-Even Analysis

Break-even analysis is a somewhat simplistic way to attempt to get a handle on the risk of a project. Using this method, the analyst determines which cash flow variable (generally revenue) is most uncertain, then models the project's NPV and determines the value of the variable in question (say, revenue) that produces an NPV of zero. The analyst then determines the likelihood that the break-even revenue level will be met or exceeded. Variables other than revenue also can be analyzed in this way.

Simulation

Monte Carlo simulation, which grew out of work on the mathematics of casino gambling, ties together sensitivities and input variable probability distributions. The first step is to specify the probability distribution of each uncertain cash flow variable. This information is input to a computer program, which then chooses at random a value for each uncertain variable, based on its probability distribution. The value selected for each uncertain variable then is used along with the other input assumptions to determine the net cash flows for each year and the resulting project NPV. This process is repeated hundreds of times, and the resulting NPVs are plotted to make up a probability distribution, which may be plotted to visually show the distribution. The primary advantage of this method is that it shows the range of outcomes along with their associated probabilities rather than merely a point estimate of NPV.

Decision Trees

A decision tree is a tool used to help the analyst choose between several courses of action. The method is especially useful in more complex capital budget situations where there are alternative courses of action. For example, if a firm was analyzing a venture involving first performing research and development and then having to decide on the basis of the outcome of the R&D whether to proceed to build a facility to manufacture a product, a decision tree could be helpful. It provides a structure within which the analyst can lay out options and investigate the possible outcomes of choosing those options. This helps to form a picture of the decision points and their potential outcomes. A probability is assigned to each potential outcome. From each decision point, branches of the tree lead to possible outcomes. Each of these possible outcomes produces an expected value for NPV along with a probability. Those values are weighted to see if the project is worth initiating. An advantage of this method is that it forces decision makers to identify the probable outcomes and determine what they would do if the alternative outcomes occurred.

Answer to Question 2E-ES06

Answer A:

$500,000 + $3,500,000 + $100,000 + $100,000 + $50,000 = $4,250,000 million.

Answer B:

The scenario tells us that the after tax operating income is $1,200,000. We find the depreciation expense by dividing the building cost into the depreciation period: $3,500,000/20 = $175,000 annual depreciation expense.

Assuming that interest on the mortgage is not considered when we discount a cash flow, or it is included in (taken out to arrive at) the $1.2 million, and there is no change in working capital, we can calculate the cash flow in three ways:

1. Simply add the $1,200,000 and the $175,000 to get $1,375,000.
2. Find total net income:
   $1,200,000 After-Tax Operating Income / (1 − .35) = $1,846,150 Taxable Income

The tax on this is $646,154, getting us back to $1,200,000 net income. Add back the $175,000 depreciation to get $1,375,000.

3. Use depreciation tax shield: Start with the $1,846,154 taxable income. Adding the $175,000 depreciation, we get before tax cash flow of $2,021,154. The tax on this is $707,404, but the depreciation tax shield is $61,250, resulting in $1,375,000 cash flow.

Answer C:

The factor for a five-year annuity at 12% from our table is 3.605. So the value of five years of cash flow is $4,956,875. But the store will open, and cash flows will start one year after spending the zero period costs, so this value needs to be discounted one more year, to $4,425,781.

The NPV is $4,425,781 − $4,250,000 = $175,000.

Answer D:

Yes, Right-way should build the store. The positive NPV (even ignoring values past five years) will add to the value of the company. The benefit of the future cash flows is greater than the costs to open to the store.

Answer E:

Sensitivity analysis shows how much small changes in the inputs affect the decision. Especially if we had a computer, we could try other assumptions about the store's forecast after tax operating income, the input with the most uncertainty. The costs of construction also may be underestimated, even the tax rate and the hurdle rate may possibly change over the next five years. How much will these have to change to turn a successful, positive NPV store into an unsuccessful, negative NPV store?

Answer to Question 2E-ES07

Answer 1:

1. The net present value is calculated as follows:

New packaging process equipment	$210,000 × 1.00	$(210,000)
Sale of existing packaging equipment	$ 75,000 × 1.00	75,000
Tax benefit from sale	$ 34,000 × .9090	30,906
Depreciation tax shield—new	$ 42,000 × .4 × 3.791	63,689
Loss of annual tax shield—old	$ 40,000 × .4 × 3.170	(50,720)
Annual after-tax savings 10%@ 5 year	$ 36,000 × 3.791	<u>136,476</u>
Net present value		$ 45,351

Annual depreciation on old equipment $200,000/5 = $40,000

Book value at end of first year $200,000 − $40,000 = $160,000

Loss on sale of old equipment:

        Sale price $75,000

        Book value 160,000   ($85,000)

Tax benefit = $85,000 × 40% tax rate $34,000

Annual depreciation on new equipment $210,000/5 = $42,000

Answer 2:

The net present value at 10%, the firm's cost of capital, is positive. A positive NPV indicates that the project earns more than the firm's cost of capital, and thus should be accepted.

Answer 3:

Nonfinancial and behavioral factors that could cause the company to change the investment decision made solely on the basis of financial terms include:

- Charleson's bonus may be negatively affected by the decision to replace the packaging equipment with the new technology, since the sale yields a short-term accounting loss of $85,000. Such a loss may cause the Central Division to miss its profit targets, and Charleson to miss his bonus.
- What kind of a warranty will the new equipment have? Since the technology is new, there may be some risk of it not working reliably.
- There will be a learning curve and therefore increased training costs.

Answer 4:

a. A profit-based compensation system such as Bell Company's may not lead to optimal decisions because it is based on accounting profit, which does not necessarily capture the changes in the company's value. Also it is focused only on the short term.

b. A better alternative would be a system that is based on market value. This would align the company's goal of maximizing shareholder value with the manager's goal of maximizing his or her bonus, and focus on long term results.

Answer to Question 2E-ES08

Answer 1:

a.& b. The Capital Asset pricing Model (CAPM) when used in an investment analysis context postulates that the return on an investment should be at least equal to the risk-free rate plus a risk premium. The risk premium is based on the risk (volatility) of the investment relative to the overall market (as measured by beta) times the incremental return on the market above the risk-free rate. The model can be expressed as follows;

$$\text{Required Return} = r_f + (r_m - r_f) \times \beta$$

Where:

r_f = risk-free rate

r_m = return on the market

β = the beta value for the investment, a measure of risk

For the various projects:
Project A: Required return = 4% + (14% − 4%) x 1.4 = 18%

Since the internal rate of return (IRR) of 16% is less than the required 18%, the project should be **REJECTED**.

Project B: Required return = 4% + (14% − 4%) × 1.6 = 20%

Since the IRR of 18% is less than the required 20%, it should be **REJECTED**.

Project C: Required return = 4% + (14% − 4%) × 0.7 = 11%

Since the IRR of 12%, is greater than the required 11%, it should be **ACCEPTED**.

Project D: Required return = 4% + (14% − 4%) × 1.1 = 15%

Since the IRR of 17%, is greater than the required 15%, it should be **ACCEPTED**.

The capital asset pricing model allows firms (users) to assess the size of risk premium necessary to compensate for bearing risk. It is a way to estimate the required rate of return on a security or investment. Once the required return has been determined it lets the user know if the expected return from the investment is sufficient to warrant acceptance of the investment.

Answer 2:

Capital rationing is where funds are limited to a fixed dollar amount and must be allocated among competing projects.

Answer 3:

a. Beta = Measure of a stock's volatility in relation to market.

Market beta = A stock that moves > market, beta > 1; if < market, < 1.

High beta stocks are riskier but potential for higher returns and vice versa.

b. Factors that have an influence on the beta value for a project include:
- The industry that the division undertaking the project is in and its risk characteristics.
- Experience the division has with similar projects, if any.
- Ability of the division to realize estimated returns on projects in the past.
- Strength of the management team of the division.
- Level of competition expected.
- The geographical location of the project. Certain countries are more risky to operate in than others.
- The degree to which the project involves new technology or unproven operating conditions.

Answer to Question 2E-ES09

Answer 1:

The weighted average cost of capital for the firm can be computed as follows.

	Market Value	Proportion	Cost
Bonds	$10,400,000[1]	0.26	5.0[3]
Common Stock	$29,600,000[2]	0.74	14.0[4]
Totals	$40,000,000	1.00	

[1] $10,000 \times 1040.00 = \$10,400,000$.

[2] $2,000,000 \times \$14.80 = 29,600,000$.

[3] $Price = \$1040.00 = \dfrac{92 + 1000}{(1 + k_d)}$

So, $k_d = \dfrac{1092}{1040} - 1 + 5\%$

[4] $k_e = D_1 + g = 1.48 = 0.04 = 14\%\ P_0\ 14.80$

$WACC = 0.26 \times 0.05(1 - 0.3) + 0.74 \times 0.14 = 11.27\%$

Answer 2:

a. The ranking of projects based on the net present value, which is the preferred criterion, is as follows.

Project	Initial Outlay	IRR	NPV
E	$240,000	16.50%	$22,500
A	$450,000	17.00%	$18,800
C	$262,000	16.20%	$9,800
B	$128,000	19.50%	$2,300
F	$160,000	11.10%	–$900
D	$180,000	10.50%	–$7,000

So, the firm should accept projects E, A, C and B. The reason for using the NPV is that this criterion maximizes the value of the firm while using the IRR can give misleading results.

b. Since there is a capital constraint, the projects need to be ranked based on the profitability index, as follows.

Project	Initial Outlay	IRR	NPV	PI[1]
E	$240,000	16.50%	$22,500	0.094
A	$450,000	17.00%	$18,800	0.042
C	$262,000	16.20%	$9,800	0.037
B	$128,000	19.50%	$2,300	0.018
F	$160,000	11.10%	–$900	–0.006
D	$180,000	10.50%	–$7,000	–0.039

[1] Profitability index = NPV / Initial Outlay.

The firm should accept projects E and A which use $690,000 and provides the highest NPV per dollar invested.

Answer 3:

The weighted average cost of capital cannot be used to evaluate the project because it is not in the same line of business as the firm's current operations. It is likely that the project would alter the firm's business risk in which case using the weighted average cost of capital would be inappropriate. The firm should use a project-specific hurdle rate that reflects the project's systematic risk.

Answer 4:

a. Based on the CAPM, the project's hurdle rate $= 0.05 + 0.10 \times 1.5 = 20\%$.
The project's net present value is:

$$NPV = ((\$60{,}000 \times .833) + (\$80{,}000 \times .694 + (\$80{,}000 \times .579) +$$

$$(\$80{,}000 \times .482)) - \$200{,}000 = -\$9620.00$$

Since the NPV is negative the project should be rejected.

b. Profitability index = NPV / Initial Investment $= -9.620/200{,}000 = -0.0481$

The profitability index scales the net present value by the initial investment on the project and provides an estimate of the project's NPV per dollar invested. In this case the project generates a negative NPV of 4.81 cents per dollar invested.

Answer 5:

a. The project's payback period $= 2 + 60 / 80 = 2.75$ years.
Based on the threshold payback period that the firm uses it would accept the project because the firm recovers its initial investment in less than 3 years.

b. The project should be rejected because it has a negative NPV. The payback period leads to a suboptimal decision because it ignores the time value of money. The payback period also ignores the cash flows in later years but in this case even with year 4's net cash flows the project's NPV remains negative.

Part 2 Section F Answers

Answer to Question 2F-ES01

Answer A:

The overarching principles identified in the *IMA Statement of Ethical Professional Practice* that should guide the work of a management accountant are honesty, fairness, objectivity, and responsibility.

Answer B:

If the controller were to manipulate the revenue in accordance with the implied wishes of the chief executive officer, these standards would be violated:

Competence

- Perform professional duties in accordance with relevant laws, regulations, and technical standards.

Integrity

- Mitigate actual conflicts of interest, regularly communicate with business associates to avoid apparent conflicts of interest. Advise all parties of potential conflicts.
- Refrain from engaging in any conduct that would prejudice carrying out duties ethically.
- Abstain from engaging in or supporting any activity that might discredit the profession.

Credibility

- Communicate information fairly and objectively.
- Disclose all relevant information that could reasonably be expected to influence an intended user's understanding of the reports, analyses, or recommendations.
- Disclose delays or deficiencies in information, timeliness, processing, or internal controls in conformance with organization policy and/or applicable law.

Answer C:

To resolve this situation, the controller should follow Sterling's policy for resolving ethical issues. If there is no policy or the policy does not resolve the situation, the controller should consider:

- Discussing the issue with the immediate supervisor unless the supervisor is involved, in which case the issue should be presented to the next higher level. If the CEO is the controller's immediate supervisor, the acceptable reviewing authority may be the audit committee or the board of directors. Communication with those outside the organization is not appropriate unless there is a clear violation of the law.
- Having a confidential discussion of the issues with an IMA ethics counselor or other impartial advisor and may consult an attorney to discuss legal obligations and rights concerning the ethical conflict.

Answer to Question 2F-ES02

Answer A:

The standards from the *IMA Statement of Ethical Professional Practice* that specifically relate to Alex Raminov and the situation at Carroll Mining and Manufacturing are these:

Competence

- Perform professional duties in accordance with relevant laws, regulations, and technical standards. It appears that CMMC is not in compliance with the relevant laws and regulations regarding the dumping of toxic materials; at a minimum, Raminov has an obligation to report this situation to higher authorities in the company.

Confidentially

- Keep information confidential except when disclosure is authorized or legally required. This standard may or may not relate to the CMMC situation, depending on the requirements of the environmental regulations in effect in the jurisdiction where CMMC is operating. Raminov may be required by law to disclose the information.

Integrity

- Refrain from engaging in any conduct that would prejudice carrying out duties ethically.
- Abstain from engaging in or supporting any activity that might discredit the profession.
- If Raminov does not report the apparent illegal dumping to those in authority at CMMC, his behavior would not be considered ethical under these standards, and his lack of action would discredit the profession.

Credibility

- Communicate information fairly and objectively.
- Disclose all relevant information that could reasonably be expected to influence an intended user's understanding of the reports, analyses, or recommendations.
- Disclose delays or deficiencies in information, timeliness, processing, or internal controls in conformance with organization policy and/or applicable law.
- All of these standards make it clear that Raminov has an obligation to act objectively in this matter and report the situation to those in authority at CMMC. The risks and exposures of illegal dumping should be disclosed in the financial reports that Raminov is preparing.

Answer B:

Initially, Raminov should follow CMMC's policy regarding the resolution of an ethical conflict. If there is no policy or the policy does not resolve the issue, he should consider the courses of action recommended in the *IMA Statement of Ethical Professional Practice*.

Since Raminov's immediate supervisor appears to be involved in the dumping situation, he should submit the issue to the next higher level. If the situation is not satisfactorily resolved, Raminov should approach successive levels of authority (e.g., chief financial officer, audit committee, board of directors). He can also contact an IMA ethics counselor or other impartial advisor to discuss possible courses of action.

Raminov should consult an attorney regarding his legal obligations and rights in this ethical conflict.

Answer C:

It is not considered appropriate for Raminov to inform authorities or individuals not employed or engaged by CMMC unless he believes there is a clear violation of the law. In discussions with his attorney, Raminov should clarify his obligations under the law. If CMMC does not take action after Raminov has informed the appropriate in-house authorities, he may be obligated to inform the regulatory agency involved. He should not under any circumstances anonymously release this information to the local newspaper.

Answer to Question 2F-ES03

Answer A:

The standards from the *IMA Statement of Ethical Professional Practice* that specifically relate to Amy Kimbell and the situation at Hi-Quality Productions are these:

Competence

- Provide decision support information and recommendations that are accurate, clear, concise, and timely.
- Recognize and communicate professional limitations or other constraints that would preclude responsible judgment or successful performance of an activity.
- Amy Kimbell has an ethical conflict because she has been told to keep quiet about errors she has discovered in the original budgeting process. The incorrect data used make the decision support data provided suspect and the decisions made based on that data risky.

Integrity

- Refrain from engaging in any conduct that would prejudice carrying out duties ethically.
- Abstain from engaging in or supporting any activity that might discredit the profession.
- Amy Kimball has an ethical conflict as she has an obligation to disclose the errors in the budgets presented but has been told not to. If she does not correct the situation, she will not be carrying out her duties ethically and therefore will discredit her profession.

Credibility

- Communicate information fairly and objectively.
- Disclose all relevant information could reasonably be expected to influence an intended user's understanding of the reports, analyses, or recommendations.
- It is clear that the budget committee has not been objective in its presentation of information and therefore has distorted the decisions based on that information. Kimbell should correct the information so that future expectations are realistic.

Answer B:

Initially, Kimbell should follow Hi-Quality Productions' policy regarding the resolution of an ethical conflict. If there is no policy or the policy does not resolve the issue, she should consider the courses of action recommended in the *IMA Statement of Ethical Professional Practice*.

Kimbell should present her findings to her immediate supervisor. If her immediate supervisor is involved in the incorrect budgeting situation or if the supervisor takes no action, she should submit the issue to the next higher level. If the situation is not satisfactorily resolved, Kimbell should approach successive levels of authority (e.g., chief financial officer, audit committee, board of directors). She can also contact an IMA ethics counselor or other impartial advisor to discuss possible courses of action. Kimbell should consult an attorney regarding her legal obligations and rights in this ethical conflict.

Answer to Question 2F-ES04

Answer A:

The standards from the *IMA Statement of Ethical Professional Practice* that specifically relate to John Morgan and the situation at Pro-Kleen are these:

Competence

- Perform professional duties in accordance with relevant laws, regulations, and technical standards.

Integrity

- Refrain from engaging in any conduct that would prejudice carrying out duties ethically.
- Abstain from engaging in or supporting any activity that might discredit the profession.

Credibility

- Communicate information fairly and objectively.
- Disclose all relevant information that could reasonably be expected to influence an intended user's understanding of the reports, analyses, or recommendations.

Answer B:

Initially, Morgan should follow Pro-Kleen's policy regarding the resolution of an ethical conflict. If there is no policy or the policy does not resolve the issue, he should consider the courses of action recommended in the *IMA Statement of Ethical Professional Practice*.

Since Morgan's immediate supervisor appears to be involved in the situation, he should submit the issue to the next higher level. If the situation is not satisfactorily resolved, Morgan should approach successive levels of authority (e.g., chief financial officer, audit committee, board of directors). He can also contact an IMA ethics counselor or other impartial advisor to discuss possible courses of action. Morgan should consult an attorney regarding his legal obligations and rights in this ethical conflict.

Answer to Question 2F-ES05

Answer A:

Management accountants should not condone the commission of unethical acts by others within their organizations. It is stated that the low-quality, low-size estimates sought by Jefferson were unethical business practices. Therefore, Charlene White should take action to resolve this situation. Specific standards that relate to this situation include these:

Competence

- Perform professional duties in accordance with relevant laws, regulations, and technical standards.

Integrity

- Mitigate actual conflicts of interest, regularly communicate with business associates to avoid apparent conflicts of interest. Advise all parties of any potential conflicts.
- Refrain from engaging in or supporting any activity that might discredit the profession.

Credibility

- Communicate information fairly and objectively.
- Disclose fully all relevant information that could reasonably be expected to influence an intended user's understanding of the reports, analyses, or recommendations.

Answer B:

Initially, White should follow UFP's policy regarding the resolution of an ethical conflict. If there is no policy or the policy does not resolve the issue, she should consider the courses of action recommended in the *IMA Statement of Ethical Professional Practice.*

Since White's immediate supervisor appears to be involved in the situation, she should submit the issue to the next higher level. If the situation is not satisfactorily resolved, White should approach successive levels of authority (e.g., corporate chief financial officer, audit committee, board of directors). She can also contact an IMA ethics counselor or other impartial advisor to discuss possible courses of action. White should consult an attorney regarding her legal obligations and rights in this ethical conflict.

Answer C:

The performance evaluation system directly affected performance at the Allegheny Division. The employees were paid bonuses on the basis of profitability but had no control over revenue because of the transfer pricing that was negotiated elsewhere. The division should be evaluated as a cost center only. The evaluation criteria should include quality standards that must be met in order to preclude the behavior exhibited.

Answer to Question 2F-ES06

Answer A:

Under *competence,* Spencer has a responsibility to "maintain an appropriate level of professional competence." He must perform his duties in accordance with relevant laws, regulations and technical standards (e.g., FASB No. 5, *Accounting for Contingencies*).

Under *confidentiality,* he must keep information confidential except when disclosure is authorized or legally required and inform his subordinates of the same requirement. He must refrain from using or appearing to use confidential information for unethical or illegal advantage personally.

Under *integrity,* Spencer must "avoid actual or apparent conflicts of interest and advise all appropriate parties of any potential conflict." He must also "refrain from engaging in any activity that would prejudice his ability to carry out his duties ethically." He should also "refrain from engaging in any activity that would discredit the profession."

Finally, under *credibility,* Spencer must "communicate information both fairly and objectively." He should "disclose fully all relevant information that could reasonably be expected to influence an intended user's understanding of the reports and recommendations presented."

Answer B:

According to the *IMA Statement of Ethical Professional Practice* Spencer should first follow the established policies of the organization he is employed by in an effort to resolve the ethical dilemma. If such policies do not exist or are not effective, he should follow the steps as outlined in "Resolution of Ethical Conflict."

First, he should discuss the problems with his immediate superior except when it appears the superior is involved. Since his superior is the chief financial officer, who gave him the instructions to ignore the situation and not consider the financial ramifications of nondisclosure, he should proceed to the next higher level, which is the chief executive officer of GRQ Company. If this step is not successful in solving the dilemma, he should proceed up the chain of command, which in this case would appear to be the board of directors of GRQ.

However, he should note that except where legally prescribed, communication of such internal problems should not be discussed with authorities or individuals not employed or engaged by the organization.

Spencer should clarify relevant ethical issues by confidential discussion with an objective advisor (e.g., IMA ethics counselor) to obtain a better understanding of possible courses of action. He should consult his own attorney as to his legal obligations and rights concerning the ethical conflict.

According to the provisions of the Sarbanes-Oxley Act of 2002 (SOX), employees are to be provided with a means to report such matters to top management of the organization. When deemed appropriate, they may report these matters to the appropriate external parties (e.g., the Securities and Exchange Commission,

Justice Department, Environmental Protection Agency, etc.) as the matter dictates. Candidates should be given some credit for being aware of this provision made by SOX.

Answer to Question 2F-ES07

Answer A:

According to the *IMA Statement of Ethical Professional Practice*, Wilson in this situation has a responsibility to demonstrate:

- *Competence* by preparing complete and clear reports and recommendations after appropriate analyses of relevant and reliable information.
- *Confidentiality* by refraining from disclosing confidential information acquired in the course of their work except when authorized, unless legally obligated to do so.
- *Integrity* by communicating unfavorable as well as favorable information and professional judgments or opinions as well as refraining from engaging in or supporting any activity that would discredit the profession.
- *Objectivity* by communicating information fairly and objectively and disclose fully all relevant information that could reasonably be expected to influence an intended user's understanding of the reports, comments, and recommendations presented.

Answer B:

Wilson should first discuss this matter with his superior, the controller, unless his superior is involved; in that case, he should go to the next managerial level. If a satisfactory solution cannot be reached with his superior, Wilson should move up the chain of command. Unless his superior is involved, Wilson should inform his superior when he goes to higher levels of management. If his superior is the chief executive officer, Wilson should go to an acceptable reviewing authority, such as the audit committee, executive committee, board of directors. Wilson can clarify ethical issues by having a confidential discussion with an objective advisor (e.g., an IMA ethics counselor) to determine a possible course of action. He may also consult with his own attorney. If Wilson is unable to resolve the ethical dilemma, there may be no other course than to resign and submit an informative memorandum to an appropriate representative of the organization.

Answer to Question 2F-ES08

Answer 1:

According to the *IMA Statement of Ethical Professional Practice*, Resolution of Ethical Conflict, Mr. Grant should "submit the issue to the next management level," and he should inform his direct supervisor.

Answer 2:

Revenue for a manufacturing company is usually properly recognized when the product is delivered. The product was not delivered during the period, and the revenue cannot be recognized during the period. The reason for the delay in delivery has no bearing on the timing of the revenue recognition.

Answer 3:

a. The entry for Sales will be decreased by the $1,250,000 sale amount. The entry for Cost of Goods Sold will decrease by $715,000, resulting in a net adjustment of –$535,000 to the Income from Operations entry. The Income from Operations will be $1,982,400. The Selling Expenses and Administration Expenses are period expenses and are not affected by the timing of the sale.
b. Accounts Receivable will decrease by the amount of the sale, to $1,028,444. Inventories will rise by only the cost of goods amount of $715,000, not the full sales amount.
c. The income statement change will be accompanied by changes to the Inventory and Accounts Receivable entries on the balance sheet. The Cash Flow statement entries for Changes in Inventory and Changes in Accounts Receivable will be altered (as will the Net Income entry if using the indirect method to construct the statement). Entries to Income Taxes Payable will also be altered.

Answer 4:

According to the *IMA Statement of Ethical Professional Practice*, Mr. Grant has an ethical responsibility to keep the information confidential and refrain from using the information for unethical or illegal advantage. Although he has not divulged any confidential information, he has used that information to provide an unethical and illegal advantage to his colleagues. He has behaved unethically, and perhaps illegally, if he meets the SEC's definition of an "insider."

Answer to Question 2F-ES09

Answer 1:

Yes, under the standards of *competence* and *objectivity* Hammon must "maintain an appropriate level of professional competence" to analyze the nature of the technical problem. She must also prepare "complete and clear reports" to management, and after appropriate analysis, report to them "relevant and reliable information" about what she believes may explain the inventory unusual inventory write-downs.

The standard of professional *competence* requires Hammond to determine what may explain the write-down based on available information. It also requires members to "perform their professional duties in accordance with relevant laws, regulations and technical standards" and to "prepare complete and clear reports and recommendations after appropriate analysis of relevant and reliable information has been performed."

Under the standard of *integrity*, she needs to refrain from either actively or passively subverting the attainment of the organization's legitimate and ethical objectives. Under objectivity, she would have a responsibility to communicate the information she found fairly and objectively.

Answer 2:

According to the *IMA Statement of Ethical Professional Practice*, Hammon should follow the guidelines established by the organization to resolve such ethical dilemmas. If such do not exist, or if they fail to resolve the dilemma, she should follow the chain of command by going to her immediate superior, which in this case would appear to be the division controller. If this is not successful, she should proceed up the chain of command until the dilemma is resolved. This would include the CEO of the division as well as the controller of Canadian parent company.

She should not disclose the nature of such problems unless it is legally prescribed to anyone who is not an employee or one who is engaged by the organization. Hammon should clarify the relevant ethical issues by confidential discussion with an objective advisor (e.g., the IMA Ethics Counseling Service) to obtain a better understanding of possible courses of action. She should consult her own attorney as to her legal obligations and rights concerning the ethical conflict. However, in this case, since a distortion of the financial statements or a similar situation does not appear to exist, this step may not be necessary.

Finally, if the ethical conflict exists after exhausting all level of internal review, she may have no other recourse on significant matters than the resign from the organization and submit an informative memorandum to an appropriate representative of the organization. Depending the nature of the overall nature and extent of the ethical conflict, it may also be appropriate to notify other parties. (Doing so seems necessary in this situation, since external fraudulent financial reporting does not appear to exist.)

Answer to Question 2F-ES10

Answer A:

SouthComm may have a corporate policy against these types of payments because such a policy is in alignment with the Foreign Corrupt Practices Act (FCPA). The FCPA forbids any U.S. company doing business overseas to pay bribes to a foreign government for obtaining contracts or business. Firms or any of their representatives who violate the FCPA are subject to both civil and criminal penalties. The "commission" mentioned in this scenario is not a commission but would be classified as a bribe. So, in addition to being unethical, the bribe in this scenario would also be illegal.

Answer B:

Lane is assuming that as long as a practice such as this is done on a regular basis, that would make it acceptable. However, that is not the case. The FCPA forbids U.S.

companies from paying bribes to obtain business—regardless of the local laws or customs.

Answer to Question 2F-ES11

Answer A:

No, Morgan Company is not acting in an ethical manner. Knowingly disposing of hazardous materials without taking necessary precautions is unethical and also may be illegal. If discovered by individuals outside the company, the long-term effect on the company's reputation as well as the environment would significantly outweigh any short-term cost savings that the company may realize.

Answer B:

Morgan Company should consider these changes:

- Set a strong tone from the top regarding ethical behavior. A strong and consistent message from top management often has a noticeable effect on the corporate culture and employee behavior.
- Create an ethics code of conduct and have regular training sessions for all employees to ensure that they are all aware of the company's ethics policies.
- Establish a process for employees to report possible ethics violations, such as a whistleblower framework. This process also could be in place for employees who wish to seek advice on possible questionable issues.
- Reexamine the company's budget to ensure that it is reasonable and that favorable results can be achieved without resorting to unethical behavior.

Creating a more ethical corporate culture could result in many benefits for Morgan Company, some of which include:

- A more positive organizational culture.
- Lower turnover rate among employees.
- Higher employee productivity.
- Improved business reputation in the community.
- Improvements in business and financial performance.

Answers to Section Practice Questions

Section A: Financial Statement Analysis

Question 2A1-AT01

Topic: Basic Financial Statement Analysis

Gordon has had the following financial results for the last four years:

	Year 1	Year 2	Year 3	Year 4
Sales	$1,250,000	$1,300,000	$1,359,000	$1,400,000
Cost of goods sold	750,000	785,000	825,000	850,000
Gross profit	$500,000	$515,000	$534,000	$550,000
Inflation factor	1.00	1.03	1.07	1.10

Gordon has analyzed these results using vertical common-size analysis to determine trends. The performance of Gordon can **best** be characterized by which one of the following statements?

- ☐ **a.** The common-size gross profit percentage has decreased as a result of an increasing common-size trend in cost of goods sold.
- ☐ **b.** The common-size trend in sales is increasing and is resulting in an increasing trend in the common-size gross profit margin.
- ☐ **c.** The common-size trend in cost of goods sold is decreasing, which is resulting in an increasing trend in the common-size gross profit margin.
- ☐ **d.** The increased trend in the common-size gross profit percentage is the result of both the increasing trend in sales and the decreasing trend in cost of goods sold.

Explanation: The correct answer is: **a.** The common-size gross profit percentage has decreased as a result of an increasing common-size trend in cost of goods sold.

Gross profit percentage is calculated as shown:

Gross Profit Percentage = (gross profit) / (sales)
Gross Profit Percentage in Year 1 = $500,000 / $1,250,000 = 40%
Gross Profit Percentage in Year 2 = $515,000 / $1,300,000 = 39.6%
Gross Profit Percentage in Year 3 = $534,000 / $1,359,000 = 39.3%
Gross Profit Percentage in Year 4 = $550,000 / $1,400,000 = 39.3%

The decrease in gross profit percentage is caused by an increasing common-size (percent of sales) trend in cost of goods sold.

Question 2A1-AT02

Topic: Basic Financial Statement Analysis

In assessing the financial prospects for a firm, financial analysts use various techniques. An example of vertical, common-size analysis is

- ☐ a. an assessment of the relative stability of a firm's level of vertical integration.
- ☐ b. a comparison in financial ratio form between two or more firms in the same industry.
- ☐ c. advertising expense is 2% of sales.
- ☐ d. comparison in financial form between two or more firms in different industries.

Explanation: The correct answer is: **c.** advertising expense is 2% of sales.

Vertical analysis looks at all items in the income statement (sales adjustments, expenses, gains, losses, other revenues, and taxes) and includes a column that shows these items as a percentage of sales. This approach allows the analyst to compare the income statements of companies of different sizes, since the comparison will be done on a percentage basis rather than on an absolute dollar basis.

Question 2A1-AT03

Topic: Basic Financial Statement Analysis

When preparing common-size statements, items on the balance sheet are generally stated as a percentage of _____ and items on the income statement are generally stated as a percentage of _____.

- ☐ a. total assets; net sales
- ☐ b. total shareholders' equity; net income
- ☐ c. total assets; net income
- ☐ d. total shareholders' equity; net sales

Explanation: The correct answer is: **a.** total assets; net sales.

Common-size balance sheets express all assets, liabilities, and equities as a percentage of the balance sheet footing (total assets). Common-size income statements express all sales adjustments, expenses, gains, losses, other revenues, and taxes as a percentage of sales.

Question 2A1-LS01
Topic: Basic Financial Statement Analysis

Which of the following statements is **true** regarding common-size statements?
- ☐ **a.** Common-size statements can be used to compare companies of different sizes.
- ☐ **b.** Common-size statements indexed over two years for two companies, with both showing a 10% increase in profits, show that both companies would make equally attractive investments.
- ☐ **c.** Horizontal common-size statements can be made only for companies with at least ten years of operational data.
- ☐ **d.** All of the above.

Explanation: The correct answer is: **a.** Common-size statements can be used to compare companies of different sizes.

Common-size statements alone showing a 10% increase in profits for two companies do not indicate that both are equally attractive investments. One of the companies may have shown an increase in profits from $10 to $11, while the other may have shown an increase in profits from $1,000,000 to $1,100,000. Horizontal common-size statements do not require ten years of data.

Question 2A1-LS02
Topic: Basic Financial Statement Analysis

A common-size statement is helpful
- ☐ **a.** for figuring out how assets are allocated.
- ☐ **b.** for determining the next investment the company should make.
- ☐ **c.** for considering whether to buy or sell assets.
- ☐ **d.** in comparing companies of different sizes.

Explanation: The correct answer is: **d.** in comparing companies of different sizes.

A common-size statement shows each major section of the financial statement valued at 100%, with its elements as percentages of the total, and is helpful when comparing companies of different sizes and when making comparisons from one year to another within the same company.

Question 2A2-CQ01
Topic: Financial Ratios

Broomall Corporation has decided to include certain financial ratios in its year-end annual report to shareholders. Selected information relating to its most recent fiscal year is provided next.

Cash	$10,000
Accounts receivable	20,000
Prepaid expenses	8,000
Inventory	30,000
Available-for-sale securities	
At cost	9,000
Fair value at year-end	12,000
Accounts payable	15,000
Notes payable (due in 90 days)	25,000
Bonds payable (due in 10 years)	35,000
Net credit sales for year	220,000
Cost of goods sold	140,000

Broomall's working capital at year-end is

- a. $40,000.
- b. $37,000.
- c. $28,000.
- d. $10,000.

Explanation: The correct answer is: **a.** $40,000.

The term *working capital* as used by accountants is calculated by subtracting current liabilities from current assets.

Working Capital = Current Assets − Current Liabilities

Current assets include cash, accounts receivable, prepaid expenses, inventories, and available-for-sale securities. (Available-for-sale securities are carried at fair value, not cost.)

Current Assets = $10,000 + $20,000 + $8,000 + $30,000 + $12,000 = $80,000

Current liabilities include accounts payable and notes payable due in 90 days.

Current Liabilities = $15,000 + $25,000 = $40,000

Working Capital = $80,000 − $40,000 = $40,000

Question 2A2-CQ02
Topic: Financial Ratios

Birch Products Inc. has the following current assets:

Cash	$250,000
Marketable securities	100,000
Accounts receivable	800,000
Inventories	1,450,000
Total current assets	$2,600,000

If Birch's current liabilities are $1,300,000, the firm's

- ☐ **a.** current ratio will decrease if a payment of $100,000 cash is used to pay $100,000 of accounts payable.
- ☐ **b.** current ratio will not change if a payment of $100,000 cash is used to pay $100,000 of accounts payable.
- ☐ **c.** quick ratio will decrease if a payment of $100,000 cash is used to purchase inventory.
- ☐ **d.** quick ratio will not change if a payment of $100,000 cash is used to purchase inventory.

Explanation: The correct answer is: **c.** quick ratio will decrease if a payment of $100,000 cash is used to purchase inventory.

The quick ratio is calculated as follows:

Quick Ratio = (Cash + Marketable Securities + Account Receivables) / (Current Liabilities)

Current Assets = (Cash + Marketable Securities + Receivables)

The quick ratio could be expanded as shown:

Quick Ratio = [(Cash + Marketable Securities + Receivables) − Inventories − Prepayments] / (Current Liabilities)

The purchase of inventory for cash will decrease the numerator of the quick ratio formula without affecting the current liabilities in the denominator. This will result in a decrease in the quick ratio.

Question 2A2-CQ08

Topic: Financial Ratios

Lowell Corporation has decided to include certain financial ratios in its year-end annual report to shareholders. Selected information relating to its most recent fiscal year is provided next.

Cash	$10,000
Accounts receivable (end of year)	20,000
Accounts receivable (beginning of year)	24,000
Inventory (end of year)	30,000
Inventory (beginning of year)	26,000
Notes payable (due in 90 days)	25,000
Bonds payable (due in 10 years)	35,000
Net credit sales for year	220,000
Cost of goods sold	140,000

Using a 365-day year, compute Lowell's accounts receivable turnover in days.

- ☐ a. 26.1 days
- ☐ b. 33.2 days
- ☐ c. 36.5 days
- ☐ d. 39.8 days

Explanation: The correct answer is: **c.** 36.5 days.

The accounts receivable turnover in days is calculated as shown:

Accounts Receivable Turnover in Days = (365 days) / (Accounts Receivable Turnover per Year)

Accounts Receivable Turnover per Year = (Net Credit Sales for Year) / (Average Accounts Receivable Balance for Year)

Average Accounts Receivable Balance for Year = (Beginning Balance + Ending Balance) / 2

Average Accounts Receivable Balance for Year = ($20,000 + $24,000) / 2

Average Accounts Receivable Balance for Year = $44,000 / 2 = $22,000

Turnover per Year = $220,000 / $22,000 = 10 Times

Turnover in Days = 365 Days / 10 Times per Year = 36.5 days

Question 2A2-CQ14

Topic: Financial Ratios

Cornwall Corporation's net accounts receivable were $68,000 and $47,000 at the beginning and end of the year, respectively. Cornwall's condensed income statement is shown next.

Sales	$900,000
Cost of goods sold	527,000
Operating expenses	175,000
Operating income	198,000
Income tax	79,000
Net income	$119,000

Cornwall's average number of days' sales in accounts receivable (using a 365-day year) is

- ☐ a. 8 days.
- ☐ b. 13 days.
- ☐ c. 19 days.
- ☐ d. 23 days.

Explanation: The correct answer is: **d.** 23 days.

The average number of days in accounts receivable is calculated as shown:

Average Number of Days in Accounts Receivable
= (# Days in Year) / (Accounts Receivable Turnover per Year)

Accounts Receivable Turnover per Year
= (Net Credit Sales for Year) / (Average Accounts Receivable Balance for Year)

Average Accounts Receivable Balance for Year = (Beginning Balance + Ending Balance) / 2

Average Accounts Receivable Balance for Year = ($68,000 + $47,000) / 2

Average Accounts Receivable Balance for Year = $115,000 / 2 = $57,500

Accounts Receivable Turnover per Year = $900,000 / $57,500
= 15.65 Times per Year

Average Number of Days in Accounts Receivable = 365 days / 15.65 Times
= 23 Days

Question 2A2-CQ21
Topic: Financial Ratios

Marble Savings Bank has received loan applications from three companies in the auto parts manufacturing business and currently has the funds to grant only one of these requests. Specific data, shown next, have been selected from these applications for review and comparison with industry averages.

	Bailey	Nutron	Sonex	Industry
Total sales (millions)	$4.27	$3.91	$4.86	$4.30
Net profit margin	9.55%	9.85%	10.05%	9.65%
Current ratio	1.82	2.02	1.96	1.95
Return on assets	12.0%	12.6%	11.4%	12.4%
Debt/equity ratio	52.5%	44.6%	49.6%	48.3%
Financial leverage	1.30	1.02	1.56	1.33

Based on this information, select the strategy that should be the **most** beneficial to Marble Savings.

- ☐ **a.** Marble Savings Bank should not grant any loans as none of these companies represents a good credit risk.
- ☐ **b.** Grant the loan to Bailey as all the company's data approximate the industry average.
- ☐ **c.** Grant the loan to Nutron as both the debt to equity ratio and degree of financial leverage are below the industry average.

☐ d. Grant the loan to Sonex as the company has the highest net profit margin and degree of financial leverage.

Explanation: The correct answer is: **c.** Grant the loan to Nutron as both the debt to equity ratio and degree of financial leverage are below the industry average.

The debt to equity ratio and the degree of financial leverage both measure an organization's risk. The lower the debt to equity ratio, the lower the risk. Similarly, the lower the degree of financial leverage, the lower the risk. In the case of Nutron, both the debt to equity ratio and the degree of financial leverage measures are below industry averages. Therefore, it is the least risky of the three choices.

Question 2A2-CQ29
Topic: Financial Ratios

The following information concerning Arnold Company's common stock was included in the company's financial reports for the last two years.

	Year 2	Year 1
Market price per share on December 31	$60	$50
Par value per share	10	10
Earnings per share	3	3
Dividends per share	1	1
Book value per share on December 31	36	34

Based on the price/earnings information, investors would **most likely** consider Arnold's common stock to

☐ a. be overvalued at the end of year 2.

☐ b. indicate inferior investment decisions by management in year 2.

☐ c. show a positive trend in growth opportunities in year 2 compared to year 1.

☐ d. show a decline in growth opportunities in year 2 compared to year 1.

Explanation: The correct answer is: **c.** show a positive trend in growth opportunities in year 2 compared to year 1.

The company's P/E (price/earnings) ratio increased from year 1 to year 2. The P/E ratio is calculated by taking the market price per share and dividing it by the earnings per share.

P/E Ratio = (Market Price per Share) / (Earnings per Share)

P/E Ratio, Year 1 = $50 / $3 = $16.67

P/E Ratio, Year 2 = $60 / $3 = $20

Since the P/E ratio is increasing from year 1 to year 2, it is showing a positive trend in growth opportunities in year 2 compared to year 1.

Question 2A2-CQ30

Topic: Financial Ratios

Devlin Inc. has 250,000 shares of $10 par value common stock outstanding. For the current year, Devlin paid a cash dividend of $3.50 per share and had earnings per share of $4.80. The market price of Devlin's stock is $34 per share. Devlin's price/earnings ratio is

- ☐ a. 2.08
- ☐ b. 2.85
- ☐ c. 7.08
- ☐ d. 9.71

Explanation: The correct answer is: **c.** 7.08.

The P/E ratio is calculated by taking the market price per share and dividing it by the earnings per share.

P/E Ratio = (Market Price per Share) / (Earnings per Share)

P/E Ratio = $34 / $4.80 = 7.08

Question 2A3-CQ01

Topic: Profitability Analysis

For the year just ended, Beechwood Corporation had income from operations of $198,000 and net income of $96,000. Additional financial information is given next.

	January 1	December 31
7% bonds payable	$95,000	$77,000
Common stock ($10 par value)	300,000	300,000
Reserve for bond retirement	12,000	28,000
Retained earnings	155,000	206,000

Beechwood has no other equity issues outstanding. Beechwood's return on shareholders' equity for the year just ended is

- ☐ a. 19.2%.
- ☐ b. 19.9%.
- ☐ c. 32.0%.
- ☐ d. 39.5%.

Explanation: The correct answer is: **a.** 19.2%.

Return on shareholders' equity is calculated as shown:

Return on Shareholders' Equity = (Net Income − Preferred Stock Dividends) / (Average Shareholders' Equity)

Shareholders' Equity = Common Stock + Reserve for Bond Retirement + Retained Earnings

Average Shareholders' Equity = (Beginning Balance + Ending Balance) / 2

Average Shareholders' Equity = ($300,000 + $12,000 + $155,000
     + $300,000 + $28,000 + $206,000) / 2

Average Shareholders' Equity = ($1,001,000) / 2 = $500,500

Since there are no preferred stock dividends, return on shareholders' equity = $96,000 / $500,500 = 0.192, or 19.2%.

Question 2A3-AT01

Topic: Profitability Analysis

For a given level of sales and holding all other financial statement items constant, a company's return on equity (ROE) will

- ☐ **a.** decrease as its total assets increase.
- ☐ **b.** increase as its debt ratio decreases.
- ☐ **c.** decrease as its cost of goods sold as a percentage of sales decrease.
- ☐ **d.** increase as its equity increases.

Explanation: The correct answer is: **a.** decrease as its total assets increase.

To analyze ROE, use the DuPont model for return on investment (ROI) and multiply it by the leverage factor. This would appear as:

DuPont Model ROI = Net Income / Sales × Sales / Average Assets

Leverage Factor = Assets / Equity

ROE = DuPont Model ROI × Leverage Factor

ROE = Net Income / Sales × Sales / Average Assets × Assets / Equity

All other things being equal, the return on equity will decrease as total assets increase.

ROE will decrease as the debt ratio decreases.

As cost of goods sold as a percentage of sales decreases, profit will increase along with ROE.

As the level of equity increases, ROE will decrease.

Question 2A3-LS01

Topic: Profitability Analysis

BDU Company has net income of $500,000 and average assets of $2,000,000 for the current year. If its asset turnover is 1.25 times, what is its profit margin?

- ☐ **a.** 0.25
- ☐ **b.** 0.31

☐ c.   0.36
☐ d.   0.2

Explanation: The correct answer is: **d.** 0.2

Profit Margin = Net Income / Sales

Calculate sales by rearranging the next formula:

Asset Turnover = Sales / Assets

Sales = (Asset Turnover) (Assets)

Sales = (1.25) ($2,000,000) = $2,500,000

Profit Margin = $500,000 / $2,500,000 = 0.2

Question 2A3-LS05

Topic: Profitability Analysis

Which of the following must be considered in measuring income?

I. Estimates regarding future events.

II. Accounting methods used by the company.

III. The degree of informative disclosure about results of operations.

IV. Different needs of users.

☐ a.   I and II only

☐ b.   II and III only

☐ c.   I, II, III, and IV

☐ d.   I, II, and IV only

Explanation: The correct answer is: **c.** I, II, III, and IV.

All of the listed items must be considered in measuring income.

Question 2A3-LS09

Topic: Profitability Analysis

In the last fiscal year, LMO Company had net sales of $7,000,000, a gross profit margin of 40%, and a net profit margin of 10%. What is its cost of goods sold?

☐ a. $4,200,000

☐ b. $6,300,000

☐ c. $2,800,000

☐ d. $700,000

Explanation: The correct answer is: **a.** $4,200,000.

Calculate gross profit by rearranging the next formula:

Gross Profit Margin = Gross Profit / Net Sales

Gross Profit = (Gross Profit Margin) (Net Sales)

Gross Profit = (40%) ($7,000,000) = $2,800,000

Calculate cost of goods sold by rearranging the next formula:

Gross Profit = Sales − Cost of Goods Sold

Cost of Goods Sold = Sales − Gross Profit

Cost of Goods Sold = $7,000,000 − $2,800,000 = $4,200,000

Question 2A3-LS10

Topic: Profitability Analysis

An increase in the gross profit margin for a merchandising firm indicates that the firm

- ☐ **a.** is increasing its revenues.
- ☐ **b.** is decreasing its fixed costs.
- ☐ **c.** is doing a better job of managing cost of sales.
- ☐ **d.** has been managing its quality control better, which results in fewer returns.

Explanation: The correct answer is: **c.** is doing a better job of managing cost of sales.

An increase in the gross profit margin indicates that the firm is doing a better job of managing cost of sales.

Question 2A4-LS01

Topic: Special Issues

Which of the following are elements of earnings quality?

I. Management's discretion in choosing from among accepted accounting principles

II. Management compensation in relation to net earnings

III. The degree to which assets are maintained

IV. The effect of cyclical and other economic forces on the stability of earnings

- ☐ **a.** I, III, and IV only
- ☐ **b.** I and III only
- ☐ **c.** II and IV only
- ☐ **d.** I, II, III, and IV

Explanation: The correct answer is: **a.** I, III, and IV only.

The basic factors of earnings quality are management and accountants' discretion in choosing accounting principles, the degree to which maintenance of assets has been provided for, and the effect of cyclical and other economic forces on the stability of earnings.

Question 2A4-LS02

Topic: Special Issues

Which of the following statements is true?

- ☐ a. Economic profits are accounting profits minus explicit costs.
- ☐ b. Economic profits are accounting profits minus implicit costs.
- ☐ c. Accounting profits are economic profits minus implicit costs.
- ☐ d. Accounting profits are economic profits minus explicit costs.

Explanation: The correct answer is: **b.** Economic profits are accounting profits minus implicit costs.

Economic profits are the ability to make more than normal profits. Economic profits are calculated by subtracting implicit costs, such as opportunity costs, from accounting profits.

Question 2A4-LS03

Topic: Special Issues

Which of the following statements is true?

- ☐ a. Financial statements need not make adjustments for inflation, as earnings automatically reflect the higher prices.
- ☐ b. Financial statements generally make adjustments for inflation, so earnings may be clearly represented over time.
- ☐ c. Financial statements make adjustments for inflation every year and state the inflation rate for the year in the footnotes of the annual report.
- ☐ d. Financial statements generally do not make adjustments for inflation, so earnings may be significantly compounded over time.

Explanation: The correct answer is: **d.** Financial statements generally do not make adjustments for inflation, so earnings may be significantly compounded over time.

Question 2A4-LS04

Topic: Special Issues

A European company provides annual reports for U.S. investors purchasing ADRs of the company's stock in the United States. The company reports €1,500,000 net income. The exchange rate between the euro and the U.S. dollar is €1.19/$1. Which of the following statements is true?

- ☐ a. Annual statements sent to U.S. investors will show net income as €1,500,000.
- ☐ b. Annual statements sent to U.S. investors will show net income as $1,260,504.

☐ **c.** Annual statements sent to U.S. investors will show net income as $1,785,000.

☐ **d.** Annual statements sent to U.S. investors will show net income as $1,500,000.

Explanation: The correct answer is: **a.** Annual statements sent to U.S. investors will show net income as €1,500,000.

Financial statements generally do not make adjustments for foreign currency exchange rates, as this would show wild fluctuations due to the exchange rate rather than company performance.

Section B: Corporate Finance

Question 2B1-AT05

Topic: Risk and Return

Using the capital asset pricing model (CAPM), the required rate of return for a firm with a beta of 1.25 when the market return is 14% and the risk-free rate is 6% is

☐ **a.** 7.5%.

☐ **b.** 14.0%.

☐ **c.** 16.0%.

☐ **d.** 17.5%.

Explanation: The correct answer is: **c.** 16.0%.

The formula for the CAPM is:

$$K_e = R_f + \beta (K_m - R_f)$$

where:
K_e = required rate of return
R_f = risk-free rate (such as the return on U.S. Treasury bills or Treasury bonds)
β = beta coefficient for the company
K_m = return on a market portfolio

$K_e = 0.06 + (1.25)(0.14 - 0.06) = 0.06 + (1.25)(0.08)$
$K_e = 0.06 + 0.10 = 0.16$, or 16%

Question 2B1-AT06

Topic: Risk and Return

The expected rate of return for the stock of Cornhusker Enterprises is 20%, with a standard deviation of 15%. The expected rate of return for the stock of Mustang

Associates is 10%, with a standard deviation of 9%. The stock that would be considered riskier is

- a. Mustang, because the coefficient of variation is higher.
- b. Cornhusker, because the standard deviation is higher.
- c. Cornhusker, because the coefficient of variation is lower.
- d. Mustang, because the return is lower.

Explanation: The correct answer is: **a.** Mustang, because the coefficient of variation is higher.

The coefficient of variation can be used to measure relative risk. It is calculated by dividing the standard deviation by the expected return.

Coefficient of variation = $\sigma / \overline{R}$

where:

σ = standard deviation
$\overline{R}$ = expected return

Coefficient of variation for Mustang = 0.09 / 0.1 = 0.9
Coefficient of variation for Cornhusker = 0.15 / 0.2 = 0.75

Therefore, the stock of Mustang is riskier than the stock of Cornhusker, because its coefficient of variation is higher.

Question 2B2-LS04

Topic: Long-Term Financial Management

Which of the following statements about correlation and return variability **best** describes a portfolio with a limited number of stocks representing different industries?

- a. Low correlation and low portfolio return variability
- b. Low correlation and high portfolio return variability
- c. High correlation and high portfolio return variability
- d. High correlation and low portfolio return variability

Explanation: The correct answer is: **a.** Low correlation and low portfolio return variability.

Having fewer stocks in a portfolio representing different industries is more likely to show low correlation and low portfolio return variability. The probability that individual stocks in different industries move up and down in value at the same time or at the same rate is low.

Question 2B2-LS05

Topic: Long-Term Financial Management

If a firm's goal is to keep portfolio risk low, the **best** strategy would be to include

- ☐ **a.** investments with low betas and highly correlated returns.
- ☐ **b.** investments with high betas and low correlated returns.
- ☐ **c.** diversified investments with high betas.
- ☐ **d.** diversified investments with low betas.

Explanation: The correct answer is: **d.** diversified investments with low betas.

If the aim is to keep portfolio risk low, diversified investments having low betas should be included. Diversification reduces portfolio risk as long as the different investments are unlikely to all move in the same direction (i.e., they are not perfectly, positively correlated). Relative to beta measures, the higher the beta above 1.0, the greater the volatility in relation to market activity.

Question 2B2-CQ06

Topic: Long-Term Financial Management

Cox Company has sold 1,000 shares of $100 par, 8% preferred stock at an issue price of $92 per share. Stock issue costs were $5 per share. Cox pays taxes at the rate of 40%. What is Cox's cost of preferred stock capital?

- ☐ **a.** 8.00%
- ☐ **b.** 8.25%
- ☐ **c.** 8.70%
- ☐ **d.** 9.20%

Explanation: The correct answer is: **d.** 9.20%.

The cost of preferred stock capital is calculated as:

Cost of Preferred Stock Capital = (Preferred Stock Dividend per Share) / (Net Price of the Preferred Stock)

The dividend per share is calculated as:

Dividend per Share = (Dividend Rate) (Par Value of Stock)

Dividend per Share = (0.08) ($100) = $8 per Share

Cost of Preferred Stock Capital = $8 / ($92 − $5) = 9.20%

Question 2B2-CQ07

Topic: Long-Term Financial Management

Bull & Bear Investment Banking is working with the management of Clark Inc. in order to take the company public in an initial public offering. Selected financial information for Clark is as shown next.

Long-term debt (8% interest rate)	$10,000,000
Common equity:	
Par value ($1 per share)	3,000,000
Additional paid-in capital	24,000,000
Retained earnings	6,000,000
Total assets	55,000,000
Net income	3,750,000
Dividend (annual)	1,500,000

If public companies in Clark's industry are trading at 12 times earnings, what is the estimated value per share of Clark?

- ☐ a. $9.00
- ☐ b. $12.00
- ☐ c. $15.00
- ☐ d. $24.00

Explanation: The correct answer is: **c.** $15.00.

The earnings per share (EPS) for Clark is calculated as:

EPS = (Net Income − Preferred Stock Dividends) / (Weighted Average Number of Common Stock Shares Outstanding)

The number of shares outstanding is 3,000,000, which is derived by taking the $3,000,000 in par value common equity and dividing it by the $1 par value per share.

EPS = ($3,750,000 − $0) / (3,000,000 Shares) = $1.25 per Share

The estimated value per share of Clark stock can then be calculated as:

Estimated Value per Share = 12 ($1.25) = $15.00 per Share

Question 2B2-LS13

Topic: Long-Term Financial Management

A long-term call option to buy common stock directly from a corporation is a

- ☐ a. forward contract.
- ☐ b. warrant.
- ☐ c. convertible security.
- ☐ d. futures contract.

Explanation: The correct answer is: **b.** warrant.

By definition, a warrant is a long-term call option to buy common stock directly from a corporation. It gives warrant holders the right to purchase shares of common stock at a given price.

Question 2B2-LS15

Topic: Long-Term Financial Management

An analyst observes a 15-year, 7% option-free bond with semiannual coupons. The required yield on this bond was 7%, but suddenly it drops to 6.5%. The price of this bond

- ☐ a. will increase.
- ☐ b. will decrease.
- ☐ c. will stay the same.
- ☐ d. cannot be determined without additional information.

Explanation: The correct answer is: **a.** will increase.

There is an inverse relationship between price and yield. If the required yield falls, the bond's price will rise, and vice versa.

Question 2B2-LS23

Topic: Long-Term Financial Management

What is the after-tax cost of debt for a 6% interest-bearing bond at an anticipated tax rate of 38%?

- ☐ a. 3.80%
- ☐ b. 3.72%
- ☐ c. 4.40%
- ☐ d. 6.00%

Explanation: The correct answer is: **b.** 3.72%.

The formula for determining the after-tax cost of debt is:

After-Tax Cost of Debt = $k_d (1 - t)$

After-Tax Cost of Debt = $(0.06)(1 - 0.38) = .0372 = 3.72\%$

Question 2B2-CQ09

Topic: Long-Term Financial Management

The Hatch Sausage Company is projecting an annual dividend growth rate for the foreseeable future of 9%. The most recent dividend paid was $3.00 per share. New common stock can be issued at $36 per share. Using the constant growth model, what is the approximate cost of capital for retained earnings?

- ☐ a. 9.08%
- ☐ b. 17.33%
- ☐ c. 18.08%
- ☐ d. 19.88%

Explanation: The correct answer is: **c.** 18.08%.

The cost of capital for retained earnings, using the constant dividend growth model (Gordon's model), is calculated as:

Cost of Capital, Retained Earnings = (Next Dividend) / (Market Price) + (Expected Dividend Growth Rate)

In this case, the next dividend is calculated by taking the current dividend of $3.00 per share and multiplying it by 1 plus the constant growth rate, as shown:

Value of Next Dividend = $3 (1 + 0.09) = $3.27

Therefore, the cost of capital for retained earnings can be calculated as:

Cost of Capital, Retained Earnings = ($3.27 / $36) + (0.09) = 0.0908 + 0.09 = 0.1808, or 18.08%

Question 2B2-CQ10

Topic: Long-Term Financial Management

Angela Company's capital structure consists entirely of long-term debt and common equity. The cost of capital for each component is shown next.

Long-term debt	8% before tax
Common equity	15%

Angela pays taxes at a rate of 40%. If Angela's weighted average cost of capital is 10.41%, what proportion of the company's capital structure is in the form of long-term debt?

- ☐ a. 34%
- ☐ b. 45%
- ☐ c. 55%
- ☐ d. 66%

Explanation: The correct answer is: **b.** 45%.

Angela's weighted average cost of capital (WACC) is given at 10.41%. The formula to calculate the WACC is:

WACC = (Weighted Cost of Debt, or w_i) (After-Tax Cost of Debt) + (1 − w_i) (Cost of Common Equity)

where:

w_i = company's weighted cost (or portion) of debt

The after-tax cost of debt is calculated as:

After-Tax Cost of Debt = (1 − Tax Rate) (% Cost of Debt)
After-Tax Cost of Debt = (1 − 0.4) (0.08) = 0.6 (0.08) = 0.048, or 4.8%

This amount can then be substituted into the WACC formula and rearranged to solve for w_i as shown:

10.41% = 4.8 % (w_i) + (1 − w_i) (15%)
10.41% = 4.8 % (w_i) + 15% − 15% (w_i)
− 4.59% = −10.2% (w_i)
w_i = − 4.59% / −10.2% = 45%

Question 2B2-CQ15

Topic: Long-Term Financial Management

Thomas Company's capital structure consists of 30% long-term debt, 25% preferred stock, and 45% common equity. The cost of capital for each component is shown next.

Long-term debt	8% before tax
Preferred stock	11%
Common equity	15%

If Thomas pays taxes at the rate of 40%, what is the company's after-tax weighted average cost of capital?

- ☐ a. 7.14%
- ☐ b. 9.84%
- ☐ c. 10.94%
- ☐ d. 11.90%

Explanation: The correct answer is: **c.** 10.94%.

The weighted average cost capital (WACC) is calculated as:

WACC = (Weight of Long-Term Debt) (After-Tax Cost of Long-Term Debt)
+ (Weight of Preferred Stock) (Cost of Preferred Stock) + (Weight of Common Equity) (Cost of Common Equity)

The after-tax cost of debt is calculated as:

After-Tax Cost of Debt = (1 − Tax Rate) (Before-Tax Cost of Debt)

After-Tax Cost of Debt = (1 − 0.4) (0.08) = (0.6) (0.08) = 0.048, or 4.8%

WACC = (0.3) (0.048) + (0.25) (0.11) + (0.45) (0.15) = 0.0144 + 0.0275 + 0.0675 = 0.1094, or 10.94%

Question 2B3-AT13
Topic: Raising Capital

Arch Inc. has 200,000 shares of common stock outstanding. Net income for the recently ended fiscal year was $500,000, and the stock has a price/earnings ratio of 8. The board of directors has just declared a three-for-two stock split. For an investor who owns 100 shares of stock before the split, the approximate value (rounded to the nearest dollar) of the investment in Arch stock immediately after the split is

- ☐ a. $2,000
- ☐ b. $1,333
- ☐ c. $3,000
- ☐ d. $4,000

Explanation: The correct answer is: **a.** $2,000.

The stock split will not change the value of the firm, nor will it change the value of the investor's holding.

Original Stock Price = (P/E Ratio) (EPS)

where

EPS = Earnings per Share

EPS = Net Income / # Shares Common Stock Outstanding

EPS = $500,000 / 200,000 = $2.50

Original Stock Price = (8) ($2.50) = $20

Since the investment value does not change with the split, ($20) (100 shares) = $2,000.

After the split, the investor will have 3/2 more shares.

(100 Shares) (3/2) = 150 Shares

Each share will be worth: $2,000 / 150 shares = $13 1/3

Question 2B4-CQ08
Topic: Working Capital Management

Shown next are selected data from Fortune Company's most recent financial statements.

Marketable securities	$10,000
Accounts receivable	60,000
Inventory	25,000
Supplies	5,000
Accounts payable	40,000
Short-term debt payable	10,000
Accruals	5,000

What is Fortune's net working capital?

- ☐ a. $35,000
- ☐ b. $45,000
- ☐ c. $50,000
- ☐ d. $80,000

Explanation: The correct answer is: **b.** $45,000.

Net Working Capital = Current Assets − Current Liabilities

Current Assets = (Marketable Securities) + (Accounts Receivable) + (Inventory) + (Supplies)

Current Assets = $10,000 + $60,000 + $25,000 + $5,000 = $100,000

Current Liabilities = (Accounts Payable) + (Short-Term Debt) + (Accruals)

Current Liabilities = $40,000 + $10,000 + $5,000 = $55,000

Net Working Capital = $100,000 − $55,000 = $45,000

Question 2B4-CQ10

Topic: Working Capital Management

The Rolling Stone Corporation, an entertainment ticketing service, is considering the following means of speeding cash flow for the corporation:

Lockbox system. A lockbox system would cost $25 per month for each of its 170 banks and would result in interest savings of $5,240 per month.

Drafts. Drafts would be used to pay for ticket refunds based on 4,000 refunds per month at a cost of $2.00 per draft, which would result in interest savings of $6,500 per month.

Electronic transfer. Items over $25,000 would be transferred electronically; it is estimated that 700 items of this type would be made each month at a cost of $18 each, which would result in increased interest earnings of $14,000 per month.

Which of these methods of speeding cash flow should Rolling Stone Corporation adopt?

- ☐ a. Lockbox and electronic transfer only
- ☐ b. Electronic transfer only
- ☐ c. Lockbox, drafts, and electronic transfer
- ☐ d. Lockbox only

Explanation: The correct answer is: **a.** Lockbox and electronic transfer only.

Rolling Stone Corporation should select the option with the greatest net benefit, which is calculated by subtracting associated costs from the benefits.

Net Benefit of Lockbox System = $5,240 − ($25) (170) = $5,240 − $4250 = $990

Net Benefit of Drafts = $6,500 − ($2) (4,000) = $6,500 − $8,000 = − $1,500

Electronic transfer only

Net Benefit of Electronic Transfer = $14,000 − ($18) (700)
$$= \$14{,}000 - \$12{,}600 = \$1{,}400$$

Considering the net benefits of the different options:

Lockbox and Electronic Transfer Only: $990 + $1,400 = $2,390

Electronic Transfer Only: $1,400

Lockbox, Drafts, and Electronic Transfer: $990 − $1,500 + $1,400 = $890

Lockbox Only: $990

Lockbox and Electronic Transfer Only have the highest net benefit of the four options listed.

Question 2B6-AT14
Topic: International Finance

A U.S.-based infant clothing company, Tiny Tot, is interested in importing fabric from China. Which of the following should Tiny Tot arrange first for the Chinese company to ship the merchandise?

- ☐ **a.** Bill of lading
- ☐ **b.** Time draft
- ☐ **c.** Letter of credit
- ☐ **d.** Sight draft

Explanation: The correct answer is: **c.** Letter of credit.

A letter of credit is sent from an importer's bank to an exporter. The letter states that the bank backs the importer's obligation to pay the exporter after the bank has received proper documentation that the trade has been completed as contracted.

Question 2B6-AT18

Topic: International Finance

An appreciation of the U.S. dollar against the Japanese yen would

- ☐ a. make U.S. goods more expensive to Japanese consumers.
- ☐ b. increase the translated earnings of U.S. subsidiaries domiciled in Japan.
- ☐ c. increase the cost of buying supplies for U.S. firms.
- ☐ d. make travel in Japan more expensive for U.S. citizens.

Explanation: The correct answer is: **a.** make U.S. goods more expensive to Japanese consumers.

An appreciation of the U.S. dollar against the Japanese yen means that it would take more Japanese yen to purchase U.S. products, thus making such purchases more expensive.

Question 2B6-AT19

Topic: International Finance

Technocrat Inc., located in Belgium, currently manufactures products at its domestic plant and exports them to the United States, since production is less expensive at home. The company is considering the possibility of setting up a plant in the United States. All of the following factors would encourage the company to consider direct foreign investment in the U.S. **except** the

- ☐ a. expectation of more stringent trade restrictions by the United States.
- ☐ b. depreciation of the U.S. dollar against Belgium's currency.
- ☐ c. changing demand for the company's exports to the United States due to exchange rate fluctuations.
- ☐ d. widening of the gap in production costs between locations in the United States and Belgium.

Explanation: The correct answer is: **d.** widening of the gap in production costs between locations in the United States and Belgium.

An increasing gap would favor production at home in Belgium because it would be even less expensive.

Section C: Decision Analysis

Question 2C1-CQ01

Topic: Cost/Volume/Profit Analysis

Following are the operating results of the two segments of Parklin Corporation.

	Segment A	Segment B	Total
Sales	$10,000	$15,000	$25,000
Variable costs of goods sold	4,000	8,500	12,500
Fixed costs of goods sold	1,500	2,500	4,000
Gross margin	4,500	4,000	8,500
Variable selling and administrative	2,000	3,000	5,000
Fixed selling and administrative	1,500	1,500	3,000
Operating income (loss)	$1,000	$(500)	$500

Variable costs of goods sold are directly related to the operating segments. Fixed costs of goods sold are allocated to each segment based on the number of employees. Fixed selling and administrative expenses are allocated equally. If Segment B is eliminated, $1,500 of fixed costs of goods sold would be eliminated. Assuming Segment B is closed, the effect on operating income would be

- a. an increase of $500.
- b. an increase of $2,000.
- c. a decrease of $2,000.
- d. a decrease of $2,500.

Explanation: The correct answer is: **c.** a decrease of $2,000.

If Segment B is closed, then Parklin would gain $13,000, which is calculated as shown:

Effect of Closing Segment B = ($1,500 in B's Fixed Cost of Goods Sold)
+ ($8,500 in B's Variable Cost of Goods Sold) +
($3,000 in B's Variable Selling and Administrative)
= $13,000

The closing would cause a reduction in sales of $15,000, resulting in a decrease in profits of $15,000 − $13,000 = $2,000.

Question 2C1-CQ02
Topic: Cost/Volume/Profit Analysis

Edwards Products has just developed a new product with a variable manufacturing cost of $30 per unit. The marketing director has identified three marketing approaches for this new product.

Approach X	Set a selling price of $36 and have the firm's sales staff sell the product at a 10% commission with no advertising program. Estimated annual sales would be 10,000 units.
Approach Y	Set a selling price of $38, have the firm's sales staff sell the product at a 10% commission, and back them up with a $30,000 advertising program. Estimated annual sales would be 12,000 units.
Approach Z	Rely on wholesalers to handle the product. Edwards would sell the new product to the wholesalers at $32 per unit and incur no selling expenses. Estimated annual sales would be 14,000 units.

Rank the three alternatives in order of net contribution, from highest to lowest.

☐ a. X, Y, Z
☐ b. Y, Z, X
☐ c. Z, X, Y
☐ d. Z, Y, X

Explanation: The correct answer is: **c.** Z, X, Y.

Contribution Margin = (Selling Price per Unit − Variable Costs per Unit) (Volume)

The contribution margin for Approach X is calculated as shown:

Contribution Margin, Approach X = [($36 − (0.1 Commission) ($36) − $30)] (10,000 units)

Contribution Margin, Approach X = ($2.40) (10,000) = $24,000

The contribution margin for Approach Y is calculated as shown:

Contribution Margin, Approach Y = [($38 − (0.1 Commission) ($38) − $30)] (12,000 Units) − $30,000 Advertising

Contribution Margin, Approach Y = ($4.20) (12,000) − $30,000 = $20,400

The contribution margin for approach Z is calculated as shown:

Contribution Margin, Approach Z = ($32 − $30) (14,000 Units) = $28,000

Question 2C1-CQ04
Topic: Cost/Volume/Profit Analysis

Elgers Company produces valves for the plumbing industry. Elgers' per-unit sales price and variable costs are as shown.

Sales price	$12
Variable costs	8

Elgers' practical plant capacity is 40,000 units. Its total fixed costs aggregate $48,000, and it has a 40% effective tax rate.

The maximum net profit that Elger can earn is

- a. $48,000.
- b. $67,200.
- c. $96,000.
- d. $112,000.

Explanation: The correct answer is: **b.** $67,200.

The maximum net profit that Elger can earn can be calculated as shown:

Maximum Net Profit = (1 − Tax Rate) (Sales − Variable Costs − Fixed Costs)

Maximum Net Profit = (1 − 0.4) [($12) (40,000) − ($8) (40,000) − $48,000]

Maximum Net Profit = (0.6) ($480,000 − $320,000 − $48,000)

Maximum Net Profit = (0.6) ($112,000) = $67,200

Question 2C1-CQ09
Topic: Cost/Volume/Profit Analysis

Cervine Corporation makes two types of motors for use in various products. Operating data and unit cost information for its products are presented next.

	Product A	Product B
Annual unit capacity	10,000	20,000
Annual unit demand	10,000	20,000
Selling price	$100	$80
Variable manufacturing cost	53	45
Fixed manufacturing cost	10	10
Variable selling and administrative	10	11
Fixed selling and administrative	5	4
Fixed other administrative	2	0
Unit operating profit	$20	$10
Machine hours per unit	2.0	1.5

Cervine has 40,000 productive machine hours available. The relevant contribution margins, per machine hour for each product, to be utilized in making a decision on product priorities for the coming year, are

	Product A	Product B
a.	$17.00	$14.00
b.	$18.50	$16.00
c.	$20.00	$10.00
d.	$37.00	$24.00

Explanation: The correct answer is: **b.** $18.50; $16.00.

Contribution per machine hour is calculated as shown:

Contribution per Machine Hour = (Unit Contribution Margin) / (Machine Hours per Unit)

Unit Contribution Margin (CMU) = Selling Price − Unit Variable Costs

Unit Variable Costs, Product A = ($53 + $10) = $63

CMU, Product A = ($100 − $63) = $37

Product A's Contribution per Machine Hour = $37 / 2 Hours = $18.50 per Hour

Unit Variable Costs, Product B = ($45 + $11) = $56

CMU, Product B = ($80 − $56) = $24

Product B's Contribution per Machine Hour = $24 / 1.5 Hours = $16.00 per Hour

Question 2C1-CQ10
Topic: Cost/Volume/Profit Analysis

Allred Company sells its single product for $30 per unit. The contribution margin ratio is 45%, and fixed costs are $10,000 per month. Allred has an effective income tax rate of 40%. If Allred sells 1,000 units in the current month, Allred's variable expenses would be

- ☐ a. $9,900.
- ☐ b. $12,000.
- ☐ c. $13,500.
- ☐ d. $16,500.

Explanation: The correct answer is: **d.** $16,500.

Variable expenses are calculated as shown:

Variable Expenses = (1 − Contribution Margin Ratio) (Sales Amount)

Sales Amount = ($30) (1,000 Units) = $30,000

Variable Expenses = (1 − 0.45) ($30,000)

Variable Expenses = (0.55) ($30,000) = $16,500

Question 2C1-CQ11
Topic: Cost/Volume/Profit Analysis

Phillips & Company produces educational software. Its unit cost structure, based on an anticipated production volume of 150,000 units, is:

Sales price	$160
Variable costs	60
Fixed costs	55

The marketing department has estimated sales for the coming year at 175,000 units, which is within the relevant range of Phillips' cost structure. Phillips' break-even volume (in units) and anticipated operating income for the coming year would amount to

- ☐ a. 82,500 units and $7,875,000 of operating income.
- ☐ b. 82,500 units and $9,250,000 of operating income.
- ☐ c. 96,250 units and $3,543,750 of operating income.
- ☐ d. 96,250 units and $7,875,000 of operating income.

Explanation: The correct answer is: **b.** 82,500 units and $9,250,000 of operating income. The break-even point in units is calculated as shown:

Break-Even (Units) = (Total Fixed Costs) / (Unit Contribution Margin)

Unit Contribution Margin = (Unit Sales Price − Unit Variable Costs)

Unit Contribution Margin = $160 − $60 = $100

Total Fixed Costs = (Fixed Cost per Unit) (Production Volume)

Total Fixed Costs = ($55) (150,000 Units) = $8,250,000

Break-Even Point (Units) = $8,250,000 / $100 = 82,500 Units

Operating Income = (Unit Contribution Margin) (Total Units) − Fixed Costs

Operating Income = ($100) (175,000 Units) − $8,250,000
= $17,500,000 − $8,250,000

Operating Income = $9,250,000

Question 2C1-CQ15

Topic: Cost/Volume/Profit Analysis

For the year just ended, Silverstone Company's sales revenue was $450,000. Silverstone's fixed costs were $120,000, and its variable costs amounted to $270,000. For the current year, sales are forecasted at $500,000. If the fixed costs do not change, Silverstone's operating profits this year will be

- ☐ a. $60,000.
- ☐ b. $80,000.
- ☐ c. $110,000.
- ☐ d. $200,000.

Explanation: The correct answer is: **b.** $80,000.

The operating profit is calculated as shown:

Operating Profit = (Contribution Margin Ratio) (Total Sales $) − Fixed Costs

Forecasted Sales, Current Year = $500,000

Contribution Margin Ratio, Year Just Ended = (Sales − Variable Costs) / (sales)

Contribution Margin Ratio, Year Just Ended = ($450,000 − $270,000) / ($450,000) = 0.4

Operating Profit = (0.4) ($500,000) − $120,000 = $200,000 − $120,000 = $80,000

Question 2C2-CQ01

Topic: Marginal Analysis

Williams makes $35,000 a year as an accounting clerk. He decides to quit his job to enter a one-year MBA program full-time. Assume Williams doesn't work in the summer or hold any part-time jobs. His tuition, books, living expenses, and fees total $25,000 a year. Given this information, the annual total economic cost of Williams' MBA studies is

- a. $10,000.
- b. $35,000.
- c. $25,000.
- d. $60,000.

Explanation: The correct answer is: **d.** $60,000.

The economic cost of pursuing the MBA program full time for one year is calculated by adding the $35,000 of forgone salary and the $25,000 of expenses together, which comes to $60,000 in total.

Question 2C2-CQ03

Topic: Marginal Analysis

Daily costs for Kelso Manufacturing include $1,000 of fixed costs and total variable costs, as shown:

Unit Output	10	11	12	13	14	15
Cost	$125	$250	$400	$525	$700	$825

The average total cost at an output level of 11 units is

- a. $113.64.
- b. $125.00.
- c. $215.91.
- d. $250.00.

Explanation: The correct answer is: **a.** $113.64.

The average cost per unit for 11 units is calculated by adding up the total costs (fixed and variable) for the 11 units and dividing that amount by 11:

Average Total Cost at an Output Level of 11 Units = ($1,000 + $250) / 11
= $1,250 / 11 = $113.64

Question 2C2-CQ04

Topic: Marginal Analysis

Harper Products' cost information for the normal range of output in a month is shown next.

Output in Units	Total Cost
20,000	$3,000,000
22,500	3,325,000
25,000	3,650,000

What is Harper's short-run marginal cost?

- ☐ a. $26
- ☐ b. $130
- ☐ c. $146
- ☐ d. $150

Explanation: The correct answer is: **b.** $130.

Marginal cost is the cost of the next unit produced. It is calculated by taking the change in costs and dividing it by the change in output (volume).
Harper's marginal cost can be calculated as:

Marginal Cost = Change in Cost / Change in Volume

Marginal Cost = ($3,325,000 − $3,000,000) / (22,500 − 20,000)
     = $325,000 / 2,500 = $130

Question 2C2-CQ11

Topic: Marginal Analysis

Refrigerator Company manufactures ice makers for installation in refrigerators. The costs per unit, for 20,000 units of ice makers, are:

Direct materials	$7
Direct labor	12
Variable overhead	5
Fixed overhead	10
Total costs	$34

Cool Compartments Inc. has offered to sell 20,000 ice makers to Refrigerator Company for $28 per unit. If Refrigerator accepts Cool Compartments' offer, the plant would be idled and fixed overhead amounting to $6 per unit could be eliminated. The total relevant costs associated with the manufacture of ice makers amount to

- ☐ a. $480,000.
- ☐ b. $560,000.

☐ c. $600,000.

☐ d. $680,000.

Explanation: The correct answer is: **c.** $600,000.

The total relevant costs associated with the manufacturing of ice makers are:

Total Relevant Costs = (Unit Variable Manufacturing Costs) (Number of Units) + (Any Avoidable Fixed Costs)

Unit Variable Manufacturing Costs = (Direct Materials + Direct Labor + Variable Overhead)

Unit Variable Manufacturing Costs = ($7 + $12 + $5) = $24

Avoidable fixed costs are $6 per unit.

Therefore, the relevant costs to manufacture the ice makers
= ($24) (20,000 units) + ($6) (20,000 units).

Total Relevant Costs = $480,000 + $120,000 = $600,000

Question 2C2-CQ14

Topic: Marginal Analysis

Capital Company has decided to discontinue a product produced on a machine purchased four years ago at a cost of $70,000. The machine has a current book value of $30,000. Due to technologically improved machinery now available in the marketplace, the existing machine has no current salvage value. The company is reviewing the various aspects involved in the production of a new product. The engineering staff advised that the existing machine can be used to produce the new product. Other costs involved in the production of the new product will be materials of $20,000 and labor priced at $5,000.

Ignoring income taxes, the costs relevant to the decision to produce or not to produce the new product would be

☐ a. $25,000.

☐ b. $30,000.

☐ c. $55,000.

☐ d. $95,000.

Explanation: The correct answer is: **a.** $25,000.

The costs relevant to the decision to produce or not to produce the new product total $25,000 and are comprised of the $20,000 cost of materials and the $5,000 cost of labor. The costs associated with the old machine are irrelevant; they are sunk, historical costs.

Question 2C2-CQ15

Topic: Marginal Analysis

Current business segment operations for Whitman, a mass retailer, are presented next.

	Merchandise	Automotive	Restaurant	Total
Sales	$500,000	$400,000	$100,000	$1,000,000
Variable costs	300,000	200,000	70,000	570,000
Fixed costs	100,000	100,000	50,000	250,000
Operating income (loss)	$100,000	$100,000	$(20,000)	$180,000

Management is contemplating the discontinuance of the Restaurant segment since "it is losing money." If this segment is discontinued, $30,000 of its fixed costs will be eliminated. In addition, Merchandise and Automotive sales will decrease 5% from their current levels. What will Whitman's total contribution margin be if the Restaurant segment is discontinued?

- ☐ a. $160,000
- ☐ b. $220,000
- ☐ c. $367,650
- ☐ d. $380,000

Explanation: The correct answer is: **d.** $380,000.

Total contribution margin in dollars is calculated as shown:

Total Contribution Margin = Sales − Variable Costs

The total contribution margin for Whitman after discontinuing the Restaurant segment would be 95% of the Merchandise segment's current contribution, plus 95% of the Automotive segment's current contribution.

Total Contribution Margin, Whitman, after Discontinuing Restaurant Segment
= (0.95) ($500,000 − $300,000) + (0.95) ($400,000 − $200,000)
= $190,000 + $190,000 = $380,000

Question 2C2-CQ16

Topic: Marginal Analysis

Aril Industries is a multiproduct company that currently manufactures 30,000 units of Part 730 each month for use in production. The facilities being used to produce Part 730 have fixed monthly overhead costs of $150,000 and a theoretical capacity to produce 60,000 units per month. If Aril were to buy Part 730 from an outside supplier, the facilities would be idle and 40% of fixed costs would continue to be incurred. There are no alternative uses for the facilities. The variable production costs of Part 730 are $11 per unit. Fixed overhead is allocated based on planned production levels.

If Aril Industries continues to use 30,000 units of Part 730 each month, it would realize a net benefit by purchasing Part 730 from an outside supplier only if the supplier's unit price is less than

- ☐ a. $12.00.
- ☐ b. $12.50.
- ☐ c. $13.00.
- ☐ d. $14.00.

Explanation: The correct answer is: **d.** $14.00.

The appropriate purchase price would occur when the price for 30,000 units is equal to the variable manufacturing costs plus the avoidable fixed costs.

(P) (Units) = (Variable Manufacturing Costs) + (Avoidable Fixed Costs)

where:

P = purchase price
Units = 30,000
Variable Manufacturing Costs = ($11) (30,000 Units) = $330,000
Avoidable Fixed Costs = (0.6) ($150,000) = $90,000

(P) (30,000) = ($330,000) + ($90,000)
30,000 P = $420,000
P = $14.00

Question 2C3-CQ01

Topic: Pricing

A market research analyst determined the next market data for a commodity.

Price	Quantity Supplied	Quantity Demanded
$25	250	750
50	500	500
75	750	250
100	1,000	0

Based on this information, which one of the following statements is **correct**?

- ☐ a. At a price of $30, there will be excess demand.
- ☐ b. A market clearing price cannot be determined.

☐ **c.** At a price of $80, there will be insufficient supply.

☐ **d.** A market price of $50 cannot exist for very long.

Explanation: The correct answer is: **a.** At a price of $30, there will be excess demand.

The market clearing price of $50 occurs when supply equals demand (500 units). Any price less than $50 will create excess demand.

Question 2C3-CQ03

Topic: Pricing

An economic research firm performed extensive studies on the market for large-screen televisions (LSTs). Portions of the results are shown next.

Household Income	LST Sales (units)
$50,000	20,000
60,000	28,000
72,000	39,200
Price of LSTs	**LST Sales (units)**
$1,000	100,000
900	115,000
810	132,250

The income elasticity of demand for LSTs is

☐ **a.** 0.4.

☐ **b.** 1.5.

☐ **c.** 1.8.

☐ **d.** 2.5.

Explanation: The correct answer is: **c.** 1.8

Income elasticity of demand is defined as the percent change in quantity demanded (sales) given a percentage change in income. The percentage change in sales is calculated by taking the change in sales from 20,000 to 28,000 units, as shown:

% Change in Sales = (28,000 − 20,000) / 24,000 = 8,000 / 24,000 = 0.33

For that same change in sales units, the percentage change in income is calculated as:

% Change in Income = ($60,000 − $50,000) / $55,000
= $10,000 / $55,000 = 0.18

The income elasticity can then be calculated as shown:

Income Elasticity of Demand = % Change in Quantity Demanded / % Change in Income

Income Elasticity of Demand = 0.33 / 0.18 = 1.83

Note: These calculations are consistent with the CMA exam's use of the midpoint formula approach to calculate elasticity of demand, as explained in Section C, Topic 3.

Question 2C3-CQ04

Topic: Pricing

Jones Enterprises manufactures three products, A, B, and C. During the month of May, Jones's production, costs, and sales data were as shown.

	Products			
	A	B	C	Totals
Units of production	30,000	20,000	70,000	120,000
Joint production costs to split-off point				$480,000
Further processing costs	$–	$60,000	$140,000	
Unit sales price				
At split-off	3.75	5.50	10.25	
After further processing	–	8.00	12.50	

Based on this information, which one of the following alternatives should be recommended to Jones's management?

- ☐ **a.** Sell both Product B and Product C at the split-off point.
- ☐ **b.** Process Product B further but sell Product C at the split-off point.
- ☐ **c.** Process Product C further but sell Product B at the split-off point.
- ☐ **d.** Process both Products B and C further.

Explanation: The correct answer is: **c.** Process Product C further but sell Product B at the split-off point.

A product should be processed further if the change in the market price from processing exceeds the additional processing costs.

Product B can be sold at split-off for $5.50 (20,000) = $110,000.
Product B can be sold after further processing for $8(20,000) = $160,000.
The cost increase is $160,000 – $110,000 = $50,000.
$50,000 is less than the additional processing costs of $60,000.

Therefore, Product B should be sold at split-off.
Product C can be sold at split-off for $10.25 (70,000) = $717,500.
Product C can be sold after further processing for $12.50 (70,000) = $875,000.
The cost increase is $875,000 – $717,500 = $157,500.
$157,500 is greater than the additional processing costs of $140,000.
Based on this information, Product C should be processed further.

Question 2C3-CQ05
Topic: Pricing

Synergy Inc. produces a component that is popular in many refrigeration systems. Data on three of the five different models of this component are shown next.

	Model A	Model B	Model C
Volume needed (units)	5,000	6,000	3,000
Manufacturing costs			
Variable direct costs	$10	$24	$20
Variable overhead	5	10	15
Fixed overhead	11	20	17
Total manufacturing costs	$26	$54	$52
Cost if purchased	$21	$42	$39

Synergy applies variable overhead on the basis of machine hours at the rate of $2.50 per hour. Models A and B are manufactured in the Freezer Department, which has a capacity of 28,000 machine processing hours. Which one of the following options should be recommended to Synergy's management?

- ☐ **a.** Purchase all three products in the quantities required.
- ☐ **b.** Manufacture all three products in the quantities required.
- ☐ **c.** The Freezer Department's manufacturing plan should include 5,000 units of Model A and 4,500 units of Model B.
- ☐ **d.** The Freezer Department's manufacturing plan should include 2,000 units of Model A and 6,000 units of Model B.

Explanation: The correct answer is: **c.** The Freezer Department's manufacturing plan should include 5,000 units of Model A and 4,500 units of Model B.

Synergy would want to maximize the contribution per machine hour, multiplied by the 28,000 machine hours available.

The contribution per machine hour for each product can be calculated as shown:

Contribution per Machine Hour = (Outside Price − Product's Unit Variable Costs) / (Number of Machine Hours Required to Make It)

Machine Hours Required to Make Any Model = Variable Overhead for That Model / ($2.50/hour)

Machine Hours Required to Make Model A = ($5) / ($2.50/hour) = 2 Hours

Machine Hours Required to Make Model B = ($10) / ($2.50/hour) = 4 Hours

Machine Hours Required to Make Model C = ($15) / ($2.50/hour) = 6 Hours

Contribution per Machine Hour, Model A = ($21 − $10 Variable Direct Costs − $5 Variable Overhead) / (2 Hours)

Contribution per Machine Hour, Model A = $6 / 2 Hours = $3.00 per Machine Hour

Contribution per Machine Hour, Model B = ($42 − $24 Variable Direct Costs − $10 Variable Overhead) / (4 Hours)

Contribution per Machine Hour, Model B = $8 / 4 Hours = $2.00 per Machine Hour

Contribution per Machine Hour, Model C = ($39 − $20 Variable Direct Costs − $15 Variable Overhead) / (6 Hours)

Contribution per Machine Hour, Model C = $4 / 6 Hours = $0.67 per Machine Hour

Based on this information about contribution per machine hour, Synergy should:

First produce 5,000 units of Model A (the highest contribution margin per machine hour) using 5,000 (2) = 10,000 machine hours.

Then produce 4,500 units of Model B (the next highest contribution margin per machine hour) using 4,500 (4) = 18,000 machine hours.

The two models would use the entire capacity of 28,000 machine hours (10,000 + 18,000), so no additional products could be produced.

Question 2C3-CQ06

Topic: Pricing

Leader Industries is planning to introduce a new product, DMA. It is expected that 10,000 units of DMA will be sold. The full product cost per unit is $300. Invested capital for this product amounts to $20 million. Leader's target rate of return on investment is 20%. The markup percentage for this product, based on operating income as a percentage of full product cost, will be

- a. 42.9%.
- b. 57.1%.
- c. 133.3%.
- d. 233.7%.

Explanation: The correct answer is: **c.** 133.3%.

The price (p) of DMA is computed by using this formula:

(p − Costs)(Number of Units) = (Return on Investment %) (Investment)

(p − $300) (10,000) = [(0.2) ($20,000,000)]

(p − $300) = $4,000,000 / 10,000

$(p - \$300) = \$400$

$p = \$700$

The markup percentage of full product cost = (Price − Cost) / (Cost).

Markup Percentage of Full Product Cost = ($700 − $300) / ($300)
= $400 / $300
= 1.333, or 133.3%.

Question 2C3-CQ08
Topic: Pricing

Almelo Manpower Inc. provides contracted bookkeeping services. Almelo has annual fixed costs of $100,000 and variable costs of $6 per hour. This year the company budgeted 50,000 hours of bookkeeping services. Almelo prices its services at full cost and uses a cost-plus pricing approach. The company developed a billing price of $9 per hour. The company's markup level would be

- ☐ a. 12.5%.
- ☐ b. 33.3%.
- ☐ c. 50.0%.
- ☐ d. 66.6%.

Explanation: The correct answer is: **a.** 12.5%.

The unit cost at 50,000 hours is:

Unit Cost at 50,000 Hours = (Fixed Costs / # Hours) + Variable Cost per Hour

Unit Cost at 50,000 hours = ($100,000 / 50,000) + $6 = $2 + $6 = $8 per Hour

Given the price of $9, the markup level on cost = (Price − Cost) / (Cost).

Markup Level on Cost = ($9 − $8) / ($8) = 1/8 = 0.125, or 12.5%

Question 2C3-CQ09
Topic: Pricing

Fennel Products is using cost-based pricing to determine the selling price for its new product based on the next information.

Annual volume	25,000 units
Fixed costs	$700,000 per year
Variable costs	$200 per unit
Plant investment	$3,000,000
Working capital	$1,000,000
Effective tax rate	40%

The target price that Fennell needs to set for the new product to achieve a 15% after-tax return on investment (ROI) would be

- a. $228.
- b. $238.
- c. $258.
- d. $268.

Explanation: The correct answer is: **d.** $268.

The target price (p) is computed by using this formula:

(Total Sales − Total Variable Costs − Total Fixed Costs) (1 − Tax Rate)
= (Target ROI) (Investment)

Total Sales = (Volume) (Target Price) = (25,000) (p)

Total Variable Costs = (Volume) (Variable Cost per Unit)
= (25,000) ($200) = $5,000,000

Total Fixed Costs = $700,000

Investment includes both plant and working capital = $3,000,000 + $1,000,000
= $4,000,000.

(25,000p − $5,000,000 − $700,000) (1 − 0.4) = (0.15) ($4,000,000)

(25,000p − $5,700,000) (0.6) = $600,000

15,000p − $3,420,000 = $600,000

15,000p = $4,020,000

p = $268

Section D: Risk Management

Question 2D1-AT16

Topic: Enterprise Risk

Which of the following is **not** an example of a form of political risk associated with foreign direct investment?

- a. Uncontrolled inflation
- b. Nationalization of factories
- c. Change in government regime
- d. Civil war

Explanation: The correct answer is: **a.** Uncontrolled inflation.

Uncontrolled inflation is an economic risk, not a political risk.

Question 2D1-AT17

Topic: Enterprise Risk

All of the following are valid reasons for expansion of international business by U.S. multinational corporations, **except** to

- ☐ **a.** secure new sources for raw materials.
- ☐ **b.** find additional areas where their products can be marketed successfully.
- ☐ **c.** protect their domestic market from competition from foreign manufacturers.
- ☐ **d.** minimize their costs of production.

Explanation: The correct answer is: **c.** protect their domestic market from competition from foreign manufacturers.

Protecting the domestic market from foreign competition is not a valid reason for expansion overseas; all the other options are valid.

Question 2D1-AT18

Topic: Enterprise Risk

Risk assessment is a process

- ☐ **a.** designed to identify potential events that may affect the entity.
- ☐ **b.** that establishes policies and procedures to accomplish internal control objectives.
- ☐ **c.** that identifies risk but does not include management's response to risk
- ☐ **d.** that assesses the quality of internal controls throughout the year.

Explanation: The correct answer is: **a.** designed to identify potential events that may affect the entity.

Risk assessment involves identifying all risks and vulnerabilities to which an organization is exposed.

Question 2D1-AT19

Topic: Enterprise Risk

Within a financial risk management context, the term *value at risk* (VaR) is defined as the

- ☐ **a.** maximum value a company can lose.
- ☐ **b.** worst possible outcome given the distribution of outcomes.
- ☐ **c.** most likely negative outcome.
- ☐ **d.** maximum loss within a certain time period at a given level of confidence.

Explanation: The correct answer is: **d.** maximum loss within a certain time period at a given level of confidence.

Value at risk is defined as the maximum loss within a given period of time and given a specified probability level (level of confidence).

Section E: Investment Decisions

Question 2E1-AT06

Topic: Capital Budgeting Process

In order to increase production capacity, Gunning Industries is considering replacing an existing production machine with a new technologically improved machine effective January 1. This information is being considered:

- The new machine would be purchased for $160,000 in cash. Shipping, installation, and testing would cost an additional $30,000.
- The new machine is expected to increase annual sales by 20,000 units at a sales price of $40 per unit. Incremental operating costs are comprised of $30 per unit in variable costs and total fixed costs of $40,000 per year.
- The investment in the new machine will require an immediate increase in working capital of $35,000.
- Gunning uses straight-line depreciation for financial reporting and tax reporting purposes. The new machine has an estimated useful life of five years and zero salvage value.
- Gunning is subject to a 40% corporate income tax rate.

Gunning Industries' initial net cash outflow in a capital budgeting decision would be

- ☐ a. $160,000.
- ☐ b. $190,000.
- ☐ c. $225,000.
- ☐ d. $195,000.

Explanation: The correct answer is: **c.** $225,000.

Gunning's initial cash outflow at time zero is calculated as:

Initial Cash Outflow = (Initial Cost of New Machine) + (Shipping, Installation, and Testing Related to the New Machine) + Additional Working Capital Required

Initial Cash Outflow = $160,000 + $30,000 + $35,000 = $225,000

Question 2E1-AT07

Topic: Capital Budgeting Process

In order to increase production capacity, Gunning Industries is considering replacing an existing production machine with a new technologically improved machine effective January 1. Gunning Industries is considering this information:

- The new machine would be purchased for $160,000 in cash. Shipping, installation, and testing would cost an additional $30,000.

- The new machine is expected to increase annual sales by 20,000 units at a sales price of $40 per unit. Incremental operating costs are comprised of $30 per unit in variable costs and total fixed costs of $40,000 per year.
- The investment in the new machine will require an immediate increase in working capital of $35,000.
- Gunning uses straight-line depreciation for financial reporting and tax reporting purposes. The new machine has an estimated useful life of five years and zero salvage value.
- Gunning is subject to a 40% corporate income tax rate.

Gunning uses the net present value method to analyze investments and will employ these factors and rates:

Period	Present Value of $1 at 10%	Present Value of an Ordinary Annuity of $1 at 10%
1	0.909	0.909
2	0.826	1.736
3	0.751	2.487
4	0.683	3.170
5	0.621	3.791

Gunning Industries' discounted annual depreciation tax shield for the first year of operation would be:

- ☐ **a.** $13,817.
- ☐ **b.** $15,200.
- ☐ **c.** $20,725.
- ☐ **d.** $22,800.

Explanation: The correct answer is: **a.** $13,817.

The depreciation tax shield for a period is calculated by taking the depreciation for the period and multiplying it by the relevant tax rate.

Using straight-line depreciation, the annual depreciation charge is calculated as:

Annual Depreciation Charge, Straight-Line Depreciation
= (Depreciable Base) / (Estimated Service Life)

For Gunning, the depreciable base will include the initial cost of the machine and the shipping, installation, and testing. Therefore, the depreciable base will be calculated as:

Depreciable Base = $160,000 + $30,000 = $190,000

Annual Depreciation Charge, Straight-Line Depreciation = ($160,000 + $30,000) / (5 years)

Annual Depreciation Charge, Straight-Line Depreciation = $190,000 / 5 Years
= $38,000

The annual depreciation tax shield is calculated by taking the annual depreciation and multiplying it by the tax rate, as shown:

Annual Depreciation Tax Shield = (Annual Depreciation) (Tax Rate)
Annual Depreciation Tax Shield = ($38,000) (0.40) = $15,200

The discounted annual depreciation tax shield is calculated by taking the annual depreciation tax shield and discounting it by the appropriate present value of $1 factor, as shown:

Discounted Annual Depreciation Tax Shield
= (Annual Depreciation Tax Shield) (Present Value of $1 Factor)

Present Value of $1 Factor for 10% at the End of Year 1 = 0.909

Discounted Annual Depreciation Tax Shield = ($15,200) (0.909) = $13,817

Question 2E1-AT08

Topic: Capital Budgeting Process

Which one of the following is **most** relevant to a manufacturing equipment replacement decision?

- ☐ a. Gain or loss on the disposal of the old equipment
- ☐ b. Original cost less depreciation of the old equipment
- ☐ c. A lump-sum write-off amount from the disposal of the old equipment
- ☐ d. Disposal price of the old equipment

Explanation: The correct answer is: **d.** disposal price of the old equipment.

Relevant costs and revenues include cash flows caused by the decision. The disposal price of the old equipment is a cash inflow that decreases the initial investment required for the replacement decision.

Question 2E2-CQ01

Topic: Discounted Cash Flow Analysis

Calvin Inc. is considering the purchase of a new state-of-art machine to replace its hand-operated machine. Calvin's effective tax rate is 40%, and its cost of capital is 12%. Data regarding the existing and new machines are presented next.

	Existing Machine	New Machine
Original cost	$50,000	$90,000
Installation costs	0	4,000
Freight and insurance	0	6,000
Expected end salvage value	0	0
Depreciation method	straight line	straight line
Expected useful life	10 years	5 years

The existing machine has been in service for seven years and could be sold currently for $25,000. Calvin expects to realize a before-tax annual reduction in labor costs of $30,000 if the new machine is purchased and placed in service.

If the new machine is purchased, the cash flows for the fifth year would amount to

- ☐ a. $18,000.
- ☐ b. $24,000.
- ☐ c. $26,000.
- ☐ d. $30,000.

Explanation: The correct answer is: **c.** $26,000.

The cash flow in Year 5 of the project is calculated as shown:

Cash Flow, Year 5 = (Projected Savings − Depreciation Expense) (1 − Tax Rate) + Depreciation Expense

Annual Depreciation Expense = (Original Cost + Installation Costs + Freight And Insurance Costs) / Useful Life)

Annual Depreciation Expense = ($90,000 + $4,000 + $6,000) / 5 years = $20,000 per year

Cash Flow, Year 5 = ($30,000 − $20,000) (1 − 0.4) + $20,000 = $6,000 + $20,000

Cash Flow, Year 5 = $26,000

Question 2E2-CQ11

Topic: Discounted Cash Flow Analysis

For each of the next six years, Atlantic Motors anticipates net income of $10,000, straight-line tax depreciation of $20,000, a 40% tax rate, a discount rate of 10%, and cash sales of $100,000. The depreciable assets are all being acquired at the beginning of year 1 and will have a salvage value of zero at the end of six years.

The present value (PV) of the total depreciation tax savings would be:

- ☐ a. $8,000.
- ☐ b. $27,072.
- ☐ c. $34,840.
- ☐ d. $87,100.

Explanation: The correct answer is: **c.** $34,840.

The depreciation tax savings (or depreciation tax shield) is calculated by taking the after-tax PV of the annual depreciation charges.

Depreciation Tax Shield = (Tax Rate) (Depreciation Expense) (PV Annuity Factor)

Depreciation Tax Shield = (0.4) ($20,000) (4.355 PV Annuity, $i = 10$, $n = 6$)

Depreciation Tax Shield = (0.4) ($20,000) (4.355) = $34,840

Question 2E2-CQ14

Topic: Discounted Cash Flow Analysis

Fuller Industries is considering a $1 million investment in stamping equipment to produce a new product. The equipment is expected to last 9 years, produce revenue of $700,000 per year, and have related cash expenses of $450,000 per year. At the end of the 9th year, the equipment is expected to have a salvage value of $100,000 and cost $50,000 to remove. The Internal Revenue Service categorizes this as 5-year Modified Accelerated Cost Recovery System (MACRS) property subject to the next depreciation rates.

Year	Rate
1	20.00%
2	32.00%
3	19.20%
4	11.52%
5	11.52%
6	5.76%

Fuller's effective income tax rate is 40% and Fuller expects, on an overall company basis, to continue to be profitable and have significant taxable income. If Fuller uses the net present value method to analyze investments, what is the expected net tax impact on cash flow in Year 2 before discounting? Assume that a positive impact decreases the income tax liability while a negative impact increases the income tax liability.

- ☐ a. Positive $28,000 impact
- ☐ b. $0 impact
- ☐ c. Negative $100,000 impact
- ☐ d. Negative $128,000 impact

Explanation: The correct answer is: **a.** Positive $28,000 impact.

The net tax impact in year 2 is calculated as shown:

Net Tax Impact, Year 2 = (Revenue − Cash Expenses − Depreciation) (Tax Rate)

Depreciation Expense, Year 2 = (Equipment Cost) (Year 2 MACRS rate)

Depreciation Expense, Year 2 = ($1,000,000) (0.32) = $320,000

Net Tax Impact, Year 2 = ($700,000 − $450,000 − $320,000) (0.4)

Net Tax Impact, Year 2 = −$28,000 (which is a reduction in taxes)

Question 2E2-CQ16

Topic: Discounted Cash Flow Analysis

AGC Company is considering an equipment upgrade. AGC uses discounted cash flow (DCF) analysis in evaluating capital investments and has an effective tax rate of 40%. Selected data developed by AGC are shown next.

	Existing Equipment	New Equipment
Original cost	$50,000	$95,000
Accumulated depreciation	45,000	–
Current market value	3,000	95,000
Accounts receivable	6,000	8,000
Accounts payable	2,100	2,500

Based on this information, what is the initial investment for a DCF analysis of this proposed upgrade?

- ☐ a. $92,400
- ☐ b. $92,800
- ☐ c. $95,800
- ☐ d. $96,200

Explanation: The correct answer is: **b. $92,800**.

The initial investment is calculated as:

Initial Investment = (Original Cost of Equipment) + (Increase in Accounts Receivable) − (Increase in Accounts Payable) − (Proceeds from Sale of Existing Equipment) + (Tax Effect of Disposal of Existing Equipment)

Increase in Accounts Receivable = ($8,000 − $6,000) = $2,000

Increase in Accounts Payable = ($2,500 − $2,100) = $400

Proceeds from Sale of Existing Equipment = $3,000 (given)

Net Book Value = Original Cost − Accumulated Depreciation

Net Book Value = $50,000 − $45,000 = $5,000

Tax Effect of Disposal of Existing Equipment = (Tax Rate) (Proceeds from Sale − Net Book Value)

Tax Effect of Disposal of Existing Equipment = (0.4) ($3,000 − $5,000) = −$800

Initial Investment = $95,000 + $2,000 − $400 − $3,000 − $800 = $92,800

Question 2E3-CQ01

Topic: Payback and Discounted Payback

Hobart Corporation evaluates capital projects using a variety of performance screens; including a hurdle rate of 16% and a payback period of 3 years or less. Management is completing review of a project on the basis of the following projections

Capital investment	$200,000
Annual cash flows (after-tax)	$74,000
Straight-line depreciation	5 years
Terminal value (after-tax)	$20,000

The projected internal rate of return is 20%. Which one of the following alternatives reflects the appropriate conclusions for the indicated evaluative measures?

	Internal Rate of Return	Payback
a.	Accept	Reject
b.	Reject	Reject
c.	Accept	Accept
d.	Reject	Accept

Explanation: The correct answer is: **c.** Accept; Accept.

Since the project's internal rate of return (IRR) of 20% exceeds the hurdle rate of 16%, it should be accepted on that basis.

The project's payback = $200,000 / $74,000 = 2.7 years, which is less than the minimum 3 years required. Therefore, the project should be accepted based on payback.

Question 2E3-CQ02

Topic: Payback and Discounted Payback

Quint Company uses the payback method as part of its analysis of capital investments. One of its projects requires a $140,000 investment and has these projected before-tax cash flows:

Year 1	$60,000
Year 2	60,000
Year 3	60,000
Year 4	80,000
Year 5	80,000

Quint has an effective 40% tax rate. Based on these data, the after-tax payback period is

- ☐ **a.** 1.5.
- ☐ **b.** 2.3.
- ☐ **c.** 3.4.
- ☐ **d.** 3.7.

Explanation: The correct answer is: **d.** 3.7.

The payback is the length of time it takes to recover the initial investment.

After-Tax Cash Flow for Year 1 = $60,000 (1 − 40% Tax Rate)

After-Tax Cash Flow for Year 1 = $60,000 (0.6) = $36,000

After-Tax Cash Flow for Year 2 = $60,000 (1 − 40% Tax Rate)

After-Tax Cash Flow for Year 2 = $60,000 (0.6) = $36,000

After-Tax Cash Flow for Year 3 = $60,000 (1 − 40% Tax Rate)

After-Tax Cash Flow for Year 3 = $60,000 (0.6) = $36,000

After-Tax Cash Flows for Year 4 = $80,000 (1 − 40% Tax Rate)

After-Tax Cash Flows for Year 4 = $80,000 (0.6) = $48,000

After-Tax Cash Flows for Year 5 = $80,000 (1 − 40% Tax Rate)

After-Tax Cash Flows for Year 5 = $80,000 (0.6) = $48,000

By the end of Year 3, Quint will recover $108,000 ($36,000 + $36,000 + $36,000) of the $140,000.

By the end of Year 4, Quint will recover $156,000 ($36,000 + $36,000 + $36,000 + $48,000) of the $140,000.

Therefore, the payback occurs at some point between Year 3 and Year 4. The payback can be calculated as:

Payback = 3 Years + [($140,000 − $108,000) / ($156,000 − $108,000)]

Payback = 3 Years + ($32 / $48) = 3 Years + 0.67 Years = 3.67 Years, which is approximately 3.7 years.

Question 2E3-CQ03

Topic: Payback and Discounted Payback

Foster Manufacturing is analyzing a capital investment project that is forecasted to produce the following cash flows and net income.

Year	After-Tax Cash Flow	Net Income
0	($20,000)	$0
1	6,000	2,000
2	6,000	2,000
3	8,000	2,000
4	8,000	2,000

The payback period of this project will be

- ☐ a. 2.5 years.
- ☐ b. 2.6 years.
- ☐ c. 3.0 years.
- ☐ d. 3.3 years.

Explanation: The correct answer is: **c.** 3.0 years.

The payback is the length of time it takes to recover the initial investment. The payback period is the amount of time it takes to have the initial investment equal to the future cash flows.

The investment will recover the initial investment of $20,000 in 3 years, as shown next.

Initial Investment = −$20,000

Sum of Cash Flows, Years 1, 2 and 3 = $6,000 + $6,000 + $8,000 = $20,000

At the end of Year 3, the cash flows are equal to the initial investment

Question 2E3-LS02

Topic: Payback and Discounted Payback

Which of the following statements is **not** true of using the payback method in capital budgeting? The payback method

- ☐ **a.** provides a rough measure of project risk.
- ☐ **b.** takes into account the time value of money.
- ☐ **c.** does not distinguish between types of cash inflows.
- ☐ **d.** represents the break-even point for an investment.

Explanation: The correct answer is: **b.** takes into account the time value of money.

A disadvantage of the payback method is that it ignores the time value of money.

Question 2E4-CQ01

Topic: Risk Analysis in Capital Investment

Long Inc. is analyzing a $1 million investment in new equipment to produce a product with a $5 per unit margin. The equipment will last 5 years, be depreciated on a straight-line basis for tax purposes, and have no value at the end of its life. A study of unit sales produced these data:

Annual Unit Sales	Probability
80,000	0.10
85,000	0.20
90,000	0.30
95,000	0.20
100,000	0.10
110,000	0.10

If Long utilizes a 12% hurdle rate and is subject to a 40% effective income tax rate, the expected net present value of the project would be

- a. $261,750.
- b. $283,380.
- c. $297,800.
- d. $427,580.

Explanation: The correct answer is: **b. $283,380.**

To calculate the expected net present value (NPV) of the project, the first step is to calculate the expected annual sales, as shown:

Expected Annual Sales Volume = (Annual Sales Volume) (Associated Probability)

Expected Annual Sales Volume = (80,000) (0.1) + (85,000) (0.2) + (90,000) (0.3) + (95,000) (0.2) + (100,000) (0.1) + (110,000) (0.1)

Expected Annual Sales Volume = 8,000 + 17,000 + 27,000 + 19,000 + 10,000 + 11,000

Expected Annual Sales Volume = 92,000

Total Margin = (Sales) (Margin per Unit)

The expected margin per year would then be calculated as shown:

Expected Annual Margin = (92,000) ($5) = $460,000

The cash flow for each of the 5 years of the project is calculated as shown:

Cash Flow, Each Year = (Contribution Margin − Depreciation) (1 − Tax Rate) + Depreciation

Depreciation = $1,000,000 / 5 Years = $200,000 per Year

Cash Flow, Each Year = ($460,000 − $200,000) (1 − 0.4) + $200,000

Cash Flow, Each Year = $260,000 (0.6) + $200,000 = $156,000 + $200,000 = $356,000

The expected NPV of the project can now be calculated:

Expected NPV of Project = (Initial Investment) + (Estimated Annual Cash Flow) (Present Value Factor of Annuity, $i=12, n=5$)

Expected NPV of Project = −$1,000,000 + ($356,000) (3.605) = $283,380

Question 2E4-CQ02
Topic: Risk Analysis in Capital Investment

Parker Industries is analyzing a $200,000 equipment investment to produce a new product for the next 5 years. A study of expected annual after-tax cash flows from the project produced these data:

Annual After-Tax Cash Flow	Probability
$45,000	0.10
50,000	0.20
55,000	0.30
60,000	0.20
65,000	0.10
70,000	0.10

If Parker utilizes a 14% hurdle rate, the probability of achieving a positive net present value is best found by utilizing

- ☐ a. sensitivity analysis.
- ☐ b. scenario analysis.
- ☐ c. simulation analysis.
- ☐ d. certainty equivalents.

Explanation: The correct answer is: **c.** simulation analysis.

Repeating the simulation process many times would allow values to be plotted on a frequency distribution graph from which the probability of a positive net present value could be found.

Question 2E4-LS03
Topic: Risk Analysis in Capital Investment

What is a primary caution when using a company's cost of capital as the discount rate to evaluate a capital project?

- ☐ a. Evaluation typically rejects high-risk projects.
- ☐ b. The cost of capital may need to be risk adjusted.
- ☐ c. Low-risk projects are favored.
- ☐ d. Opportunity costs can be distorted.

Explanation: The correct answer is: **b.** The cost of capital may need to be risk adjusted.

Many firms use their company's cost of capital as the yardstick to discount the cash flows on new investments. But in situations where new projects are more or less risky than is normal for the firm, use of the company rate can lead to erroneously accepting or rejecting a project.

Question 2E4-LS04

Topic: Risk Analysis in Capital Investment

Which type of real option would a firm be **most** likely to choose if there is a high probability that competitors can enter a market and capture profitable future cash flows?

Note that this discussion refers to competitors entering, exiting or otherwise changing the markets. The earlier discussion concerning whether our firm has exclusive right to exercise its real options (including all four of these choices) is not the same as responding to a competitive action in the marketplace.

- ☐ **a.** Adapt
- ☐ **b.** Abandon
- ☐ **c.** Postpone
- ☐ **d.** Expand

Explanation: The correct answer is: **a.** Adapt.

The ability of a firm to vary output or production methods in response to demand allows the firm to swap or exchange its output mix as demand changes. Given the myriad tumultuous and competitive market situations, companies often build flexibility into their manufacturing operations so they can respond quickly to any changes and produce the most valuable set of outputs.

Section F: Professional Ethics

Question 2F1-AT01

Topic: Ethical Considerations for Management Accounting and Financial Management

As management accountants progress in the profession, they often have the responsibility to supervise the work of less experienced workers. Which of the following is an ethical responsibility of the supervisor?

- ☐ **a.** Hire new workers who will fit in socially with existing staff.
- ☐ **b.** Maximize the profit or minimize the cost of the department.
- ☐ **c.** Ensure that workers handle confidential information appropriately.
- ☐ **d.** Encourage the workers to develop relations with customers.

Explanation: The correct answer is: **c.** Ensure that workers handle confidential information appropriately.

Per the *IMA Statement of Ethical Professional Practice,* a management accountant has the responsibility to keep information confidential except when disclosure is authorized or legally required. A management accountant also has the responsibility to inform all relevant parties regarding appropriate use of confidential information. This includes monitoring subordinates' activities to ensure compliance.

Question 2F1-AT02

Topic: Ethical Considerations for Management Accounting and Financial Management

Sam Smith has been offered a pair of tickets to the pro football team if Smith purchases a computerized inventory control system from a specific vendor. Which of the following steps should Smith take?

- ☐ a. Refuse any further conversations with the vendor.
- ☐ b. Review his company's policies on gifts from vendors.
- ☐ c. Sign the contract for the system if the price of the ticket is less than $50.
- ☐ d. Consult with the Audit Committee of the board of directors.

Explanation: The correct answer is: **b.** Review his company's policies on gifts from vendors.

According to the *IMA Statement of Ethical Professional Practice,* when faced with ethical issues, an individual should follow his or her organization's established policies on the resolution of such a conflict.

Question 2F1-AT03

Topic: Ethical Considerations for Management Accounting and Financial Management

John Moore was recently hired as assistant controller of a manufacturing company. The company controller, Nancy Kay, has forecasted a 16% increase in annual earnings. However, during the last quarter of the year, John estimates that the company will report only a 12% increase in earnings. When he reports this to Nancy, she tells him that meeting the numbers won't be a problem. She explains that there are several jobs in production that will finish after the end of the fiscal year, and she will record the associated revenue in the accounting system for the current year.

What is the first step that John Moore should take at this time?

- ☐ a. Notify the audit committee of the issue.
- ☐ b. Contact his lawyer to determine his rights.
- ☐ c. Discuss the issue with the chief financial officer of another company, who does not know any employees at John's company.
- ☐ d. Follow his organization's established policies regarding the resolution of this type of conflict.

Explanation: The correct answer is: **d.** Follow his organization's established policies regarding the resolution of this type of conflict.

Before taking any steps, John Moore should check to see if his organization has established policies regarding how to handle this type of conflict. If such policies exist, he should follow them.

Question 2F2-AT01

Topic: Ethical Considerations for the Organization

The Foreign Corrupt Practices Act is a U.S. law that prohibits U.S. companies from

- ☐ **a.** making "corrupt" payments to foreign officials for the purpose of obtaining or retaining business.
- ☐ **b.** making products in overseas markets that do not comply with the same safety and environmental regulations as for domestically produced products.
- ☐ **c.** exporting to countries that do not comply with U.S. human rights regulations.
- ☐ **d.** selling products for corrupt, unethical, or illegal purposes.

Explanation: The correct answer is: **a.** making "corrupt" payments to foreign officials for the purpose of obtaining or retaining business.

The 1977 Foreign Corrupt Practices Act is a U.S. law that forbids U.S. companies from obtaining contracts or business through the payment of bribes.

Question 2F2-AT02

Topic: Ethical Considerations for the Organization

Which of the following actions will most likely result in a successful foreign business venture in Islamic countries?

- ☐ **a.** Employ Islamic people.
- ☐ **b.** Behave in a manner that is consistent with Islamic ethics.
- ☐ **c.** Have property in an Islamic nation.
- ☐ **d.** Adhere to Islamic beliefs.

Explanation: The correct answer is: **b.** Behave in a manner that is consistent with Islamic ethics.

Successful operation by a company operating in a foreign country is a function of how well the company adapts to the host country's culture. Successful adaptation includes behaving in a manner that is consistent with the host country's ethics.

APPENDIX A

Time Value of Money Tables

Present Value of $1

Periods	1%	2%	3%	4%	5%	6%	7%	8%	9%	10%	11%	12%	13%	14%	15%	16%	18%	20%
1	0.990	0.980	0.971	0.962	0.952	0.943	0.935	0.926	0.917	0.909	0.901	0.893	0.885	0.877	0.870	0.862	0.847	0.833
2	0.980	0.961	0.943	0.925	0.907	0.890	0.873	0.857	0.842	0.826	0.812	0.797	0.783	0.769	0.756	0.743	0.718	0.694
3	0.971	0.942	0.915	0.889	0.864	0.840	0.816	0.794	0.772	0.751	0.731	0.712	0.693	0.675	0.658	0.641	0.609	0.579
4	0.961	0.924	0.888	0.855	0.823	0.792	0.763	0.735	0.708	0.683	0.659	0.636	0.613	0.592	0.572	0.552	0.516	0.482
5	0.951	0.906	0.863	0.822	0.784	0.747	0.713	0.681	0.650	0.621	0.593	0.567	0.543	0.519	0.497	0.476	0.437	0.402
6	0.942	0.888	0.837	0.790	0.746	0.705	0.666	0.630	0.596	0.564	0.535	0.507	0.480	0.456	0.432	0.410	0.370	0.335
7	0.933	0.871	0.813	0.760	0.711	0.665	0.623	0.583	0.547	0.513	0.482	0.452	0.425	0.400	0.376	0.354	0.314	0.279
8	0.923	0.853	0.789	0.731	0.677	0.627	0.582	0.540	0.502	0.467	0.434	0.404	0.376	0.351	0.327	0.305	0.266	0.233
9	0.914	0.837	0.766	0.703	0.645	0.592	0.544	0.500	0.460	0.424	0.391	0.361	0.333	0.308	0.284	0.263	0.225	0.194
10	0.905	0.820	0.744	0.676	0.614	0.558	0.508	0.463	0.422	0.386	0.352	0322	0.295	0.270	0.247	0.227	0.191	0.162
11	0.896	0.804	0.722	0.650	0.585	0.527	0.475	0.429	0.388	0.350	0.317	0.287	0.261	0.237	0.215	0.195	0.162	0.135
12	0.887	0.788	0.701	0.625	0.557	0.497	0.444	0.397	0.356	0.319	0.286	0.257	0.231	0.208	0.187	0.168	0.137	0.112
13	0.879	0.773	0.681	0601	0.530	0.469	0.415	0.368	0.326	0.290	0.258	0.229	0.204	0.182	0.163	0.145	0.116	0.093
14	0.870	0.758	0.661	0.577	0.505	0.442	0.388	0.340	0.299	0.263	0.232	0.205	0.181	0.160	0.141	0.125	0.099	0.078
15	0.861	0.743	0.642	0.555	0.481	0.417	0.362	0.315	0.275	0.239	0.209	0.183	0.160	0.140	0.123	0.108	0.084	0.065
16	0.853	0.728	0.623	0.534	0.458	0.394	0.339	0.292	0.252	0.218	0.188	0.163	0.141	0.123	0.107	0.093	0.071	0.054
18	0.836	0.700	0.587	0.494	0.416	0.350	0.296	0.250	0.212	0.180	0.153	0.130	0.111	0.095	0.081	0.069	0.051	0.038
20	0.820	0.673	0.554	0.456	0.377	0.312	0.258	0.215	0.178	0.149	0.124	0.104	0.087	0.073	0.061	0.051	0.037	0.026
22	0.803	0.647	0.522	0.422	0.342	0.278	0.226	0.184	0.150	0.123	0.101	0.083	0.070	0.056	0.046	0.038	0.026	0.018
24	0.788	0.622	0.492	0.390	0.310	0.247	0.197	0.158	0.126	0.102	0.082	0.066	0.053	0.043	0.035	0.028	0.019	0.013

Present Value of an Annuity

Periods	1%	2%	3%	4%	5%	6%	7%	8%	9%	10%	11%	12%	13%	14%	15%	16%	18%	20%
1	0.990	0.980	0.971	0.962	0.952	0.943	0.935	0.926	0.917	0.909	0.901	0.893	0.885	0.877	0.870	0.862	0.847	0.833
2	1.970	1.942	1.913	1.886	1.859	1.833	1.808	1.783	1.759	1.736	1.713	1.690	1.668	1.647	1.626	1.605	1.566	1.528
3	2.941	2.884	2.829	2.775	2.723	2.673	2.624	2.577	2.531	2.487	2.444	2.402	2.361	2.322	2.283	2.246	2.174	2.106
4	3.902	3.808	3.717	3.630	3.546	3.465	3.387	3.312	3.240	3.170	3.102	3.037	2.974	2.914	2.855	2.798	2.690	2.589
5	4.853	4.713	4.580	4.452	4.329	4.212	4.100	3.993	3.890	3.791	3.696	3.605	3.517	3.433	3.352	3.274	3.127	2.991
6	5.795	5.601	5.417	5.242	5.076	4.917	4.767	4.623	4.486	4.355	4.231	4.111	3.998	3.889	3.784	3.685	3.498	3.326
7	6.728	6.472	6.230	6.002	5.786	5.582	5.389	5.206	5.033	4.868	4.712	4.564	4.423	4.288	4.160	4.039	3.812	3.605
8	7.652	7.325	7.020	6.733	6.463	6.210	5.971	5.747	5.535	5.335	5.146	4.968	4.799	4.639	4.487	4.344	4.078	3.837
9	8.566	8.162	7.786	7.435	7.108	6.802	6.515	6.247	5.995	5.759	5.537	5.328	5.132	4.946	4.772	4.607	4.303	4.031
10	9.471	8.983	8.530	8.111	7.722	7.360	7.024	6.710	6.418	6.145	5.889	5.650	5.426	5.216	5.019	4.833	4.494	4.192
11	10.37	9.787	9.253	8.760	8.306	7.887	7.499	7.139	6.805	6.495	6.207	5.938	5.687	5.453	5.234	5.029	4.656	4.327
12	11.26	10.58	9.954	9.385	8.863	8.384	7.943	7.536	7.161	6.814	6.492	6.194	5.918	5.660	5.421	5.197	4.793	4.439
13	12.13	11.35	10.63	9.986	9.394	8.853	8.358	7.904	7.487	7.103	6.750	6.424	6.122	5.842	5.583	5.342	4.910	4.533
14	13.00	12.11	11.30	10.56	9.899	9.295	8.745	8.244	7.786	7.367	6.982	6.628	6.302	6.002	5.724	5.468	5.008	4.611
15	13.87	12.85	11.94	11.12	10.38	9.712	9.108	8.559	8.061	7.606	7.191	6.811	6.462	6.142	5.847	5.575	5.092	4.675
16	14.72	13.58	12.56	11.65	10.84	10.11	9.447	8.851	8.313	7.824	7.379	6.974	6.604	6.265	5.954	5.668	5.162	4.730
18	16.398	14.992	13.754	12.659	11.690	10.828	10.059	9.372	8.756	8.201	7.702	7.250	6.840	6.467	6.128	5.818	5.273	4.812
20	18.046	16.351	14.877	13.590	12.462	11.470	10.594	9.818	9.129	8.514	7.963	7.469	7.025	6.623	6.259	5.929	5.353	4.870
22	19.660	17.658	15.937	14.451	13.163	12.042	11.061	10.201	9.442	8.772	8.176	7.645	7.170	6.743	6.359	6.011	5.410	4.909
24	21.243	18.914	16.936	15.247	13.799	12.550	11.469	10.529	9.707	8.985	8.348	7.784	7.283	6.835	6.434	6.073	5.451	4.937
26	22.795	20.121	17.877	15.983	14.375	13.003	11.826	10.810	9.929	9.161	8.488	7.896	7.372	6.906	6.491	6.118	5.480	4.956
28	24.316	21.281	18.764	16.663	14.898	13.406	12.137	11.051	10.116	9.307	8.602	7.984	7.441	6.961	6.534	6.152	5.502	4.970
30	25.808	22.396	19.600	17.292	15.372	13.765	12.409	11.258	10.274	9.427	8.694	8.055	7.496	7.003	6.566	6.177	5.517	4.979
32	27.270	23.468	20.389	17.874	15.803	14.084	12.647	11.435	10.406	9.526	8.769	8.112	7.538	7.035	6.591	6.196	5.528	4.985
34	28.703	24.499	21.132	18.411	16.193	14.368	12.854	11.587	10.518	9.609	8.829	8.157	7.572	7.06	6.609	6.21	5.536	4.99
36	30.108	25.489	21.832	18.908	16.547	14.621	13.035	11.717	10.612	9.677	8.879	8.192	7.598	7.079	6.623	6.22	5.541	4.993
40	32.835	27.355	23.115	19.793	17.159	15.046	13.332	11.925	10.757	9.779	8.951	8.244	7.634	7.105	6.642	6.233	5.548	4.997

APPENDIX B

ICMA Learning Outcome Statements—Part 2

Revised August 2015
Source: Institute of Certified Management Accountants

PART 2 – Financial Decision Making

Section A. Financial Statement Analysis (25%—Levels A, B, and C)

Part 2—Section A.1. Basic Financial Statement Analysis

a. for the balance sheet and income statement prepare and analyze common-size financial statements; i.e., calculate percentage of assets and sales, respectively; also called vertical analysis
b. for the balance sheet and income statement prepare a comparative financial statement horizontal analysis; i.e., calculate trend year over year for every item on the financial statement compared to base year
c. calculate the growth rate of individual line items on the balance sheet and income statement

Part 2—Section A.2. Financial Ratios

The candidate should be able to:

Liquidity

a. calculate and interpret the current ratio, the quick (acid-test) ratio, the cash ratio, the cash flow ratio, and the net working capital ratio
b. explain how changes in one or more of the elements of current assets, current liabilities, and/or unit sales can change the liquidity ratios and calculate that impact
c. demonstrate an understanding of the liquidity of current liabilities

Leverage

d. define solvency
e. define operating leverage and financial leverage

f. calculate degree of operating leverage and degree of financial leverage
g. demonstrate an understanding of the effect on the capital structure and solvency of a company with a change in the composition of debt vs. equity by calculating leverage ratios
h. calculate and interpret the financial leverage ratio, and determine the effect of a given change in capital structure on this ratio
i. calculate and interpret the following ratios: debt to equity, long-term debt to equity, and debt to total assets
j. define, calculate and interpret the following ratios: fixed charge coverage (earnings to fixed charges), interest coverage (times interest earned), and cash flow to fixed charges
k. discuss how capital structure decisions affect the risk profile of a firm

Activity

l. calculate and interpret accounts receivable turnover, inventory turnover and accounts payable turnover
m. calculate and interpret days sales outstanding in receivables, days sales in inventory, and days purchases in accounts payable
n. define and calculate the operating cycle and cash cycle of a firm
o. calculate and interpret total assets turnover and fixed asset turnover

Profitability

p. calculate and interpret gross profit margin percentage, operating profit margin percentage, net profit margin percentage, and earnings before interest, taxes, depreciation, and amortization (EBITDA) margin percentage
q. calculate and interpret return on assets (ROA) and return on equity (ROE)

Market

r. calculate and interpret the market/book ratio, the price/earnings ratio and price to EBITDA ratio
s. calculate and interpret book value per share
t. identify and explain the limitations of book value per share
u. calculate and interpret basic and diluted earnings per share
v. calculate and interpret earnings yield, dividend yield, dividend payout ratio and shareholder return

General

w. identify the limitations of ratio analysis
x. demonstrate a familiarity with the sources of financial information about public companies and industry ratio averages
y. evaluate the financial strength and performance of an entity based on multiple ratios

Part 2—Section A.3. Profitability analysis

a. demonstrate an understanding of the factors that contribute to inconsistent definitions of "equity," "assets" and "return" when using ROA and ROE
b. determine the effect on return on total assets of a change in one or more elements of the financial statements
c. identify factors to be considered in measuring income, including estimates, accounting methods, disclosure incentives, and the different needs of users
d. explain the importance of the source, stability, and trend of sales and revenue
e. demonstrate an understanding of the relationship between revenue and receivables and revenue and inventory
f. determine and analyze the effect on revenue of changes in revenue recognition and measurement methods
g. analyze cost of sales by calculating and interpreting the gross profit margin
h. distinguish between gross profit margin, operating profit margin and net profit margin and analyze the effects of changes in the components of each
i. define and perform a variation analysis (percentage change over time)
j. calculate and interpret sustainable equity growth

Part 2—Section A.4. Special issues

The candidate should be able to:

a. demonstrate an understanding of the impact of foreign exchange fluctuations
   1. identify and explain issues in the accounting for foreign operations (e.g., historical vs. current rate and the treatment of translation gains and losses)
   2. define functional currency
   3. calculate the financial ratio impact of a change in exchange rates
   4. discuss the possible impact on management and investor behavior of volatility in reported earnings
b. demonstrate an understanding of the impact of inflation on financial ratios and the reliability of financial ratios
c. define and explain off-balance sheet financing
   1. identify and describe the following forms of off-balance sheet financing: (i) leases; (ii) special purpose entities; (iii) sale of receivables; and (iv) joint ventures
   2. explain why companies use off-balance sheet financing
   3. calculate the impact of off-balance sheet financing on the debt to equity ratio
d. describe how to adjust financial statements for changes in accounting treatments (principles, estimates, and errors) and how these adjustments impact financial ratios
e. distinguish between book value and market value; and distinguish between accounting profit and economic profit
f. identify the determinants and indicators of earnings quality, and explain why they are important

Section B. Corporate Finance (20%—Levels A, B, and C)

Part 2—Section B.1. Risk and return

The candidate should be able to:

a. calculate rates of return
b. identify and demonstrate an understanding of systematic (market) risk and unsystematic (company) risk
c. identify and demonstrate an understanding of credit risk, foreign exchange risk, interest rate risk, market risk, industry risk and political risk
d. demonstrate an understanding of the relationship between risk and return
e. distinguish between individual security risk and portfolio risk
f. demonstrate an understanding of diversification
g. define beta and explain how a change in beta impacts a security's price
h. demonstrate an understanding of the Capital Asset Pricing Model (CAPM) and calculate the expected risk-adjusted returns using CAPM

Part 2—Section B.2. Long-term financial management

The candidate should be able to:

a. describe the term structure of interest rates, and explain why it changes over time
b. define and identify the characteristics of common stock and preferred stock
c. identify and describe the basic features of a bond such as maturity, par value, coupon rate, provisions for redeeming, conversion provisions, covenants, options granted to the issuer or investor, indentures, and restrictions
d. identify and evaluate debt issuance or refinancing strategies
e. value bonds, common stock, and preferred stock using discounted cash flow methods
f. demonstrate an understanding of duration as a measure of bond interest rate sensitivity
g. explain how income taxes impact financing decisions
h. define and demonstrate an understanding of derivatives and their uses
i. identify and describe the basic features of futures and forwards
j. distinguish a long position from a short position
k. define options and distinguish between a call and a put by identifying the characteristics of each
l. define exercise price, strike price, option premium and intrinsic value
m. demonstrate an understanding of the interrelationship of the variables that comprise the value of an option; e.g., relationship between exercise price and strike price, and value of a call
n. define swaps for interest rate and foreign currency
o. define and identify characteristics of other sources of long-term financing, such as leases, convertible securities, and warrants
p. demonstrate an understanding of the relationship among inflation, interest rates, and the prices of financial instruments

- q. define the cost of capital and demonstrate an understanding of its applications in capital structure decisions
- r. determine the weighted average cost of capital and the cost of its individual components
- s. calculate the marginal cost of capital
- t. explain the importance of using marginal cost as opposed to historical cost
- u. demonstrate an understanding of the use of the cost of capital in capital investment decisions
- v. demonstrate an understanding of how income taxes impact capital structure and capital investment decisions
- w. use the constant growth dividend discount model to value stock and demonstrate an understanding of the two-stage dividend discount model
- x. demonstrate an understanding of relative or comparable valuation methods, such as price/earnings (P/E) ratios, market/book ratios, and price/sales ratios

Part 2—Section B.3. Raising capital

The candidate should be able to:

- a. identify the characteristics of the different types of financial markets and exchanges
- b. demonstrate an understanding of the concept of market efficiency, including the strong form, semi-strong form, and weak form of market efficiency
- c. describe the role of the credit rating agencies
- d. demonstrate an understanding of the roles of investment banks, including underwriting, advice, and trading
- e. define initial public offerings (IPOs)
- f. define subsequent/secondary offerings
- g. describe lease financing, explain its benefits and disadvantages, and calculate the net advantage to leasing using discounted cash flow concepts
- h. define the different types of dividends, including cash dividends, stock dividends, and stock splits
- i. identify and discuss the factors that influence the dividend policy of a firm
- j. demonstrate an understanding of the dividend payment process for both common and preferred stock
- k. define share repurchase and explain why a firm would repurchase its stock
- l. define insider trading and explain why it is illegal

Part 2—Section B.4. Working capital management

The candidate should be able to:

Working capital

- a. define working capital and identify its components
- b. calculate net working capital
- c. explain the benefit of short-term financial forecasts in the management of working capital

Cash

d. identify and describe factors influencing the levels of cash
e. identify and explain the three motives for holding cash
f. prepare forecasts of future cash flows
g. identify methods of speeding up cash collections
h. calculate the net benefit of a lockbox system
i. define concentration banking
j. demonstrate an understanding of compensating balances
k. identify methods of slowing down disbursements
l. demonstrate an understanding of disbursement float and overdraft systems

Marketable securities

m. identify and describe reasons for holding marketable securities
n. define the different types of marketable securities, including money market instruments, T-bills, treasury notes, treasury bonds, repurchase agreements, Federal agency securities, bankers' acceptances, commercial paper, negotiable CDs, Eurodollar CDs, and other marketable securities
o. evaluate the trade-offs among the variables in marketable security selections, including safety, marketability/liquidity, yield, maturity, and taxability
p. demonstrate an understanding of the risk and return trade-off

Accounts receivable

q. identify the factors influencing the level of receivables
r. demonstrate an understanding of the impact of changes in credit terms or collection policies on accounts receivable, working capital and sales volume
s. define default risk
t. identify and explain the factors involved in determining an optimal credit policy

Inventory

u. define lead time and safety stock; identify reasons for carrying inventory and the factors influencing its level
v. identify and calculate the costs related to inventory, including carrying costs, ordering costs and shortage (stockout) costs
w. explain how a just-in-time (JIT) inventory management system helps manage inventory
x. identify the interaction between high inventory turnover and high gross margin (calculation not required)
y. demonstrate an understanding of economic order quantity (EOQ) and how a change in one variable would affect the EOQ (calculation not required)

Short-term credit and working capital cost management

z. demonstrate an understanding of how risk affects a firm's approach to its current asset financing policy (aggressive, conservative, etc.)

aa. identify and describe the different types of short-term credit, including trade credit, short-term bank loans, commercial paper, lines of credit, and bankers' acceptances

bb. estimate the annual cost and effective annual interest rate of not taking a cash discount

cc. calculate the effective annual interest rate of a bank loan with a compensating balance requirement and/or a commitment fee

dd. demonstrate an understanding of factoring accounts receivable and calculate the cost of factoring

ee. explain the maturity matching or hedging approach to financing

ff. demonstrate an understanding of the factors involved in managing the costs of working capital

General

gg. recommend a strategy for managing current assets that would fulfill a given objective

Part 2—Section B.5. Corporate restructuring

The candidate should be able to:

a. demonstrate an understanding of the following:
  i. mergers and acquisitions, including horizontal, vertical, and conglomerate
  ii. leveraged buyouts

b. identify defenses against takeovers (e.g., golden parachute, leveraged recapitalization, poison pill (shareholders' rights plan), staggered board of directors, fair price, voting rights plan, white knight)

c. identify and describe divestiture concepts such as spin-offs, split-ups, equity carve-outs, and tracking stock

d. evaluate key factors in a company's financial situation and determine if a restructuring would be beneficial to the shareholders

e. validate possible synergies in targeted mergers and acquisitions

f. define bankruptcy

g. differentiate between reorganization and liquidation

h. value a business, a business segment, and a business combination using discounted cash flow method

i. evaluate a proposed business combination and make a recommendation based on both quantitative and qualitative considerations

Part 2—Section B.6. International finance

The candidate should be able to:

a. demonstrate an understanding of foreign currencies and how foreign currency affects the prices of goods and services

b. identify the variables that affect exchange rates

c. calculate whether a currency has depreciated or appreciated against another currency over a period of time, and evaluate the impact of the change
d. demonstrate how currency futures, currency swaps, and currency options can be used to manage exchange rate risk
e. calculate the net profit/loss of cross-border transactions, and evaluate the impact of this net profit/loss
f. recommend methods of managing exchange rate risk and calculate the net profit/loss of your strategy
g. identify and explain the benefits of international diversification
h. identify and explain common trade financing methods, including cross-border factoring, letters of credit, banker's acceptances, forfaiting, and countertrade
i. demonstrate an understanding of how transfer pricing affects effective worldwide tax rate

Section C. Decision Analysis (20%—Levels A, B, and C)

Part 2—Section C.1. Cost/volume/profit analysis

The candidate should be able to:

a. demonstrate an understanding of how cost/volume/profit (CVP) analysis (break-even analysis) is used to examine the behavior of total revenues, total costs, and operating income as changes occur in output levels, selling prices, variable costs per unit, or fixed costs
b. calculate operating income at different operating levels
c. differentiate between costs that are fixed and costs that are variable with respect to levels of output
d. explain why the classification of fixed vs. variable costs is affected by the time-frame being considered
e. calculate contribution margin per unit and total contribution margin
f. calculate the breakeven point in units and dollar sales to achieve targeted operating income or targeted net income
g. demonstrate an understanding of how changes in unit sales mix affect operating income in multiple-product situations
h. calculate multiple-product breakeven points given percentage share of sales and explain why there is no unique breakeven point in multiple-product situations
i. define, calculate and interpret margin of safety and margin of safety ratio
j. explain how sensitivity analysis can be used in CVP analysis when there is uncertainty about sales
k. analyze and recommend a course of action using CVP analysis
l. demonstrate an understanding of the impact of income taxes on CVP analysis

Part 2—Section C.2. Marginal analysis

The candidate should be able to:
   a. identify and define relevant costs (incremental, marginal, or differential costs), sunk costs, avoidable costs, explicit and implicit costs, split-off point, joint production costs, separable processing costs, and relevant revenues
   b. explain why sunk costs are not relevant in the decision-making process
   c. demonstrate an understanding of and calculate opportunity costs
   d. calculate relevant costs given a numerical scenario
   e. define and calculate marginal cost and marginal revenue
   f. identify and calculate total cost, average fixed cost, average variable cost, and average total cost
   g. demonstrate proficiency in the use of marginal analysis for decisions such as (a) introducing a new product or changing output levels of existing products, (b) accepting or rejecting special orders, (c) making or buying a product or service, (d) selling a product or performing additional processes and selling a more value-added product, and (e) adding or dropping a segment
   h. calculate the effect on operating income of a decision to accept or reject a special order when there is idle capacity and the order has no long-run implications
   i. identify and describe qualitative factors in make-or-buy decisions, such as product quality and dependability of suppliers
   j. calculate the effect on operating income of a make-or-buy decision
   k. calculate the effects on operating income of a decision to sell or process further; and of a decision to drop or add a segment
   l. identify the effects of changes in capacity on production decisions
   m. demonstrate an understanding of the impact of income taxes on marginal analysis
   n. recommend a course of action using marginal analysis

Part 2—Section C.3. Pricing

The candidate should be able to:

   a. identify different pricing methodologies, including market comparables, cost-based, and value-based approaches
   b. differentiate between a cost-based approach (cost-plus pricing, mark-up pricing) and a market-based approach to setting prices
   c. calculate selling price using a cost-based approach
   d. demonstrate an understanding of how the pricing of a product or service is affected by the demand for and supply of the product or service, as well as the market structure within which it operates
   e. demonstrate an understanding of the impact of cartels on pricing

    f. demonstrate an understanding of the short-run equilibrium price for the firm in (1) pure competition; (2) monopolistic competition; (3) oligopoly; and (4) monopoly using the concepts of marginal revenue and marginal cost
    g. identify techniques used to set prices based on understanding customers' perceptions of value, competitors' technologies, products and costs
    h. define and demonstrate an understanding of target pricing and target costing and identify the main steps in developing target prices and target costs
    i. define value engineering
    j. calculate the target operating income per unit and target cost per unit
    k. define and distinguish between a value-added cost and a nonvalue-added cost
    l. define the pricing technique of cost plus target rate of return
    m. calculate the price elasticity of demand using the midpoint formula
    n. define and explain elastic and inelastic demand
    o. estimate total revenue given changes in prices and demand as well as elasticity
    p. discuss how pricing decisions can differ in the short-run and in the long-run
    q. define product life cycle; identify and explain the four stages of the product life cycle; and explain why pricing decisions might differ over the life of a product
    r. evaluate and recommend pricing strategies under specific market conditions

Section D. Risk Management (10%—Levels A, B, and C)

Part 2—Section D.1. Enterprise risk

The candidate should be able to:
    a. identify and explain the different types of risk, including business risk, hazard risks, financial risks, operational risks, and strategic risks
    b. demonstrate an understanding of operational risk
    c. define legal risk, compliance risk, and political risk
    d. demonstrate an understanding of how volatility and time impact risk
    e. define the concept of capital adequacy (i.e., solvency, liquidity, reserves, sufficient capital, etc.)
    f. explain the use of probabilities in determining exposure to risk and calculate expected loss given a set of probabilities
    g. define the concepts of unexpected loss and maximum possible loss (extreme or catastrophic loss)
    h. identify strategies for risk response (or treatment), including actions to avoid, retain, reduce (mitigate), transfer (share), and exploit (accept) risks
    i. define risk transfer (e.g., purchasing insurance, issuing debt)
    j. demonstrate an understanding of the concept of residual risk and distinguish it from inherent risk
    k. identify and explain the benefits of risk management
    l. identify and describe the key steps in the risk management process
    m. explain how attitude toward risk might affect the management of risk
    n. demonstrate a general understanding of the use of liability/hazard insurance to mitigate risk (detailed knowledge not required)
    o. identify methods of managing operational risk

p. identify and explain financial risk management methods
q. identify and explain qualitative risk assessment tools including risk identification, risk ranking, and risk maps
r. identify and explain quantitative risk assessment tools including cash flow at risk, earnings at risk, earnings distributions, and earnings per share (EPS) distributions
s. identify and explain Value at Risk (VaR) (calculations not required)
t. define enterprise risk management (ERM) and identify and describe key objectives, components and benefits of an ERM program
u. identify event identification techniques and provide examples of event identification within the context of an ERM approach
v. explain the role of corporate governance, risk analytics, and portfolio management in an ERM program
w. evaluate scenarios and recommend risk mitigation strategies
x. prepare a cost-benefit analysis and demonstrate an understanding of its uses in risk assessment and decision making
y. demonstrate an understanding of the COSO ERM conceptual framework

Section E. Investment Decisions (15%—Levels A, B, and C)

Part 2—Section E.1. Capital budgeting process

The candidate should be able to:

a. define capital budgeting and identify the steps or stages undertaken in developing and implementing a capital budget for a project
b. identify and calculate the relevant cash flows of a capital investment project on both a pretax and after-tax basis
c. demonstrate an understanding of how income taxes affect cash flows
d. distinguish between cash flows and accounting profits and discuss the relevance to capital budgeting of incremental cash flow, sunk cost, and opportunity cost
e. explain the importance of changes in net working capital in capital budgeting
f. discuss how the effects of inflation are reflected in capital budgeting analysis
g. define hurdle rate
h. identify and discuss qualitative considerations involved in the capital budgeting decision
i. describe the role of the post-audit in the capital budgeting process

Part 2—Section E.2. Discounted cash flow analysis

The candidate should be able to:

a. demonstrate an understanding of the two main discounted cash flow (DCF) methods, net present value (NPV) and internal rate of return (IRR)
b. calculate NPV and IRR
c. demonstrate an understanding of the decision criteria used in NPV and IRR analyses to determine acceptable projects

    d. compare NPV and IRR focusing on the relative advantages and disadvantages of each method, particularly with respect to independent versus mutually exclusive projects and the "multiple IRR problem"
    e. explain why NPV and IRR methods can produce conflicting rankings for capital projects if not applied properly
    f. identify assumptions of NPV and IRR
    g. evaluate and recommend project investments on the basis of DCF analysis

Part 2—Section E.3. Payback and discounted payback

The candidate should be able to:

    a. demonstrate an understanding of the payback and discounted payback methods
    b. identify the advantages and disadvantages of the payback and discounted payback methods
    c. calculate payback periods and discounted payback periods

Part 2—Section E.4. Risk analysis in capital investment

The candidate should be able to:

    a. identify alternative approaches to dealing with risk in capital budgeting
    b. distinguish among sensitivity analysis, scenario analysis, and Monte Carlo simulation as risk analysis techniques
    c. explain why a rate specifically adjusted for risk should be used when project cash flows are more or less risky than is normal for a firm
    d. explain how the value of a capital investment is increased if consideration is given to the possibility of adding on, speeding up, slowing up, or discontinuing early
    e. demonstrate an understanding of real options and identify examples of the different types of real options: e.g., abandon, delay, expand, and scale back (calculations not required)

Section F. Professional Ethics (10%—Levels A, B, and C)

Ethics may be tested in conjunction with any topic area.

Part 2—Section F.1 Ethical considerations for management accounting and financial management professionals

Using the standards outlined in **IMA's Statement of Ethical Professional Practice**, the candidate should be able to:

    a. identify and describe the four overarching ethical principles
    b. evaluate a given business situation for its ethical implications

c. identify and describe relevant standards that may have been violated in a given business situation and explain why the specific standards are applicable
d. recommend a course of action for management accountants or financial managers to take when confronted with an ethical dilemma in the business environment
e. evaluate and propose resolutions for ethical issues such as fraudulent reporting, manipulation of analyses, results, and budgets

Using the Fraud Triangle model, the candidate should be able to:

f. identify the three components of the triangle
g. use the model to explain how a management accounting and financial management professional can identify and manage the risk of fraud

Part 2—Section F.2. Ethical considerations for the organization

The candidate should be able to:

a. identify the purpose of the U.S. Foreign Corrupt Practices Act
b. identify the practices that the U.S Foreign Corrupt Practices Act prohibits, and explain how to apply this act to typical business situations
c. apply relevant provisions of IMA's Statement on Management Accounting, "Values and Ethics: From Inception to Practice" to a business situation
d. discuss corporate responsibility for ethical conduct
e. explain why it is important for an organization to have a code of conduct
f. demonstrate an understanding of the ways ethical values benefit an organization
g. demonstrate an understanding of the differences between ethical and legal behavior
h. demonstrate an understanding of role of "leadership by example" or "tone at the top" in determining an organization's ethical environment
i. explain the importance of human capital to an organization in creating a climate where "doing the right thing" is expected (i.e., hiring the right people, providing them with training, and practicing consistent values-based leadership)
j. explain how an organization's culture impacts its behavioral values
k. explain the importance of an organization's core values in explaining its ethical behavior
l. discuss the importance of employee training to maintaining an ethical organizational culture
m. describe the following methods to monitor ethical compliance: human performance feedback loop and survey tools
n. explain the importance of a whistleblowing framework (e.g., ethics helpline) to maintaining an ethical organizational culture
o. identify the requirements of SOX Section 406 - Code of Ethics for Senior Financial Officers
p. discuss the issues organizations face in applying their values and ethical standards internationally
q. demonstrate an understanding of the relationship between ethics and internal controls

Bibliography and References

American Institute of Certified Public Accountants, www.aicpa.org

Anderson, David R., Dennis J. Sweeney, Thomas A. Williams, Jeff Camm, and R. Kipp Martin. *Quantitative Methods for Business*, 11th ed. Mason, OH: South-Western, 2010.

Arens, Alvin A., Randal J. Elder, and Mark S. Beasley. *Auditing and Assurance Services: An Integrated Approach*, 13th ed. Upper Saddle River, NJ: Prentice-Hall, 2009.

Bergeron, Pierre G. *Finance: Essentials for the Successful Professional*. Independence, KY: Thomson Learning, 2002.

Bernstein, Leopold A., and John J. West. *Financial Statement Analysis: Theory, Application, and Interpretation*, 6th ed. Homewood, IL: Irwin, 1997.

Blocher, Edward J., David E. Stout, Paul E. Juras, and Gary Cokins. *Cost Management: A Strategic Emphasis*, 6th ed. New York: McGraw-Hill, 2013.

Bodnar, George H., and William S. Hopwood. *Accounting Information Systems*, 10th ed. Upper Saddle River, NJ: Prentice-Hall, 2010.

Brealey, Richard A., Stewart C. Myers, and Franklin Allen. *Principles of Corporate Finance*, 10th ed. New York: McGraw-Hill, 2011.

Brigham, Eugene F., and Michael C. Ehrhardt. *Financial Management: Theory and Practice*, 14th ed. Mason, OH: Cengage, 2013.

Campanella, Jack (ed.). *Principles of Quality Costs: Principles, Implementation, and Use*, 3rd ed. Milwaukee: ASQ Quality Press, 1999.

Committee of Sponsoring Organizations of the Treadway Commission (COSO), www.coso.org

Committee of Sponsoring Organizations of the Treadway Commission (COSO). *Enterprise Risk Management—Integrated Framework*. 2004.

Daniels, John D., Lee H. Radebaugh, and Daniel Sullivan. *International Business: Environments and Operations*, 14th ed. Upper Saddle River, NJ: Prentice-Hall, 2012.

Evans, Matt H. Course 11: The Balanced Scorecard, www.exinfm.com/training/pdfiles/course11r.pdf

Flesher, Dale. *Internal Auditing: Standards and Practices*. Altamonte Springs, FL: Institute of Internal Auditors, 1996.

Financial Accounting Standards Board, www.fasb.org

Financial Accounting Standards Board. *Statements of Financial Accounting Concepts*. Norwalk, CT: Author.

Forex Directory. "U.S. Dollar Charts," www.forexdirectory.net/chartsfx.html

Garrison, Ray H., Eric W. Noreen, and Peter Brewer. *Managerial Accounting*, 14th ed. Boston: McGraw-Hill/Irwin, 2011.

Gelinas, Ulric J. Jr., Richard B. Dull, and Patrick Wheeler. *Accounting Information Systems*, 9th ed. Cincinnati, OH: South-Western College Publishing, 2011.

Gibson, Charles H. *Financial Reporting and Analysis*, 13th ed. Mason, OH: South-Western Cengage Learning, 2013.

Goldratt, Elihayu M., and Jeff Cox. *The Goal: A Process of Ongoing Improvement*, 25th anniversary revised ed. Great Barrington, MA: North River Press, 2011.

Grant Thorton, LLP, www.grantthornton.ca

Greenstein, Marilyn, and Todd M. Feinman. *Electronic Commerce: Security, Risk Management, and Control*. Boston: McGraw-Hill Higher Education, 2000.

Hartgraves, A. L., and Wayne J. Morse. *Managerial Accounting*, 6th ed. Lombard, IL: Cambridge Business Publishers, 2012.

Hildebrand, David K., R. Lyman Ott, and J. Brian Gray. *Basic Statistical Ideas for Managers*, 2nd ed. Belmont, CA: Thomson Learning, 2005.

Hilton, Ronald W., Michael W. Maher, and Frank H. Selto. *Cost Management: Strategies for Business Decisions*, 4th ed. Boston: McGraw-Hill Irwin, 2007.

Horngren, Charles T., Srikant M. Datar, and Madhav Rajan. *Cost Accounting: A Managerial Emphasis*, 14th ed. Upper Saddle River, NJ: Prentice-Hall, 2012.

Hoyle, Joe B., Thomas F. Schaefer, and Timothy S. Doupnik. *Advanced Accounting*, 10th ed. Boston: McGraw-Hill Irwin, 2010.

Institute of Internal Auditors. "International Standards for the Professional Practice of Internal Auditing," https://na.theiia.org/standards-guidance/mandatory-guidance/Pages/Standards.aspx

Institute of Management Accountants, www.imanet.org

Institute of Management Accountants. *Enterprise Risk Management: Frameworks, Elements, and Integration*. Montvale, NJ: Author, 2006.

Institute of Management Accountants. *Enterprise Risk Management: Tools and Techniques for Effective Implementation*. Montvale, NJ: Author, 2007.

Institute of Management Accountants. *IMA Statement of Ethical Professional Practice*. Montvale, NJ: Author, 2005.

Institute of Management Accountants. *Managing Quality Improvements*. Montvale, NJ: Author, 1993.

Institute of Management Accountants. *Value and Ethics: From Inception to Practice*. Montvale, NJ: Author, 2008.

International Accounting Standards Board, www.ifrs.org

Investopedia.com, www.investopedia.com

Kaplan, Robert S., and David P. Norton. *The Balanced Scorecard: Translating Strategy into Action*. Boston: Harvard Business School Press, 1996.

Kaplan, Robert S., and David P. Norton. *The Strategy-Focused Organization: How Balanced Scorecard Companies Thrive in the New Business Environment*. Boston: Harvard Business School Press, 2001.

Kaplan, Robert S., and David P. Norton. "Using the Balanced Scorecard as a Strategic Management System." *Harvard Business Review* (January–February 1996).

Kieso, Donald E., Jerry J. Weygandt, and Terry D. Warfield. *Intermediate Accounting*, 14th ed. Hoboken, NJ: John Wiley & Sons, 2012.

Larsen, E. John. *Modern Advanced Accounting*, 10th ed. New York: McGraw-Hill, 2006.

Laudon, Kenneth C., and Jane P. Laudon. *Management Information Systems*, 11th ed. Upper Saddle River, NJ: Pearson Prentice Hall, 2010.

Mackenzie, Bruce, et al. *Interpretation and Application of International Financial Reporting Standards*. Hoboken, NJ: John Wiley & Sons, 2012.

McMillan, Edward J. *Not-for-Profit Budgeting and Financial Management*. Hoboken, NJ: John Wiley & Sons, 2010.

Moeller, Robert R. *COSO Enterprise Risk Management*, 2nd ed. Hoboken, NJ: John Wiley & Sons, 2011.

Moyer, R. Charles, James R. McGuigan, and Ramesh P. Rao. *Contemporary Financial Management*, 13th ed. Mason, OH: Cengage, 2014.

MSN Money. "Currency Exchange Rates," http://investing.money.msn.com/investments/exchange-rates/

Nicolai, Loren A., John D. Bazley, and Jefferson P. Jones. *Intermediate Accounting*, 11th ed. Mason, OH: Cengage, 2010.

Olve, Nils-Göran, and Anna Sjöstrand. *The Balanced Scorecard*, 2nd ed. Oxford, UK: Capstone, 2006.

Rosenberg, Jerry M. *The Essential Dictionary of International Trade*. New York: Barnes & Noble, 2004.

Sarbanes-Oxley, www.sarbanesoxleysimplified.com/sarbox/compact/htmlact/sec406.html

Sawyer, Lawrence B., Mortimer A. Dittenhofer, and Anne Graham (eds.). *Sawyer's Internal Auditing: The Practice of Modern Internal Auditing*, 5th ed. Altamonte Springs, FL: Institute of Internal Auditors, 2003.

Securities and Exchange Commission, www.sec.gov/rules/final/33-8177.htm

Shim, Jae K., and Joel G. Siegel. *Schaum's Outlines: Managerial Accounting*, 2nd ed. New York: McGraw-Hill, 2011.

Siegel, Joel G., Jae K. Shim, and Stephen W. Hartman. *Schaum's Quick Guide to Business Formulas: 201 Decision-Making Tools for Business, Finance, and Accounting Students*. New York: McGraw-Hill, 1998.

Simkin, Mark G., and Carolyn A. Strand Norman. Hoboken, NJ: John Wiley & Sons, 2011.

Simkin, Mark G., Jacob M. Rose, and Carolyn S. Norman. *Core Concepts of Accounting Information Systems*, 12th ed. Hoboken, NJ: John Wiley & Sons, 2012.

Stiglitz, Joseph E. *Globalization and Its Discontents*. New York: Norton, 2002.

Subramanyam, K. R., and John L. Wild. *Financial Statement Analysis*, 10th ed. New York: McGraw Hill, 2009.

U.S. Department of Justice. Foreign Corrupt Practices Act, Antibribery Provisions, www.usdoj.gov/criminal/fraud/fcpa/guide.pdf

U.S. Securities and Exchange Commission, www.sec.gov

Van Horne, James C., and John M. Wachowicz Jr. *Fundamentals of Financial Management*, 13th ed. Harlow, UK: Pearson Education

Warren, Carl S., James M. Reeve, and Jonathan Duchac. *Financial and Managerial Accounting*, 12th ed. Mason, OH: Cengage, 2013.

Wessels, Walter J. *Economics*, 5th ed. New York: Barron's, 2012.

XE.com, www.xe.com

Index of Learning Outcome Statements

LOS 2.A.1.a:
For the balance sheet and income statement, prepare and analyze common-size financial statements; i.e., calculate percentage of assets and sales, respectively; also called vertical analysis...7, 653

LOS 2.A.1.b:
For the balance sheet and income statement, prepare a comparative financial statement horizontal analysis; i.e., calculate trend year over year for every item on the financial statement compared to base year...10, 653

LOS 2.A.1.c:
Calculate the growth rate of individual line items on the balance sheet and income statements...10, 653

LOS 2.A.2.a:
Calculate and interpret the current ratio, the quick (acid-test) ratio, the cash ratio, the cash flow ration, and the net working capital ratio...18, 653

LOS 2.A.2.b:
Explain how changes in one or more of the elements of current assets, current liabilities, and/or unit sales can change the liquidity ratios and calculate that impact...22, 653

LOS 2.A.2.c:
Demonstrate an understanding of the liquidity of current liabilities...22, 653

LOS 2.A.2.d:
Define solvency...18, 653

LOS 2.A.2.e:
Define operating leverage and financial leverage...23, 24, 653

LOS 2.A.2.f:
Calculate degree of operating leverage and degree of financial leverage...24, 654

LOS 2.A.2.g:
Demonstrate an understanding of the effect on the capital structure and solvency of a company with a change in the composition of debt vs. equity by calculating leverage ratios...26, 654

LOS 2.A.2.h:
Calculate and interpret the financial leverage ratio, and determine the effect of a given change in capital structure on this ratio...25, 654

LOS 2.A.2.i:
Calculate and interpret the following ratios: debt to equity, long-term debt to equity, and debt to total assets...26, 27, 654

LOS 2.A.2.j:
Define, calculate, and interpret the following ratios: fixed charge coverage (earnings to fixed charges), interest coverage (times interest earned), and cash flow to fixed charges...28, 654

LOS 2.A.2.k:
Discuss how capital structure decisions affect the risk profile of a firm...654

LOS 2.A.2.l:
Calculate and interpret accounts receivable turnover, inventory turnover, and accounts payable turnover...31, 32, 34, 654

LOS 2.A.2.m:
Calculate and interpret days sales outstanding in receivables, days sales outstanding in inventory, and days purchases in accounts payable...32, 33, 34, 654

LOS 2.A.2.n:
Define and calculate the operating cycle and the cash cycle of a firm...31, 35, 654

LOS 2.A.2.o:
Calculate and interpret total assets turnover and fixed asset turnover...33, 654

LOS 2.A.2.p:
Calculate and interpret gross profit margin percentage, operating profit margin percentage, net profit margin percentage, and earnings before interest, taxes, depreciation, and amortization (EBITDA) margin percentage...24, 41, 654

LOS 2.A.2.q:
Calculate and interpret return on assets (ROA) and return on equity (ROE)...43, 46, 654

LOS 2.A.2.r:
Calculate and interpret the market/book ratio, the price/earnings ratio, and price to EBITDA ratio...33, 654

LOS 2.A.2.s:
Calculate and interpret book value per share...39, 654

LOS 2.A.2.t:
Identify and explain the limitations of book value per share...39, 654

LOS 2.A.2.u:
Calculate and interpret basic and diluted earnings per share...35, 36, 654

LOS 2.A.2.v:
Calculate and interpret earnings yield, dividend yield, dividend payout ratio, and shareholder return...35, 37, 654

LOS 2.A.2.w:
Identify the limitations of ratio analysis...19, 654

LOS 2.A.2.x:
Demonstrate a familiarity with the sources of financial information about public companies and industry ratio averages...19, 20, 23, 26, 27, 28, 32, 654

LOS 2.A.2.y:
Evaluate the financial strength and performance of an entity based on multiple ratios...50, 654

LOS 2.A.3.a:
Demonstrate an understanding of the factors that contribute to inconsistent definitions of "equity," "assets," and "return" when using ROA and ROE...59, 655

LOS 2.A.3.b:
Determine the effect on return on total assets of a change in one or more elements of the financial statements...61, 655

LOS 2.A.3.c:
Identify factors to be considered in measuring income, including estimates, accounting methods, disclosure incentives, and the different needs of users...68, 655

LOS 2.A.3.d:
Explain the importance of the source, stability, and trend of sales and revenue...67, 655

LOS 2.A.3.e:
Demonstrate an understanding of the relationship between revenue and receivables and revenue and inventory...68, 655

LOS 2.A.3.f:
Determine and analyze the effect on revenue of changes in revenue recognition and measurement methods...67, 655

LOS 2.A.3.g:
Analyze cost of sales by calculating and interpreting the gross profit margin...62, 655

LOS 2.A.3.h:
Distinguish between gross profit margin, operating profit margin, and net profit margin and analyze the effects of changes in the components of each...62, 655

LOS 2.A.3.i:
Define and perform a variation analysis (percentage change over time)...655

LOS 2.A.3.j:
Calculate and interpret sustainable equity growth...64, 655

LOS 2.A.4.a:
Demonstrate an understanding of the impact of foreign exchange fluctuations...655

LOS 2.A.4.a.1:
Identify and explain issues in the accounting for foreign operations (e.g., historical vs. current rate and the treatment of translation gains and losses)...93, 655

LOS 2.A.4.a.2:
Define functional currency...90, 92, 655

LOS 2.A.4.a.3:
Calculate the financial ratio impact of a change in exchange rates...92, 655

LOS 2.A.4.a.4:
Discuss the possible impact on management and investor behavior of volatility in reported earnings...92, 655

LOS 2.A.4.b:
Demonstrate an understanding of the impact of inflation on finical ratios and the reliability of financial ratios...87, 655

LOS 2.A.4.c:
Define and explain off–balance sheet financing...84, 655

LOS 2.A.4.c.1:
Identify and describe the following forms of off–balance sheet financing: (i) leases; (ii) special purpose entities; (iii) sale of receivables; and (iv) joint ventures...655

LOS 2.A.4.c.2:
Explain why companies use off–balance sheet financing...655

LOS 2.A.4.c.3:
Calculate the impact of off–balance sheet financing on the debt to equity ratio...85, 655

LOS 2.A.4.d:
Describe how to adjust financial statements for changes in accounting treatments (principles, estimates, and errors) and how these adjustments impact financial ratios...82, 655

LOS 2.A.4.e:
Distinguish between book value and market value; distinguish between accounting profit and economic profit...81, 86, 655

LOS 2.A.4.f:
Identify the determinants and indicators of earnings quality, and explain why they are important...83, 655

LOS 2.B.1.a:
Calculate rates of return...112, 656

LOS 2.B.1.b:
  Identify and demonstrate an understanding of systemic (market) risk and unsystemic (company) risk...119, 656

LOS 2.B.1.c:
  Identify and demonstrate an understanding of credit risk, foreign exchange risk, interest rate risk, market risk, industry risk, and political risk...111, 656

LOS 2.B.1.d:
  Demonstrate an understanding of the relationship between risk and return...113, 656

LOS 2.B.1.e:
  Distinguish between individual security risk and portfolio risk...117, 656

LOS 2.B.1.f:
  Demonstrate an understanding of diversification...119, 656

LOS 2.B.1.g:
  Define beta and explain how a change in beta impacts a security's price...122, 656

LOS 2.B.1.h:
  Demonstrate an understanding of the Capital Asset Pricing Model (CAPM) and calculate the expected risk-adjusted returns using CAPM...122, 656

LOS 2.B.2.a:
  Describe the term structure of interest rates, and explain why it changes over time...133, 656

LOS 2.B.2.b:
  Define and identify the characteristics of common stock and preferred stock...141, 143, 152, 656

LOS 2.B.2.c:
  Identify and describe the basic features of a bond such as maturity, par value, coupon rate, provisions for redeeming, conversion provisions, covenants, options granted to the issuer or investor, indentures, and restrictions...133, 656

LOS 2.B.2.d:
  Identify and evaluate debt issuance or refinancing strategies...141, 656

LOS 2.B.2.e:
  Value bonds, common stock, and preferred stock using discounted cash flow methods...140, 145, 146, 154, 656

LOS 2.B.2.f:
  Demonstrate an understanding of duration as a measure of bond interest rate sensitivity...137, 656

LOS 2.B.2.g:
  Explain how income taxes impact financing decisions...130, 656

LOS 2.B.2.h:
  Define and demonstrate an understanding of derivative and their uses...167, 656

LOS 2.B.2.i:
Identify and describe the basic features of futures and forwards...171, 172, 656

LOS 2.B.2.j:
Distinguish a long position from a short position...171, 656

LOS 2.B.2.k:
Define options and distinguish between a call and a put by identifying the characteristics of each...168, 656

LOS 2.B.2.l:
Define exercise price, strike price, option premium, and intrinsic value...132, 169, 656

LOS 2.B.2.m:
Demonstrate an understanding of the interrelationship of the variables that comprise the value of an option; e.g., relationship between exercise price and strike price, and value of a call...170, 656

LOS 2.B.2.n:
Define swaps for interest rate and foreign currency...173, 656

LOS 2.B.2.o:
Define and identify characteristics of other sources of long-term financing, such as leases, convertible securities, and warrants...173, 656

LOS 2.B.2.p:
Demonstrate an understanding of the relationship among inflation, interest rates, and the prices of financial instruments...137, 656

LOS 2.B.2.q:
Define the cost of capital and demonstrate an understanding of its applications in capital structure decisions...155, 657

LOS 2.B.2.r:
Determine the weighted average cost of capital and the cost of its individual components...156, 657

LOS 2.B.2.s:
Calculate the marginal cost of capital...164, 657

LOS 2.B.2.t:
Explain the importance of using marginal cost as opposed to historical cost. ..157, 657

LOS 2.B.2.u:
Demonstrate an understanding of the use of the cost of capital in capital investment decisions...167, 657

LOS 2.B.2.v:
Demonstrate an understanding of how income taxes impact capital structure and capital investment decisions...167, 657

LOS 2.B.2.w:
Use the constant growth dividend discount model to value stock and demonstrate an understanding of the two-stage dividend discount model...146, 657

LOS 2.B.2.x:
Demonstrate an understanding of relative or comparable valuation methods, such as price/earnings (P/E) ratios, market/book ratios, and price/sales ratios...148, 657

LOS 2.B.3.a:
Identify the characteristics of the different types of financial markets and exchanges...188, 657

LOS 2.B.3.b:
Demonstrate an understanding of the concept of market efficiency, including the strong form, semi-strong form, and weak form of market efficiency...190, 657

LOS 2.B.3.c:
Describe the role of credit rating agencies...190, 657

LOS 2.B.3.d:
Demonstrate an understanding of the roles of investment banks, including underwriting, advice, and trading...189, 657

LOS 2.B.3.e:
Define initial public offerings (IPOs)...189, 657

LOS 2.B.3.f:
Define subsequent/secondary offerings...190, 657

LOS 2.B.3.g:
Describe lease financing, explain its benefits and disadvantages, and calculate the net advantage to leasing using discounted cash flow concepts...185, 657

LOS 2.B.3.h:
Define different types of dividends, including cash dividends, stock dividends, and stock splits...192, 657

LOS 2.B.3.i:
Identify and discuss the factors that influence the dividend policy of a firm...193, 657

LOS 2.B.3.j:
Demonstrate an understanding of the dividend payment process for both common and preferred stock...191, 194, 657

LOS 2.B.3.k:
Define share repurchase and explain why a firm would repurchase its stock...194, 657

LOS 2.B.3.l:
Define insider trading and explain why it is illegal...191, 657

LOS 2.B.4.a:
Define working capital and identify its components...201, 657

LOS 2.B.4.b:
Calculate net working capital...201, 657

LOS 2.B.4.c:
Explain the benefit of short-term financial forecasts in the management of working capital...201, 657

LOS 2.B.4.d:
Identify and describe factors influencing the levels of cash...203, 658

LOS 2.B.4.e:
Identify and explain the three motives for holding cash...204, 658

LOS 2.B.4.f:
Prepare forecasts of future cash flows...658

LOS 2.B.4.g:
Identify methods of speeding up cash collections...205, 658

LOS 2.B.4.h:
Calculate the net benefit of a lockbox system...207, 658

LOS 2.B.4.i:
Define concentration banking...209, 658

LOS 2.B.4.j:
Demonstrate an understanding of compensating balances...209, 658

LOS 2.B.4.k:
Identify methods of slowing down disbursements...209, 658

LOS 2.B.4.l:
Demonstrate an understanding of disbursement float and overdraft systems...209, 658

LOS 2.B.4.m:
Identify and describe reasons for holding marketable securities...212, 658

LOS 2.B.4.n:
Define the different types of marketable securities, including money market instruments, T-bills, treasury notes, treasury bonds, repurchase agreements, Federal agency securities, bankers' acceptances, commercial paper, negotiable CDs, Eurodollar CDs, and other marketable securities...213, 658

LOS 2.B.4.o:
Evaluate the trade-offs among the variables in marketable security selections, including safety, marketability/liquidity, yield, maturity, and taxability...211, 212, 658

LOS 2.B.4.p:
Demonstrate an understanding of the risk and return trade-off...212, 658

LOS 2.B.4.q:
Identify the factors influencing the level of receivables...215, 658

LOS 2.B.4.r:
Demonstrate an understanding of the impact of changes in credit terms or collection policies on accounts receivable, working capital and sales volume...216, 658

LOS 2.B.4.s:
Define default risk...217, 658

LOS 2.B.4.t:
Identify and explain the factors involved in determining an optimal credit policy...217, 658

Index of Learning Outcome Statements

LOS 2.B.4.u:
Define lead time and safety stock; identify reasons for carrying inventory and the factors influencing its level...221, 658

LOS 2.B.4.v:
Identify and calculate the costs related to inventory, including carrying costs, ordering costs and shortage (stockout) costs...219, 658

LOS 2.B.4.w:
Explain how a just-in-time (JIT) inventory management system helps manage inventory...223, 658

LOS 2.B.4.x:
Identify the interaction between high inventory turnover and high gross margin (calculation not required)...224, 658

LOS 2.B.4.y:
Demonstrate an understanding of economic order quantity (EOQ) and how a change in one variable would affect the EOQ (calculation not required)...219, 658

LOS 2.B.4.z:
Demonstrate an understanding of how risk affects a firm's approach to its current asset financing policy (aggressive, conservative, etc.)...201, 658

LOS 2.B.4.aa:
Identify and describe the different types of short-term credit, including trade credit, short-term bank loans, commercial paper, lines of credit, and bankers' acceptances...224, 659

LOS 2.B.4.bb:
Estimate the annual cost and effective annual interest rate of not taking a cash discount...225, 659

LOS 2.B.4.cc:
Calculate the effective annual interest rate of a bank loan with a compensating balance requirement and/or a commitment fee...228, 659

LOS 2.B.4.dd:
Demonstrate an understanding of factoring accounts receivable and calculate the cost of factoring...229, 659

LOS 2.B.4.ee:
Explain the maturity matching or hedging approach to financing...201, 659

LOS 2.B.4.ff:
Demonstrate an understanding of the factors involved in managing the costs of working capital...201, 659

LOS 2.B.4.gg:
Recommend a strategy for managing current assets that would fulfill a given objective...223, 659

LOS 2.B.5.a.i:
Demonstrate an understanding of mergers and acquisitions, including horizontal, vertical, and conglomerate...235, 659

LOS 2.B.5.a.ii:
Demonstrate an understanding of leveraged buyouts...242, 659

LOS 2.B.5.b:
Identify defenses against takeovers (e.g., golden parachute, leveraged recapitalization, poison pill (shareholders' rights plan), staggered board of directors, fair price, voting rights plan, white knight)...236, 659

LOS 2.B.5.c:
Identify and describe divestiture concepts such as spin-offs, split-ups, equity carve-outs, and tracking stock...237, 243, 659

LOS 2.B.5.d:
Evaluate key factors in a company's financial situation and determine if a restructuring would be beneficial to the shareholders...238, 659

LOS 2.B.5.e:
Validate possible synergies in targeted mergers and acquisitions...238, 659

LOS 2.B.5.f:
Define bankruptcy...241, 659

LOS 2.B.5.g:
Differentiate between reorganization and liquidation...241, 659

LOS 2.B.5.h:
Value a business, a business segment, and a business combination using discounted cash flow method...240, 659

LOS 2.B.5.i:
Evaluate a proposed business combination and make a recommendation based on both quantitative and qualitative considerations...240, 659

LOS 2.B.6.a:
Demonstrate an understanding of foreign currencies and how foreign currency affects the prices of goods and services...247, 659

LOS 2.B.6.b:
Identify the variables that affect exchange rates...251, 659

LOS 2.B.6.c:
Calculate whether a currency has depreciated or appreciated against another currency over a period of time, and evaluate the impact of the change...253, 660

LOS 2.B.6.d:
Demonstrate how currency futures, currency swaps, and currency options can be used to manage exchange rate risk...252, 253, 660

LOS 2.B.6.e:
Calculate the net profit/loss of cross-border transactions, and evaluate the impact of this net profit/loss...254, 261, 660

LOS 2.B.6.f:
Recommend methods of managing exchange rate risk and calculate the net profit/loss of your strategy...254, 660

LOS 2.B.6.g:
Identify and explain the benefits of international diversification...254, 660

Index of Learning Outcome Statements

LOS 2.B.6.h:
Identify and explain common trade financing methods, including cross-border factoring, letters of credit, banker's acceptances, forfaiting, and countertrade...258, 660

LOS 2.B.6.i:
Demonstrate an understanding of how transfer pricing affects effective worldwide tax rate...262, 660

LOS 2.C.1.a:
Demonstrate an understanding of how cost/volume/profit (CVP) analysis (break-even analysis) is used to examine the behavior of total revenues, total costs, and operating income as changes occur in output levels, selling prices, variable costs per unit, or fixed costs...279, 660

LOS 2.C.1.b:
Calculate operating income at different operating levels...281, 660

LOS 2.C.1.c:
Differentiate between costs that are fixed and costs that are variable with respect to levels of output...276, 660

LOS 2.C.1.d:
Explain why the classification of fixed vs. variable costs is affected by the timeframe being considered...278, 660

LOS 2.C.1.e:
Calculate contribution margin per unit and total contribution margin...280, 281, 660

LOS 2.C.1.f:
Calculate the breakeven point in units and dollar sales to achieve targeted operating income or targeted net income...281, 660

LOS 2.C.1.g:
Demonstrate an understanding of how changes in unit sales mix affect operating income in multiple-product situations...283, 660

LOS 2.C.1.h:
Calculate multiple-product breakeven points given percentage share of sales and explain why there is no unique breakeven point in multiple-product situations...284, 660

LOS 2.C.1.i:
Define, calculate and interpret margin of safety and margin of safety ratio...285, 660

LOS 2.C.1.j:
Explain how sensitivity analysis can be used in CVP analysis when there is uncertainty about sales...285, 660

LOS 2.C.1.k:
Analyze and recommend a course of action using CVP analysis...286, 660

LOS 2.C.1.l:
Demonstrate an understanding of the impact of income taxes on CVP analysis...283, 660

LOS 2.C.2.a:
: Identify and define relevant costs (incremental, marginal, or differential costs), sunk costs, avoidable costs, explicit and implicit costs, split-off point, joint production costs, separable processing costs, and relevant revenues...291, 303, 661

LOS 2.C.2.b:
: Explain why sunk costs are not relevant in the decision-making process...291, 661

LOS 2.C.2.c:
: Demonstrate an understanding of and calculate opportunity costs...293, 661

LOS 2.C.2.d:
: Calculate relevant costs given a numerical scenario...293, 661

LOS 2.C.2.e:
: Define and calculate marginal cost and marginal revenue...303, 661

LOS 2.C.2.f:
: Identify and calculate total cost, average fixed cost, average variable cost, and average total cost...303, 661

LOS 2.C.2.g:
: Demonstrate proficiency in the use of marginal analysis for decisions such as (a) introducing a new product or changing output levels of existing products, (b) accepting or rejecting special orders, (c) making or buying a product or service, (d) selling a product or performing additional processes and selling a more value- added product, and (e) adding or dropping a segment...293, 294, 297, 299, 300, 661

LOS 2.C.2.h:
: Calculate the effect on operating income of a decision to accept or reject a special order when there is idle capacity and the order has no long-run implications...292, 661

LOS 2.C.2.i:
: Identify and describe qualitative factors in make-or-buy decisions, such as product quality and dependability of suppliers...295, 661

LOS 2.C.2.j:
: Calculate the effect on operating income of a make-or-buy decision...294, 661

LOS 2.C.2.k:
: Calculate the effects on operating income of a decision to sell or process further; and of a decision to drop or add a segment...296, 661

LOS 2.C.2.l:
: Identify the effects of changes in capacity on production decisions...292, 661

LOS 2.C.2.m:
: Demonstrate an understanding of the impact of income taxes on marginal analysis...661

LOS 2.C.2.n:
: Recommend a course of action using marginal analysis...293, 661

Index of Learning Outcome Statements **683**

LOS 2.C.3.a:
Identify different pricing methodologies, including market comparables, cost-based, and value-based approaches...310, 313, 661

LOS 2.C.3.b:
Differentiate between a cost-based approach (cost-plus pricing, mark-up pricing) and a market-based approach to setting prices...313, 321, 661

LOS 2.C.3.c:
Calculate selling price using a cost-based approach...314, 661

LOS 2.C.3.d:
Demonstrate an understanding of how the pricing of a product or service is affected by the demand for and supply of the product or service, as well as the market structure within which it operates...322, 661

LOS 2.C.3.e:
Demonstrate an understanding of the impact of cartels on pricing...333, 661

LOS 2.C.3.f:
Demonstrate an understanding of the short-run equilibrium price for the firm in (1) pure competition; (2) monopolistic competition; (3) oligopoly; and (4) monopoly using the concepts of marginal revenue and marginal cost...326, 662

LOS 2.C.3.g:
Identify techniques used to set prices based on understanding customers' perceptions of value, competitors' technologies, products and costs...317, 662

LOS 2.C.3.h:
Define and demonstrate an understanding of target pricing and target costing and identify the main steps in developing target prices and target costs...317, 662

LOS 2.C.3.i:
Define value engineering...319, 662

LOS 2.C.3.j:
Calculate the target operating income per unit and target cost per unit...317, 321, 662

LOS 2.C.3.k:
Define and distinguish between a value-added cost and a nonvalue-added cost...319, 662

LOS 2.C.3.l:
Define the pricing technique of cost plus target rate of return...321, 662

LOS 2.C.3.m:
Calculate the price elasticity of demand using the midpoint formula...329, 662

LOS 2.C.3.n:
Define and explain elastic and inelastic demand...328, 662

LOS 2.C.3.o:
Estimate total revenue given changes in prices and demand as well as elasticity...331, 662

LOS 2.C.3.p:
Discuss how pricing decisions can differ in the short-run and in the long-run...310, 662

LOS 2.C.3.q:
Define product life cycle; identify and explain the four stages of the product life cycle; and explain why pricing decisions might differ over the life of a product...320, 662

LOS 2.C.3.r:
Evaluate and recommend pricing strategies under specific market conditions...320, 662

LOS 2.D.1.a:
Identify and explain the different types of risk, including business risk, hazard risks, financial risks, operational risks, and strategic risks...353, 662

LOS 2.D.1.b:
Demonstrate an understanding of operational risk...353, 662

LOS 2.D.1.c:
Define legal risk, compliance risk, and political risk...353, 662

LOS 2.D.1.d:
Demonstrate an understanding of how volatility and time impact risk...354, 662

LOS 2.D.1.e:
Define the concept of capital adequacy (i.e., solvency, liquidity, reserves, sufficient capital, etc.)...353, 662

LOS 2.D.1.f:
Explain the use of probabilities in determining exposure to risk and calculate expected loss given a set of probabilities...356, 662

LOS 2.D.1.g:
Define the concepts of unexpected loss and maximum possible loss (extreme or catastrophic loss)...351, 662

LOS 2.D.1.h:
Identify strategies for risk response (or treatment), including actions to avoid, retain, reduce (mitigate), transfer (share), and exploit (accept) risks...356, 662

LOS 2.D.1.i:
Define risk transfer (e.g., purchasing insurance, issuing debt)...356, 662

LOS 2.D.1.j:
Demonstrate an understanding of the concept of residual risk and distinguish it from inherent risk...356, 359, 662

LOS 2.D.1.k:
Identify and explain the benefits of risk management...359, 662

LOS 2.D.1.l:
Identify and describe the key steps in the risk management process...357, 662

LOS 2.D.1.m:
Explain how attitude toward risk might affect the management of risk...355, 662

LOS 2.D.1.n:
Demonstrate a general understanding of the use of liability/hazard insurance to mitigate risk (detailed knowledge not required)...357, 662

LOS 2.D.1.o:
Identify methods of managing operational risk...357, 662

LOS 2.D.1.p:
Identify and explain financial risk management methods...357, 663

LOS 2.D.1.q:
Identify and explain qualitative risk assessment tools including risk identification, risk ranking, and risk maps...355, 663

LOS 2.D.1.r:
Identify and explain quantitative risk assessment tools including cash flow at risk, earnings at risk, earnings distributions, and earnings per share (EPS) distributions...352, 663

LOS 2.D.1.s:
Identify and explain Value at Risk (VaR) (calculations not required)...351, 663

LOS 2.D.1.t:
Define enterprise risk management (ERM) and identify and describe key objectives, components and benefits of an ERM program...358, 663

LOS 2.D.1.u:
Identify event identification techniques and provide examples of event identification within the context of an ERM approach...354, 663

LOS 2.D.1.v:
Explain the role of corporate governance, risk analytics, and portfolio management in an ERM program...360, 663

LOS 2.D.1.w:
Evaluate scenarios and recommend risk mitigation strategies...356, 663

LOS 2.D.1.x:
Prepare a cost-benefit analysis and demonstrate an understanding of its uses in risk assessment and decision making...357, 663

LOS 2.D.1.y:
Demonstrate an understanding of the COSO ERM conceptual framework...358, 663

LOS 2.E.1.a:
Define capital budgeting and identify the steps or stages undertaken in developing and implementing a capital budget for a project...371, 663

LOS 2.E.1.b:
Identify and calculate the relevant cash flows of a capital investment project on both a pretax and after-tax basis...374, 663

LOS 2.E.1.c:
Demonstrate an understanding of how income taxes affect cash flows...376, 663

LOS 2.E.1.d:
Distinguish between cash flows and accounting profits and discuss the relevance to capital budgeting of incremental cash flow, sunk cost, and opportunity cost...372, 663

LOS 2.E.1.e:
Explain the importance of changes in net working capital in capital budgeting...373, 663

LOS 2.E.1.f:
Discuss how the effects of inflation are reflected in capital budgeting analysis...373, 663

LOS 2.E.1.g:
Define hurdle rate...386, 663

LOS 2.E.1.h:
Identify and discuss qualitative considerations involved in the capital budgeting decision...381, 663

LOS 2.E.1.i:
Describe the role of the post-audit in the capital budgeting process...372, 663

LOS 2.E.2.a:
Demonstrate an understanding of the two main discounted cash flow (DCF) methods, net present value (NPV) and internal rate of return (IRR)...385, 663

LOS 2.E.2.b:
Calculate NPV and IRR...390, 394, 663

LOS 2.E.2.c:
Demonstrate an understanding of the decision criteria used in NPV and IRR analyses to determine acceptable projects...393, 394, 663

LOS 2.E.2.d:
Compare NPV and IRR focusing on the relative advantages and disadvantages of each method, particularly with respect to independent versus mutually exclusive projects and the "multiple IRR problem."...397, 664

LOS 2.E.2.e:
Explain why NPV and IRR methods can produce conflicting rankings for capital projects if not applied properly...398, 664

LOS 2.E.2.f:
Identify assumptions of NPV and IRR...398, 664

LOS 2.E.2.g:
Evaluate and recommend project investments on the basis of DCF analysis...664

LOS 2.E.3.a:
Demonstrate an understanding of the payback and discounted payback methods...405, 664

LOS 2.E.3.b:
Identify the advantages and disadvantages of the payback and discounted payback methods...407, 664

LOS 2.E.3.c:
Calculate payback periods and discounted payback periods...405, 408, 664

LOS 2.E.4.a:
Identify alternative approaches to dealing with risk in capital budgeting...412, 664

Index of Learning Outcome Statements

LOS 2.E.4.b:
Distinguish among sensitivity analysis, scenario analysis, and Monte Carlo simulation as risk analysis techniques...412, 416, 417, 419, 664

LOS 2.E.4.c:
Explain why a rate specifically adjusted for risk should be used when project cash flows are more or less risky than is normal for a firm...419, 664

LOS 2.E.4.d:
Explain how the value of a capital investment is increased if consideration is given to the possibility of adding on, speeding up, slowing up, or discontinuing early...416, 664

LOS 2.E.4.e:
Demonstrate an understanding of real options and identify examples of the different types of real options: e.g., abandon, delay, expand, and scale back (calculations not required)...416, 664

LOS 2.F.1.a:
Identify and describe the four overarching ethical principles...437, 664

LOS 2.F.1.b:
Evaluate a given business situation for its ethical implications...446, 664

LOS 2.F.1.c:
Identify and describe relevant standards that may have been violated in a given business situation and explain why the specific standards are applicable...447, 665

LOS 2.F.1.d:
Recommend a course of action for management accountants or financial managers to take when confronted with an ethical dilemma in the business environment...440, 447, 665

LOS 2.F.1.e:
Evaluate and propose resolutions for ethical issues such as fraudulent reporting, manipulation of analyses, results, and budgets...447, 665

LOS 2.F.1.f:
Identify the three components of the (fraud) triangle...665

LOS 2.F.1.g:
Use the (fraud triangle) model to explain how a management accounting and financial management professional can identify and manage the risk of fraud...665

LOS 2.F.2.a:
Identify the purpose of the U.S. Foreign Corrupt Practices Act...460, 665

LOS 2.F.2.b:
Identify the practices that the U.S Foreign Corrupt Practices Act prohibits, and explain how to apply this act to typical business situations...460, 665

LOS 2.F.2.c:
Apply relevant provisions of IMA's Statement on Management Accounting, "Values and Ethics: From Inception to Practice" to a business situation...460, 462, 665

LOS 2.F.2.d:
Discuss corporate responsibility for ethical conduct...453, 665

LOS 2.F.2.e:
Explain why it is important for an organization to have a code of conduct...455, 665

LOS 2.F.2.f:
Demonstrate an understanding of the ways ethical values benefit an organization...455, 665

LOS 2.F.2.g:
Demonstrate an understanding of the differences between ethical and legal behavior...456, 665

LOS 2.F.2.h:
Demonstrate an understanding of role of "leadership by example" or "tone at the top" in determining an organization's ethical environment...456, 665

LOS 2.F.2.i:
Explain the importance of human capital to an organization in creating a climate where "doing the right thing" is expected (i.e., hiring the right people, providing them with training, and practicing consistent values-based leadership)...457, 665

LOS 2.F.2.j:
Explain how an organization's culture impacts its behavioral values...457, 665

LOS 2.F.2.k:
Explain the importance of an organization's core values in explaining its ethical behavior...456, 665

LOS 2.F.2.l:
Discuss the importance of employee training to maintaining an ethical organizational culture...457, 665

LOS 2.F.2.m:
Describe the following methods to monitor ethical compliance: human performance feedback loop and survey tools...459, 665

LOS 2.F.2.n:
Explain the importance of a whistleblowing framework (e.g., ethics helpline) to maintaining an ethical organizational culture...459, 665

LOS 2.F.2.o:
Identify the requirements of SOX Section 406—Code of Ethics for Senior Financial Officers...461, 665

LOS 2.F.2.p:
Discuss the issues organizations face in applying their values and ethical standards internationally...460, 665

LOS 2.F.2.q:
Demonstrate an understanding of the relationship between ethics and internal controls...459, 665

Index

This index identifies the page on which a key term or concept is introduced in context. It is not meant as a comprehensive index of all references to that term or concept.

Accelerated depreciation, 378
Accounting changes, 82
Accounting profit, 81
Accounts receivable (A/R), 215
Accounts receivable turnover ratio, 31
Accrued expenses, 224
ACH (automated clearing house), 208
Acid-test ratio, 19
Acquisitions, 235
Activity level, 277
Add or drop a segment, 297
Adjusted book value method, 240
Agency cost, 131
Agent, 131
Allowable cost, 317
American option, 169
Annuity investment, 391
A/R (accounts receivable), 215
Assets
   current, 18
   depreciable, 39
   international, diversification of, 264
   unproductive, 39
Asset-based borrowing, 227
Asset turn, 59
At-the-money options, 169
Automated clearing house (ACH), 208
Availability float, 206

BA (bankers' acceptance), 227, 259
Bad debts, 217

Bankers' acceptance (BA), 227, 259
Bankruptcy, 241
Beta, 122
Binomial lattice model, 171
Black-Scholes option model, 171
Bond(s), 132
   administration of, 134
   duration, 137
   interest rate, 135
   liquidation and rankings of, 139
   maturity of, 135
   principal (par value, face value), 135
   ratings of, 136
   redeeming/retiring, 136
   refinancing, 141
   secured and unsecured, 139
   terminology, 134
   types of, 133
   valuation of, 140
   yield of, 137
Bond price-yield curve, 138
Book value, 131
Book value per share, 86
Book value per share of common stock, 132
Book value weights, 163
Break-even graph, 279
Break-even point, 280
Buffer (safety) stock, 221

Call option, 169
Call option payoff, 169

Call provision
  bonds, 136
  preferred stock, 154
Cap (market capitalization), 114, 141
Capital
  cost of, 155
  debt, 156
  equity, 156
Capital Asset Pricing Model (CAPM), 122, 161, 419
Capital budget, 370
Capital budgeting
  applications, 370
    project and time dimensions in, 370
  stages of, 371
Capital investments (capital expenditures), 369
Capital leases, 186
Capital markets, 188
Capital structure, 23
Capital structure ratios, 26
CAPM (Capital Asset Pricing Model), 122, 161, 419
Carrying costs, 219
Cartels, 333
Cash discount, 216
Cash dividend, 192
Cash flows
  incremental, 372
  management of, 205
  uniform, 391
Cash flow ratio, 21
Cash flow to fixed charges ratio, 28
Cash inflows, 205
Cash management, 203
Cash outflows, 205
Cash ratio, 20
CE (certainty equivalent), 114
Centralized payables, 210
Certainty equivalent (CE), 114
Change in demand, 323
Change in quantity demanded, 323
Change in quantity supplied, 325
Change in supply, 325
Chapter 7 Bankruptcy, 241
Chapter 11 reorganizations, 241
Clearing float, 209
Coefficient of variation (CV), 116

COGS (cost of goods sold), 41
Collateralized account receivable, 227
Collateralized inventory, 227
Collection float, 205
Collection points, 206
Collection system, 205
Commercial paper (CP), 227
Commitment fee, 228
Common-size statements, 6
  horizontal, 10
  vertical, 7
Common stock, 132, 143, 144
Common stock valuation, 145
Comparative advantage, in global trade, 256
Comparative P/E ratio method, 240
Compensating balance, 209, 228
Competence, 438
Complements, 324
Concentration banking system, 209
Concentration flows, 205
Concurrent engineering, 319
Confidentiality, 439
Consignment, 258
Consolidation, 235
Constant dividend growth model, 146
Constant dividend payout ratio, 193
Contribution margin, 280
Contribution margin per unit, 281
Contribution margin ratio, 282
Contribution margin statement, 284
Conversion provision, bonds, 136
Convertible debt, 187
Convertible preferred stock, 188
Convexity, 138
Corporate charter rules, 236
Correlation, 118
Correlation coefficient, 118
Cost, 275
Cost approach, 88
Cost-based pricing, 313
Cost behavior, 277
Cost driver, 275
Cost object, 276
Cost of capital, 155, 386
  calculating, 156
  cost of common equity, 159
  debt, 157

Index **691**

in investment decisions, 167
marginal, 164
preferred stock, 158
weighted average, 163
Cost of common equity, 159
Cost of equity, 159
Cost of goods sold (COGS), 41
Cost of sales analysis, 41
Cost-plus pricing, 313
Cost/volume/profit (CVP) analysis, 275
Counterpurchase, 260
Countertrade, 260
Coupon rate (coupon yield), 135
Covariance, 117
Covenant, 134
negative, 134
positive, 134
CP (commercial paper), 227
Credibility, 439
Credit
revolving, 226
trade, 225
Credit period, 215
Credit terms, 215
Cross-border factoring, 260
Cumulative dividend feature, 191
Cumulative voting, 143
Currency exchange rates, 249
Currency futures, 252
Currency options, 252
Currency swap, 252
Current assets, 18
Current budget (operating budget), 369
Current (working) capital, 18, 201
Current investments (current expenditures), 369
Current liabilities, 18
Current rate method, 95
Current ratio, 19
Current yield (bonds), 137
CV (coefficient of variation), 116
CVP (cost/volume/profit) analysis, 275
CVP (break-even) graph, 279

Days' purchases in accounts payable, 34
Days' sales in receivables, 32
DB (declining-balance) depreciation, 379
DCF (discounted cash flow), 145, 239, 385

DDM (dividend discount model), 145
Debt(s)
bad, 217
cost of, 157
Debt as leverage, 23
Debt capital, 156
Debt financing, 129
Debt to equity ratio, 26
Debt to total assets ratio, 27
Declining-balance (DB) depreciation, 379
Default risk, 217
Degree of financial leverage (DFL), 24
Degree of operating leverage (DOL), 24
Demand, 322
elasticity of, 328
price elasticity of, 328
Demand curve, 322, 323, 327, 328
Demand schedule, 322
Depreciable assets, 39
Depreciable basis, 377
Depreciation, 376
Depreciation pattern, 378
Depreciation tax shield, 381
Depreciation time period, determining, 377
Derivative, 167
Derivatives and Hedging (ASC Topic 815), 168
DFL (degree of financial leverage), 24
Direct effect (cash flows), 374
Disbursement float, 209
Disbursement system, 209
Discounted cash flow (DCF), 145, 239, 385
Discounted payback method, 408
Discount terms, 216
Disequilibrium, 327
Diversification, 119
of international assets, 264
portfolio risk and, 120
Divestitures, 237
Dividend discount model (DDM), 145
Dividend growth model, 160, 162
Dividends in kind, 192
Dividend payout ratio, 37
Dividend yield, 37
DOL (degree of operating leverage), 24
DuPont model, 44, 47, 60

Earnings before interest, taxes, depreciation, and amortization (EBITDA), 40
Earnings per share (EPS), 35
Earnings persistence, 85
Earnings quality, 83
Earnings yield, 87
EBITDA (earnings before interest, taxes, depreciation, and amortization), 40
e-commerce, 211
Economic exposure, 254
Economic order quantity (EOQ), 219
Economic profit, 81
Effective annual interest rate, 228
Elasticity of demand, 328
Electronic commerce (e-commerce), 211
Electronic payment system, 208
Employee stock ownership plan (ESOP), 242
Enterprise risk, 349
Enterprise risk management (ERM), 358
Enterprise Risk Management–Integrated Framework (*ERM Framework*; COSO), 351, 358
EOQ (economic order quantity), 219
EPS (earnings per share), 35
Equilibrium, 326
Equilibrium price, 327
Equipment financing loans, 185
Equity, cost of, 159
Equity capital, 156
Equity carve-outs, 238
Equity financing, 130
Equity growth, 38
ERM (enterprise risk management), 358
ERM Framework (*Enterprise Risk Management–Integrated Framework*; COSO), 351, 358
Error corrections, 82
ESOP (employee stock ownership plan), 242
Estimates, in income analysis, 69
Ethical issues, 453
   corporate responsibility for ethics, 453
   government legislation of, 460
   in international business, 262, 460
   measuring and improving compliance, 458

Ethical principles, 437
European option, 169
Exchange rate(s), 90, 249
Exercise date, option, 169
Exercise price, option, 169
Expected return, 115
Expenses, accrued, 224
Expense analysis, 42
Expiration date, option, 169
Expropriation, 263

Face value, bond, 135
Factor, 260
Factoring, 229
Fairness, 437
Fair price provisions, 236
Fair Value Measurements and Disclosures (ASC Topic 820), 171
Fair value standards, 88
Federal Reserve Board tools, for controlling money supply, 251
Fedwire, 209
Financial distress, 131
Financial leverage, 23
Financial leverage ratio, 25, 60
Financial ratios
   accounts receivable turnover, 31
   acid test, 19
   book value per share, 86
   cash, 20
   cash flow, 21
   cash flow to fixed charges, 28
   days' purchases in accounts, 34
   days' sales in receivables, 32
   debt, 27
   debt to equity, 26
   fixed-charge coverage, 28
   inventory turnover, 32
   long-term debt to equity, 27
   market to book value, 86
   price to earnings, 87
   times interest earned, 28
   total debt to total capital, 26
Financing leases, 186
Fixed asset turnover ratio, 33
Fixed-charge coverage ratio, 28
Fixed cost, 276
Fixed exchange rate, 249

Flexible exchange rate, 250
Floating exchange rate, 250
Foreign currency, accounting for, 89
Foreign currency exchange, 247, 249
Foreign currency loans, 261
Foreign exchange futures, 252
Foreign investment, risk and rate of return, 254
Foreign subsidiaries, accounting for, 92
Forfaiting, 260
Forward contract, 171
Fraud triangle, 442
Free trade, 263
Functional currency, 92
Fundamental value, 132
Futures contract, 172
FX futures, 252

Going-concern value, 131
Golden parachutes, 236
Gordon constant growth model, 147
Greenmail, 237
Gross profit, 40
Gross profit margin, 41
Gross working capital, 201

Haircut, 230
Historical method (VaR), 352
Historical rate of return, 160
Holding cash, motives for, 204
Holding period return (HPR), 112
Honesty, 437
Horizontal common-size statements, 10
HPR (Holding period return), 112
Human performance feedback loop, 459
Hurdle rate, 386

"Implementing Target Costing" (*SMA*), 316
Income, demand and, 324
Income approach, 88
Income effect, 323
Income measurement analysis, 68
Income taxes, 167
    and CVP analysis, 283
    depreciation, 376
    and marginal analysis, 302

Incremental cash flows, 372
Indenture (deed of trust), 133
Inherent risk, 356
Initial public offering (IPO), 189, 242
Insider trading, 191
Integrity, 439
Interest rate, effective annual, 228
Internal rate of return (IRR), 393
    calculating the, 394
    NPV and, 397
International trade, financing of, 258
In-the-money options, 169
Intrinsic value, 132
Inventory, 218
Inventory control, 218
Inventory management, 218
Inventory turnover ratio, 32
Invested capital, definitions of, 39
IPO (initial public offering), 189, 242
IRR. *see* Internal rate of return
Item, 218

JIT (just-in-time) system, 223
Joint costs, 296
Joint products, 296
Joint services, 296
Joint ventures, 31
Just-in-time (JIT) system, 223

Kanban, 223

LBO (leveraged buyout), 237, 242
Leading P/E ratio, 149
Lead time, 221
Leases, 30, 185
    capital, 186
    financing, 186
    operating, 186
Legal issues, in global business, 262
Legally insolvent organizations, 241
Letter of credit, 258
Letter stocks, 243
Leveraged buyout (LBO), 237, 242
Leverage ratios, 25, 60
Liabilities, current, 19
Life-cycle costing, 320
Linear programming, 301
Line of credit, 226

Liquidating dividends, 192
Liquidation (liquidating value), 144, 153
Liquidation value, 131
Liquidation value per share, 131
Liquidity, 17, 203
Litigation defense, 236
"Lobster traps," 237
Lockbox system, 206
Long position, 171
Long-term debt to equity ratio, 27

MACRS table, 379
Mail float, 206
Majority-rule voting, 143
Majority voting, 143
Make versus buy, 293
Managed floating exchange rate system, 251
Marginal analysis, 291
Marginal cost of capital (MCC), 164
Margin of safety (MOS), 285
Marketable securities, 211, 213
Market approach, 88
Market-based pricing, 313
Market capitalization (cap), 114, 141
Market clearing price (equilibrium price), 327
Market efficiency, 190
Market equilibrium, 326
Market to book value ratio, 86
Market value, 132
  per share, 143, 192
  stock, 141
Market value weights, 163
Maturity date, option, 169
MCC (marginal cost of capital), 164
Mergers, 235
Minimum rate of return, 386
Monte Carlo analysis, 417
Monte Carlo simulation, 171, 352
MOS (margin of safety), 285

NAL (net advantage of leasing), 187
Negative covenant, 134
Net advantage of leasing (NAL), 187
Net effect (cash flows), 374
Net income, 40
Net operating income, 277

Net present value (NPV), 387
Net profit margin, 42
Net working capital, 201
Notional amount, 167
NPV (net present value), 387

Objectivity, 437
Off-balance sheet financing, 29, 84
Open account, 259
Operating activity analysis, 31
Operating budget (current budget), 369
Operating cycle, 31
Operating income, 40, 276
Operating leases, 186
Operating leverage, 23
Operating profit margin, 41, 62
Opportunity, in fraud triangle, 443
Option(s), 136, 169
Ordering costs, 219
Out-of-the-money options, 169
Outstanding share, 141

"Pacman" defense, 236
Par value, bond, 135
Passive residual dividend policy, 193
Payable through draft (PTD), 210
Payback method
  advantages and disadvantages of the, 407
  defined, 405
  interpreting the, 407
Payback period (PP), 405
P/B (price-to-book) ratio, 150
Peak load pricing, 321
P/E (price/earnings) ratio, 87, 149
Percentage of sales method, 201
Perfectly elastic demand, 328
Perfectly inelastic demand, 328
Poison pills, 236
Poison put, 236
Portfolio, 117
Portfolio rate of return, 119
Portfolio risk, 117
  systematic, 120
  unsystematic, 121
Positive covenant, 134
PP (payback period), 405
PPP (Purchasing power parity), 251
Precautionary motive, 204

Preemptive rights, common stock, 144
Preferred shareholders' book value, 39
Preferred stock, 152, 158, 188
Premium, option, 169
Prepayment, 259
Present value (PV), 388
Pressure, in fraud triangle, 443
Price decreases, 328
Price/earnings (P/E) ratio, 87, 149
Price elasticity of demand, 328
Price increases, 324, 326
Price/sales (P/S) ratio, 151
Price-to-book (P/B) ratio, 150
Pricing, 309
   cost-based, 313
   cost-plus, 313
   market-based, 313
   peak load, 321
   supply and demand based, 310
Pricing decision, 309
Primary market, 189
Probability distribution, 115
Processing float, 206
Product life-cycle costing, 320
Profit margin, 59
Promissory note, 226
Protectionism, free trade and, 263
Proxy statement, 144
P/S (price/sales) ratio, 151
PTD (payable through draft), 210
Purchases, in foreign currency, 91
Purchasing power parity (PPP), 251
Put option, 169
Put option payoff, 170
PV (present value), 388

Quality function deployment (QFD), 320
Quantity demanded, change in, 323
Quantity supplied, change in, 325
Quick ratio, 19

Rate of return, 112
Ratios, 17
   current, 19
   financial. *see* Financial ratios
   financial leverage, 25, 60
Rationalization, in fraud triangle, 443
RCOE (Return on Common Equity), 59

Receivables, 31
Refinancing, bonds, 141
Relative price, 252
Relative valuation, 148
Relevant range, 276
Remeasurement, of currency, 93
Reorder point (ROP), 222
Required rate of return (RRR), 386
Residual risk, 356
Resolving Ethical Issues, 440
Resource prices, and supply, 326
Responsibility, 438
Return (rate of return), 112
Return, expected, 115
Return on assets (ROA), 39, 43, 58
Return on capital investment (ROCI), 38
Return on Common Equity (RCOE), 59
Return on equity (ROE), 39, 43, 46, 59
Return on investment (ROI), 39, 43, 58
Revenues, 67, 276
Revenue driver, 276
Reverse split, 192
Revolving credit, 226
Risk, 111
   default, 217
   return and, 113
Risk analysis, 411
Risk appetite, 355
Risk assessment, 355
Risk aversion, 114
Risk identification, 354
Risk response, 356
ROA (return on assets), 39, 43, 58
ROCI (return on capital investment), 38
ROE (return on equity), 39, 43, 46, 59
ROI (return on investment), 39, 43, 58
ROP (reorder point), 222
RRR (required rate of return), 386

Safety (buffer) stock, 221
Sales, in foreign currency, 90
Sale-leaseback transactions, 243
Scenario analysis, 417
SEC (Securities and Exchange
   Commission), 189
Secondary market, 135, 190
Secured bond, 139
Secured short-term loan, 227

Securities, marketable, 211
Securities and Exchange Commission (SEC), 189
Security market line (SML), 123
Securities registration, 190
Selling off the crown jewels, 237
Sell or process further, 296
Sensitivity analysis
  in CVP analysis, 285
  in risk analysis, 412
SGR (sustainable growth ratio), 38
Shareholder wealth, 114
Shareholder wealth maximization (SWM), 114
Short position, 171
Short-term credit, types of, 224
Short-term credit management, 228
Short-term loan
  secured, 227
  unsecured, 226
Sight draft, 258
Simulations, 416
Sinking fund provision, bonds, 136
SL (straight-line) depreciation, 378
SML (security market line), 123
Solvency, 18
Special order pricing, 292
Speculative motive, 204
Spin-offs, 237
Split-ups, 238
Stable dollar, 193
Standards, 439
Standard deviation, 115
Statement of Ethical Professional Practice (IMA), 431, 435
Statutory voting, 143
Stock, 141
  common, 132, 143, 145
  inventory and, 218
  preferred, 152, 158, 188
Stock control, 218
Stock dividend, 192
Stock repurchases, 194
Stock splits, 192
Straight-line (SL) depreciation, 378
Strike price, option, 169
Substitution effect, 323
Sum-of-the-years' digits (SYD), 378

Supply, change in, 325
Supply and demand, 322
Supply and demand based pricing, 310
Supply curve, 325–327
Supply schedule, 325
Sustainable equity growth, 38
Sustainable growth rate, 64
Sustainable growth ratio (SGR), 38
Swap, 173
SWM (shareholder wealth maximization), 114
SYD (sum-of-the-years' digits), 378

Target costing, 315, 316
Targeted stocks, 243
Target price, 317
Target rate of return on investment, 321
Target value weights, 163
Taxes, supply and, 326
Tax effect (cash flows), 374
Technically insolvent organizations, 241
Technology, supply and, 326
Temporal method, 93
Tender offer, 236
Term loans, 183
Time draft, 258
Times interest earned ratio, 28
Total asset turnover, 59
Total asset turnover ratio, 33
Total cost, 276
Total debt to total capital ratio, 26
Tracking stocks, 243
Trade credit, 225
Traditional voting, 143
Trailing P/E ratio, 149
Transactions exposure, 254
Transaction motive, 204
Transfer of accounts receivable, 29
Transfer pricing, 262
Translation exposure, 253
Trend analysis, 10
Trust receipt, 230

Underlying (underlier), 167
Uniform cash flow, 391
Unit, 218
Unit contribution margin, 281
Unit elastic demand, 330

Unproductive assets, 39
Unsecured bond (debenture), 139
Unsecured short-term loan, 226

Valuation, 131
Value
  book, 131
  fundamental, 132
  going-concern, 131
  intrinsic, 132
  liquidation, 131
  market, 132
Value-added costs, 319
Value at risk (VaR), 389
Value engineering, 319
"Values and Ethics: From Inception to Practice" *(SMA)*, 453
VaR (value at risk), 389
VaR (variance-covariance method), 352
Variable cost, 276
Variable dividend growth model, 147
Variable interest entities (VIEs), 30

Variance-covariance method (VaR), 352
Variation analysis, 10
Vertical common-size statements, 7
VIEs (Variable interest entities), 30
Voting rights
  common stock, 143
  preferred stock, 153

Weighted average cost of capital (WACC), 163
Weighted marginal cost of capital (WMCC), 164
Whistleblower framework, 459
White knight defense, 236
Window dressing, 22
WMCC (weighted marginal cost of capital), 164
Working (current) capital, 18, 201
Working capital management, 202

Zero balance account (ZBA), 210
Zero dividend growth model, 146